Learn French

THIS BOOK INCLUDES:

Learn French for Beginners

French Short Stories for Beginners

Learn French for Intermediate users

Learn French for Advanced Users

French Short Stories

Speak French

The Complete French Language Books Collection to Learn Starting from Zero, Have Fun and Become Fluent like a Native Speaker

TABLE OF CONTENTS

Learn French for Beginners

French Short Stories for Beginners

Learn French for Intermediate Users

Learn French for Advanced Users

French Short Stories

Speak French

Learn French for Beginners

The complete beginners guide to speak French in just 7 days starting from zero. Includes the most common words and phrases

Introduction

Learning French is a long-term undertaking and part of the challenge facing any learner is to remain motivated beyond the first few weeks and throughout the whole process. At the beginning, learning a new language is fresh and exciting and you will make rapid progress. However, as the first weeks turn into months, you can expect to feel your initial progress slow a little and you may lose sight of why you started learning French in the first place. In moments like this, **you need to find ways to rekindle your enthusiasm and remember why you originally decided to start learning French**.

Therefore, when you first start out, it is a good idea to be specific about your motivations. Think about why you want to learn French. Is it because it will help your career? Do you have a particular attachment to France? Do you live in France and want to integrate better with the community? What are the specific benefits you look forward to in your life once you can speak French? It is a good idea to jot down a list of your reasons for learning French, so that when the inevitable moment of disillusionment arrives, you can come back to your list to re-engage with your core motivations.

Set Specific Goals.

Once you have clearly articulated your reasons for learning French, it will help you to set a long-term language goal. Whatever stage you are at in learning a language, without a goal of some kind how will you ever know when you have succeeded? **When setting your goal, try to be more specific than simply: "I will speak French fluently!"** I like to express my goals in terms of what I will be able to do, rather than a notional idea of fluency. Goals expressed in this way might look like:

I will be able to watch and enjoy a French film without subtitles by Christmas

I will be able to go on holiday to France next summer and get by without English

I will pass my B1-level exam in February

Having some kind of goal articulated will give you something more concrete to work towards than simply "learn French", be a source of motivation, and help you make better decisions about your learning.

Chapter 1- French Alphabet and Pronunciation

You undoubtedly had to memorize the alphabet when you were a kid. Picture yourself back in kindergarten, except this time, instead of an English or Spanish teacher, you have a French one. If you want to show your teacher that you are motivated and eager to learn, pay special attention to L' Alphabet.

The French Alphabet

One thing that both English and French have in common is that their alphabets have 26 letters. But many of them are said in very different ways.

Before you get too deep into the French language, you should know that it has "accentuated vowels" and special symbols that don't exist in English. For example:

- *è* (grave accent): is pronounced similarly to the "e" in the word "bet." In addition, it can be found in the letters "a" and "u".

- *é* (acute accent): pronounced as "ei" is found above the letter "e".

- *ê* (circumflex accent): found on top of all vowels, elongates the pronunciation of the vowel, similar to how the "ay" in "play" is drawn out.

- The French sound /ə/, which is unique and sounds like a short "u".

- *ç* (call cedilla): modifies the sound of the letter "k" to an "s" For instance, in French, the term "*garçon*" can signify either "boy" or "waiter.". It is pronounced in this mode /GHAR son/".

- The diaeresis comes after the second of two vowels in a row and is called a "*tréma*" in French. It's to show that the letters have separate sounds. For instance, the term for Christmas in French is *Noël*, which is pronounced /no EL/.

Use free tools like Google Translate to listen to these unique French sounds online. This method will help you understand them better.

Now, say the letters below based on what is written below them. Keep in mind that the terms utilized to express the sounds are derived from the Standard American English accent.

Aa/ah/

Matches the "a" in "father".

Bb/bé/

Matches the "e" in "bed".

Cc/sé/

Matches the "k", but if there is a cedilla, it becomes the sound "s".

Dd/dé/

Matches the "d" in "day"

Ee/ə/

Matches the "a" in "again".

Ff/ef/

Matches the "f" in "food".

Gg/ g/

Matches the "s" in "measure" if it comes after "e" or "i". Other than that, it Matches the "g" in "girl".

Hh/ashe/

It is often not pronounced. For example, "*heureux*", which is French for "happy", is pronounced as/EUH reuh/.

Ii/ee/

Matches the "ee" in "seen".

Jj/dji/

Matches the second "g" in "garage".

Kk/ka/

Matches the "k" in "kite".

Ll/el/

Matches the "l" in "love".

Mm/em/

Matches the "m" in "man".

Nn/en/

Matches the "n" in "neck".

Oo/o/

Matches the "o" in "holiday".

Pp/pe/

Matches the "pe" in "pellet".

Qq/ku/

Matches the "k" in "kick".

Rr/er/

Matches the "r" in "error".

Ss/ess/

Matches the "s" in "sat".

Tt/te/

Matches the "t" in "tent".

Uu/y/

A uniquely French sound, which is similar to the "oo" in "too".

Vv/ve/

Matches the "v" in "vow".

Ww/doblé vee/

Matches the "w" in "weekend".

Xx/iks/

Matches the "x" in "xylophone".

Yy/y/

Pronounced as/I grec/ when alone. Other than that, it is like the sound "ea" in "each".

Zz/zed/

Matches the "z" in "zebra".

French Pronunciation Guidelines

- If there are two sounds /k/ together, only the first one doesn't change. For example, "accept" is pronounced, *accepter* /AK sep tee/.

- The sound /ks/ changes to /z/ or/gz/, as in exact /EG zakt/.

- If "e" or "i" comes before the sounds /k/ or /g/, they change to /s/ and/ʒ/ respectively.

- If the letters "*gu*" is followed by "e" or "i," the "u" is silent, as in *guerre* which is pronounced /GEH/ ("war").

- If the "s" is between two vowels, it changes to a /z/. For example, *chose* ("thing") becomes /shooz/.

- The "*t*" transforms to an "s" when it is followed by "ie," "ia," or "io", as *patient* ("patient"), which is pronounced /PEH syun/.

- If /il/ at the end of a word comes after a vowel, it changes to /ee/, as in *œil* /uh Y/ ("eye").

- If "*ill*" is not at the beginning of a word, it changes to /ee/, as in "oreille" which is pronounced /ooh REYH/ ("ear").

- If there is no vowel before "ill," the sound "i" is made, like in the word *fille* ("girl") which is pronounced /fee yh/. But in the words *distiller*/distile/ ("to distill") and *mille*/mil/ ("thousand"), the /l/ is pronounced.

- If the letter "*o*" comes after the letter "y," it is said as "wa," as in *voyage* ("travel"), which is pronounced, /VWA yaj/.

- When the letters "*i*," "*u*," and "*y*" come before a vowel in a word, they change into "glides," as *pied* /pye/ ("foot"), *oui* /wi/ ("yes"), and *huit* /oo weet/ ("eight").

6

- The "*e*" at the end is not said, as in *bouche*/boosh/ ("mouth").

- In French, a process known as "liaison" refers to what takes place when a sound that is normally silent is spoken exactly before the word that comes precedes it. For example, "*vous avez*" is rendered /vou zavee/ ("you have").

- Also, the liaison is in the vowel that comes after a word that ends with a silent "e." For example, *reste à côté* is pronounced as/rest ah cotei/ ("stay next").

- *Enchaînement* is a French phenomenon that moves the sound of a consonant from the end of a word to the beginning of the word that comes before it. For example, ("she is") *elle est* is said as /e le/.

- The majority of the time, you don't say the last e in a French word. For instance, *jambe* /jamb/ (leg), *bouche* /bush/ (mouth), *lampe* /lamp/ (lamp).

- If the letter "*e*" gets followed by two consonants, it sounds like /*ei*/ without the glide from e to i, but it is more open. For instance: *pelle* /pèl/ (shovel), *lettre* /lètr/ (letter).

- Learn the French sounds that don't make any sound, which are the final -*b* that follows an m- (such as *plomb* /plon/ (the 'om' sounds more like the 'on' in wrong)/ [metal]), final -*d* (such as *chaud* /shoh/ [warm]), final -*p* (such as *trop* /tro/ [very much]), final -*s* (such as *trés* /treh/ [very much]), final -*t* (such as *part* /par/ [part]), final -*x* (such as *prix* /pri/ [price]), and the final -*z* (such as *assez* /ase/ [enough]).

How to Properly Pronounce the Single Vowels

/***a***/: Like the initial "a" in "marmalade", but less open /a/. This vowel sound is most comparable to the open vowel sound of â.

Examples: *table* (table), *chat* (cat), *sac* (bag), *baggage* (luggage), *rat* (rat), *matin* (morning), *bras* (arm)

/***e***/: Like the 2nd /a/ in "*marmalade*," this tone is similar to the English indefinite article "a", but it has a more pronounced sound. Similar sounds include "*e*" /eu/ and "*eu*" /oeu/ that are both pronounced similarly to more open e and eu.

Examples: *deux* (two), *oeuvre* (master works), *cheveu* (hair), *soeur* (sister), *beurre* (butter), *heure* (hour)

Don't forget that the e at the end of French terms is always mute. For instance: *Notre Dame, Anne*

When speaking French, it's common to slip over the e in the central position of a word. Case in point: *boulevard, Mademoiselle*

/***i***/: the more short version of the English for the /ee/ sound.

Examples: *courir* (to run), *pipe* (pipe), *midi* (midday), *minute* (minute), *nid* (nest)

/***o***/: In French, the letter o can represent two distinct sounds. The initial /o/ is open, like the o in "not," "more," and "for" in English.

The 2nd sound resembles the English used in the words "low" and "go" sound, which is more closed /o/.

In French, most /o/ sounds have an open form. Only at the end of a word does it become closed.

Examples of the open /o/: *botte* (botte), *homme* (man),

Examples of the closed /o/: *indigo* (indigo), *vélo* (bicycle), *développer* (to develop)

/eau/, /au/, /ô/: These phonologically are comparable to the closed /o/ sound. For instance: *auto* (car), *contrôle* (control), and *eau* (water)

/**u**/: There is no equivalent in English to the French pronunciation of u. A /u/ like in "push" is pronounced very differently in French compared to it is in English. In French, however, the letter u is used for the vowel combination /ou/, but not as in the English word "push.".

Examples: *minute*, *voiture* (car), *humain* (human)

/**y**/:- this is pronounced very similarly to the double /i/ sound that is found in French.

Examples: *loyer*/loi ier/ (lease), *noyer*/noi ier/ (to drown), *rayer*/rai ier/ (to scratch), *pays*/pai i/ (country)

Practice pronouncing the following:

si => sou => su

rue => rit => roue

sous => assure => assis

écrou => écrit => écru

repu => tous => asile

tisse => sucre => rousse

git => joue => jus

revit => revue => couve

Accentuated Vowels

One of the most obvious differences between English and French is that the latter uses accented characters. Most vowel sounds, with the exception of /*y*/, can be accentuated.

/**è**/ -this is pronounced like the /e/ in pet. The grave accent is also placed on top of a as well as u to create *à* and *ù*, respectively, although these do not change the pronunciation.

Examples: *Hélène*/hei len/ (Helen), *où*/oo/ (where)

/**é**/ -the special character above the e is called the acute accent and it is only used over e.

Example: *égoïste*/ei go ist/ (selfish), *comédie*/ko mei dee/ (comedy)

/**ê**/ -the circumflex accent, which is the special character over e, can also be placed on top of all the other vowels. What it does is that it lengthens the sound.

Example: *à côté de*/ah co tei deuh/ (beside), *s'il te plaît*/silt te ple/ (please)

/**ë**/ -this special character is called the dieresis mark and it is put over a vowel to show that the sound is a separate syllable from the other vowel next to it. For instance, if you have two vowels put together such as ai, it is usually pronounced as /e/, but if you place a dieresis on top of the /i/, the sound becomes /ai/.

Example: *naïf*/na eef/ (naive), *haïr*/a eer/ (to hate).

8

Vowel Combination Pronunciation

/**ou**/ -this vowel combination sounds like something in between the sounds of the u in bush and the oo in cool.

Example: *cou*/coo/ (neck), *genou*/g like the ge in 'garage' and 'e' like 'a' in english:/geuh noo/ (knee)

/**au**/ and/**eau**/ -this is pronounced the same way as/ô/.

Example: *bateau*/bah toh/ like the 'o' in 'go'/ (ship), *eau*/oh/ like the 'o' in 'go'/ (water)

/**oi**/ -to pronounce this vowel combination, make the/wa/ sound.

Example: *doigt*/doo wa/ (finger), *oie*/oo wa/ (goose)

/**ai**/ -this is pronounced the same way as/ê/.

Example: *j'ai*/zhei/'j' sounds like 'ge' in 'garage'/ (I have), *maison*/mei son/('on' sounds like 'on' in 'wrong')/ (house)

/**ui**/ -to produce the sound of this vowel combination, the diphthong/oo wee/.

Example: *fruit*/froo ee/ (fruit), *aujourd'hui*/oo zhoor dui/('j' like 'ge' in 'garage')/(today)

/**eu**/ and/**oeu**/ -pronounced the same way as the short/u/ sound.

Example: *bleu*/blu/ (blue), *feu*/fu/ (fire)

/**er**/,/**et**/ and/**ez**/ -these vowl combinations have a sound that is similar to/é/.

Example: *boulanger*/boo lan ge/('g' like 'ge' in 'garage')/ (baker), *hier*/ee yer/ (yesterday)

Practice pronouncing the following:

mêle => meule => molle

coeur => corps => caire

sol => sel => seule

Plaire => pleure => implore

l'or => l'air => leur

peur => port => père

gueule => guerre => encore

Nasal Vowel Pronunciation

/**on**/ - it is not possible to find an exact English sound that is similar to this unique French sound. However, the closes vowel would probably be the long/o/ such as the o in long (but without fully pronouncing the/ng/ sound).

Example: *oncle*/ohng kl/ (uncle), *bon*/bohn/ (good)

/**an**/ and/**am**/ -if a vowel combination is followed by the letter n or m, it does not immediately mean that the sound would be nasal, unless the n or m is the final letter of the word. However, if there is only one vowel before the n or m, the vowel is a nasal sound.

Example: *détient*/dei ti ahn/ (holds), *sens*/sahns/ (sense)

/*en*/ and/*em*/ -the closest sound that is similar to these French nasal vowels would be the a in swan.

Example: *souvent*/soo vahn/ (often), *ensemble*/ahn sahm bl/ (together)

/*in*/,/*ain*/,/*ein*/, and/*aim*/ -the closest sound in the English language that is similar to this one would be the an in hang.

Example: *main*/mahn/ (hand), *pain*/pahn/ (bread)

/*un*/ and/*um*/ -to produce the nasal vowel sound, find the sound between/*o*/ and/*e*/.

Example: *un*/unh/ (one or a), *brun*/brunh/ (brown)

Practice pronouncing the following:

bain => banc => bond

sain => cent => son

daim => dans => don

fin => faon => fond

gain => gant => gond

geint => jean => jonc

lin => lent => long

main => ment => mont

pain => paon => pont

rein => rang => rond

thym => tant => ton

vin => vent => vont

Exercise

Here is a list of words that will let you practice most of the sounds in the French alphabet. Use a sound recorder and a free online application such as Google Translate to compare your pronunciation with that of a native speaker.

Consonant Sounds

- *Beau*
- *Doux*
- *Fête*
- *Guerre*
- *Cabas*

- *Loup*
- *Femme*
- *Nous*
- *Agneaux*
- *Passé*

- *Roue*
- *Option*
- *Choux*
- *Tout*

Semi-Vowel Sounds

- *Travail*
- *Oui*

Vowel Sounds

- *Là*
- *Pâte*
- *Aller*
- *Faite*
- *Maître*
- *Monsieur*
- *Régie*

Nasal Vowel Sounds

- *Sans*
- *Pain*

- *Vous*
- *Hasard*
- *Joue*

- *Huit*

- *Jeune*
- *Queue*
- *Haut*
- *Minimum*
- *Roue*
- *Sûr*

- *Parfum*
- *Nom*

Chapter 2 - General Greetings

It is customary to offer a firm handshake as a greeting when meeting a new acquaintance for the first time. This may be someone who you have been introduced to or someone that you meet and begin a dialogue. Let's say you run into someone that you have previously met and know a little bit. You would then greet them and give a small kiss on either cheek. These are simple niceties that are always practiced by the French. If you know someone really well, then the usual greeting is one kiss on each cheek, but this is typically reserved for people like family.

The following phrases will help you introduce yourself to someone and to say hello, no matter what time of day it is. The written French in the middle of the page is correct French and to the right, you will find the phonetic pronunciation of the words so that you can say them easily:

| Good Morning | *Bonjour* | Bon Joor |

(This can be used as hello as well)

| Hi! | *Salut!* | Saloo |

(As a general rule, the final letter of a word is not pronounced unless it is immediately followed by another word that starts with a vowel.)

Check out these additional greetings. Say them aloud.

I am pleased to meet you.	*Enchanté*	Onshontay
What's up?	*Quoi de neuf?*	Kwah de neuhf?
Goodbye	*Au Revoir*	Orh revwar
See you later!	*À tout à l'heure!*	Ah toot ah lheuhr
I am sorry I am late.	*Je suis désolé d'être en retard.*	Jeuh swee dezolay detra on retar

Note: This is a perfect example of how *être* (to be) is used in a sentence. In this case it means literally, "I am sorry to be late", but it's the same way you would say, " I am sorry I am late."

This is a useful phrase that you can use when you need to ask someone on an adjoining seat to let you through or if you bump into someone by accident and wish to say that you are sorry.

| Excuse me! | *Excusez Moi!* | Excusay mwa! |

Quiz Time!

Easy right? In the span of 5 minutes, you have learned to say eight phrases. Learning French is nothing without repetition. Can you pass this brief quiz?

Scenario: you are meeting a friend for lunch and you are 10 minutes late. What are two phrases you would likely use to greet him?

*Try to work from your memory only by using a voice recorder on your phone or handheld device, then check what you said against the phrases previously provided. How did you do? Ready to move on?

Answer: while there is no wrong answer, the preferable choice would be: "*Salut! Je suis désolé détre an retard* ".

Let's look at some more nice introductions. Perhaps you want to introduce your friend or family member to someone and in this case you would use the following phrase:

This is my husband	*Voici mon mari*	Vwassee mon maree
This is my wife	*Voici ma femme*	Vwassee ma famm
This is my daughter	*Voici ma fille*	Vwassee ma fee yh
This is my son	*Voici mon fils*	Vwassee mon feece

Of course if you are introducing your whole family, you would not need to say Voici each time but could shorten it by saying:

Voici mon mari, ma femme et mon fils

Or change the sentence according to who you are introducing. The word *ET* means AND and is pronounced as "AY". Voici mes amis! These are my friends. This is the easiest way to break the ice and to get to know everyone without having to break into the formality of the French language. People today recognize these greetings and introductions and they can be used so easily.

Now, it's time to put some words together to make sentences. There is not much use in saying "hello" if you can't follow it up with asking how someone is, or asking a question. When you are on holiday, you may want to get somewhere and the "hello" will allow you to approach someone, but you will need to go further by putting words together in such a way that whoever you approach will understand what you want. If you are on the plane to France and want to practice your French on the stewardess, here are some phrases that you can try just to see how your accent is understood.

The verb that I will introduce you to is *VOULOIR* or "to want to". However, merely saying that you want something in English is considered a bit rude. It's the same in French. You would never use the equivalent of "I WANT" which would be "je veux". The polite way of saying this in French is to use the equivalent of "I would like". Remember niceties go a long way in any language.

| I would like a coffee | *Je voudrais un café* | Juh voodray un cafay |

It is usual in France to be served coffee that is black unless you ask for milk. Thus, when the stewardess asks you if you would like a drink and you tell her that you would like a coffee, you will also need to specify that you want milk or cream.

| With milk please | *Avec du lait s'il vous plaît* | Ahvec du lay sihl voo pley |

Having learned that it is polite to say I would like rather than I want, you also need to know another nicety. One would never use the expression "What?" when you do not hear something that has been said. It's a very bad reflection of upbringing and the better option is to say "*Comment*?" (pronounced comm on?) or to even ask the person you are speaking to, to repeat that which was said, using the phrase.

13

Can you repeat that please?	*Pouvez-vous répéter cela s'il vous plaît?*	Poovei voo repettay sella seel voo play

Perhaps your fellow passenger is French and you would like to practice your pronunciations. Introduce yourself using the salutations shown above and then try some phrases if the person in the neighboring seat seems friendly.

May I practice my French with you?	*Puis-je pratiquer mon français avec vous?*	Pwee juh pratikay mon froncay aveck vous?
Do you know what time it is?	*Savez-vous quelle heure il est?*	Ssavay voo kell urr eel è

General conversation that may follow on the plane could involve phrases that use French, but also explains a little bit about yourself. You will need to listen to the replies and be aware of how to ask a French person to slow down so that you can understand a little better.

Can you speak slower please?	*Pouvez-vous parler plus lentement s'il vous plaît?*	Poovay voo parlay ploo lanteuhman ('an' like 'an' in 'want') seel voo play

Now that you have a general understanding of French greetings, why not try these common phrases out!

Hello!/ Good Day/ Good Morning/ Good Afternoon	*Bonjour!*	Boh-joor!
Good Evening!	*Bonsoir!*	Boh-swahr
Hello (answering phone)	*Allô*	ah-lo
Hello Sir	*Bonjour Monsieur*	Boh-joor meuh ssieuh
Hello Ma'am	*Bonjour Madame*	Boh-joor Mah-dahm
Nice to meet you!	*Enchanté*	An-shon-tay!
How are you?	*Comment vas-tu?*	Koh-mahn vah-too?
	ça va?	sah-vah?
	comment allez-vous?	koh-mahn tallay-voo?
I'm fine,	*Ça va bien.*	sah-vah bee-yen.
I'm fine, thanks!	*Bien, merci!*	Bee-yen, mayr-see
And You?	*Et toi?*	Ei twah
	Et vous?	Ei voo
What's up?	*Quoi de neuf?*	Kwah de nuff?
Welcome!	*Bienvenue!*	Bee-yen-veuh-nu!
I'm happy to see you!	*Je suis ravi de te voir.*	Jeuh-swee rah-vee deh the euh-

		vwar.
Have a good holiday!	*Bonnes vacances!*	Bohn vah-kahns!
(have a) Safe trip!	*Bon voyage!*	Bohn vowa ya ge!
See you later!	*à plus tard!*	ah ploo tahr!
See you soon!	*à bientôt*	ah bee-yen toh!
Goodbye!	*Au revoir!*	Oh ruh-vwar!
Good night!	*Bonne nuit!*	Bohn-nwee!
See you tomorrow!	*à demain!*	Ah de-mahn
Enjoy your weekend!	*Bon weekend!*	Bohn week-end!
Have a good week!	*Bonne semaine!*	Bohn seh-mane!
Yes	*Oui*	Wee
No	*Non*	Nohn (on like '<u>long</u>')
Please	*S'il vous plaît*	Seel voo play
Thanks!	*Merci*	Mair-see
No thank you.	*Non merci.*	Nohn mair-see
Sorry	*Pardon*	Pahr-dohn
Sorry to disturb you	*Je suis désolé de vous déranger*	Jeuh-swee-day-zoh-lay-de-voo-day-rahn-jei
Good luck!	*Bonne chance!*	Bohn-shawns!
Have fun!	*Amuse-toi bien!*	Ah-muze-twa bee-yen!
Cheers!	*Santé!*	Sahn-tay!
All the best!	*Bonne continuation!*	Bohn kohn-tee-nwah-see-ohn!

Learning these words by heart will help you when you speak French because you will be able to catch snatches of words in replies you get. Thus, the more words you know, the more likely you are to be able to understand the conversation. The problem with conjugating French is that all of the verbs change when you associate them with different genders, so it's best to keep things simple at this time. In sentences throughout the book, however, you will see that verbs are used differently when referring to different people. If you want to learn more about how this works, it may be a good idea to invest in a verb conjugation book, although as a tourist, you really don't need to dig that deeply into the language to make yourself heard and understood.

I know we have touched on this before, but I feel it bears repeating. The biggest problem many people have with the French language is that every object is either masculine or feminine and that, quite often, the sex of the object doesn't really make much sense. If you ask a French man why a certain word is masculine or why it's feminine, they will usually answer you with a shrug. It's a very old language and is well established and even French people make mistakes with the prefixes used to describe the sex of something. **Le, la** and **les** are used to describe the word that we use in our language that is "the". However, **le** is masculine and thus refers to masculine objects, **la** is feminine and **les** is plural. You can't

15

make a mistake when talking about a person as the sex is obvious but when you start to speak and listen to French, you will find that things such as a table, a bedroom, a bookcase and even a car, all have a masculine or feminine prefix because in the French language that's the way that the words are ordered.

You are fairly safe using the salutations that we have used in this chapter because they don't really refer much to the sex of someone. *Bonjour* is universal, as is *Salut!* It is only when you start to construct sentences to try and explain something to a French person that the sexes come into play. Over the next chapter, I hope that you will be able to use the information to ask questions about the accommodations that you have in France.

Quiz Time!

Here we are at the end of the first lesson. I know it seems like we have gone over a lot of information, but let's make sure you are actually retaining some of this info. Take this short quiz to find out!

1. How do you say hello?

2. How do you pardon yourself after bumping into someone?

3. How would you introduce your friends?

4. How would you request a coffee?

5. How do you say "Good Night"?

Answer Key:

1. *Salut!/ Bonjour!*

2. *Excusez Moi!*

3. *Voici mesa mis*

4. *Je Voudrais un café*

5. *Bonne nuit!*

Chapter 3 - Numbers

Did you know that around 10 million Americans speak French, while about 35% of the French speak English; the number of times people kiss each other on the cheek in France depends on the region but can be up to 5; you can find over 400 varieties of French cheese; each year 75 million tourists visit France; 20% of the French people live in the regions around Paris; France is second in the world for film production. Numbers and ordinals can tell you a lot about the place and help you learn some pretty fascinating facts.

Naturally, not being able to use numbers means staying forever away from all the exciting details of France and the French people, which you could otherwise learn. And besides not knowing the numbers in French means not being able to shop any Parisian couture or write down the phone number of an interesting French person you met!

0 is written as *Zéro* is pronounced (zay-roh)

1 is written as *Un* and is pronounced (ahn)

2 is written as *Deux* and is pronounced (deuh)

3 is written as *Trois* and is pronounced (trwah)

4 is written as *Quatre* and is pronounced (kat)

5 is written as *Cinq* and is pronounced (sahnk)

6 is written as *Six* and is pronounced (seess)

7 is written as *Sept* and is pronounced (set)

8 is written as *Huit* and is pronounced (weet)

9 is written as *Neuf* and is pronounced (neuhf)

10 is written as *Dix* and is pronounced (deess)

11 is written as *Onze* and is pronounced (ohnz)

12 is written as *Douze* and is pronounced (dooz)

13 is written as *Treize* and is pronounced (trehz)

14 is written as *Quatorze* and is pronounced (kah-tohrz)

15 is written as *Quinze* and is pronounced (kanz)

16 is written as *Seize* and is pronounced (sez)

17 is written as *Dix-sept* and is pronounced (dee-set)

18 is written as *Dix-huit* and is pronounced (deez-weet)

19 is written as *Dix-neuf* and is pronounced (deez-neuhf)

20 is written as *Vingt* and is pronounced (vahn)

21 is written as *Vingt et un* and is pronounced (vahn tay ahn)

22 is written as *Vingt-deux* and is pronounced (vahn deuh)

23 is written as *Vingt-trois* and is pronounced (vahn trwah)

30 is written as *Trente* and is pronounced (trawnt)

31 is written as *Trente et un* and is pronounced (trawnt ay uhn)

32 is written as *Trente-deux* and is pronounced (trawnt deuh)

40 is written as *Quarante* and is pronounced (kah-rawnt)

50 is written as *Cinquante* and is pronounced (sank-awnt)

60 is written as *Soixante* and is pronounced (swah-ssawnt)

70 is written as *Soixante-dix* and is pronounced (swah-ssawnt deess)

71 is written as *Soixante et onze* and is pronounced (swah-ssawnt ay ohnz)

72 is written as *Soixante-douze* and is pronounced (swah-ssawnt dooz)

80 is written as *Quatre-vingts* and is pronounced (ka-truh vahn)

81 is written as *Quatre-vingt-un* and is pronounced (ka-truh vahn ahn)

82 is written as *Quatre-vingt-deux* and is pronounced (ka-truh vahn duh)

90 is written as *Quatre-vingt-dix* and is pronounced (ka-truh vahn deess)

91 is written as *Quatre-vingt-onze* and is pronounced (ka-truh vahn ohnz)

92 is written as *Quatre-vingt-douze* and is pronounced (ka-truh vahn dooz)

100 is written as *Cent* and is pronounced (sawn)

101 is written as *Cent un* and is pronounced (sawn ahn)

200 is written as *Deux cents* and is pronounced (duh sawn)

201 is written as *Deux cent un* and is pronounced (duh sawn ahn)

1,000 is written as *Mille* and is pronounced (meel)

2,000 is written as *Deux mille* and is pronounced (duh meel)

1,000,000 is written as *Un million* and is pronounced (ahn meel-ee-ohn)

Chapter 4 - What's Today's Date?

January in the French language is translated to *Janvier*

February in the French language is translated to *Février*

March in the French language is translated to *Mars*

April in the French language is translated to *Avril*

May in the French language is translated to *Mai*

June in the French language is translated to *Juin*

July in the French language is translated to *Juillet*

August in the French language is translated to *Août*

September in the French language is translated to *Septembre*

October in the French language is translated to *Octobre*

November in the French language is translated to *Novembre*

December in the French language is translated to *Décembre*

Monday in the French language is translated to *Lundi* (masc)

Tuesday in the French language is translated to *Mardi* (masc)

Wednesday in the French language is translated to *Mercredi* (masc)

Thursday in the French language is translated to *Jeudi* (masc)

Friday in the French language is translated to *Vendredi* (masc)

Saturday in the French language is translated to *Samedi* (masc)

Sunday in the French language is translated to *Dimanche* (masc)

Today in the French language is translated to *aujourd'hui*

Yesterday in the French language is translated to *hier*

The day before yesterday in the French language is translated to *avant-hier*

Tomorrow in the French language is translated to *demain*

The day after tomorrow in the French language is translated to *après-demain*

Next week in the French language is translated to *la semaine prochaine*

Last month in the French language is translated to *le mois dernier*

In August in the French language is translated to *en août*

All of these different forms will be covered more in detail later on.

What's today's date

In English, days are counted with ordinal numbers (the first, second, third, etc.), while French uses cardinal numbers except for the 1st day of the month, which is *le premier (mai)* when followed by the month only, or *le dimanche 1 (un/ premier) mai* if preceded by the day of the week. You will, therefore, only need to reapply numbers as you have already learned them with no additional endings: *le vingt (20) mai, le douze (12) janvier*.

Depending on where you are from, you may also be accustomed to "on the 24th of June" or "on June 24th", in French, only one order prevails:

- on the 24th of June/ on June 24th – *le 24 juin, or: le (lit. "the") 24 (vingt-quatre, unchanged form) juin* (uncapitalized, no introduced by any preposition)

'*On the 14th of September*' = *Le* (definite article) + Day of the month + month:

I need to have this back on June 14th – *J'ai besoin que tu me redonnes ça le 14 (quatorze) juin*

We celebrate Christmas on December 24th – *Nous célébrons Noël le 24 (vingt-quatre) décembre*

Learning a new language can be daunting, but at least the French thought about keeping this one simple: no regional differences, no added prepositions in between, and only the presence of the definite article le at the beginning! What about adding, say, Saturday into the mix? The day of the week will only need to come right between the article le and the day's number, as you will see here:

I need to have this back on Saturday, June 14th - *J'ai besoin que tu redonnes ça le samedi 14 juin.*

We will celebrate Christmas on Monday, December 24th – *Nous célèbrerons Noël le lundi 24 décembre.*

Exercise:

Here are five French sentences to correct. For each, note down the mistake that was made in the sentence and how you would rewrite it. Do not hesitate to go back to the grammar point associated with it at any point if you feel the need to do so. You will find the answers to the sentences after the learning objective, as well as all relevant explanations for each:

- *Je suis revenu d'Angleterre au jeudi 3 octobre.*

I came back from England on Thursday, October 3rd.

- *Le Mardi 6 Janvier, nous serons en vacances.*

On Tuesday, January 6th, we'll be on holidays.

- *Vous devez soumettre le dossier le 22 de juin.*

You must turn in the file on June 22nd.

- *Je ne serai pas disponible le dimanche le 4 mai.*

I won't be available on Sunday, May 4th.

- *Son anniversaire était le 8ième de novembre.*

His birthday was on November 8th.

Learning objectives:

- Know the name of each month and day of the week
- Know how to introduce dates in French with the proper article

- Know whether or not to capitalize days and months in French

Exercise: Explanations

- *Je suis revenue d'Angleterre au jeudi 3 octobre.*

The article here is not right: the French only use le, which refers to either the day of the week (jeudi being a masculine word) or to any day if it is not specified ("day" being jour in French, also a masculine word). The correct sentence would, therefore, be: *Je suis revenue d'Angleterre le jeudi 3 octobre.*

- *Le Mardi 6 Janvier, nous serons en vacances.*

The problem with this sentence is the capitalization, which may seem tempting when English is your first language: note, however, that French never capitalizes either days of the week or months, although French speakers make that mistake occasionally. The correct sentence would, therefore, be: *Le mardi 6 janvier, nous serons en vacances.*

- *Vous devez soumettre le dossier le 22 de juin.*

There is one extra preposition that should not be here, especially if you are already accustomed to saying "the 22nd of June". Adding an additional preposition in French would sound like the logical solution, but saying dates in French doesn't require any. The correct sentence would, therefore, be: *Vous devez soumettre le dossier le 22 juin.*

- *Je ne serai pas disponible le dimanche le 4 mai.*

Similarly to the previous sentence, the second le shouldn't be here, as the generally observed word order here is: le (+ day of the week, if specified) + day of the month + month. The correct sentence would, therefore, be: *Je ne serai pas disponible le dimanche 4 mai.*

- *Son anniversaire était le 8ième de novembre.*

This is one crucial aspect in which French is markedly different than English: while English uses ordinal numbers (the first, the second, etc.), French uses 'normal' or cardinal numbers instead: le sept décembre, le vingt-deux janvier... The correct sentence would, therefore, be: *Son anniversaire était le 8 (huit) novembre.*

Twenty years ago = il y a vingt ans

You have already encountered *il y a* when talking about 'there is/ there are'. It is also how the French translate 'ago' from English, adding the number of days, weeks, or years right afterward:

They rebuilt the cathedral three weeks ago – *Ils ont reconstruit la cathédrale il y a trois semaines.*

I sent them the cheque twenty days ago, but I haven't received any answer – *Je leur ai envoyé le chèque il y a vingt jours, mais je n'ai pas reçu de réponse.*

For four days, forty minutes = pendant quatre jours, quarante minutes

He enjoys reading for thirty minutes before going to bed – *Il aime lire pendant trente minutes avant d'aller au lit.*

I'll be out of the country for five days – *Je serai hors du pays pendant cinq jours.*

Chapter 5 - Seasons

Can you imagine spending your next summer in the South of France? Touring the beaches of *Cannes* and *St. Tropez*, tasting the delicate wines of *Nice* and *Marseille*...A summer in France can turn into an unforgettable holiday that many dream of. What about spending your spring break in Paris? You could marvel at the Eifel tower through the blooming flower beds along the streets. Spend entire days in the green paradise of *Parc des Buttes-Chaumont*, reading a great book or maybe even your guide to the French capital. A fall trip to France can be a real once in a lifetime experience for food enthusiasts – this is when you can see wild mushrooms being picked and when the olive and fig harvest are richest. Winter in France, on the other hand, is uniquely romantic and offers great ski resorts that you can enjoy even if you don't practice any extreme sports. But for you to get a taste of all of that greatness, you first need to learn the seasons in French.

l'été is pronounced as (lei-tei) Summer

    en été is pronounced as (awn ay-tay) in the summer

l'automne is pronounced as (loh-tohn) Fall

    en automne is pronounced as (aw noh-tohn) in the fall

l'hiver is pronounced as (lee-vair) Winter

    en hiver is pronounced as (aw nee-vair) in the winter

le printemps is pronounced as (luh prahn-tawn) Spring

    au printemps is pronounced as (oh prahn-tawn) in the spring

Chapter 6 - Color and Shapes

The French love their country and have a great appreciation for everyone who is just as excited about France. But imagine you had to describe the French flag to anyone, or the intricate shapes of the Triumphal arch in Paris – would you be able to do it without knowing the words for colors and shapes? Besides, if you want to blend in with the locals, instead of stand out like a tourist, on your next visit to the country you need to be up to code with all the latest trends of artistic French fashion. Your key to French style is learning the words for shapes and colors, thus being able to absorb all the trending cuts and hues with ease. France is a country of diversity and art, which you will be able to view differently after learning about shapes and colors.

In French, adjectives also have a gender.

An example of this is *vert/e* (green).

Vert is the male form of the word *"green"* and *verte* is the female form.

Many terms in French correspond to the nouns they represent on the basis of both number and gender. Maroon and orange represent the just exceptions, as are colors whose names are altered utilizing terms such as *clair-light* and *foncé-dark*. Many of the adjectives are also positioned following the main substantive.

For example, *un carré brun* is a brown square and *une boîte noire* is a black box.

Rouge is pronounced as (rooge) Red

orange is pronounced as (oh-rahnge) Orange

jaune is pronounced as (jon) Yellow

vert/e is pronounced as (vehr/t) Green

bleu/e is pronounced as (bluh) Blue

pourpre, violet/te is pronounced as (poor-pruh, vee-oh-leh/let) Purple

blanc/he is pronounced as (blawn/sh) White

brun/e, marron is pronounced as (brahn/brewn, mah-rohn) Brown

noir/e is pronounced as (nwahr) Black

rose is pronounced as (roze) Pink

doré/e is pronounced as (doh-ray) Golden

argenté/e is pronounced as (ahr-zhawn-tay) Silver

gris/e is pronounced as (gree/z) Gray

le carré is pronounced as (kah-ray) square

le cercle is pronounced as (sair-kluh) circle

le triangle is pronounced as (tree-awn-gluh) triangle

l'octogone is pronounced as (ok-toh-gohn) octagon

une boîte is pronounced as (bwaht) box

le cône is pronounced as (kohn) cone

le cylindre is pronounced as (see-lahn-druh) cylinder

la sphère is pronounced as (sfair) sphere

le cube is pronounced as (kewb) cube

le rectangle is pronounced as (rayk-tawn-gluh) rectangle

l'ovale is pronounced as (oh-vahl) oval

Chapter 7 - Family and Animals

Studies have shown the French people form very strong bonds with their families and friends. For instance, a survey held in 2013 noted that 93% of the people surveyed felt they had at least one close family member who they could rely on. That same year France proved once again how important family and love are, by legalizing same-sex marriage. But the French people don't only love other humans – they are also enthusiastic about animals. There are about 17 dogs per every 100 people in France which is one of the highest ratios in the world!

la famille is pronounced as (fah-mee-yh) Family

des parents is pronounced as (pahr-awn) Relatives

les grands-parents is pronounced as (grawn-pahr-awn) Grand-parents

les parents is pronounced as (pahr-awn) Parents

la mère, maman is pronounced as (mehr, ma-mawn) Mom

la belle-mère is pronounced as (bell-mehr) Stepmother/Mother-in-Law

le père, papa is pronounced as (pehr, pa-pa) Dad

le beau-père is pronounced as (boh-pehr) Stepfather/Father-in-Law

la fille is pronounced as (fee-yh) Daughter

le fils is pronounced as (feess) Son

la soeur is pronounced as (sir) Sister

la demi-soeur is pronounced as (duh-mee-sir) Half/Step Sister

la belle-soeur is pronounced as (bell-sir) Sister-in-Law

la belle-fille is pronounced as (bell-fee-yh) Stepdaughter/Daughter-in-Law

le frère is pronounced as (frehr) Brother

le demi-frère is pronounced as (duh-mee-frehr) Half/Step Brother

le beau-frère is pronounced as (boh-frair) Brother-in-Law

le beau-fils is pronounced as (boh-feess) Stepson/Son-in-Law

les jumeaux is pronounced as (ju-moh) Twins (m)

les jumelles is pronounced as (ju-mell) Twins (f)

l'oncle is pronounced as (ohnkl) Uncle

la tante is pronounced as (tawnt) Aunt

la grand-mère is pronounced as (grawn-mehr) Grandmother

le grand-père is pronounced as (grawn-pehr) Grandfather

la cousine is pronounced as (koo-zeen) Cousin (f)

le cousin is pronounced as (koo-zahn) Cousin (m)

la femme is pronounced as (fam) Wife

le mari is pronounced as (mah-ree) Husband

la femme is pronounced as (fam) Woman

l'homme is pronounced as (ohm) Man

la fille is pronounced as (fee-yh) Girl

le garçon is pronounced as (gar-sohn) Boy

la nièce is pronounced as (nee-ess) Niece

le neveu is pronounced as (nuh-vuh) Nephew

les petits-enfants is pronounced as (puh-tee-zawn-fawn) Grandchildren

la petite-fille is pronounced as (puh-teet fee-yh) Granddaughter

le petit-fils is pronounced as (puh-tee feess) Grandson

des parents éloignés is pronounced as (pahr-awn ay-lwawn-yay) Distant Relatives

Célibataire is pronounced as (say-lee-bah-tair) Single

marié(e) is pronounced as (mah-ree-ay) Married

séparé(e) is pronounced as (say-pah-ray) Separated

divorcé(e) is pronounced as (dee-vor-say) Divorced

veuf/ veuve is pronounced as (vuhf/ vuhv) Widower/ Widow

Animals

le chien/ la chienne is pronounced as (shee-ahn/ shee-enn) Dog

le chat/ la chatte is pronounced as (shah/ shaht) Cat

le chiot is pronounced as (shee-oh) Puppy

le chaton is pronounced as (shah-tohn) Kitten

le cochon is pronounced as (koh-shohn) Pig

le coq is pronounced as (kohk) Rooster

le lapin is pronounced as (lah-pahn) Rabbit

la vache is pronounced as (vahsh) Cow

le cheval is pronounced as (chuh-val) Horse

le canard is pronounced as (kah-nahr) Duck

la chèvre is pronounced as (shev-ruh) Goat

l'oie is pronounced as (lwah) Goose

le mouton is pronounced as (moo-tohn) Sheep

l'agneau is pronounced as (lah-n-yoh) Lamb

l'âne is pronounced as (lah-n) Donkey

la souris is pronounced as (soo-ree) Mouse

Chapter 8 - Gender and Articles

Gender and articles in the French language go hand in hand, because they are dependent on each other throughout the communication process. Take note that each noun in the French language has a gender: masculine or feminine.

Gender

The nouns were determined to be masculine or feminine not by how "male" or "female" they are (except in the case of the sex of most living things, such as the rooster and the hen), but by how the word is pronounced, spelled, and how it was developed.

There is no exact "formula" to determine whether a noun is masculine or feminine, and the only way to become familiar with this is to constantly expose yourself to as much French input as possible. Upon encountering a noun, you must also memorize its gender.

Persons

When a noun represents a person, the sex of the person determines the gender (but keep in mind that there are still exceptions to this "rule"). Generally, the female form of the noun is created by placing an -e to a masculine noun. For example:

Tony is a student. => *Tony est un étudiant.*

Sarah is a student. => *Sarah est une étudiante.*

If a masculine noun already ends with an -e, there is no need to add another -e to make it feminine. The noun, therefore, can be applicable to both. For example:

Benedict is a poet. => *Benedict est poète.*

Jane is a poet. => *Jane est poète.*

Animals

The masculinity or femininity of the French nouns for animals is not always based on the animal's gender. For instance, snails are often "masculine", because the French always refer to them as "*un escargot*" regardless as to whether it is a male or female snail. On the other hand, ants are always "*la fourmi*" even if there are also girl and boy ants.

Take note that many animals in the French language are irregular masculine and feminine forms. For example:

Male lion: => *le lion*

Female lion => *la lionne*

Male dog: => *le chien*

Female dog: => *la chienne*

Ideas and Objects

Nouns that represent abstractions and nonliving things are arbitrary, although in general you can infer their gender based on the ending of the word.

In general, nouns ending in -aire, -age, -é, -et, -ien, -in, -nt, - le, -eau, -asme, and -isme are masculine.

For example:

- **-aire**: *un dictionnaire* (a dictionary), *le proriétaire* (the owner)
- **-age**: *un sondage* (a survey), *le reportage* (the report)
- **-é**: *un café* (a coffee shop), *le comité* (the committe)
- **-et**: *un billet* (a ticket), *le sujet* (the subject)
- **-ien**: *un magicien* (a magician), *le musicien* (the musician)
- **-in**: *un bain* (a bath), *le cousin* (the cousin)
- **-nt**: *un accident* (an accident), *le monument* (the monument)
- **-le**: *un vignoble* (a vineyard), *le diable* (the devil)
- **-eau**: *un bateau* (a boat), *le bureau* (the office)
- **-asme and -isme**: *le sarcasme* (sarcasm), *le romantisme* (romanticism), *l' optimisme* (optimism)

Generally speaking, nouns ending in -ade, -aison, -té, -ette, -ance/ -ence, -ve, -ure, -ille/ -elle are feminine.

For example:

- **-ade**: *une salade* (a salad), *la limonade* (the lemonade)
- **-aison**: *une raison* (a reason), *la saison* (the season)
- **-té**: *la liberté* (liberty), *la beauté* (beauty)
- **-ette**: *une fourchette* (the fork), *la baguette* (the baguette)
- **-ance and -ence**: *la résistance* (the resistance), *la conférence* (the conference)
- **-ve**: *la larve* (the larva), *la lessive* (the washing)
- **-ure**: *une coiffure* (a hairstyle), *la blessure* (the injury)
- **-ille and -elle**: *la veille* (vigil), *la bouteille* (the bottle), *la dentelle* (lace), *la vaisselle* (the dishes)

Determining the gender of the nouns in French is imperative since all modifiers should agree in it. For instance, the forms of adjectives and past participles should be based on whether a noun is masculine or feminine.

For example:

A white dog. (the French noun "dog" is masculine)   *Un chien blanc.*

A white car. ("car" is feminine in French)   *Une voiture blanche.*

A cold morning. ("morning" is masculine in French)   *Un matin froid.*

A cold night. (in French, "night" is feminine)   *Une nuit froide.*

The Articles

In the English language, the articles are "a", "an", and "the". In French, articles play a major role in communication, for it is not possible to use a noun alone.

The articles in French are classified as either definite or indefinite, which is same as in English. One major difference is that French articles characterize the masculinity or femininity of the noun that it precedes. It is therefore wise to memorize not just nouns, but also the articles that accompany them.

The Indefinite Articles

An indefinite article is a determiner that pertains to a nonspecific reference. The indefinite articles in English are "a", "an", and "some". In French, they are "***un***", "***une***", and "***des***", respectively.

"***Un***" is used for masculine nouns. For example:

A cat (male) => *Un chat*

A telephone => *Un téléphone*

A knife => *Un couteau*

"***Une***" is used for feminine nouns. For example:

A cat (female) => *Une chatte*

A television => *Une télévision*

A fork => *Une fourchette*

"***Des***" is used for plural nouns. For example:

Some tomatoes => *Des tomates*

Some sausages => *Des saucisses*

To talk about multiple nouns you have to repeat the indefinite article before every noun. For example:

Un couteau et une fourchette. (A knife and a fork.)

The Definite Articles

A definite article is a determiner that is used to indicate a specific or certain noun or to refer to a noun that has already been mentioned or specified. "The" is the English definite article. In French, these are "***le***", "***la***", "***l'***", and "***les***".

"***Le***" is placed before a masculine singular noun that begins with a consonant. For example:

The cheese => *Le fromage*

The rooster => *Le coq*

The dictionary => *Le dictionnaire*

"**La**" is placed before a feminine singular noun that begins with a consonant. For example:

The lemonade => *La limonade*

The hen => *La poule*

The philosophy => *La philosophie*

"**L'**" is placed before a singular noun that begins with a vowel or with a silent "h". It is the contracted form of "le" and "la". For example:

The man => *L'homme*

The school => *L'école*

The hospital => *L'hôpital*

"**Les**" is placed before plural nouns. It does not have a contracted form. If it precedes a word that begins with a vowel sound or a silent "h", the "s" in "les" (which is usually silent), is pronounced with a /z/ sound. For example:

The men => *Les hommes*

The hens => *Les poules*

The hospitals => *Les hôpitaux*

To talk about multiple nouns you have to repeat the definite article before every noun. For example:

Acheter le livre bleu et les chaussures noires. (Buy the blue book and the black shoes.)

The Partitive Articles

A partitive article refers to only a part of the object and not the object as a whole. It is used whenever the exact amount of an item cannot be determined. In English, they are "any" and "some". Often, they can be omitted; you will still be understood if you choose to say either "He has water" or "He has some water".

However, these articles cannot be omitted in the French language. Every time you encounter a situation wherein "some" or "any" is needed in the sentence, you must use them.

For masculine singular nouns, "**du**" is used. For example:

I have (some) paper. => *J' ai du papier.*

For feminine singular nouns, "**de la**" is used. For example:

Do you have (any) lemonade? => *Avez-vous de la limonade?*

For singular nouns that begin with a vowel or a silent "**h**", "**de l'**" is used. For example:

She has (some) water? => *a-t-elle de l'eau?*

For plural nouns, "**des**" is used. For example:

There are children in the park. => *Il y a des enfants dans le parc.*

Exercise

1. State the correct article before each French noun:

_chanteur   _vin

_étudiant   _argent

_avenue   _chapeau

_prénom   _espoir

_boulevard   _fraise

_vocabulaire   _boisson

_maison   _prison

_vacances

2. Rewrite the following nouns in the feminine form:

Acteur   Mari

Chat   Chanteur

Neveu

3. Rewrite the following nouns in the masculine form:

Vraie   Bleue

Belle   Curieuse

Vieille

Chapter 9 - Nouns and Pronouns

The French call the noun "nom", which is also the same word for "name". After all, nouns are used to give names to people, animals, places, things, ideas, events, and so on.

French nouns, just like English nouns, are characterized as either common or proper, singular or plural, and count or mass.

Common and Proper Nouns

A common noun is a generic term for all the members of a class of words. Never put a capital letter at the beginning of a word. Example: a cat is "un chat".

A proper noun is a term that denotes a specific thing, and the first letter of the word is always capitalized. For example: Benedict and Jane is *"Benedict et Jane"*.

Singular and Plural Nouns

As you know, singular denotes "one" and plural denotes "more than one". To form the plural form of a single noun in French, just add a -s to the end of the word like in English. For example: *le chat* (the cat) becomes *les chats* (the cats). Take note that you can also use the indefinite article *"des"*, such as by saying *"des chats"*.

However, French singular nouns that end in **-s**, **-x**, and **-z** do not need to be changed to turn them into the plural form. Instead, the article before it is changed. For example: *le bras* (the arm) becomes *les bras* (the arms), *la croix* (the cross) becomes *les croix* (the crosses), and *le nez* (the nose) becomes *les nez* (the noses).

Generally, for French singular nouns that end in **-eu**, **-eau**, and **-ou**, an **-x** is attached to the end to turn them into plural form. For example: *le bateau* (the boat) becomes *les bateaux* (the boats), *le cheveu* (the hair) becomes *les cheveux* (the hairs). Keep in mind that there are exceptions, such as *le cou* (the neck), which becomes *les cous* (the necks).

French singular nouns that end in **-ail**, and **-al** can be pluralized by replacing them with **-aux**. For example: *l'animal* (the animal) becomes *les animaux* (the animals), and *un travail* (the job) becomes *des travaux* (the jobs). Again, there are exceptions, such as *un carnaval* (a carnival) to *des carnavals* (the carnivals), and *un chandail* (a sweater) to *des chandails* (the sweaters).

Plural Masculine Form for Adjectives

You do not have to change the masculine plural form of adjectives that have **-s** or **-x** at the end. For example: *un cheveu gris* (a gray hair) to *des cheveux gris* (the gray hairs).

However, for masculine plural forms of adjectives that have **-al** or **-eau** at the end, you will need to change them to **-aux** or **-eux**, respectively. For example: *le beau bateau* (the beautiful boat) to *les beaux bateaux* (the beautiful boats).

Subject Pronouns

A sentence should always have a subject that does something and a verb to show what that subject is doing. There are 3 types of subjects, namely the 1st person, 2nd person, and the 3rd person.

In English, the singular forms are "I", "You", and "He" or "She", respectively. In French, these are *"Je"*, *"Tu"* or *"Vous"* and *"Il"* or *"Elle"*.

The plural forms in English are "We", "You", and "They", while in French, these are *"Nous"* or *"On"*, *"Vous"*, and *"Ils"* or *"Elles"*.

- ***Je*** (I) becomes ***J'*** if it is followed by a vowel sound or a silent "h". For example: *J'habite à Paris.* (I live in Paris).

- You use *"**tu**"* (you) when you are talking to your friends, to children, or to close family members. For example: *Tu es Sarah?* (Are you Sarah?). *"**Vous**"* is used in a formal conversation. For example: *Voulez-vous (ceci)?* (Do you want (it)?)

- *"**Il**"* and *"**Elle**"* are French for "He" and "She" respectively. For example: *Il mange un gâteau et elle boit du thé.* (He is eating cake and she is drinking tea).

- *"**Nous**"* is the French pronoun for "we". For example: *Nous aimons ce vin.* (We like this wine). The more colloquial pronoun for "we" is *"**on**"*. For example: *On habite ici* (We live here).

- *"**Ils**"* and *"**Elles**"* are used for plural masculine and feminine subjects, respectively. For example: *Ils sont amoureux d'elle* (They (the men) are in love with her). *Elles aiment regarder des films romantiques* (They (the women) love to watch romantic movies).

- In situations wherein all of the members of a group are not female (such as a group having two men and three women), or if you do not know the sex of the members of the group, then *"**ils**"* is used.

- Familiarize yourself with the inflection of verbs (called "Conjugation") depending on the subject.

Infinitive (or base form): *habiter* (to live in)

Subject Pronouns and Conjugation:

J' => *habite*

Tu => *habites*

Il, Elle => *habite*

Nous => *habitons*

Vous => *habitez*

Ils, Elles => *habitent*

Exercise

1. Turn these singular nouns into plural, including the proper article before each.

- *Tante (f)*
- *Vélo (m)*
- *Chambre (f)*
- *Tatou (m)*
- *Livre (m)*
- *Voiture (f)*
- *Bijou (m)*
- *Boisson (f)*
- *Enfant (m)*
- *Chaise (f)*
- *Cheval (m)*
- *Soeur (f)*
- *L'arbre (m)*
- *Pou (m)*

2. Translate these English sentences into French, following the proper subject pronouns. You may use a dictionary to help guide you in verb conjugations:

- I live in the United States.

- I am American.

- He eats at that restaurant.

- She does not like the food.

- They are singing a Christmas song.

- (While talking to your cousin): You are beautiful!

- (While talking to a stranger): You are good at drawing.

Chapter 10 - Adjectives, Adverbs, Conjunctions, and Prepositions

Before we get to the conversational pillars of French, we need to talk about some major parts of speech.

Adjectives

Adjectives are a huge part of speaking any language. They allow you to describe nouns and objects. French adjectives are relatively easy for the most part. However, their only tricky asset is that the vast majority of them have to match their respective objects which they describe in terms of plurality and gender. This can make for quite a mess when you're newer to French.

Take, for example, the French adjective *joli*, meaning "pretty" or "cute". If I wanted to say "He is pretty", I would say "*Il est joli*". However, if I wanted to say "she is pretty", I would instead say "*Elle est jolie*". Notice the addition of the *e* to make it feminine.

Depending upon what exactly the adjective is, there are different ways to make one feminine. For example, the vast majority of adjectives can be made feminine simply by the addition of an -*e* to the end of it.

A key difference between English and French adjectives is that French adjectives nearly always go after the noun in question, which can really trip you up at first. After a while, it starts to make sense in its own way - after all, it's just another manner of communication. However, avoid falling into the trap of accidentally using an adjective incorrectly because you don't know any better.

Some adjectives do go before the noun though. It can be hard to remember which ones exactly, but just think of the following acronym: beauty, age, goodness, size. Adjectives which have to do with those typically can go before the adjective rather than after.

Additionally, you very much need to be wary of the meanings of your adjectives. Certain adjectives can go before and after a noun. However, this can create two diametrically different meanings depending upon the placement. Take, for example, curieux.

If you place *curieux* before the noun, it means weird or strange. However, if you place it after the *noun*, it means curious or inquisitive. In other words, the correct adjective placement can be the difference between giving praise to your kid and calling them a total weirdo. Be more careful than to call your kid a total weirdo, my friend.

Adverbs

Adverbs describe verbs and adjectives. Adverbs are incredibly easy to form. You may notice a parallel between French adverbs and Spanish adverbs if you've spent any time study Spanish, by chance: you form adverbs by taking the adjective you'd like to make into an adverb, putting it into its feminine form, and appending *ment* to it, similar to how you form adverbs in Spanish.

Take, for example, the adjective *lent*, meaning slow. Now, let's put it in its feminine form, which gives us *lente*. Then, we just add *ment*, the French equivalent of the English "-ly", and we've got lentement meaning slowly. In a sentence:

"*Pouvez-vous parler lentement? Je ne parle pas bien français.*" ("Would you speak slowly? I don't speak

French well.")

Overall, the process of creating adverbs in French is super easy.

Conjunctions

Conjunctions are an integral part of any language. I say this because we haven't talked about them at all, yet there's not really a part of language which is dedicated to providing logical order to sentences so much as the conjunctions are.

There are quite a few conjunctions in the French language. More than quite a few, actually. There are a ton of them. Let's start with the coordinating conjunctions. What coordinating conjunctions are are conjunctions that serve to connect two different clauses without placing some sort of emphasis on one or the other. In French, there are actually seven different coordinating conjunctions.

Mais - but

Et - and

Ou - or

Or – yet/however

Ni - neither, nor (used in pairs)

Car - because

Donc - thus, so

These all have their own particular uses, and you can likely figure out approximately how to use them based off of their English translations. Indeed, basing their usage off of their English translations is a relatively safe way to use these powerful parts of speech.

Next, there are subordinating conjunctions. These are a bit more complicated to use, so if something a little weird, I'll put an example by it in parentheses.

Comme - like, as (*Il est courageux comme le lion* - he is courageous like the lion)

Quand - when

Lorsque - when

Que - that (*Je sais bien que tu as raison* - I know for certain that you're right.)

Si - if

And then there are just some general ones that you need to know:

Avant que - before the event of (*Je suis parti avant qu'elle soit arrivée.* - I left before she arrived.)

Autant que – as much/ as many as

Bien que - although

Tel(le)(s) que - such that

This is just scratching the surface, really. There are absurd amounts of French conjunctions out there. But with the knowledge that I've given you thus far, you should be able to make your way around moderately well.

Prepositions

We've already learned a couple of prepositions in French, such as *à* (meaning to, at, or in) and **de** (meaning of or from). However, there are even more that we haven't talked about! A lot of these things which have relatively direct English translations, but others are ones which will take a bit more explanation. Let's dive in.

à cause de – because of (negative)

à travers - through

après - after

au lieu de - instead of something

avant - before

avec - with

chez - *chez* is a tricky one. It can mean "at the location of x person's house", where *chez moi* means "at my home"or "to my home"; it can also mean "at a company's name" as in *"J'ai mangé chez McDonald's"*; lastly, it can simply mean "for" - *"Quel marche chez toi?"* meaning "What worked for you?"

contre - against something

dans - in (used if followed by article)

depuis - since, for (in reference to a length of time)

dès – from/ as soon as

en - in (used if not followed by article)

entre - between

environ - approximately

grâce à - thanks to (positive)

jusqu'à - up to, until

par - by, alongside, through

pendant - during, for (in reference to a length of time)

pour - for

sous - under

sur - on

vers - towards something,

Those are a ton of prepositions to hopefully get you started. You need to be using a lot of this to the extent that you can. Be writing to yourself in private journals and things of the like; try your hand at reading online news and forums. Work with what you've learned.

Chapter 11 - The Present Tense in French

Verb overview

Being able to master different tenses in French is a critical skill as it will enable you to share your experience, talk about what you are currently doing, or future projects and life experiences that interest you. As much as English conjugations are extremely simple from a French-speaker perspective—for instance, the present tense only requires adding an "s" to the third person, e.g., "he buys" or, worst of all, an 'e' and 's' as in "he fishes"— French has a special ending for all pronouns, and, one of its major features, exceptions to many rules.

In this section, you are provided with the most essential guidelines to know how verbs are conjugated in the present tense (our *présent*/préza̧/). Rather than putting the emphasis on learning each one by heart, there are examples in context, indications on when to use the present, and the most common exceptions that you will need to know and recognize when speaking French.

The most important piece of information to keep in mind is the following: barring exceptions—after all, why would there be a French rule without exceptions? There are three major categories of verbs in French. If you ever need to find one of these verbs quickly, a concise mini-dictionary has been compiled at the end of this book for you to brush up your knowledge of French when you need it the most!

- 1er groupe: verbs ending in -er:

- *manger* (to eat),
- *parler* (to speak/talk),
- *arriver* (to arrive),
- *acheter* (to buy),
- *penser* (to think)
- *travailler* (to work)
- *visiter* (to visit)
- *chercher* (to look for, to search)
- *donner* (to give)
- *ressembler* (to look like)

Major exceptions: *aller* (to go), belonging to the third group—which is detailed in all following sections given how important it is in French to be able to use it correctly.

- 2ème groupe: verbs ending in -ir, except a couple that belongs to the third category:

- *finir* (to finish),
- *choisir* (to choose)

- 3ème groupe: verbs with all other endings + some ending in -ir:

- *dormir* (to sleep)
- *venir* (to come)
- *sentir* (to feel; to smell)
- *courir* (to run)
- *voir* (to see)
- *devoir* (to have to; must)
- *savoir* (to know)
- *vouloir* (to want)
- *pouvoir* (to be able to; can)
- *falloir* (to have to, used in impersonal sentences)
- *apprendre* (to learn)
- *prendre* (to take, grasp)
- *attendre* (to wait)
- *vendre* (to sell)
- *faire* (to do, make)
- *boire* (to drink)
- *lire* (to read)
- *dire* (to say)
- *rire* (to laugh), etc.

Auxiliaries:

- *être* – to be
- *avoir* – to have

For now, get used to knowing how French verbs are classified according to their endings:

- the first group deals with -er verbs, except for aller—which encompasses the notion of an 'irregular verb';
- the second group deals exclusively with verbs ending in -ir, but not all of them; and
- the third group deals with some of these -ir verbs and all of the others presenting different endings (*savoir or vendre*, for instance).

You may want to start listing them on a separate piece of paper to note down their conjugation patterns—that way, you will be prepared for anything on your language learning journey!

The two auxiliaries used in French, *être* and *avoir*, are both very irregular—you will have to learn their conjugation separately but will acquire them much more swiftly given how often you will encounter them in French!

Present Tense

Its conjugation and uses

The French *présent* will help you describe the actions you are doing every day, actions you are currently doing, or facts about yourself. It is its major difference with English that clearly separates 'I do' from 'I'm doing', whereas French tends to chunk them into a single tense, the present tense.

Here are some example sentences to get you acquainted with some of its uses in context as well as the ways it is conjugated:

When I go to the supermarket, I always buy a bottle of water – *Quand je vais (aller) au supermarché, j'achète (acheter) toujours une bouteille d'eau.*

I know what you are thinking about – *Je sais (savoir) ce que tu penses (penser).*

We finish writing this report – *Nous finissons (finir) d'écrire ce rapport.*

I'm eating salad today – *Je mange (manger) de la salade aujourd'hui.*

I'm 22 – *J'ai (avoir) 22 ans.* (When saying your age, 'avoir' is compulsory in French)

You will probably have noticed that English tends to use either the simple present or progressive present to talk about different categories of events; in French, whether you are saying "I'm reading a very good book" or "I run every other morning", the simple present or the *présent simple* is used: *Je lis (lire) un très bon livre/ Je cours (courir) le matin tous les deux jours.*

In Section 3, there is more detail into the quintessential past tense in French: the *passé composé*, which serves to translate the preterite in oral speech. For now, there is one crucial detail you will find useful: when introducing an action that you have been doing for quite some time, and that is still going on in the present, French uses the simple present tense instead of past tense:

I have been working in England for four years now – *Cela fait maintenant quatre ans que je travaille en Angleterre.* As detailed later, the verb *travailler* is here conjugated at the first-person singular in the present, with no apparent trace of any past conjugation.

Those examples covered the present tense conjugations for verbs belonging to all three groups; you will first begin with the group composed of -*er* verbs:

1st group:

MANGER/ ACHETER – the first thing to do is take the -*r* ending off:

Je mange/ J'achète (the accent is only here for pronunciation purposes for *acheter* and isn't seen on any other French verb)

Tu manges/ Tu achètes (the second-person singular always requires an 's' for virtually every tense)

Il mange/ Il achète (for first group verbs, the first- and third-person singular are the same)

Nous mangeons/ Nous achetons (+ ons with nous; here, manger keeps its 'e' because of pronunciation; otherwise, it is deleted)

Vous mangez/ achetez (a 'ez' is added with vous in most tenses, but for obvious reasons, it is not doubled in verbs where an 'e' is already present, such as these)

Ils mangent/ Ils achètent ('ent' is added to the ending, with the second 'e' being naturally not present)

As a rule, for first group verbs, note down:

- take off the -r, and add to the 'e': ø (nothing), +s, ø (nothing), (e)ons, +(e)z, +(e)nt

For second group verbs ending in -ir, such as *finir* (to finish, end), or *choisir* (to choose):

2nd group:

FINIR/ CHOISIR – as with the first group, delete the -r immediately

Je finis/ Je choisis (here, add a compulsory 's' to the first-person singular)

Tu finis/ Tu choisis (the second-person singular always requires an 's' for every tense)

Il finit/ Il choisit (for second group verbs, add a 't' for the third-person singular)

Nous finissons/ Nous choisissons (add 'ssons' to the ending of the verb)

Vous finissez/ Vous choisissez (keeping the 'ss' from above, add 'ez' which is the hallmark of the *vous* person in French)

Ils finissent/ Ils choisissent (keeping the 'ss) from above, add 'ent' which is the hallmark of the *ils* person in French)

As a rule, for second group verbs, note down:

- take off the -r, and add to the 'i': +s, +s, +t, +ssons, +ssez, +ssent

You will now delineate the most important verbs in the third group category. Please note that owing to the many endings of these verbs and the presence in that category of many irregular verbs, it will be the hardest part of your learning. For now, it may be more prudent to get an overall grasp of 3rd-group verb conjugations before attempting to learn each by heart.

3rd group:

VENDRE/ ATTENDRE – first of all, take off the -re ending from these verbs:

Je vends/ J'attends – add an 's' to the first-person singular

Tu vends/ Tu attends – regular 's' which characterizes the second-person singular

Il vend/ Il attend – here, it would be superfluous to add 't' since there already is a 'd' at the end

Nous vendons/ Nous attendons – add 'ons' to the 'end' ending, similarly to how nous works for most verbs in most tenses

Vous vendez/ Vous attendez – add 'ez' to the 'end' ending, similarly to how vous works for most verbs in most tenses

Ils vendent/ Ils attendent – add '(e)nt' to the 'end' ending, as you would do with ils with verbs from other groups

- Exception for *PRENDRE: nous prenons, vous prenez, ils prennent;* the rest is regular *(je prends, tu prends, il prend)*
- Overview: -re, then: +s, +s, ø (nothing), +ons, +ez, +ent

FAIRE/ LIRE/ DIRE – delete off the -re ending:

Je fais/ Je lis/ Je dis

Tu fais/ Tu lis/ Tu dis

Il fait/ Il lit/ Il dit

Nous faisons/ Nous lisons/ Nous disons – because it would be confusing to add 'ons' to the -i radical already present, they are linked together with an extra 's'

Vous faites*/ Vous lisez/ Vous dites* – here, only *lire* follows the normal rule, while the other two do not

Ils font*/ Ils lisent/ Ils disent – the last two verbs, *lisent* and *disent*, are given the traditional 'ent' ending that goes with ils in the French present tense.

- Exception for *RIRE*: *nous rions* (no linking 's'), *vous riez, ils rient*
- Overview: -re, then: +s, +s, +t, +(s)ons, +(s)ez, +(s)ent

VOIR/ SAVOIR/ VOULOIR

Je vois/ Je sais/ Je veux – These three verbs are all irregular in their own ways, so you will, unfortunately, have to learn them by heart

Tu vois/ Tu sais/ Tu veux – same as their first person

Il voit/ Il sait/ Il veut – both 's' and 'x' get replaced with the usual ending for *il* in the present, which is 't'

Nous voyons*/ Nous savons*/ Nous voulons* – again, the radicals get irregular while their endings do not.

Vous voyez*/ Vous savez*/ Vous voulez* – the same phenomenon occurs

Ils voient/ Ils savent/ Ils veulent* – the 'ent' ending gets attached to the radical

- Note: *vouloir*, which here has a 'x' as a first-person and second-person ending, has the same conjugation pattern as *pouvoir: je peux, tu peux, il peut, nous pouvons, vous pouvez, ils peuvent.*
- Overview: each has their own radical, which then gets added: +s/x, +s/x, +t, +(consonant)ons, +(consonant)ez, +(consonant)ent

ALLER, the only -*er* verb which doesn't belong to the first group:

Je vais

Tu vas

Il va

Nous allons

Vous allez

Ils vont

- Overview: aller is indeed the perfect example of an irregular verb in French!

You can do it! The two French auxiliaries, *être* and *avoir*, will only be covered before some short example sentences that describe why the verbs are given certain endings:

ÊTRE, to be – irregular, no matter the tense

Je suis

Tu es

Il est

Nous sommes

Vous êtes

Ils sont

AVOIR, to have – irregular, no matter the tense

J'ai

Tu as

Il a

Nous avons

Vous avez

Ils ont

While French conjugations are rife with exceptions, you normally will have started identifying some common patterns to help you understand written French. For instance:

- Even you may not know the conjugated verb réussissons (from *réussir,* to make it, to manage), you can already identify the person, which would be *nous,* or we. If you look at it more closely, you will also realize that two 's's were added at that person between the radical and the ending—which group do you think it might belong to then?

- Similarly, *chantez* (from *chanter,* to sing) has to go with the plural vous. Is it from the third group? Why?

- One verb that is yet to be seen in detail is *venir,* which in this case belongs to the third group—which person could *vient* belong to? What about *viens*?

Special case: to be doing something – *être en train de faire quelque chose*

Être en train de + infinitive verb is a very convenient French expression that is the equivalent of English 'to be doing something'. Now, you have just seen that the French *présent simple* or simple present can usually retranscribe the meaning alright, but the precision that someone is in the middle of doing something while another action happens can always come in handy:

I was doing my French exercises while he stormed into the room – *J'étais en train de faire mes exercices de français quand il est rentré en trombe dans la pièce.*

Why are you always waving at the sky? (Granted, you may not use this one that much, but it serves this purpose well) – *Pourquoi es-tu toujours en train de faire signe au ciel?*

He couldn't hear you; he was loading the dishwasher into the car – *Il ne pouvait pas t'entendre, il était en train de mettre le lave-vaisselle dans la voiture.*

- to storm into... – *rentrer en trombe* (idiomatic expression)

- room – *pièce* (f), *salle* (f)

- to wave – *faire signe*

- sky – *ciel* (m)

- hear you – *t'entendre,* with 't" being the pronoun for you (don't worry, this phenomenon will be explained in detail later in the book!)

- car – *voiture* (f)
- dishwasher – *lave-vaisselle (m)*, or literally 'cleans-dishes'

Bonus: washing machine – *lave-linge* (m) or *machine à laver* (f), literall 'washes-clothes' and 'machine, appliance to wash'

Emotions and sensations: using *être* and *avoir*

Being able to describe what you are feeling is also a very important part of your journey and will enhance your ability to communicate with people and get to exchange thoughts with them.

An interesting phenomenon takes place in French: for all sensations that have to do with the body, with which English would use "to be" (to be hungry, thirsty, tired, afraid), it is *avoir* which is used in French; don't hesitate to note these down as you see them, as you will certainly use them very often:

- To be hungry – *avoir faim* ("have hunger") – *J'ai faim, J'ai eu faim* (present and passé composé conjugation; you will get to the latter in a following section with detail as to how it is formed)
- To be thirsty – *avoir soif* ("have thirst") – *J'ai soif, J'ai eu soif*
- To be tired – *avoir sommeil* ("have sleep")/*être fatigué* – *J'ai/ ai eu sommeil*
- To be afraid – *avoir peur* ("have fear") – *J'ai peur/ J'ai eu peur*
- To be right – *avoir raison* ("have reason") – *J'ai raison/ J'ai eu raison*

For different adjectives that refer to thoughts or beliefs, *être* is either used similarly to English or in French has verbs that too correspond to their English counterparts:

To be certain, sure – *être certain(e), sûr(e)*

To believe – *croire, penser* (respectively 3rd group and 1st-group)

To think – *penser* (1st-group verb)

To suppose – *supposer* (1st-group verb)

To understand – *comprendre* (3rd-group verb)

To know – *savoir, connaître* (3rd-group verbs)

To decide – *décider* (1st-group verb)

Exercise:

For each of the following sentences, conjugate the verb in parentheses in the present tense, according to its associated pronoun. Corrections will be given after the learning objective as well as some facts about the language, which will help you enhance your knowledge in French:

- *Je ne… (comprendre) pas ce qu'il a voulu dire.*
- I don't understand what he meant.
- *Il… (penser) qu'il faut plutôt que nous restions ici.*
- He thinks we better stay here.
- *Nous… (croire; same pattern as for 'voir') ce que tu nous dis.*

45

- We believe what you tell us.
- *... (Supposer)-vous qu'il rentrera tard ce soir?*
- Do you suppose he'll come back late tonight?
- *Je... (savoir) ce que j'ai vu.*
- I know what I saw.

Learning objectives:

- Be able to use French to talk about what you are currently doing or like to do regularly
- Be able to categorize most verbs in their respective groups
- Know common verbs to express what you like doing or what you feel to the person/s you're talking with
- Know some common patterns in the present tense—which person always gets an 's' or an '(e)nt' ending, for example
- Be able to conjugate the two auxiliaries of French, *être* and *avoir*, which will come in handy when the *passé compose* is covered—one of the most important tenses in French

Exercise: Correction
- *Je ne comprends pas ce qu'il a voulu dire.*

Being a 3ʳᵈ-group verb, *comprendre* requires an 's' when used in conjunction with *je*. A common mistake would be not to add it and conjugate it as a 1ˢᵗ-group verb.

- *Il pense qu'il faut plutôt que nous restions ici.*

1ˢᵗ-group verbs do not require any additional ending at both the first and third persons in the present.

- *Nous croyons ce que tu nous dis.*

Being an irregular verb like most 3ʳᵈ-group verbs, *croire* follows the same conjugation patterns as *voir (je crois/vois, tu crois/vois, il croit, nous croyons, vous croyez, ils croient)*.

- *Supposez-vous qu'il rentrera tard ce soir?*

Vous in the present tense is always associated with the *-ez* ending.

- *Je sais ce que j'ai vu.*

Savois would undoubtedly sound hilarious—but like many other 3ʳᵈ-group verbs, *savoir* undergoes transformations for the first three persons and conjugates itself as follows: *je sais, tu sais, il sait, nous savons, vous savez, ils savent*.

- to mean – *vouloir dire*: *vouloir dire* is an extremely common idiomatic expression, and both words cannot be separated from each other. It literally means 'want to say'.
- we better stay here – *il faut plutôt...*: *falloir* in passing has already been mentioned as an important 3rd-group verb that is only used in impersonal constructions. It translates as 'It is necessary that' + subjunctive, which mood is covered in Section 5. It also can be a substitute for 'must', as in: We must hurry up now – *Il faut que nous nous dépêchions maintenant.*

- in passing – *en passant*
- rather, as in – *plutôt* 'I rather prefer staying at home' – *Je préfère plutôt rester à la maison.*
- at home, home – *à la maison*; idiomatic expression
- *tard* – late
- to come back – *revenir, rentrer* (*rentrer* is only used when someone/something is coming back inside of a place, e.g., back home, back to the building, etc... *Revenir* is more general and can be used in all contexts.)
- tonight – *ce soir*
- *j'ai vu* – verb *voir*, 'to see', conjugated in the *passé compose*

Chapter 12 - Past and Future Tenses

French is a rather easy language to learn, but the hardest thing about it when you're coming from an English-speaking background is most certainly its numerous convoluted verb tenses.

There are at least four basic French past tenses, and just as many basic French future tenses. Only knowing two past tenses and two future tenses in French is sufficient for basic communication.

Let's take these one at a time.

Passé composé

Passé composé, which literally translates to "*compound past*," is the more prevalent form of the French past tense. It's utilized to talk about something that has already happened, either right now or in the past. It's a straightforward tense to construct.

The auxiliary verb and the "past participle" are the 2 elements to form the passé composé. While *avoir* is the more common auxiliary verb, *être* is acceptable in some contexts. The past participle is the verb's past tense. The past perfect tense is formed by combining the past participle with an auxiliary verb; if "I'm eating" is the present continuous, then "I have eaten" is the past perfect tense. French is similarly working.

In that case, how do you create the past participle? It's very easy.

When using a verb ending in **-ir**, the **-ir** is substituted for the **-i**. For instance, *finir* become *fini*

Verbs ending in **-er** are changed by adding a **-é** after removing **-er**. As a result, *mangé* would replace *manger*.

The ending **-re** is dropped and the ending **-u** is added to verbs ending in **-re**. Thus, *vendu* instead of *vendre*.

To form the *passé composé*, all you do is conjugate the auxiliary verb to the person speaking (normally *avoir*), and then get the past participle. So "I have eaten" in French would become "*J'ai mangé*". "He has sold the strawberries" would be "*Il a vendu les fraises*".

Simple enough, right? Now the question becomes "when do we use être as opposed to *avoir*?"

Well, there's actually a system for this: just remember DR. and MRS. VANDERTRAMP. Seriously. That's the mnemonic.

When you're using intransitive verbs which indicate either motion (going somewhere) or a change of state (changing in some essential way), you use *être* as your auxiliary verb.

The following are the verbs which will use être:

Devenir translated into English: to become something

Rentrer translated into English: to enter something again

Monter translated into English: to go up something (e.g., the bus)

Rester translated into English: to stay

Sortir translated into English: to leave, exit, or go out

Venir translated into English: to come

Aller translated into English: to go somewhere

Naître translated into English: to be born to somebody

Descendre translated into English: to go down something or descend

Entrer translated into English: to enter into something

Retourner translated into English: to return to something

Tomber translated into English: to fall down or trip

Revenir translated into English: to return to something or to come back

Arriver translated into English: to arrive to/at something

Mourir translated into English: to die

Partir translated into English: to leave somewhere

An important thing to note about using être as an auxiliary verb is that you must adjust the *passé composé* to match the gender and person. So "he left" would be "*il est venu*", but "she left" would be "*elle est venue*", and "they left" would be "*ils sont venus*".

When using avoir as the auxiliary verb, however, this is not the case. With avoir, it is not necessary for the subject and the participle to be the same. If a direct object pronoun is used before the verb, then the past participle of avoir must also agree with the pronoun. (Stay tuned for further details).

Imparfait

Here, then, is an explanation of the most prevalent French past tense. But there's another incredibly important one that we have yet to cover at all. This tense is known as the *imparfait*. The *imparfait*, or "imperfect", doesn't refer at all to a completed event. Rather, it refers to a given ongoing event or state in the past ("I was happy", "I was young") or a repeated event ("I used to watch..."). This concept doesn't have a direct correlative in English, but the English tense "past continuous" or "past progressive" can certainly get across the same exact point.

The imperfect is simple to form.

For **-er** verbs, you just drop the ending and add -ais, -ais, -ait, -ions, -iez, or -aient.

For **-re** verbs is more complicated, they can slightly change. Exmples: *prendre = je prenais..., croire = je croyais..., dire = je disais*

For **-ir** verbs of the third group behave like -er verbs, you just replace -ir with -ais, -ais, -ait, -ions, -iez, or -aient (dormir = je dormais..., mourir = je mourais..., venir = je venais).

The similar procedure is used for the 2° group of **-ir** verbs, but you add an "*iss*' ' before it. Example: *finir = je finissais, grandir = je grandissais.*

For instance, if you were planning on saying "When I was young, I would play often.", you would say "*Quand j'étais jeune, je jouais souvent.*"

The imperfect is notoriously difficult to master, but it will come in handy quite often for you, so it's worth teaching anyway.

These are the main cases in which you'd want to use the imperfect over the passé composé:

- Actions or states which occurred often and not just once

- Descriptions of either emotional or physical states: personal feelings, one's age, the given time and weather.

- Any states or actions where the duration is ongoing but unknown.

- Used alongside the passé composé in order to give more depth or information.

- Polite suggestion and wishes - *"Pourrais-tu m'aider?"*: "Could you help me?" (literally "Would you have the ability to give me help?")

- As part of a conditional clause.

Futur Proche

Futur proche literally means "close future" and refers to events which will most certainly happen, and soon. The futur proche is insanely easy to create. All that you do is combine *aller* (to go) conjugated to the person alongside the infinitive of the verb to be carried out in the near future.

Je vais faire les magasins.

"I'm going to go shopping."

Ils vont jouer au basket.

"They're going to go play basketball."

You can combine this, of course, with dates or times to explicitly state when an action is going to be undertaken.

Vas-tu aller à la librairie demain?

"Are you going to the bookstore tomorrow?"

This is, of course, a very simple tense, but you'll find it incredibly useful. When you're out and about and scratching surface-type conversations with native French speakers, it's unlikely that as a tourist or newcomer, you're going to need to tell them your grand far-future life goals. However, if you need to, that's what the next tense is for.

Futur Simple

The *simple future* tense is, well, simple. It's a very no-nonsense tense that is a little more complicated than the previous tense, and it can be quite easy to sound like you have no idea what you're talking about. However, it's worth learning anyway, because it's a rather common tense.

The futur simple implies something that will happen at some point in the future. The way that you form it is by taking the *entire infinitive* of a verb as the stem, and then adding *-ai, -as, -a, -ons, -ez, or -ont* depending upon who is talking. If the verb ends in **-re**, then and only then do you remove something from the verb, taking off the final -e before adding your ending.

Note that some verbs are irregular, such as *être* and *avoir*. These have the future stems of *ser-* and *aur-*, respectively.

So let's try this with the verb chanter, meaning "to sing". Here's how we'd do it:

Chanter - to sing, futur simple

Conjugation	Meaning	Pronunciation
Je chanterai	I will sing	Jeuh shahn-teh-reh
Tu chanteras	You will sing	Tuh shahn-teh-rah
Il/elle/on chantera	He/she/it/one will sing	Il/el/ohn shahn-teh-rah
Nous chanterons	We will sing	Noo shahn-teh-rohn
Vous chanterez	You all/you (p.) will sing	Voo shahn-teh-rey
Ils/elles chanteront	They will sing	Il/el shahn-teh-rohn

Simple enough, right? The futur simple isn't a terribly difficult tense to use in and of itself, and it's rather easy to set up.

Chapter 13 - The Imperative and Subjunctive Mood and Passive Voice

The Imperative Mood

The imperative mood is one of the easiest moods to navigate for foreign learners given its similar endings across all group verbs and the fact that most of it is the same as present tense conjugations—not to mention the few persons that can be conjugated in the imperative!

- *Prends ton manteau* – Take your coat

- *Allez donc voir à la réception si personne n'a trouvé vos clés* – Go see at the reception if somebody found your keys

- *Sois plus courageux* – Be braver

1st-group verbs: *MANGER – (tu) Mange! (nous) Mangeons! (vous) Mangez!*

- Important note: indeed, do not add an 's' in the imperative mood for tu.

2nd-group verbs: *FINIR – Finis! Finissons! Finissez!*

3rd-group verbs:

- verbs with present tense forms: *DORMIR/ COURIR/ SENTIR/ VOIR/ CROIRE/ VENIR/ FAIRE/ DIRE/ LIRE/ PRENDRE* and its derivatives (*apprendre, surprendre, reprendre, méprendre,* etc...)

(Dors, dormons, dormez; vois, voyons, voyez...)

- common auxiliaries (*pouvoir, vouloir, devoir*) are generally never conjugated in the imperative

- *falloir*, being a strictly impersonal verb, cannot be conjugated in the imperative

- verbs and auxiliaries with different forms: *SAVOIR* (sache, sachons, sachez); *ÊTRE* (sois/swa/, soyons/swayõ/, soyez/swayé/); *AVOIR* (aie/è/, ayons/éyõ/, ayez/éyé/); *ALLER* (va, allons, allez)

What about you train yourself to use some imperative forms before moving on to the next major conjugation in French, the subjunctive mood:

- ...(croire) ce que tu veux, ce n'est pas moi qui ai pris ton ordinateur.

- Believe what you think, I wasn't the one who took your computer.

- *Tu dois prendre des forces: ... (manger) plus de soupe!*

- You've got to gain strength: eat more soup!

- *... (être) plus forts contre l'adversité!*

- Let us be stronger against adversity!

- Answers: *Crois/ Mange* (with the 's', remember?)/ *Soyons*

The Subjunctive Mood

While you will surely not have to use the subjunctive mood when speaking French, it is used in a couple of contexts, which you should at least be aware of—its construction may especially be confusing if you have never been exposed to it, so this section will at least give you more tools to understand French more closely.

The most important thing to remember is that verbs in the subjunctive are always preceded by *que*, which is why it is included in the conjugation tables for you to remember this particularity of French.

- after verbs expressing doubt, desire, possibility:

You will most likely encounter the subjunctive, and have to use it, after those particular:

- *aimer que*, conditional – *J'aimerais que nous puissions aller au cinéma tous ensemble* – I would like all of us to be able to go to the cinema together.

- *souhaiter que*, conditional – *Il souhaiterait que nous en terminions avec cette affaire le plus rapidement possible* - He'd prefer that we get that matter wrapped up as fast as possible.

- *préférer que*, conditional – *Je préférerais que tu ne touches à rien; je n'ai pas encore fait estimer ces vases* – I'd rather you didn't touch anything; I haven't yet had these vases estimated.

- *espérer que*, only in the past – *Ils espéraient que leur patron leur donne une augmentation, mais en vain* – They were hoping that their boss would give them a raise, but to no avail.

- *douter que*, indicative – *Nous doutons qu'il puisse venir* – We doubt he may come/ We doubt he is able to come.

- after impersonal constructions

Impersonal constructions suggesting obligation or necessary conditions are commonly followed by the subjunctive or the infinitive depending on how it is worded; please pay close attention to the following examples:

Il faut que (subj) – *Il faut que tu sois en forme pour ton entretien d'embauche demain (être)* – You have to be in top form for your job interview tomorrow.

Il faut (infinitive) – *Il faut prendre des précautions contre la grippe en hiver (prendre)* – One must take precautions against the flu in winter.

Il est préférable que (subj) – *Il est préférable qu'il prenne quelques jours de vacances* – It would be better if he took some time off.

Il est préférable de (infinitive) – *Il est préférable de poser des questions si l'on n'a pas compris quelque chose* - It's better to ask quetions if you haven't understood something.

As these examples highlight, those impersonal constructions can be used in two ways: the infinitive form in French is rather general and will englobe everyone or a group of people, while the subjunctive form is conjugated according to a particular subject (ex: *que tu sois en forme pour ton entretien d'embauche*). First is an overview of these constructions before diving into how to conjugate verbs in the subjunctive:

- *Il faut que/ Il faut* (obligation, similar to 'must')

- *Il est préférable que/ Il est préférable de* ('it is preferrable to', literally)

53

- *Il est nécessaire que/ Il est nécessaire de* (obligation; il faut is preferred and more common)

- *Il est (très/ peu) probable que* ('it is (very/ hardly) likely that'; exclusively used with que and a subjunctive)

Conjugations

1st-group verbs will be the easiest ones to learn by far since only the *nous* and *vous* persons see their endings change compared to the simple present:

MANGER/ CHANTER – take off the **-r**:

Que je mange – que je chante

Que tu manges – que tu chantes – s being often the hallmark of the tu person

Qu'il mange – qu'il chante

Que nous mangions – que nous chantions – + ions

Que vous mangiez – que vous chantiez

Qu'ils mangent – qu'ils chantent

ALLER – pay close attention to the additional '**i**' in the radical, which will move a bit:

Que j'aille/jay/ – que tu ailles/tu ay/ – qu'il aille/il ay/ – que nous allions/nouz-alyõ/ – que vous alliez/vouz-alyé/ – qu'ils aillent/ilz-ay/

The 2nd-group verbs have the same endings as the two verbs above, with one exception: the *ss* radical that you have already encountered with them (*vous finissiez*), will be here used for all persons:

FINIR – CHOISIR

Que je finisse – que je choisisse

Que tu finisses – que tu finisses

Qu'il finisse – qu'il choisisse

Que nous finissions – que nous choisissions

Que vous finissiez – que vous choisissiez

Qu'ils finissent – qu'ils choisisses

3rd-group verbs, preceded by their reputation, will probably prove the most arduous for you. The subjunctive conjugation will now be detailed for you to see how each works.

You may want to note down how most of the following verbs possess a radical for the *je, tu, il* and *ils* persons, while using another one for the *nous* and *vous* persons:

- *dormir, courir, sentir* – take off the -ir ending and add the endings you have seen so far: *que je dorme/ coure/ sente, que tu dormes,qu' il dorme, que nous dormions, que vous dormiez, qu' ils dorment*

- *voir* – take off the -*r* here and conjugate as above, but remember to add the '*i*' for *nous* and *vous*, which single out these persons from the present of this verb: *que je voie, que tu voies, qu' il voie, que nous voyions, que vous voyiez, qu' ils voient*

- *apprendre, prendre, surprendre* – radical turns into prenn(e) and pren-: *que je prenne, que tu prennes, qu'il prenne, que nous prenions, que vous preniez, qu'ils prennent*

- *vendre* – radical turns into vend(e) – *que je vende, que tu vendes, qu' il vende, que nous vendions, que vous vendiez, qu' ils vendent*

- *venir* – irregular radicals (vienne/ ven-): *que je vienne, que tu viennes, qu'il vienne, que nous venions, que vous veniez, qu'ils viennent*

- *devoir* – irregular radicals (doive/ dev-): *que je doive, que tu doives, qu'il doive, que nous devions, que vous deviez, qu'ils doivent*

- *savoir* – savoir turns into sach(e): *que je sache, que tu saches, qu'il sache, que nous sachions, que vous sachiez, qu'ils sachent*

- *vouloir* – irregular radicals (veuille/ voul-): *que je veuille, que tu veuilles, qu'il veuille, que nous voulions, que vous vouliez, qu'ils veuillent*

- *pouvoir* – pouvoir turns into puiss(e): *que je puisse, que tu puisses, qu'il puisse, que nous puissions, que vous puissiez, qu'ils puissent*

- *faire* – turns into fass(e) – *que je fasse, que tu fasses, qu' il fasse, que nous fassions, que vous fassiez, qu' ils fassent*

- *dire, lire* – the 'r' turns into an 's' – *que je dise/ lise, que tu dises, qu' il dise, que nous disions, que vous disiez, qu' ils disent*

Être – *que je sois, que tu sois, qu' il soit, que nous soyons, que vous soyez, qu' ils soient*

Avoir – *que j'aie, que tu aies, qu' il aie, que nous ayons, que vous ayez, qu' ils aient*

The Passive Voice

Using the passive voice in the present or past tense is incredibly easy and will build on your knowledge of present conjugations for the auxiliaries involved.

Whereas the *passé composé* required different auxiliaries depending on the action described (movement-oriented or not), it is the auxiliary *être* here that does all the work, just like English. When the agent is introduced by by in English, it is *par/par/* that is used in French:

- Past (passé composé): *j'ai été, tu as été, il/elle a été, nous avons été, vous avez été, ils ont été*

- Present: *je suis, tu es, il est, nous sommes, vous êtes, ils sont*

- Future: *je serai, tu seras, il sera, nous serons, vous serez, ils seront*

You may also want to note that since être is utilized in the passive voice, any adjectives or past participates following it must bear the mark for gender or number if the subject is female or plural:

He was accused of shoplifting – *Il a été accusé de vol à l'étalage.* (*a été* here is the passé composé form of *être*, since it refers to a past action).

We (female) were tested rigorously by a group of professionals – *Nous avons été testées rigoureusement par un groupe de professionnels.*

I (male) will be interviewed at 3:00 p.m. tomorrow – *Je serai interviewé à quinze heures demain.*

Many buildings are being built in my neighborhood – *De nombreux bâtiments sont en train d'être construits dans mon quartier.*

- neighborhood – *un quartier* (m)/kartyé/

- building – *un bâtiment* (m)
- to build – *bâtir, construire* (2nd group, 3rd group); the circumflex accent is compulsory no matter the conjugation

Être is indeed very versatile when it comes to passive; however, you may also encounter a particular construction that is typical to French.

Se faire: a very idiomatic construction

Se faire has two different meanings in French:

- it may help to express an action that is performed on oneself (*se faire mal*, to hurt oneself; *se faire violence*, to restrain oneself from doing something, to force oneself to do something)

I hurt myself while cutting down wood – *Je me suis fait mal en coupant du bois*

Some of the guests had to stop themselves from binging on the cake – *Quelques invités ont dû se faire violence pour ne pas s'empiffrer de gâteau*

- it may be employed strictly for passive structures when the result of the action is negative for a living subject (an animal or human being):

I was scammed two months ago – *Je me suis fait arnaquer il y a deux mois*

He was robbed of 500 euros – *Il s'est fait voler cinq cents euros*

We were cut off by an impolite driver – *Nous nous sommes fait couper la route par un conducteur malpoli*

- to scam someone – *arnaquer* (1st group) *quelqu'un*
- to be, get scammed – *se faire arnaquer*

- it may also be used for very specific actions that someone commonly does for someone else (*se faire prescrire des médicaments*, to be prescribed medicine; *se faire renvoyer/être renvoyé*, to be expelled)

My niece's dog was prescribed antibiotics – *Le chien de ma nièce s'est fait prescrire des antibiotiques* (only se faire works in this case)

Many students were expelled from prestigious universities after too many protests across the country – *Beaucoup d'étudiants se sont fait renvoyer d'universités prestigieuses après de trop nombreuses manifestations à travers le pays (être renvoyé may also be used here: ont été renvoyés...)*

Impersonal constructions: translating the passive/One should not...

The passive voice in French will be majorly used when referring to an action performed by someone or something onto someone or something; for instance, the traditional The mouse is eaten by the cat.

However, it so happens that passive voice constructions in English can be much more general (English is spoken in many countries), and it is this particularity that this book will help you translate into French.

For these cases where the passive voice refers to a general phenomenon or sort of 'truth of life', French will heavily privilege using an active voice (with regular, so to speak, conjugations), and will retranscribe the general quality of that statement with the pronoun ***on*** ('it, we').

What is great about *on*—as you have already seen—is that it can accommodate a rather fluid number of people without singling them out specifically or giving out too many details; in essence, using it in such contexts is how French retranscribes that vagueness or absence of information as to who does what:

English is spoken in many countries – *On parle anglais dans de nombreux pays*

Beef is commonly served with rice and carrots – *On sert généralement du boeuf avec du riz et des carottes*

It is often thought that walking under a ladder brings bad luck – *On pense souvent que marcher endessous d'une échelle porte malheur*

- to bring bad luck – *porter malheur* ('carry, bring bad luck')

Once the other kind of sentences where *on* is used as an impersonal pronoun are covered, you will be perfectly fluent in understanding all its nuances—yes, that pronoun can be confusing, and you may at first be tempted to think that there is a 'we' person in there that doesn't have anything to do with the content of the sentence... but it is now one more path cleared for you to reach greater heights on your language learning journey!

One must/ can/ should... = where French and English intertwine

You are in luck! Impersonal sentences conveying orders or recommendations may be translated in two ways in French:

- *Il faut que...* ('one has to'), *il est nécessaire que/ de...* which has already been covered extensively in the Subjunctive subsection

- *on ne doit pas* ('one should not'), which has the advantage of requiring very little conjugation and being extremely similar to English.

One must always pay attention to the small beauties of life – *Il faut toujours prêter attention aux petites merveilles de la vie./ On doit toujours prêter attention...*

Anything, something, nothing...

anything (not... anything): *rien*

- I don't know anything about this new play – *Je ne sais rien de cette nouvelle pièce de théâtre*

anything (in an affirmative statement): *n'importe quoi/npo'rte-kwa/*

- We have no idea what caused this; it could be anything – *Nous n'avons aucune idée de ce qui a causé ça; ça pourrait être n'importe quoi*

not... any: *ne/ n'* [verb/auxiliary] *aucun(e)(s)* [noun, if there is one]

- I don't have any idea how to get there – *Je n'ai aucune idée de comment aller là-bas*

nothing: *rien*

something: *quelque chose*

anywhere (not... anywhere): *nulle part*

- I can't seem to find my keys anywhere – *Je n'arrive pas à trouver mes clés* (anywhere here wouldn't be translated into French)/ *Je ne trouve mes clés nulle part* (*nulle part* as not)

anywhere (in an affirmative statement): *n'importe où*

- It's like looking for a needle in a haystack: my new glasses could be anywhere – *C'est comme chercher une aiguille dans une botte de foin: mes nouvelles lunettes pourraient être n'importe où*

nowhere: *nulle part*

- I find holidays much more relaxing when you are in the middle of nowhere – *Je trouve les vacances beaucoup plus relaxantes quand on est au milieu de nulle part* (*milieu*, m = middle)

somewhere: *quelque part*

- But there should be at least one open restaurant somewhere! – *Mais il doit bien y avoir un restaurant d'ouvert quelque part*

anytime: *n'importe quand*

- You may contact us anytime between 9:00 a.m. and 3:00 p.m. – *Vous pouvez nous contacter n'importe quand entre neuf heures du matin et trois heures de l'après-midi/ entre neuf heures et quinze heures*

sometime: *un de ces jours*

- We should schedule an appointment sometime – *Nous devrions convenir d'un rendez-vous* (formal)/ *fixer un rendez-vous* (more common) *un de ces jours*

somehow: *d'une certaine manière*, when expressing disbelief, is conveyed through the conditional or through *de manière/ de façon surprenante* (lit. in a surprising way):

- He somehow managed to not follow any instruction – *Il a réussi, de façon surprenante, à ne suivre aucune instruction*

somewhat: *quelque peu/kèlke-peu/*, invariable

- I found his indications somewhat misleading – *J'ai trouvé ses indications quelque peu trompeuses*

Chapter 14: Greetings, Sayings, and Daily Expressions

When you first settle into a foreign location, you may feel lonely and homesick. You may keep thnking about the good old days when you were with your childhood friends and relatives in your home country.

However, moving to France, whether temporarily or permanently is not so bad. In fact, this new experience can be great for you. It would teach you new things, such as new skills and behaviors. It would also expose you to new cultures as well as allow you to form connections with new people.

The following greetings, sayings, and daily expressions may come in handy whenever you find yourself in a situation where you have to communicate with another person. Just keep practicing your French. Soon enough, you will be able to adjust and feel at home.

1. *Je t'aime tellement* is translated into English as I love you so much

2. *Tu me manques* is translated into English as I miss you

3. *Je suis désolé* is translated into English as I am sorry

4. *Je vous aime* bien is translated into English as I like you

5. *Tu es si gentil* is translated into English as You're so sweet

6. *Mon plaisir / Vous êtes les bienvenus* is translated into English as My pleasure / You are welcome

7. *Joyeux anniversaire!* is translated into English as Happy Birthday!

8. *Joyeux Noël!* is translated into English as Merry Christmas!

9. *Bonnes vacances!* is translated into English as Happy Holidays!

10. *Bonne année!* is translated into English as Happy New Year!

11. *Joyeux anniversaire!* is translated into English as Happy Anniversary!

12. *Joyeux Thanksgiving!* is translated into English as Happy Thanksgiving!

13. *Joyeuses Pâques* is translated into English as Happy Easter

14. *Joyeux Halloween!* is translated into English as Happy Halloween!

15. *Joyeuse Saint-Valentin!* is translated into English as Happy Valentine's Day!

16. *Bienvenue à la maison* is translated into English as Welcome Home

17. *Félicitations!* is translated into English as Congratulations!

18. *Bonjour* is translated into English as Hello

19. *Bon après-midi / bonne journée* is translated into English as Good afternoon / Good Day

20. *Bonsoir* is translated into English as Good evening

21. *Bonne nuit* is translated into English as Good night

22. *Au revoir* is translated into English as Goodbye

23. *Mes condoléances* is translated into English as My condolences

24. *Mes condoléances* is translated into English as Get well soon

25. *Bon voyage* is translated into English as Have a safe trip

26. *Profitez!* is translated into English as Enjoy!

27. *Bonne chance* is translated into English as Good luck

28. *Dieu vous bénisse* is translated into English as God bless you

29. *Ça fait longtemps* is translated into English as It has been a long time

30. *Je te déteste* is translated into English as I hate you

31. *Prends soin de toi* is translated into English as Take care

32. *A plus tard* is translated into English as See you later

33. *Je suis à la maison* is translated into English as I'm home

34. Je ne peux pas rentrer à la maison is translated into English as I can't go home

35. *Merci de laisser* un message is translated into English as Please leave a message

36. *Je t'appellerai plus tard* is translated into English as I will call you later

37. *Je suis occupé* is translated into English as I am busy

38. *Comment s'est passée ta journée?* is translated into English as How was your day?

39. *C'est une belle journée* is translated into English as It is such a beautiful day

40. *Je me sens très fatigue* is translated into English as I feel very tired

41. *Je suis heureux aujourd'hui* is translated into English as I am happy today

42. *Je suis triste aujourd'hui* is translated into English as I feel sad today

43. *Je suis nerveux* is translated into English as I am nervous

44. *Je me sens très déprimé* is translated into English as I feel depressed

45. *Je suis intéressé* is translated into English as I am interested

46. *Je suis déçu* is translated into English as I am disappointed

47. *Elle est jalouse* is translated into English as She is jealous

48. *Qu'est-ce qu'on a pour le dîner?* is translated into English as What do we have for dinner?

49. *Veuillez enlever vos chaussures* is translated into English as Please take off your shoes

50. *Non, je ne l'ai pas fait* is translated into English as No, I did not do it

51. *Peut-être que vous l'avez laissé dans votre placard* is translated into English as Maybe you left it in your closet

52. *À qui parlez-vous au téléphone?* is translated into English as Who are you talking to on the phone?

53. *Qu'a-t-il dit?* is translated into English as What did he say?

54. *Où as-tu mis mes clés de voiture?* is translated into English as Where did you put my car keys?

55. *Quand était la dernière fois que vous êtes allé chez le dentiste?* is translated into English as When was the last time you went to the dentist?

56. *Quel est le problème avec vous?* is translated into English as What is wrong with you?

57. *Nous avons eu un dîner parfait la nuit dernière* is translated into English as We had a perfect dinner

date last night

58. *Je suis content que vous vous en sortiez bien* is translated into English as I'm glad you two are doing great

59. *Allez-y* is translated into English as Go ahead

60. *Arrêtez de faire des excuses* is translated into English as Stop making excuses

61. *Pouvez-vous mettre le film en pause pendant un moment?* is translated into English as Can you pause the movie for a while?

62. *Un dollar* is translated into English as One dollar

63. *Deux oiseaux* is translated into English as Two birds

64. *Trois garcons* is translated into English as Three boys

65. *Quatre filles* is translated into English as Four girls

66. *Cinq balles* is translated into English as Five balls

67. *Six chapeaux* is translated into English as Six hats

68. *Sept portes* is translated into English as Seven doors

69. *Huit arbres* is translated into English as Eight trees

70. *Neuf chaises* is translated into English as Nine chairs

71. *Dix équipesis* translated into English as Ten teams

72. *Aïe! Tu m'as lancé dans les pieds* is translated into English as Ouch! You jerked me in the feet

73. *Wow! Je ne savais pas que tu ferais ça* is translated into English as Wow! I didn't know you would do that

74. *Ouf! C'était fermé* is translated into English as Whew! That was close

75. *Le temps est chaud et ensoleillé* is translated into English as The weather is hot and sunny

76. *Il fait très froid dehors* is translated into English as It's very cold outside

77. *Rendez-vous à l'entrée du centre commercial* is translated into English as Let's meet at the entrance of the mall

78. *Avez-vous vu la sortie?* is translated into English as Have you seen the Exit?

79. *Pouvez-vous allumer le téléviseur, s'il vous plaît?* is translated into English as Can you please turn on the TV?

80. *Pourquoi as-tu éteint les lumières?* is translated into English as Why did you turn off the lights?

81. *C'est encore lundi* is translated into English as It's Monday again

82. *Je suis programmé pour mon examen dentaire ce mardi* is translated into English as I am scheduled for my dental check-up this Tuesday

83. *Le mercredi, nous ne portons pas d'uniforme* is translated into English as On Wednesdays, we don't wear uniform

84. *Avez-vous des projets jeudi?* is translated into English as Do you have plans on Thursday?

85. *Dieu merci, c'est vendredi* is translated into English as Thank goodness it's Friday

86. *Je ne peux pas attendre samedi soir* is translated into English as I can't wait for Saturday night

87. *Vas-tu à l'église ce dimanche?* is translated into English as Are you going to church this Sunday?

88. *Aujourd'hui c'est mon anniversaire* is translated into English as Today is my birthday

89. *Elle était très en colère hier* is translated into English as She was very upset yesterday

90. *J'espère que tout ira bien demain* is translated into English as I hope everything will be alright tomorrow

91. *Avez-vous déjeuné?* is translated into English as Did you have breakfast?

92. *Je vais prendre un bain maintenant* is translated into English I will take a bath now

93. *Je dînerai ce soir.* is translated into English as I'll have dinner tonight.

94. *Bois ton café* is translated into English as Drink your coffee.

95. *Ne vas-tu pas à l'école?* is translated into English as Aren't you going to school?

96. *Avez-vous déjà vu le film?* is translated into English as Did you already see the film?

97. *La fin était vraiment fabuleuse* is translated into English as The ending was really fabulous

98. *J'ai vu la bande-annonce* is translated into English as I saw the trailer

99. *Je pense que c'est ennuyeux* is translated into English as I think it's boring

100. *Voulez-vous prendre un café?* is translated into English as Do you want to have coffee?

101. *Avez-vous entendu les nouvelles?* is translated into English as Have you heard the news?

102. *Je l'apprécie vraiment* is translated into English as I really appreciate it

103. *Je ne comprends pas* is translated into English as I don't understand

104. *Qu'en penses-tu?* is translated into English as What do you think?

105. *Que voulez-vous dire?* is translated into English as What do you mean?

106. *Tu devrais rentrer tôt à la maison* is translated into English as You should go home early

107. *Pourquoi n'ai-je pas pensé à cela?* is translated into English as Why didn't I think of that?

108. *Veux-tu aller au cinéma avec moi?* is translated into English as Would you like to go to the movies with me?

109. *J'espère que tu te sentiras bientôt mieux* is translated into English as I hope you feel better soon

110. *Vous avez absolument raison* is translated into English as You are absolutely right

111. *Je ne pense pas* is translated into English as I don't think so

112. *Je suis désolé de l'entendre* is translated into English as I am sorry to hear that

113. *Je préfère dormir que de sortir* is translated into English as I would rather sleep than go out

114. *Je me sens paresseux pour me lever* is translated into English as I feel lazy to get up

115. *Je ne pouvais pas y croire* is translated into English as I could not believe this

116. *Je suis très heureux de vous parler de cela* is translated into English as I am so excited to tell you about this

117. *Pourquoi ne pas rejoindre notre équipe de football?* is translated into English as How about joining our football team?

118. *Merci de m'avoir invite* is translated into English as Thank you for inviting me

119. *Je promets que je ne le referai plus* is translated into English as I promise I won't do it again

120. *Il semble y avoir un problème avec notre connexion internet* is translated into English as There seems to be a problem with our internet connection

121. *Ce n'est pas ta faute* is translated into English as It is not your fault

122. *Ne répétez plus les mêmes erreurs* is translated into English as Don't repeat the same mistakes again

123. *Je souhaite que cela ne soit jamais arrive* is translated into English as I wish it never happened

124. *La nouvelle était vraiment choquante* is translated into English as The news was really shocking

125. *À mon avis, elle ne dit pas la vérité* is translated into English as In my opinion, she is not telling the truth

126. *Je crains que nous ne puissions pas arriver à temps* is translated into English as I'm worried we can't get there on time

127. *Je n'ai pas le choix* is translated into English as I have no choice

128. *Que pensez-vous de notre nouveau patron?* is translated into English as What do you think of our new boss?

129. *Pouvez-vous me donner votre opinion sur l'histoire?* is translated into English as Can you give me your thoughts about the story?

130. *J'aurais dû prendre mes vitamins* is translated into English as I should have taken my vitamins

131. *Je regrette de ne pas avoir été préparé à mon examen* is translated into English as I regret that I have not been prepared for my exam

132. *Je dois aller au travail demain* is translated into English as I have to go to work tomorrow

133. *Je m'en fous* is translated into English as I don't care

134. *Faites ce que vous voulez* is translated into English as Do whatever you want

135. *Êtes-vous sûr de ne pas en avoir besoin?* is translated into English as Are you sure you won't need them?

136. *On dirait qu'il va pleuvoir* is translated into English as It looks like it is going to rain

137. *Pourriez-vous s'il vous plaît l'expliquer?* is translated into English as Could you please explain it?

138. *Je suppose qu'il a déjà trente ans* is translated into English as I guess he is already thirty years old

139. *Nous n'avons pas pu y arriver à cause du traffic* is translated into English as We were not able to make it because of traffic

140. *Pouvez-vous expliquer pourquoi vous n'avez pas assisté à la réunion?* is translated into English as Can you explain why you did not attend the meeting?

141. *N'oubliez pas d'acheter les articles d'épicerie figurant sur la liste* is translated into English as Don't forget to buy the grocery items on the list

142. *Tu viens à la maison à quelle heure?* is translated into English as What time are you coming home?

143. *Combien coûte votre location?* is translated into English as How much is your rental?

144. *Viens à l'intérieur* is translated into English as Come on, inside

145. *Laissez vos chaussures à la porte, s'il vous plaît* is translated into English as Leave your shoes at the door, please

146. *Tu peux le faire!* is translated into English as You can do it!

147. *Oiseaux d'une plume volent ensemble* is translated into English as birds of a feather flock together

148. *retour à la case départ* is translated into English as back to square one

149. *la curiosité a tué le chat* is translated into English as curiosity killed the cat

150. *pleurer sur le lait renversé* is translated into English as cry over spilled milk

151. *tourner autour du pot* is translated into English as beat around the bush

153. *épargner pour un jour de pluie* is translated into English as save for a rainy day

Chapter 15 - Get to Know Each Other

You can go fairly far with just a little French. A simple *"bonjour"* with a few basic words to say who you are will definitely sound better than embarrassed silence. Your attitude will play a major role: keep positive. A French person will notice very quickly that you are a foreigner and will be happy to speak in French with you as he or she most probably speaks very little English. So don't focus on making perfect sentences or avoiding mistakes, just try to be understood! The person you are talking to will be thankful and will see your effort of trying to speak in his/her language as a very positive sign coming from you. Hey, you are making the step forward!

Here you will learn how to introduce yourself and your friends, how to use various expressions, how to describe people, and what to say after the first few words. So, put on a fake mustache, grab your bottle of red, and start talking!

"You say goodbye, and I say hello"

You could always use *"bonjour"* or *"bonsoir"* (good evening) with anyone you meet. Depending on the situation, a wide choice of words is available:

Bonjour is said in English as good morning/ good afternoon

Bonsoir is said in English as good evening, good night

Salut: hi (not fitting for adults you don't know well, your future mother in law won't appreciate it). You can also use "salut" to say goodbye.

Ciao: even less formal, fits for goodbye.

Au revoir: formal goodbye

Bonne journée: bye bye or have a good day

Bonne soirée: bye bye have a good evening

Bonne nuit is said in English as good night

Ça fait longtemps: it's been a while

à bientôt is said in English as see you soon

À tout à l'heure is said in English as see you shortly

Bisou bisou!: kiss kiss

How are you?

There again, the choice is yours.

Comment ça va? is said in English as how are you?

Ça va?: shorter, obviously.

Comment allez-vous? is said in English as how are you, addressing an entire group or an individual that you don't know well(polite form)

Ça roule?/ ça gaze?: literally is it rolling?Is it gauze? Asking a young person or someone you know well if things are ok.

Your answers might be the following:

Ça va bien, merci. Et toi/vous? is said in English as I'm doing well, thanks. And you?

Ça va is said in English as I'm ok

Ça va pas mal is said in English as I'm not bad

Comme çi comme ça is said in English as So so

Ça ne va pas bien is said in English as I'm not ok/things are not doing well.

Tout baigne is said in English as Everything is fine (not formal, you can use it only with persons you know very well)

Polite phrases

Merci is said in English as thank you

Merci beaucoup is said in English as thank you very much

S'il te/vous plaît is said in English as please

De rien is said in English as you are welcome

Excusez-moi/ excusez-moi is said in English as excuse me

Pardon is said in English as sorry

Introducing yourself

Quel est ton/votre nom? is said in English as What is your name?

Comment t'appelles-tu / comment vous appelez vous? is said in English as Same, lit.: how are you called?

Je m'appelle Philippe is said in English as My name is Philippe.

Je suis Lucie is said in English as I am Lucie

In a more formal situation, you might want to introduce yourself in a more polite way:

J'aimerais me présenter, je m'appelle Isabelle is said in English as I would like to introduce myself; my name is Isabelle.

Je ne pense pas que nous nous connaissions, je m'appelle Jean is said in English as I don't think we know each other ; my name is Jean.

Je suis heureux de faire votre connaissance is said in English as It's nice to meet you.

Pareillement is said in English as too/same here (agreement to what the person just said)

Voici Jérôme is said in English as This is Jérôme.

Je vous présente mon ami is said in English as Meet my friend.

S'il vous plaît, permettez-moi de vous présenter Sarah is said in English as Please let me introduce you to Sarah.

J'aimerais que vous fassiez la connaissance de Pau is said in English as I would like you to meet Paul.

Connaissez-vous Daniel? Do you know Daniel?

Prénom: first name

Nom (de famille) is said in English as last name

Nom de jeune fille is said in English as maiden name

Le nom de mon fils/fille is said in English as my son's/ daughter's name

C'est l'abréviation pour... is said in English as it's short for

Vous pouvez m'appeler par mon prénom is said in English as You can call me by my first name.

Describing people

If you need to tell people about your girlfriend's beauty or your boyfriend's awesome stature, you will need a few words that describe these attributes. Here are a few that might come in handy.

Petit(e) is said in English as small

Grand(e) is said in English as tall

Maigre is said in English as skinny

Gros(se) is said in English as fat (less impolite than in English)/large

Lourd(e) is said in English as heavy

Jeune is said in English as young

Vieux is said in English as old

Âge moyen is said in English as middle aged

Beau/belle is said in English as handsome/beautiful

Moche is said in English as ugly

Musclé(e) is said in English as muscular

Canon is said in English as hot/fit (not formal)

Thon is said in English as ugly (don't stand in front of him/her, you might get a slap in your face)

Le visage is said in English as face

Les yeux is said in English as eyes

Le nez is said in English as nose

La bouche is said in English as mouth

Les oreilles is said in English as ears

La/les joue(s) is said in English as cheek(s)

Le cou is said in English as neck

Les épaules is said in English as shoulders

Le(s) bras is said in English as arm(s)

La poitrine is said in English as chest/breasts

Le ventre is said in English as belly

Les fesses/ le cul is said in English as buttocks/butt

La/les jambe(s) is said in English as leg(s)

Le(s) pied(s) is said in English as foot/feet

Do you want to describe what you like in hair? Do this, keeping in mind that the hair found on your head are always plural: les cheveux. Hair found on your arms or on your shoulders (for the less fortunate) can be either singular or plural: le(s) poil(s).

Noirs: black

Bruns/châtains: brown

Roux: red

Blonds: blond

Blonds platine: platinum blond

Gris: gray

Blancs: white

Raides: straight

Ondulés: wavy

Bouclés: curly

Crépus: kinky

Chauve/ tête d'œuf: bald/ lit. Egg's head (not very polite, of course).

Describing eyes might be a good idea. Here are a few words to help you out;

Marron/brun: brown

Noisette: hazel

Vert: green

Bleu: blue

Maquillage: make up

Cils: eyelashes

Sourcils: eyebrows

Yeux en amande: almond eyes

Chapter 16 - Eating, Drinking and Visiting

Now that you have safely landed in France or any other French-speaking country, and hopefully on time, you now deserve to move on to the real thing: enjoy yourself without too much trouble. French culture has so much to offer, it would be a shame not to enjoy it, and that in French. So get ready to learn everything an English speaking tourist needs to know in order to have a great time!

In a restaurant:

Nothing better than going to a French restaurant in France. It even feels better if you are able to order your meal, understand what that strange looking plate is made of, make your compliments to the chef, get some more wine, and even ask for the bill. Who knows, you might be able to get to know some people, and exchange about culture, food, and language! *Bon appétit!*

Réserver une table is said in English as to book a table

Pour ce soir is said in English as for tonight

Pour 2 personnes is said in English as for two

Au nom de is said in English as in the name of

Une table en terrasse is said in English as a table on the terrace

A l'intérieur is said in English as inside

Le menu/la carte is said in English as the menu

La carte des desserts/ des boissons is said in English as the dessert/ drinks menu

Que recommandez-vous? is said in English as What do you recommend?

Le plat du jour is said in English as dish of the day

Commander is said in English as to order

Être prêt is said in English as to be ready

Végétarien/végétalien is said in English as vegetarian/vegan

Nous allons prendre is said in English as We are going to have

Le vin rouge/blanc de la maison is said in English as the house red/white wine

Un verre is said in English as a glass

Une bouteille is said in English as a bottle

La même chose is said in English as the same thing

De l'eau du robinet/ en carafe is said in English as tap water

L'eau gazeuse is said in English as sparkling water

L'eau plate is said in English as plain water

Délicieux is said in English as delicious

Formidable is said in English as amazing

Miam miam is said in English as yummy

Aigre-doux is said in English as sweet and sour

Epicé is said in English as spicy

Mes compliments au chef is said in English as my compliments to the chef

Sel/poivre is said in English as salt/pepper

Une serviette is said in English as a napkin

Un couteau is said in English as a knife

Une fourchette is said in English as a fork

Une cuillère is said in English as a spoon

Une paille is said in English as a straw

Une tasse is said in English as a cup

Une petite/grande assiette is said in English as a small/large plate

Un plateau is said in English as a tray

Du pain is said in English as some bread

Le plat is said in English as dish

La viande is said in English as meat

Le poulet is said in English as chicken

Le bœuf is said in English as beef

Le veau is said in English as veal

Le canard is said in English as duck

Le porc is said in English as pork

L'agneau is said in English as lamb

La saucisse is said in English as sausage

Le poisson is said in English as fish

Fruits de mer is said in English as seafood

Du riz is said in English as some rice

Des pâtes is said in English as some pasta

Des frites is said in English as french fries

Des légumes is said in English as vegetable

La pomme de terre is said in English as potato

La tomate is said in English as tomato

La salade is said in English as salad

Le menu/plat enfant: kids menu/dish

Entrée is said in English as starter

Plat de résistance is said in English as main dish

Dessert is said in English as dessert

La glace is said in English as ice cream

Le gâteau is said in English as cake

Digestif is said in English as digestive (strong) alcohol after a meal

L'addition is said in English as the bill

Payer en liquide is said in English as pay cash

Payer avec la carte is said in English as pay with a credit card

Quelle cuisson pour votre viande? is said in English as How would you like your meat to be cooked?

Bleu is said in English as very rare

Saignant is said in English as rare

À point is said in English as medium

Bien cuit is said in English as well done

Le service est inclus is said in English as service is included

Serveur/serveuse is said in English as waiter/waitress

Un pourboire is said in English as a tip

Offert is said in English as free of charge

Froid is said in English as cold

Brûlé is said in English as burned

Je ne veux pas payer is said in English as I don't want to pay

Je veux parler au patron is said in English as I want to speak to the boss

Acting like a pro in a bar or café

Bars and cafés are probably the best places to practice your language skills. This is where the atmosphere is laid back, good music is playing (sometimes), and holding a drink in your hand may very well be a secret weapon for some people (it certainly is for me) to push back their linguistic barriers. So go on, share some relaxed conversation, practice your small talk, pay a round, and don't forget the main goal: have fun! *Santé!* (cheers!)

Practical hint: service in French bars and restaurants are always included unless specified so. Do leave a tip if you find the service to be of higher quality or if you want to impress that sexy waitress.

Prendre/boire un verre is said in English as have a drink

Boire un coup is said in English as have a drink, less formal

L'apéro is said in English as *aperitif*, a truly magical word in French

Qu'est-ce que vous prenez? is said in English as What will you have?

Un verre de... is said in English as a glass of...

Une bière pression is said in English as a draft beer

Un panaché is said in English as a shandy (mix of beer and lemonade)

Une bouteille de... is said in English as a bottle of...

Trinquer is said in English as to drink to

Santé/ à la tienne/ à la vôtre/tchin-tchin is said in English as cheers!

Une/ma tournée is said in English as a/my round

Un/e autre is said in English as another

La même chose is said in English as the same

Être gai/e, pompette is said in English as to be tipsy

Être saoul/e, ivre is said in English as to be drunk

Être bourré is said in English as to be wasted

Avoir la gueule de bois is said in English as to have a hangover

La bière is said in English as beer

Le vin is said in English as wine

Un demi is said in English as 25cl beer

Un demi de vin rouge/blanc is said in English as 50cl of red/white wine

Une girafe is said in English as a huge beer container with a tap at the bottom. Useful for a group.

Un café noir/au lait is said in English as a coffee black/ with milk

Un thé/au lait/au citron is said in English as tea/ with milk/with lemon juice

Un chocolat chaud is said in English as a hot chocolate

Le lait is said in English as milk

Un jus d'orange/de pomme is said in English as orange/apple juice

Un soda is said in English as a soda

Un coca light is said in English as diet coke

Une limonade is said in English as lemonade

Le garçon is said in English as the bar waiter

La serveuse is said in English as the bar waitress

Activities

Now that you have arrived well, rested your bones in a nice bed, had some tasty food in your belly, you are now ready to get down to business. France being the most visited country in the world, you will have enough to do. But how are you going to express your needs? Just read the following--you will find the most useful words for your touristic activities.

Touriste: tourist

Bruyant: noisy

Faire le touriste: being all touristy

Guide touristique: guide book/ tour guide

Visiter: to tour

Découvrir: to discover

Louer: to rent

Acheter: to buy

Caution: deposit

Assurance: insurance

Recommandé: recommend

L'église: church

Le château: castle

La grotte: cave

Les ruines: ruins

La forêt: forest

Le chemin de randonnée: hiking trail

La piste cyclable: bike way

La rivière: river

La plage: beach

La montagne: mountain

La ville: city

Le musée: museum

La campagne: country side

Le parc d'attraction: theme park

Le parc nautique: water park

La piscine couverte/découverte: indoor/outdoor swimming pool

La discothèque/la boite: disco/club

Aller à un concert: to go to a concert

Itinéraire: itinerary

Planifier: to plan

Flâner: to stroll

Ne rien faire/ glander: to do nothing/ familiar

Prendre une photo/un selfie: take a picture/a selfie

Se baigner: to go for a swim

Se promener: to walk around

Faire une marche/une promenade: to hike

Courir: to run

Faire du jogging: to jog

Faire du vélo: to bike

Jouer: to play

Money!

Money is of course a central subject when it comes to traveling. You will need to have some knowledge about it to get through lots of situations. How do you find a bank, an exchange office, or tell someone that this wonderful painting is way too expensive? Let's look at some important sentences you will need.

L'argent: money

Combien ça coûte?: How much does it cost?

Cher/ ce n'est pas donné: expensive

Pas cher/ bon marché: cheap

Carte bancaire: credit card

Payer: pay

Payer en espèce/liquide: to pay cash

Payer par chèque: pay by check

Un billet de...: a ...note

Une pièce de...: a... coin

La monnaie: change

Chèque de voyage: traveler's cheque

Le distributeur (automatique de billet): ATM

Code: PIN code

La banque: bank

Le bureau de change: foreign exchange office

Changer de l'argent: to change money

Le taux de change: the exchange rate

Retirer: to withdraw

Déposer: to make a deposit

Virer/ faire un virement: to transfer money

Dépenser: to spend

Economiser: to save money

Être à découvert: to be overdrawn

Emprunter: to borrow

Prêter: to lend

Clothes shopping!

Would you know your way around a clothes shop in France? Well let me tell you that even though I speak perfect French, I still encounter lots of challenges when going to such god-forsaken places. Guys, you can skip this section if you want to (and practice ordering a *"bière pression"*, while she's getting the credit card). Girls, rejoice!

Essayer: to try/ to try on

Pantalon: pants

La cabine d'essayage: the changing room

La taille: size

Trop grand(e)/petit(e): too big/ too small

Autre couleur: other color

Une réduction: a discount

À quelle heure fermez-vous le magasin ce soir: At what time do you close the shop tonight?

Les heures d'ouverture/ de fermeture: opening/closing times

En solde: on sale

Se faire rembourser: to be reimbursed

Un avoir: a credit note

Le bon d'achat: a voucher

Le ticket de caisse: receipt

Le miroir: mirror

Rendre: to return

Aller: to fit

Cette jupe vous va bien: This skirt fits you well.

Les chaussures: shoes

Les baskets: sneakers

Les chaussettes: socks

Le pantalon: pants

La jupe: skirt

La robe: dress

Le T-shirt: practice your accent!

Le débardeur: longshoreman

Le pull: sweater

La veste: jacket

Le manteau: coat

L'imperméable: raincoat

Le chapeau: hat

La casquette: baseball cap

La culotte: panties

Soutien-gorge: bras

Sous-vêtements: underwear

Maillot de bain: bathing suit

Les lunettes: glasses

Speeding up the process

Reading in a foreign language can be so overwhelmingly difficult at first, and listening to the foreign language is just much more beginner-friendly in comparison.

But if you're using the French subtitles to learn from things like TV shows and YouTube videos, you are learning French not only through listening but reading as well. Reading does not always have to mean reading from dusty, old books. In fact, it can be done in all sorts of non-traditional ways like when we use French subtitles to learn specific lines and moments from shows we are watching. And it can be even more useful when done in larger quantities.

The goal is to figure out how to increase the amount of French that you read on a daily basis for yourself. This chapter is going to focus on the reasons why you should read more French every day as well as ways that you may use to ease into extended reading as well as extensive listening.

Why not spend the rest of the day reading or you may listen for as long as you like when your studies are done for the day? Firstly, it will assist you in rapidly converting a greater portion of that stream of indecipherable French language into words that you are able to comprehend. Second, it offers an additional option to remain involved in studying and ultimately living via French for a number of hours each day in a way that is both entertaining and comprehensive. Thirdly, some of the most accomplished polyglots in the world, such as Alexander Arguelles, Luca Lampariello, and Steve Kaufmann, are strong proponents of using reading as a technique to acquire foreign languages. Lastly, and most significantly, reading a lot in a foreign language is one of the best methods to construct and readily preserve a large range of vocabulary in that language.

When you first start learning French, reading original French materials may be extremely time-consuming and challenging. At what point precisely should you begin reading items other than subtitles in French? If you want to become fluent in French over the next few years, the best time to start learning is as soon as you possibly can. The more opportunity you give yourself to practice reading and writing French, the better. Reading will become another routine for you much more quickly if you do it frequently while you are young.

Let's pretend for argument's purpose that you did make the decision to engage in a substantial amount of reading, for instance by playing a video game in French. Do you often pause the game to check up on every new word as it comes up throughout the whole thing? When do you have a chance to relax, and enjoy the game? When you first begin working with such a vast volume of material in a foreign language, the experience might feel entirely overwhelming. After only a day or two however, you may feel completely exhausted and frustrated from your efforts. This is when well-thought-out approaches to learning a language might come in helpful.

Intensive vs. Extensive Reading

It's necessary to have an understanding of the distinction between extensive reading and intensive reading. When doing intensive reading, the objective is to analyze and research each and every new word and grammatical point included in a chosen text that is relatively brief in length. The Anki and the Goldlist Method are two useful tools that may be used to examine the information gained from this site. This type of reading is only meant to take between 20-45 minutes to complete.

On the other hand, the purpose of extensive reading is to increase one's ability to enjoy reading for extended periods of time. In contrast to extensive reading, there is no need to make an effort to evaluate knowledge using Anki or any of the other available methods. When you are reading a text that is simple for your level, you are able to read a considerably bigger quantity of pages for many hours with only a few pauses in between, however, when you are reading a text that is tough for your level, you are only able to study a limited number of pages before your mind starts to give up.

When you are still in the beginning or intermediate stages of learning a language, it may be quite challenging to track down significant reading resources that are appropriate for your skill level. According to some estimates, you need to have a comprehension rate of 98% of a given book before you are able to engage in truly prolonged reading.

When it comes to picking up new terms from a lengthy reading assignment, you should, ideally, depend primarily on context alone. However, in point of fact, there will be a great number of terms that you have neither seen nor heard before, and this is true regardless of the starting material that you select. In order for you to comprehend what is going on in the text, it is quite probable that you will need to go back through the content you read for the first time with the assistance of a dictionary or an English translation.

Just like how there's no magical point where you're ready for native French materials, there's also no magical point where you're ready for extensive reading. In order to successfully bridge the gap between intensive reading and extensive reading, a long series of efforts at reading must be made. There are principles of extensive reading, however, that you can use at any level to make this process much more enjoyable and faster overall.

Limiting Anki Reviews

The next thing to do is to make certain that you have sufficient time to read by making a few minor tweaks to Anki's schedule so that you aren't forced to study cards for more than two hours on a daily basis. In order to accomplish this, you will first need to ensure that you actually have enough time to read. Regardless of how much time you can devote every day towards learning French, lengthy Anki review sessions are completely unnecessary. There comes a point where your time is much better spent doing things like extensive reading.

Anki review sessions consist of doing both new cards, which are indicated by the color blue in Anki, and review cards, which are indicated by the color green in Anki. Exercises that have been generated but have not yet been used in review sessions are referred to as "new cards." Review cards have been looked at for at least one other time previously. An Anki session that consists of 10 new cards and 10 review cards will be defined as a 10/10 session from this point on, making the total number of exercises here 20.

You have the ability in Anki to set the amount of exercises that need to be done on a daily basis to 10/10, or any other number that you want. Simply opening Anki, clicking on the gear icon to the right of your deck, and selecting 'Options' from the drop-down menu that appears is all that is required to do this. First, increase the number of 'New cards/day' to 10, then navigate to the 'Reviews' page and reduce the number of 'Maximum reviews/day' to 10.

If you want to increase those numbers, our suggestion for beginning is set at ten review sessions out of ten total, and we urge exercising caution if you do so. If you wish to do additional Anki reviews, a greater number like 20/20 might perhaps be completed if the work is split up into two or more smaller sessions and spread out over the day. If you are feeling really inspired to do more Anki on some days, go for it! However, doing such a huge quantity every day will be an extremely tough habit to keep up with. Still, if you are feeling exceptionally inspired to complete more Anki, go for it!

At the time of this book's creation, Anki's default "Maximum reviews/day" setting was 100; nevertheless, if you retain this option, your daily review sessions in Anki alone can rapidly start reaching 90 minutes. This does not account for the time needed to read or listen to the information before making the cards.

An excessive quantity of Anki card practice on a daily basis is counterproductive. If using more Anki makes you feel demotivated, you won't be able to learn as much or make as much progress. In order to prepare for the more challenging courses, you need not endure torturous ultra-marathons of Anki reviews.

You can complete a more enormous amount of Anki cards in the long run if you prevent burnout by simply practicing short sessions consistently as a habit. You can do more cards in each session. In order to develop this consistency with Anki, sessions should last no more than an hour, and you shouldn't push yourself to do more just so you can make faster progress. Keep yourself from being bored and stop just before you reach that point. This will keep you interested for the following round.

If you find that you struggle to concentrate during the 10/10 sessions, try beginning with the 5/5 sessions instead. You should work on improving both your French skills and your ability to concentrate intently by practicing. If you get out of bed and immediately check your social media accounts when you first go online in the morning, you will probably have a very tough time concentrating on your studies, as well as reading and listening to raw French, if this is already a habit of yours.

You might find that you have more focus and energy when you start your day with things like morning walks, meditation, inspirational audiobooks, and exercise. Their importance should not be underestimated in the slightest. How you start your day can determine whether your time and energy will be sapped by all the distractions of the world or will be channeled 100% into doing the things that matter the most to you.

Principles of Extensive Reading

Now that you have enough time available to start extensive reading, let's take a look at five principles to help make reading a much more pleasurable and overall effective learning experience. The more pleasurable it is the more time you'll naturally want to spend doing it which equates to you learning faster.

Perhaps the biggest improvement you can make to your reading comprehension and speed is to read silently. While reading aloud can certainly be beneficial to pronunciation, it is a telltale sign of intensive reading. But in extensive reading, it's completely unnecessary for the most part. Continuously reading aloud makes reading painfully slow and unnatural which in fact pushes you further away from extensive reading.

Think about reading in your native language. Have you been reading this chapter aloud? Have you been moving your lips to form the words with your mouth? If English is your native language, the answer to these questions is most likely no. The reason we can read so well in our native language is not because we practice reading everything aloud. It's because of the massive volume we have read extensively throughout the years, and the overwhelming majority of it was read silently.

For French, try aiming to read silently 95% of the time and save the other five percent for speaking new words aloud with proper pronunciation. In this way, it will be more akin to how you learned to read so well in your native language. You already have more than enough new words to say aloud as a beginner or intermediate learner, and reading aloud anymore than this is just going to slow you down.

The second principle of extensive reading is to read for general meaning, pleasure, and curiosity rather than 100% complete comprehension. In general, once you understand the overall meaning of a sentence, move right along to the next. Don't try to read it aloud or re-read it in an attempt to memorize new vocabulary and grammar structures. These are short-term memory tactics that have little impact on what is stored in your long-term memory. You naturally learn faster when you allow yourself to naturally read. Forgetting words means that you are learning them.

Extensive reading is most effective when it is the means to an end and not the other way around. The end goal in mind should be the content you're really interested in. And when French is the means to that end, you get really good at the language as a result through the sheer volume of comprehensible input you receive through reading.

Our third principle of extensive reading is to find something to read that is not the news. Reading the news from time to time can be quite beneficial in learning the geography, politics, and current events of French speaking countries, but you may not find this information compelling enough to do it extensively.

It's very typical of French learners and language learners in general to try to read the news in the target language, as it seems like a reasonable and logical goal to aim towards. However, the reality is that maintaining a daily routine of reading conventional books and other forms of traditional reading material may be an extremely challenging task. It's possible that after a few weeks or months, it will feel like there is an infinite stream of French to work through. This is due to the fact that most new pieces are not related to one another. There is no overarching narrative that compels you to read all the way through to the conclusion in order to find out what occurs.

That drive you get from a great story is what compels you to continue reading through the most difficult moments. This is why we highly recommend reading any and all kinds of fictional stories from start to finish. This could be anything from short stories, popular novels like Harry Potter, or even stories told through video games. And if you aren't a fan of physical books or video games, you could even start extensive reading by going through a TV show or movie line by line using the French subtitles. Of course, non-fiction can work just as well if you have a particular topic that fascinates you like European history as an example.

If you are easily distracted while at the computer, however, you may have more success with a physical copy of a book or at least a printed copy of some reading material found online. At first, it might seem unnecessary to take the extra time and money to acquire physical copies when almost everything is immediately available through the internet. But what you gain in exchange is very much worth the effort. It is a wonderful experience to be able to physically touch in one's hands books written in a foreign language and doing so allows one to maintain the best possible degree of focus while reading through the material. The experience of turning real pages is far more gratifying than that of clicking virtual links on the internet at any moment.

The fourth principle we would like to introduce is to use bi-lingual texts whenever possible. Of course, the dictionary is useful at any level in figuring out the meaning of new words, but having a copy of the text translated in your native language can drastically increase your reading speed. Reading in new languages is an incredible amount of work in the beginning, and you will want every advantage you can get to speed up the process.

Translations can help you focus on getting to the next part of the story rather than trying to comprehend the French text 100%. When you read the translation of the text in your native language, you instantly comprehend the meaning of the text 100% and are ready to continue forward. This can help prevent you from getting hung up on why certain language was used in the French text. As long as you are engaging the target language in the text and trying to understand it before reading the translation, it does not matter how often you use the English text even if it's initially sentence by sentence.

The fifth and final principle of extensive reading is to track your progress using a notebook. It is by no means required just like bi-lingual texts, but keeping a written log of how much you read every day is like magic in helping you build confidence in your reading ability. These feelings of improvement and growth are the foundation of a long-term habit of extensive reading. It will give you a deep sense of accomplishment each day to see how much progress you made and to compare it with how much you have made on previous days. That tingly and fuzzy feeling you will receive makes it all the easier to come back the next day and chip away at whatever material you're reading through.

Use each page, chapter, short story, written article, and whatever means you can to track your reading speed and progress. Obviously printed materials are going to be much more straightforward to track using pages, but sometimes you have to be a bit creative. For instance, even if you decide to first practice extensive reading using the French subtitles to a TV show, it's very much worth keeping a record of how many minutes of video time you clear each day. Any record at all can make your growth and process both tangible and visible.

Extensive Listening

On the other hand, extensive listening may be accomplished by selecting anything to view and then pushing the play button. This will conclude the discussion. There is no need to pay attention to the terms that have a high frequency here. You do it just for the enjoyment of the experience. When you are in need of a break from reading or when you are exhausted at the end of the day are two ideal moments for lengthy listening, but these are not the only occasions that qualify.

A binging session is strongly suggested! The more you listen, the better your comprehension abilities will be, and you could even pick up a bit or two here and there just from paying attention to the context. The portions that are beyond your comprehension serve as a driving force to get you back here the next day, eager to absorb more information.

The true test will be whether or not you can commit to watching more French television than you do English episodes. If you are serious about reaching an expert or even near-native level in French within a few years, you need to make this practice of immersing yourself in the language of its native speakers a priority above your other pastimes. You need to train your eyes and hearing every day, and you should put in as much time as you can, hour by hour and minute by minute.

It might be challenging to decide which of one's previous pastimes and interests should be given up in order to devote more time to learning French. Nevertheless, it is far simpler to begin by focusing on one's "dead time," also known as downtime, throughout the day. Take a book with you everywhere you go so that you may make the most of your "downtime" and "uptime" respectively. You may convert time spent walking, biking, or driving into listening time by ensuring that your mobile device is always filled with hours of French entertainment to listen to at this period.

It is not necessary to live in a completely French-speaking environment in order to achieve fluency in the language; however, the results you get will be substantially more rewarding once you begin to predominantly communicate in French.

Try out different things by making your own French plans that fit your needs. You may begin the day by using Anki and engaging in intensive reading and listening, and then go on to engaging in extended reading and listening later in the day. You might also try giving yourself a break whenever you feel the need to by alternating between tasks that are intensive and ones that are extensive. You might also get right into intensive reading and listening without any further preparation. Put your own thoughts to the test and discover what you find to be the most educational and enjoyable along the trip.

Lang-8, Italki, and HelloTalk

Output practicing is another option that might help you fill up some of the gaps in your timetable. Let's take a look at three distinct methods that can help you get in touch with native speakers and get corrections.

Lang-8 is a free language exchange website that allows users to publish postings in the language that they desire to practice in order to improve their proficiency in that language. The website can be found at http://lang-8.com. Users on this platform are free to discuss virtually any topic they choose. You might write about whatever has been going through your head all day, or you can focus on particular subjects that are of interest to you. You will be rewarded with corrections in exchange for providing corrections to the posts written by other users in your native language.

It's possible that using Lang-8 will be the most efficient method of getting fixes both in terms of time and money. It is incredibly useful to be able to visit the website whenever you want, write for ten to twenty minutes, make a few simple adjustments for other users, and then depart to go about the rest of your day. You are able to come back to Lang-8 the following day, or even later on the same day, in order to find modifications to your post.

Italki (https://www.italki.com) may be the better solution for you if you are prepared to spend a few dollars every session to chat with tutors face to face. To make use of Italki, you will need to look for a teacher that you find appealing, arrange for a time slot that is open, and then go on to Skype (https://www.skype.com) immediately before the time that you and your instructor have agreed upon. The expense may be worth it to you if you feel that the benefits of face-to-face talk and tutoring outweigh the disadvantages.

The immensely popular software HelloTalk (https://www.hellotalk.com) has made it possible to communicate in a variety of languages via texting in ways that were previously unavailable. The vast majority of people who are interested in learning a foreign language have a very favorable opinion of this app since it is likely the most practical option to interact directly with native speakers of practically any language. It is an excellent platform for initiating organic conversations with individuals hailing from a variety of nations all around the world. You will have the opportunity to make new acquaintances while conversing in each other's native language and offering and receiving corrections as you go along. Texting takes the weight off of having face-to-face talks when meeting new people, so if you want to meet more people, this might be the best option for you.

Living the Language

In the beginning stages of learning French (beginner and early intermediate), Anki is an excellent tool for internalizing the fundamentals of the language. However, in the long run, it is not the most effective tool for growing vocabulary and general language proficiency. If you try to put every new word you discover into Anki, it will slow down both your reading and listening to a rate that is comparable to that of a snail's pace. Also, even if you were to limit your use of Anki to just one hour per day at the intermediate to advanced levels, it may be an immeasurably more enjoyable way to spend that hour than it would be to review the thousands of words by doing things like reading more native French material, listening to more native French material, or even chatting with native speakers.

Reading thousands of pages, as opposed to hundreds, is what will help you master a subject. This is the winning strategy. If you want to feel like you're actually living the language instead of merely learning it, favor substantial reading and listening.

After hundreds of pages of reading and many hours of listening to French, you will have experienced all there is to. You'll soon have the same lightning-fast comprehension as native speakers. And the French you learn will feel as comfortable on your tongue as your first language. The thought of being a polyglot may even intrigue you at that moment.

Chapter 17 - Making Sentences

Where things start to come together

This is it. Keep cool; this is where magic starts happening.

Ok, so it's perhaps not that exciting, but still, this is the point where you start speaking French:

nominal groups (Phrases)

We have seen that the smallest meaningful unit of a language is the word. A word communicates one idea/concept. That can be an action (verb), an object/person (noun), a characteristic (adjective), etc.

Next up comes the phrase. A phrase is a group of words that make sense together (i.e.: are organized in a grammatically correct fashion), but which do not form a complete sentence.

A nice car	*Une jolie voiture*
Bob and Jack	*Bob et Jack*
A group of words	*Un groupe de mots*
The smallest meaningful unit of a language	*La plus petite unité linguistique dotée de sens*

As you can see, these words go together and have a meaning, but they don't tell you anything about what's happening (action). We call these "nominal groups", that is to say "groups of nouns"

They are comprised of articles, nouns and adjectives and can be used as a unit:

A nice car passed in the street.

We passed a nice car in the street.

It works the same way in French, of course, but there are some differences when it comes to word order:

Word order

Not world order. Word order.

In English, adjectives are nearly always placed before the noun:

A **black** cat

A **red** car

A **great** game

In French however, *descriptive adjectives* tend to be placed AFTER the noun:

*Un chat **noir***

*Une voiture **rouge***

*Un jeu **amusant***

But, wait a minute, how can that be? In the table above, adjectives were in the same place as in English.

Those are exceptions. As a rule of thumb, French adjectives are placed before the noun (as in English) when they describe:

Adjective describing...	English	French
Beauty	A nice car	*Une jolie voiture*
Age	An old lady	*Une vieille dame*
Good/bad	A good bed – a bad bed	*Un bon lit – un mauvais lit*
Size	A big house	*Une grande maison*

All other types of adjectives – possessive (my, your, etc.), demonstrative (this, that, etc.)... – go before the noun.

Plural

In grammar, we talk of the "number" of a noun, verb or pronoun to indicate if we are speaking of one item or several. It's pretty simple, there are only two cases:

Singular = only 1 item/person

Plural = more than 1 item/person

We use plural forms when talking about several items instead of just one:

One house=>two houses

The principle is the same in French:

Une maison=>Deux maisons

In English as in French, the main mark of the plural is an extra "s" at the end of the nouns.

There are however some exceptions in French depending on the word's ending:

All words ending with "-*eau*" make their plural with "*x*" instead of "s"

- *Un chapeau => Des chapeaux* (One hat, several hats)

Most words ending with "-*au*" or "-*eu*" make their plural with "*x*" instead of "s" (there are a few exceptions but let's not worry about those now)

A few words ending with "-*ou*" make their plural with "*x*":

- *Hiboux* (howls), *choux* (cabbages), *genoux* (knees), *bijoux* (jewels), *cailloux* (stones), *poux* (louses)

We have already covered verbs and pronouns before, but let's have a quick look at them again:

English	French	Number
I am	*Je suis*	Singular – only me
You are	*Tu es*	Singular – only you
He/she/it is	*Il/elle est*	Singular – only that other person or object
We are	*Nous sommes*	Plural – several people including

		the person speaking.
		Can also be singular when you talk to someone you don't know
You are	*Vous êtes*	Plural – several people including the person spoken to, but not the person speaking.
They are	*Ils/elles sont*	Plural – several people excluding the person spoken and the person speaking.

Note: *elles* refers to a group exclusively consisting of females. If there is a male in the group, the pronoun "*ils*" is used instead:

Jane, Mary and Cindy = *elles*

Jane, Mary and Paul = *ils*

This is the object of some feminist claims but it is merely a grammatical convention and also applies to objects:

A car and a truck = they

Une voiture (f.) et un camion (m.) = ils

We can argue whether it is fair or sexist or whatever. At the time of this writing, that's the way it is.

Agreement

In grammar, *agreement* refers to the way words change in relationship to other words in the sentence:

Number - plural

As we have seen, nouns change depending on the number.

Unfortunately, it doesn't stop here. In French, *articles* and *adjectives* also agree on number with the noun:

The small house=>The small houses

La petite maison=>Les petites maisons

This also applies when the adjective is located after the verb:

The house is small=>The houses are small

La maison est petite=>Les maisons sont petites

You have to keep track of the number throughout your sentences. It is a common source of spelling errors.

Gender

As you might remember, we have talked about gender in the English vs. French chapter. Briefly, every noun has a specific gender, either male or female.

Now that you know a bit more about the various parts of speech and that you have acquired some French vocabulary, we are going to have a look at how it works in practice.

If you remember the section on articles, you remember that:

Un = a (masculine form)

Une = a (feminine form)

In French, articles and adjectives agree in number AND in gender with the noun. Here are a few examples that should help you understand how it works:

Masculine nouns	English	Feminine nouns	English
Un chapeau	A hat	*Une voiture*	A car
Des chapeaux	Hats	*Des voitures*	cars
Un petit village	A small village	*Une grande ville*	A big city
Des petits villages	Small villages	*Des grandes villes*	Big cities
Un sujet important	An important subject	*Une question importante*	An important question
Des sujets importants	important subjects	*Des questions importantes*	important questions
L'effet positif	The positive effect	*La beauté sensuelle*	The sensual beauty
Les effets positifs	The positive effects	*Les beautés sensuelles*	The sensual beauties
Le monde bleu	The blue world	*La galaxie bleue*	The blue galaxy
Les mondes bleus	The bleu worlds	*Les galaxies bleues*	The blue galaxies
Un bon moment	A good time	*Une manière élégante*	An elegant manner
Des bons moments	Good times	*Des manières élégantes*	Elegant manners

Simple sentence structure

Once again, French and English are pretty much the same. A basic sentence is made of:

- subject
- verb
- complement (optional)

You are learning French.

Vous apprenez le français.

Simple, right?

Subject + Verb + Complement

Now let's have a closer look at each one of these items:

Subject

The subject of a sentence is who/what the sentence is about:

The person/animal/object performing the action (or being in the state) described by the verb is the subject.

Sounds complicated but it isn't.

<u>The small dog</u> jumps over the fence.

What jumps over the fence? The small dog. Therefore "the small dog" is the **subject** of the sentence.

<u>Bob</u> is feeling lonely.

Who is feeling lonely? Bob is. Thus **Bob** is the **subject** of the sentence.

It is important to note that the subject can be a single word (i.e.: Bob) or a group of words (i.e.: the small dog).

The same applies to French.

<u>Le petit chien</u> saute la barrière.

<u>Bob</u> se sent seul.

Verb

By now, you should know what a verb is. If you need a refresher, just check out the previous chapter.

Complement (optional)

The rest of the sentence. A complement completes the sentence and gives more information about the action or state described by the verb:

The small dog jumps **over the fence**.

<u>Over the fence</u> completes the sentence and explains where the small dog jumped. That's the complement. It could have been just about anything else, like

The small dog jumps **with joy**.

Chapter 18 - Creating a Simple Learning Plan

Your Core Daily French Practice

We have looked at a variety of techniques and tips for learning French in this book, but how much and how often should you actually study? I have learnt that success in language learning depends largely on being consistent, and that going for days (or even weeks) without studying makes it difficult to progress. Therefore, **I try to make language learning a part of my lifestyle and this means aiming to study every day.** Now, in reality, I do take days off - sometimes a few days off! However, when you consider that learning a language is a long-term project, it seems smarter to set out with the intention of studying every day and to allow yourself some flexibility within that, than to do the opposite, which is to "fit it in" whenever you have time.

To make sure language learning is part of my lifestyle, I have a daily core study time. This is a session of around 45 minutes (sometimes more, sometimes less) which I like to do first thing in the morning, before my day begins. Having my core study time early in the morning helps make sure the study gets done, because once the working day begins it is hard to carve out time for anything else! I sit in a quiet room where I will not be distracted and I use the time to do what you might call the "hard work" - concentrated and focused study, as opposed to activities such as browsing language videos on YouTube, which is usually a shallow activity full of distraction.

Now, the key is to make your core study time regular, because it is in the act of revisiting the language every day that you learn new things and deepen your understanding of what you already know. Along with consistency, the other most important aspect of this approach to learning languages is the creation of time for in-depth study. You may have plenty of dead time throughout your day - on the bus, during your lunch hour - and this can be useful time for extra practice, but dead time is often short and prone to distraction. I have found nothing to be as valuable as quiet, uninterrupted time for language learning in which you can truly focus, and that is why I create this core study time every day and make it a priority.

What I have described here is the routine that works particularly well for me - I can focus well in the morning, and 45-60 minutes is a productive amount of time. However, I would be the first to say you should adapt this to fit your personal preferences. If the most practical and productive study time for you is 15 minutes in the evening before bed, then that is precisely what you should do. The important thing is to study consistency and to create an environment in which you can focus.

Finding Time to Speak

The way I view speaking practice is not so much for learning new things (although you certainly will), but rather to consolidate what you have already learnt. Speaking with people is your opportunity to take the language you have learnt on your own and put it into practice, so that speaking starts to become natural and you learn to express yourself better in French. Once you feel ready to start speaking and have experienced your first conversations in French, you may well become addicted to the feeling of communicating in another language, which is a wonderful thing!

However, the practicalities of creating the time to speak French with people is not always easy, and for this reason there is an ongoing risk that you go for weeks or months without speaking with anyone, for no reason other than you do not get around to organising it. Unless you are lucky enough to be surrounded by French speakers, you will have to be proactive in creating your own opportunities to speak French. In my own learning, I realised a long time ago that if I do not schedule my speaking time, it will not happen!

Therefore, **I have a rule of scheduling multiple lessons and language exchanges at a time, usually deciding on the next four or five dates in advance, so that they go into my diary and are fixed. As a consequence, my speaking happens.** I recommend you do the same.

Studying in Your Dead Time

If you have adopted the principle of core study time, then you are off to a great start. The good news, though, is that there is almost certainly plenty of extra time throughout your day which you can take advantage of to spend more time with French. Dead time refers to those moments in the day when you cannot be productive and have no choice but to wait. Commuting is the classic example, but you may also spend time walking, eating, or waiting for meetings to start. People use this time differently, but there is a fair chance that in such situations you either reach for your phone, daydream, or some combination of the two!

Periods of dead time throughout your day can add up to considerable amounts of time - easily an hour or more per day - and this time can be a great asset for your language learning if you make use of it in a smart way. While your core study time is best used for focused study, your dead time is ideal for less intense, more entertaining activities. **For most people, the trick to taking advantage of your dead time is to use your smartphone or tablet to make your language learning material portable.** By all means, you can carry your textbook around with you all day, but technology has given us many options for accessing the material we want anywhere:

- Download podcasts in French
- Use electronic flashcards to review your vocabulary
- Read the news in French on Le Monde website
- Buy French short story books for your Kindle (I have a written series of short story books for beginners which are referenced at the start of this book.)
- Take pictures on your phone of the chapter you are currently working on in your textbook so you always have it with you
- Take a picture of the grammar tables you are trying to memorize

The great thing about using your dead time to study French is that everyone has dead time, it does not have to be scheduled, and it can quickly add up to large amounts of time. The trick is to develop the habit of recognizing when you are at a loose end and to use the time for French rather than Facebook!

What Should the First Year of French Look Like?

Let's imagine you have a goal of achieving a good level of proficiency in French in one year. What would that year look like, and how would you need to study differently over the course of that year in order to reach your goal? This is a frequently-asked question which is helpful for developing the mindset of a good language learner, and so in this closing section I will describe my experience of how the study process changes as your level improves.

At the beginning you know little or no French, and so your first task is to learn the basics. It is helpful to gain as complete a picture as possible of the basics of the language, and the best way to do that is to work quickly through an entry-level book such as this from cover to cover, spending your time listening to the sounds of the language, and looking at the basic explanations of grammar. It is preferable to be fairly superficial at this stage, as the value lies in getting a general picture of the language rather than memorizing every detail.

Conclusion

I'd like to thank you and congratulate you for transiting my lines from start to finish.

I genuinely hope that over the course of this book, I've managed to set you up for success. I fully believe that I have, but the proof will be in the pudding of you learning and applying French in your day to day life. I fully expect that you can do that.

This is obviously not all there is to the French language, grammar or vocabulary, but if you have made it this far, you should have laid strong foundations upon which to base your future studies of the French language, and be well on your way to fluency. Learning French doesn't have to take ten years, or even one. In fact, you may be surprised to discover that you already know a lot of French.

Yes, French is full of strange rules and oddities, excruciatingly precise verb forms and the bizarre issue of "masculine" and "feminine" nouns. Is a chair masculine or feminine? What about a car? (both are feminine, by the way.)

French grammar can be a headache, even for a native speaker, but if you pay attention to this guide, you will quickly realize that English and French are far more alike than you might have guessed at first. For a native English speaker, French is a surprisingly simple language to learn. Or rather, it should be.

Chapter 19 - Five Things to Get Right as a Beginner

Now, let's look at the five steps I recommend you follow in order to get off to the best possible start learning French.

1. Find a Good Teacher

While it is perfectly possible to learn a language through self-study, and many independent language learners do so, I recommend that you find yourself a good teacher when you begin learning French, especially if this is your first foreign language. A good teacher will help provide some structure to your learning, give you feedback on your mistakes, encourage you, and, most importantly, help fine-tune your pronunciation. For many students, simply having another human being to interact and practice speaking French with is enough to provide a motivational boost.

What makes a good teacher? A good teacher is somebody who can help you learn faster than you might be able to on your own. He or she should be encouraging and create an environment in which you feel comfortable speaking French without worrying about making mistakes. Your teacher should allow you to have a say in what you learn, and in the material you use, and treat your lesson time as much as a conversation as a formal class. They should occasionally correct your grammar and pronunciation, but not too much - allowing you the opportunity to speak freely without interruption is also important. Lastly, your teacher does not necessarily have to be a native French speaker. In my experience, many of the best language teachers are non-native speakers of a language; their experience of learning the language themselves can give them a special insight into your learning journey.

Finding the kind of teacher described above might sound like a tall order, but I assure you that you will know it when you find her! I am often asked how to spot a good teacher and this description will give you some points to consider. In addition to local listings and adverts for language teachers, you should also consider taking lessons online, as they offer you much more flexibility in scheduling and can also be more affordable.

Tip:

There are many websites you can use to find French teachers online, but the company I recommend and use personally is Italki, who allow you to choose from both informal tutors and professional teachers. For special offers, and other options for finding affordable speaking practice, please visit my resource page at: http://iwillteachyoualanguage.com/resources

2. Learn Key Phrases and Important Verbs

As we said before, learning lists of words as a general language learning strategy will get you nowhere, but there is significant value in learning the most common French words and phrases at the beginning. Why? For two reasons: firstly, because learning common words and phrases will allow you to start communicating; secondly, because these words and phrases are so common that you will encounter them everywhere and quickly learn to use them naturally without much effort.

Learning set phrases sometimes involves learning grammatical constructions that you do not yet understand, such as in the phrase: Qu'est-ce que c'est? - "What is it?", which may appear terrifying to a beginner! However, there is a world of difference between understanding the grammar of a phrase, and simply using the phrase in order to get what you want. You do not need to understand the mechanics of why you say something in a certain way. Indeed, "why" may not always be a helpful question to ask when there is material to learn! If a phrase appears to be useful, then simply learn the phase as-is.

Examples of other potential confusing, yet extremely important, expressions might be:

- *Je m'appelle...* - My name is...

- *Est-ce que vous pouvez...?* - Can you...? (asking someone to do something)

- *Est-ce que je peux...?* - Can I...? (asking if you are allowed to do something)

You can find a full list of the essential French phrases I suggest you start with in Appendix 1 at the end of this book. Be sure to use the Audio Vault to check your pronunciation.

3.Learn the Fundamentals

Perhaps you have bad memories of learning a language at school, where after sitting through years of French classes you were still barely able to string a sentence together. Learning a new language should never be like this, not least because you can make faster progress as a beginner than at any other stage of the language learning journey. Make the most of the energy and motivation you feel right now to get a good grounding in the fundamentals of French grammar - conveniently, everything that is covered in this book!

Some parts of French grammar, such as the conjugation of verbs in the present tense, are essential and must simply be memorised, since without the ability to conjugate basic verbs you will be unable to communicate in French. My core recommendation in this book, however, is that you do not stop there - you should familiarise yourself with all the main grammatical concepts in French right from the beginning, rather than waiting months for them to appear in a school syllabus. You may not need to use these concepts yourself for some time, but by becoming aware that the concepts exist you give yourself a more complete picture of the grammar of the language and prime your brain to learn grammar much more easily further down the line.

There is nothing as motivating as making quick progress as a beginner in a new language, and the sense of progress and achievement itself will encourage you to keep going. For this reason, the best time to work hard and learn the basics is at the start.

4.Get a Good French Textbook

It is commonly said that a language cannot be taught, it must be learnt. However good a teacher may be and however effectively they guide you in your learning, the desire to learn must exist within the student or nothing will be learnt at all. In other words, you must take responsibility for your learning, and in order to do this you need the right tools. Whether or not you have a French teacher, I strongly recommend you have a good self-study textbook so that you can learn independently: look up grammar, practice reading, learn new words, complete grammar drills, and so on, outside your lesson time.

Personally, when I learn a new language, the first challenge I set myself is always to work through a good textbook cover-to-cover before taking any lessons, in order to familiarise myself with the main concepts of the language. I find it is far more efficient to learn the basics in my own time, instead of hiring a teacher to essentially give me the same information I already have in my textbook.

When trying to find the right textbook for you, I suggest you take a trip to your local bookshop so you can physically look through a selection of titles. Here are a few things to consider:

- **Determine which level of book you need.** Language textbooks usually start with A1, for beginners, and go up to C2, for advanced students. Choose a book that covers a suitable range, and avoid the temptation to choose something too advanced.

- **Why are you learning French?** Do you want to learn the basics for a trip? Do you hope to use French for business? Are you aiming for all-around fluency? Knowing this will help you choose a suitable textbook, or avoid an unsuitable one!

- **Look for a textbook with plenty of dialogues.** You will have noticed that I have mentioned the importance of exposure to French many times in this book. The more input you receive via reading and listening the faster you will grow your vocabulary and break out of beginner French. Dialogues in textbooks are great for this because they (usually) give you examples of spoken French in realistic situations that are not too difficult to understand. Ensure that the dialogues come with accompanying audio.

- **Choose a book you like.** This sounds like a trivial point, but many people will be tempted to learn French using a hand-me-down textbook, their old book from school, or something they found lying around the office! It is vitally important you actually like your chosen textbook, or else you will not look forward to picking it up every day to study with. Look at a variety of textbooks and choose one you find aesthetically pleasing and that you can imagine yourself working with on a daily basis.

Look inside the textbook first and see if the material is written in a straightforward way that is easy to understand. Make sure the book contains enough descriptive details that you feel you have all the information you need (some textbooks are nothing more than exercises, with no explanation). Lastly, you may also like to choose two different books, so you can see alternative explanations and switch between the two if you get bored.

5. Seek some French speakers to converse with

Ultimately, the best way to master a new tongue is to put what you've learned into practice. Studying by yourself with a textbook for months will not guarantee speaking fluency in the target language. Conversely, if you create regular opportunities to practice speaking French, even as a beginner, the confidence you will gain combined with the extra exposure to real spoken French, will turn you into a versatile speaker of French over time. I consider "speaking practice" to be distinct and separate from lessons with your teacher, because there is a different dynamic and you typically have to work harder to make the conversation successful.

To find people to practice French with you should look both online and in your local area. French meetup groups or societies are often a good place to start, especially if you live near a large town or city:

- Alliance Française: https://www.alliancefr.org/
- Meetup.com: https://www.meetup.com/

You might also simply search online for "French conversation" or "French language exchange" to see what pops up near you.

If you struggle to find options near you then you can use one of the many websites and apps which help you connect with language exchange partners online, through Skype calls or text chat. For a complete list, please visit my resource page:

- http://iwillteachyoualanguage.com/resources

Lastly, I run a private Facebook community for language enthusiasts, in which many people have found fantastic language exchange partners. You can join for free at:

- https://www.facebook.com/groups/fluencymastermind/
- Or search on Facebook: fluency mastermind

The internet has revolutionised language learning and created countless opportunities that never existed before to practice with people from all over the world. If you are unfamiliar with these opportunities, I encourage you to look into the websites I have listed above, you may be pleasantly surprised! Connecting with real people to practice French with is the most enjoyable and human element of language learning, and there has never been a better time to get started!

Conclusion.

I hope that through reading this book you gained a wealth of new knowledge on the French language and are already well on your way to speaking French. You have now been exposed to all facets of the French language that a beginner and even an intermediate French speaker needs to know. You can now speak in present tense, past tense and future tense and you have an arsenal of nouns to fit your every need. Now that you can form a full sentence with ease, the only thing left to do is practice! Practice is everything, especially with pronunciations. In order to keep teaching your tongue and lips to pronounce these new sounds, you must say them aloud each day. Read through the dictionary of phrases in chapter eight or the words in chapter seven each day and in no time you will be spitting them out with ease.

It may seem like a lot to remember, but as you begin to memorize certain sections like verbs and such you will begin to notice what sounds right and what sounds wrong, That is why reading aloud is so beneficial. You can teach your brain to hear you speaking and in time it will notice when you have made a mistake.

Keep this book close beside you and jump to whatever section you need a refresher on, whenever you may need it. If you forget something, don't panic as you have all of the information right at your fingertips. While you are practicing or watching French films, keep this book close at hand so that you can check something you may have forgotten. Come back to these exercises and these practice questions, to keep yourself sharp, or to spruce up your pronunciation every once in a while, and you will never be lost in the French language. If you ever take a break from French, this book will be here to help you out when you come back!

Thank you for reading the entirety of this book, and I hope you are excited to continue your language journey. Now that you have learned everything you need to know as a beginner, the next step is to begin reading short stories to increase your vocabulary. As you practice, seeing new stories will help you to test your comprehension and pronunciation skills. Expose yourself as much as you can to French daily so that it stays fresh in your mind and in your memory. Enjoy your travels as a newly French speaking person!

Share this book with friends and family of your choosing and soon you will be able to have secret conversations in French that nobody else will understand. Share this book with your spouse and you will be able to have secret French conversations at full volume in front of your kids, the possibilities are endless!

If you liked this book, a review on amazon is always appreciated so that many others like yourself can discover and enjoy the wealth of knowledge hidden within these pages.

FREE AUDIO OF "LEARN FRENCH FOR BEGINNERS"

Download your fee audio from our website:

www.dupontlanguageinstitute.com

or follow this QR code:

To download the file:

Username: AC-01
Password: ?xd@IG!ySbLa

To open the file:

Password: 9!@atFbLk95mJ4!f

French short stories
for beginners

Learn French in a fast and easy way and grow your
vocabulary with 15 captivating short stories

Introduction

You have to familiarise yourself with the linguistic distinctions between English and French before diving headfirst into French classes. Remember that there are many grammatical and lexical parallels between English and French, making the study of the latter less daunting than it may first appear.

In this book, we are presenting short stories that you can read to practice French language. Each story has its own topic, where important vocabulary is presented before the story. Then, you have the story, which you can read at your own leisure.

Most importantly, you can begin to practice the language that we have discussed throughout this book in an engaging manner. As such, here is a suggested methodology that you can apply to the study of these short stories.

1.- Next, read through the story, paragraph by paragraph. Since you will find the Spanish and English version, you will be able to visualize the structures and conjugations that we have studied throughout this volume. That way, you will be able to make a mental note of the way each structure is presented in real-life. This makes learning grammar and sentence structure a lot more digestible.

2.- Then, go through every one of the paragraphs. When you reach the end of the story, go back to any parts that you feel weren't clear or perhaps you have questions about. You can focus on these parts so that you can get the extra practice that you need. Once you feel comfortable with the entire story, you can then move on to the questions.

3.- The questions following the story are both meant to test your reading comprehension and give you an opportunity to practice your writing skills. This exercise will provide you with the chance to use your imagination as it pertains to writing skills.

4.- The suggested responses at the end of the story are meant to serve as a guide. So, you can compare your own answers to the suggested ones. Of course, these are only suggested answers. That means you can very well come up with your own answers according to the passage that you have read.

5.   Finally, please review the vocabulary presented at the end of the story. The words in that vocabulary have been selected in order to help you warm up for the content in the story. You will find both the French and English words in the list. That way, you won't have to guess their meaning. You can read through the list, and make a note of the words that you find new or challenging.

If you keep studying French, you'll start to pick up on subtleties that set it apart from English. As long as you keep these distinctions in mind and don't let them throw you off, switching back and forth between English and Spanish is OK. Maintaining regular practice is the key to fluency and accuracy in this lovely language.

1. Métiers

Alain est chauffeur de taxi dans une ville quelque part dans le continent africain. Tous les matins, il se lève tôt. Alain travaille pour George. George est le propriétaire du taxi. Il emploie Alain pour conduire le taxi. Tous les jours, Alain a un versement minimum à donner à George. Alain est aussi responsable de la maintenance de la voiture. Alain récupère la voiture au garage. Il lave la voiture. Il monte dans la voiture. Il met sa ceinture de sécurité. Il démarre la voiture. Il part travailler. Alain va en ville pour trouver des clients.

Alain is a taxi driver in a city somewhere in the African continent. Every morning he wakes up early. Alain works for George. George is the owner of the taxi. He uses Alain to drive the taxi. Every day, Alain has a minimum payment to give to George. Alain is also responsible for the maintenance of the car. Alain gets the car from the garage. He's washing the car. He gets into the car. He puts on his seatbelt. He starts the car. He goes to work. Alain goes to town to find customers.

Une jeune femme debout au bord du trottoir appelle le taxi. Alain arrête la voiture devant la jeune femme. Il abaisse la vitre de la voiture.

A young woman standing at the sidewalk calls the taxi. Alain stops the car in front of the young woman. He lowers the window of the car.

-Bonjour! dit la jeune femme. J'aimerais aller à l'hôtel de ville s'il vous plaît.

-Hello! said the young woman. I would like to go to the city hall please.

La jeune femme monte dans le taxi. Alain redémarre la voiture et se dirige vers l'hôtel de ville. La jeune femme sort un rouge à lèvres de son sac. Elle enlève ses lunettes de soleil. Elle regarde le rétroviseur et met du rouge à lèvres. Elle remet ses lunettes.

The young woman gets into the cab. Alain restarts the car and heads for City Hall. The young woman pulls a lipstick out of her bag. She takes off her sunglasses. She looks at the mirror and puts on lipstick. She puts on her glasses.

-Est-ce que je peux fumer? demande-t-elle à Alain.

- Oui, vous pouvez fumer.

-Merci.

-Can I smoke? she asks Alain.

-Yes, you can smoke.

-   Thank you.

La jeune femme sort un paquet de cigarettes de son sac. Elle prend une cigarette et un briquet. Elle allume la cigarette et fume. La voiture arrive à l'hôtel de ville. La jeune femme paie les frais de taxi. Elle sort de la voiture.

The young woman takes a pack of cigarettes from her bag. She takes a cigarette and a lighter. She lights the cigarette and smokes. The car arrives at City Hall. The young woman pays the taxi fees. She gets out of the car.

Alain conduit la voiture vers la station essence. Alain met de l'essence dans la voiture. Puis il repart. En route, un homme hèle le taxi. Alain s'arrête devant lui.

Alain drives the car to the gas station. Alain puts gas in the car. Then he leaves. On the way, a man hails the taxi. Alain stops in front of him.

-*Bonjour monsieur! dit l'homme.*

-*Bonjour monsieur! Où allez-vous?*

-*Je suis de passage dans cette ville, répond l'homme. J'aimerais aller à un endroit. Je ne sais pas où se trouve le lieu. Mais j'ai un plan de l'endroit.*

-*Montrez-moi le plan.*

-Hello sir! said the man.

-Hello sir! Where are you going?

-I'm passing through this city, the man replies. I would like to go to a place. I do not know where the place is. But I have a plan of the place.

-Show me the plan.

L'homme déplie le plan. Alain le regarde. Le plan montre le chemin pour aller vers un magasin en ville.

The man unfolds the plan. Alain looks at him. The map shows the way to go to a store in town.

-*Montez dans la voiture, monsieur, dit Alain. Je vous emmène.*

-Get in the car, sir, said Alain. I am taking you.

L'homme s'installe dans la voiture. Alain démarre et part.

The man settles in the car. Alain starts and leaves.

-*Votre voiture est confortable, dit le client.*

-Your car is comfortable, says the customer.

-*Merci, répond Alain. Mais ce n'est pas la mienne.*

-Thank you, Alain answers. But it's not mine.

-*Vous louez cette voiture?*

-You rent this car?

-*Je travaille pour le propriétaire de cette voiture.*

-I work for the owner of this car.

-*D'accord.*

-Okay.

-*D'où venez-vous? demande Alain.*

-Where are you from? asks Alain.

-*Vous êtes français?*

-You're French?

-*Non, je suis belge.*

-No, I'm Belgian.

-*Belge?*

-Belgian?

-Oui, je viens de Belgique. Depuis quand travaillez-vous pour le propriétaire de cette voiture?

-Yes, I come from Belgium. Since when do you work for the owner of this car?

-Depuis plus d'un an, répond Alain.

-For more than a year, answers Alain.

-Et votre salaire mensuel est-il satisfaisant? demande l'homme.

-And is your monthly salary satisfactory? the man asks.

-Moyennement satisfaisant.

-Moderately satisfactory.

-Pardonnez-moi. Je suis trop indiscret.

-Excuse me. I am too indiscreet.

-Ce n'est rien, monsieur. Le salaire moyen chez nous est bas. Ce n'est pas un secret.

-It's nothing, sir. The average salary here is low. It's not a secret.

-Mais c'est votre vie privée.

-But that's your private life.

-Je vous dis que ce n'est pas grave. Si vos questions me gênent, je ne vous réponds pas.

-I tell you it does not matter. If your questions bother me, I do not answer you.

-D'accord.

-Okay.

-Nous sommes arrivés.

-We have arrived.

Alain stationne devant le magasin. Le client donne de l'argent à Alain.

Alain is parked in front of the store. The customer gives money to Alain.

-Dites-moi, pourriez-vous passer me prendre tout à l'heure? demande le client à Alain.

-Tell me, could you pick me up later? the customer asks Alain.

-A quelle heure? répond Alain.

-At what time? Alain answers.

-Dans trois ou quatre heures.

-In three or four hours.

-Je vais vous donner mon numéro de téléphone. Appelez-moi quand vous voulez partir.

-I'll give you my phone number. Call me when you want to leave.

-D'accord, merci. Quel est votre nom, monsieur?

-Ok thank you. What is your name, sir?

-Alain.

-Alain.

-Moi, c'est Ethan.

-Me, it's Ethan.

Ethan enregistre le numéro du chauffeur de taxi dans le répertoire de son téléphone.

Ethan records the number of the taxi driver in his phone book.

-Merci Alain. Je vous appelle donc dans trois ou quatre heures.

-Thank you Alain. So I'll call you in three or four hours.

-Bien monsieur. A tout à l'heure.

-Well sir. Right away.

Alain démarre la voiture et part. Il rentre chez lui pour prendre le déjeuner. Alain enlève son blouson. Il fait chaud. Alain enlève ses chaussures. Il s'assoupit sur le canapé du salon. Trente minutes plus tard, sa femme le réveille. Alain remet ses chaussures et se lave le visage. Il met un chapeau et repart travailler.

Alain starts the car and leaves. He goes home to have lunch. Alain takes off his jacket. It's hot. Alain takes off his shoes. He falls asleep on the sofa in the living room. Thirty minutes later, his wife wakes him up. Alain puts on his shoes and washes his face. He puts on a hat and goes back to work.

Le téléphone d'Alain sonne. Il décroche:

Alain's phone rings. He hung up:

-Allô!

-Hello!

-Alain? C'est moi, Ethan. Je vais partir dans trente minutes. Pourriez-vous passer me prendre s'il vous plaît?

-Alain? It's me, Ethan. I will leave in thirty minutes. Could you pass me please?

-Oui, monsieur. Où êtes-vous?

-Yes sir. Where are you?

-Je suis au même endroit où vous m'avez laissé. Au magasin.

-I'm in the same place where you left me. At the store.

-D'accord, monsieur. Je passe vous prendre.

-OK sir. I'm going to pick you up.

-Merci Alain. Je vous attends devant le magasin.

-Thank you Alain. I'm waiting for you in front of the store.

-Ok! A tout à l'heure!

-Okay! Right away!

Trente minutes plus tard, Ethan monte dans le taxi.

Thirty minutes later, Ethan gets in the cab.

-Savez-vous où je peux trouver un distributeur automatique de billets? Je n'ai plus d'argent dans mon portefeuille.

-Do you know where I can find a cash machine? I have no more money in my wallet.

-*Je vous y emmène tout de suite.*

-I'll take you there right away.

Alain stationne devant une banque. Ethan sort de la voiture. Il se dirige vers le distributeur automatique de billets. Il sort sa carte bancaire de son portefeuille. Il insère la carte bancaire dans le DAB. Il entre la somme d'argent à retirer. Ethan reçoit de l'argent. Il retire sa carte bancaire. Il range l'argent dans son portefeuille. Il met le portefeuille dans sa poche. Puis il revient dans le taxi.

Alain is parked in front of a bank. Ethan gets out of the car. He goes to the ATM. He takes out his credit card from his wallet. He inserts the bank card into the ATM. He enters the sum of money to withdraw. Ethan receives money. He withdraws his credit card. He puts the money in his wallet. He puts the wallet in his pocket. Then he comes back in the taxi.

Quiz

1. Where does Alain live and work?
a. Europe
b. Belgium
c.Africa

2. Alain works as a ----
a. Taxi driver
b. Hotel attendant
c.Teacher

3. The woman who boards Alain's car requests to?
a. Use the mirror
b. Apply lipstick
c. smoke

4. What was the name of the customer at the store?
a. Alain
b. Dan
c. Ethan

Answers

1.c
2.a
3.c
4.c

Vocabulary

- *Chauffeur de taxi* --- taxi driver
- *Versement* --- payment
- *Conduire le taxi* --- drive the cab
- *Alain récupère la voiture* --- Alain picks up the car
- Ceinture de sécurité --- seat belt
- *Il part travailler* --- he goes to work
- *Debout* --- standing
- *Bord du trottoir* --- curb
- *Il abaisse la vitre de la voiture* --- he rolls down the car window
- *Hôtel de ville* --- town hall
- *Rouge à lèvres* --- lipstick
- Lunettes de soleil --- sunglasses
- *Rétroviseur* --- rear-view mirror
- *Est-ce que je peux fumer?* --- Can I smoke in the car?
- *Paquet* --- pack
- *Briquet* --- cigarette lighter
- *Frais de taxi* --- taxi fares
- *Station essence* --- gas station
- *Un homme hèle le taxi* --- a man hails the cab
- *Où allez-vous?* --- where are you going?
- *L'homme déplie le plan* --- the man unfolds the map
- *Magasin* --- shop
- *Ce n'est pas la mienne* --- it's not mine
- *Vous louez cette voiture?* --- do you rent this car?
- *Belge* --- Belgian
- *Pardonnez-moi* --- forgive me
- *Bas* --- low
- *Vie privée* --- private life
- *Alain stationne* --- Alain parks
- *Il fait chaud* --- it's warm
- *Il s'assoupit* --- he dozes off
- *Distributeur Automatique de Billets* (DAB) --- Automated Teller Machine (ATM)
- *Portefeuille* --- wallet
- *Carte bancaire* --- debit card
- *Poche* --- pocket

2. Une Tarte Aux Pommes

J'ouvre les yeux au moins vingt secondes avant que le réveil ne sonne. Je m'appelle Henri et j'ai cinquante ans. J'ai trois enfants, Marie, Mathieu et Quentin, des enfants très intelligents et dont je suis fier. Les deux aînés sont partis continuer leurs études universitaires à l'étranger. Marie est en Allemagne et Mathieu en France. Pour ce qui est de Quentin, le petit dernier, nous ne savons pas ce qu'il projette de faire, mais pour le moment il est parti vivre en colocation avec un de ses amis et nous le voyons encore pendant les weekends, ou quand il n'a pas cours. C'est fou ce que les enfants grandissent vite, le temps file à toute allure.

I open my eyes at least 20 seconds before the alarm rings. My name is Henri and I'm 50 years old. I have three children, Marie, Mathieu and Quentin, very intelligent children, of whom I am proud. The two elders left to continue their college studies abroad. Marie is in Germany and Mathieu in France. As for Quentin, the youngest, we do not know what he's planning to do, but for the moment he's gone off to live with a friend of his and we see him on weekends or when he's not at his classes. It's crazy how children grow up fast, time flies.

Ma femme Zoé dort encore. Sans trop tarder, je me lève et je vais dans la salle de bain me laver le visage pour effacer les traces de l'oreiller. Je porte un débardeur et un short, il est six heures du matin. Je prends la serviette suspendue sous le miroir et je m'essuie le visage avec.

Zoe still sleeps. Without too much delay I get up and go to the bathroom to wash my face to remove the traces of the pillow. I wear a tank top and a shirt ; it is 6am in the morning. I find the towel under the mirror and I wipe my face with it.

Je me change avant de me diriger vers la cuisine pour prendre mon petit déjeuner. J'entends Zoé se lever.

I change before heading to the kitchen for breakfast. I hear Zoé getting up.

"Tu es bien matinal aujourd'hui.

'You are early today.'

– Oh, je n'avais plus sommeil, dis-je en ouvrant le frigo.

'Oh, I was no longer sleepy,' I say opening the fridge.

– Il y a des céréales aux fruits rouges si ça te dit, chéri.

'We have red fruit cereals if you want, darling.'

– Mhhh, non c'est bon, je vais juste manger des biscottes. Fais-nous du café plutôt.

'Mhhh, no it's good, I'm just going to eat crackers. Make us some coffee instead.'

– Oui, chef, dit-elle en sautillant.

'Yes, sir.' She said, hopping.

– Tu n'as toujours pas de nouvelles des enfants?

'You still have no news from the children?

– Non.

'No.'

– Marie, Mathieu, et Quentin?

'Marie? Mathieu, and Quentin?'

– *Ils sont sûrement occupés. Quentin a appelé hier soir quand tu étais encore au travail. Il passera dimanche, il veut nous présenter sa petite copine, Clémence.*

'They are probably busy. Quentin called last night when you were still at work. He will come on Sunday, he wants to introduce his girlfriend, Clemence.'

– *Eh bien, comme je le pensais, le temps passe vite. Et dire qu'il y a un an, on déposait Mathieu à l'aéroport et voilà que Quentin a une petite copine! dis-je en riant.*

'Well, as I said time flies. Thinking that just a year ago we were dropping off Mathieu at the airport, and now Quentin has a girlfriend!"l I said with a little chuckle.

– *Nous avons bien fait de prendre cet appartement. A nous deux, la maison était bien trop grande. En plus, notre portier Marcello est extrêmement sympathique.*

'We did well by taking this apartment, the house was way too big just for the two of us. Moreover, we have a friendly doorman."

– *Oui, c'est sûr. Mais il se fait vieux, il devrait partir à la retraite pour enfin pouvoir se reposer.*

Yes, but Marcello is getting old, he has to rest and retire.'

– *Il n'a pas de famille apparemment. Et puis son travail ne le fatigue pas tant que ça je pense."*

'But he does not have a family, and it seems like his work is not so much tiring.'

Le téléphone sonne. Zoé s'empresse de regarder le nom affiché sur l'écran. Déçue, elle le tend à Henri: c'est un de ses amis qui l'appelle.

The phone rings. Zoé hastens to see the name displayed on the screen. Disappointed she hands it to me, it is one of my friends calling.

"*Bon, je vais faire une tarte, je sors faire quelques courses pour acheter les ingrédients.*

'Good, I'm going to make a pie. I will go out shopping to buy the ingredients.'

– *Moi aussi je veux sortir faire un tour.*

'I'm going out for a walk.'

– *Allons-y ensemble alors.*

'We will go together then.'

– *D'accord. Préparons-nous alors", dis-je.*

'Okay. Let's get ready,' I said.

Nous avons eu un déjeuner calme. C'était délicieux, j'adore les lasagnes, surtout avec des champignons. En début d'après-midi, on a regardé quelques feuilletons. Puis j'ai enfilé mes lunettes pour lire les journaux pendant qu'elle continuait à regarder ses séries.

We had a quiet lunch, it was delicious, I really like lasagna, especially with mushrooms. In the early afternoon we watched a few soap operas and she continued watching her shows while I put on my glasses to read the newspapers.

"*Bon, je vais aller faire ma tarte. Je n'ai pas envie de commencer trop tard, je serai fatiguée ensuite et je n'aime pas remettre à demain, dit-elle en se levant.*

'Good, I'll go make my pie. I do not want to start too late, I will be tired and I do not want to postpone it until tomorrow.' She said, standing up.

– Moi je pense faire une petite sieste.

'Yes, I'm going to take a nap.'

– Est-ce que tu ne serais pas mieux dans le lit?

'Wouldn't it better to sleep on the bed?'

– Oh que non, le canapé est bien mieux, crois-moi.

'Oh no, the sofa is better, believe me.'

– Si tu le dis."

'If you say so.'

Je ne sais plus quelle heure il est quand j'ouvre les yeux. Il commence à faire nuit. Je me lève et vais vers la cuisine. Ça sent le gâteau. Zoé est justement en train de sortir la tarte du four. Elle en profite pour humer la douce odeur de tarte sortant du four.

I do not know what time it is when I open my eyes ; it is getting dark. I get up and go to the kitchen. It smells like pie, Zoe is just taking out the pie from the oven. She seizes the opportunity to smell the odor that the pie gives off.

"Et voilà, je n'ai pas perdu la main! dit-elle en souriant comme une enfant.

'And here, I did not lose the knack!' she said, smiling like a child.

– Ça a l'air bon.

'It looks good.'

– C'est l'odeur qui t'a réveillé? Tu semblais dormir tellement bien que je n'ai pas osé te réveiller.

'Is it the smell that woke you up? You seemed to sleep so well that I did not dare to wake you up.'

– Je me suis assoupi un instant et puis hop!"

'I fell asleep for a moment and then hop!'

Je m'assieds et la regarde découper deux morceaux de la tarte.

I sat down and watched her cut out two pieces of the pie.

"Tu veux qu'on l'appelle?

'Do you want to make a call?'

– Qui donc?

'Who?'

– Mathieu voyons. Je sais que c'est son anniversaire et que c'est pour ça que tu as fait cette tarte. Une tarte aux pommes, hein? C'est ce qui m'a mis la puce à l'oreille.

'Mathieu. I know it's his birthday and that's why you made this pie. An apple pie, huh?' That's what set me thinking she would like to call him.

– C'est sa préférée… Il doit être occupé, je ne veux pas le déranger.

'It's his favorite … He must be busy, I do not want to disturb him.'

– Mais non, c'est vendredi, il doit sûrement avoir un peu de temps. Et puis on ne le dérangera pas longtemps. On va juste lui souhaiter un joyeux anniversaire! dis-je en déverrouillant mon smartphone. En plus il est connecté! ajoutais-je.

'But no, it's Friday, he must surely have some time. And then we will not disturb him for a long time. We're just going to wish him a happy birthday!' I say unlocking my smartphone. 'In addition he is connected!' I added.

– *Vraiment? Appelle-le alors!", dit-elle en se rapprochant de moi.*

'Really? Call him then!' she said, coming closer to me.

Ça bipe un moment, il ne décroche pas. On essaye une seconde fois, rien.

It beeps for a moment, he does not pick up. We try a second time, nothing.

On attend cinq minutes avant de retenter, au cas où il serait sorti un instant, et on rappelle. Cette fois, il décroche.

We wait five minutes before retrying in case it takes a moment and we call back. This time he picks up.

"Allô? Bonjour papa.

'Allo? Hello, Dad.'

– *Bonjour fiston, ça va? On t'appelle juste pour...*

'Hello son, how are you? We call you for...'

– *Joyeux anniversaire chééérii!", s'empresse Zoé par-dessus mon épaule gauche.*

'Happy birthday honeeeeeey.' says Zoé over my left shoulder

J'entends Mathieu rire, je ris à mon tour.

I hear Mathieu laughing, I laugh in turn.

«Oui, voilà, joyeux anniversaire fiston, c'est pour te dire que nous t'aimons et que nous pensons à toi.

'Yes, voilà, happy birthday son, we love you.'

– *Tu nous manques!*

'We miss you!'

– *Vous me manquez aussi... Et merci de ne pas avoir oublié. Et désolé de ne pas vous avoir appelé souvent.*

'I miss you too... And thank you for not having forgotten. And sorry for not calling you often.'

– *Ce n'est rien, tu dois être occupé.*

'It's nothing, you must be busy.'

– *Appelle-nous quand tu as le temps, OK?*

'Well call us when you have time. OK?'

– *Ça marche!*

'I'll do it!'

– *On a fait une tarte aux pommes, tu t'en rappelles? C'est ta préférée.*

'We did an apple pie, remember? It's your favorite.'

– *Mhhhh, oui oui. Ça fait longtemps que je n'en ai pas mangé. Tiens je vais m'en acheter une après.*

'Mhhhh, yes yes. I have not eaten it for a long time. Maybe I'll buy some after.'

– *Sinon, ça va?*

'Then, how are you doing?'

– *Oui, mais je dois vous laisser. Je vais sortir avec des amis.*

'Good, but I have to leave. I am going out with friends.'

– *Pas de souci, vas-y. Nous sommes heureux de t'avoir eu au téléphone aujourd'hui! dis-je.*

'No worries, go ahead. We are happy we could talk to you today!'

– *Moi aussi mes parents chéris! Ah, et Marie m'a appelé, elle m'a dit qu'elle pourrait sûrement venir me voir d'ici peu. Elle n'a encore rien dit, mais vous la connaissez avec ses mystères.*

'So did I, my dear parents! Ah, and Marie called me, she told me she could probably come and see me. She has not said anything yet but, you know, her and her mysteries.'

– *Quelle bonne nouvelle, appelez-nous quand vous serez ensemble, lança Zoé.*

'That's good news, call us then,' said Zoé.

– *Oui, maman! Promis! Bises!*

'Yes mom! Promised! Hugs!'

– *Bisous!*

'Kisses!'

– *Au revoir fiston."*

'-See you, son.'

Quand il a raccroché, Zoé a pris un morceau de tarte et me l'a tendu. C'est bon, je suis heureux. On a eu notre fils au téléphone et on a pu lui souhaiter un joyeux anniversaire.

When he hung up Zoe took a piece of pie and handed it to me. 'It's good, I'm happy, we had our son on the phone and we could wish him a happy birthday.'

Quiz

1. How old is Henri
a. 20 years
b. 50 years
c. 30 years

2. Where does Marie stay?
a. France
b. Belgium
c. German

3. What is the name of Quentin's girlfriend?
a. Zoe
b. Marie
c. Clemence

4. Who had a birthday?
a. Marie
b. Quentin

c. Mathieu

Answers

1.b
2.c
3.c
4.c

Vocabulaire / Vocabulary

- *secondes* --- seconds
- *réveil* --- alarm
- *fier* --- proud
- *aînés* --- elders
- *coloc'* --- shared appartment
- *c'est fou* --- it's crazy
- *serviette* --- towel
- *la cuisine* --- kitchen
- *petit déjeuner* --- breakfast
- *oreiller* --- pillow
- *débardeur* --- tank top
- *short* --- shorts
- *sommeil* --- sleep
- *céréales* --- cereal
- *dimanche* --- Sunday
- *sympathique* --- nice
- *retraite* --- retirement
- *écran* --- screen
- *tarte aux pommes* --- apple pie
- *une sieste* --- a nap
- *morceau* --- piece
- *canapé* --- sofa
- *joyeux anniversaire* --- happy birthday

3. End of The Holidays - Fin des Vacances

Avec la liste d'achats pour l'uniforme de l'école en main, Peter et Henry montent dans la voiture pour se rendre en ville.

With the school uniform shopping list in hand, Peter and Henry get into the car to drive to town.

Quand ils arrivent, ils vont d'abord dans un magasin de sport pour acheter des baskets. Henry essaie 4 paires différentes --- une paire entièrement blanche, une paire bleue et blanche, une paire rouge et noire et une paire blanche et verte. Peter pense que les bleues et blanches sont les plus belles, mais Henry préfère les rouges et noires, parce qu'elles lui rappellent son équipe de football préférée. Elles coûtent plus cher, mais Peter est d'accord pour la paire rouge et noire.

When they arrive, they go first to a sports shop to buy some trainers. Henry tries on 4 different pairs – one all white pair, one pair that is blue and white, one pair that is red and black, and finally a white and green pair. Peter thinks the blue and white look best but Henry wants the red and black, because they remind him of his favorite football team. They cost more, but Peter agrees to the red and black pair.

Pendant qu'ils sont dans le magasin de sport, ils achètent les chaussettes de sport blanches de Henry.

While they are in the sports shop, they buy Henry's white PE socks.

Ils se rendent ensuite dans un grand magasin bien connu pour chercher les cinq autres articles, y compris les chaussures.

They then go to a well-known department store to look for the other five items, including the shoes.

Ils trouvent tout de suite les polos blancs et parviennent à trouver et à mettre les cinq chemises dont Henry a besoin dans le panier. Près des polos se trouvent les sweatshirts de différentes couleurs: bleu marine, vert, violet, jaune et, heureusement, rouge. Il y a donc un sweat-shirt rouge de la taille d'Henry qui va dans le panier.

They find the white polo shirts straightaway and are able to put the five shirts Henry needs into the shopping basket. Near to the polo shirts are the sweatshirts in different colours: navy blue, green, purple, yellow and, thankfully, red. So, a red sweatshirt in Henry's size goes into the shopping basket.

Les chaussettes grises sont tout aussi faciles à trouver --- il y en a beaucoup dans la bonne taille. Cinq paires vont dans le panier.

The grey socks are just as easy to find – there are plenty in the right size. Five pairs go into the shopping basket.

Il y a aussi un grand choix de pantalons --- ou du moins c'est ce que Peter pense. Il les regarde presque tous sur les étagères mais ne trouve qu'un seul de la bonne taille pour Henry. Peter le met dans le panier et essaie de trouver un vendeur. Mais Peter décide de ne pas s'inquiéter car Henry portera ses shorts pendant les premières semaines d'école, ils pourront ensuite en commander en ligne et attendre qu'ils arrivent.

There are plenty of trousers to choose from as well – or so Peter thinks. He looks at nearly every pair on the racks and only finds one pair that are the right size for Henry. Peter puts them in the basket and tries to find an assistant. But then Peter decides not to worry as Henry will wear shorts for the first few weeks back at school, and they can order a pair online and wait for them to arrive.

Ils vont à la caisse et paient les articles du panier.

They go to the till and pay for the items in the basket.

C'est maintenant le tour des chaussures. Ils vont au rayon chaussures où il y a beaucoup de choix. Certaines avec des lacets, d'autres avec des scratchs. Peter décide que les chaussures à lacets sont mieux et Henry essaie une paire dans laquelle il dit être vraiment à l'aise. Elles ont aussi l'air élégantes. Peter paie donc également pour les chaussures.

And now the shoes. They go to the shoe department where there are many pairs to choose from. Some with laces, some with Velcro straps. Peter decides that laced shoes are better and Henry tries on a pair that he says are really comfortable. They look smart as well. So, Peter pays for the shoes as well.

Avec tous ces sacs à transporter, Peter suggère d'aller boire un verre avant de rentrer chez eux. Henry demande s'il peut avoir quelque chose à manger, car les courses lui donnent faim.

With lots of bags to carry, Peter suggests they go for a drink before going home. Henry asks if he can have something to eat as shopping makes him hungry.

Café et gâteau pour Peter, Coca-Cola et gâteau pour Henry.

Coffee and cake for Peter, Coca-Cola and cake for Henry.

Quiz

1) Quelles est la paire de baskets préférées d'Henry?
a) La paire blanche
b) La paire bleue et blanche
c) La paire rouge et noire
d) La paire blanche et verte
1) Which is Henry's favourite pair of trainers?
a) The white pair
b) The blue and white pair
c) The red and black pair
d) The white and green pair

2) Dans quelle couleur les sweatshirts ne sont-ils pas disponibles?
a) Bleu marine
b) Vert
c) Rouge
d) Orange
2) Which colour are the sweatshirts not available in?
a) Navy blue
b) Green
c) Red
d) Orange

3) Pourquoi Peter ne s'inquiète pas pour les pantalons?
a) Ils ont l'air solides
b) Ils pourront en commander en ligne plus tard
c) Ils ont des lacets
d) Ils ont des scratchs
3) Why does Peter not worry about the trousers?
a) They look resistant
b) They can order some online later
c) They have laces

d) They have Velcro straps

Answers:

1.C
2. D
3. B

Vocabulaire / Vocabulary

- *Achats* --- Shopping
- *D'accord* --- Agrees
- *Tout de suite* --- Straightaway
- *Assistant* --- Assistant
- *Suggère* --- Suggests
- *Paire* --- pair

4. Homonyms and Homophones --- Les copines – The Girlfriends

Un groupe d'amies se retrouve après le travail pour aller au cinéma. Elles sont toutes mariées, avec des enfants. Elles se retrouvent une fois par semaine pour profiter d'un moment rien qu'à elles, sans mari, sans enfant, pour se détendre et échanger des potins. Elles ne se sont pas vues depuis un mois, car elles sont parties en vacances, chacune de leur côté. Ravies de se retrouver, elles sont impatientes de se raconter leur été...

A group of friends meet up after work to go to the movies. They are all married, with children. They meet once a week to enjoy a moment just for themselves, without a husband, without children, to relax and exchange gossip. They have not seen each other for a month, because they have gone on vacation, everyone on his own. Delighted to meet again, they are eager to tell each other their summer ...

– Oh, les filles! J'ai failli recevoir une amende pour excès de vitesse tellement j'étais pressée d'arriver, souffle l'une d'entre elles qui arrive en courant.

- Oh, girls! I almost got a fine for excess speed because I was in a hurry to get there, blows one of them who comes running.

– Ah! Moi je suis arrivée avec un quart d'heure d'avance! Je cours depuis ce matin pour ne pas manquer ce rendez-vous.

- Ah! I arrived a quarter of an hour in advance! I have been running since this morning in order not to miss this appointment.

– Et moi j'ai faim! Je n'ai mangé qu'une amande et bu un verre d'eau depuis ce matin. Il est temps de se mettre à table! Répond la troisième femme.

- And I'm hungry! I have only eaten an almond and drunk a glass of water since this morning. It's time to sit down and eat! The third woman answers.

– Au secours! Comment tu fais pour tenir?

- Help! How are you doing to hold?

– Eh bien pourtant crois-moi, j'ai des réserves: deux semaines de vacances à l'hôtel avec pension complète! On n'a pas arrêté de manger, et pas que des légumes verts!

- Well, believe me, I have reserves: two weeks of vacation at the hotel with full board! We did not stop eating, not just green vegetables!

– Et toi Charlotte, tu es rentrée quand?

- And you Charlotte, when did you come back?

– Ah mais moi, je suis partie au mois de mai avec ma mère. Nous sommes allées vers la mer en Bretagne et le Mont Saint-Michel. Je suis restée dans le coin cet été.

- Ah, but I left in May with my mother. We went to the sea in Brittany and Mont Saint-Michel. I stayed in the area this summer.

– Génial. Et toi, Sabine, quand pars-tu?

- Awesome. And you, Sabine, when do you leave?

– Je voulais partir au mois de septembre et me mettre au vert, mais finalement on va rester. On a fait

une croix sur les vacances. Mon mari est sans emploi et mon fils ne veut pas bouger, car il a cours.

- I wanted to leave in September and go green, but finally we will stay. We forgot about holidays. My husband is unemployed and my son does not want to move because he has school.

– Je vois. Ce n'est pas de chance. Mais tu pourras toujours faire des balades à vélo dans la région et profiter des magnifiques champs de blé. Tu peux aussi venir profiter un peu de la piscine chez moi, la rassure Charlotte.

- I see. It's no luck. But you can still go cycling in the area and enjoy the beautiful wheat fields. You can also enjoy a little pool at home, reassures Charlotte.

– Merci, c'est gentil. Alors on commande? Il paraît que ce restaurant est bon et pas cher. En plus, j'ai gagné un bon d'achat cette semaine! Avec le coût de la vie, aucun complexe!

- Thanks, that's nice. So we order? It seems that this restaurant is good and not expensive. In addition, I won a voucher this week! With the cost of living, no complex!

– Je ne te le fais pas dire, enchérit Sabine. J'avais regardé pour inscrire les enfants en camps de vacances, mais en voyant le prix, j'ai fait un bond. Allez, que cela ne nous coupe pas l'appétit! Je vais prendre des spaghettis, j'adore les pâtes. Je sens que je vais ressortir d'ici comme un vrai poids lourd à quatre pattes!

"I'm not telling you," Sabine said. I had looked to enroll the kids in vacation camps, but seeing the price, I jumped. Come on, let's not lose our appetite! I'm going to have spaghetti, I love pasta. I feel like I'm coming out of here like a real heavyweight on all fours!

– Ne dis pas de bêtises, voyons, tu n'as que la peau sur les os. On dirait que tu te nourris de petits pois! Tu goûtes le magret de canard avec moi? C'est très fin.

- Do not talk nonsense, see, you have only the skin on the bones. Looks like you're eating peas! Do you taste the duck breast with me? It's very fine.

– En parlant de petits pois! Savez-vous ce que m'a fait ma fille pendant les vacances? Elle a perdu une dent en mangeant des petits pois! Il faut le faire! Si elle avait croqué dans un morceau de pain dur comme le fer, j'aurais compris! Et à dix-sept ans, perdre une dent, vous imaginez le drame! Elle ne voulait plus ouvrir la bouche jusqu'à la fin des vacances. Elle est pleine de complexes cette petite. Je devrais l'emmener voir un psy, qu'en pensez-vous?

- Speaking of peas! Do you know what my daughter did to me during the holidays? She lost a tooth while eating peas! It has to be done! If she had crunched in a piece of hard bread like iron, I would have understood! And at seventeen, lose a tooth, you imagine the drama! She did not want to open her mouth until the end of the holidays. She is full of this small complexes. I should take her to see a shrink, what do you think?

– Mais non! C'est juste une adolescente! Inscris-la à un cours de chant, ça va l'obliger à être moins timide. Elle a une belle voix!

- But no! She's just a teenager! Make her join a singing class, it will force her to be less shy. She has a beautiful voice!

– Bon, mais revenons à notre menu. Moi, c'est régime. Je ne bois plus une goutte de vin, un pot d'eau ça ira. Mais vous, vous buvez quoi?

- Good, but let's go back to our menu. Me, I am on diet. I no longer drink a drop of wine, a pot of water will be fine. But you? what do you drink?

– Tu devrais, ça fait circuler le sang!

- You should, it makes the blood circulate!

– *Cent euros la bouteille, ils exagèrent!*

- One hundred euros a bottle, they exaggerate!

– *Au fait Isabelle, ton amoureux t'emmène bientôt devant l'autel?*

- By the way, Isabelle, your lover is taking you to the altar soon?

– *Chères amies, vous serez les premières invitées à la fête, ne vous en faites pas; car pour le moment, il n'a pas l'air très tenté par le mariage. Je pensais qu'il ferait sa demande cet été à Venise, un soir sur une ballade romantique… j'ai attendu, mais rien!*

- Dear friends, you will be the first guests at the party, do not worry; because for the moment, he does not seem very tempted by the marriage. I thought he would propose this summer in Venice, one night over a romantic ballad … I waited, but nothing!

– *Ah, les hommes! Tu sais, ne sois pas trop impatiente. Le mariage, c'est un mythe. Le père de mes enfants perd sa paire de lunettes tous les matins, et il ronfle si fort que parfois ça me tente d'aller dormir sous la tente.*

- Ah, men! You know, do not be too impatient. Marriage is a myth. The father of my children loses his glasses every morning, and he snores so hard that sometimes it tempts me to go to sleep under the tent.

– *Eh bien, dit l'une d'entre elles, levons nos verres aux joies du mariage, et au plaisir de se moquer de nos maris et enfants entre copines!*

- Well, said one of them, let's raise our glasses to the joys of marriage, and the pleasure of making fun of our husbands and children between friends!

Résumé De L'histoire

Un groupe de mères de famille et épouses, copines depuis longtemps, se retrouve toutes les semaines pour passer un moment agréable ensemble, loin de leurs responsabilités et de leur mari. Elles en profitent généralement pour se raconter les histoires de la maison. C'est le retour des vacances et elles ne se sont pas vues depuis un mois. Elles profitent d'un dîner au restaurant pour se raconter leurs vacances!

Summary Of The Story

A group of long-time girlfriends, all wives and mothers, get together every week to have a moment to themselves, away from their daily routines, responsibilities and respective husbands. It's generally a good time for them to speak about the little stories that happen at home. They are now just getting back from vacation and haven't seen each other in a month. A friendly dinner at the restaurant is a good opportunity for them to talk about what happened during their vacation.

Quiz

1. Lequel de ces mots désigne une couleur?
a) vert
b) vers
c) verre

2. Comment écrit-on le chiffre "100"?

a) sang
b) cent
c) sens

3. Quand le prix est élevé, on dit que c'est...
a) chair
b) chère
c) cher

4. Janvier est un...
a) mois
b) moi
c) moit

5. Dans la phrase «le père perd sa paire», quel est le verbe?
a) père
b) perd
c) paire

Answers

1. A
2. B
3. C
4. A
5. B

Vocabulaire / Vocabulary

- *amande* --- almond
- *amende* --- a fine
- *au secours!* --- help!
- *autel* --- altar (church)
- *balade* --- stroll, walk
- *ballade* --- ballad
- *bon / bonne* --- good
- *bond* --- leap
- *camp* --- camp
- *car* --- because
- *cent* --- hundred
- *ce/cette* --- this
- *champs* --- field
- *chant* --- song, singing
- *cher / chère* --- dear
- *cours* --- lessons
- *coût* --- cost, price
- *crois* --- *croire* – to believe

- *croix* --- cross
- *dans* --- in
- *dent* --- tooth
- *eau* --- water
- *faim* --- hunger
- *faire* --- to do, to make
- *fer* --- iron
- *fête* --- party
- *fin/ fine* --- delicate, thin
- *goûtes* --- goûter – to taste
- *goutte* --- droplet
- *hôtel* --- hotel
- *mai* --- May
- *mer* --- sea
- *mère* --- mother
- *moi* --- me
- *mois* --- month
- *mont* --- mount, hill
- *un os, des os* --- a bone, bones
- *paire* --- pair
- *pâtes* --- pasta
- *perd* --- perdre – to lose
- *père* --- father
- *peu* --- a little, a few
- *peux* --- pouvoir – can, to be able to
- *poids* --- weight
- *pois* --- pea
- *pot* --- pot, jar
- *qu'en* --- que --- that
- *quand* --- when
- *quart* --- quarter
- *sang* --- blood
- *sans* --- without
- *sens* --- sense
- *sept* --- seven
- *tente* --- tenter --- to tempt, to attempt
- *tente* --- tent
- *verre* --- glass
- *vers* --- toward
- *vert* --- green
- *vois* --- voir – to see
- *voix* --- voice

5. À l'aventure!

Cécile, Karine, Bérangère et Frédérique sont un groupe d'amies. Elles se connaissent depuis l'école primaire. Elles font toujours tout ensemble. Quand elles étaient petites, elles étaient toujours dans la même équipe de sport, et elles faisaient toutes les mêmes activités extra-scolaires. Ensuite, au collège, elles sont restées unies, elles passaient tous leurs week-ends ensemble. À l'adolescence, quand elles ont eu leur premier téléphone, elles se voyaient toute la journée à l'école, et ensuite passaient beaucoup de temps à se téléphoner tous les soirs.

Cécile, Karine, Bérangère and Frédérique are a group of friends. They know each other since elementary school. They always do everything together. When they were small, they were still in the same sports team, and they all did the same extra-curricular activities. Then, in college, they remained united, they spent all their weekends together. As a teenager, when they had their first phones, they saw each other all day at school, and then spent a lot of time calling each other every night.

Au lycée, elles ont toutes les quatre choisi la même filière, et ont toutes décidé de passer un baccalauréat littéraire. Depuis trois ans, elles parlent de partir voyager. Elles veulent toutes aller voyager ensemble. Elles passent des heures à regarder des sites internet de voyage, et à rêver devant les prospectus d'agences de voyage.

In high school, they all four chose the same path, and all decided to pass a literary baccalaureate. For three years they have been talking about traveling. They all want to travel together. They spend hours watching websites travel, and dreaming about travel agency flyers.

Cet été, elles ont enfin toutes passées leur baccalauréat avec succès. Elles ont dix-huit ans, et elles veulent partir en vacances ensemble pour la première fois. Elles travaillent pendant les vacances depuis deux ans pour économiser.

This summer, they finally all passed their baccalaureate successfully. They're eighteen, and they want to go on vacation together for the first time. They have been working on vacation for two years to save money.

Karine et Cécile font les marchés tous les étés depuis qu'elles ont seize ans pour économiser de l'argent. Frédérique travaille au cinéma du village tous les week-ends, et de temps en temps elle aide aussi ses parents dans leur boutique de vêtements. L'été, elle aide aussi sur les marchés. Bérangère travaille comme serveuse dans un restaurant pendant les week-ends et les vacances d'été.

Karine and Cecile have been doing the shopping every summer since they were sixteen to save money. Frédérique works in the village cinema every weekend, and from time to time she also helps her parents in their clothing shop. In the summer, it also helps the markets. Bérangère works as a waitress at a restaurant during weekends and summer holidays.

Après deux ans d'efforts, elles ont enfin assez d'argent pour partir! Elles ont dix-huit ans, le lycée est terminé. C'est l'occasion de partir à l'aventure avant d'aller à l'université! Pour la première fois, les quatre filles vont être séparées. Karine part à la faculté de lettres dans la ville d'à côté, Bérangère va étudier les langues étrangères à 200 kilomètres de là, Cécile entre dans une école préparatoire à Paris, et Frédérique a choisi de faire un master en histoire de l'art à Besançon.

After two years of effort, they finally have enough money to go! They are eighteen, the school is over. This is the opportunity to go on an adventure before going to university! For the first time, the four girls will be separated. Karine goes to the faculty of letters in the city next door, Bérangère goes to study foreign languages 200 kilometers away, Cécile enters a preparatory school in Paris, and Frédérique chose to do a master's degree in art history in Besançon.

Cet été, c'est leur chance de partir en vacances ensemble à l'aventure, leurs premières vacances d'adultes. Elles parlent de partir à l'aventure toutes les quatre depuis tellement longtemps, et enfin, elles peuvent planifier!

This summer, it's their chance to go on vacation together on an adventure, their first adult vacation. They talk about going on an adventure all four for so long, and finally, they can plan!

Ce jour-là, elles se sont toutes réunies dans leur café préféré. C'est le début de l'été, elles ont reçu les résultats du bac il y a une semaine, et elles veulent partir au mois d'août. Elles sont toutes les quatre à leur table préférée, elles ont commandé des cafés, et elles ont décidé de planifier leurs vacances.

That day, they all gathered in their favorite cafe. It's the beginning of the summer, they received the results of the bac a week ago, and they want to leave at least August. They are all four at their favorite table, they ordered coffee, and they decided to plan their holidays.

"Ça y est les filles" dit Karine, "pendant les vacances, nous partons ensemble à l'aventure! Alors, où voulez-vous aller?"

"That's girls," said Karine, "during the holidays, we go on an adventure together! So where do you want to go? "

«Super! À l'aventure! Je suis prête à aller n'importe où...» dit Bérangère «mais pas dans un pays trop froid.»

"Great! To the adventure! I'm ready to go anywhere ... "said Bérangère" but not in a country too cold."

"Bon d'accord..." répond Karine "n'allons pas dans un pays trop froid. De toute façon, c'est l'été, j'ai envie d'avoir chaud! Allons plutôt dans un endroit avec de belles plages, du soleil, des piscines..."

"Okay ..." Karine answers "do not go to a cold country. Anyway, it's summer, I want to be hot! Let's go instead to a place with beautiful beaches, sun, pools ... "

«Enfin! Génial! Partons à l'aventure!» commence Cécile «par contre, je ne veux pas aller dans un pays où il y a trop d'insectes. J'ai trop peur des araignées!»

" Finally! Awesome! Let's go on an adventure! Begins Cecile, "but I do not want to go to a country where there are too many insects. I'm too scared of spiders! "

«Ok pas de problème!» répond Karine. «Allons dans un endroit chaud, et sans trop d'insectes!»

"OK no problem! Karine answers. "Let's go to a warm place, and without too many insects! "

«Moi, peu importe! Je veux partir avec vous les filles!» ajoute Frédérique «Enfin, je n'aime pas les araignées non plus. Et je suis allergique au pollen, alors je ne veux pas partir à la campagne. Je ne veux pas aller dans un pays trop chaud. Et je n'aime pas prendre l'avion.»

"Me, no matter! I want to go with you girls! "Finally, I do not like spiders either. And I'm allergic to pollen, so I do not want to go to the countryside. I do not want to go to a country too hot. And I do not like to fly."

«Ah...» Karine commence à se demander où elles vont bien pouvoir partir en vacances. "Bon, je suppose qu'il y a plein d'endroits sympas où nous pouvons aller sans prendre l'avion!»

"Ah ..." Karine begins to wonder where they'll be able to go on vacation. "Well, I guess there are lots of cool places to go to without a plane! "

«Ah, moi non plus je n'aime pas prendre l'avion» dit Cécile «Et le bateau me rend malade. La voiture, ça va. Par contre je ne sais pas conduire.»

"Ah, I do not like to fly either" says Cecile "And the boat makes me sick. The car is fine. But I do not know how to drive. "

Karine est la seule à avoir le permis de conduire. Les autres filles ont eu leurs dix-huit ans plus tard, elles n'ont pas encore eu le temps de le passer. Elle n'a pas très envie de conduire toute seule pendant des heures... et puis, elle n'a pas de voiture. D'habitude, elle emprunte la voiture de ses parents.

Karine is the only one with a driving license. The other girls were eighteen years later, they have not had time to pass it yet. She does not really want to drive alone for hours ... and then she does not have a car. She usually borrows her parents' car.

"Ah, moi aussi le bateau me rend malade... On pourrait partir en bus!» ajoute alors Bérangère.

"Ah, me too the boat makes me sick ... We could go by bus!" Adds Bérangère.

Karine réfléchit pendant un moment... Elle ne pensait pas que leurs options seraient aussi limitées!

Karine thinks for a moment ... She did not think their options would be so limited!

«Alors vous voulez aller dans un pays pas trop froid, pas trop chaud, où il n'y a pas d'insectes, pas de campagne, et vous ne voulez pas prendre l'avion, ni le bateau?" dit-elle aux autres filles.

"So you want to go to a country not too cold, not too hot, where there are no insects, no countryside, and you do not want to fly or the boat? She said to the other girls.

«Oui voilà!" répondent Bérangère, Cécile et Frédérique.

"Yes that's it! "Answer Bérangère, Cécile and Frédérique.

«Dites les filles... si on restait ici pendant les vacances?"

"Tell the girls ... if we stayed here during the holidays? "

Reading Comprehension

1. Why is this story entitled "*L'aventure*"? Are the characters really going on an adventure?

2. Can you name all the characters in the story and explain who they are in French?

3. "*L'école primaire*" is primary school is French. Do a research and find out what comes after in France.

4. Karine is the only character to have her driving license. Research when teenagers in France are allowed to drive. Is it different in your country?

Quiz

1. Who are the girls to each other?
a. Best friends
b. Sisters
c. Cousins

2. How old are they?
a. Sixteen
b. Seventeen
c. Eighteen

3. What is different this summer?

a. They just turned eighteen.
b. They all passed their baccalaureate.
c. They can go on holidays together.

4. How do they plan on funding their holiday?
a. They worked during holidays.
b. Their parents are paying.
c. They plan on working abroad.

5. Where does Bérangère want to go?
a. Anywhere, as long as it's hot
b. Anywhere, as long as it's far
c. Anywhere, as long as it's not too hot

6. What does Cécile dislike?
a. Cécile hates the cold
b. Cécile hates insects
c. Cécile hates the heat

7. Why does Frédérique dislike the countryside?
a. She's scared of spiders.
b. She doesn't like walking.
c. She's allergic to pollen.

8. Who hates taking the plane?
a. Frédérique and Cécile
b. Frédérique and Karine
c. Frédérique and Bérangère

9. Why can't they take a boat?
a. Cécile prefers to drive.
b. Cécile and Bérangère feel ill on boats.
c. Bérangère is scared of boats.

Answers:

1.a
2.c
3.b and c
4.a
5.a
6.b
7.c
8.a
9.b

Vocabulaire / Vocabulary

- *Petit* --- Small
- *Uni* --- United
- *En voyageant* --- Traveling
- *Rêver* --- to dream
- *Sauver* --- to save
- *Vêtements* --- Clothing
- *Aventure* --- Adventure
- *Vacances* --- Vacation
- *Favori* --- Favorite
- *Du froid* --- Cold

6. Le Chemin de l'Épanouissement

Louis prit à cœur les conseils de son oncle et commença à explorer différentes formations et opportunités éducatives. Il savait que l'acquisition de nouvelles compétences et connaissances lui ouvrirait des perspectives pour sa future carrière. Après mûre réflexion, il décida de s'inscrire à un cours de gestion d'entreprise qui lui fournirait une vision plus large des différentes industries et des principes de leadership.

Louis took his uncle's advice to heart and began exploring different courses and educational opportunities. He knew that gaining new skills and knowledge would open up prospects for his future career. After careful consideration, he decided to enroll in a business management course that would provide him with a broader understanding of various industries and leadership principles.

Pendant ce temps, Laura, étant une partenaire attentionnée, encourageait Louis dans sa quête de croissance personnelle et professionnelle. Elle comprenait son désir de trouver l'épanouissement dans son travail et était impatiente de le voir heureux et épanoui. Ensemble, ils recherchèrent différents cours et universités proposant des horaires flexibles pour s'adapter à la vie professionnelle chargée de Louis.

Meanwhile, Laura, being a supportive partner, encouraged Louis in his pursuit of personal and professional growth. She understood his desire to find fulfillment in his work and was eager to see him happy and fulfilled. Together, they researched different courses and universities that offered flexible schedules to accommodate Louis's busy work life.

Louis découvrit bientôt une université réputée qui proposait un programme du soir destiné aux professionnels en activité. Le programme se concentrait sur l'administration des affaires et offrait un programme complet couvrant divers aspects de la gestion, notamment la finance, le marketing, les ressources humaines et la planification stratégique. Excité par cette opportunité, Louis s'inscrivit au programme et attendit avec impatience son premier jour de cours.

Louis soon discovered a reputable university that offered an evening program for working professionals. The program focused on business administration and provided a comprehensive curriculum covering various aspects of management, including finance, marketing, human resources, and strategic planning. Excited about the opportunity, Louis enrolled in the program and eagerly awaited his first day of class.

Alors que Louis se lançait dans son parcours éducatif, il se sentait revigoré par les nouveaux défis et l'occasion d'apprendre auprès de professeurs et d'experts du secteur expérimentés. Il se plongea dans ses études, embrassant les cours et participant activement aux discussions en classe. Grâce à ses études, il acquit une vision précieuse des différents modèles commerciaux, des stratégies innovantes et des techniques de gestion efficaces.

As Louis embarked on his educational journey, he found himself energized by the new challenges and the chance to learn from experienced professors and industry experts. He dove into his studies, embracing the coursework and actively participating in class discussions. Through his studies, he gained valuable insights into different business models, innovative strategies, and effective management techniques.

Pendant cette période, Louis maintint une relation étroite avec son oncle David. Ils discutaient souvent des progrès de Louis dans ses études, et David lui offrait conseils et soutien chaque fois qu'il rencontrait des difficultés. David soulignait l'importance du réseautage et de la création de liens avec des professionnels de différentes industries, car cela pouvait ouvrir des portes vers des opportunités passionnantes.

Throughout this time, Louis maintained a close relationship with his uncle David. They frequently discussed Louis's progress in his studies, and David offered guidance and support whenever Louis encountered difficulties. David emphasized the importance of networking and connecting with professionals in various industries, as it could open doors to exciting opportunities.

Motivé par les conseils de son oncle, Louis s'impliqua activement avec ses camarades de classe et ses professeurs, se constituant ainsi un solide réseau de personnes partageant les mêmes ambitions. Il participa à des salons de l'emploi et à des événements sectoriels, saisissant chaque occasion d'élargir ses contacts professionnels et de se familiariser avec différentes perspectives de carrière. Grâce à ces relations, Louis apprit l'existence de stages et d'offres d'emploi correspondant à ses intérêts et à ses aspirations.

Motivated by his uncle's advice, Louis actively engaged with his classmates and professors, building a strong network of like-minded individuals. He attended career fairs and industry events, seizing every chance to expand his professional contacts and gain exposure to different career paths. Through these connections, Louis learned about internships and job openings that aligned with his interests and aspirations.

Alors que Louis poursuivait ses études et s'immergeait dans le monde des affaires, il découvrit une passion pour l'entrepreneuriat et l'innovation. Il était fasciné par l'idée de créer sa propre entreprise et de développer des solutions révolutionnaires pouvant avoir un impact positif sur la vie des gens. Cet intérêt naissant alimenta sa détermination à exceller dans ses études et à acquérir les compétences et connaissances nécessaires pour poursuivre ses rêves d'entrepreneur.

As Louis continued his studies and immersed himself in the business world, he discovered a passion for entrepreneurship and innovation. He became fascinated by the idea of starting his own business and developing groundbreaking solutions that could make a positive impact on people's lives. This newfound interest fueled his determination to excel in his studies and acquire the necessary skills and knowledge to pursue his entrepreneurial dreams.

Au fil du temps, les efforts et le travail acharné de Louis portèrent leurs fruits. Il obtint son diplôme avec mention du programme de gestion d'entreprise, doté d'une solide base de connaissances et d'un réseau solide de professionnels issus de diverses industries. Avec un sentiment renouvelé de confiance et de détermination, Louis était prêt à se lancer dans son parcours entrepreneurial.

Over time, Louis's dedication and hard work paid off. He graduated with honors from the business management program, equipped with a wealth of knowledge and a strong network of professionals in various industries. With a newfound sense of confidence and purpose, Louis was ready to embark on his entrepreneurial journey.

Soutenu par Laura, qui poursuivait également ses propres objectifs professionnels en tant que journaliste, Louis commença à planifier méticuleusement son entreprise. Ensemble, ils ont fait des séances de remue-méninges, effectué des recherches de marché et élaboré un plan d'affaires complet. Ils savaient que la construction d'une entreprise prospère nécessitait dévouement, persévérance et engagement envers l'apprentissage continu.

Supported by Laura, who had also been pursuing her own professional goals as a journalist, Louis began meticulously planning his business venture. Together, they brainstormed ideas, conducted market research, and developed a comprehensive business plan. They knew that building a successful business required dedication, perseverance, and a commitment to continuous learning.

S'appuyant sur ses expériences et les leçons apprises lors de ses études, Louis réussit à lancer avec succès sa propre start-up - une entreprise technologique axée sur la création de solutions durables et respectueuses de l'environnement. Sa passion pour l'innovation et son engagement à avoir un impact positif ont résonné auprès des investisseurs, et il a obtenu des financements pour concrétiser ses idées.

Drawing from his experiences and the lessons he learned during his studies, Louis successfully launched his own startup—a technology company focused on creating sustainable and eco-friendly solutions. His passion for innovation and his commitment to making a positive impact resonated with investors, and he secured funding to bring his ideas to life.

Alors que l'entreprise de Louis prospérait, il continuait de s'appuyer sur le soutien et la sagesse de son oncle David, qui est devenu à la fois un mentor et un investisseur dans son projet. Leur passion commune pour l'ingénierie et l'innovation leur permettait de collaborer sur des projets, combinant l'expertise technique de David avec la vision entrepreneuriale de Louis.

As Louis's business flourished, he continued to lean on the support and wisdom of his uncle David, who became both a mentor and an investor in his venture. Their shared passion for engineering and innovation allowed them to collaborate on projects, combining David's technical expertise with Louis's entrepreneurial vision.

Au fil du temps, la start-up de Louis devint un nom reconnu dans l'industrie, recevant des éloges pour ses produits durables et son approche novatrice. Le travail acharné, la détermination et la volonté d'apprendre des autres avaient transformé sa vie et sa carrière.

As time passed, Louis's startup became a recognized name in the industry, receiving accolades for its sustainable products and innovative approach. Louis's hard work, determination, and willingness to learn from others had transformed his life and career.

En regardant en arrière, Louis réalisa que sa décision de poursuivre une formation complémentaire et de suivre sa passion pour l'entrepreneuriat avait été un tournant dans sa vie. Il était passé du sentiment d'être surchargé de travail et incertain quant à son avenir à la découverte de l'épanouissement, du succès et d'un sens profond.

Looking back, Louis realized that his decision to pursue further education and follow his passion for entrepreneurship had been a turning point in his life. He had gone from feeling overworked and uncertain about his future to finding fulfillment, success, and a sense of purpose.

Au final, le parcours de Louis à la découverte de soi et de sa croissance professionnelle n'avait pas seulement bénéficié à lui-même, mais avait également inspiré les autres à suivre leurs propres aspirations. À travers son dévouement, il avait prouvé que, avec la bonne mentalité, un apprentissage continu et le soutien des êtres chers, chacun pouvait créer son propre chemin vers le succès et avoir un impact significatif sur le monde.

In the end, Louis's journey of self-discovery and professional growth not only benefited him but also inspired others to follow their own aspirations. Through his dedication, he proved that with the right mindset, continuous learning, and the support of loved ones, anyone could create their own path to success and make a meaningful impact on the world.

Quiz

1.Quelle formation Louis décide-t-il de suivre pour sa croissance professionnelle?
A) Ingénierie informatique
B) Gestion d'entreprise
C) Marketing digital
D) Sciences politiques

2.Quel rôle Laura joue-t-elle dans la vie de Louis?
A) Sa sœur

B) Sa meilleure amie

C) Sa collègue de travail

D) Sa petite amie

3.Quelle est la profession de Laura?

A) Avocate

B) Médecin

C) Journaliste

D) Architecte d'intérieur

4.Comment Louis réussit-il à financer sa start-up?

A) En remportant un jeu télévisé

B) En remportant une loterie

C) En empruntant de l'argent à sa famille

D) En obtenant des investissements des entrepreneurs

5.Quel est le domaine d'activité de la start-up de Louis?

A) Agriculture biologique

B) Énergie renouvelable

C) Industrie de la mode

D) Secteur du divertissement

Answers:

1.B

2.D

3.C

4.D

5.B

Vocabulaire / Vocabulary

- *l'épanouissement* (m): fulfillment
- *les perspectives (f)*: prospects, opportunities
- *les compétences* (f): skills
- *les connaissances* (f): knowledge
- *la carrière* (f): career
- *les formations* (f): courses, training
- *les opportunités éducatives* (f): educational opportunities
- *la gestion d'entreprise* (f): business management
- *les industries* (f): industries
- *les principes de leadership* (m): leadership principles
- *la partenaire* (f): partner
- *la vie professionnelle chargée*: busy work life
- *l'université* (f): university
- *le programme du soir*: evening program
- *l'administration des affaires* (f): business administration

- *les aspects* (m): aspects
- *la finance*: finance
- *le marketing*: marketing
- *les ressources humaines* (f): human resources
- *la planification stratégique*: strategic planning
- *les professeurs* (m): professors
- *les experts du secteur* (m): industry experts
- *les études* (f): studies
- *les modèles commerciaux* (m): business models
- *les stratégies innovantes* (f): innovative strategies
- *les techniques de gestion* (f): management techniques
- *l'oncle* (m): uncle
- *les progrès* (m): progress
- *les conseils* (m): advice
- *le soutien* (m): support
- *le réseautage*: networking
- *les relations* (f): relationships
- *les stages* (m): internships
- *les offres d'emploi* (f): job openings
- *les intérêts* (m): interests
- *les aspirations* (f): aspirations
- *les défis* (m): challenges
- *les séances de remue-méninges* (f): brainstorming sessions
- *les recherches de marché* (f): market research
- *le plan d'affaires*: business plan
- *l'entrepreneuriat* (m): entrepreneurship
- *l'innovation* (f): innovation
- *les investisseurs* (m): investors
- *la start-up* (f): startup
- *les solutions durables* (f): sustainable solutions
- *l'environnement* (m): environment
- *les éloges* (m): accolades
- *le travail acharné*: hard work
- *la volonté d'apprendre*: willingness to learn
- *le sens profond*: sense of purpose

7. Laura entre en fac de médecine

Aujourd'hui, c'est le jour du conseil de classe. Laura est en terminale scientifique, option S.V.T, c'est-à-dire, Science et Vie de la Terre. L'année prochaine, elle espère entrer en faculté de médecine. Mais les places sont chères, et il lui faut d'abord obtenir l'approbation du conseil de classe. Le conseil de classe réunit tous les professeurs et les parents d'élèves une fois tous les trois mois. Laura est déléguée de sa classe et participe donc à chaque conseil de classe.

Today is the day of the class council. Laura is in the scientific terminale, option S.V.T, that is to say, Science and Life of the Earth. Next year, she hopes to enter the Faculty of Medicine. But the places are expensive, and she must first obtain the approval of the class council. The class council brings together all teachers and parents once every three months. Laura is a class delegate and therefore participates in each class council.

Elle entre dans la salle. Tout le monde s'installe. On peut voir une légère anxiété sur son visage. Le conseil de classe va-t-il oui ou non approuver sa demande? Le proviseur prend la parole.

She enters the room. Everyone settles. You can see a slight anxiety on her face. Will the class council approve or not her application? The headmaster speaks.

— Nous allons débuter ce dernier conseil. Messieurs dames les professeurs, parents d'élèves et délégués de classe, je vous prie de bien vouloir prendre place.

- We will start this last tip. Gentlemen teachers, parents and class delegates, please take a seat.

Ça y est, le conseil est lancé. Après trente minutes de discussions sur les camarades qui la précèdent dans la liste, c'est enfin au tour du cas de Laura.

That's it, the council is launched. After thirty minutes of discussions of the friends who precede her in the list, it is finally the case of Laura.

— Bien, dit le proviseur, qu'en est-il du cas de Laura Mallet?

- Well, says the headmaster, what about the case of Laura Mallet?

Le professeur principal de Laura est celui qui enseigne la S.V.T.

Laura's main teacher is the one who teaches S.V.T.

— Écoutez, pour ma part, Laura est une élève remarquable, studieuse, concentrée, appliquée. Elle souhaite tenter sa chance dans une fac de médecine. Selon moi, elle y a largement sa place. Il faudra redoubler d'efforts mais, moi, je donne un avis très favorable

- Listen, for my part, Laura is a remarkable student, studious, concentrated, applied. She wants to try her luck in a medical school. In my opinion, she has found her niche. She will have to take more effort but for me, I give a very favorable opinion.

Les autres professeurs donnent à leur tour leurs points de vue. Il n'y a rien à craindre pour Laura, elle fait partie des meilleurs. Réponse définitive du conseil de classe: Avis Très Favorable, avec les Félicitations.

The other teachers give their views in turn. There is nothing to fear for Laura, she is one of the best. Final reply from the class council: Very favorable opinion, with congratulations.

Voilà une bonne chose de faite. Ainsi les candidatures que Laura a envoyées auront plus de chances d'être acceptées. Sans se poser de questions, elle indique sur la plateforme en ligne des candidatures pour les études supérieures, ses choix et vœux pour la poursuite de son parcours scolaire. Les réponses sont à attendre pour la fin de l'année, dans le courant de l'été.

That's a good thing done. So the applications that Laura sent will be more likely to be accepted. Without asking any questions, she indicated on the online platform applications for higher education, her choices and wishes for the continuation of her academic career. Answers are expected by the end of the year, during the summer.

Quelques mois plus tard... Juillet. Laura a été acceptée dans la quasi-totalité des facultés dans lesquelles elle a postulé et, qui plus est, dans l'une des meilleures facs du pays! Mais la partie n'est pas encore gagnée. Il lui faut désormais passer le fameux concours de médecine. Il y a plus de quatre mille inscrits, et seulement deux cents élèves seront acceptés. C'est un vrai parcours du combattant, car une fois entré en fac de médecine, il faut pouvoir y rester. Le programme est très compliqué, et il est interdit de redoubler.

A few months later ... July. Laura has been accepted in almost all of the faculties in which she has applied and, moreover, in one of the best universities in the country! But the game is not won yet. She must now pass the famous medicine test. There are over four thousand applicants, and only two hundred students will be accepted. It's a real obstacle course, because once you enter medical school, you have to be able to stay there. The program is very complicated, and it is forbidden to repeat.

Ainsi, le 1er septembre, Laura se rend à la faculté de Paris I, la Sorbonne. Elle a obtenu son bac avec la mention Félicitations du jury et une moyenne générale de 19/20, l'excellence en fait! L'université de la Sorbonne se trouve dans le célèbre quartier Latin, juste à côté du Panthéon, non loin du boulevard Saint-Michel et de la Cathédrale Notre-Dame de Paris. D'abord, une visite de l'université s'impose. Les lieux sont magnifiques, de style Haussmannien, une réelle beauté architecturale. Deux heures plus tard, le concours a commencé. Laura se trouve dans un gigantesque amphithéâtre où près de cinq cents personnes sont assises et passent aussi le concours. Laura doit remplir dix pages de questionnaires à choix multiple. Pour cela, elle a quatre heures. Les questions sont particulièrement difficiles et nécessitent plusieurs minutes de réflexion. Quatre heures plus tard, le concours est terminé. Laura ne se rend absolument pas compte si sa prestation a été bonne ou non. Les réponses arriveront dans un mois. En fonction de sa place dans le concours, elle sera admise dans l'une ou l'autre faculté de médecine du pays.

Thus, on September 1st, Laura goes to the faculty of Paris I, the Sorbonne. She obtained her bachelor degree with the Congratulations of the jury and a general average of 19/20, excellence in fact! The Sorbonne University is located in the famous Latin Quarter, just next to the Pantheon, not far from the boulevard Saint-Michel and Notre Dame Cathedral. First, a visit to the university is required. The places are beautiful, Haussmann style, a real architectural beauty. Two hours later, the test begins. Laura is in a gigantic amphitheater where nearly five hundred people sit and also take the test. Laura must complete ten pages of multiple-choice questionnaires. For that, she has four hours. The questions are particularly difficult and require several minutes of reflection. Four hours later, the test is over. Laura does not know if her performance was good or not. Answers will arrive in a month. Depending on her place in the graduatory, she will be admitted to one or other of the country's medical schools.

Un mois plus tard, Laura reçoit un courrier de la Sorbonne dans sa boîte aux lettres. Stressée, elle déchire l'enveloppe et sort le papier officiel! REÇUE! Elle est dixième sur quatre mille, ce qui veut dire qu'elle a sa place dans la meilleure faculté de médecine de France, à la Sorbonne! La semaine suivante, c'est la rentrée scolaire.

A month later, Laura receives a letter from the Sorbonne in her mailbox. Stressed, she rips the envelope and takes out the official paper! APPROVED! She is tenth out of four thousand, which means that she has her place in the best faculty of medicine in France, at the Sorbonne! The following week is back to school.

Premier jour de rentrée. Laura se retrouve à nouveau dans l'amphithéâtre du concours. Mais cette fois-ci, ils ne sont que cent, l'autre moitié des reçus est dans une autre classe. Laura découvre son emploi du temps, seulement dix-huit heures de cours dans la semaine. Mais le reste du temps, il faudra qu'elle apprenne énormément de choses toute seule. Tous les samedis matin, c'est heure de colle. Une heure de colle à la fac, c'est une heure d'interrogation au tableau par l'un des professeurs. C'est très difficile et très angoissant car les professeurs sont généralement très sévères.

First day of school. Laura finds herself again in the test's amphitheater. But this time, they are only one hundred, the other half of the attendees are in another class. Laura finds out about her schedule, only eighteen hours of classes in the week. But the rest of the time, she will learn a lot of things alone. Every Saturday morning, it's test time. An hour of test at the university is an hour of questioning on the board by one of the professors. It is very difficult and very distressing because the teachers are usually very strict.

Laura aura des examens régulièrement, presque toutes les semaines. Et elle devra passer des partiels tous les trimestres, c'est-à-dire tous les trois mois. Maintenant, le plus dur reste à faire, garder sa place à la fac, et surtout, devenir médecin!

Laura will have regular exams almost every week. And she will have to go partial every quarter, that is to say every three months. Now, the hardest thing remains to be done, keep his place in college, and most importantly, become a doctor!

Résumé

Laura est en Terminale Scientifique, option Science et Vie de la Terre. Elle veut rejoindre l'année prochaine une faculté de médecine, et si possible la meilleure de France, à la Sorbonne, Université de Paris I. Mais pour cela, elle doit obtenir l'approbation de son conseil de classe. Comme elle est déléguée de classe, elle peut donc assister au conseil. Résultat, le conseil approuve sa demande en lui donnant un avis favorable. Désormais, il lui reste à passer le concours d'entrée. C'est chose faite, et elle est reçue. Il lui faudra maintenant conserver sa place en réussissant divers examens et partiels qu'impose l'université et, enfin, devenir médecin.

Laura is in Scientific Terminale, option Science and Life of the Earth. She wants to join next year a faculty of medicine, and if possible the best in France, at the Sorbonne, University of Paris I. But for this, she must obtain the approval of the class council. As a class delegate, she can attend the council. As final result, the Board approves her request with a favorable opinion. From now on, it remains for her to pass the entrance examination. It's done, and it's approved. She will now have to keep her place by passing various exams and partial ones imposed by the university and finally becoming a doctor.

Quiz

1. Quelle est la filière que suit Laura?
a. Bac Professionnel
b. Scientifique, option Science de l'ingénieur
c. Littéraire
d. Scientifique, option Science et Vie de la Terre

2. Quelle faculté souhaite intégrer Laura l'année prochaine?
a. Faculté de Médecine
b. Faculté de Physique
c. Faculté de Langues

d. Faculté de Mathématiques

3. Quelles sont les conditions pour entrer en faculté pour Laura?
a. Avoir l'autorisation de ses parents
b. Avoir une autorisation de la faculté
c. Être parmi les deux cents premiers du concours d'entrée
d. Être parmi les mille premiers du concours d'entrée

4. Que se passe-t-il tous les samedis matin pour Laura?
a. Elle fait du sport
b. Elle fait ses devoirs
c. Elle en profite pour dormir plus longtemps
d. Elle a une heure de colle et d'interrogations au tableau

Answers

1. d
2. a
3. c
4. d

Vocabulaire / Vocabulary

- *terminale* --- final year (in highschool)
- *approbation* --- approval
- *délégué de classe* --- class representative
- *anxiété* --- anxiety, stress
- *demande* --- request
- *prier [quelqu'un de faire quelque chose]* --- to kindly request sb to do sth
- *lancer* --- to initiate
- *camarade* --- classmate
- *professeur principal* --- head teacher
- *concentré* --- focused
- *appliqué* --- diligent
- *largement* --- widely, plenty, easily
- *craindre* --- to fear
- *études supérieures* --- postgraduate studies
- *dans le courant de* --- during
- *la quasi-totalité de* --- nearly all, the majority of
- *concours* --- competitive examination
- *parcours du combattant* --- uphill battle, obstacle course
- *moyenne générale* --- grade point average, overall average
- *ne pas se rendre compte* --- not realizing, having no idea of
- *prestation* --- performance
- *en fonction de* --- according to, depending on
- *admettre [participe passé: admis]* --- to admit, to accept

- *boîte aux lettres* --- mailbox
- *rentrée scolaire* --- start of the school year
- *emploi du temps* --- time schedule
- *tableau* --- board
- *partiel* --- exam (based on a module)
- *trimestre* --- quarter

8. Éducation

Avec un travail exigeant et un partenaire aimant, la routine quotidienne d'Emily était bien chargée. Cependant, dans le but d'un avenir plus prometteur, elle décida de s'inscrire à un programme de troisième cycle en informatique dans une université renommée. Emily avait déjà terminé ses études de premier cycle en littérature anglaise, une matière qu'elle adorait, mais elle savait que, du point de vue de l'employabilité, cela ne suffisait pas comparé aux diplômes techniques.

With a demanding job and a loving partner, Emily's daily routine was tightly packed. However, in pursuit of a brighter future, she decided to enroll in a graduate program for computer science at a renowned university. Emily had already completed her undergraduate studies in English literature, a subject she adored, but she knew that in terms of employability, it fell short compared to technical degrees.

Cette fois, Emily était déterminée à faire la différence. Armée d'expérience et de détermination, elle ne laisserait pas passer cette opportunité éducative. Poursuivre un master en informatique était sans aucun doute un défi, mais les récompenses promises en valaient la peine. Les cours qu'elle avait suivies pendant ses études de premier cycle semblaient être un jeu d'enfant comparé à la complexité de ce programme. Des études diligentes et une persévérance inébranlable seraient ses alliées.

This time, Emily was determined to make a difference. Armed with experience and determination, she was not going to let this educational opportunity slip away. Pursuing a master's degree in computer science was undoubtedly a challenge, but the rewards it promised were worth the effort. The coursework she had completed during her undergraduate studies seemed like child's play compared to the complexity of this program. Diligent study and unwavering perseverance were going to be her allies.

Dans ce programme, Emily découvrit que les manuels scolaires avaient une valeur supérieure aux cours eux-mêmes. Certains professeurs avaient une tendance aux discours interminables, ce qui rendait incroyablement difficile de rester concentré en classe. Elle comprit rapidement que consacrer du temps à la lecture des chapitres du livre lui fournissait souvent le double des informations par rapport aux heures passées en amphi. Heureusement, les assistants d'enseignement étaient d'une grande aide. Ils avaient le don d'expliquer les concepts complexes en utilisant un langage simple et accessible.

In this program, Emily discovered that the textbooks held more value than the lectures themselves. Some professors had a penchant for long-winded speeches, making it incredibly challenging to stay focused during class. She soon realized that dedicating time to reading chapters from the book often provided twice the information compared to the hours spent in the lecture hall. Fortunately, the teaching assistants were a godsend. They had a knack for explaining intricate concepts using simple and relatable language.

Pour que les informations s'ancrent réellement, Emily savait qu'elle devait fournir des efforts sérieux en dehors de la salle de classe. Les groupes d'étude formés par des étudiants dévoués jouaient un rôle essentiel pour la motiver et la maintenir sur la bonne voie. Dans ces groupes, ils partageaient des notes méticuleuses prises pendant les cours et passaient en revue méticuleusement le matériel qu'ils pensaient retrouver aux examens. Cependant, tout n'était pas sérieux, il y avait également des pauses lors des sessions d'étude, utilisées comme opportunités pour discuter et relâcher le stress et la frustration accumulés.

To ensure the information truly sank in, Emily knew she had to put in serious work outside the classroom. Study groups formed by dedicated students played a pivotal role in motivating her and keeping her on track. In these groups, they shared meticulous notes taken during lectures and meticulously reviewed the material they believed would appear on the exams. However, it wasn't all seriousness and no play. They took breaks during their study sessions, using them as opportunities to chat and release pent-up stress and frustration.

À l'approche de la fin de la première année, la tension remplissait la salle de classe pendant les derniers cours. Le prochain test consisterait uniquement en des questions d'essai, il n'y aurait pas de choix multiples pour s'appuyer. La méthode du bachotage serait vaine. Pour obtenir une bonne note, il fallait réellement comprendre la matière. Emily et ses camarades de classe avaient payé des frais de scolarité considérables, mais tout le monde n'allait pas réussir l'examen. Le succès serait réservé à ceux qui assistaient assidûment aux cours, participaient activement aux groupes d'étude et se plongeaient profondément dans le matériel du cours.

As the end of the first year approached, tension filled the classroom during the final lectures. The upcoming test would consist solely of essay questions; there would be no multiple-choice to fall back on. Cramming was a futile strategy. In order to achieve a good grade, one had to genuinely comprehend the subject matter. Emily and her fellow classmates had paid substantial tuition fees, yet not everyone would pass the test. Success would be reserved for those who diligently attended lectures, actively participated in study groups, and extensively delved into the course material.

C'était semblable à l'apprentissage d'une langue étrangère. Ceux qui excellent dans l'acquisition linguistique sont ceux qui se plongent totalement dans la langue cible. Ils dévorent autant de matériel écrit que possible et consacrent chaque moment libre à écouter la langue parlée. L'immersion prend le pas sur leurs anciens passe-temps et modes de vie. C'est cet engagement qui les pousse à atteindre la fluidité.

It was akin to learning a foreign language. Those who excel in language acquisition are the ones who fully immerse themselves in the target language. They devour as much written material as possible and spend every free moment listening to the language being spoken. Immersion takes precedence over their previous hobbies and lifestyles. It is this commitment that propels them to achieve fluency.

Maintenant, la question n'est pas de savoir si Emily a réussi l'examen final. La véritable question se trouve en vous. Êtes-vous prêt à faire tout ce qu'il faut pour atteindre la fluidité? Allez-vous vous immerger pleinement dans la langue, relever les défis et vous consacrer à la quête du savoir?

Now, the question is not whether Emily passed the final exam. The true question lies within you. Will you do whatever it takes to achieve fluency? Will you fully immerse yourself in the language, embrace the challenges, and dedicate yourself to the pursuit of knowledge?

Bonne étude! Et merci de vous lancer dans cette aventure linguistique!

Happy studying! And thank you for embarking on this linguistic adventure!

Quiz

1.Quel programme d'études Emily a-t-elle décidé de suivre?
A) Sciences politiques
B) Littérature anglaise
C) Informatique
D) Médecine

2.Quel type de questions étaient présentes dans le test de fin d'année?
A) Questions à choix multiple
B) Questions à développement
C) Questions de calcul
D) Questions de dessin

3.Comment Emily a-t-elle trouvé les manuels scolaires par rapport aux cours?
A) Moins utiles
B) Plus difficiles à comprendre
C) Plus intéressants
D) Plus ennuyeux

4.Quel rôle les groupes d'étude ont-ils joué pour Emily?
A) Aucun rôle
B) Source de distraction
C) Motivation et soutien
D) Source de compétition

5.Quelle est la clé de la réussite selon l'histoire?
A) La chance
B) Le talent inné
C) L'argent
D) L'engagement et le travail acharné

Answers:

1.C
2.B
3.C
4.C
5.D

Vocabulaire / Vocabulary

- *Travail exigeant* - demanding job
- *Partenaire aimant* - loving partner
- *Routine quotidienne* - daily routine
- *Programme de troisième cycle* - graduate program
- *Université renommée* - renowned university
- *Études de premier cycle* - undergraduate studies
- *Littérature anglaise* - English literature
- *Diplômes techniques* - technical degrees
- *Faire la différence* - make a difference
- *Opportunité éducative* - educational opportunity
- *Master en informatique* - master's degree in computer science
- *Récompenses prometteuses* - promising rewards
- *Cours de premier cycle* - undergraduate coursework
- *Études diligentes* - diligent study
- *Persévérance inébranlable* - unwavering perseverance
- *Manuels scolaires* - textbooks
- *Discours interminables* - long-winded speeches
- *Rester concentré* - to stay focused

- *Expliquer des concepts complexes* - to explain intricate concepts
- *Langage simple et accessible* - simple and relatable language
- *Travail sérieux en dehors de la salle de classe* - serious work outside the classroom
- *Groupes d'étude* - study groups
- *Notes méticuleuses* - meticulous notes
- *Passer en revue* - to review
- *Salle de classe* - classroom
- *Questions d'essai* - essay questions
- *Bachotage* - cramming
- *Comprendre réellement la matière* - genuinely comprehend the subject matter
- *Frais de scolarité considérables* - substantial tuition fees
- *Assister assidûment aux cours* - diligently attend lectures
- *Plonger profondément dans le matériel du cours* - extensively delve into the course material
- *Acquisition linguistique* - language acquisition
- *Langue cible* - target language
- *Dévorer du matériel écrit* - devour written material
- *Écouter la langue parlée* - listen to the language being spoken
- *L'immersion* - immersion
- *Engagement* - commitment
- *Fluidité* – fluency

9. Le Dortoir

The Dorms

Jessica pensait que le dortoir était confortable. Elle n'a eu aucun souci avec sa chambre la première semaine et tous ses amis étaient également contents de leur chambre. Le bâtiment était rempli d'étudiants en première année. Ils avaient tous des intérêts et des parcours différents et chacun voulait en apprendre plus sur les différentes formations de la fac. Les étudiants plus anciens étaient hébergés dans un autre bâtiment à l'autre bout du campus.

Jessica thought the dorms were nice. In the first week, she didn't have any issues with her room, and her friends were happy with their rooms as well. The building was filled with freshmen. They all had different interests and backgrounds, and everyone wanted to learn more about their college majors. The upper classmen were housed in another building on the opposite side of campus.

Le dortoir des premières années comptait quatre étages. Au rez-de-chaussée et au quatrième il y avait des espaces communs avec des canapés. Là les étudiants pouvaient se retrouver entre les cours ou en fin de journée afin de se détendre et d'étudier. Ces étages disposaient également des équipements de cuisine rudimentaires où l'on pouvait réchauffer son repas ou faire du café. Les étudiants habitaient dans de petites chambres au premier, deuxième et troisième étage. Chaque chambre accueillait deux lits.

The freshman dorms had five floors. On the first floor and the fifth floor, there were common areas with sofas. Here students could gather together between classes or at the end of the day to relax and study. These floors also had basic kitchen appliances to warm food or make coffee. The students lived on the second, third and fourth floors in small rooms. Each room had two beds.

La colocataire de Jessica n'était pas encore arrivée alors elle a pu choisir son lit. Elle a choisi le lit de gauche dans sa chambre. Elle préférait celui-ci car il était mieux éclairé par la fenêtre. Son lit était très confortable et elle avait même acheté quelques coussins en plus pour un confort supplémentaire.

Jessica's roommate had not arrived yet so she got to pick which bed she wanted. She chose the bed on the left of her assigned room. She preferred that one because it had better lighting from the room's window. Her bed was very comfortable and she even bought some extra pillows for added comfort.

Durant la première semaine toutes les affaires de Jessica ont été soigneusement rangées à leur place au fur et à mesure qu'elle ouvrait ses cartons. Elle a rangé toutes ses fournitures scolaires dans son bureau, quelques-uns de ses vêtements dans les tiroirs et a accroché le reste sur des cintres dans un petit placard. Le rangement à chaussures s'est révélé très utile. Elle a affiché quelques photos ramenées de chez elle sur son mur et a accroché un rideau rose pastel à la fenêtre.

During the first week, all of Jessica's belongings were put neatly in their place as she unpacked her bags. She arranged all her school supplies in her desk, stored some of her clothing in drawers, and hung the rest on hangers in a small closet. The shoe rack was especially helpful. She hung a few photos from home on her wall and draped a pastel pink curtain over the window.

Après sa première semaine, Jessica a commencé à se sentir à l'aise dans sa nouvelle chambre. Sa colocataire n'était toujours pas arrivée et Jessica avait hâte de la rencontrer. Elle a fait une demande à la réception et la femme derrière le comptoir a consulté son ordinateur et a dit à Jessica que sa colocataire devrait arriver le lendemain.

After her first week Jessica began to feel comfortable in her new room. Her roommate had not shown up yet and Jessica was eager to meet her. She made an inquiry and the woman behind the information desk checked her computer and then told Jessica her roommate should be arriving the following day.

Il restait encore sept jours avant le début des cours mais Jessica voulait être prête. Elle s'est réveillée le lendemain matin et s'est mise au travail en rassemblant tout ce dont elle aurait besoin dans les mois à venir. Elle a imprimé ses horaires de cours et a acheté tous les manuels dont elle aurait besoin pour chaque matière. Elle a même fait le tour du campus pour savoir où aurait lieu chacun de ses cours. Elle était alors confiante dans la réussite de son premier jour de fac.

There were still seven days until classes would begin, but Jessica wanted to be prepared. She woke the next morning and went to work gathering what she would need in the months ahead. She printed her course schedule, and bought all the books she would need for each course. She even walked around campus to find where each of her classes would be held. This gave her confidence that her first day of college would be a successful one.

Stéphanie a demandé à Jessica si elle voulait prendre un verre dans un café qui était populaire auprès des nouveaux étudiants. Maintenant qu'elle avait tout réglé, le café lui semblait être une magnifique façon de se détendre. Le café était mignon et il y avait beaucoup de premières années assis derrière les petites tables rondes, en pleine conversation. Jessica a reconnu certains des étudiants de son dortoir.

Stephanie had asked Jessica if she wanted to have a cup of coffee at a shop that was popular among new students. Now that she had everything in order, coffee sounded like a wonderful way to relax. The shop was cute, and there were a number of freshmen seated at small round tables deep in conversation. Jessica recognized several of the freshmen from her dorm.

Après le café, les deux amies sont allées dans une librairie qui était juste à quelques pâtés de maison de celui-ci. Elles aimaient toutes les deux la lecture mais n'ont pas emmené de livres avec elles car ceux-ci étaient trop grands pour être emportés dans leur sac. C'était sympa d'avoir une nouvelle amie qui partageait son amour de la lecture.

After coffee, the two friends went to a bookstore that was just a few blocks away from the café. They both enjoyed reading, but hadn't brought any books with them as they were too large to carry in luggage. It was nice to have a new friend who shared a love of reading

La librairie était ancienne et avait de grandes étagères antiques en bois. L'atmosphère y était agréable et des sièges confortables étaient à disposition des clients qui voulaient passer un peu de temps à lire dans le silence du magasin. Il y avait des centaines de livres, dans tous les genres, et les deux filles ont passé le reste de leur après-midi à en choisir quelques-uns à ramener chez elles.

The bookstore was old and had big, wooden, antique shelving. It had a lovely atmosphere, and there was comfortable seating for customers who wanted to spend some time and read in the quiet building. There were hundreds of books, in all genres, and the two girls spent the rest of their afternoon choosing a few to take home.

Heureuses de leurs nouvelles lectures et fatiguées par autant de marche, Jessica et Stéphanie sont rentrées dans leur chambre au dortoir pour la nuit. Devant sa porte, Jessica a entendu du bruit provenant de la chambre. C'était sûrement sa nouvelle colocataire. Jessica est entrée et a vu quelqu'un sous un grand tas de vêtements. Tout était désordonné: les vêtements, les chaussures et les autres affaires s'éparpillaient chaotiquement par terre. Jessica dit d'une voix forte: "Bonjour", et sa nouvelle colocataire se redressa. Jessica n'en croyait pas ses yeux. C'était Lucie!

Happy with their new reading material, and tired from so much walking, Jessica and Stephanie went back to their dorm rooms for the night. Outside her door, Jessica heard a noise from inside her room. It was probably her new roommate. Jessica entered and saw someone underneath a large pile of clothes. Everything was a mess, clothes, shoes, and other belongings in complete chaos on the floor. Jessica said in a loud voice, 'Hello,' and her new roommate sat up. Jessica couldn't believe her eyes. It was Lucie!

Elles se sont enlacées et ont crié de joie. Jessica a aidé Lucie à ranger ses affaires et la chambre était rapidement redevenue propre et ordonnée. Lucie a raconté à Jessica ses derniers jours en Géorgie et Jessica lui a raconté ses premiers jours à la fac. Jessica a promis à Lucie de lui montrer le campus le lendemain et de la présenter à tous ceux qu'elle avait rencontrés.

They gave each other a big hug and shouted with excitement. Jessica helped Lucie with her things and before long the room was once again clean and tidy. Lucie told Jessica about her last few days in Georgia and Jessica told Lucie about her first days at college. Jessica promised Lucie that the following day she would show her around campus and introduce her to everyone she had met.

Quiz

1. Where were the upper classmen housed?
a. In the same house as freshmen
b. another building on the opposite side of campus
c.Within campus

2. The dorm had common areas with sofas in which floors?
a. first floor
b. Second floor
c. Third floor

3. When was Jessica's roommate to arrive?
a. In a week's time after the enquiry
b. The next day
c. She had no roomate

4. What was Stephanie and Jessica out to take?
a Tea
b. Coffee
c. Lunch

Answers

1. b
2. a
3. b
4. b

Vocabularies

- thought --- *Pensait*
- beds --- *des lits*
- comfortable --- *confortable*
- arranged --- *arrangé*
- confidence --- *confiance*
- seated --- *assise*
- Reading --- *en train de lire*
- Night --- *nuit*
- Shouted --- *a crié*

10. Weather And Temperature

The Big Soccer Match

Bonjour! Mon nom est Javier et j'ai seize ans. Mes amis et moi, nous aimons vraiment jouer au football dans le parc de notre quartier. Nous jouons presque tous les jours après l'école. Parfois, nous jouons tout l'après-midi. Ma mère s'énerve parce que je joue beaucoup avec mes amis.

Hello! My name is Javier and I am sixteen years old. My friends and I, we really play at the football in the park of our quarter. We play almost every day after school. Sometimes we spend the whole afternoon. My mother gets upset because I play a lot with my friends.

Aujourd'hui, le ciel est nuageux. Les nuages sont gris. Je pense qu'il va bientôt pleuvoir. Le ciel est sombre et il y a un peu de vent. Mes amis sont inquiets parce qu'il va bientôt pleuvoir. Nous avons un grand match aujourd'hui contre les garçons d'un autre quartier. Ils viennent parce qu'ils veulent nous défier.

Today it is cloudy. Clouds are heavy. I think it will rain soon. The sky is dark and there is a bit of wind. My friends are worried because it's going to rain soon. We have a great match today against the boys from another district. They come because they want to challenge us.

Nous avons une très bonne équipe. Nous sommes rapides, nous avons de la force et nous sommes agiles. Nous voulons jouer et battre l'autre équipe. Nous sommes sûrs que nous allons nous en sortir. Nous avons tout l'énergie nécessaire pour gagner.

We have a very good team. We are quick, we have strength and we are agile. We want to play and beat the other team. We are sure that we will get through this. We all have the energy we need to win.

Mais le temps est mauvais aujourd'hui. Je souhaite une journée ensoleillée et chaude. Avec un temps agréable, il est facile d'avoir un bon match. L'équipe est vivante et a très envie de bien faire. Il y a des jours où le ciel est nuageux, mais sans pluie. Ça, c'est une bonne chose. Pas de problème. Mais le problème d'aujourd'hui, c'est la pluie. S'il pleut, on ne peut pas jouer.

But the weather is bad today. I would like a sunny and warm day. With a pleasant weather, it is easy to have a good match. The team is alive and very keen to do well. Ithere are cloudy days, but no rain. That is a good thing. No problem. But today's problem is the rain. If it rains, we can't play.

Nous sommes prêts et attendons l'autre équipe. Ils sont en route. Je pense qu'ils seront là dans une demi-heure. Je pense que ça nous laisse assez de temps avant que la pluie arrive. Il y a beaucoup de vent. Mais ce n'est pas grave. Il n'y a pas de problème avec le vent. L'important, c'est qu'il ne pleuve pas...

We are ready and waiting for the other team. They are on their way. I think they'll be there in half an hour. I think it takes us enough time before the rain comes. There is a lot of wind. But it's not serious. There is no problem with the wind. The important is that it doesn't rain...

Mes amis et moi, nous ne détournons pas le regard du ciel. Qu'est-ce que nous allons faire s'il pleut?

My friends and I, we don't take our eyes off the sky. What are we going to do if it rains?

S'il pleut, le match est annulé. Si le match est annulé, il faudra attendre une semaine de plus pour jouer. Les garçons ne peuvent venir dans notre quartier que le mercredi après-midi. Nous ne pouvons pas jouer un autre jour non plus.

If it rains, the game is canceled. If the game is canceled, we'll have to wait another week to play. The boys can only come to our neighborhood on Wednesday afternoons. We can't play on another day either.

Oh non! Je sens une goutte d'eau. C'est impossible! Les autres enfants ne sont pas encore arrivés. Il ne peut pas pleuvoir!

Oh no! I feel a drop of water. This is impossible! The other children haven't arrived yet. It can't be raining!

Enfin, les autres enfants arrivent. Nous sommes tous prêts à jouer. La pluie n'a pas encore commencée. Nous avons de la chance. C'est juste nuageux et sombre, mais il n'y a pas de pluie. Nous commençons le jeu. L'autre équipe est très bonne, mais nous sommes meilleurs. Ils marquent un but, puis nous en marquons un. Le score est un à un. Le match est passionnant. Les deux équipes sont fortes.

Finally, the other children arrive. We're all ready to play. The rain hasn't started yet. We're lucky. It's just cloudy and dark, but there's no rain. We start the game. The other team is very good, but we're better. They score a goal, then we score one. The score is one-to-one. The match is exciting. Both teams are strong.

Et puis...

And then...

La pluie!

The rain!

Nooooooooooooon...

Nooooooooooooo...

Tout le monde court pour se mettre à l'abri de l'eau. Il pleut très fort. C'est incroyable. On dirait un torrent d'eau.

Everyone runs for cover from the water. It's raining very hard. It's unbelievable. It looks like a torrent of water.

Le jeu est annulé avec le score un à un. Nous devons attendre une semaine de plus pour définir le gagnant. On n'y peut rien. Mais je suis content parce que nous avons joué. Même si nous n'avons joué que trente minutes, nous avons quand même joué aujourd'hui. Je sais que ma mère est fâchée parce que je rentre à la maison tout mouillé. Peu importe. Je suis heureux. Mes amis et moi, nous sommes satisfaits parce que nous avons bien joués. La semaine prochaine, nous aurons une autre chance de gagner le match. Je sais que nous allons réussir. Nous jouons toujours en équipe. Nous donnons toujours nos meilleurs efforts. C'est ce qui compte.

The game is canceled with the score tied at one each. We have to wait another week to determine the winner. There's nothing we can do about it. But I'm happy because we played. Even if we only played for thirty minutes, we still played today. I know my mother is upset because I'm coming home all wet. It doesn't matter. I'm happy. My friends and I are satisfied because we played well. Next week, we'll have another chance to win the match. I know we'll succeed. We always play as a team. We always give our best efforts. That's what matters.

Résumé de l'histoire

Aujourd'hui, nous avons un match de football important contre les garçons d'un autre quartier. Ils sont très bons, mais nous sommes les meilleurs. Le problème que nous avons aujourd'hui, c'est le temps qu'il fait. Le ciel est nuageux et il va bientôt pleuvoir. Ce n'est pas une journée ensoleillée et chaude. C'est un jour nuageux et sombre. J'ai peur qu'il pleuve avant que l'autre équipe arrive. Ils arrivent et nous commençons le jeu. Chaque équipe marque un but, mais tout à coup, la pluie tombe. Il pleut très fort.

Nous ne pouvons plus jouer. Mais je suis heureux parce que j'ai eu la chance de jouer. La semaine prochaine, nous aurons une autre chance de jouer contre la même équipe. Je sais que nous allons gagner!

Summary Of The Story

Today, we have an important soccer game against the boys from another neighborhood. They are very good, but we are the best. The problem we have today is the weather. The sky is cloudy, and it will soon rain. It is not a sunny and warm day. It is a cloudy and dark day. I'm afraid it will rain before the other team comes. They come and we start the game. Each team scores a goal, but suddenly, the rain comes. It is raining very hard. We can no longer play. But I am happy because I had the opportunity to play. Next week, we will have another opportunity to play against the same team. I know we are going to win!

Quiz:

1. Quel sport pratique les garçons?
a. Basket-ball
b. Baseball
c. Football
d. Tennis

2. Quel est le problème aujourd'hui?
a. La pluie
b. La chaleur
c. Le vent
d. Le soleil

3. Où jouent les garçons aujourd'hui?
a. Dans un stade
b. A l'extérieur
c. Dans un gymnase
d. A l'école

4. Comment est le ciel?
a. Ensoleillé
b. Chaleureux
c. Beau
d. Nuageux

5. Quel est le score du jeu?
a. Un à un
b. Un à zéro
c. Zéro à zéro
d. Deux contre un

Answers

1.C
2.A
3.B

4.D
5.A

Vocabulaire / Vocabulary

- *Bonjour*: hello
- *Nom*: name
- *Amis*: friends
- *Aimons*: enjoy
- *Vraiment*: very much
- *Jouer*: to play
- *Nuageux*: cloudy
- *Nuage*: cloud
- *Gris*: grey
- *Pleuvoir*: rain, raining
- *Ciel*: sky
- *Sombre*: dark
- *Vent*: wind
- *Inquiets*: worried
- *Match*: game
- *Garçons*: boys
- *Quartier*: neighborhood
- *Défier*: challenge
- *Équipe*: team
- *Rapides*: fast
- *Force:* strength
- *Battre*: to beat
- *Sûrs:* certain
- *Énergie*: energie
- *Temps*: weather
- *Ensoleillée*: sunny
- *Chaude*: warm
- *Agréable*: pleasant
- *Facile*: easy
- *Vivante*: cheerful
- *Envie*: willingness
- *Aujourd'hui*: today
- *Jouer*: to play
- *Attendons*: waiting
- *En route:* on the way
- *Demi-heure*: half an hour
- *Assez de temps*: enough time
- *Détournons*: look away
- *Regard*: sights
- *Nous faisons*: we do

- *Annuler*: cancel
- *Semaine*: week
- *Non plus*: either
- *Goutte d'eau*: raindrop
- *C'est impossible*: it's impossible
- *Enfin*: finally
- *Nous commençons*: we begin
- *Autre*: other
- *Marquent*: score
- *But*: goal
- *Passionnant*: exciting
- *Tout le monde*: everyone
- *Court*: run
- *A l'abri*: shelter
- *Très fort*: very hard
- *Incroyable*: incredible
- *Torrent*: downpour
- *Score*: score
- *Gagnant*: winner
- *On n'y peut rien*: we can't do anything about it
- *Mère*: mother
- *Fâchée*: upset
- *Parce que*: because
- *Peu importe*: it doesn't matter
- *Satisfaits*: satisfied
- Semaine prochaine: next week
- *Efforts*: efforts
- *C'est ce qui compte*: that's what counts

11. Journée à la plage

Célia et son mari Ludovic vont à la plage tous les dimanches depuis cinq ans. Ils adorent la plage! Ils emmènent toujours leurs deux enfants, Cécile et Christophe, et leur chienne Pamplemousse.

Célia and her husband Ludovic have been going to the beach every Sunday for five years. They love the beach! They always bring their two children, Cécile and Christophe, and their bitch Pamplemousse.

Avant, ils habitaient loin de la plage. Ils avaient un appartement tout petit dans une grande ville. Ils habitaient au dernier étage, il y avait six étages à monter sans ascenseur. L'appartement était sombre, et trop petit pour une famille, mais c'était en plein centre-ville. Célia et Ludovic travaillaient tous les deux en ville, et ils prenaient le métro tous les matins.

Before, they lived far from the beach. They had a very small apartment in a big city. They lived on the top floor, there were six floors to climb without a lift. The apartment was dark, and too small for a family, but it was right in the center of town. Celia and Ludovic both worked in the city, and they took the metro every morning

Un jour, ils en ont eu assez, et ils ont décidé de partir. Célia et Ludovic ont trouvé du travail dans le sud de la France, et ils sont partis. Ils ont acheté une grande maison à la campagne, avec un grand jardin pour leurs enfants et Pamplemousse. Ils ont même une piscine. Leur maison est quatre fois plus grande que leur ancien appartement en ville. Ils ont beaucoup de place, et ils passent beaucoup de temps dans leur grand jardin quand il fait beau.

One day, they had enough, and they decided to leave. Célia and Ludovic found work in the south of France, and they left. They bought a big house in the countryside, with a big garden for their children and Grapefruit. They even have a pool. Their house is four times bigger than their old apartment in town. They have lots of room, and they spend a lot of time in their big garden when the weather is nice.

Leur nouvelle maison est seulement à une demi-heure en voiture de la plage. Alors depuis, ils profitent au maximum. Leurs voisins les voient partir tous les week-ends avec leurs parasols, leurs bouées et leur pique-nique.

Their new house is only a half hour drive from the beach. So since then, they enjoy the maximum. Their neighbors see them leaving every weekend with their umbrellas, buoys and picnics.

Ce dimanche, Ludovic et les enfants sont déjà dans la voiture, ils attendent Célia. Ils veulent partir tôt pour passer toute la journée à la plage. Ils attendent déjà depuis quinze minutes.

This Sunday, Ludovic and the children are already in the car, they are waiting for Célia. They want to leave early to spend the whole day at the beach. They have been waiting for fifteen minutes already.

Cécile et Christophe ont préparé le pique-nique avec leur père. Ils ont fait des sandwichs jambon-fromage, et des sandwichs poulet-mayonnaise. Christophe adore le poulet, mais Cécile n'aime pas.

Cécile and Christophe prepared the picnic with their father. They made ham-cheese sandwiches, and chicken-mayonnaise sandwiches. Christophe loves chicken, but Cecile does not like it.

Ils ont aussi emmené des sodas, des jus de fruits, et beaucoup de glaçons. Il fait très chaud aujourd'hui. Il y a beaucoup de soleil. Ils ont aussi pris à manger pour Pamplemousse, bien sûr.

They also brought sodas, juices, and lots of ice cubes. It's very hot today. There's a lot of sun. They also had to eat for Grapefruit, of course.

Ils veulent aller nager et jouer sur la plage, ensuite pique-niquer vers midi, puis se promener et peut-

être même aller acheter une glace dans la soirée.

They want to go swimming and play on the beach, then have a picnic around noon, then go for a walk and maybe even buy ice cream in the evening.

Leur père a pris un ballon pour jouer sur la plage, et des balles pour leur chienne Pamplemousse. Ils sont tous prêts à partir, sauf Célia. Ludovic s'impatiente.

Their father took a ball to play on the beach, and bullets for their bitch Grapefruit. They are all ready to leave, except Célia. Ludovic gets impatient.

S'ils ne partent pas bientôt, il y aura du monde sur la route, et il ne trouvera pas de place de parking pour garer la voiture.

If they do not leave soon, there will be people on the road, and there will be no parking space to park the car.

Il déteste partir en retard. Les enfants commencent à s'ennuyer.

He hates leaving late. The children are getting bored.

"Où est maman?" demande Christophe.

"Where is Mom? Asks Christophe.

«Tu connais ta mère, elle est toujours en retard!" lui répond son père.

"You know your mother, she's always late! His father replies.

C'est vrai, leur mère Célia perd toujours toutes ses affaires, et elle est toujours en retard. Elle est encore dans la maison. Son mari et ses enfants attendent dans la voiture depuis trente minutes maintenant.

That's right, their mother Celia always loses all her belongings, and she is always late. She is still in the house. Her husband and children have been waiting in the car for thirty minutes now.

Célia est encore en train de préparer le sac de plage. Elle a préparé les serviettes de plage, les bouteilles d'eau, les crèmes solaires... mais elle cherche encore ses lunettes de soleil. Elle ne peut pas partir sans ses lunettes de soleil! Elle ne va rien voir.

Celia is still preparing the beach bag. She has prepared beach towels, water bottles, sunscreens ... but she is still looking for her sunglasses. She cannot leave without her sunglasses! She will not see anything.

Célia regarde par la fenêtre, et voit son mari et ses enfants qui lui font signe de la voiture. Ils ont l'air impatients. Célia regarde l'heure: ils l'attendent depuis déjà quarante minutes.

Celia looks out the window, and sees her husband and children beckoning him to the car. They look impatient. Celia looks at the time: they have been waiting for forty minutes already.

Célia décide de partir quand même sans ses lunettes de soleil, ses enfants et son mari attendent, et même leur chienne s'impatiente. Pamplemousse aboie, et les voisins ne vont pas être contents.

Celia decides to leave anyway without her sunglasses, her children and her husband are waiting, and even their dog is getting impatient. Grapefruit barks, and the neighbors are not going to be happy.

Elle sort de la maison avec le sac de plage, les serviettes de plage, la crème solaire et les bouteilles d'eau. Elle rentre enfin dans la voiture, ils vont pouvoir partir pour la plage.

She comes out of the house with the beach bag, beach towels, sunscreen and bottled water. She finally gets back in the car, they will be able to leave for the beach.

«Je ne trouve pas mes lunettes de soleil!" s'exclame Célia en rentrant dans la voiture.

"I can not find my sunglasses! Exclaims Celia as she enters the car.

Ludovic et les enfants éclatent de rire. Même Pamplemousse a l'air de s'amuser. Tout le monde rit pendant cinq minutes, ils n'arrêtent plus de rire!

Ludovic and the children burst out laughing. Even Grapefruit seems to be having fun. Everyone laughs for five minutes, they stop laughing!

Célia ne comprend pas ce qu'il y a de si amusant. Elle ne trouve pas ses lunettes de soleil. Ce n'est pas très drôle.

Celia does not understand what's so much fun. She can not find her sunglasses. It's not very funny.

"Regarde-toi dans le miroir!" dit Ludovic à sa femme.

"Look in the mirror! Ludovic said to his wife.

Célia se regarde dans le miroir de la voiture, et les lunettes sont là, sur sa tête...

Celia looks at herself in the mirror of the car, and the glasses are there, on her head ...

"Je n'aurais jamais pensé à chercher là!"

"I never thought of looking there! "

La famille rit joyeusement, et se met enfin en route pour la plage.

The family laughs happily, and finally sets off for the beach.

Reading Comprehension

1. Can you name the five characters in this story? Who are they?

2. The story is called *"Journée à la plage"*. If you don't know what this means, check your dictionary. Then, write down all the words related to *"plage"* you find in the text.

3. Why is everybody laughing at the end?

4. Write down all the words that mark the time. Did the family wait for a long time?

5. *"en train de"*: at first glance, what do you think this means? Now check the expression in a dictionary. Beware, some words are "false friends" in French!

6. Look up the meaning of *"en avoir assez"*. Find synonyms in French.

Quiz

Careful! There may be more than one good answer.

1. Who is Célia?
a. Célia is Ludovic and Pamplemousse's mother.
b. Célia is Cécile and Ludovic's mother.
c. Célia is Cécile and Christophe's mother.

2. Who is Cécile?
a. Cécile is Ludovic's daughter.
b. Cécile is Christophe's mother.

c. Cécile is Christophe's sister.

3. Who is Ludovic?
a. Ludovic is Célia's son.
b. Ludovic is Célia's husband.
c. Ludovic is Christophe and Cécile's father.

4. Who is Pamplemousse?
a. Cécile's sister
b. Célia's daugher
c. The family's dog

5. Where is the family at the time of the story?
a. At the beach
b. At home
c. In the car

6 . What is Célia looking for?
a. Her sunglasses
b. Her beach towels
c. Sunscreen

7."Christophe adore le poulet, mais Cécile n'aime pas." means:
a. Christophe and Cécile both love chicken.
b. Christophe loves chicken, but Cécile does not.
c. Cécile loves chicken, but Christophe does not.

8. What type of sandwiches does the family make?
a. Ham/cheese and chicken/mayo
b. Ham/mustard and chicken/mayo
c. Sausage/pickles and chicken/mustard

9. Find the word "to laugh" in the text:
a. éclater
b. rire
c. s'amuser

Answers:

1. c.
2. a and c.
3. b and c.
4. c
5. b and c.
6. a.
7.b.
8. a.
9. b.

Vocabulaire / Vocabulary

- *L'amour* --- Love
- *Chienne* --- Bitch
- *Montée* --- Climb
- *Matin* --- Morning
- *Jardin* --- Garden
- *Voisins* --- Neighbors
- *Sandwichs* --- Sandwichs
- *Espace* --- Space

12. Cousins d'Auvergne, le terroir Français!

Hugo a treize ans. Il vit avec ses parents, ses deux grandes sœurs et son petit frère, dans un superbe appartement du septième arrondissement parisien, entre les Invalides et la Tour Eiffel. Son père est juriste et sa mère restauratrice d'art au musée d'art contemporain de Beaubourg. Les deux grandes sœurs d'Hugo ont dix-huit et quinze ans. La plus âgée poursuit des études d'avocat, et l'autre entre dans le prestigieux lycée parisien Henri IV.

Hugo is thirteen years old. He lives with his parents, his two sisters and his little brother, in a superb apartment in the seventh arrondissement of Paris, between the Invalides and the Eiffel Tower. His father is a lawyer and his mother restorer of art at the Museum of Contemporary Art in Beaubourg. Hugo's two big sisters are eighteen and fifteen. The oldest is studying law, and the other enters the prestigious Parisian high school Henri IV.

C'est une famille bourgeoise et fière de l'être. L'un des grands-pères d'Hugo s'occupait de nombreux hôtels parisiens, l'une de ses grands-mères était actrice de cinéma. Hugo aime beaucoup Paris et surtout le quartier où il habite. Pas très loin, il y a le Grand Palais où il y a toujours de superbes expositions. Et juste derrière, il y a la plus belle avenue du monde, les Champs-Élysées. Les parents d'Hugo ont beaucoup d'argent et adorent partir à l'étranger pendant les vacances.

It is a bourgeois family and proud of it. One of Hugo's grandfathers took care of many Parisian hotels, one of his grandmothers was a film actress. Hugo loves Paris a lot and especially the neighborhood where he lives. Not far away, there is the Grand Palais where there are always beautiful exhibitions. And right behind, there is the most beautiful avenue in the world, the Champs-Élysées. Hugo's parents have a lot of money and love to go abroad during the holidays.

Et justement les vacances d'hiver approchent. Cette année, ils ont prévu d'aller passer quinze jours dans la célèbre ville du père Noël, à Rovaniemi, en Finlande. Il paraît qu'il y a énormément de neige là-bas, et qu'il fait nuit toute la journée à cette période. On peut faire des randonnées en chiens de traîneau, faire du ski, voir des loups, des ours, des rennes et même des élans.

And precisely the winter holidays are approaching. This year, they have planned to spend a fortnight in the famous Santa Claus city, Rovaniemi, Finland. It seems that there is a lot of snow there, and it is night all day at this time. You can go on dog sled rides, go skiing, see wolves, bears, reindeer and even moose.

Le soir même du début des vacances de Noël, toute la famille est à l'aéroport Charles-De-Gaulle pour le départ. Mais voilà, il y a un énorme problème. L'avion ne va pas pouvoir partir car il y a des tempêtes de neige sur toute la Finlande et un volcan en éruption en Islande rend le voyage dangereux. Tous les avions sont contraints de rester au sol. Deux choix s'offrent à eux. Attendre, mais cela pourrait durer une semaine entière. Ou rentrer chez eux.

The very evening of the beginning of the Christmas holidays, the whole family is at the airport Charles-De-Gaulle for the departure. But there is a huge problem. The plane will not be able to leave because there are snowstorms all over Finland and an erupting volcano in Iceland makes the trip dangerous. All planes are forced to stay on the ground. Two choices are available to them. Wait, but it could last a whole week. Or go home.

— Nous allons devoir faire autrement les enfants!

- We will have to do otherwise children!

— Non!

- No!

Tout le monde est déçu, le voyage s'annonçait tellement bien.

Everyone is disappointed, the trip promised to be so good.

— Bon, les enfants, je viens d'avoir tonton Fernand au téléphone, il nous invite chez lui en Auvergne.

- well, children, I just finish to talk to uncle Fernand on the phone, he invites us to his home in Auvergne

— Quoi, l'Auvergne? En pleine campagne?!

- What, Auvergne? In the middle of the countryside?!

— Il n'y a rien à faire là-bas, c'est nul! Il n'y a personne!

- There is nothing to do there, it sucks! There is nobody!

— Mais non, vous allez voir!

- No, you'll see!

C'est ainsi qu'Hugo, ses parents, ses sœurs et son frère ont rejoint la bonne vieille région de l'Auvergne. C'est vrai que pour des Parisiens avertis, l'Auvergne, c'est le bout du monde. Lorsqu'ils sont arrivés, il faisait nuit. Mais la nuit, dans les villages d'Auvergne, les lumières sont éteintes. Et la nuit noire, les Parisiens ne connaissent pas trop, ils ont l'habitude du ciel orangé dans lequel on ne voit que la lune et non les étoiles.

This is how Hugo, his parents, his sisters and his brother joined the good old region of Auvergne. It is true that for sophisticated Parisians, Auvergne is the end of the world. When they arrived, it was dark. But at night, in the villages of Auvergne, the lights are out. And the dark night, Parisians do not know too much, they are used to the orange sky in which we see only the moon and not the stars.

Heureusement, la cheminée fonctionnait, il faisait chaud dans la maison. Le lendemain matin, ils ont pris un petit-déjeuner auvergnat, avec des œufs, de la charcuterie locale, du jambon d'Auvergne notamment, du lait et du beurre de la ferme, du jus d'orange et des croissants. Et ils se sont levés avec une superbe surprise, il a neigé dans la nuit, presque cinquante centimètres.

Fortunately, the fireplace worked, it was hot in the house. The next morning they had an Auvergnat breakfast with eggs, local cold cuts, ham from Auvergne, milk and butter from the farm, orange juice and croissants. And they got up with a great surprise, it snowed in the night, almost fifty centimeters.

— Cet après-midi, on ira skier!

- This afternoon, we will go skiing!

Comme il n'y a pas beaucoup de monde en Auvergne, ils ont eu la station de ski pour eux seuls. C'était super. Mais Hugo aurait préféré aller en Finlande. Et Jérémy, leur cousin, a un look et un caractère de paysan qu'Hugo ne supporte pas. Il n'a jamais visité Paris, n'a jamais pris l'avion, il est monté une fois dans le train, il ne connaît donc pas le métro non plus, ni le TGV (le train à grande vitesse). Par contre, il parle tout le temps de son troupeau de vaches, de ses tracteurs et de sa magnifique région.

Since there are not many people in Auvergne, they had the ski resort for them alone. It was great. But Hugo would have preferred to go to Finland. And Jeremy, their cousin, has a peasant look and character that Hugo does not support. He has never visited Paris, never taken a plane, he got once on the train, so he does not know the metro either, nor the TGV (the high speed train). On the other hand, he talks all the time about his herd of cows, his tractors and his beautiful region.

Le lendemain, ils sont allés à Clermont-Ferrand pour regarder un match de Rugby avec l'équipe du coin. Ça, c'était incroyable. Il y avait une ambiance surprenante. Et comme Clermont-Ferrand a gagné, et bien tout le monde a fait la fête. Finalement, c'était drôle, la campagne. Ensuite, ils ont fait une randonnée sur les volcans d'Auvergne, et ils ont fait de la luge. Puis le soir, ça a été jeux de société, super soirée finalement.

The next day, they went to Clermont-Ferrand to watch a Rugby match with the local team. That was incredible. There was a surprising atmosphere. And because Clermont-Ferrand won, everyone was partying. Finally, the Holidays in the countryside were funny. Then they went on a hike along the volcanoes of Auvergne, and they went sledging. Then in the evening, it was time for board games, great evening after all.

Les vacances touchaient à leur fin. C'était si bien qu'Hugo n'avait pas envie de partir. Mais toutes les bonnes choses ont une fin et il faut retourner à l'école. À son retour, chacun de ses camarades a raconté ses vacances.

The holidays were coming to an end. It was so good that Hugo did not want to leave. But all good things have an end and you have to go back to school. Upon his return, each of his classmates recounted his holidays.

— Moi je suis partie aux États-Unis.

- I went to the United States.

Hugo était déjà allé aux USA deux fois.

Hugo had been to the USA twice before.

— Moi au Japon!

- Me in Japan!

Déjà fait aussi.

Already done too.

— Et moi j'ai visité St-Pétersbourg!

- And I visited St Petersburg!

Hugo irait pour les prochaines vacances.

Hugo would go for the next vacation.

— Moi, j'ai fait un long périple en voiture dans toute l'Italie.

- I went on a long car trip all over Italy.

Et ça aussi, Hugo l'avait fait. Et ainsi de suite, tout le monde a raconté son voyage. Hugo avait presque honte. Lui, il était resté en France. Puis son tour est venu de raconter.

And that too, Hugo did it. And so on, everyone told about his trip. Hugo was almost ashamed. He had stayed in France. Then his turn came to tell.

— Et bien, moi, j'ai rendu visite à mes cousins..., dit-il, un peu gêné.

- Well, I visited my cousins ..., he said, a little embarrassed.

— Ah bon? Où ça?

- Is that so? Where?

— En Auvergne...

- In Auvergne ...

— En Auvergne...?!

- In Auvergne ...?!

— *C'est dans quel pays ça, l'Auvergne?*

- In what country, Auvergne?

— *Je ne connais pas moi l'Auvergne, dis-nous où ça se trouve Hugo! C'est en Asie?*

- I do not know Auvergne, tell us where is it, Hugo! It's in Asia?

— *Mais non, l'Auvergne, c'est en France!*

- No, Auvergne is in France!

En fait personne ne connaissait l'Auvergne, parce que tous ses amis partaient tout le temps à l'étranger, et jamais en France. C'est alors qu'Hugo s'est mis à raconter ses vacances et toute la classe l'a écouté pendant près d'une heure! Finalement, l'Auvergne, c'était mieux que la Finlande!

In fact nobody knew Auvergne, because all his friends went abroad all the time, and never in France. It was then that Hugo started telling his vacation and the whole class listened to him for almost an hour! Finally, Auvergne was better than Finland!

Résumé

Hugo est un jeune garçon dans une famille nombreuse. Ses parents sont riches, ils habitent dans le septième arrondissement de Paris, entre la Tour Eiffel et les Invalides. Tous les ans, ils partent plusieurs fois en vacances à l'étranger. Cette année, ils doivent partir en Finlande, à Rovaniemi, pour les vacances de Noël. Mais finalement, le voyage est annulé à la dernière minute car les avions ont interdiction de décoller à cause du temps. Ils sont contraints d'abandonner leur idée. Finalement ils se rendent en Auvergne chez leur oncle. Au départ, tout le monde est très déçu. Mais finalement, c'étaient les meilleures vacances qu'ils n'aient jamais passées!

Summary Of The Story

Hugo is a young boy in a large family. His parents are wealthy; they live in the seventh district of Paris, between the Eiffel Tower and Les Invalides. Every year, they go on vacation abroad multiple times. This year, they were supposed to go to Rovaniemi, Finland, for Christmas vacation. However, the trip is canceled at the last minute because flights are prohibited from taking off due to the weather. They are forced to give up on their plan. Eventually, they head to their uncle's place in Auvergne. Initially, everyone is very disappointed. But in the end, it turns out to be the best vacation they've ever had!

Quiz

1. Quelle est la profession du père d'Hugo?
a. Avocat
b. Guide touristique
c. Juriste
d. Boulanger

2. Où Hugo part-il en vacances cette année?

a. Aux États Unis

b. À Saint-Pétersbourg

c. En Auvergne

d. En Finlande

3. Pourquoi le voyage d'Hugo est-il annulé?

a. Les avions sont interdits de décoller

b. Ils ont changé d'avis

c. Ils n'ont plus d'argent

d. Ils ont loupé leur avion

4. Parmi ces activités, laquelle Hugo a faite pendant ses vacances?

a. Ils sont allés à la piscine

b. Ils ont skié

c. Ils ont visité l'usine de Michelin

d. Ils ont regardé un match de foot

Answers

1. c

2. d

3. a

4. b

Vocabulaire / Vocabulary

- *juriste* --- lawyer, jurist
- *restauratrice* [*masculin = restaurateur*] --- restorer
- *prestigieux* --- prestigious, esteemed
- *surtout* --- especially, above all
- *exposition* --- exhibition, exhibit
- *à l'étranger* --- abroad
- *approcher* --- to get close, to be coming
- *traîneau* --- sleigh
- *renne* --- reindeer
- *élan* --- moose
- *énorme* --- huge, very big
- *tempête de neige* --- snowstorm, blizzard
- *contraindre* --- to force, to compel
- *autrement* --- differently
- *décevoir* [*participe passé: déçu*] --- to disappoint
- *tonton* --- uncle (informal)
- *c'est nul!* --- it sucks!
- *averti* --- forewarned
- *cheminée* --- fireplace
- *charcuterie* --- cold cooked meat

- *notamment* --- in particular, notably
- *station de ski* --- ski resort
- *du coin* --- nearby, local
- *ambiance* --- atmosphere, vibe
- *luge* --- sledge, sled
- *jeu de société* --- board game
- *toucher à sa fin* --- to come to an end
- *périple* --- journey
- *et ainsi de suite* --- and so on
- *honte* --- shame

13. Past and Future - Les voyageurs du temps – The Time Travelers

Lorsqu'ils étaient à l'école ensemble et qu'ils avaient dix ans, un petit groupe d'enfants écrivit dans un cahier, qu'ils enterrèrent plus tard dans un parc, ce qu'ils voulaient faire quand ils seraient grands. Ils s'étaient promis de se retrouver quand ils auraient grandi et qu'ils auraient trente ans, pour déterrer le cahier. Leurs parents vivaient tous dans le même quartier. C'était en 1998. Nous sommes désormais en 2018, vingt ans plus tard. Le groupe d'enfants a tenu sa promesse: ils sont devenus des adultes aujourd'hui et se retrouvent à l'occasion d'une fête pour déterrer le cahier. L'un d'entre eux prend la parole:

When they were in school together at the age of ten, a small group of children wrote in a notebook, which they later buried in a park, what they wanted to do when they would be grown up. They had promised to meet when they would have grown up and they would be thirty, to unearth the notebook. Their parents all lived in the same neighborhood. It was 1998. We are now in 2018, twenty years later. The group of children kept its promise: they became adults today and meet at a party to dig up the notebook. One of them speaks:

- Ça fait bizarre de se retrouver tous ici. Voyons déjà si notre boîte avec le cahier est toujours enterrée sous cet arbre...

- It's weird to be all here. Let's see if our box with the notebook is still buried under this tree ...

Il prend sa pelle et creuse. Oui! La boîte est toujours là! Nerveusement, le groupe se resserre autour du trésor qu'ils viennent de déterrer...

He takes his shovel and digs. Yes! The box is still there! Nervously, the group tightens around the treasure they have just dug up ...

- Si je me souviens bien, c'est moi qui ai écrit la première page, dit Noémie, une jeune femme aux cheveux roux.

"If I remember correctly, I wrote the first page," said Noémie, a young woman with red hair.

- Alors à toi l'honneur, lui répond l'homme à la pelle. Il lui tend le vieux cahier.

"Then the honor to you," replies the man with a shovel. He hands her the old notebook.

- Je ne me souviens plus de ce que j'ai écrit. Elle lit à voix haute sa page: "Je m'appelle Noémie, j'ai dix ans, et quand je serai grande, je serai maman! Je veux plein d'enfants, des filles et des garçons. Ils seront tous gentils et bien élevés, et nous ferons plein de choses ensemble." Wow! Dit-elle. Je n'arrive pas à croire que je voyais déjà les choses comme ça! C'est fou!

- I do not remember what I wrote. She reads aloud her page: "My name is Noémie, I'm ten, and when I grow up I'll be a mother! I want lots of kids, girls and boys. They will all be nice and well behaved, and we will do a lot of things together. Wow! She says. I cannot believe I already saw things like that! It's crazy!

- Et alors? Tu as eu des enfants? Lui demande une autre jeune femme à côté d'elle.

- So what? Did you have children? Ask another young woman next to her.

- Deux! Et j'ai appris hier que j'étais enceinte du troisième! C'était le destin!

- Two! And I learned yesterday that I was pregnant with the third! It was destiny!

Le groupe applaudit cette bonne nouvelle, tout en embrassant chacun leur tour la jeune femme pour la féliciter.

The group applauds these good news, while embracing each one in turn the young woman to congratulate her.

- Noémie, dis-nous qui a écrit la page suivante, lui demande l'homme à la pelle.

- Noemie, tell us who wrote the next page, asks her the man with the shovel.

- C'est... Sophie! Forcément, nous étions très proches à l'époque!

- It's ... Sophie! Of course, we were very close at the time!

Sophie prend le cahier et lit:

Sophie takes the notebook and reads:

- «Je ne sais pas trop quoi écrire sur ce cahier, mais je le fais parce que si je ne le fais pas, les autres diront encore que je n'en fais qu'à ma tête. Alors j'espère juste que dans vingt ans, ils me laisseront tranquille et que je pourrai faire ce que je veux! J'aimerais bien devenir chef, pour pouvoir décider toute seule et faire ce que je voudrai quand je voudrai." Ha ha! Super! Elle éclate de rire.

- "I do not really know what to write on this notebook, but I do it because if I don't do it, the others will still say that I am stubborn. So I just hope that in twenty years they will leave me alone and that I will be able to do what I want! I would like to become a chef so that I can decide alone and do what I want and when I want. Ha ha! Great! She bursts out laughing.

- Alors Sophie, tu es chef? Lui demande Noémie.

- So Sophie, are you a chef? Asks Noémie.

- Presque. Je suis maîtresse d'école! Comme ça, c'est moi qui décide toute la journée ce que font tous les enfants de ma classe! Je leur dis quand ranger leurs affaires et quand s'asseoir! Alors oui, c'est moi le chef!

- Almost. I am a school teacher! That way, it's me who decides all day what all the children in my class do! I tell them when to store their things and when to sit down! So yes, I'm the boss!

- C'est super, jusque-là on a deux sur deux. Réussite totale. Qui est le prochain?

- It's great, until now we have two out of two. Total success. Who's next?

- Attends, je regarde... c'est toi, Marc! Sophie tend le cahier à l'homme qui tient la pelle. Il la pose et s'essuie les mains avant de le prendre.

- Wait, I'm looking ... it's you, Marc! Sophie hands the notebook to the man holding the shovel. He puts it down and wipes his hands before taking it.

- Moi, je me souviens très bien de ce que j'avais écrit. J'ai dû écrire que je serai pompier. Je me souviens en avoir rêvé toute mon enfance! Alors, il est écrit... «Moi, je suis Marc et je serai pompier quand je serai grand. J'éteindrai des feux et je sauverai des chats dans les arbres. J'aurai un casque avec une grande visière. PS: Si je ne me souviens plus où j'ai caché la réserve de bonbons pour ne pas que mon frère les mange tous quand je retrouverai ce cahier, ils sont cachés dans la paire de bottes en caoutchouc de papy». Et voilà, je vous l'avais dit: pompier! Mais cela dit, je ne suis jamais devenu pompier; mais j'ai bien un casque avec une grande visière: je suis soudeur!

- I remember very well what I had written. I had to write that I would be a fireman. I remember dreaming it for all my childhood! So, it's written ... "Me, I'm Marc and I'll be a fireman when I grow up. I will extinguish fires and save cats in the trees. I will have a helmet with a large visor. PS: If I do not remember where I hid the candy store so that my brother will not eat them all when I find this notebook, they are hidden in the pair of grandpa rubber boots. And here I was, firefighter! But having said that, I never became a firefighter; but I have a helmet with a big visor: I am a welder!

- *Et ton frère a-t-il trouvé la cachette de bonbons? Demande son ami.*

- And did your brother find the hiding place of the candies? Asks his friend.

- *Non, mais je me souviens de cette histoire! Mon grand-père les a trouvés et il les a tous mangés! J'avais retrouvé les emballages vides dans la poche de sa veste de pêche!*

- No, but I remember this story! My grandfather found them and he ate them all! I found the empty packaging in the pocket of his fishing jacket!

Tout le groupe éclate de rire.

The whole group laughs.

- *Allez, c'est à toi Thomas. Vas-y, lis-nous ton histoire.*

- Come on, it's yours, Thomas. Go ahead, tell us your story.

Un jeune homme blond avec de grosses lunettes prend le cahier.

A young blond man with big glasses takes the notebook.

- *Ah oui... Regardez... Moi je n'avais rien écrit, mais j'étais fan de bandes dessinées à l'époque et j'avais fait un dessin plutôt pas mal de l'Incroyable Hulk! Il dit: "je suis l'Incroyable Thomas et je serai dessinateur de bandes dessinées."*

- Oh yes ... Look ... I did not write anything, but I was a fan of comics at the time and I did a pretty good drawing of the Incredible Hulk! He says, "I am the Incredible Thomas and I will be a cartoonist. "

- *Et l'es-tu devenu? Demande Noémie.*

- And have you become one? Noémie asks.

- *Non, mais en revanche, je suis éditeur et j'en publie! J'ai ma propre collection de bandes dessinées. Je choisis les dessinateurs et les histoires. Il ne reste plus que toi, Louis. À toi de nous lire ta page. Il passe le cahier au dernier garçon.*

- No, but on the other hand, I'm an editor and I publish! I have my own collection of comics. I choose the designers and the stories. All we have left is Louis. It's up to you to read us your page. He passes the notebook to the last boy.

- *Alors, moi ça dit: «Je suis Louis, je suis un visiteur du passé. Quand tu trouveras ce texte, c'est que j'aurai fait un voyage spatio-temporel dans le futur, pour te révéler ton avenir. Je sais déjà que tu vas avoir un prix Nobel de physique pour tes inventions géniales et que tu vas révolutionner la science. Tu seras un visionnaire et en avance sur ton temps! Alors bonne chance à toi, futur moi". Ha ha! C'est tout à fait moi!*

- So, it says to me: "I am Louis, I am a visitor of the past. When you find this text, it is because I will have made a spatio-temporal journey in the future, to reveal to you your future. I already know that you will have a Nobel Prize in physics because of your brilliant inventions and that you will revolutionize science. You will be a visionary and ahead of time! So good luck to you, future me". Ha ha! It's totally me!

- *Et alors, Louis? Demande Marc. L'as-tu eu, ton prix Nobel?*

- And then, Louis? Marc asks. Did you get it, your Nobel Prize?

- *Un prix Nobel de physique futuriste, non. Mais j'ai eu un diplôme d'archéologie!*

- A Nobel Prize in futuristic physics, no. But I had an archeology degree!

- Ah! Alors le petit Louis qui avait dix ans a vu juste! Il pouvait vraiment lire l'avenir! Regarde-toi aujourd'hui, à déterrer le passé! Tu le mérites, ton Prix Nobel!

- Ah! So little Louis, when he was ten, was right! He could really read the future! Look at yourself today, digging up the past! You deserve it, your Nobel Prize!

Résumé De L'histoire

Un groupe de trentenaires qui s'étaient perdus de vue depuis vingt ans se retrouve mystérieusement autour d'un arbre, pour déterrer une boîte qu'ils avaient enterrée lorsqu'ils étaient encore enfants. Mais que contient cette boîte? Quels mystères renferme-t-elle? La découverte de ce trésor leur réserve de véritables révélations. Ce n'est pas une boîte, c'est une machine à voyager dans le temps...

Summary Of The Story

A group of old friends in their thirties finds themselves gathered around a tree. Twenty years have passed since the last time they saw each other, and they are now ready to dig up a box they had buried there when they were kids. What's inside the box? What mysteries are hidden inside? The discovery of this treasure holds true revelations for the group. It is not just a regular box, it is a time machine...

Quiz

1.La boîte contenant le cahier a été enterrée...
a) Il y a 10 ans
b) Il y a 20 ans
c) Il y a 30 ans

2. Les bonbons cachés ont-ils été découverts?
a) oui
b) non
c) on ne sait pas

3. Sophie...
a) voulait être chef
b) voulait être institutrice
c) voulait être maman

4. Louis voulait être...
a) voyageur
b) Prix Nobel
c) archéologue

5. Louis est aujourd'hui...
a) voyageur
b) Prix Nobel
c) archéologue

Answers

1. B
2. A
3. A
4. B
5. C

Vocabulaire / Vocabulary

- *lorsqu'ils étaient à l'école* --- when they were in school
- *ils avaient dix ans* --- they were ten years old
- *écrivit dans un cahier* --- wrote in a notebook
- *enterrèrent* --- they burried
- *ce qu'ils voulaient faire* --- what they wanted to do
- *quand ils seraient grands* --- when they would be grown ups
- *ils s'étaient promis* --- they promised each other
- *quand ils auraient grandi* --- when they would have grown up
- *ils auraient trente ans* --- they would be thirty years old
- *leurs parents vivaient* --- their parents lived
- *c'était en 1998* --- it was in 1998
- *le groupe d'enfants a tenu sa promesse* --- the group of kids kept its promise
- *ils sont devenus des adultes* --- they became adults
- *cahier* --- notebook
- *enterré / enterrée* --- burried (passive)
- *pelle* --- shovel
- *ils viennent de déterrer* --- they just unburried
- *c'est moi qui ai écrit* --- it's me who has written
- *ce que j'ai écrit* --- what I have written
- *quand je serai grande* --- when I grow up
- *je serai maman* --- I will be a mum
- *ils seront tous gentils* --- they will all be kind
- *nous ferons* --- we will do
- *je voyais* --- I was seeing
- *tu as eu des enfants* --- you had kids
- *j'ai appris hier* --- I learned yesterday
- *enceinte* --- pregnant
- *c'était le destin* --- it was destiny
- *applaudit* --- applaudir – to applaud
- *qui a écrit* --- who wrote
- *nous étions très proches* --- we were very close
- *les autres diront* --- the others will say
- *ils me laisseront tranquille* --- they will leave me alone
- *je pourrai faire* --- I will be able to do
- *ce que je voudrai* --- what I will want
- *ranger* --- to clean, to tidy up
- *ce que j'avais écrit* --- what I had written
- *j'ai dû écrire* --- I must have written

163

- *je serai pompier* --- I will be a fireman
- *j'éteindrai des feux* --- I will extinguish fires
- je sauverai des chats --- I will save cats
- *j'aurai un casque* --- I will have a helmet
- *je retrouverai ce cahier* --- I will find this notebook
- *botte en caoutchouc* --- rubber boot
- *je vous l'avais dit* --- I told you
- *je ne suis jamais devenu* --- I never became
- *casque* --- helmet
- *visière* --- visor
- *ton frère a-t-il trouvé* --- has your brother found
- *mon grand-père les a trouvés* --- my grandfather found them
- *il les a tous mangés* --- he ate them all
- *j'avais retrouvé les emballages* --- I had found the wrappings
- *blond* --- blonde
- *je n'avais rien écrit* --- I had not written anything
- *j'étais fan* --- I was a fan
- *bande dessinée* --- comic book
- *j'avais fait un dessin* --- I had drawn a picture
- *je serai dessinateur* --- I will be an illustrator
- *l'es-tu devenu* --- did you become (it)
- *éditeur / éditrice* --- publisher
- *quand tu trouveras* --- when you will find
- *j'aurai fait un voyage* --- I will have traveled
- *avenir* --- what's ahead, future, destiny
- *tu vas avoir* --- you will have
- *physique* --- physics
- *tu vas révolutionner* --- you will revolutionize
- *tu seras* --- you will be
- *visionnaire* --- visionary
- en avance sur ton temps --- ahead of your time
- *l'as-tu eu* --- did you get it
- *futuriste* --- futuristic
- *archéologie* --- archeology
- *avait dix ans* --- was ten years old
- *a vu* --- has seen
- *il pouvait* --- he could
- *mérites* --- *mériter* – to deserve

14. Channel Tunnel

Si vous souhaitez vous aventurer dans une quête mystique vers le Pays de l'Enchantement, traverser le Pont Enchanté est la manière magique de procéder. Le voyage est aussi enchanteur que la destination elle-même. Pour entamer votre quête, suivez simplement le sentier sinueux à travers la forêt mystique qui mène au pont. Le chemin est bien indiqué par des panneaux ensorcelés, vous guidant à chaque étape.

If you're looking to embark on a mystical adventure to the Land of Enchantment, traversing the Enchanted Bridge is the magical way to go. The journey is as enchanting as the destination itself. To begin your quest, simply follow the winding path through the mystical forest that leads to the bridge. The route is well-marked with enchanted signs, guiding you every step of the way.

Une fois arrivé à l'entrée, le processus est un jeu d'enfant, empreint de merveille et d'émerveillement. Si vous avez effectué une réservation, vous aurez accès à la guérite enchantée. Récitez simplement votre code de réservation et le gardien de la porte vous dévoilera l'heure de départ de votre moyen de transport magique. Le personnel du Pont Enchanté veille avec diligence à ce que les voyageurs munis de réservations soient pris en charge comme il se doit. Il est recommandé d'arriver 45 minutes avant l'heure de départ prévue, mais pendant la saison estivale animée, prévoyez un peu plus de temps en raison de l'afflux d'autres aventuriers.

Once you arrive at the entrance, the process is a breeze, filled with wonder and awe. If you've made a reservation, you'll be granted access to the ethereal toll booth. Just recite your reservation code, and the gatekeeper will reveal the departure time of your magical transport. The Enchanted Bridge staff diligently ensure that travelers with reservations are accommodated accordingly. It is recommended to arrive 45 minutes prior to your scheduled departure, but during the bustling summer season, be sure to allow extra time for the influx of fellow adventurers.

Pour ceux qui n'ont pas de réservation, craignez moins! Vous avez la possibilité de payer sur place. Vous serez emporté(e) par le prochain moyen de transport magique disposant d'une place libre. Quel que soit le chemin que vous choisissez, un code de lettre scintillant vous sera attribué. Souvenez-vous de ce code, car il est la clé de votre voyage.

For those without reservations, fear not! You have the option to pay upon arrival. You'll be whisked away on the next available magical transport with an open seat. Whichever path you choose, a shimmering letter code will be bestowed upon you. Remember this code, for it holds the key to your journey.

Au-delà de la guérite, se trouve le terminal mystique, orné d'écrans scintillants révélant le moyen de transport en cours de chargement et son code de lettre correspondant. Les écrans vous informent également du moment où votre lettre devrait être appelée. Ces informations enchanteresses vous permettent de décider si vous souhaitez vous délecter d'une tasse de thé magique ou vous lancer dans une quête grandiose à la recherche d'un festin plus substantiel.

Beyond the toll booth lies the mystical terminal, adorned with shimmering screens that reveal the current loading transport and its corresponding letter code. The screens also provide insight into when your letter is expected to be summoned. This enchanting information allows you to decide whether to indulge in a magical cup of tea or embark on a grand quest for a more substantial feast.

Lorsque votre lettre est appelée, retournez auprès de votre fidèle destrier et suivez les panneaux enchanteurs. Passez par les portes du royaume du contrôle des passeports et parcourez la zone de sécurité ensorcelée avant de rejoindre la file d'attente pour vous aventurer sur le moyen de transport magique. Ces files d'attente sont étroitement gérées, et il est primordial de se comporter avec une conduite appropriée et d'attendre patiemment son tour.

When your letter is called, return to your trusty steed and follow the enchanting signs. Pass through the gates of the passport control realm and navigate the bewitching security area before joining the queue to venture onto the magical transport. These queues are tightly managed, and it is of utmost importance to conduct oneself with proper decorum and wait patiently in line.

Lorsque l'heure d'embarquer sur le moyen de transport arrive, avancez avec précaution, car l'entrée du moyen de transport magique est à la fois petite et étroite. Progressez avec prudence jusqu'à ce qu'un aimable membre de l'équipage du Pont Enchanté vous indique où garer votre noble destrier. Pendant le stationnement, soyez attentif aux instructions de sécurité ensorcelantes pour la sécurité de tous les voyageurs. N'oubliez pas, la magie éblouissante est strictement interdite.

As the time to board the transport arrives, traverse the path with care, as the entrance to the magical transport is both small and narrow. Proceed cautiously until a gracious member of the Enchanted Bridge crew directs you to park your noble steed. While parking, be attentive to the mesmerizing security instructions for the safety of all travelers. Remember, flash magic is strictly forbidden.

Pendant la traversée, il est conseillé de rester auprès de votre destrier magique et de laisser une fenêtre légèrement entrouverte. Les enchanteurs effectueront des contrôles de sécurité sur le véhicule enchanté avant que les moteurs ne vrombissent, signifiant le début de votre expédition de 35 minutes. Le temps se dissipera comme un rêve éphémère tandis que vous vous délecterez de l'ambiance enchanteresse. Certains aventuriers choisissent de fermer les yeux et de se reposer, se préparant à poursuivre leur voyage extraordinaire, tandis que d'autres se délectent de collations enchantées ou se lancent dans des jeux fantaisistes.

During the crossing, it is advised to remain by your magical steed and leave a window slightly ajar. The enchanters will conduct security checks on the charmed vehicle before the engines rumble to life, signifying the commencement of your 35-minute expedition. Time will drift away like a fleeting dream as you revel in the enchanting ambiance. Some adventurers choose to close their eyes and rest, preparing for the continuation of their extraordinary journey, while others delight in partaking of enchanted snacks or engaging in whimsical games.

Une fois arrivé de l'autre côté du pont, préparez-vous à de nouveaux enchantements de sécurité avant que les portes ne s'ouvrent et que vous puissiez poursuivre votre quête magique. Le voyage à travers le Pont Enchanté est un moment d'émerveillement et de joie, vous transportant sans heurts vers des royaumes inconnus.

Once you reach the other side of the bridge, prepare yourself for further security enchantments before the doors open, and you are free to continue your magical quest. The journey across the Enchanted Bridge is an experience of pure wonder and delight, transporting you seamlessly to realms unknown.

S'aventurer à travers le Pont Enchanté est un exploit étonnamment facile, garantissant que chaque voyageur vivra une expérience de voyage magique hors du commun.

Venturing across the Enchanted Bridge is a marvelously effortless feat, ensuring that every traveler's magical voyage is nothing short of extraordinary.

Quiz

1. Quelle est la méthode recommandée pour réserver votre passage à travers le Pont Enchanté?
A) Réciter un sort magique
B) Envoyer un pigeon voyageur
C) Téléphoner à l'enchanteur du pont
D) Effectuer une réservation en ligne

2. Combien de temps dure le voyage à travers le Pont Enchanté?
A) 10 minutes
B) 45 minutes
C) 1 heure
D) 3 heures

3. Quelles activités sont recommandées pendant le voyage à travers le Pont Enchanté?
A) Pratiquer la magie noire
B) Faire une sieste
C) Jouer du violon
D) Faire une séance de méditation

4. Comment les passagers doivent-ils se comporter dans les files d'attente pour le moyen de transport magique?
A) Danser et chanter
B) Se téléporter directement dans le transport
C) Patienter calmement
D) Organiser une course de sorciers

5. Que doivent faire les passagers lorsqu'ils atteignent l'autre côté du Pont Enchanté?
A) Effectuer une danse de la victoire
B) Participer à un banquet enchanteur
C) Effectuer un rituel de bienvenue
D) Continuer leur quête magique

Answers:

1.D
2.B
3.B
4.C
5.D

Vocabulaire / Vocabulary

- *Pont Enchanté* - Enchanted Bridge
- *Quête* - Quest
- *Aventure* - Adventure
- *Pays de l'Enchantement* - Land of Enchantment
- *Destrier* - Steed
- *Enchanteur/Enchanteuse* - Enchanter/Enchantress
- *Guérite* - Toll booth
- *Code de réservation* - Reservation code
- *Terminal* - Terminal
- *Lettre code* - Letter code
- *Voyage* - Journey
- *Transport magique* - Magical transport

- *Écran* - Screen
- *Chargement* - Loading
- *File d'attente* - Queue
- *Parking* - Parking
- *Instructions de sécurité* - Security instructions
- *Fenêtre* - Window
- *Contrôle de sécurité* - Security check
- *Moteurs* - Engines
- *Traversée* - Crossing
- *Sieste* - Nap
- *Enchanté* - Enchanting
- *Quête magique* - Magical quest
- *Expédition* - Expedition
- *Collation* - Snack
- *Destination* - Destination
- *Réservation* - Reservation
- *Réservation code* - Reservation code
- *Moyen de transport* - Means of transport
- *Rêve* - Dream
- *Ambiance* - Ambiance

15. Le monde des animaux de compagnie – The world of pets

Il y a beaucoup d'animaux dans le monde. Il y a des animaux sauvages et des animaux domestiques. Les animaux sauvages sont ceux qui vivent dans la forêt ou dans la jungle. Ces animaux ne sont pas amis des humains. Ces animaux vivent dans leur habitat naturel. Par conséquent, ils ne se mélangent pas aux humains. Il est préférable de les laisser dans leur habitat naturel.

There are many animals in the world. There are wild animals and domestic animals. Wild animals are those that live in the forest or in the jungle. These animals are not friendly towards humans. They live in their natural habitat. Consequently, they don't interact with humans. It's preferable to leave them in their natural habitat.

Le lion, l'ours, le tigre, l'éléphant, le rhinocéros, l'hippopotame et les loups sont quelques exemples d'animaux sauvages. Ces animaux ne sont pas des animaux de compagnie. Il y a aussi d'autres animaux comme les oiseaux et les reptiles qui sont également sauvages.

The lion, the bear, the tiger, the elephant, the rhinoceros, the hippopotamus, and the wolves are some examples of wild animals. These animals are not pets. There are also other animals like birds and reptiles that are also wild.

Il y a aussi beaucoup d'animaux domestiques. Ces animaux sont de bons animaux de compagnie ou servent à aider les humains dans leur travail. Par exemple, les chevaux et les vaches sont des animaux qui aident les humains. Les autres animaux qui vivent à la ferme sont les cochons, les poulets et les canards. Ces animaux sont également élevés pour servir de nourriture.

There are also many domestic animals. These animals are good companions or help humans in their work. For example, horses and cows are animals that assist humans. Other animals that live on farms are pigs, chickens, and ducks. These animals are also raised for food.

Dans une maison ordinaire, il y a des animaux de compagnie comme des chiens, des chats, des oiseaux et des poissons. Ces animaux sont une compagnie parfaite pour les humains. Les chiens, en particulier, sont de bons animaux de compagnie pour les enfants. Bien sûr, un très gros chien n'est pas une bonne idée pour les jeunes enfants. Les chats sont aussi de bons animaux de compagnie même s'ils sont plus indépendants. Les chats ont besoin de leur propre espace. Les poissons ne font pas de bruit tandis que les oiseaux chantent le matin.

In a regular household, there are companion animals like dogs, cats, birds, and fish. These animals are perfect companions for humans. Dogs, in particular, are good companionship animals for children. Of course, a very large dog is not a good idea for young children. Cats are also good companionship animals even though they are more independent. Cats need their own space. Fish don't make noise while birds sing in the morning.

Il y a des gens qui ont des animaux exotiques comme des souris, des araignées et des serpents domestiques. Il est important d'être prudent avec ce type d'animaux de compagnie parce qu'ils ne sont pas faciles à soigner et peuvent blesser d'autres personnes. Certains serpents sont venimeux. Certaines araignées le sont aussi. Les souris ne sont pas dangereuses, mais beaucoup de gens ne les aiment pas.

Some people have exotic animals like mice, spiders, and domesticated snakes. It's important to be cautious with this type of companion animal because they are not easy to care for and can harm other people. Some snakes are venomous. Certain spiders are too. Mice are not dangerous, but many people don't like them.

J'ai deux chiens. Ce sont mes meilleurs amis. Ils s'appellent Bruno et Tyson. Bruno est brun. Il est petit et très joueur. Tyson, lui, est noir. Il est grand et très fort, mais il n'est pas agressif. En fait, il est très mignon avec les enfants. Ce que mes chiens aiment le plus, c'est courir dans le parc avec les enfants de mon quartier.

I have two dogs. They are my best friends. Their names are Bruno and Tyson. Bruno is brown. He is small and very playful. Tyson, on the other hand, is black. He is big and very strong, but he's not aggressive. In fact, he's very gentle with children. What my dogs love the most is running in the park with the kids from my neighborhood.

Je pense acheter un nouvel animal, mais je n'ai plus de place dans ma maison. J'aimerais bien avoir un chaton, mais avec deux chiens, je pense qu'un chaton ne serait pas une bonne idée. Je pense à un autre animal comme un hamster. Les hamsters sont des animaux inoffensifs qui ne font pas de bruit. Ils ne sortent pas de leur cage non plus. Ce sont de très bons animaux pour une petite maison.

I'm thinking of getting a new pet, but I don't have any more space in my house. I would like to have a kitten, but with two dogs, I think a kitten wouldn't be a good idea. I'm considering another animal like a hamster. Hamsters are harmless animals that don't make noise. They also don't come out of their cage. They are very good pets for a small house.

Et vous? Vous avez un animal de compagnie? Quels animaux vous aimez? Si vous avez de jeunes enfants à la maison, les chiens sont de bons animaux de compagnie. Les chiens sont des animaux de compagnie idéaux pour les enfants. Si vous n'avez pas beaucoup d'espace, un hamster est l'animal de compagnie qu'il vous faut. Un autre bon animal de compagnie pour vous est le poisson. Ils ne prennent pas beaucoup de place et sont faciles à entretenir. Ce qu'il y a de mieux avec les hamsters et les poissons, c'est qu'ils ne font pas de bruit et ne salissent pas la maison.

And you? Do you have a companion animal? What animals do you like? If you have young children at home, dogs are good companion animals. Dogs are ideal companion animals for children. If you don't have much space, a hamster is the companion animal you need. Another good companion animal for you is a fish. They don't take up much space and are easy to care for. What's great about hamsters and fish is that they don't make noise and don't make a mess in the house.

Résumé de l'histoire

Il y a des animaux sauvages et des animaux domestiques. Les animaux sauvages ne vivent pas avec les humains. Ils vivent dans leur habitat naturel. Les animaux sauvages sont heureux chez eux. Il y a d'autres animaux qui vivent avec les humains. Dans une ferme, il y a beaucoup d'animaux qui aident les humains. Il y a aussi des animaux qui sont élevés comme nourriture pour les humains. Ces animaux sont utiles et importants. Il y a aussi d'autres animaux qui servent d'animaux de compagnie pour les humains. Les animaux domestiques sont de bons amis pour les enfants. Les chiens sont de bons animaux de compagnie tout comme les petits animaux comme les hamsters et les poissons, particulièrement pour les petites maisons.

Summary of the story

There are wild animals and domestic animals. Wild animals do not live with humans. They live in their natural habitat. Wild animals are happy in their own place. There are other animals that work with humans. On a farm, there are many animals that help humans. There are also animals that are raised for food. These animals are useful and important. There are also other animals that serve as pets for humans. Pets are company for humans and are good friends of children. Dogs are good pets, but small animals such as hamsters and fish are also good pets, especially in small houses.

Quiz

1. Quels sont les animaux sauvages?
a. Lion, chien, tigre
b. Lion, vache, cheval
c. Lion, tigre, ours
d. Lion, tigre, cochon

2. Qui sont les animaux domestiques?
a. Chien et chat
b. Chien et loup
c. Chien et ours
d. Chien et serpent

3. Quels animaux sont des animaux domestiques?
a. Animaux sauvages
b. Animaux de la ferme
c. Animaux qui vivent avec les humains dans leur maison
d. Animaux de travail

4. Quel sera mon nouvel animal de compagnie?
a. Chien
b. Chat
c. Cheval
d. Hamster

5. Combien de chiens ai-je?
a. Deux
b. Trois
c. Quatre
d. Cinq

Answers

1. C
2. A
3. C
4. D
5. A

Vocabulary

- *Monde*: world
- *Animaux*: animals
- *Sauvages*: wild
- *Domestiques*: domestic
- *Forêt*: woods
- *Jungle*: jungle
- *Amis*: Friends
- *Humains*: humans
- *Habitat*: habitat
- *Les laisser*: leave them
- *Exemples*: examples
- *Lion*: lion
- *Ours*: bear
- *Tigre*: tiger
- *Éléphant*: elephant
- *Rhinocéros*: rhinoceros
- *Hippopotame*: Hippopotamus
- *Loups*: wolves
- *Reptiles*: reptiles
- *Précisément*: precisely
- *Chevaux*: horses
- *Vaches*: cows
- *Ferme*: farm
- *Cochons*: pigs
- *Poulets*: hens
- *Canards*: ducks
- *Élevés*: raised
- *Chiens*: dogs
- *Chats*: cats
- *Oiseaux*: birds
- *Poissons*: fish
- *Parfaite*: perfect
- *Compagnie*: company
- *En particulier*: in particular
- *Indépendants*: independent
- *Espace*: space
- *Exotiques*: exotic
- *Souris*: mice
- *Araignées*: spiders
- *Blesser*: to hurt
- *Dangereuses*: dangerous
- *Brun*: brown
- *Joueur*: playful
- *Noir*: black
- *Fort*: strong

- *Aggresif*: aggressive
- *Mignon*: cute
- *Parc*: park
- *Pense*: thinking
- *J'aimerais*: I would like
- *Chaton*: kitten
- *Hamster*: hamster
- *Inoffensifs*: harmless
- *Cage*: cage
- *Idéaux*: ideal
- *Salissent*: dirty

Conclusion

I hope this book was able to help you on your journey to learn French as a second language. This guide was intended to give you a leg up into the French-speaking world, in order to communicate your most basic needs in a short period of time.

If you take the time and commit to your daily lessons continually, do your exercises and drill the sentences in your mind, you will definitely learn a lot within the space of two weeks.

The next step is to keep on going. Drill these words and phrases even more, and use the language! Find a French speaker, take a weekend trip to Paris, or Montreal, and start speaking French! Practice makes perfect and don't forget to review the lessons from time to time.

FREE AUDIO OF "FRENCH SHORT STORIES FOR BEGINNERS"

Download your fee audio from our website:

www.dupontlanguageinstitute.com

or follow this QR code:

To download the file:

Username: AC-002
Password: 2kL+uWFMG8}G

To open the file:

Password: 86)(ykgAYn64!_8G

Learn French

An easy method for intermediate users to be able to have a fluent French conversation in just 7 days. Includes intermediate grammar rules, exercises and common everyday life sentences

Introduction

All successful language learners once started at the beginning, as complete beginners, wondering whether or not they had the ability to learn a foreign language. The one quality you can be sure all these learners had --- before they became successful --- was motivation. If you can foster a passion for French, if you can make it so important to you that it almost becomes your single defining purpose, if you can get clear on what it will mean to you to one day wake up and know that you are fluent in the language, then let me tell you, there is nothing that will stop you reaching that goal.

Having picked up this book on learning French, you have probably already thought about why you want to learn the language. It may help, though, to take a moment to be clear about these motives before moving on, and even write them down. Researchers have shown that those who write their goals down are far more likely to achieve those goals, and the best part is that it only takes a moment to do so.

I would like to propose a variation on the goal-setting exercise that can help you evoke your true feelings about French and why you wish to learn it. It can be a helpful exercise at the start of a language learning journey, but also at various points along the way, when you might be searching for motivation.

Close your eyes.

You wake up, and you realize the hard work has paid off. You are now fluent in French after working hard at it for many months.

Words roll off your tongue. You can express yourself effortlessly. You understand what others are saying to you.

You "belong".

How does it feel? What does it mean to you to have achieved this?

Consider jotting down your response to this task in a notebook --- it may have unexpected consequences in the future!

Becoming clear about your true motivation to learn French can have the power to transform your whole language learning journey. Your reason for learning French may be different from mine or from that of others reading this book. This motivation is personal to you and is the fuel that will power your journey to fluency in French. As tempting as it might be to skip ahead, it is important to stop and become clear on why you are learning the language first.

What Are the Benefits of Learning French?

Bearing all of this in mind, let's look at some of the main benefits that are available to everyone as a speaker of French. I encourage you to think about which of these benefits most motivate you and combine them with your own personal reasons for learning the language. You may well find some inspirations you had not yet considered!

Learning French Is Good for The Brain

It is widely accepted that there are several cognitive and physiological benefits associated with learning any second language and there are many advantages in choosing French specifically. It is estimated that over half the world's population uses more than one language on a daily basis and many monolingual

English speakers, brought up speaking the global language of business and travel, are often not aware that this is quite normal. But in fact, in other parts of the world (including much of the French-speaking world) bilingualism is the norm.

Travel in France, Belgium, Switzerland, French Canada & Africa

France consistently ranks as the top tourist destination worldwide, ahead of countries like the United States and China. Although most individuals in popular tourist destinations in France can speak English, many have just basic skills. Learning French would tremendously facilitate any trip to France, especially if you plan to independently explore the nation, as you cannot rely solely on the citizens to be able to converse in English when purchasing tickets, traveling the train, or dining in restaurants.

Furthermore, being able to speak the local language will enable you to have much closer contact with the people you meet and will make your trip a much more enriching experience. This is also true in the French-speaking parts of Belgium and, to a lesser extent, Switzerland, although the latter country has a strong tradition of multilingualism and it is probably easier to find people who speak English there.

Communicate with People All Over the World

While French has long since been replaced by English as the global *lingua franca*, it is still widely spoken in many places all over the world in former French colonies, notably in large parts of Africa. It is estimated that globally, there are 110 million native speakers of French and that a further 190 million speak French as a second language. This means that learning French will equip you to communicate with large numbers of people worldwide.

Gain Advantages in Business

If you do business with French speakers, you will gain their respect by speaking their language. It was Nelson Mandela who said *"If you talk to a man in a language he understands, that goes to his head. If you talk to him in his language, that goes to his heart"*. Being able to conduct meetings and other business transactions in the native language of your partners without relying on English has a clear benefit, but simply being able to engage in small talk in French will have a dramatic effect on your relationship and command respect.

Acquire a More In-Depth Knowledge of the Culture of France

It is impossible to study a new tongue without also knowing about the history and traditions of the country whose language you are studying since language and culture are inextricably linked. France is a nation that looks back on its long and eventful past with great passion and possesses a rich cultural legacy. It is safe to say that the French are incredibly proud of their history and cultural heritage, and this feeling of pride is well warranted on their part. The French language serves as the key that unlocks the door to this culture as well as the cultures of other countries that speak French. It is certainly possible to admire French culture without being able to speak the language itself; nevertheless, learning French will provide you with a degree of insight and personal happiness that is significantly deeper.

Open the Doors to French Art, Literature and Film

France is a country with a great tradition of art and literature. Reading novels or watching films in translation is nothing like experiencing them in the language in which they were written. Being able to understand French will open the doors to some of the world's great literary and artistic achievements.

French musicians and filmmakers extend their country's tradition of artistic excellence into the present day. One famous example is the annual Cannes Film Festival. It is one of the most exciting occasions in the film business since it features cutting-edge works of cinema from all over the globe. The festival's highest honor, the Palme d'Or, is presented annually to the best film.

For all these reasons, it is clear that choosing to learn French is a decision that will bring real and tangible benefits to your life. By now you are probably excited to get started, as all these benefits, and more, await you as you progress through this book and begin your journey to mastering French.

Chapter 1 - Greetings and Other Useful Day To Day Phrases

The first thing that tourists and beginners usually turn to when it comes to learning a language quickly would be the greetings and commonly used phrases. This is actually a great way to start practicing French. Furthermore, it lets the learner take a peek into the culture of the French people. This chapter contains a large collection of greetings and phrases that you will find quite useful in everyday conversation.

Formal Greetings

Good day (Hello) in the French language is translated to *Bonjour!*

Good morning in the French language is translated to *Bon matin!*

Good afternoon in the French language is translated to *Bon après-midi!*

Good evening in the French language is translated to *Bonsoir!*

Good night in the French language is translated to *Bonne nuit!*

How are you? in the French language is translated to *Comment allez-vous?*

Very well, thank you in the French language is translated to *Très bien, merci.*

And you? in the French language is translated to *Et vous?*

Goodbye (temporarily) in the French language is translated to *Au revoir.*

Goodbye (permanently) in the French language is translated to *Adieu!*

(Have a) good day! in the French language is translated to *Bonne journée*

You can choose to say "*bonjour*" in the morning and in the afternoon. After 6 o'clock in the evening, you can say "*bonsoir*".

Informal Greetings

Hi! => *Salut!*

Is everything okay? => *Tout va bien?*

How are you? => *Ça va?*

Great! => *Très bien!*

Forms of Address

Mr. in the French language is translated to (*M*) *Monsieur, Messieurs*

Mrs. in the French language is translated to (*Mme*) *Madame, Mesdames*

Miss in the French language is translated to (*Mlle*) *Mademoiselle, Mesdemoiselles*

Introductions

Formal: What is your name? in the French language is translated to *Comment vous appelez-vous?*

Informal: What's your name? in the French language is translated to *Comment t'appelles-tu?*

Quel est son prénom? in the French language is translated to What is his/her first name?

My name is... in the French language is translated to *Je m'appelle...*

Charmed. in the French language is translated to *Enchanté*

Who is it? in the French language is translated to *Qui est-ce?*

How old are you? in the French language is translated to *Quel âge avez-vous?*

What is your nationality? in the French language is translated to *Quelle est votre nationalité?*

Where do you live? in the French language is translated to *Où habitez-vous?*

What do you do for a living? in the French language is translated to *Que faites-vous dans la vie?*

Where do you work? in the French language is translated to *Où travaillez-vous?*

What are your favorite hobbies? in the French language is translated to *Quels sont vos loisirs préférés?*

Common Phrases

Pardon? Repeat that please. in the French language is translated to *Pardon? Répétez, s'il vous plaît.*

I don't understand. in the French language is translated to *Je ne comprends pas.*

I don't know. in the French language is translated to *Je ne sais pas.*

Can you speak slower, please? in the French language is translated to *Pouvez-vous parler plus lentement, s'il vous plaît?*

Excuse me. in the French language is translated to *Excusez-moi.*

(If you) please. in the French language is translated to *S'il vous plaît.*

One moment, please. in the French language is translated to *Un moment, s'il vous plait.*

I am sorry. in the French language is translated to *Je suis désolé/désolée.*

That's okay! in the English language is translated to *Ce n'est pas grave!*

Thank you very much! in the English language is translated to *Merci beaucoup.*

You are welcome in the English language is translated to *Je vous en prie*

It's nothing. in the French language is translated to *De rien.*

You are welcome in the French language is translated to *Pas de quoi.*

Key Question Words

It is imperative to know these key question words when asking for specific information:

How many... in the French language is translated to *Combien de...*

How much... in the French language is translated to *Combien*

At what time... in the French language is translated to *À quelle heure*

How... in the French language is translated to *Comment*

Where... in the French language is translated to *Où*

Why... in the French language is translated to *Pourquoi*

What... in the French language is translated to *Qu'est-ce que*

When... in the French language is translated to *Quand*

Who... in the French language is translated to *Qui*...

Which.../ What... in the French language is translated to *Quel(s)/Quelle(s)*

Talking about Directions and Places

"Where is...?" is a question that you need to master in French when you are traveling. Here are some common phrases:

Where is the Eiffel Tower? in the French language is translated to *Où est la tour Eiffel?*

Where is the bathroom? in the French language is translated to *Où sont les toilettes?*

Where is the bus going? in the French language is translated to *Où va ce bus?*

Where does this road lead? in the French language is translated to *Où mène cette rue?*

Use the preposition *"à"* when you want to convey the idea that you are traveling to or are currently staying in a specific location.

For example, if you are going to say "I am going to Paris", say: *Je vais à Paris.*" On the other hand, "we are in Paris," translates to "*Nous sommes à Paris.*"

Put the definite article after *"à"* if you wish to talk about staying at or visiting certain places (such as museums and cathedrals). For example:

Pierre is going to the museum. => *Pierre va au musée.*

Sarah wants to go to the cathedral. => *Sarah veut aller à la cathédrale.*

Go to the coffee shop. => *Aller au café.*

To say that the place is within eyesight, you can use these phrases:

Question: *Où est le bâtiment?* (Where is the building?)/ *Où sont les bâtiments?* (Where are the buildings?)

Answer: *Le voici!* (Here it is!) or *La voilà!* (There it is!)/ *Les voilà!* (There they are!)

Talking about the Weather

"*Le temps*" is the French word for the weather. It is often a favorite topic among native French speakers, particularly if the weather is bad.

The French names for the seasons are as follows:

Spring in the French language is translated to *le printemps*

Summer in the French language is translated to *l'été*

Fall in the French language is translated to *l'automne*

Winter in the French language is translated to *l'hiver*

To ask "What is the weather like?", say: *Quel temps fait-il?*

To answer, say: *Il fait...* and then describe it as:

Warm => *Chaud*

Cold => *Froid*

Nice => *Beau*

Mild => *Doux*

Cool => *Frais*

Bad => *Mauvais*

Sunny => *Du soleil*

Windy => *Du vent*

If it is raining, say: => *Il pleut.*

If it is snowing, say: => *Il neige.*

To talk about the temperature, you say: *La température est de vingt cinq degrés.* (It is 25 degrees [Celsius]).

Talking about Where you Live

"*Habiter*" is the French word for living in a space, while "*vivre*" refers to both time and space.

For instance, if you say "they lived in the 19th century", you make use of "*vivre*", hence: "*ils vivaient au dix-neuvième siècle.*" Keep in mind that vivre is an irregular verb.

If you wish to talk about where you live, you use "*habiter*", such as:

J'habite dans un appartement. (I live in an apartment.)

Nous habitons une maison. (We live in a house.)

Exercise

Practice saying the French or English counterpart of these greetings and phrases without looking at the notes:

- Good day (Hello)
- Good morning
- Good afternoon
- Good evening

- Good night
- How are you?
- Very well, thank you.
- And you?
- Goodbye (temporarily)
- Goodbye (permanently)
- *Bonne journée*
- Hi!
- Is everything okay?
- Great!
- Formal: What is your name?
- Informal: What's your name?
- *Quel est son prénom?*
- My name is...
- Charmed.
- Who is it?
- How old are you?
- What is your nationality?
- Where do you live?
- What do you do for a living?
- *Où travaillez-vous?*
- What are your favorite hobbies?
- Pardon? Repeat that please.
- I don't understand.
- I don't know.
- Can you speak more slowly, please?
- Excuse me.
- (If you) please.
- Un moment, s'il vous plaît.
- I am sorry.
- That's okay!
- Thank you very much!
- You are welcome
- It's nothing.

Chapter 2 - What You Need to Know About French: A Linguistic Background

French is a member of the Romance family of languages and it is closely related to languages such as Italian and Spanish. It does not have as many native speakers as Spanish or Portuguese, but as previously mentioned, millions of individuals all around the world use French as either their primary language or their secondary language.

Romance language speakers generally find it easy to acquire other Romance languages because they are related in grammar, vocabulary, and other ways. Once you have learnt one of these languages, learning one or more of the others is greatly facilitated. If Romance languages can be considered brothers and sisters of French, then languages like English can be thought of as cousins. They are located further apart on the linguistic family tree but also have much in common.

Today's standard French is most closely related to the northern French dialects. However, French has evolved into a language that is truly spoken all over the world as a result of France's influence and reach throughout the colonial period. French is spoken not only in France, but also in numerous African countries that were historically part of France, as well as in Belgium, Switzerland, Canada, the United States of America, and a few other places besides. It is the working language of many international organisations and is recognised as an official language in 29 nations. After World War II, English replaced French as the international language, which had been in use since the seventeenth century.

Let me introduce some of the key features of French.

Word Gender

As we noted in the previous section, French makes use of grammatical gender, meaning that nouns are considered either masculine or feminine. Whereas in English we use 'the' to introduce a noun, in French you will need to choose either *le* or *la* for masculine and feminine nouns respectively. There are several examples …

Masculine:
- *le café* --- the café
- le supermarché --- the supermarket
- *le vin* --- the wine
- le poisson --- the fish

Feminine:
- *la terre* --- the earth
- *la danse* – dance
- *la nourriture* – food
- *l'actrice* --- the actress

French Verb Tenses

The use of verbs is another area in which French and English differ from one another. In English, there is not a lot of variation in the form that verbs take. In the present tense, the only variation is in the 3rd person (he/she) form, where an "s" is added:

- I say

- You say

- He/she says

- We say

- They say

However, in French, as we saw in the previous section, there are many variations that occur based on who really performs the action.

French verb tenses (talking about events in the past, present or future) also differ somewhat from English. For instance, when discussing events that occurred in the past, French makes a fundamental distinction between:

- An occurrence that took place just once at a specific instance in time

- Something that has been present for a considerable amount of time or that occurs frequently

This can be expressed in a variety of different ways in English, but it is much easier to do it in French. As a result, students of French can acquire familiarity with its tenses very quickly. In point of fact, it is likely a great deal simpler for native English speakers to become fluent in French tenses than it is for native French speakers to become conversant in the intricate tenses system of the English language.

One last thing to take into consideration is that the subjunctive is frequently used in French. This usage is practically extinct in the English language and can only be found in sentences such as "It is important that we be on time" (not "are on time"). However, not only the subjunctive is rarely needed at the beginner stages of French, but even when you do come to learn the subjunctive, you will discover that it often occurs in predictable places, and as part of common expressions, which will help you become accustomed to its usage quickly. In conclusion, the subjunctive tense in French is not as difficult to utilize as it is in Italian and Spanish, two languages in which it is utilized far more frequently.

French Pronunciation and Spelling

Even if there is absolutely nothing to be afraid of, it's possible that some students of French will be nervous about the pronunciation of the language. There is a relatively small set of sounds that can be challenging for native English speakers, but with a little practice, most people can master them. Because there is no equivalent sound in English phonology, the French "r" is likely the sound that causes the most consternation among native English speakers. It is articulated at the back of the throat with the throat just slightly open, and the sound is comparable to that of someone clearing their throat, but it is softer and more delicate.

Another trap that people who speak English are susceptible to falling into is the fact that French makes a distinction between "*u*" and "*ou*" (as in tu and vous), whereas English simply has the sound in "you," which is neither one nor the other. This can lead to some very interesting circumstances as when you think you are saying "neck" (*cou*), you may actually pronounce *cul*, which means "arse", which could wind up being rather awkward! This can result in some rather funny scenarios as when you believe you are saying "neck" (*cou*), you may actually speak cul! Luckily for us, the majority of the remaining vowels and consonants in French are significantly simpler for speakers of English to articulate. You are going to learn everything there is to know about these sounds, including how to perfect them, in the following part, so try not to worry too much about it right now!

Finally, French spelling, which can appear inconsistent at first glance, needs attention. Even if the spoken language of France has evolved considerably since it was first recorded in writing, the written form of the language has not kept pace. As a result, many French words now contain letters that are silent. At first glance, written French may appear daunting due to the numerous accents and other markings (known as diacritics) atop and below the letters. This should not bother you, as there is nothing too challenging beyond a few idiosyncratic spellings to memorize, and you can take solace in the fact that we have far poorer spelling in English!

This section has given you an overview of some of the linguistic areas you can expect to find when you start learning French. We will look at all of these aspects in more detail as we continue, starting with French pronunciation.

Chapter 3 - How Does it Work?

So many people all the time everywhere make an extreme error in learning languages: they fail to look at it in the context of a language and instead try to turn it into a game of memorization. This doesn't work. There are good and bad ways to learn language, and if at the end of the day, all you have to show for yourself are a few phrases memorized off of some flash cards, then frankly, you're learning the language in a bad way.

I've been trying to communicate how to learn languages for a very long time and I'm still having a hard time determining whether I think language learning is an art or a science. Regardless, the truth is that there is no one perfect way to learn a language, because we all learn in terribly different ways, which makes it nigh impossible to pin down one singular way which would most work.

However, there are certain natural mechanisms for picking up languages that people of average intelligence and greater ability can utilize in order to pick up language really easily.

We don't come out of the womb learning a language. We come out as a blank slate. We have the *ability* to speak language, but it's unformed; a baby born in China will learn a form of Chinese, and a baby born in England will learn English.

Babies can't read flash cards. And while our natural propensity to learn a language demonstrably goes down as a person ages, there are numerous reasons for this which aren't normally accounted for.

A child has to learn a language in order to survive and communicate, and has an easy time learning a language due to the fact that it's completely immersed in it.

There are language learning gurus out there who are polyglots because they put themselves in similar situations in order to learn language: they immerse themselves nearly entirely in the language by traveling from place to place and making it so that they have to speak and understand the language to survive and communicate.

Now, it's likely not feasible for you to up and relocate to Quebec or France just in order to learn a language. But that's not to say that we can't trigger the same sort of intuitive language learning processes that these language learning gurus and these children are tapping into.

In other words, this entire method is based around the idea that if you have the proper springboard and the proper background, you can do any number of things with the language that you wish simply by natural self guided immersion and active effort in learning the language.

My goal in this book isn't to give you a vocabulary list to memorize, nor is it to give you a precise grammatical explanation of every single thing (though I'll certainly try to give accurate and succinct explanations), but rather it's to help you streamline the natural language learning processes so that you don't, well, forget every last thing that you learn in the process of reading this book.

The way that they taught you to learn languages in high school was wrong. Cut and dry, 100%, it was not the right way to go about it. Well, it was and it wasn't. It was right in some capacities --- you likely had to listen to and repeat phrases in the class, which was solid basic immersion. But the idea of regurgitating vocab words onto a test is bizarre and ludicrous and just a way to ensure that you forget the very words you learned the following year.

The only way to avoid this sort of situation is by actively using the vocabulary and words that you've learned, but the reality is that a lot of high schools --- especially ones with less funding --- don't try particularly hard with their pen pal projects or anything of that nature.

Anyhow, the purpose of this book is to streamline the process of learning a language intuitively. There are a few different ways in which I'm going to try earnestly to do this. The first is by explaining the differences between English and French.

You may be wondering, "why would you do that? Why not start with the similarities?"

Well, the simple answer is because any language has more happening in common with another language than it has happening differently. This may sound bizarre, but think about it --- every language is just a form of communication. There are various differences between them but ultimately, they're all attempting to accomplish the same essential key concept: the usage of verbal cues in order to denote or tell a given thing.

However, for all the similarities, languages can also be incredibly different. For example, if I were going to try to tell the similarities between English and Japanese, the list would be incredibly short, by mere virtue of the fact that English and Japanese have little truly in common. Grammatically, they are incredibly different beasts. On top of this, the vocabulary is very different. It's much easier to make you understand the ways in which Japanese and English are different than try to expect you to latch onto the things that are.

When you're told things that are similar between languages, you latch onto those concepts. You're unaware of the vast amount of differences and you may, in fact, make very simple mistakes. One common such mistake in French is the combination of the existence and state verb *être* with the present participle of another verb.

In English, we use this to construct the present continuous tense. For example:

I am eating.

He is playing.

They are walking.

However, this isn't such the case in French. The equivalent phrases would be along the lines of:

Je suis mangant.

Il est jouant.

Ils sont marchant.

But this isn't correct at all, and in fact sound particularly bizarre and out of place to other French speakers. The correct way would be to conjugate the infinitive of the directly referenced verb (to eat, to play, to walk) for the present indicative and completely leave the *être* (to be) verb out of it:

Je mange.

Il joue.

Ils marchent.

There are a great number of differences between English and French as such that you'll somewhat naturally pick up as we go along, but that I'll point out regardless.

One particular sound is the sound made in "*je*" and "*le*" and similar words. You may be tempted, especially if you have experience in other Romance languages where the sounds are very cut and dry, to pronounce these as "jeh" and "leh", as in "JEffrey" or "LEt's go", but you can't do that. This sound is actually much closer to the *oo* sound in *book* (U.S. English).

For phonetic purposes, this specific sound will be represented with the letters *uu*.

It's also important to bear in mind going forward that every *r* in Modern French is pronounced in a very guttural trill, quite similar to the German *r*, though not quite as intense. (though it's particularly hard for a language to be anywhere near as intense as German is, truthfully.) The only exception is generally in rural communities in Quebec or among the elderly in Southern France. Otherwise, the sound is guttural and produced from airflow at the back of the throat. It can be difficult to ascertain at first, but you can find YouTube videos concerning the French *r* to help you to understand it.

So if I were to write the following phrase:

Je prends un sandwich. (I'll take/have a sandwich.)

I would write the pronunciation for it as such:

juu PRAHND uh(n) sand-WEECH

The *n* in parentheses denotes that the consonant should be barely uttered and heard.

There are still more differences between French and English, and it's really important to bear these in mind as you go forward, too.

First off, they are not pronounced similarly, at all. There will be several cognates that you'll run into that look quite similar to the English phrase but are pronounced nothing the same. Take, for example, the word "horrible". In French, the *h* is silent, the *r* would be guttural, and the *ble* consonant, which would sound like "bull" in English, sounds like "bluu" in French. So we go from *HOR-ih-bull* to *or-EEH-bluu*. *Il y a une grande différence entre les deux!* (There's a big difference between the two!)

That's not even including *false cognates* which you need to be incredibly wary of. Take for instance the word *terrible*. It also exists in French, where in a literary sense, it means something very similar to the English "terrible". However, if you were to ask a French person how they're doing, and they said "*pas terrible*", you may think they're saying "not bad" or "not terrible", but this isn't the case. In fact, *terrible* (tuu-REEH-bluu) in the colloquial sense means "great". So "*pas terrible*" really means "not great" or "not the best".

Going beyond that, a lot of things are somewhat topsy turvy in French. Take the phrase "*yaourt aux fruits*". This means "yogurt with fruit". However, "*aux*" is a contraction of "*à les*", meaning "to the" or "at the". The typical French word for "with" would indeed be "*avec*", as in "*Je vais aller au centre commercial avec mes copains*" ("I'm going to the mall with my friends."). However, "with" doesn't have as many uses in French as it does in English, and to express the innate quality of something, or the idea of something belonging to something else in a categorical sense, you use à rather than avec.

One last super important difference that we're going to cover at this given moment is saying your occupation. In English, we say "I am *a professor*" or "I am *a butcher*". However, the French leave this article out. To them, an occupation is an intrinsic quality, which somewhat makes sense if you think about it. So instead of saying "*Je suis un professeur*" (I am a professor), the French would rather say "*Je suis professeur*" (literally 'I am professor').

Basic sentence structure

Anyhow, let's get to the meat of this chapter, because there's still quite a bit left to cover: subjects and verbs. This is the basis of every single sentence we speak. I'm sure that, by now, you know what a subject is. A subject is the word which denotes the performer of an action.

My dog is big.

In this sentence, *my dog* is the subject, where *is* is the verb (to be). Every language has a specific order in which they put subjects, objects, and verbs (an object being the direct recipient of an action, such as "I love cats", where "cats" is the object).

Subject pronouns

In English, we use sentence pronouns quite often. In fact, we use them in nearly every sentence!

So what is a sentence pronoun? A sentence pronoun is anything which replaces giving the direct name of something in the sentence. Take for example the sentence "John plays basketball."

Normally, if we've already brought John up as the topic of conversation, we can contextually replace his name and still have it be clear that we're talking about him specifically. We would do this by saying "he plays basketball."

Then, we use *we, I,* and *you* per standard, because there's not really a first or second direct *noun*. All direct nouns are by their nature in the third person. If your name were Janet, and you were asking me for directions, I wouldn't say "Janet needs to go to the light and turn left." The *you* would imply that I'm speaking *directly* to you, and the fact that I'm talking to you directly conversely implies that I need to use *you* in the first place, because the fact that I'm talking directly *to* someone and not directly *of* someone puts the sentence in the second person. Thus, I would say "You need to go to the light and turn left."

In English, we have several different subject pronouns. However, we still have less than French, miraculously.

Here are the ones that we mainly use in English:

I-first person singular.

you-second person singular.

He, she, it-third person singular

we-first person plural

they-third person plural

French, likewise, has numerous. They also have something we don't: a second person plural. We do have them, but they're informal and unstandardized. For example, in the Southern U.S. you may hear "y'all", and up north and in Britain you'll often hear "you guys". However, we don't have a singular word to refer to multiple people, and they do.

They also have the concept of *formality*. This means that in the second person singular formation, they will use different words depending entirely upon who they're talking to. For example, if you're talking to somebody you just met, someone older than you, or someone in a position of authority over you, you will always use the formal second-person pronoun, which coincidentally is also the second person plural. You use the informal second-person form, the equivalent of English "you" and German "du", when you're around people younger than you, family members, or people that you have met more than once.

The French pronouns are as follows:

- *Je (juu)*-first person singular
- *Tu (too)*-second person singular
- *Il/elle (il/el)*-third person singular
- *Nous (noo)*-first person plural
- *Vous (voo)*-second person plural / first person singular formal
- *Ils/elles (il/el)*-third person plural, ils for males/mixed gender, elles for females

If you haven't figured it out, in French, you nearly never say the last syllable. The only case in which you do is if it's followed by a vowel, and even then, there are a lot of exceptions. You'll pick up on this a lot more as you actually work with the language and discover the parameters and tendencies of it. We'll talk more about the difference between *ils* and *elles* momentarily.

On

On is a super important term in French that you're going to run into a lot. It has a direct translation to the English *one*.

When talking to a boss, one says "*vous*".

Quand on parle au patron, on dit << vous >>.

However, it also has an implicit meaning of "we" in reference to an unspecific group.

In France, we drink wine.

En France, on boit du vin.

What's more, in colloquial French, people will often use *on* instead of *nous* in order to avoid the more verbose nous conjugations. Compare the following sentences which mean we're going to go to the movies:

On va aller au cinéma. (ohn va AL-ley oh seen-ey-mah, in practice the *va* and *aller* sound like one word: ohn v'AL-ley oh seen-ey-mah)

Nous allons aller au cinéma. (nooz AL-lohn AL-ley oh seen-ey-mah)

The first is much easier to say and remember. This will become far more obvious the more that you work with French and get to more complex conjugations, such as the imperfect tense.

This pronoun deserved its own place because it's very unique and doesn't quite have a direct approximate in English. It is always conjugated like the *il/elle* third person pronouns, as it's a third person pronoun itself.

Verb conjugation

Verbs are always conjugated in one way or another. However, English actually has one of the easiest verb conjugation systems of any language. The only thing which makes English verb conjugation particularly difficult is the tendency of it to be irregular and for there to be a lot of verbs to cover terribly specific situations. For example, take the phrase "to wait for". You would think, given the commonness of this particular verb and situation, it would be a verb of its own accord. However, this isn't the case. French, however, *does* have a verb for this --- *attendre*. "*J'attends mes amis.*" corresponds to "I'm waiting for my friends."

Anyway, English's verb conjugation is indeed rather simple. However, it still exists in some ways. The normal way that we conjugate regular verbs is to, in the raw indicative form, to add an -s to the third person singular. Like so:

I eat, you eat, he/she/it eats, we eat, they eat.

Or, if it's a present continuous verb, we'll use the auxiliary verb "to be" (which is irregular) before the gerund of the given verb, as we talked about earlier:

I am eating, you are eating, he/she/it is eating, we are eating, they are eating.

French has a more nuanced system of conjugation than English. There are more endings and forms and even tenses. The saving grace, however, is they tend to follow a pattern all on their own. Once you learn this pattern, verbs become far easier.

The present indicative and the present continuous form a singular tense in French, known simply as the *présent*, which of course means "present". The present can be conjugated in many ways but tends to follow a pattern, as you'll see momentarily.

There are three categories of French verbs: *-re* verbs, *-er* verbs, and *-ir* verbs. Most verbs are *regular*, which means that they follow specific patterns of usage and spelling. There is some contention here, in that quite a few verbs are *irregular*... including the ones which are arguably the most common.

That's not to discourage you at all, though, as even the irregular verbs follow a very similar pattern to the regular verbs. So without further ado, let's conjugate some verbs!

First, we're going to focus on *-er* verbs, with the specific example of *parler*, meaning "to speak".

Parler --- to speak

Conjugation	Meaning	Pronunciation
*Je parl**e***	I speak	Juu pahrl
*Tu parl**es***	You speak	Too pahrl
*Il/elle/on parl**e***	He/she/it/one speaks	Il/el/ohn pahrl
*Nous parl**ons***	We speak	Noo pahr-lohn
*Vous parl**ez***	You all/you (f.) speak	Voo pahr-ley
*Ils/elles parl**ent***	They speak	Il/el pahrl

The way that conjugation works is by dropping the final two letters of the regular verb, always *-er*, *-ir*, or *-re*, and replacing them with the given suffix. The suffixes for each pronoun are italicized.

As you can see, the endings for *-er* verbs are *-e*, *-es*, *-e*, *-ons*, *-ez*, and *-ent*.

Now is a better time than any to make a mental note for you: you do NOT pronounce the *-ent* suffix on *-er* verbs. Ever. The verb sounds functionally the same as the third person *singular* conjugation.

Anyway, now let's do an *-ir* verb. The endings for *-ir* verbs are *-is*, *-is*, *-it*, *-issons*, *-issez*, and *-issent*. You don't pronounce the *-ent* here, either. However, it doesn't sound like the third person singular, because the third person singular ends in a *t* sound (if followed by a vowel) or none at all, where the third person plural ends in an *s* sound.

Finir --- to finish

Conjugation	Meaning	Pronunciation
Je finis	I finish	Juu fee-nee
Tu finis	You finish	Too fee-nee
Il/elle/on finit	He/she/it/one finishes	Il/el/ohn fee-nee
Nous finissons	We finish	Noo fee-nee-sohn
Vous finissez	You all/you (f.) finish	Voo fee-nee-sey
Ils/elles finissent	They finish	Il/el fee-nees

And lastly, we're going to work with regular -re verbs. -Re verbs can be somewhat tricky, because they change the scheme up a bit. The third person singular doesn't add *anything* to the stem. Thus, the -re verb endings are as follows: -s, -s, *nothing*, -ons, -ez, -ent. Let's practice this using the verb *vendre*, meaning "to sell".

Vendre --- to sell

Conjugation	Meaning	Pronunciation
Je vends	I sell	Juu vahnd
Tu vends	You sell	Too vahnd
Il/elle/on vend	He/she/it/one sells	Il/el/ohn vahn
Nous vendons	We sell	Noo vahnd-ohns
Vous vendez	You all/you (f.) sell	Voo vahnd-ey
Ils/elles vendent	They sell	Il/el vahnd

Do you see how this is working? These verbs all follow a very certain manner of spelling, but it certainly does have an order that you can really easily pick up on. And if it seems difficult now, don't worry --- it will most definitely make more sense with practice.

I'd like to move onto articles, but we can't quite yet. This is because we need to cover some major *irregular* verbs. These are verbs that you may use which don't follow the same rules as the verbs prior. These are verbs that you'll learn with practice. The first one that we're going to cover is "to be", or *être*. Here's how you conjugate it.

Être --- to be

Conjugation	Meaning	Pronunciation
Je suis	I am	Juu swee
Tu es	You are	Too ey
Il/elle/on est	He/she/it/one is	Il/el/ohn ey
Nous sommes	We are	Noo sohm
Vous êtes	You all/you (f.) are	Vooz eht
Ils/elles sont	They are	Il/el sohn

You use *être* pretty much as you would expect to use it. There are certain places where the translation of "to be" don't quite work across English to French, though, but we'll get there in a second.

You use *être* in order to describe something or somebody, as well as to tell where you are. It actually corresponds largely to "to be" in English, but there are certain cases where it does. For example, in English, we'd say "I'm 20 years old". *Mais en français*, we'd say "I have 20 years". There are a few other examples I'll list off momentarily, after going into the conjugation of "to have".

Avoir --- to have

Conjugation	Meaning	Pronunciation
J'ai (Je ai contraction)	I have	Jey
Tu as	You have	Too ah
Il/elle/on a	He/she/it/one has	Il/el/ohn ah
Nous avons	We have	Noo ah-vohn
Vous avez	You all/you (f.) have	Voo ah-vey
Ils/elles ont	They have	Il/el ohn

So to say *I'm twenty years old* in French, you'd say *j'ai vingt ans* (jey VAHNT ahn) --- "I have twenty years".

There are some embarrassing mix-ups between *être* and *avoir* which might happen. You need to be mindful and aware of these. Consider, for example, the sentence "I am full". You might be tempted to translate this directly: *je suis plein*. But this is a HORRIBLE idea! Why? Because *"Je suis plein" does* mean "I'm full"... as in "I'm full with a baby."

Instead, you'd say *J'ai plein*, or roughly "I have fullness".

This likewise plays out with "I'm hot". If you were to say *"Je suis chaude"* as a woman, you'd be telling somebody you're aroused. Rather, you'd want to say *"J'ai chaud"* --- "I have hot". This means that the temperature is hot, or that you feel an uncomfortable heat.

Avoir is used for a few other phrases similarly to describe personal feelings. *J'ai faim* would mean "I'm hungry", though it literally means I have hunger.

The next verb we have to cover is *faire*. *Faire* technically means "to do" or "to make", but it has a ton of idiomatic expressions as well. Here's how you conjugate faire:

Faire --- to do, to make

Conjugation	Meaning	Pronunciation
Je fais	I do, I make	Juu feh
Tu fais	You do, you make	Too feh
Il/elle/on fait	He/she/it/one does, he/she/it/one makes	Il/el/ohn feh
Nous faisons	We do, we make	Noo feh-zohn
Vous faites	You all/you (f.) do, you all/you (f.) make	Voo feht
Ils/elles font	They do, they make	Il/el fohn

There are many cases where you'll use "*faire*", like so.

Où est Timothie? (Where is Timothy?)

Dans sa chambre. Il fait ses devoirs. (He's in his room. He's doing his homework.)

It's also has quite a few idiomatic uses. For example, if it's a nice day out, you would say "*Il fait beau*" --- literally "It's doing handsome". If it's hot, you'd say "*il fait chaud*" and if it's cold, you'd say "*il fait froid*". In other words, if you're using an adjective to describe the weather, you'd use *il fait...* before it. However, if you're describing a current weather action, like rain or snow, you use the verb for those: *neiger* and *pleuvoir* specifically. "It's snowing" would be "*Il neige*" (Il nehj) and "It's raining" would be "*Il pleut*" (Il ploo).

Another verb that we need to cover is *aller*, which means "to go". You need to understand this verb in order to understand the near future tense later.

Aller --- to go

Conjugation	Meaning	Pronunciation
Je vais	I go	Juu vey
Tu vas	You go	Too vah
Il/elle/on va	He/she/it/one goes	Il/el/ohn vah
Nous allons	We go	Nooz al-LOHN
Vous allez	You all/you (p.) go	Vooz al-LEY
Ils/elles vont	They go	Il/el vohn

You would use *aller* exactly as you'd expect to. If you're going to a place, you of course would use a preposition to denote it. The preposition is generally à:

Je vais à la bibliothèque. (juu vey-z-ah lah beeb-leeh-oh-tek)

I'm going to the library.

There's one more irregular verb I'm going to specifically hop into in this chapter before we head into the next one about the wonderfully confusing world of French pronunciation: *venir*, or "to come". The cool thing about *venir* is that once you understand it, you understand the verbs which spring from it --- *revenir*, meaning "to come back/come again"; *devenir*, meaning "to become"; *souvenir*, meaning "to remember". Here's how you would conjugate *venir* and its derivatives:

Venir --- to come

Conjugation	Meaning	Pronunciation
Je viens	I come	Juu vee-ahn
Tu viens	You come	Too vee-ahn
Il/elle/on vient	He/she/it/one comes	Il/el/ohn vee-ahn
Nous venons	We come	Noo vuu-nohn
Vous venez	You all/you (p.) come	Voo vuu-ney
Ils/elles viennent	They come	Il/el vee-ehn

Venir is often paired with "*de*", meaning "from" or "of". Observe:

D'où viens-tu? ("Where are you from?", literally "from where are you coming?")

Je viens des États-Unis. ("I come from the United States.")

There are a few more big verbs, but we'll cover them later on in the book. For now, just try to get some practice with *-er*, *-ir*, and *-re* verbs. I've included some regular *-er*, *-ir*, and *-re* verbs in order to help you get the hang of it through practice and dedication.

Manger – to eat

Parler – to speak

Bouger – to move

Finir – to finish

Punir – to punish

Agir – to act

Écrir – to write

Dire – to say

Lire – to read

Articles

Before we move on to the next chapter, it's absolutely necessary that we cover articles. Articles make up a huge part of French. Every single noun must have an article before it, no exceptions. Well, some exceptions, but they're very few.

What are articles? They're not what you read in the paper or on Facebook, shared by a zealous family member. No, *articles* are the part of speech which refers to the marker for a noun. That is to say, look at the following sentences:

I eat some apples.

I eat the apples.

I eat an apple.

Some, the, and *an* are the markers here, because they tell you the specificity of the thing. *Some* means that you're eating any given apples. *The* implies that you're eating a very specific, previously referenced set of apples. *An* implies that you eat any given apple.

In French, this is expanded upon, much like verb conjugation.

Before we talk about that, we need to talk about *gendered nouns*. Every noun in French has a gender. This doesn't mean that an *apple* is a woman, of course. It's not going to bear your child or anything. The genders of nouns are a totally grammatical separation --- a holdover from Vulgar Latin, more or less. The genders are also intrinsic to French. A lot of words would be a lot weirder and a lot of phraseologies would be a lot stranger if gendered nouns were slowly phased out.

The idea of gendered nouns may seem extremely bizarre to an English speaker, and indeed, it can be a little strange at first. None of our nouns have genders. But after practice and dedication, you'll start to learn what makes a noun a certain gender and be able to more or less guess what gender a noun is with some degree of accuracy.

It's important to note that the gender of a noun will correlate to it in subject pronouns, like so:

"*Comment tu trouves la pomme*?" (How do you like the apple?)

"*Elle est un peu acide.*" (It's a tad tart.)

"Apple" is feminine --- *la pomme* --- and so when we reference it in the sentence following, we have to use the feminine pronoun.

Anyhow, back to the main topic of articles.

Firstly, we have *definite articles*. These correspond to "the". There are four different definite articles:

Le --- masculine singular: *Le pont* ("the bridge")

La --- feminine singular: *La vache* ("the cow")

Les --- plural: *Les enfants* ("the children")

L' --- followed by vowel: *L'art* ("the art")

You use definite articles when you're talking about a specific instance of something. Basically, in the same way that you'd use "the" in English. You also use it when you're referring to something in a broader sense, where in English we'd normally drop the article altogether.

For example, if you wanted to say "I like oranges", you'd use the definite articles --- *J'aime les oranges* --- where in English we don't use an article at all in that sentence.

After definite articles, we have *partitive* articles. These basically mean "some of" or "any". These are as follows:

Du --- masculine singular: Du vin ("some wine")

De la --- feminine singular: *De la pizza* ("some pizza")

Des --- plural: *Des framboises* ("some raspberries")

De l' --- before vowel: *De l'eau* ("some water")

Generally, partitive articles are used in reference to food or drink.

The last form of article in French is the *indefinite* article. This correlates to "a" or "an" in English. This has two forms:

Un --- masculine singular: Un lion ("A lion")

Une --- feminine singular: *Une langue* ("A language")

That about sums up articles in French. We can go a bit further with them, but that involves the next part, which is...

Negation

Okay, I lied. There's actually one more major thing we have to cover before we go onto the next part. That's the concept of "negation". Negation means simply taking something and then turning it negative. We negative things in English by adding "do not". For example:

"I don't like to walk."

"He doesn't talk."

"We don't look."

You can also negate things in French. You do so by surrounding the verb with *ne pas*. The *ne* indicates a negative statement, where the *pas* means specifically "not".

So to take those sentences we just wrote and translate them:

"*Je n'aime pas marcher.*" (Juu nehm pah mahr-chey)

"*Il ne parle pas.*" (Il nuu pahrl pah)

"*Nous/on ne regardons/regarde pas.*" (Noo/ohn nuu ruu-gahr-dohn/ruu-gahrd pah)

See how that works?

Now, how do articles come into play? Well, if you have a negative statement, it's important to take note that the article will change if you're negating a sentence with partitive or indefinite articles. However, it doesn't change in sentences with definite articles.

Here's a sentence with an indefinite article:

J'ai un stylo. (I have a pen.)

And here it is, negated:

Je n'ai pas de stylo. (I don't have a pen.)

This change, however, does not occur in sentences with definite articles.

As-tu vu le film? (Have you seen the film?)

Non, je n'ai pas vu le film. (No, I haven't seen the film.)

While we're on the topic of negation, there are a few special cases where you don't use "*ne...pas*", and where "*pas*" actually changes.

These are as follows:

Ne...rien - "nothing"

Ne...jamais - "never"

Ne...pas encore - "not yet"

Ne...plus - "not any longer"

Ne...personne - "nobody"

So you could use these as follows:

Je ne veux rien. ("I want nothing," or "I don't want anything.")

Il ne l'a pas encore fait. ("He hasn't done it yet.")

Nous ne sommes plus contents. ("We aren't happy anymore.")

They're a little obtuse to learn and understand at first, but they're not too terribly difficult to grasp once you get the hang of them, and they can make your writing far more expressive, too.

Chapter 4 - Starting From Zero

Your early efforts at studying French through native French materials such as films are absolutely recommended for beginners, but if you don't acquire the basics of French as you grow, both your understanding and your language abilities will be rather limited. Supplementing your learning with just a few basic French grammar lessons can greatly speed up your ability to break down and understand language used by native speakers. This includes the ability to distinguish between formal, polite, and casual speech. Also, learning a bit about French phonetics and practicing proper pronunciation from the very start will make it much easier for native speakers to understand you.

This chapter will attempt to provide a brief glimpse into the uses and limitations of language learning materials. You will also find a collection of advice you might find useful as a beginner or if you are currently working your way through a French language course or book at any level.

There are so many ways to learn the basics to any foreign language these days, and we don't wish to dictate an exact process of how to get started. That should be your choice.

Get enthusiastic about something first! Some people spend months focusing solely on phonetics to mimic a native speaker's pronunciation. Some may be looking for more immediate results and will dive straight into communicating with native French speakers on day one. Some people prefer a more structured method, so they use language-learning platforms such as Duolingo.

With the advent of the internet and resources like YouTube, it is now feasible to educate oneself in any subject, including foreign languages, without ever setting foot in a classroom or touching a textbook. However, we suggest using a coursebook or textbook, with the caveat that you should limit yourself to just one. In fact, comprehensive introductions to every foreign language can be found in a good coursebook. Good grammatical explanations and a large vocabulary of simple examples are included in these introductions.

French textbooks and other learning materials create a protective learning environment, but students should break out of their comfort zone and interact with native speakers as soon as feasible. Language and culture outside of that sphere are the real things. You may just require the first of a series of two, three, four, or more coursebooks to study French before moving on to materials written for native speakers. This may be accomplished quickly and easily by making it a daily habit to read and listen to authentic French from the get-go.

Taking Steps Every Single Day

The results of studying French for a total of 90 minutes per week, three times per week, will be below average. If you only give yourself a modest amount of time to study French each week, it will take you twenty years to attain any level of proficiency in the language, and you will struggle to comprehend and converse in it during that period.

Becoming fluent in a language requires daily practice of a set of abilities that involve not only the acquisition of knowledge but also the use of one's eyes, ears, tongues, hands, and brain. Even if you just have thirty minutes to devote to French study on the busiest days, that's better than nothing. It's possible that you won't pick up much new information on that particular day, but if you keep taking these relatively insignificant but nonetheless persistent acts, you will eventually develop new routines that will facilitate the significant adjustment in your way of life.

Developing and sticking to a routine that allows you to study French on a regular basis will be one of your first defiances. Concentrate on maintaining the habit of learning a new language every day at any cost. The formation of habits requires consistency. After you have established that studying French will be a consistent priority for you, you may expand upon your daily routine by including additional learning activities such as reading and listening to French spoken by native speakers.

If you are serious about reaching a high level of French proficiency, you should not take this practice lightly. You are attempting to become fluent in a totally new culture while also acquiring a foreign language. If you want to be able to communicate in French as well as you can in your native language, it's time to start taking things seriously. Show up every single day and learn what you can.

Phonetic Awareness

Regardless of whatever material you choose to begin learning with, incorporating phonetics early on in your program is highly recommended. Learning to speak with correct pronunciation should be a part of every program to master the French language or any other language. French phonetic knowledge and training will make your speech much easier for native speakers to fully comprehend. And they will notice the hard work you put into not just being able to communicate with them but also sounding similar to them. That is sure to make conversations much more comfortable and pleasant.

When practicing pronunciation, repeating words after a native speaker and attempting to mimic them is generally good practice, but without phonetic awareness and training, you are likely to still speak with a rather thick accent. When we start communicating in a new language, we automatically and unconsciously project and apply the phonetic rules from our native tongue to the new language we are learning. After such a lengthy period of time spent speaking our native language, the speech patterns of that language become ingrained in us.

As a result, there are sounds in French that you might not be able to recognize by ear and thus be unable to mimic without some basic phonetic awareness and training. Unfortunately, some French language learners decide to skip this step without realizing its true importance, and the consequences of this decision can be found in their speech. For example, you can tell who took the time to practice and master basic vowel sounds like [y], [œ], and [ø] and who did not.

The good news is that this knowledge and training is easy to obtain and master with a little time and effort. It's as easy as studying the sounds of French vowels and consonants and consistent practice. Anki exercises, listening to native French materials, or even occasionally reading aloud offer such training methods.

The International Phonetic Alphabet (IPA) symbols may be new to you if you have never studied phonetics before. It can be a little overwhelming when looking at the entire IPA system, yet there is no need to study each individual letter and diacritic. You will only need to learn the symbols for the new sounds in French and a few in English that will help you to make these new sounds. These symbols and their sounds will become familiar to you in just a few short days or weeks of practice.

French Vowels

Our written explanation is meant only as a brief introduction to French phonetics so that you are more aware of how to produce the new sounds with your mouth and tongue. You can find a free recording of a native French speaker saying any word discussed in this chapter or virtually any French word at Forvo (https://forvo.com). The next few sections can be initially challenging and possibly overwhelming at first glance, so we recommend grabbing a cup of coffee or two as you work your way through.

To produce the [y] sound like in "*tu*" (you), start with the [i] vowel sound (the "ee" in "see") which you already know how to produce. Make that sound aloud and hold it for a few seconds. While producing this sound, round your lips like you would when you make the "wh" sound (like in "who") without moving your tongue at all. Your tongue will naturally want to move backwards, but if you keep it still, you will make the [y] sound.

To do the [œ] sound like in "*œuf*" (egg), first make the [ɛ] sound (the "e" in "bed"). Now, round your lips. That creates the [œ] sound.

And to make the [ø] sound like in "*deux*" (two), we will need the [e] sound found in "play". At the end of the word "play", you can hear [eɪ], which is two vowel sounds (also known as a diphthong). Make and hold the [e] sound and then round your lips. That makes the [ø] sound.

There are other somewhat new vowel sounds in French, which are closer to their English counterparts, but these can be learned easily through simple mimicry. It is the three rounded vowels [y], [œ], and [ø] that will require the most attention if you are a native speaker of English. If practiced on a daily basis in the context of new vocabulary, however, these vowels and all French vowels will come to you just as naturally as the English ones do.

French Consonants

Looking at the new consonants in French, there are [ɲ], [ɥ], and [ʁ]. To make the [ɲ] found in words like "*agneau*" (lamb), simply put the middle of your tongue on the roof of your mouth. It sounds like you're trying to say "nyah".

The [ɥ] sound in words like "*huit*" (eight) can be made by first starting with the English word "shoe". Say the word aloud and hold the last vowel sound which will be [u]. From this [u], switch to the [i] sound (the "ee" in "see") quickly. This rapid sliding of the tongue makes the [ɥ] sound.

The infamous French guttural "R" [ʁ] is a common complaint amongst native English speakers learning French and other European languages, but such complaints will bring you no closer to perfect pronunciation. They are a waste of your time and energy. Resolve to conquer the French "R" today.

There are four common variations that are used, and you'll hear them all when you listen to native French speakers. They are the uvular trill [ʀ], the voiced uvular fricative [ʁ], the uvular approximant [ʁ], and the voiceless uvular fricative [χ]. Which ones are used varies from person to person, but they are all made with the uvula and back of the tongue. And they all make a gargling sound as if you were trying to spit something up. We recommend using the voiced uvular fricative [ʁ], as it is the most common in France.

It's also highly recommended to listen to the differences between these four sounds to gather a more complete understanding that our written explanation cannot provide. Perhaps one of the best demonstrations of these guttural sounds online can be found at https://www.youtube.com/watch?v=hI2Pso1dDjM. As an added bonus, this video also provides demonstrations for the other sounds discussed in this chapter.

Let's quickly go through some other pronunciation mistakes that non-native French speakers may not pick up on. The French "P", "T", and "K" letters are shorter than they are in English. Instead of saying "pah", "tah", and "kah", drop the "ah" and keep them short.

The French "L" uses only the tip of the tongue and much less tongue comparatively to the English "L". Try saying "la" but using only the tip of your tongue. These small adjustments should be much easier compared to all the other sounds that we have covered.

There are many silent letters in French, and more often than not the last letter at the end of a word is silent. And in fact, every "H" in French is silent. But there are muted "H"s like in "*herbe*" (grass) and aspirated "H"s in words like "*hallion*" (rag). Muted "H"s contract to make "*l'herbe*" (the grass), but aspirated "H"s do not like in "*le haillon*" (the rag).

And finally, unlike English, contractions in French are mandatory. "Le homme" is incorrect. You must use "*l'homme*".

If you are not a beginner but were unaware of some of these phonetic rules, there is no need to worry. You can always rewrite any unnatural speaking habits in French that you may have developed thus far. This new phonetic awareness will slowly shape your pronunciation over time when paired with deliberate practice. Some learners even go as far as to record themselves to compare with a native speaker or to check on their progress from time to time.

French Dialects

Of course, pronunciation and also a considerable amount of vocabulary change depending on which country you go to. At the time of writing this book, French is the official language in 29 different countries, but Parisian French is considered the standard. It is what most French learning materials will teach you. Even within the country of France, however, you will find several dialects such as the southern Marseille and Toulouse varieties. Nonetheless, French people understand the full range of dialects within their country, and so can you in time.

Start with the standard Parisian French and branch outward as you read and listen to native materials from French speakers from all across the world. In Europe, you'll find a common European French spoken in countries like Belgium, Switzerland, and Luxembourg with minor differences in dialects and region-specific vocabulary.

It is when you step outside of Europe that you will find a massive variety of dialects and region-specific vocabularies depending on which of the other French speaking countries you visit. For example, while Haiti does list their official language as French, the French-based creole language called Haitian Creole is what you will hear spoken on the street.

In Africa, there is no single, unified African French language. West and Central, East, Maghreb, and Djibouti speak different dialects of French alongside Arabic and other local indigenous languages which results in a tremendous variety of vocabulary and expressions.

Canadian French and Québécois (Quebec French) have very notable differences compared to the French spoken in Europe and elsewhere. They have been more heavily influenced by Great Britain and the United States, and as a result, they have adopted many more English words into their colloquial speech. Because of its regional vocabulary as well as its distinct pronunciation, dialogue between native Canadian French speakers is often not understood by native French speakers from elsewhere.

On the other hand, French speaking Canadians are regularly exposed to European French through TV, movies, and the news, so this Canadian dialect can be toned down when speaking with non-Canadian francophones. This lighter version of Canadian French can be mostly understood by European French speakers although things may need to be repeated from time to time.

These regional differences are not so much different than English, however. If you grow up in an English speaking country, you can travel to any other English speaking country in the world and still be able to communicate with almost anyone. You may need to learn a few new words to prevent any future confusion or misunderstandings, but everyone will be able to understand you regardless of your dialect. Although fully understanding all the local slang is another matter entirely.

That's Too Many Rules!

All of these pronunciation rules and dialects can be quite overwhelming, but there's no need to review and memorize all of this information like you would cram for a school test. Because you are now more aware of the phonetics of French, you'll slowly start to notice these new sounds more and more when listening to native French speakers. You will begin to build a natural intuition for how to pronounce words and gradually incorporate this information into your spoken French. You can always refer back to the rules whenever you are confused about anything.

French pronunciation is just one small example of how potentially easy it is to get lost trying to study and review large lists of rules and information in an effort to memorize them all. The way you get better at these rules, however, is not to memorize the rules at all. It's to practice them subconsciously by reading and listening to native French as much as possible every single day.

By covering the basics of French pronunciation, we hope we have provided a short but sufficient demonstration of the uses and limitations of language learning materials. We attempted to condense the phonetics of French down to the most important points, and we could easily continue this discussion by getting into more complex topics such as spelling and liaison. But at a certain point such as this, the advanced rules like these are more effectively learned through intuition and large amounts of input just like how native speakers learn. So, instead of studying rule by rule, learn it naturally word by word.

This same principle applies to the grammar lessons contained within your grammar course or coursebook.

Stop Taking Textbooks So Seriously!

Instead of being your obedient and trustworthy servant, your textbook ought to be the one that served you. It should not be allowed to take control of you.

Allow these books to serve you for a little while, and then put them away. If practicing your grammar and doing drills isn't something that interests you, don't waste your time with them. Don't put forth unnecessary mental effort by trying to answer the book's comprehension questions. Do not repeat the same words over and again. It is not necessary to commit conjugation and declension tables to memory.

Grab the gist of it, and then leave! Find answers to your questions on grammar and vocabulary in as little as five minutes. You can get more than enough practice by making Anki a daily habit and reading and listening to native French resources every day.

Feed Anki the new knowledge you wish to practice throughout your coursebook time. Anki flashcard exercises are a great way to break down and master large chunks of text, whether it's a monologue, conversation, or lengthy section containing new vocabulary words, phrases, grammar structures, verb conjugations, etc.

To avoid falling asleep before the next chapter, it is not necessary to create an Anki card for every new word and verb conjugation. Take it as far as you can until boredom sets in, and then move on. Reading and listening to authentic French content is far more essential than using a coursebook or even Anki.

One of the Most Frequent Errors

This is where most people go wrong when first learning a language. It's a common blunder that kills the dreams of many eager beginners trying to learn a foreign language. You can jump right into learning from authentic French resources without waiting to finish your first course or textbook. You are under no obligation to complete the program! Learn from it what you can till boredom sets in.

If we force ourselves to study topics we are not truly interested in, our brains send us signals of boredom to warn us that we will eventually burn out. That's the cleverness of our brains. When anything stops operating, they are aware of it. We are not necessarily ignorant or lazy if we have trouble learning new things. It means to halt one's current activity and switch gears.

If you feel like you need to learn all this important material before you can learn from entertaining materials like French films and TV series, you may feel that you have only yourself to blame for being bored. However, you would be completely wrong to think that way. The key to never growing tired and giving up is to learn straight from materials that are enjoyable.

If you find yourself losing interest and concentration, switch to new reading material. Skip between in your French textbook and focus on the things that really interest you. You should continue your education at whatever place best suits your needs. Learning is maintained when you tune into your intrinsic motivation and act on it. That's the key to always being eager to take in new information and develop your skills.

When possible, you should go right into learning from native sources. Motivation is increased more than practically anything else when you make the personal link between what you are learning in French learning resources and what you see and hear in local materials. In this way, you will be able to master all the serious French you believe you need to know.

Early Output or No?

It will be up to you to decide how early on in the process of learning a new language to incorporate output and conversations with native speakers. This is a heated topic in the world of language acquisition right now, but I'll try to sum up the key argument in one statement. Since it's impossible for native speakers to correct all of our faults, early output offers a unique approach to learning through trial and correction, but we also run the risk of developing unnatural speaking habits early on.

The timing of your output practice implementation is ultimately up to you. Speaking and writing French every day should be a top priority if you want to achieve rapid progress and start having meaningful conversations with native French speakers as soon as feasible. Some polyglots even begin communicating with their teachers exclusively in the target language, and others have achieved remarkable fluency with input-only methods.

How About More Advanced Textbooks?

After reading just one textbook, you may feel like you still don't understand the fundamentals, and in some ways, that's probably true. In French-speaking countries, how do people handle the basics of life like bills, housing, banking, and employment? You'll need to learn some new words and phrases if you ever hope to live and work abroad. You could want to go so far as to buy a second textbook just to be safe and avoid coming across as a typical hapless tourist. Just do it.

Dedicated language students may enjoy a set of course books or textbooks because of the potential for growth and the novelty of the learning process. With each successive chapter, the student is exposed to new grammatical structures that expand his or her conceptual framework and vocabulary. Coursebooks provide novel ideas and grammatical structures in an approachable manner, making the first few months of study a lively and intriguing time.

However, those who have progressed to the intermediate level of language study may attest to what lies beyond the first few textbooks. We know we're still far from fluent in the language, so we've started investing in more advanced books that go into greater detail about grammar, phrases, and idioms. We're putting in extra time each day, studying for longer than the recommended three hours. A new language can be very context-dependent, and explanations of more complex grammar are becoming increasingly verbose. More vocabulary needs to be learned and reviewed constantly. The initial few thousand came easily with a little effort, but then there are 30,000 that we feel we are required to regularly examine. This is a significant increase from before!

It's really simple to get stuck in a rut when learning a new language. Without realizing it, learning can stagnate, bore, and be ineffective for months or even years. What happened to having fun? Time is of the essence. It's possible that "I have to study more!" will be the last thing you say before losing all interest in studying.

This book is here to tell you that learning a language in conjunction with these enjoyable activities can yield far greater success and enjoyment in the long run. Of course, the logical order of operations is to reverse the two.

An Alternative Course

If you find yourself encountering a linguistic structure in your native French texts that you aren't familiar with, try using one of these advanced resources as a reference. Wouldn't it be great if you could just drop by, pick up the essentials of the grammar structure or word you need, and go on? Learning new vocabulary and grammar structures in the context of a story you care about is much more likely to stick in your memory long after you've forgotten a series of dry grammar explanations. This is the impact of a proper setting.

Perhaps you won't even need an intermediate or advanced French textbook. These days, most inquiries may have their answers found online within two minutes. The vast majority of words and phrases, as well as many example sentences, may be found in online dictionaries. If further clarification is needed, most common sentence forms may be found with a quick internet search and given adequate explanations.

Chapter 5 - The Sounds of French

An Easy Guide to the Pronunciation of French

Let's quickly review a crucial principle for foreign language pronunciation before we go into French pronunciation. Starting a second language later in life makes it harder to pronounce than a native. Even if a person marries a foreigner, moves to their country, and speaks the language every day for twenty years, they will still have an accent. Accents are learned by language exposure, not immersion. Because of this, people learning a new language must realize that speaking with a perfect accent is not a realistic goal and that no matter how long it takes to learn, people will probably know you are not a native speaker the moment you open your mouth. Regardless of learning time.

It is unfortunate that many students have a tendency to focus an excessive amount of their efforts on correcting their pronunciation, which can actually delay their progress. Some of these students may even acquire an inferiority complex over their accents, which is also sad. It is essential to keep in mind that perfect pronunciation at a native level should not be your objective when learning a language. You should instead place more emphasis on having a clear and understandable pronunciation; if you are able to do so, then you have already accomplished one more step towards learning a new language.

Most languages have alphabets and some, such as Spanish and Turkish, have alphabets where each letter corresponds exactly to one sound. This makes reading these alphabets easy, because each word sounds the way it is written. Speakers of other languages, such as English, are not so lucky. Think about words ending in "-ough." The words "cough", "though", "through", "bough" and "enough" are written the same way, but have five different pronunciations! Some sounds, like the common "th" sound in English, do not even exist in many other languages, which explains why French speakers learning English are prone to saying "one", "two", "tree".

For English speakers learning French as a second language, things are no different. There are some entirely new sounds, and without mastering these sounds, your pronunciation can sound just as strange. However, this is not a cause for concern; it just requires practice. Think of it as like learning any other new skill, such as roller-skating. At the beginning, it feels very unnatural and you have to think carefully about every movement to make sure you do not fall over. When you start out, you feel clumsy and it might be quite difficult to stay standing. However, if you keep practicing, you will soon be able to skate without consciously thinking about it at all. It is a bit like this when you learn to pronounce the sounds of a new language. At first, you have to concentrate on the sounds you are making, but very soon, you will start speaking naturally without having to think about it. Now let's take a more detailed look at the sounds of French.

I have known many people who become self-conscious of their pronunciation in a foreign language. If you take a second to think of the many foreign movie stars, sportsmen or politicians you may have heard speak on TV or radio in English, I am sure you were much more interested in what they had to say than critiquing their accent!

In fact, it is more likely you found their foreign accent endearing, and nice to listen to. Try to keep this in mind as you move forward with your French, and especially if you have a tendency to worry about your pronunciation. The content of what you have to say is far more important!

The Basics of French Pronunciation --- The Sounds of French

In order to even begin a serious discussion about pronunciation in any language, you must be aware that what you read and what you pronounce are not always the same, as we know is the case with English and French. To this end, there is a useful tool called the International Phonetic Alphabet (IPA) (https://en.wikipedia.org/wiki/International_Phonetic_Alphabet) that can be a useful reference. I do not recommend you learn the IPA at first, but if you do find yourself getting stuck with pronunciation, it might be a useful tool to explore, as it helps you focus clearly on the sound that is being used.

French Consonants

Let's start with the consonants. Many consonant sounds in French are almost identical to English, although if you listen very carefully you will hear that there are sometimes subtle differences. If you can train yourself to notice these differences and reproduce them yourself, your pronunciation will sound less foreign.

Take a look at the examples below and listen to the audio files to hear the pronunciation.

/b/ --- *bateau* (like in the English word 'boat')

bon / good

beau / handsome

besoin / need

/d/ --- *dîner* (like in the English word 'dinner')

dans / in

donner / give

différent / different

/g/ --- *gare* (like in the English word 'gift')

général / general

gros / big

groupe / group

/f/ --- *flic* (like in the English word 'fall')

un film / film

fait / fact

faire / to do

/l/ --- *lait* (like in the English word 'lazy')

longtemps / long

leurs / their

loin / far

/m/ --- *mêler* (like in the English word 'mix')

mon / mine

merci / thank you

un monde / world

/n/ --- *nous* (like in the English word 'nice')

non / no

un nom / name

nouveau / new

/s/ --- *sac* (like in the English word 'sack')

Note: Always pronounced /s/ when beginning or ending a word as in "*son*" and "*bonus*," but /z/ when placed between two vowels, as in "*nasal*".

si / if

sans / without

besoin / need (pronounced /z/ in this word)

/ʃ/ --- *chat* (like in the English word 'machine')

Note: "*ch*" in French is always soft like the '*sh*' in the English word 'shoot', not the 'ch' the English 'chocolate'.

une chose / thing

une chance / chance

chercher / to look for

/v/ --- *vous* (like in the English word 'vile')

voir / to see

vrai / true

vite / quick

/z/ --- *zoo* (like in the English word 'zoo')

Note: The letter "*z*" rarely appears at the beginning of a word. It often appears at the end, but in this case, it is usually silent. For example: *nez* / nose; *assez* / enough.

zéro / zero

magazine / magazine

bizarre / bizarre

There are also a few consonant sounds in French which are unique cases and not so common in English:

/ʒ/ --- *japonais* (rare in English, as in "treasure")

je / I

toujours / always

juste / right

/ɲ/ --- *poignet* (as in "nuke" or the "ñ" in "español" in Spanish)

gagner / to win

These three consonants are aspirated when stressed in English. To generate the sound, you must expel air from your mouth. Try putting a small piece of paper on your hand, hold it next to your mouth and say 'paper' loudly. The paper moves, right? But in French, these sounds are not aspirated. Try making the same sound but without blowing any air so the paper on your hand does not move and you will be somewhere close to the French pronunciation.

All of the sounds we have looked at so far are different in French than in English, but not drastically so. There is, however, one infamous sound in French that has nothing even vaguely similar in English phonology and that is what we are going to look at next.

Chapter 6 - The Future Tense in French

Using the French *future* may not be one of the most important first steps to take on your language learning journey, but it remains very useful to learn and know in a couple of cases. Whether you want to discuss future plans with native speakers or understand short pieces of writing, knowing how it is formed will help you navigate French with more ease.

The most important piece of information to remember about French is that, contrary to English, it adds an ending to verbs as opposed to adding an auxiliary before the verb. However, it is by far one of the simplest tenses to learn, given that in most case its endings are similar throughout the different categories of verbs. Below are a couple of examples of how it is formed with each person:

What will you do when you're older? – *Que feras-tu (tu – faire) quand tu seras (tu – être) plus grand?*

You'll have many occasions to perfect your French once you arrive there – *Tu auras (tu – avoir) de nombreuses occasions de perfectionner ton français dès que tu arriveras (tu – arriver) là-bas.*

We'll start learning a new language in a few months – *Nous commencerons (nous – commencer) à apprendre une nouvelle langue dans quelques mois.*

I'll first visit a museum, and then I'll go for a walk in the old town – *Je visiterai (je – visiter) d'abord un musée, puis j'irai (je – aller) faire un tour dans la vieille ville.*

I'll finish reading the report while they choose a new project – *Je finirai (je – finir) de lire le rapport pendant qu'ils choisiront (ils – choisir) un nouveau projet.*

Example paragraph: (The French is listed first to get you acquainted with its different forms)

Quand je serai (être) en France, je pense que j'aurai (avoir) besoin de visiter au moins trois musées durant mon séjour. En même temps, il y a quelques parcs intéressants en ville et j'espère que je pourrai (pouvoir) trouver une occasion d'y passer un peu de temps. Tu crois que nous aurons (avoir) le temps de visiter d'autres choses en plus? En tout cas, je n'hésiterai (hésiter) pas non plus à goûter un peu de cuisine française, puisqu'elle est réputée à travers le monde. Pour l'instant, je m'en tiendrai (s'en tenir) à quelque chose de plus simple.

When I'll be in France, I think I'll need to visit at least three museums during my stay. At the same time, there are a couple of interesting parks in town, and I hope I'll be able to find an opportunity to spend some time there. Do you think we will have the time to visit other things as well? Anyway, I won't hesitate either to taste some French cuisine since it is acclaimed all across the world. For now, I'll stick to something simpler.

- language – *langue (f)*
- in a few days/weeks/months – *dans quelques jours/semaines/mois*
- the old town – *la vieille ville*
- while (simultaneity) – *pendant que...*
- to need to do something – *avoir besoin de faire quelque chose*
- at least – *au moins*
- stay – *séjour (m)*

- to spend some time – *passer un peu de temps*

- He enjoys spending some time in good company on sunny days – *Il aime passer un peu de temps en bonne compagnie pendant les beaux jours.*

- as well – *en plus* (if nothing is added); *en plus de..., ainsi que...* (if there are more than one element in the sentence):

- That you are able to speak German as well will prove advantageous to the both of us – *Que vous soyez capable de parler allemand en plus va être advantageux pour nous deux.*

- I can speak German as well as English – *Je peux parler l'allemand en plus de l'anglais / ainsi que l'anglais.*

- There are some repairs to be done to the roof and to the windows as well – *Il y a des réparations à faire au niveau du toit, ainsi qu'au niveau des fenêtres. / Il y a des réparations à faire au niveau du toit, et en plus des fenêtres.*

- (all) across the world – *à travers le monde*

As in many cases in French, there are a lot of common patterns barring the usual exceptions: for example, what do *visiterai, commencerons,* or *finirai* have in common? They are all formed from the complete verb stem, plus an additional ending to point out who is doing the action. You may also have noticed that some of these examples tend to weave the future with the present tense in English while French focuses solely on future tenses for both: it is very much an advanced concept, but you may want to take note of it now if it interests you. This will be detailed right after the conjugation patterns for you to see it more clearly. For now, here are some common patterns:

1st group:

MANGER / PARLER – keep the full stem of the word, then add:

Je mangerai / Je parlerai --- + ai

Tu mangeras / Tu parleras --- + as

Il mangera / Il parlera --- + a

Nous mangerons / Nous parlerons --- + ons

Vous mangerez / Vous parlerez --- + ez

Ils mangeront / Ils parleront --- + ont

In short, there are only a couple of endings to remember, but nothing to change or delete! Some of these endings are already known to you, such as *ons*, which is the hallmark of the first-person plural *nous*: the fact that there are so many similarities between tenses makes for a much more enjoyable experience!

2nd group:

FINIR / CHOISIR – keep the full stem of the word, then add:

Je finirai / Je choisirai --- + ai, exactly as the previous ones

Tu finiras / Tu choisiras --- + as, exactly as the previous ones

Il finira / Il choisira --- + a, exactly as the previous ones

Nous finirons / Nous choisirons --- + ons

Vous finirez / Vous choisirez --- + ez

Ils finiront / Ils choisiront --- + ont

In short, the second group follows the same pattern as the first one.

3rd group:

DORMIR / SENTIR – the same as the two above (*Je dormirai, Tu sentiras, Il dormira...*)

VENIR / COURIR – for these, the endings remain the same (*ai, as, a, ons, ez, ont*), but the radical undergoes some transformations, which you may want to keep in mind:

Je viendrai / Je courrai

Tu viendras / Tu courras

Il viendra / Il courra

Nous viendrons / Nous courrons

Vous viendrez / Vous courrez

Ils viendront / Ils courront

VOIR / SAVOIR / VOULOIR – similar to the two verbs above, they retain the same endings for all persons, but their radicals change:

Je verrai / Je saurai / Je voudrai – voir turns into verr-, savoir into saur-, and vouloir into voudr-

Tu verras / Tu sauras / Tu voudras

Il verra / Il saura / Il voudra

Nous verrons / Nous saurons / Nous voudrons

Vous verrez / Vous saurez / Vous voudrez

Ils verront / Ils sauront / Ils voudront

Want to start testing your knowledge in real time? Consider the verb *pouvoir* (to be able to; can), which in the future tense also changes its radical: it is no longer *pouv-* but *pourr-*. How do you conjugate it? Same for *devoir* (to have to), whose radical becomes *devr-*. There are quite a lot of extra 'r's in the future tense!

APPRENDRE / VENDRE, and all other verbs ending in -endre (*attendre*, to wait; *prendre*, to take) have their conjugation pattern in regular: here, the 'e' is superfluous and so must be taken off before conjugating it, but then you only need to apply the endings seen above (*j'apprendrai, tu apprendras, il apprendra, nous apprendrons, vous apprendrez, ils apprendront; je vendrai, tu vendras...*)

BOIRE / LIRE / DIRE / RIRE – simply take off the 'e' and start conjugating!

FAIRE – *faire*, as you may have noticed in one of the previous examples (*tu feras*), undergoes a transformation as far as its radical is concerned: it becomes *fer-*, and then:

Je ferai

Tu feras

Il fera

Nous ferons

Vous ferez

Ils feront

Major exceptions: *ALLER / AVOIR / ÊTRE* (to go, to have, to be)

J'irai / J'aurai / Je serai – the trio here is *ir-, aur-, and ser-*

Tu iras / Tu auras / Tu seras

Il ira / Il aura / Il sera

Nous irons / Nous aurons / Nous serons

Vous irez / Vous aurez / Vous serez

Ils iront / Ils auront / Ils seront

You have now—as any student of French shall do while learning the language—encountered a couple of irregularities and exceptions in this section, but you have also observed one essential rule of French, which you should never forget: it sometimes happens to be easy! All endings for the future tense are indeed straightforward and replicable to verbs of all the three different groups! The only major point to keep in mind is that some radicals get to change when conjugating the *futur*.

Having to retain all of these new radicals, which sometimes even barely resemble the infinitive form, can be overwhelming; however, there is a hidden bonus: any verb in French that you may encounter and that has a regular ending, but a seemingly untraceable radical is almost sure to be conjugated in the future! In more ways than one, French is also built from an appreciation for little things... So, now that you have gained a clearer view of how to form the future, you may either want to just go right to the Conditional Mood section, which will prove useful when asking polite requests in day-to-day French, or take a look at the following example sentences and exercises designed to test your newly acquired knowledge!

Exercise:

Below are five French sentences to correct. For each, note down the mistake that was made in the sentence and how you would rewrite it. Do not hesitate to go back to the grammar point associated with it at any point if you feel the need to do so. You will find the answers to the sentences after the learning objective, as well as all relevant explanations for each. For each French sentence containing two verbs conjugated in the *futur*, only one is incorrect:

– *Ils veniront (venir) quand ils le pourront (pouvoir).*

They'll come when they can.

– *Nous finiront (finir) de réviser notre français quand nous seront (être) complètement bilingues!*

We will finish revising our French when we are completely bilingual!

– *Qu'as-tu prévu pour demain? – Tu voiras (voir).*

What have you planned for tomorrow? – You'll see.

- *Nous devrions (devoir) nous arrêter à la poste à 9 heures 30.*

We'll have to stop by the post office at 09:30.

- *Nous serrons (être) déjà partis à la mer lorsque vous arriverez (arriver).*

We'll already have gone to the beach when you arrive.

Learning objectives: By now, you should

- Be able to form the future for most verbs by add a couple of key endings: + *ai, as, a, ons, ez, ont*

- Know that some verbs change their radical in the future tense

- Be able to use the French futur in simple sentences to describe what you'll do, what'll you be, and so much more.

Exercise: Correction

- *Ils veniront (venir) quand ils le pourront (pouvoir).*

It is the first verb here that isn't conjugated right: the ending is indeed the right one, but its radical changes in the future and become *viendr-*, just as *pouvoir* turns into *pourront* with *ils*. The correct sentence would, therefore, be: *Ils viendront quand ils le pourront.*

- *Nous finiront (finir) de réviser notre français quand nous seront (être) complètement bilingues!*

Finiront and *seront* are the problem here: they indeed both sound right, but *nous* requires an 's' rather than a 't', which is the province of *ils / elles* instead. The correct sentence would, therefore, be: *Nous finirons de réviser notre français quand nous serons complètement bilingues!*

- *Qu'as-tu prévu pour demain? – Tu voiras (voir).*

Voir is yet another one of those verbs whose radical changes in the future tense. The correct sentence would, therefore, be: *Qu'as-tu prévu pour demain? – Tu verras.*

- *Nous devrions (devoir) nous arrêter à la poste à 9 heures 30.*

The radical is correct here, the ending is fine and matches what *nous* requires in all tenses... but there is an excess 'i' in between the radical and the ending! It is, in fact, the mark of the conditional mood, which you will see right afterward because most of it relies on the conjugations for the *futur*. The correct sentence would, therefore, be: *Nous devrons nous arrêter à la poste à 9 heures 30.*

- *Nous serrons (être) déjà partis à la mer lorsque vous arriverez (arriver).*

The second verb is well conjugated, but the first one not so much: there is indeed an extra 'r', which especially shouldn't be here since *serrons* is actually the future form of *serrer* that means 'to grip, grasp'. However, that sentence was particularly easy since you have already seen *serons* in the third example; the correct sentence would, therefore, be: *Nous serons déjà partis à la mer lorsque vous arriverez.*

Grammar and Vocabulary: Advanced knowledge

Learning the *futur* should not have been that daunting of a task, so now for some peculiarities of French that may be of interest to you, especially if you only meant to relearn the notion and now want some more engrossing facts about how French works:

we'll start learning – *nous commencerons à apprendre*: using gerunds, or forms ending with (the French equivalent of -ing) -*ant* isn't common at all after a verb in French; instead, French links the first verb to the second one in its infinitive form with a preposition. With *commencer*, it is *à*, and it is compulsory.

For instance, he started cooking at 4:00 p.m., although it was too early – Il a commencé à cuisiner à quatre heures de l'après-midi, même s'il était trop tôt.

go for a walk – *aller faire un tour:* this French idiomatic expression is very commonly used, and you may find it essential soon on your language learning journey. It is also a common synonym for 'go outside'.

Additional note: remember the many trenches you had to navigate when learning all the intricacies of the *passé composé*? Since *aller* is itself a verb of movement, you would obviously use *être* with it (*Je suis allé faire un tour en ville* – I went for a walk in town).

stop revising – *arrêter de réviser*: somewhat similarly to *commencer,* which was covered just above, *arrêter* requires a preposition when introducing an infinitive verb afterward, which for this verb is *de.*

have gone to – *être parti à*

Finally, there is a final grammatical point to see for the most dedicated learners out there. Consider the following sentences that you have already encountered:

They'll come when they can – *Ils viendront quand ils le pourront.*

What will you do when you're older? – *Que feras-tu quand tu seras grand?*

'Be' and 'Can' are respectively left in the present tense in English, while French focuses on all similar occurrences on the fact that 'be able to come' will happen, or not, in the future, and so will 'being older'. That is why you have *ils le pourront* and *tu seras grand* conjugated with *pouvoir* and *être* respectively. It is also conversely a source of many mistakes on the part of French students learning English who would rather write: "What will you do when you will be older?", or get suddenly confused when they listen to The Beatles sing "Will you still need me, will you still feed me, when I'm sixty-four?"

Chapter 7 - Imperatif – Commands

In French, commands are expressed with the verb in the imperative form. Commands typically omit the subject pronoun.

a) The "*vous*" form.

The polite "*vous*" from French, which ends in -ez, is quite significant.

Travaillez bien! --- translates to - work well!

Écoutez attentivement! --- translates to - listen attentively!

N'utilisez pas votre telephone! --- translates to - do not use your phone!

Discuss it! --- translates to - do not discuss!

b) The «*tu*» form.

The familiar form "*tu*" is transformed into an imperative form by removing the last -s from verbs that finish in -*er*.

Appelle ton ami! --- translates to - call your friend!

Cherche-la! --- translates to - look for her!

Va à la plage! --- translates to - go to the beach!

NB: *Vas-y!* --- translates to - go ahead (the -s is added back to create the liaison)

The -s is not removed from most other verbs.

Prends une pause! --- translates to - take a break!

Écris une lettre! --- translates to - write a letter!

Ne t'en va pas! --- translates to - don't leave!

c) The use of «let's» in French.

To express the meaning "let us," the verb must be rephrased in the first-person plural present indicative form (nous), and the subject pronoun must be removed from the sentence.

Organisons une fête! --- translates to - Let's organize a party!

Dansons ensemble! --- translates to - Let's dance together!

Allons-y! --- translates to - Let's go!

d) The case of reflexive verbs.

After the verb, the reflexive pronoun is inserted with a hyphen when the word is a reflexive verb:

Retrouvons-nous à la gare! --- translates to - Let's meet at the train station!

e) Underline the verb in imperative then give their infinitive.

Ex: *enlevez --- enlever*

Chez le docteur: «Enlevez votre chemise. Baissez la tête. Respirez. Toussez. Remettez vos vêtements. Prenez cette ordonnance et allez au dispensaire pour vous faire soigner. Revenez me voir dans une semaine.»

De bonnes résolutions: «soyons respectueux envers nos parents; obéissons à nos professeurs; travaillons sans faiblir; cherchons à nous perfectionner sans cesse.

Conseils d'une mère à sa fille: «si tu veux être toujours bien vêtue, prends soins de tes vêtements, lave-les souvent, repasse-les, raccommode le moindre accroc, suspens-les à des cintres, protège-les contre les mites et les cafards.

The conjugation

Formulae: To put a verb in imperative you simply start by putting it in present, then you eliminate the first person singular plus the verb (*Je + verb*) and the third person singular and plural plus the verb (*Il/elle/ils/elles + verb*). It now remains the second person singular (tu + verb) and plural (*vous + verb*) and the first-person plural (*nous + verb*). Here you can remove all the pronoun (*tu – vous – nous*) and only keep the conjugated form of the verb in present. These three that remains therefore form the imperative. For the imperative or commands has only three persons in French. Actually, is two persons but because French has two types of second person (*tu – vous*) it now makes it three.

I need to remind you that a command is addressed to the person I am talking to that means "you" and if I'm part of it, that will be to "us". That's why I, He, She, They cannot be used here.

Now let's see how this works in practical.

Put the verb «*parler*» in imperative.

Phase 1: *Le présent de l'indicatif*

parler			
Je	Parle	Nous	Parlons
Tu	Parles	Vous	Parlez
Il /elle	parle	Ils/elles	parlent

Phase 2: removal of subject pronouns

			Parlons
	parles		parlez

Phase 3: removal of «s from the second person singular.

Positive form

| Parle |
| Parlons |
| parlez |

Negative form

| Ne parle pas |
| Ne parlons pas |
| Ne parlez pas |

«parler» <-> parle ≠ ne parle pas --- «aller» <-> va ≠ ne va pas

Parlons ≠ ne parlons pas --- allons ≠ n'allons pas

Parlez ≠ ne parlez pas --- allez ≠ n'allez pas

The case of the verbs in: «*ir*», «*re*» et «*oir*»

The verbs «*finir*», «*sortir*», «*prendre*», «*voir*» and «*faire*»

Le présent de l'indicatif

finir	faire	voir	Sortir
Je finis	Je fais	Je vois	Je sors
Tu finis	Tu fais	Tu vois	Tu sors
Il/elle finit	Il/elle fait	Il/elle voit	Il/elle sort
Nous finissons	Nous faisons	Nous voyons	Nous sortons
Vous finissez	Vous faites	Vous voyez	Vous sortez
Ils/elles finissent	Ils font	Ils/elles voient	Ils/elles sortent

L'impératif présent

Positive form

Finis	Fais	Vois	Sors
Finissons	Faisons	Voyons	Sortons
finissez	faites	voyez	sortez

Negative form

Ne finis pas	Ne fais pas	Ne vois pas	Ne sors pas
Ne finissons pas	Ne faisons pas	Ne voyons pas	Ne sortons pas
Ne finissez pas	Ne faites pas	Ne voyez pas	Ne sortez pas

the irregular verbs «être» and «avoir»

Positive form

avoir	être
aie	sois
ayons	soyons
ayez	soyez

Negative form

N'aie pas	Ne sois pas
N'ayons pas	Ne soyons pas
N'ayez pas	Ne soyez pas

Put in l'impératif.

a) *Dérouler sa ligne, rester, immobile, attendre.* (1st person plural)

b) *Préparer son sac, embrasser sa mère et partir.* (2nd person plural)

c) *Casser du bois fin, allumer le feu, l'entretenir.* (2nd person plural)

d) *Surveiller, attendre, courir, écouter* (2nd person singular)

e) *Faire ce qu'on dit, dire ce qu'on sait, finir avant ce soir.* (1st person plural)

f) *Tu approches: Vendredi, à la pleine lune, sur la colline, les filles-génies dansent. Tu vas sur la colline lorsque la terre est froide. Quand le tam-tam bat son plein, quand le cercle est bien animé, quand sans arrêt une danseuse remplace une autre danseuse, tu*

g) *t'approches.*

Solutions.

a) *Déroulons, restons, attendons*

b) *Préparez, embrassez, partez*

c) *Cassez, allumez, entretenez-le*

d) *Surveille, attends, cours, écoute*

e) *Faisons, disons, finissons*

f) *Approche / Vas*

g) *Approche-toi)*

Imperative for reflexive verbs

(Se laver, se lever, se réveiller, s'occuper de, se presser, se voir, s'entendre etc.)

NB: «se» here can be replaced by : me – te – le – la – lui – nous – vous – les or moi – toi – elle – eux – elles.

Positive form

Se laver	*Se lever*	*Se réveiller*	*Se voir*	*S'entendre*
Lave-toi	*Lève-toi*	*Réveille-toi*	*Vois-toi*	*Entends-toi*
Lavons-nous	*Levons-nous*	*Réveillons-nous*	*Voyons-nous*	*Entendons-nous*
Lavez-vous	*Levez-vous*	*Réveillez-vous*	*Voyez-vous*	*Entendez-vous*

Negative form

Se laver	*Se lever*	*Se réveiller*	*Se voir*
Ne te lave pas	*Ne te lève pas*	*Ne te réveille pas*	*Ne te vois pas*
Ne nous lavons pas	*Ne nous levons pas*	*Ne nous réveillons pas*	*Ne nous voyons pas*
Ne vous lavez pas	*Ne vous levez pas*	*Ne vous réveillez pas*	*Ne vous voyez pas*

Exercises

a. In positive form, the pronoun: *toi – nous – vous* are positioned after the verb.

□ true □ false

b. The formulae for negative form is:

□ Ne + pronoun + pas + verb

□ Ne + verb + pronoun +pas

□ Ne + pronoun + verb + pas

1. Complete the table

infinitif	Présent de l'indicatif	Impératif
Dormir	*Tu ....*	....
Apprendre	*Tu ....*	....

Chanter	*Tu ....*	*..........................*
Regarder	*Tu ....*	*..........................*
Danser	*Nous ....*	*..........................*
Jouer	*Vous ....*	*..........................*

2. Put in imperative.

Il est temps de nettoyer :

Tu laves la voiture → ....*la voiture.*

Tu balayes le sol → ....*le sol.*

Tu essuies les vitres → ....*les vitres.*

Prépare-toi pour la journée :

Tu te lèves tôt → ....*tôt.*

Tu te douches → ....*toi.*

Tu te brosses les dents → ....*les dents.*

3. Put in imperative.

Préparer un repas :

Vous choisissez une recette → Choisissez une recette.

Vous vérifiez les ingrédients nécessaires → .... *les ingrédients nécessaires.*

Vous achetez les produits manquants → .... *les produits manquants.*

Vous préparez les ustensiles → .... *les ustensiles.*

Vous suivez les étapes de la recette → .... *les étapes de la recette.*

Vous préchauffez le four → .... *le four.*

Vous servez le repas chaud → .... *le repas chaud.*

Vous dégustez avec plaisir → .... *avec plaisir.*

Vous rangez la cuisine → .... *la cuisine.*

Vous lavez les plats → .... *les plats.*

4. Put in imperative at the 2nd person plural

Crêpes sucrées :

Prenez (prendre) une poêle.

.... *(Mélanger) de la farine, du sucre et des œufs dans un bol.*

.... *(Verser) un peu de lait pour obtenir une pâte lisse.*

.... *(Chauffer) la poêle à feu moyen.*

.... (Verser) une louche de pâte dans la poêle chaude.

.... (Retourner) la crêpe après 2 minutes.

.... (Dorer) l'autre côté.

.... (Répéter) le processus pour les autres crêpes.

.... (Garnir) de sucre, de confiture ou de Nutella.

.... (Déguster) tant qu'elles sont chaudes.

5. Tell us how to cook a typical meal in your country

....
....
....
....
....

6. Put in imperative at the 2nd person singular

Ouvre (ouvrir) ton livre à la page 50.

.... (Lire) le premier paragraphe.

.... (Souligner) les mots que tu ne comprends pas.

.... (Écrire) une note en marge.

.... (Tourner) à la page suivante.

.... (Résumer) le contenu en quelques phrases.

.... (Fermer) le livre une fois fini.

.... (Ranger) le livre dans ton sac.

7. Write an SMS to a friend to tell him how to get to a cinema or supermarket.

....
....
....
....

8. Put in imperative

Rappels amicaux :

a- *Si tu as le temps, ... (Passer) par la librairie et .... (Chercher) le livre que j'avais réservé ....(ne pas oublier) de demander une facture. Merci.*

b- *Cher voisin, ...(ne pas arroser) les plantes cette semaine, elles ont eu assez d'eau. Merci!*

c- *N'oublie pas, ... (Retirer) de l'argent avant de venir à la soirée. À tout à l'heure.*

d- .... (Envoyer) moi les photos de la dernière randonnée. Hâte de les voir!

e- Chérie, si le plombier appelle, ...(ne pas lui dire) le prix que nous avions convenu, je lui parlerai directement.

f- Les gars, ... (Montrer) à Max où sont les outils. À demain.

9. Transform the sentences as in the example.

Example: *Nous ne devons pas rentrer tard. → Ne rentrons pas tard!*

Prudence!

Vous ne devez pas sortir seul. →

Tu ne dois pas aller dans ce quartier. →

Nous ne devons pas passer dans ce souterrain. →

Tu ne dois pas traverser là. →

Nous ne devons pas prendre cette rue. →

Vous ne devez pas partir à pied. →

Tu ne dois pas faire demi-tour. →

Vous ne devez pas tourner ici. →

10. Transform as in the examples

Example: *Ils ne sont pas contents → Soyons contents!*

Elle est inquiète. → Ne sois pas inquiète!

a. *Vous êtes distraits. →* ....

b. *Tu n'es pas honnête. →* ....

c. *Ils n'ont pas faim. →* ....

d. *Elle n'est pas rassurée. →* ....

e. *Vous avez raison. →* ....

f. *Tu es fatigué. →* ....

g. *Ils sont énervés. →* ....

h. *Vous n'êtes pas attentifs. →* ....

11. Put in imperative (in 2nd person singular)

Se préparer. → ....

S'installer. → ....

Se dépêcher. → ....

Se détendre. → ....

Se coucher. → ....

Se promener. → ....

Se concentrer. → ....

Se divertir. → ....

12. Put in order

1- pas / Ne / éloignez / vous

2- Ne / assieds / t' / pas

3- Ne / pas / approche / t'

4- battons / nous / Ne / pas

5- pas / vous / Ne / arrêtez

6- Ne / perds / te / pas

7- t' / pas / inquiète / Ne

8- nous / pas / Ne / disputons.

13. Put in negative form.

Parfume-toi, mais ne te parfume pas trop!

Mangez bien, mais .... tout le gâteau!

Regarde-nous, mais .... avec étonnement!

Entraînez-vous, mais .... trop fort!

Souriez toujours, mais .... en te moquant!

Travaille dur, mais .... sans prendre de pauses!

14. Put in imperative

Mangez (manger), il y a assez pour tout le monde.

.... (écouter) bien, c'est important.

.... (ne pas toucher) aux objets fragiles.

Les enfants, ... (être) sages pendant notre absence.

.... (ne pas prendre) trop de sucre, c'est mauvais pour la santé.

Messieurs, ... (ne pas parler) fort, il y a une réunion à côté.

.... (revenir) tôt, il se fait nuit.

.... (lire) les instructions avant d'utiliser l'appareil.

Si tu veux savoir, ... (demander) à la réception.

Il commence à pleuvoir, ... (ouvrir) le parapluie et .... (se mettre) à l'abri.

.... (s'éloigner) des machines en marche.

.... (croire) en tes rêves, ils peuvent se réaliser.

15. Transform in imperatif as in the examples.

Examples:

Je chante ou je danse? → Ne chante pas, danse!

Vous voyagez ou vous restez? → Ne voyagez pas, restez!

Je regarde ou j'écoute? → ....

Nous achetons ou nous vendons? → ....

Je prends un café ou un thé? → ....

Nous cuisinons ou nous commandons de la nourriture? → ....

Je monte ou je descends? → ....

Vous étudiez ou vous jouez? → ....

16. Transform in imperative as in the example

<u>Example</u>: *Tu ne dois pas pleurer. → Ne pleure pas!*

Vous devez regarder ce film. → ....

Tu ne dois pas oublier ton sac. → ....

Nous devons prendre le bus tôt. → ....

Vous ne devez pas parler fort. → ....

Tu dois finir tes devoirs. → ....

Nous ne devons pas nous disputer. → ....

Vous devez écrire cette lettre. → ....

Tu dois écouter la musique. → ....

Vous ne devez pas jeter ces papiers. → ....

Tu dois respecter les règles. → ....

Solutions

a. true

b. Ne + pronoun + verb + pas

1. Complete the table

infinitif	Présent de l'indicatif	Impératif
Dormir	Tu dors	Dors
Apprendre	Tu apprends	Apprends
Chanter	Tu chantes	Chantes
Regarder	Tu regardes	Regardes
Danser	Nous dansons	Dansez
Jouer	Vous jouez	Jouez

2. Put in imperative.

Il est temps de nettoyer :

Tu laves la voiture → Lave la voiture

Tu balayes le sol → Balaye le sol

Tu essuies les vitres → Essuie les vitres

Prépare-toi pour la journée :

Tu te lèves tôt → Lève-toi tôt

Tu te douches → Douche-toi

Tu te brosses les dents → Brosse-toi les dents

3. Put in imperative.

Préparer un repas:

Vous choisissez une recette → Choisissez une recette.

Vous vérifiez les ingrédients nécessaires → Vérifiez les ingrédients nécessaires.

Vous achetez les produits manquants → Achetez les produits manquants.

Vous préparez les ustensiles → Préparez les ustensiles.

Vous suivez les étapes de la recette → Suivez les étapes de la recette.

Vous préchauffez le four → Préchauffez le four.

Vous servez le repas chaud → Servez le repas chaud.

Vous dégustez avec plaisir → Dégustez avec plaisir.

Vous rangez la cuisine → Rangez la cuisine.

Vous lavez les plats → Lavez les plats.

4. Put in imperative at the 2nd person plural

Crêpes sucrées :

Prenez une poêle.

Mélangez de la farine, du sucre et des œufs dans un bol.

Versez un peu de lait pour obtenir une pâte lisse.

Chauffez la poêle à feu moyen.

Versez une louche de pâte dans la poêle chaude.

Retournez la crêpe après 2 minutes.

Dorez l'autre côté.

Répétez le processus pour les autres crêpes.

Garnissez de sucre, de confiture ou de Nutella.

Dégustez tant qu'elles sont chaudes.

6. Put in imperative at the 2nd person singular

(Lire) → Lis le premier paragraphe.

(Souligner) → Souligne les mots que tu ne comprends pas.

(Écrire) → Écris une note en marge.

(Tourner) → Tourne à la page suivante.

(Résumer) → Résume le contenu en quelques phrases.

(Fermer) → Ferme le livre une fois fini.

(Ranger) → Range le livre dans ton sac.

8. Put in imperative

Rappels amicaux.

*a- Si tu as le temps, **passe** par la librairie et **cherche** le livre que j'avais réservé **n'oublie pas** de demander une facture. Merci.*

*b- Cher voisin, **n'arrose pas** les plantes cette semaine, elles ont eu assez d'eau. Merci!*

*c- N'oublie pas, **retire** de l'argent avant de venir à la soirée. À tout à l'heure.*

*d- **Envoie** moi les photos de la dernière randonnée. Hâte de les voir!*

*e- Chérie, si le plombier appelle, **ne lui dis pas** le prix que nous avions convenu, je lui parlerai directement.*

*f- Les gars, **montrez** à Max où sont les outils. À demain.*

9. Transform the sentences as in the example.

Example: *Nous ne devons pas rentrer tard.* → *Ne rentrons pas tard!*

Prudence!

Vous ne devez pas sortir seul. → *Ne sortez pas seul!*

Tu ne dois pas aller dans ce quartier. → *Ne va pas dans ce quartier!*

Nous ne devons pas passer dans ce souterrain. → *Ne passons pas dans ce souterrain!*

Tu ne dois pas traverser là. → *Ne traverse pas là!*

Nous ne devons pas prendre cette rue. → *Ne prenons pas cette rue!*

Vous ne devez pas partir à pied. → *Ne partez pas à pied!*

Tu ne dois pas faire demi-tour. → *Ne fais pas demi-tour!*

Vous ne devez pas tourner ici. → *Ne tournez pas ici!*

10. Transform as in the examples

<u>Example</u>: *Ils ne sont pas contents* → *Soyons contents!*

Elle est inquiète. → *Ne sois pas inquiète!*

a. Vous êtes distraits. → *Ne soyez pas distraits!*

b. Tu n'es pas honnête. → *Sois honnête!*

c. Ils n'ont pas faim. → *Ayez faim!*

d. Elle n'est pas rassurée. → *Sois rassurée!*

e. Vous avez raison. → *N'ayez pas raison!*

f. Tu es fatigué. → *Ne sois pas fatigue!*

g. Ils sont énervés. → *Ne soyez pas énervés!*

h. Vous n'êtes pas attentifs. → *Soyez attentifs!*

11. Put in imperative (in 2nd person singular)

Se préparer. → *Prépare-toi!*

S'installer. → *Installe-toi!*

Se dépêcher. → *Dépêche-toi!*

Se détendre. → *Détends-toi!*

Se coucher. → *Couche-toi!*

Se promener. → *Promène-toi!*

Se concentrer. → *Concentre-toi!*

Se divertir. → *Divertis-toi!*

12. Put in order

1- pas (4) / Ne (1) / éloignez (3) / vous (2)

2- Ne (1) / assieds (3) / t' (2) / pas (4)

3- Ne (1) / pas (4) / approche (3) / t' (2)

4- battons (3) / nous (2) / Ne (1) / pas (4)

5- pas (4) / vous (2) / Ne (1) / arrêtez (3)

6- Ne (1) / perds (3) / te (2) / pas (4)

7- t' (2) / pas (4) / inquiète (3) / Ne (1)

8- nous (2) / pas (4) / Ne (1) / disputons.(3)

13. Put in negative form.

*Parfume-toi, mais **ne te parfume pas** trop!*

*Écoute-moi, mais **ne m'écoute pas** en criant!*

*Mangez bien, mais **ne mangez pas** tout le gâteau!*

*Regarde-nous, mais **ne nous regarde pas** avec étonnement!*

*Entraînez-vous, mais **ne vous entraînez pas** trop fort!*

*Souriez toujours, mais **ne souriez pas** en te moquant!*

*Travaille dur, mais **ne travaille pas** sans prendre de pauses!*

14. Put in imperative

*Mangez (manger), il y a assez pour tout le monde. → **Mangez**, il y a assez pour tout le monde.*

***Écoutez** bien, c'est important.*

***Ne touchez pas** aux objets fragiles.*

*Les enfants, **soyez** sages pendant notre absence.*

***Ne prenez pas** trop de sucre, c'est mauvais pour la santé.*

*Messieurs, **ne parlez pas fort**, il y a une réunion à côté.*

***Revenez** tôt, il se fait nuit.*

***Lisez** les instructions avant d'utiliser l'appareil.*

*Si tu veux savoir, **demande** à la réception.*

*Il commence à pleuvoir, **ouvre** le parapluie et **mets-toi** à l'abri.*

***Éloignez-vous** des machines en marche.*

***Crois** en tes rêves, ils peuvent se réaliser.*

15. Transform in imperative as in the examples.

Je regarde ou j'écoute? → Ne regarde pas, écoute!

Nous achetons ou nous vendons? → N'achetez pas, vendez!

Je prends un café ou un thé? → Ne prends pas un café, prends un thé!

Nous cuisinons ou nous commandons de la nourriture? → Ne cuisinez pas, commandez de la nourriture!

Je monte ou je descends? → Ne monte pas, descends!

Vous étudiez ou vous jouez? → N'étudiez pas, jouez!

16. Transform in imperative as in the example

<u>Example:</u> *Tu ne dois pas pleurer. → Ne pleure pas!*

Vous devez regarder ce film. → **Regardez ce film!**

Tu ne dois pas oublier ton sac. → **N'oublie pas ton sac!**

Nous devons prendre le bus tôt. → **Prenons le bus tôt!**

Vous ne devez pas parler fort. → **Ne parlez pas fort!**

Tu dois finir tes devoirs. → **Finis tes devoirs!**

Nous ne devons pas nous disputer. → **Ne nous disputons pas!**

Vous devez écrire cette lettre. → **Écrivez cette lettre!**

Tu dois écouter la musique. → **Écoute la musique!**

Vous ne devez pas jeter ces papiers. → **Ne jetez pas ces papiers!**

Tu dois respecter les règles. → **Respecte les règles!**

Chapter 8 - Instruments for the Construction of Phrases

A or An

In French, *une* refers to feminine nouns and *un* to masculine nouns; both are used in place of the English a/an depending on the gender of the word being referred to. Examples of this type of item include:

- *un ticket* (a ticket)
- *une carte postale* (a postcard)

Adjectives

"Je cherche un hôtel confortable." translates to English as I am looking for a comfortable hotel.

In French, an adjective always follows the noun, however, there are a few exceptions to this rule. The prepositions *"grand"* (meaning "big") and *"petit"* (meaning "small") are used before the nouns that they describe. You should be familiar with these two exceptions.

In contrast to the English language, French is capable of having adjectives in both their singular and plural forms. This demonstrates that in order to provide an accurate description of a noun that is expressed in the plural form, you must employ an adjective that is written in the plural form. Another extra layer of complexity has been added to the matter by the fact that you are also responsible for ensuring that you are utilizing the correct masculine or feminine form of adjectives. In most cases, the feminine form of an adjective will have a "-e" at the end. Examples are the French words *petit* (masculine) and *petite* (feminine), which both indicate small.

Future Tense

"Je vais arriver demain." translates to I am going to arrive tomorrow.

The future can be formed in other ways by using the present tense of the word "go" in conjunction with another verb.

I am going	*Je vais*
You are going	*Tu vas (informal) or Vous allez (formal)*
He/she is going	*Il/elle va*
We are going	*Nous allons*
They are going	*Ils/elles vont*

Gender

Nouns in French are assigned a gender, which can be either feminine or masculine, depending on the context. There isn't necessarily a connection between the gender of a word and the gender of the thing it refers to. For instance, the word for table in French is *une table*, which is a feminine form of the word. The gender of the noun has a significant impact on the way the sentence is constructed, particularly with regard to the articles and adjectives

Have

"*J'ai deux frères.*" (I have two brothers.)

In the same way that it does in English, the verb form shifts depending on the subject that is being used.

I have	*J'ai*
You have	*Tu as (informal) or Vous avez (formal)*
S/he has	*Elle/Il a*
We have	*Nous avons*
They have	*Ils/Elles ont*

Locations

"*Mon passeport est dans mon sac.*" (My passport is in my bag.)

A preposition, such as "dans" or "in," can be placed before the location or the place to indicate where something is located, just like it is done in the English language.

My and Your

"*Voici mon mari et voici ma fille.*" (This is my husband and this is my daughter.)

In French, the pronouns "my" and "your" take on distinct forms depending on the gender and number of the noun they're referring to.

Mon passeport (masc.)	My passport
Ma voiture (fem.)	My car
Mes bagages (plural)	My luggage
Votre passeport (masc.)	Your passport
Votre voiture (fem.)	Your car
Vos bagages (plural)	Your luggage

No matter whether the noun is masculine or feminine, "*mon*" should be used instead of "*ma*" when the noun begins with a "h" or other vowel sounds.

Ton, ta, and *tes - son, sa, ses* are the French informal "your" and "his/her"; they are formed in the same way as "my" in English.

Negative Form

"Je ne sais pas." (I do not know.)

Adding "ne" before the verb and "pas" at the end of a phrase makes it negative in French.

Plural Form

"Je voudrais deux billets." (I would like two tickets.)

The -s at the end of a word in written French is usually dropped when spoken. The presence of an adverb (such as *"beaucoup de"* or "a lot of"), a numeral (such as *"deux billets"* or "two tickets) or the plural article (such as *"les"* = plural form of "the") might help you discern whether a spoken French word is singular or plural.

"Je voudrais deux billets mensuels." (I would like two monthly tickets.)

When the noun it modifies is plural, as we've already established, the corresponding adjective must also be changed to the plural form. Adding a -s to the end of an adjective is the standard method for accomplishing this.

Pointing at something

"C'est le bon train." (That is the right train.)

It is possible to point to anything by saying *"c'est"* which directly translates to "it is". This is the easiest technique to point at something. You can also turn a statement into a question that may be answered with a yes or a no by just replacing the period at the end of the phrase with a question mark. Example: "C'est le bon train?" which literally translates to "Is that the right train?" in English.

Questions

Who	*Qui*	*Qui est-ce?*
		Who is it?
What	*Qu'est-ce que*	*Qu'est-ce que c'est?*
		What is it?
Which	*Quel (masc.)*	*Lequel(le)?*
	Quelle (fem.)	Which one?
When	*Quand*	*Quand part le vol?*
		When does the flight leave?
Where	*Où*	*Où est le bar?*
		Where is the bar?
How	*Comment*	*Comment êtes-vous venu?*
		How did you get here?

How much/ How many	*Combien*	*Combien de billets?*
		How many tickets?
Why	*Pourquoi*	*Pourquoi riez-vous?*
		Why are you laughing?

Some

"*Je voudrais des pommes, du pâté et de l'eau.*" (I would like some apples, some pate and some water.)

In French, the word meaning "some" has three different words. The gender and number of the noun to which "some" refers determine which form is used. The preposition "*du*" is used for male-singular nouns. The preposition "*de (la)*" is used with a noun feminine-singular. As a rule, "*des*" is added to plural nouns.

Somebody's

"*La chambre de Marie*" (Marie's room)

The preposition "*de*" (of) before a word indicates that something is of ownership by a certain person.

The

"*Je prends les escargots, le bifteck et la tarte Tatin.*" (I will have the snails, the steak and the tarte Tatin.)

When referring to a noun in French, the article "the" has three different equivalents, one for each gender and one for single and plural nouns. The article *"le"* is used with masculine and singular nouns. The article *"la"* indicates the single feminine form of a word. The article *"les"* indicates the plural form of a noun.

"*L'hôtel près de la gare n'est pas cher.*" (The hotel near the train station is not expensive.)

When either "*le*" or "*la*" is used in front of a word that begins with an "h" or a vowel, they are both transformed into "*l*".

Yes - No Questions

"*Ici?*" (Here?)

To ask a question that can be answered with yes or no, simply construct a statement and raise the intonation of the sentence like you would in English. This basic principle may be used for as few as one word.

Importance of Liaisons

As a result of the frequent usage of word liaisons in French, those who are not native speakers sometimes have trouble translating spoken French into written French and back again. There are two main features of French word liaisons:

The word's pronunciation begins with the consonant of the word that comes before it that does not make a sound. The next word usually starts with the letter H or a vowel.

Different pronunciations are used for liaised consonants. Consonants whose pronunciation most frequently shifts comprise:

D – became a /t/

F – became a /v/

S – became a /z/

X – became a /z/

Even though they now liaise, the consonants *g, n, p, r, t,* and *z* are still produced in the exact same manner.

In the French language, word liaisons may also be broken down into three distinct groups. These include:

1. *Liaisons obligatoires* or Required Liaisons – Words that connect here are often associated with one another because of their function or significance. These words can be matched with any of the following:

   a) Pronoun + verb, example: *vous avez* /vuzavé/

   b) Noun preceded by an article

   c) Adjective + noun, example: *bon ami* /bonɛmi/

   d) Number + noun, example: *très occupé* /trɛzokuhpé/

   e) 2 different single-syllable prepositions, example: *chez eux* /shɛzuh/

Experts in the French language agree that Required Liaisons is the most straightforward for non-native speakers to memorize as they attempt to master the nuances of the language.

2. *Liaisons interdites* or Forbidden Liaisons – This may remind you of the title of an old movie, but it truly describes those letters that no human being has ever been able to successfully pronounce. You can frequently spot these letters in the following locations:

   a) After a person's complete name has been mentioned. Example: *Thomas est parti* /toma-ɛy-parti/ (rough translation: Thomas left)

   b) After the preposition *et* /ɛt/ (and). Example: *et en* /ɛyén/ some speakers might pronounce a hint of the letter 'n' at the end.

   c) Before the *H* aspirate or h-aspiré. Example: *en haut* /ənô/ (top)

   d) When adverbs of questioning form precede it. Example: *Comment est-il* /komän-ɛitil/ (How is it?)

e) When it is preceded by the *toujours* /tuʒuʁ/ (always or still). Example: *toujours ici*/ tuʒuʁisi/ (still here).

3. *Liaisons facultatives* or Optional Liaisons – These "liaisons" are terms that have morphed into their current form throughout the course of time. As a result of the fact that the liaisons frequently depend on the level of formality among speakers, it is more challenging for novices to thoroughly learn the French language. The following are some examples of situations in which optional liaisons may take place:

   a) Whenever a plural noun comes before the letter. Example: *femmes arrivent* /fɛmzariv/

   b) When the present tense form of the verb *être* (to be) comes before a noun in the sentence, which is il est /élés/. Example: *il est idiot* /éléytidio/ (it is foolish).

   c) When *il est* is placed before adjective. Example: *il est heureux* /éléyuru/ (he is happy).

Keep in mind that liaisons are not the same as *enchaînement*. The silent consonants of isolated words are emphasized in liaising because of the vowel that follows them. Even when the term *enchaînement* is used by itself, the last consonant is always said. When one term is joined to another that starts with a vowel, the last consonant is moved to the beginning of the following word and pronounced with the first vowel letter of the new word.

Can be found *Enchaînement* in the following instances:

• *Avec* /ävɛk/ (along with). When the word is added to avec, it would then be pronounced as /ävɛ-kəl/ (roughly translated to 'with it').

• *Elle* /ɛl/ (it) – this is often used with the preposition est, and the prepositional phrase would then be pronounced as /ɛ-lé/ (she is).

Many additional words can also be chained together to form new words. The speaker just needs to keep in mind that the last letter of the first word is joined to the first vowel of the second word to pronounce these properly.

Order of Words

The standard sequence of a sentence in any language is (SVO) subject-verb-object, as is the case in English. If you are unsure about the correct sentence structure to utilize, you may always fall back on how you would ordinarily speak English. By doing so, you will be easily understood by most people.

Chapter 9 - Comprehension of Verb Forms in the French

English verbs are easy to conjugate since they stay the same in most tenses and just need a letter like "s" to alter the tense or subject. French verbs must be conjugated practically every time the verbal tense changes. Learn about French verb categories before starting to conjugate them.

Categories comprise:

1. *Regular -ER verbs* include *accompagner* (to accompany), *danser* (to dance), and others. English infinitive verbs have French equivalents. Depending on the pronoun, they are conjugated in 6 ways. The following demonstrates how each French pronoun conjugates the infinitive French verb *accompagner*:

Pronoun	Conjugation rules	Final word
Je	Delete the final letter in the phrase.	*Accompagne*
Tu	Substitute the *s* instead of the letter *r*.	*Accompagnes*
Il	The same conjugation as the pronoun *Je* is used here.	*Accompagne*
Nous	Change -er in -ons.	*Accompagnons*
Vous	Switch the -r using the -z in his place.	*Accompagnez*
Ils	Change -r with the -nt	*Accompagnent*

2. *Regular -IR verbs* --- Verbs like these are words that finish in -ir and are also the French corresponding of infinitive English verbs that need the use of the word 'to' preceding the verb. The pronoun that is linked to the verb also plays a role in the conjugation of the verb. Consider, for example, the construction-related verb *bâtir* (to build):

Pronoun	Conjugation rules	Final word
Je	Substitute the s instead of the letter r.	*Bâtis*
Tu	The same conjugation as the pronoun *Je* is used here.	*Bâtis*
Il	Substitute -r using -t in his place	*Bâtit*
Nous	Change -er in -ssons	*Bâtissons*
Vous	Change -r with -ssez	*Bâtissez*
Ils	Substitute -r with -ssent	*Bâtissent*

3. *Regular -RE verbs* --- are infinitive verbs ending in -re. The verb pronoun determines conjugation. For instance: *défendre* (to defend):

Pronoun	Conjugation rules	Final word
Je	Simply change the -re to a -s at the end	*Défends*

Tu	The same conjugation as the pronoun *Je* is used here	*Défends*
Il	Delete the final letter *-re* in the phrase	*Défend*
Nous	Change *-re* with *-ons*	*Défendons*
Vous	Simply change the *-re* to a *-ez* at the end	*Défendez*
Ils	Remove *-re* and add *-ent*	*Défendent*

4. Stem-changing verbs --- as English verb categories, French stem-changing verbs have two stems that modify spelling or syllable accent based on whether they are used with singular or plural pronouns. These are termed boot verbs because when pronouns are placed three to a column, identical verbs for each pronoun commonly make a boot shape.

Take *geler (freeze)*. This is conjugated like regular verbs, but the stem word's spelling changes somewhat, typically by replacing the initial *"e"* with a *"é"*. Present-tense conjugation is as follows:

je gèle	*nous gelons*
tu gèles	*vous gelez*
il gèle	*ils gèlent*

An interwoven line around conjugations with *"è"* as the initial vowel forms a boot or shoe. This approach helps non-native French speakers recall how stem-changing verbs are conjugated in common usage based on the verb's tense and pronoun.

5. Irregular verbs --- verbs that finish in *-er, -ir,* or *-re* like regular verbs, but they nonetheless take the same form as normal verbs. On the other hand, in contrast to normal French verbs, irregular French verbs do not follow a set pattern for their conjugation. In other instances, the spelling of the term could be altered entirely in order for it to be consistent with the pronoun that is being used with it. One example of this is the French verb *être*, which means "to be." These words are at the top of the list of the most frequently used French verbs, and they may be conjugated in a variety of different ways depending on the context:

Je suis, which is often abbreviated as *j'suis* at times

Tu es

Il est

Nous sommes

Vous êtes

Ils sont

Given that there are more than a thousand French verbs, it may take time for students of the language to fully grasp how French verbs are conjugated. However, once a person has mastered the fundamentals of conjugating the most frequently used verbs in French, he will typically find it simpler to go to the more sophisticated forms of the language.

Chapter 10 - How to Improve Your French Accent

We have already looked in detail at French pronunciation, so now let's consider how you can apply everything you have learned and start to improve your *accent*.

For a start, what is the difference between pronunciation and accent? Are they not the same?

Pronunciation is the way the individual sounds of a language are produced. In order to be understood, you need to pronounce words correctly. You might not sound like a native speaker but if you have good pronunciation, you will be able to pronounce all the language sounds and words clearly and understandably. An accent, on the other hand, is a way of pronouncing words that differs by region, country or social group. As a French learner, you will naturally speak with a foreign accent at first, but the better your accent is the more "native like" you will sound. Perfecting your French accent is difficult, but it can certainly be improved with the right approach.

This chapter will be of interest if you have ever found yourself wondering:

Is my accent any good?

Do I sound too "foreign"?

What I can do to improve my accent?

Let's start with some perspective.

A Lot of Listening!

Natsuko, a Japanese girl of eight years old, once came to me to learn guitar. She was completely unfamiliar with the language after just moving to the UK. As could be expected from a youngster of her age, she spoke great English with a good rounded British accent after only one year of school in her new country. It was a privilege to see Natsuko every Tuesday of her first school year and witness her growth as a student.

Since Natsuko did not yet know any English, she had to rely on listening to the language around her to figure out what was going on. How much of the school year do you think she spent listening to English? In her first year of school, I estimate she spent around 1,500 hours listening to English between her six-hour school days, a few extra-curricular activities, and six weeks of school breaks.

Now, if an eight-year-old child needs 1,500 hours of exposure to a new language in order to develop native-like pronunciation in the language, it is likely that we, as adults, need at least that, if not more. After all, Natsuko had the benefit of teachers and classmates supporting her all-day long. In your case, let's be generous and say you would need to amass around 2,000 hours of meaningful exposure to French in order to develop a native-like accent when speaking. It took Natsuko one year of attending school full-time. How long would it take you to reach 2,000 hours of listening?

15 min per day: 21.9 years

30 min per day: 10.95 years

45 min per day: 7.3 years

60 min per day: 5.48 years

90 min (the length of a movie) per day: 3.65 years

Now, does this mean you need to spend 2,000 hours listening to French before you can start speaking? Not at all. You will be able to have a perfectly enjoyable conversation in French well before that. It is also not necessary for you to have a native-like accent in French, like Natsuko had in English --- you certainly do not. However, if you do have ambitions to speak natural French it is helpful to have a sense of perspective about how long it might take, and a real-life example to contemplate. The main lesson I took from watching Natsuko's English transform over the course of a year was this: You must spend a lot of time listening to your new language.

However, you have an advantage over an eight-year-old student and can cut down on the 2,000 hours required by bringing study abilities to the table. A child may be sponge-like in their ability to pick up new sounds, and have a wonderful lack of inhibition that allows them to embrace any learning opportunity, but as an adult, you can grasp learning opportunities on an intellectual level that can allow you to learn far faster.

Tips for Improving Your Accent

The first step in developing a good French accent is to learn to listen to and notice the rhythm and melody of a French accent. Listening comes before speaking. If you cannot hear it, you cannot say it. Here are some practical steps to follow to develop a good French accent:

1. Pay special attention to how fascinating native French speakers speak words and phrases. Play them back in your head and say them loudly.

2. Record yourself saying these words and phrases, and listen back. (The phone in your pocket is great for this. Look for the voice recorder app.) The discrepancy between your inner and outer perceptions of your own voice can take you aback.

3. If you have a French friend or teacher, ask them to record the same vocabulary and send them to you in a voice message. Pay close attention to the differences, and copy them yourself.

4. Try hard to copy the rhythm and melody of the phrases you learn. Repeated listening may reveal hidden melodies or rhythms. Incorporate movement, sound, and song into your study methods.

5. Learn songs. Singers use clear articulation to convey the meaning of song lyrics, making them a valuable tool for studying accents and pronunciation. If you're trying to memorize French lyrics, you'll have to put in some serious mental work to link the words to the music, so you'll be paying careful attention to how the words sound. Your accent will gradually fade as your pronunciation rapidly improves, which takes more time, but it's well worth the effort.

Chapter 11 - Taking Advantage of What You Already Know: Cognates

When learning French as a beginner, one of your most important jobs is to grow your vocabulary. There is simply no escaping the fact that you have to learn a large number of new words in order to speak a foreign language. Of course, grammar is also important, but enlarging your vocabulary is the fastest way to improve your ability to express yourself effectively in French.

Think of it this way: With lots of grammar and no vocabulary, you cannot express anything. However, with lots of vocabulary and no grammar, you can express a lot. If you dedicate yourself to mastering French grammar principles but lack a working vocabulary, you will remain unable to communicate effectively. However, if you put in the effort to acquire a broad vocabulary, you will likely be able to communicate well in most settings, despite the fact that your grammar may be less than acceptable.

Although reaching a high level of proficiency in French requires you to know several thousand words, you can do a lot as a beginner with just a small vocabulary. An important language learning strategy, then, as a beginner, is not to learn every single word you come across, but rather to focus on learning important vocabulary you can use to communicate right away --- but more on this later.

The first question is: How should you go about learning all the words you need to know to start speaking French? Different languages have different challenges but, as we have already seen, the one advantage English speakers have learning French is that the two languages share a lot of common vocabulary. These are words you already know in English that are the same (or very similar) in French, and these mutually-intelligible words are known as *cognates*. The greatest number of these have come to English from French over the last 1,000 years, and a few common examples are:

révolution --- revolution

théâtre --- theatre

géographie --- geography

As you can see, apart from the addition of an accent or two, or a slightly different spelling, these words are almost identical. In addition, more recently, French has begun to borrow words rather extensively from English, and many English words are now in daily use in the French language, for example *sandwich, weekend, hamburger, hot dog, football*. Other words have been absorbed into French and have taken on new (and sometimes slightly bizarre) meanings:

baskets --- trainers, running shoes (from the idea of "basketball shoes" or sneakers)

hand --- handball (shortened form, the word "handball" is also used)

foot – football (shortened form of "football", the same as for "handball")

This shared vocabulary makes French much easier to learn than languages like Chinese or Vietnamese since there are far more cognates (incidentally, Vietnamese does have quite a few words that come from French due to the French colonization of the country --- but that is another story!). It even makes French easier to learn than other closely related languages like German or Italian since the number of words shared by English and French is so high.

Another factor that will help you as a new learner of French is that there are groups of words that follow more or less predictable patterns, so if a word ends in a particular way in English, there is a good chance that it will have a corresponding ending in French.

Here are some common patterns to remember:

- *ty* becomes *-té*

personality --- *personnalité*

society --- *société*

equality --- *égalité*

- *ly* becomes *-ement*

finally --- *finalement*

particularly --- *particulièrement*

temporarily --- *temporairement*

currently --- *actuellement*

- *tion* stays *-tion*

ambition --- *ambition*

coalition --- *coalition*

cessation --- *cessation*

- *ssion* becomes *-ssion*

recession --- *récession* (economic)

oppression --- *oppression*

admission --- *admission*

You may have heard of so-called *false friends*. Words that appear similar or even share the same etymological origin but have distinct meanings in French and English are called "false friends". For example, *actuellement* means "at the moment, presently" and *éventuellement* means "possibly, potentially".

However, false friends are relatively few and far between, and the result is that you start out with a large bulk of "free" vocabulary that does not need to be learnt. If you do not know a word, you can often just try to guess and you will find that more often than not, it works!

Chapter 12 - Traveling and Going About

We are now getting to some pretty useful things, especially if you are planning a trip to France or any French speaking country. Foreigners are usually easily helped by locals to find their way, especially if they speak a little French. So don't hesitate to leave your GPS in your pocket and use the opportunity of looking for your way to talk to people and ask them for guidance. If you stick to English when asking your way to others, it might very well be considered as a rude attitude. Don't forget that you are asking a "favor", so the least you can do is to try to ask in French.

But that won't be much of a problem, since you are now reading this chapter about "indications" (directions). So let's start with the basics, and what you should definitely start your sentence with: "*excusez-moi*".

Excusez-moi: is translated into English excuse me

Pardon: is translated into English pardon me

Je cherche: is translated into English I'm looking for

Où est/sont: is translated into English Where is/are

Dans quelle rue se trouve: is translated into English In which street is the ... located?

Est-ce que ... est loin d'ici? is translated into English Is the ... far from here?

Où puis-je trouver: is translated into English Where can i find

Comment est-ce que je vais à/au...: is translated into English How do I get to the...

Pouvez-vous m'aider: is translated into English Can you help me

Pouvez-vous me montrer: is translated into English Can you show me

Pouvez-vous me dire: is translated into English Can you tell me

Est-ce que ... est loin/près d'ici? is translated into English Is the... far/close from here?

Pouvez-vous m'emmener: is translated into English Can you take me to

Centre ville: is translated into English city center

Le prochain/ la prochaine: is translated into English the next

À gauche: is translated into English on the left

À droite: is translated into English to the right

Tout droit: is translated into English go straight

Traverser: is translated into English to cross

Demi tour: is translated into English U turn

Derrière: is translated into English behind

À coté: is translated into English next to

Devant: is translated into English in front of

En face: is translated into English opposite

Bout de la rue: is translated into English end of the road

Le feu rouge: is translated into English the traffic light

Le rond point: is translated into English the roundabout

Une carte: is translated into English a map

Nord/sud/est/ouest: is translated into English North, south, east, west

What do you need exactly? Here is a list of things you might suddenly have the need for. Good luck!

Les toilettes: is translated into English toilets

La gare: is translated into English train station

Le supermarché: is translated into English the supermarket

La piscine: is translated into English swimming pool

Le distributeur de billets: is translated into English ATM

La boulangerie: is translated into English bakery (that's a very useful one)

Le magasin: is translated into English the shop

La pharmacie: is translated into English the pharmacy

L'hôpital: is translated into English the hospital

Le restaurant: is translated into English the restaurant

At the train station

How do I book a train ticket in French? How do I find out which track I should go to? How do I complain if my train has been canceled? Don't worry, in this section we will go through a certain number of easy sentences to help you survive in the train station.

Prendre le train: is translated into English to take the train

Un ticket: is translated into English a ticket

Aller simple: is translated into English one way

Aller retour: is translated into English round trip

Première/seconde classe: is translated into English first/second class

Tarif spécial: is translated into English special fare

Réduction: is translated into English discount

Combien coûte: is translated into English how much is...

À quelle heure part/arrive: is translated into English at what time leaves/arrive?

Le quai: is translated into English the platform

Être en retard: is translated into English to be late

Le train est en retard: is translated into English the train is late

Rater le train: is translated into English to miss the train

Composter: is translated into English to validate a ticket

Annuler: is translated into English to cancel

Échanger: is translated into English to exchange

Remboursable: is translated into English refundable

Les renseignements: is translated into English information (desk)

La grève: is translated into English the strike (happens more than you think)

Les horaires: is translated into English timetable

Le TGV: is translated into English High speed train

Le wagon restaurant: is translated into English bar compartment

Hotels

How do I book a hotel room in French? What do I say to the friendly receptionist who doesn't speak a word of English? How do I get my breakfast in my room? How do I cancel my expensive booking? Here again, we will take a look at some basic sentences that will help you to answer these questions. Do note, though, that in touristic areas, hotel staff are supposed to speak some English, so don't get robbed through expensive extras just because you absolutely want to get things done in French. Do try to get friendly contacts with employees; it might very well be helpful.

L'hôtel: the hotel

La réception: reception

Une chambre disponible: an available room

Réserver une chambre: book a room

Lit simple/double: single/double bed

Quel est le prix d'une chambre double? how much is a double room?

Un lit de bébé: a cot

Un lit d'appoint: a spare bed

Admis: allowed

Une clé: a key

Une clé magnétique: magnetic card

Petit-déjeuner compris: breakfast included

Demi-pension: half board

Pension complète: full board

Servi: served

Le service en chambre / d'étage: room service

Réserver en ligne: to book online

Sous le nom: under the name

Une chambre avec vue: room with a view

A partir de quelle heure?: from what time?

Prendre possession de la chambre: check in

Libérer la chambre: check out

Code Wifi: Wifi code

Ne marche pas: doesn't work

La douche: the shower

Trop chaud/ froid: too hot/cold

L'ascenseur: the elevator

Premier étage: second floor (US)

Annuler une réservation: cancel a booking

Remboursé: refunded

Garer la voiture: park the car

Se lever tôt: to wake up early

Faire la grasse matinée: to sleep in

Faire la sieste: to take a nap

Ne pas déranger: do not disturb

Merci de faire ma chambre: please clean up my room

Le savon: soap

La serviette: towel

La robe de chambre: robe

La télécommande: remote control

Service de blanchisserie: cleaning service

Centre de bien être: wellness center

Supplément: extra charge

Service voiturier: valet service

L'auberge de jeunesse: youth hostel

Appartement de location: private renting appartment

Camping: camping

Surviving French airports

Not an easy task, friends... Now that we have already gotten to know the word "grève", let's carry on with more fun! This section will help you in finding your way through check in, security, duty free and boarding hassle. Information at both Paris' airports is written in English, but you might come across some folks not speaking English, or simply not in the mood. Keep your cool attitude, smile, and surprise them by your awesome French vocabulary. *C'est parti*!

L'aéroport: the airport

Prendre l'avion: taking the plane

Rater l'avion: to miss the plane

Le retard: the delay

Le comptoir d'enregistrement: the check-in desk

Un aller simple/retou: one-way ticket/ a round trip

Combien coûte: how much

Par personne: per person

La porte d'embarquement: the boarding gate

La compagnie aérienne: the airline company

Les départs: the departures

Les arrivées: the arrivals

Les horaires: time schedule

Les bagages/ valises: luggage/ suitcases

Assistance personnelle: personal assistance

À votre disposition: at your disposal

Annulé: cancelled

Échanger: exchange

La douane: customs

Nationalité: nationality

Tamponner: to stamp

Postuler pour un visa: apply for a visa

Formulaire de déclaration: declaration form

Les renseignements: information

Le parking dépose-minute: drop-off point

Le parking souterrain: underground parking

La sortie: exit

L'entrée: entrance

La grève: the strike

Objets trouvés: lost property

Perdre ses bagages: to lose your luggage

Le contrôle des passeports: passports control

atterrir: to land

décoller: to take off

La ceinture de sécurité: the seat belt

L'altitude: the altitude

Les turbulences: turbulence

L'équipage: the crew

La sortie de secours: the emergency exit

La cabine: the cabin

Le plateau: the tray

Le siège: the seat

Le couloir: the aisle

Le hublot: the window

L'hôtesse de l'air: the air hostess

Le steward: the steward

La soute: the hold

La correspondance: the connection

Chapter 13 - Seeing the Sites

During the course of your trip to France you will no doubt visit places of interest and will need to go through the formality of buying tickets or seeking information that is useful to you. For example, you may have bought several postcards in the gift shop and not know if the shop sells stamps. Some do for the convenience of travelers and also have a post box so that you can post your postcards as soon as they are written. You may also want to buy books on the historical place that you have visited.

Sometimes, you may not see clearly what entry costs and may have to inquire before you make your mind up whether you want entry to that place of not. Thus, knowing how to ask is very important.

One ticket please	*Un billet s'il vous plaît*	Uhn bee aye si voo play
How much does a child ticket cost?	*Combien coûte un billet enfant?*	Combee ann coot uhn bee aye onfon?
Two adults and one child please	*Deux adultes et un enfant s'il vous plaît*	Pronunciation: Duhz adoolt ay uhn onfon si voo play

If you get stuck for your numbers you can indicate the numbers on your fingers and then say the word adult or enfant so that they know how many tickets you want for each.

Now, supposing you have bought postcards and you want to ask if the shop has stamps. This is asked using the following phrase.

| Do you have stamps? | *Avez-vous des timbres?* | Avay voo day tambr? |

If you want to know the history of a building that you are visiting, then chances are that you will not understand the French spoken by a guide. Some of these places do have headphones so that you can listen to a commentary in your own language. Other than that, tourist information brochures may be printed in different languages as well. You may also be able to buy DVDs and these are very useful because you can choose the language that you want and take a little bit of history home with you.

There are various ways that you can visit historical places. Sometimes you are permitted to go around the attraction following specific paths which are indicated. You may also be able to go around with a guide during high season. If this is your preference, you may have to ask at what time the tour begins:

| At what time does the guided tour begin? | *À quelle heure commence la visite guidée?* | Ah kell hur commonse la viseet geeday |

You may also want to know whether this costs extra and whether the guide speaks in English.

| Are the guided tours in English? | *Les visites guidées sont-elles en anglais?* | lay viseet geeday sontayl on onglay? |

It is worth noting when you go to visit the Eiffel Tower, there are different tariffs depending upon which level you want to go up to. Here's a free tip! The best choice is the second level because this is high enough to see the city, and a café and restaurant is available there so that you can enjoy your time at leisure once you have reached this level. However, the prices do change from time to time so you need to look at the boards to see what the prices currently are for each level. There is also a shop so that you can buy souvenirs.

Second level please	*Deuxième étage s'il vous plaît*	Duh zee em etage si voo play

Of course, this isn't the only site to see in a city like Paris. You will need to travel around a bit. Use the map that you get from the tourist information office or from stations that serve the metro, as this will give you all the information that you need in order to know which metro station you will need to get to each of the attractions. Similar to within any city within France, the maps that you get allow you to plan your days and to make the most of your time, getting from one attraction to another. It is a good idea to have one of these maps from day one so that you can spend some time planning to get the most out of the visit. By doing this, you can also work out what you will see and where you will eat along the way.

Common useful phrases to know when you are out seeing the sites:

Referring to your map, you may be able to ask these questions to get help from a passer-by:

Can you help me?	*Pouvez-vous m'aider?*	Poo-vay voo meh-day
I cannot find this road.	*Je ne peux pas trouver cette route*	Juh nuh purh pa troovay sett root
Am I allowed to take photographs?	*Est-ce que je peux prendre des photos?*	Eska juh purh prond day photo?
Can you take a photo of me and my husband?	*Pouvez-vous prendre une photo de moi et mon mari?*	Poo-vay voo prend oon photo duh mwa ay mon marry?
Does the museum have a shop?	*Le musée a-t-il un magasin?*	Luh muzay – a teel uhn magazan?
Can you change this note for coins?	*Pouvez-vous changer ce billet pour des pièces de monnaie?*	Poovay voo chonjay suh bee ay pour day pee es de monay?
Are children permitted to visit?	*Les enfants sont-ils autorisés à visiter?*	Lays onfon sonteel autoreesay a viseetay?
At what time does the art gallery close?	*À quelle heure ferme la galerie?*	A kell hur fairm la gallairee?
Is there a lot to see?	*Est-ce qu'il y a beaucoup de choses à voir?*	S-keel yah bo-coo duh shoze-ah vwah?
Are there any restaurants near our hotel?	*Y a-t-il des restaurants près de notre hôtel?*	Yah-teel day rez-toh-rahn preh duh nohtr oh-tel?
May I have a restaurant guide?	*Puis-je avoir un guide de restaurant?*	Pweez-ah-vwahr on geed-day rez-toh-rahn?
Do you have guided tours?	*Avez-vous des visites guidées?*	Ah-vay voo dez vee-zit gee-day
I'd like to book a place for the next tour.	*J'aimerais réserver une place pour la prochaine visite.*	Jzem-rah ray-zah-vay oon plahs poor lay pro-shane vee-zit.
Museum	*Musée*	Mue-zay

Zoo	Zoo	zoo
Park	*Parc*	pahrk
Natural Park	*Parc Naturel*	pahrk nah-tu- rehl
Castle	*Château*	Sha-toh
Monument	*Monument*	Mohn-yu-mahn
Cinema	*Cinéma*	see-nay-mah
Concert	*concert*	kohn-ser
Stadium	*stade*	stahd
Circus	*cirque*	sirk
Aquarium	*Aquarium*	Ah-kwah-ree-um

By the time that you have seen all the sites, you will be ready to sit down and dine in style. Bear in mind that if you are eating in a posh restaurant, it's a good idea to dress for dinner. There are convenience foods available where you can dress more casually. However, after a long day of visiting all the sites, it's time to slow down and enjoy French cuisine at its best. You may even find that your hotel caters for babysitting, but do book up early if you need this service since you really don't want to be disappointed at the last moment.

Quiz Time!

1. How do you say Natural park?

2. How would you ask for help?

3. How would you request 1 ticket?

4. How would you request a "Second Level" ticket?

5. How would you inquire about a guided tour?

Solutions

1. *Parc Naturel*

2. *Pouvez vous m'aider s'il vous plaît?*

3. *Un billet s'il vous plait*

4. *Un billet pour le deuxième étage s'il vous plaît*

5. *Où sont les visites guidées s'il vous plaît)*

Chapter 14. How to Reassure Someone

Expressions	Meaning
Ça va aller/ Ça ira	It will be ok
Ce n'est rien	It's nothing
Ne vous inquiétez pas	Do not worry
Ne t'en fais pas	Do not worry
Ce n'est pas grave	It does not matter

Let's see a conversation where your friend has an interview. He is scared and you reassure him.

Augustin - Salut! Comment vas tu?

(Hi! How are you?)

Benoit - Salut! Ça va. Et toi?

(Hi! Fine. And you?)

Augustin - Moi! Pas mal.

(Me! Not good)

Benoit - Pourqoui? Qu'est-ce qui s'est passé?

(Why? What happened?)

Augustin - J'ai un entretien demain. J'ai peur d'échouer.

(I have an interview tomorrow. I am scared of failing.)

Benoit - Tu es très intelligent. Tu es capable de réussir. Ne t'en fais pas.

(You are very intelligent. You are capable of succeeding. Do not worry.)

Augustin - Il y aura beaucoup de gens, ça m'angoisse. 60 personnes ont postulé et il n'y a qu'une place.

(There will be a lot of people, it worries me. 60 people applied and there is only one place.)

Benoit - Ça ira! Faire de ton mieux.

(It will be fine! Do your best.)

Augustin - Oui. Je dois faire de mon mieux parce que c'est un emploi que je cherchais depuis longtemps.

(Yes. I have to do my best because it is a job I have been looking for for a long time.)

Benoit - Eh! Bien! Bon courage! As-tu besoin de mon aide?

(Hey! Well! Good luck! Do you need my help?)

Augustin - Merci pour demander. Mais c'est un entretien technique.

(Thanks for asking. But it's a technical interview.)

Benoit - Tu as trop d'expérience. Ça sera facile pour toi!

(You have too much experience. It will be easy for you!)

Augustin - C'est pas facile. De nos jours, il y a beaucoup de compétition entre les gens. Et tous les gens ont des compétences. Je suis inquiète. J'ai besoin de cet emploi. Je veux épouser Beatrice. Pour commencer une nouvelle vie, je dois gagner suffisamment d'argent.

(It is not easy. Nowadays, there is a lot of competition between people. And all people have skills. I'm worried. I need this job. I want to marry Beatrice. To start a new life, I have to earn enough money.)

Benoit - Ne t'inquiète pas. Pense positivement. Tout ce que tu peux faire est de faire des efforts. Laisse le reste sur ton destin.

(Do not worry. Think positively. All you can do is make an effort. Leave the rest on your destiny.)

Augustin - Oui. Merci. Je dois aller maintenant sinon je serai en retard.

(Yes. Thank you. I have to go now or I will be late.)

Benoit - Ça va. Rappelle-moi si besoin. Au revoir!

(It's okay. Call me back if needed. Goodbye!)

Augustin - Au revoir!

(Goodbye!)

Vocabulary Words

Word	Meaning	Pronunciation
Malgré de	Despite	Maa – l – gray – d
Création	Creation	K – ray – a – ti – oh
Véhicules	Vehicules	Way – hi – kooh – l
Discret	Discreet	Di – s – k – ray
Discuter	To discuss	Di – s – kooh – tay
Divorce	Divorce	Di – voh – r – c
Douche	Shower	Dooh – sh
Documentaliste	Archivist	Do – kooh – moh – taa – li – s – t
Écho	Echo	Ay – koh
Énervé	Annoyed	Ay – neh – r – way
Enfant	Child	Oh – n – foh
Équilibre	Balance	Ay – ki – li – b – r
Escalade	Climbing	Eh – s – kaa – laa – d
Éteindre	To switch off	Ay – tah – n – d – r
Exercice	Exercise	Eh – k – s – r – si – s
Facile	Easy	Faa – si – l

Famille monoparentale	One-parent family	Faa – mi – mo – no – paa – roh – n – taa – l
Kilomètre	Kilometer	Ki – lo – meh – t – r
Fatigant	Tiring	Faa – ti – goh
Fauteuil	Armchair	Foh – t – uh – i
Fenêtre	Window	F – uh – neh – th – r
Fiche	Card	Fi – sh
Fichier	File	Fi – sh – i – ay
Fin	End	Fah
Finir	To finish	Fi – ni – r
Fleur	Flower	F – l – uh – r
Flic	Cop	F – li – k
Frapper	To knock	F – raa – pay
Frisé	Curly	F – ri – zay
Gronder	To tell off	G – roh – n – day
Habitant	Occupant	Aa – bi – toh
Handicapé	Disabled	Aa – n – di – kaa – pay
Hébergement	Accomodation	Ay – beh – r – j – moh
Héros	Heroes	Ay – roh
Histoire	Story	I – s – tuah – r
Hôpital	Hospital	O – pi – taa – l
Incroyable	Incredible	Ah – k – roh – aa – b – l
Inventer	To invent	Ah – voh – n – ti – r
Jaune	Yellow	Joh – n
Journée	Day	Jooh – r – nay
Juste	Just	Jooh – s – t
Définitivement	Definitely	Day – fi – ni – ti – v – moh
Sensibiliser	To make aware	So – n – si – bi – li – zay
Voies	Roads/ Streets	Vuah
Fosses	Pits	Foh – s
Diminuer	To diminish	Di – mi – nooh – ay
Crainte	Fear	K – rah – n – t
Soyez prudent	Take care	So – yay – prooh – doh
Influence	Influence	Ah – f – looh – oh – s

Chapter 15. How to Express Dissatisfaction

Expressions	Meaning
Ce n'est pas normal!	This is not normal!
C'est inacceptable!	This is unacceptable!
On ne peut pas accepter ça!	We can't accept that!
C'est intolérable!	It's intolerable!
On ne peut pas tolérer ça!	We can't tolerate that!
C'est scandaleux!	It's scandalous!
C'est lamentable!	It's a shame!
Je trouve ça lamentable!	I find it lamentable!
Tu exagères!	You exaggerate!
Je ne m'attendais pas à ça!	I did not expect that!

Let's see an example where you write a letter to the restaurant manager expressing your dissatisfaction about the service.

(In French)

Caroline Régime,

Avenue Jean Louise,

1200, Lyon

Monsieur responsable,

Passage Jean Louise,

1200, Lyon

Le 20 Mars, 2020

Sujet: Exprimer mécontentement du service.

Avec tout le respect que je dois, je voudrais apporter à votre attention que je suis mécontente avec le service de votre restaurant.

J'ai visité votre restaurant le 18 Mars. Premièrement, j'y suis allée parce que j'ai lu des bonnes critiques.

L'aura avait l'air sympa. Mais quand j'ai demandé au serveur quelques suggestions sur un plat populaire, il était un peu grossier. Aussi la plupart de plats n'étaient pas disponibles. Ce n'était pas normal! En plus j'ai du attendre pour 40 minutes pour la nourriture. Je ne m'attendais pas à ça. Mais, la nourriture était bonne. C'est la seule raison pour laquelle j'écris cette lettre. Je souhaite que vous amélioriez le service.

Cordialement,
Caroline

(In English)

Caroline Régime,

Avenue Jean Louise,

1200, Lyon

Mr. Manager,

Passage Jean Louise,

1200, Lyon

March 20, 2020

Subject: Express service dissatisfaction

With all due respect, I would like to bring to your attention that I am unhappy with the service of your restaurant.

I visited your restaurant on March 18. First, I went there because I read good reviews. The aura looked nice. But when I asked the waiter for a few suggestions on a popular dish, it was a bit rude. Also most of the dishes were not available. It was not normal! Besides, I had to wait 40 minutes for food. I did not expect that. But, the food was good. That's the only reason I'm writing this letter. I want you to improve the service.

Cordially,

Caroline

Express Intention/ objectif/ goal

Expressions	Meaning
Pour	For
Afin de	In order to
Avoir objectif de	Aim to
Envisager de	Plan to
Prévoir de	Plan to

The conjugation of the verb *"Prévoir"*

Je prévois (I plan)

Tu prévois (You plan)

Il/ Elle/ On prévoit (He plans/ She plans/ We plan)

Nous prévoyons (We plan)

Vous prévoyez (You plan)

Ils/ Elles prévoient (They plan)

The conjugation of the verb *"Envisager"*

J'envisage (I plan)

Tu envisages (You plan)

Il/ Elle/ On envisage (He plans/ She plans/ We plan)

Vous envisagez (You plan)

Nous envisageons (We plan)

Ils/ Elles envisagent (They plan)

Let's see some examples:

- *J'apprends le français pour aller au Canada.*

(I'm learning French to go to Canada)

- *J'apprends le français afin d'aller au Canada.*

(I am learning French in order to go to Canada.)

- *J'ai pour objectif d'aller au Canada.*

(My goal is to go to Canada.)

- *J'envisage d'aller au Canada.*

(I plan to go to Canada.)

- *Je prévois d'aller au Canada.*

(I plan to go to Canada.)

- *Je révise les verbes pour avoir des bonnes notes dans l'examen.*

(I revise the verbs to get good marks in the exam.)

- *Je révise les verbes afin d'avoir des bonnes notes dans l'examen.*

(I revise the verbs in order to have good marks in the exam.)

- *J'envisage d'avoir de bonnes notes dans l'examen.*

(I plan to have good marks in the exam.)

- *Je prévois d'avoir de bonnes notes dans l'examen.*

(I plan to have good marks in the exam.)

Vocabulary Words

Word	Meaning	Pronunciation
Lavabo	Washbasin	Laa – va – bo
Littérature	Literature	Li – tay – raa – tooh – r
Loin	Far	Luah
Maigrir	To lose weight	May – g – ri – r
Mariage	Marriage	Maa – ri – aa – j
Merveilleux	Wonderful	M – uh – r – vi – uh
Message	Message	May – saa – j
Meuble	Furniture	Muh – b – l
Nager	To swim	Naa – jay
Naissance	Birth	Nay – soh – n – s
National	National	Naa – si – o – naa – l
Neige	Snow	Neh – j

Noisette	Hazelnut	Nuah – zeh – t
Nombril	Belly button	Nom – b – ri – l
Numéro	Number	Nooh – may – ro
Ordinateur	Computer	O – r – di – naa – t – uh – r
Oublier	To Forget	Ooh – b – li – ay
Parfait	Perfect	Paa – r – fay
Passeport	Passport	Paa – s – po – r
Passer	To spend time	Paa – say
Ajouter	To add	Aa – jooh – tay
Valeurs morales	Moral values	Vaa – l – uh – r – moh – raa – l
Carence	Deficiency	Kaa – roh – n – s
Réagir	To react	Ray – aa – ji – r
Protéine	Protein	Pr – o – tay – i – n
Calcium	Calcium	Kaa – l – si – om
Vitamine	Vitamin	Vi - taa – mi – n
Système actuel	Current system	Si – s – t – uh – m – aa – k – tooh – el
Arrêt cardiaque	Cardiac arrest	Aa – ray – kaa – r – di – a – k
Alimentation	Food	Aa – li – mon – taa – si – oh
S'attaquer	To tackle	Saa – taa – kay
Par instance	For instance	Paa – r – ah – n – s – toh – s
Science	Science	Si – oh – n – s
Malnutrition	Malnutrition	Maa – l – nooh – tri – si – oh
Diabète	Diabetes	Di – a – beh – t
Obésité	Obesity	O – bay – si – tay
Carrière	Career	Kaa – ri – eh – r
Façonner	To shape	Faa – so – nay
Formation	Training	Fo – r – maa – si – oh
Confiance	Trust/ Confidence	Kon – fi – oh – s
Théorique	Theoretical	Th – ay – o – ri – k
Motivation	Motivation	Mo – ti – va – si – oh
Par	By	Paa – r
Administration des affaires	Business Administration	Aa – d – mi – ni – s – traa – si – oh – day – z – aa – fay – r

Pour conclure	To conclude	Pooh – r – ko – n – k – looh – r
Vie réelle	Real life	V – ray – el
Relever	To raise	Ruh – luh – vay
Peu importe	No matter	P – ah – m – poh – r – t
En ligne	Online	Oh – li – n – yuh

Conclusion

I'd like to tell you how impressed I am with how well you followed my instructions. Throughout this book, I've done my best to put you in a position to succeed, and I hope I've done so. I firmly believe I have, but the proof will be in the pudding of studying and applying French in your everyday life. I completely expect you to do that.

This is not just about the French language, grammar or vocabulary, but if you have done so far, you should have laid a solid foundation for basing your future learning of the French language and being well on your path to fluency. It doesn't take ten years, or even one, to learn French. You might be shocked to discover that you already know a lot of French.

Yes, French is full of odd rules and peculiarities, exaggeratingly precise verb forms and the mysterious problem of "masculine" and "feminine" nouns. Is a chair masculine or feminine? What about a car? (both are feminine, by the way.)

French grammar can be a hassle, even for a native speaker, but if you pay attention to this guide, you can quickly realize that English and French are much more similar than you may have thought at first. Many native English speakers find French to be a simple foreign language to learn. If anything, it should be.

FREE AUDIO OF "LEARN FRENCH for intermediate users"

Download your fee audio from our website:

www.dupontlanguageinstitute.com

or follow this QR code:

To download the file:

Username: AC-book-3
Password: C~*w2T?LwyHh

To open the file:

Password: 6YfNo!$=gT6?cE45

Learn French

The complete learning guide for advanced users to learn French like a pro and be fluent like a native speaker. Includes advanced grammar and exercises and advanced sentences

Introduction

After getting beyond the initial unfamiliarity, French is one of the simplest languages for English speakers to learn.

French is simple for English people to learn since they share so much terminology. Since English has borrowed from French for over 1000 years, beginners will find that many terms are the same and others only slightly different.

Even better, many of these terms are daily words you use. Some examples:

bus --- bus

table --- table

réservation – reservation

responsable – responsible

French purists and the Académie Française are upset that the French are now importing English vocabulary in huge numbers. Many modern words are the same in French but with a French accent. Some examples:

email --- email (purists insist on saying *couriel*, from *courier électronique*, 'electronic mail')

sandwich --- sandwich

internet --- internet

week-end --- weekend

Many French terms and idioms are known to English speakers, while others are being adopted. Some examples might be *vin de table, c'est la vie, raison d'être, nom de plume* and many more.

Finally, English has reinterpreted certain French words. Example: *"chef"*. Chef means "boss" in French, and a *"chef de cuisine"* runs a kitchen. However, English-speaking kitchens and restaurants have kept several French words for roles like *sous-chef, sommelier*, and so on, while *"chef"* in English now means "boss of the kitchen" rather than "boss".

The happy result of the close relationship of the two languages is that any English speaker taking up French starts off already knowing thousands of words that do not need to be learnt. So, one of the biggest tasks of learning a new language --- acquiring new vocabulary --- is considerably reduced! However, French and English share a significant number of *faux amis*, false friends, or words that appear alike but have different meanings, due to their proximity. French "sensible" means "sensitive". You'll soon learn to recognize these hidden traps, so don't worry.

There are other parts of French that tend to throw students off, but none of them are as challenging as they would at first seem to students of the language. The gender of French nouns was something you likely spent a lot of time in class studying about. You can't tell the gender of a word just by looking at it, but these strategies can help you remember or guess correctly more often than not. Feminine nouns often end in -aison, -sion, -tion, or -xion, whereas male nouns typically end in consonants. There are always exceptions, but perhaps these suggestions will help students get started without taking on too much.

Verbs are another challenge that any student of French will have to tackle, but just as with noun gender, learning verbs is not as difficult as some would have you believe. The important thing to know about French verbs is that they "inflect". In other words, their appearance shifts depending on who is carrying out the action. Take a look at conjugations of the verbs *toucher* and *finir* below, for example:

toucher is translated into English as to touch

je touche is translated into English as I touch

tu touches is translated into English as you touch

il/elle touche is translated into English as he/she touches

nous touchons is translated into English as we touch

vous touchez is translated into English as you (pl.) touch

ils/elles touchent is translated into English as they touch

finir is translated into English as to finish

je finis is translated into English as I finish

tu finis is translated into English as you finish

il/elle finit is translated into English as he/she finishes

nous finissons is translated into English as we finish

vous finissez is translated into English as you (pl.) finish

ils/elles finissent is translated into English as they finish

However, it's important to keep in mind that despite the spelling differences, and that they're based on who's performing the activity, all three versions are pronounced precisely the same. This makes things more simpler than they initially appear, at least when speaking.

In addition to conjugating verbs, you will also have to learn how to put these verbs in different tenses, such as the past, present and future. However, the basic French tenses, while different from English, are not particularly challenging to understand. Several of the 'difficult' tenses follow the same logic as English, so once you know how to make the fundamental tenses, the more complex ones are easy to pick up as well.

In this book, we will explain all of the more difficult aspects of French one by one and show you why none of these things are as hard as they might seem at first.

Chapter 1 - Beginning A Conversation

Learning vocabulary is a dull way of trying to speak a new language. In this guide, we want to start with a basic conversation.

Common Greeting Terms

Monsieur --- Sir For any male

Madame, Madam --- For a married woman

Mademoiselle, Miss --- For an unmarried woman

Conversational phrases

French convertional phrases:

1. *Salut, d'où venez-vous?*
2. *Je viens de Paris.*
3. *Quel âge avez-vous?*
4. *J'ai vingt-cinq ans.*
5. *Qu'est-ce que vous aimez faire pendant votre temps libre?*
6. *J'aime lire des livres et regarder des films.*
7. *Avez-vous des frères ou sœurs?*
8. *Oui, j'ai un frère aîné et une sœur cadette.*
9. *Quelle est votre couleur préférée?*
10. *Ma couleur préférée est le bleu.*
11. *Quel est votre plat préféré?*
12. *J'adore les pâtes à la carbonara.*
13. *Vous travaillez ou étudiez?*
14. *Je travaille comme enseignant.*
15. *Quel temps fait-il aujourd'hui?*
16. *Il fait beau et ensoleillé.*
17. *Vous avez des projets pour le week-end?*
18. *Oui, je vais rendre visite à des amis.*
19. *Quelle est votre saison préférée?*
20. *J'aime l'automne pour ses couleurs chaudes.*
21. *Avez-vous des animaux de compagnie?*

22. *Oui, j'ai un chat nommé Minou.*

23. *Comment était votre journée?*

24. *Ma journée s'est bien passée, merci!*

25. *À bientôt!*

* conversation hint: Use **tu** with people that are close to you, like family and friends. **Vous** is formal and used with your boss or elders.

English translation of previous conversations:

1.   Hi, where are you from?
2.   I'm from Paris.
3.   How old are you?
4.   I am twenty-five years old.
5.   What do you like to do in your free time?
6.   I like reading books and watching movies.
7.   Do you have brothers or sisters?
8.   Yes, I have an older brother and a younger sister.
9.   What is your favorite color?
10. My favorite color is blue.
11. What is your favorite dish?
12. I love carbonara pasta.
13. Do you work or study?
14. I work as a teacher.
15. What's the weather like today?
16. It's nice and sunny.
17. Do you have any plans for the weekend?
18. Yes, I'm going to visit some friends.
19. What is your favorite season?
20. I like autumn for its warm colors.
21. Do you have any pets?
22. Yes, I have a cat named Minou.
23. How was your day?
24. My day went well, thank you!
25. See you soon!

Chapter 2 - Rules of The French Alphabet And Pronunciation

Alphabet

26 are the letters that make up the French alphabet. The letters w and k are utilized very seldom, mostly in measurements such as kilo. Punctuation looks the same as English except quotation marks, which are written like this: « *Je suis fatigué.* »

Not every French dialect makes use of all of the language's 17 vowels: /a/, /ɑ/, /e/, /ɛ/, /ɛː/, /ə/, /i/, /o/, /ɔ/, /y/, /u/, /œ/, /ø/.

A single consonant at the end of a French word is silent since pronunciation is based on spelling. In contrast, the final f, k, q, and l are spoken when they appear in words. Depending on the context of the word, the last c may be pronounced or left silent.

The next word in a sentence, when it starts with a vowel, takes the last consonant of the previous word, for example, *vous avez* is pronounced: vou-Za-vay.

The t of et is never pronounced. Doubling the n at the end of the word makes the n to be pronounced as in chien to chienne.

Pronunciation

Most French words have the accent or stress in the last syllable.

Diacritical marks

In proper French writing, you will come across various diacritical marks such as the acute accent (*é*), the grave accent (*à, è, ù*), the circumflex (*â, ê, î, ô, û*), the diaeresis (¨), and the cedilla (ç). Each of these marks serves a distinct purpose.

The acute accent, or <u>accent aigu</u> (é), is used exclusively over the letter "*e*" and represents the sound /e/. In modern French, it has replaced many instances where "e" followed by a consonant, often "s" in the past, used to be used. For example, "*écouter*" replaces the older form "escouter."

The grave accent, or accent grave (*à, è, ù*), is employed over "*a*" or "*u*" Its main function is to differentiate between homophones, such as "*à*" (meaning "to") and "*a*" (meaning "has"), or "*ou*" (meaning "or") and "*où*" (meaning "where"). When placed on top of an "e," it indicates the sound /ɛ/.

The circumflex, or accent <u>circonflexe</u> (*â, ê, î, ô, û*), signifies the sounds /ɑ/, /ɛ/, and /o/ when placed over the letters "a," "e," and "o," respectively. However, in modern Parisian French, the distinction between the sounds /a/ and /ɑ/ represented by "a" and "â" is becoming less common, and they are often pronounced the same as [a]. In Belgian French, "*êis*" is pronounced as [ɛː].

The <u>cedilla</u> (ç) appears under the letter "c" and alters its pronunciation to /s/ instead of /k/. For example, "*je lance*" means "I throw" with the "c" pronounced as [s] before "e," whereas "*je lançais*" means "I was throwing" without the cedilla, and "c" is pronounced as [k] before "a". When "ç" is placed in front of the vowels "a," "o," or "u," it softens the sound from the hard /k/ to the softer /s/. For instance, "*ça*" is pronounced as /sa/. However, it's important to note that the cedilla (ç) is never used before the vowels "e," "i," or "y," as these vowels always have the soft /s/ sound (e.g., *ce, ci, cycle*).

Additionally, in French, the diacritical mark tilde (˜) is placed above the letter "n" to indicate Spanish origin for a word or name. Like other diacritics, the tilde has no effect on the alphabetical order.

Ligatures

Ligatures are combinations of two letters, œ and æ, which are treated as equivalent to the sequences "*oe*" and "*ae*" respectively.

Œ:

In certain words, ⟨oe⟩ is contracted into the mandatory ligature Œ. Some of these words are native to French and have pronunciations such as /œ/ or /ø/. For instance, "sœur" meaning "sister" is pronounced /sœʁ/, and "œuvre" meaning "work (of art)" is pronounced /œvʁ/. Œ is also used in words of Greek origin, such as "cœlacanthe" for "coelacanth." In cases where œ appears after the letter "c," the pronunciation of "c" can vary, being /k/ in some instances (e.g., "cœur") and /s/ in others (e.g., "cœlacanthe").

Æ:

The ligature Æ is rare and primarily appears in certain words of Latin and Greek origin, like "tænia," "ex æquo," "cæcum," and "æthyse" (referring to a plant known as dog's parsley).

French vowels

/i/ - as in "*vie*"

/e/ - as in "*fée*"

/ɛ/ - as in "*sel*"

/a/ - as in "*gars*"

/y/ - as in "*vu*" (This sound is not present in English)

/ø/ - as in "*le*" (This sound is not present in English)

/œ/ - as in "*veulent*" (This sound is not present in English)

/u/ - as in "*doux*"

/o/ - as in "*faux*"

/ɔ/ - as in "*homme*"

/ɑ/ - as in "*bas*"

French Consonants:

/p/ - pronounced as in "*plage*"

/b/ - pronounced as in "*bon*"

/t/ - pronounced as in "*terre*"

/d/ - pronounced as in "*dîner*"

/k/ - pronounced as in "*cou*"

/g/ - pronounced as in "*gare*"

/f/ - pronounced as in "*flic*"

/v/ - pronounced as in "*vous*"

/l/ - pronounced as in "*le*"

/s/ - pronounced as in "*sac*"

/z/ - pronounced as in "*zoo*"

/ʃ/ - pronounced as in "*chat*"

/ʒ/ - pronounced as in "*japonais*"

/m/ - pronounced as in "*mêler*"

/n/ - pronounced as in "*nous*"

/ɲ/ - pronounced as in "*agneau*" (This sound is found only in French)

/ŋ/ - pronounced as in "*camping*" (This phoneme is present in French but with Americanized influence)

/R/ - pronounced as in "*rue*" (The "R" sound is modified in French)

Articles

Where English only has two indefinite articles and one definite, French has up to seven.

There are three distinct types of the definite article that correlate to the article "the" in English: *Le, La and Les*. There is also the singular l' used before vowels

The gender and number (singular or plural) of the word determine the use that is appropriate.

The singular male nouns utilize *Le*.

Le garcon, le président

The singular feminine nouns use *La*

La fille, la dame

Plural nouns of any gender utilize *Les*

Les garçons, les filles.

Before any vowel, the letter *L'* is always written in the singular, regardless of gender

L'enfant

Similar to the articles "a/an" and "some" in English, there are three different forms of the indefinite article in French.

They are *Un, une* and *des*.

Partitive articles are used in the singular with non-count nouns:

They are: *du, de la* and *de l'*

Un is used with singular masculine nouns.

Un garcon, un président

Une is used with singular feminine nouns

Une fille, une dame

Des is used with plural nouns, whatever gender they may be

Des garçons, des filles,.

The partitive forms are used in the singular

Du café, de la bière

Nouns and Adjectives

French assigns a specific gender (either masculine or feminine) to any word, be it a task, creature, or a country.

Nouns ending in −O (singular) and −I (plural) are masculine, while those ending in −A (singular) and −E (plural) are feminine.

Chapter 3 - The Imperative and Subjunctive Mood and Passive Voice

The Imperative Mood

The imperative mood is one of the easiest moods to navigate for foreign learners given its similar endings across all group verbs and the fact that most of it is the same as present tense conjugations—not to mention the few persons that can be conjugated in the imperative!

- *Prends ton manteau* – Take your coat

- *Allez donc voir à la réception si personne n'a trouvé vos clés* – Go see at the reception if somebody found your keys

- *Sois plus courageux* – Be braver

1ˢᵗ -group verbs: *MANGER – (tu) Mange! (nous) Mangeons! (vous) Mangez!*

Important note: indeed, do not add an 's' in the imperative mood for *tu*.

2ⁿᵈ -group verbs: FINIR – *Finis! Finissons! Finissez!*

3ʳᵈ -group verbs:

- verbs with present tense forms: *DORMIR/ COURIR/ SENTIR/ VOIR/ CROIRE/ VENIR/ FAIRE/ DIRE/ LIRE/ PRENDRE* and its derivatives (*apprendre, surprendre, reprendre, méprendre, etc...*)

- (*Dors, dormons, dormez; vois, voyons, voyez...*)

- common auxiliaries (*pouvoir, vouloir, devoir*) are generally never conjugated in the imperative

- *falloir*, being a strictly impersonal verb, cannot be conjugated in the imperative

- verbs and auxiliaries with different forms: *SAVOIR (sache, sachons, sachez); ÊTRE (sois/swa/, soyons/swayõ/, soyez/swayé/); AVOIR (aie/è/, ayons/éyõ/, ayez/éyé/); ALLER (va, allons, allez)*

What about you train yourself to use some imperative forms before moving on to the next major conjugation in French, the subjunctive mood:

- *...(croire) ce que tu veux, ce n'est pas moi qui ai pris ton ordinateur.*

Believe what you think, I wasn't the one who took your computer.

- *Tu dois prendre des forces: ... (manger) plus de soupe!*

You've got to gain strength: eat more soup!

- *... (être) plus forts contre l'adversité!*

Let us be stronger against adversity!

- Answers: Crois/ Mange *(with the 's', remember?)*/ Soyons

The Subjunctive Mood

While you will surely not have to use the subjunctive mood when speaking French, it is used in a couple of contexts, which you should at least be aware of—its construction may especially be confusing if you have never been exposed to it, so this section will at least give you more tools to understand French more closely.

The most important thing to remember is that verbs in the subjunctive are always preceded by que, which is why it is included in the conjugation tables for you to remember this particularity of French.

- after verbs expressing doubt, desire, possibility:

You will most likely encounter the subjunctive, and have to use it, after those particular:

- *aimer que*, conditional – *J'aimerais que nous puissions aller au cinéma tous ensemble* – I would like all of us to be able to go to the cinema together.

- *souhaiter que*, conditional – *Il souhaiterait que nous en terminions avec cette affaire le plus rapidement possible* – He'd prefer that we get that matter wrapped up as fast as possible.

- *préférer que*, conditional – *Je préfèrerais que tu ne touches à rien; je n'ai pas encore fait estimer ces vases* – I'd rather you didn't touch anything; I haven't yet had these vases estimated.

- *espérer que*, only in the past – *Ils espéraient que leur patron leur donne une augmentation, mais en vain* – They were hoping that their boss would give them a raise, but to no avail.

- *douter que*, indicative – *Nous doutons qu'il puisse venir* – We doubt he may come/ We doubt he is able to come.

- after impersonal constructions

Impersonal constructions suggesting obligation or necessary conditions are commonly followed by the subjunctive or the infinitive depending on how it is worded; please pay close attention to the following examples:

Il faut que (subj) – *Il faut que tu sois en forme pour ton entretien d'embauche demain (être)* – You have to be in top form for your job interview tomorrow.

Il faut (infinitive) – *Il faut prendre des précautions contre la grippe en hiver (prendre)* – One must take precautions against the flu in winter.

Il est préférable que (subj) – *Il est préférable qu'il prenne quelques jours de vacances* – It would be better if he took some time off.

Il est préférable de (infinitive) – *Il est préférable de poser des questions si l'on n'a pas compris quelque chose* – It's better to ask quetions if you haven't understood something.

As these examples highlight, those impersonal constructions can be used in two ways: the infinitive form in French is rather general and will englobe everyone or a group of people, while the subjunctive form is conjugated according to a particular subject (ex: *que tu sois en forme pour ton entretien d'embauche*).

First is an overview of these constructions before diving into how to conjugate verbs in the subjunctive:

- *Il faut que/ Il faut* (obligation, similar to 'must')

- *Il est préférable que/ Il est préférable de* ('it is preferrable to', literally)

- *Il est nécessaire que/ Il est nécessaire de* (obligation; il faut is preferred and more common)

- *Il est (très/ peu) probable que* ('it is (very/ hardly) likely that'; exclusively used with que and a subjunctive)

Conjugations

The 1st group of verbs is the easiest to learn since only the "nous" and "vous" forms under go changes compared to the simple present tense:

For verbs like *MANGER/CHANTER*, you need to remove the -r:

que je mange - que je chante

que tu manges - que tu chantes (often identified by the -s for the "tu" form)

qu'il mange - qu'il chante

que nous mangions - que nous chantions (+ ions)

que vous mangiez - que vous chantiez

qu'ils mangent - qu'ils chantent

For the verb *ALLER*, pay close attention to the additional 'i' in the stem, which will shift slightly:

que j'aille /ʒ'aj/ - que tu ailles /t(y) aj/ - qu'il aille /il aj/

que nous allions /nuz-alyõ/ - que vous alliez /vu-za-lje/ - qu'ils aillent /ilz-aj/

The 2nd -group verbs have the same endings as the two verbs above, with one exception: the ss radical that you have already encountered with them (*vous finissiez*), will be here used for all persons:

FINIR – CHOISIR

Que je finisse – que je choisisse

Que tu finisses – que tu choisisses

Qu'il finisse – qu'il choisisse

Que nous finissions – que nous choisissions

Que vous finissiez – que vous choisissiez

Qu'ils finissent – qu'ils choisissent

The 3rd group of verbs, known for their complexity, might prove to be the most challenging for you. Let's delve into the details of their subjunctive conjugations so you can understand how each one works.

You'll notice that most of the verbs listed below have different stems for the "*je*," "*tu*," "*il*", and "*ils*" forms, as opposed to the "*nous*" and "*vous*" forms:

1. Verbs ending in -ir like *dormir, courir, sentir*:

Remove the -ir ending and add the endings you've already seen:

que je dorme - que tu dormes - qu'il dorme -

que nous dormions - que vous dormiez - qu'ils dorment.

2. The verb *voir*:

Remove the -r and conjugate as above, but remember to add an 'i' for the "*nous*" and "*vous*" forms:

que je voie - que tu voies - qu'il voie -

que nous voyions - que vous voyiez - qu'ils voient.

Verbs like *apprendre, prendre, surprendre:*

3. The radical changes to "*prenn(e)*" and "*pren-*":

que je prenne - que tu prennes - qu'il prenne -

que nous prenions - que vous preniez - qu'ils prennent.

4. The verb *vendre*:

The radical becomes "*vend(e)*":

que je vende - que tu vendes - qu'il vende,

que nous vendions - que vous vendiez - qu'ils vendent.

5. The verb *venir*:

It has irregular radicals "*vienne/ven-*":

que je vienne - que tu viennes - qu'il vienne,

que nous venions - que vous veniez - qu'ils viennent.

6. The verb *devoir*:

It has irregular radicals "*doive/dev-*":

que je doive - que tu doives - qu'il doive, -

que nous devions - que vous deviez - qu'ils doivent.

7. The verb *savoir*:

The radical changes to "*sach(e)*":

que je sache - que tu saches - qu'il sache,

que nous sachions - que vous sachiez - qu'ils sachent.

8. The verb *vouloir*:

It has irregular radicals "*veuille/voul-*":

que je veuille - que tu veuilles - qu'il veuille -

que nous voulions - que vous vouliez - qu'ils veuillent.

9. The verb *pouvoir*:

It becomes "*puiss(e)*":

que je puisse - que tu puisses - qu'il puisse,

que nous puissions - que vous puissiez - qu'ils puissent.

10. The verb *faire*:

It turns into "*fass(e)*":

que je fasse - que tu fasses - qu'il fasse -

que nous fassions - que vous fassiez - qu'ils fassent.

11. Verbs like *dire, lire*:

The 'r' becomes an 's':

que je dise/lise - que tu dises - qu'il dise -

que nous disions - que vous disiez - qu'ils disent.

Finally, the irregular verbs "*être*" and "*avoir*" have unique forms in the subjunctive:

- *Être: que je sois, que tu sois, qu'il soit, que nous soyons, que vous soyez, qu'ils soient.*
- *Avoir: que j'aie, que tu aies, qu'il aie, que nous ayons, que vous ayez, qu'ils aient.*

The Passive Voice

Using the passive voice in the present or past tense is incredibly easy and will build on your knowledge of present conjugations for the auxiliaries involved.

Whereas the passé composé required different auxiliaries depending on the action described (movement-oriented or not), it is the auxiliary être here that does all the work, just like English. When the agent is introduced by by in English, it is par/par/ that is used in French:

- Past (passé composé): *j'ai été, tu as été, il/elle a été, nous avons été, vous avez été, ils ont été*
- Present: *je suis, tu es, il est, nous sommes, vous êtes, ils sont*
- Future: *je serai, tu seras, il sera, nous serons, vous serez, ils seront*

You may also want to note that since *être* is used in the passive voice, any adjectives or past participates following it must bear the mark for gender or number if the subject is female or plural:

He was accused of shoplifting – Il a été accusé de vol à l'étalage. (*a été* here is the *passé composé* form of *être*, since it refers to a past action).

We (female) were tested rigorously by a group of professionals – *Nous avons été testées rigoureusement par un groupe de professionnels.*

I (male) will be interviewed at 3:00 p.m. tomorrow – *Je serai interviewé à quinze heures demain.*

Many buildings are being built in my neighborhood – *De nombreux bâtiments sont en train d'être construits dans mon quartier.*

1) neighborhood – *un quartier* (m)/kartyé/

2) building – *un bâtiment* (m)

3) to build – *bâtir, construire* (2nd group, 3rd group); the circumflex accent is compulsory no matter the conjugation

Être is indeed very versatile when it comes to passive; however, you may also encounter a particular construction that is typical to French.

Se faire: a very idiomatic construction

Se faire has two different meanings in French:

--- it may help to express an action that is performed on oneself (*se faire mal*, to hurt oneself; *se faire violence*, to restrain oneself from doing something, to force oneself to do something)

I hurt myself while cutting down wood – *Je me suis fait mal en coupant du bois*

Some of the guests had to stop themselves from binging on the cake – *Quelques invités ont dû se faire violence pour ne pas s'empiffrer de gâteau*

- it may be employed strictly for passive structures when the result of the action is negative for a living subject (an animal or human being):

I was scammed two months ago – *Je me suis fait arnaquer il y a deux mois*

He was robbed of 500 euros – *Il s'est fait voler cinq cents euros*

We were cut off by an impolite driver – *Nous nous sommes fait couper la route par un conducteur malpoli*

• to scam someone – *arnaquer* (1st group) *quelqu'un*

• to be, get scammed – *se faire arnaquer*

- it may also be used for very specific actions that someone commonly does for someone else (*se faire prescrire des médicaments*, to be prescribed medicine; *se faire renvoyer/être renvoyé*, to be expelled)

My niece's dog was prescribed antibiotics – *Le chien de ma nièce s'est fait prescrire des antibiotiques* (only se faire works in this case)

Many students were expelled from prestigious universities after too many protests across the country – *Beaucoup d'étudiants se sont fait renvoyer d'universités prestigieuses après de trop nombreuses manifestations à travers le pays* (être renvoyé may also be used here: *ont été renvoyés...*)

Impersonal constructions: translating the passive/One should not...

The passive voice in French will be majorly used when referring to an action performed by someone or something onto someone or something; for instance, the traditional The mouse is eaten by the cat.

However, it so happens that passive voice constructions in English can be much more general (English is spoken in many countries), and it is this particularity that this book will help you translate into French.

For these cases where the passive voice refers to a general phenomenon or sort of 'truth of life', French will heavily privilege using an active voice (with regular, so to speak, conjugations), and will re-transcribe the general quality of that statement with the pronoun on ('it, we').

What is great about on — as you have already seen — is that it can accommodate a rather fluid number of people without singling them out specifically or giving out too many details; in essence, using it in such contexts is how French re-transcribes that vagueness or absence of information as to who does what:

English is spoken in many countries – *On parle anglais dans de nombreux pays*

Beef is commonly served with rice and carrots – *On sert généralement du boeuf avec du riz et des carottes*

It is often thought that walking under a ladder brings bad luck – *On pense souvent que marcher en-dessous d'une échelle porte malheur*

- to bring bad luck – *porter malheur* ('carry, bring bad luck')

Once the other kind of sentences where on is used as an impersonal pronoun are covered, you will be perfectly fluent in understanding all its nuances—yes, that pronoun can be confusing, and you may at first be tempted to think that there is a 'we' person in there that doesn't have anything to do with the content of the sentence... but it is now one more path cleared for you to reach greater heights on your language learning journey!

One must/ can/ should... = where French and English intertwine

You are in luck! Impersonal sentences conveying orders or recommendations may be translated in two ways in French:

- *Il faut que...* ('one has to'), *il est nécessaire que/ de...* which has already been covered extensively in the Subjunctive subsection

- *on ne doit pas* ('one should not'), which has the advantage of requiring very little conjugation and being extremely similar to English.

One must always pay attention to the small beauties of life – *Il faut toujours prêter attention aux petites merveilles de la vie./ On doit toujours prêter attention...*

Anything, something, nothing...

anything (not... anything): *rien*

- I don't know anything about this new play – *Je ne sais rien de cette nouvelle pièce de théâtre*

anything (in an affirmative statement): *n'importe quoi*/npo'rte-kwa/

- We have no idea what caused this; it could be anything – *Nous n'avons aucune idée de ce qui a causé ça; ça pourrait être n'importe quoi* not... any: *ne/ n'* [verb/auxiliary] *aucun(e)(s)* [noun, if there is one]

- I don't have any idea how to get there – *Je n'ai aucune idée de comment aller là-bas*

nothing: *rien*

something: *quelque chose*

anywhere (not... anywhere): *nulle part*

- I can't seem to find my keys anywhere – *Je n'arrive pas à trouver mes clés* (anywhere here wouldn't be translated into French)/ *Je ne trouve mes clés nulle part* (*nulle part* as not)

anywhere (in an affirmative statement): *n'importe où*

- It's like looking for a needle in a haystack: my new glasses could be anywhere – *C'est comme chercher une aiguille dans une botte de foin: mes nouvelles lunettes pourraient être n'importe où*

nowhere: *nulle part*

- I find holidays much more relaxing when you are in the middle of nowhere – *Je trouve les vacances beaucoup plus relaxantes quand on est au milieu de nulle part* (*milieu*, m = middle)

somewhere: *quelque part*

- But there should be at least one open restaurant somewhere! – *Mais il doit bien y avoir un restaurant d'ouvert quelque part*

anytime: *n'importe quand*

- You may contact us anytime between 9:00 a.m. and 3:00 p.m. – *Vous pouvez nous contacter n'importe quand entre neuf heures du matin et trois heures de l'après-midi/ entre neuf heures et quinze heures*

sometime: *un de ces jours*

- We should schedule an appointment sometime – *Nous devrions convenir d'un rendez-vous* (formal)/ *fixer un rendez-vous* (more common) *un de ces jours*

somehow: *d'une certaine manière*, when expressing disbelief, is conveyed through the conditional or through *de manière/ de façon surprenante* (lit. in a surprising way):

- He somehow managed to not follow any instruction – *Il a réussi, de façon surprenante, à ne suivre aucune instruction*

somewhat: *quelque peu/kèlke-peu/*, invariable

- I found his indications somewhat misleading – *J'ai trouvé ses indications quelque peu trompeuses*

Chapter 4 - Get Into The Mindset

There are two different primary mindsets to language acquisition in the world right now. There are more in other subsets, but the two most commonly encountered are the academic sort --- the sort which has you sitting in a classroom, possibly all day, drilling you with vocabulary lessons and grammatical concepts in an academic context --- and the immersive sort --- these are the ones which are generally espoused by polyglots, so I think that taking time in order to establish how you can work within this framework is super important.

I don't think there's anything explicitly wrong with the academic manner. But I do think it has its shortcomings as a form of language pedagogy intended for simple and natural language learning.

The reason that we use classrooms in order to teach things and we teach in such book-based ways in general is that teaching the myriad lessons which are taught at an institution like so demands that one have dedicated linear study. For a great many things, this works well. Mathematics, a musical instrument, chemistry, and so forth. For linguistics, it can work, but it's very far detached from our natural forms of language learning.

What actually works best for linguistics, many have found --- it's not a universal thing, remember, but it's just the thing which works best for the majority of people --- is an immersion based learning experience. Or in other words, an experience where they're surrounded by the language and are practicing it not just in the context of tests and flash cards, but in the television they watch, the applications on their phone, the people that they talk to, and so on.

I've spoken to a lot of people in my life who have tried to learn this or that language. They always tell me that "I'm just not cut out for learning languages" or something like that, and it's absurd.

I'm going to be honest: the traditional methods for language learning require a certain amount of passivity. We aren't made to learn language passively. It's not something that we're created to do. And when people are sitting in classrooms learning drab vocab which may or may not be something they'll actually talk about, I can't help feel like there's a lack of proper action or motivation. Often, too, that's what will kill the person's ability to learn: an utter lack of motivation due to the fact that they couldn't care less about the thing they're learning.

Let me make this clear: language learning is not easy. It can be made easier, but it's not easy. Saying that you expect to learn a language in a month or with only ten minutes of practice a day is a lot like those diet pills that proclaim themselves to be some kind of snake oil that will make you shed 100 pounds in a year: it doesn't happen. Full stop. It is possible to learn a language very quickly --- in two to three months --- with absolute dedication and what actually totals out to a lot of hard work, just like it's possible to lose 100 pounds in a year. However, it is not a passive activity.

Language learning happens in three ways:

1) Receiving input

2) Generating output

3) Receiving feedback/correction

It's through these three alone that you're going to learn a language. The input could be anything. It could be a gigantic "For Dummies" book that walks through every step of the language for beginners, or it could be a barebones explanatory sheet that teachers the person the basics before putting them on their own.

The output happens in one way only: you personally creating the phrases from the concepts that you know and from the things that you know. This is the only way that output can happen.

Receiving feedback and correction happens through somebody more proficient in the language than you are correcting you on this topic or that of the language after hearing you speak. They could be anybody from a teacher to a pen-pal to a girlfriend who was fluent in the language. It doesn't matter, what matters is that somehow and some way you're getting it.

So with those aspects of language learning fleshed out, now what we need to settle is how we can get those. The fact is that a lot of people, and in fact a lot of traditional language learning systems, will put up a fight against these natural language learning mechanisms. But I refuse to do that.

Here are the things that I'm going to emphasize from a standpoint of your demeanor towards language learning:

- *Passion* for the language
- *Connection* to the content
- *Immersion* rather than arbitrary rote memorization
- *Confidence* in your ability to speak
- *Willingness* to go out of your comfort zone.

You need a passion for the language if you want to learn it. Even a fake one, if you have to conjure one up out of thin air. At the beginning, learning a language is going to be awful. You're not going to know anything, you're going to be extremely lost and confused. You have to care enough about the language that you're working with that you can just keep on going with it even through rough patches and plateaus.

You need a connection to the content if you genuinely want to retain it. I find that in a lot of people, the only way for them to remember something is if they find that to some degree they care about it. This doubles up on the first point by reinforcing the idea that if you care about something, you're more likely to both work hard on it and to retain it.

You need immersion rather than rote memorization because immersion is going to teach you to use the language everywhere and use context to figure out new words and sounds. This is how we naturally learn our first languages and it's how we can naturally learn even more if we manage to tap into that primitive "lightbulb" notion of making things click and making gears simply turn. This builds upon the first and second points because I insist that you immerse yourself in topics that you care about, and help you to seek them out.

You need confidence in your ability to speak. Not in your ability to speak the language, you're going to be awful at the language for a long time. You need to accept that. "A long time" could be any number of measures from a month to several years. You have to realize that your reinforcement and your feedback is only going to come by speaking to people you've never spoken to before in a language that you're not entirely comfortable in. By getting out of that comfort zone and getting comfortable "being wrong", as well as by accepting that you will often flub up in seemingly simple ways, you will become a better speaker of the language even faster.

Lastly, you need willingness to go out of your comfort zone. This is something that only you can give yourself. I can harp on how important this and that thing is all that I want, but ultimately it's up to you to summon the willpower to actually make something happen for yourself in the context of language learning.

You'll need to summon a lot of willpower, in fact. This method is "fast and easy", but it's most certainly not a timesaver. If you want to learn a language in 10 minutes per day, you should relegate yourself to barely knowing the language in 4 years' time. If you want to learn it faster, you have to accept that your entire world will be in that language now, to the extent that you can make it so, and you have to accept that you're going to be spending an hour or two working in that language, translating both to and from, and that's not even including any time that you spend talking to your tutor.

But if you follow through with this method, I can guarantee you that you'll be a great speaker of whatever language it is that you want to speak.

Chapter 5 - Learn From What You Love

You will never be ready to read or listen to something written or recorded by a native speaker. Neither when you finish those six volumes of French textbooks. This imaginary point in time where you will magically be ready to understand everything doesn't exist. But the truth is that you don't even need to understand half of everything. You just need some simple rules which you will find in this chapter.

If you really want to reach an advanced level of French within a few years, it is absolutely necessary to read, listen, and watch native French materials for multiple hours every day. Although if your goals aren't set on reaching a high level of French in such a short time frame, start with however much time you can commit to every day.

Doing more than 90 minutes or so every day of coursebook study and Anki review, however, is not recommended. When strict study time begins to exceed this amount of time, you'll begin to run into problems similar to those mentioned in the last two chapters. For that reason, after this strict study period ends, we encourage reading, listening, watching, and learning from native French materials as much as possible every day.

The 20-Minute Rule

The common French used in video games, comics, novels, websites, movies, and television shows may be analyzed and used as a learning resource. However, you know what a massive undertaking it is if you have ever attempted to study any of these things attentively. Just how can one maintain concentration long enough to analyze an entire internet article or even a short tale sentence by sentence? How can you handle French-only websites without going crazy? In what ways are TV shows readable for academic purposes?

How can you maintain the motivation to keep up with these unrealistic study schedules after only two days? The situation continues to worsen. You may lose your early enthusiasm for learning a new language by forcing yourself to study for long periods of time until you would rather do anything else.

You spend around 20 minutes immersed in the French language content of your choice, without the benefit of English subtitles or translations. Be on the lookout for unfamiliar terms that have appeared more than once in your reading, seeing, and listening. Do not pause the reading, watching, or listening to note down the unfamiliar terms that are repeated twice or more. For future use, make sure to include things like page numbers, playback times, audio track numbers, and screenshots.

When studying anything written originally in French, you are permitted to use a dictionary as often as necessary. When you're just reading the text, there is far less context to keep you focused as opposed to when there is video or audio content, and this is particularly true when there are quite a few terms that you are unfamiliar with.

After around 20 minutes, pause to go at your list of recurring terms. Use grammar guides and the internet's dictionaries to dissect these words and lines and understand their meanings. Now that you understand the context of these often-used words and phrases, you may use Anki to study the portions you choose most relevant. A passage in this book might be anything from a single large phrase to many sentences to a short conversation.

The Power of Context

But why pick just one or two passages to practice using Anki and not three or more passages? There are two main reasons behind this choice. First, the process of creating the Anki cards for just one or two passages already takes a significant amount of time and work. And second, it is to set a strict limit on how much you review through Anki.

To maximize your time for studying native French via reading and listening, you should use Anki as little as possible. More manageable word and context lists may be made with the aid of the 20-Minute Rule.

The acquisition of linguistic competence is facilitated by exposure to new vocabulary, phrases, and grammatical points in a variety of settings. Each subsequent contact likewise reinforces their memory in our minds.

This is why Anki allows you to practice with no texts at all, allowing you to get right back into reading and listening. If there are any terms or grammatical rules that you have looked up several times but still don't understand, you may wish to keep Anki for later. Using Anki or even the Goldlist Method to review every single new word or phrase you have learned can severely slow down the time it takes you to reach fluency.

As you read, listen, and mine a single source of native French for vocabulary and phrases, a remarkable process begins to unfold. By rereading the same sections over the course of several days or weeks, you will eventually get familiar with the topic's lexical staples. If you already have a solid grasp of high-frequency words, you could have an easier time grasping new information from that source.

Learning new vocabulary and expressions in the context of a compelling tale or plot makes it much easier to retain. Each and every sentence has the potential to stand out and become a memorable quote. Context is everything.

Forget the Rest!

There is no need to translate entire drama episodes or online articles. Learning everything on your high frequency word list should be a large enough chunk of work as is. But if you feel you can handle more, by all means go through as many lines or sentences as you can before mental fatigue eventually surfaces. That fatigue signals that it's time to take a quick mental break before moving on to new content.

Don't bother watching movies or reading articles only once. To maximize your learning, avoid watching the same video, movie, or TV show many times in a row. That's not very entertaining. The vast internet library of original French content, though, could be more entertaining.

French Is Not Too Fast

Using English subtitles to watch French TV shows, movies, dramas, and videos is an English reading activity with some background noise. You will learn nothing outside a few basic words. Even if you use them to zone out after a long day of studying French or to help you concentrate on the tale, native speakers will always speak too quickly.

If you don't make an effort every day to comprehend their rapid speech, you'll never catch what they're saying. However, it will be difficult for you to understand them at the beginning and intermediate levels since they utilize hundreds of words that you do not yet know. To respond to this question, you must regard listening comprehension as a talent. Building this ability requires using the words you do know in context to fill in the gaps where your vocabulary may be lacking.

Only through determined effort will you be able to master the foreign tongue. You should take advantage of every opportunity that helps you improve your reading and listening skills. The common belief that mastery in any field requires around 10,000 hours of dedicated effort has been widely disproven. However, most people agree on the need for regular practice.

Most students of a foreign language have the most trouble with listening comprehension because they are not exposed to nearly enough understandable information to master the language as native speakers really speak it. While the audio components of language classes are helpful, you may need more exposure to local speakers to grasp the language truly.

You should listen for the complete 20 minutes before reading the subtitles, even if they will help you understand the most important parts of the movie. Subtitles are real-time practice since they don't include the native speakers you'll hear in the actual world.

Most of us don't come from families where we'd be exposed to French for eight to twelve hours a day for ten years or more. The cost of hiring a tutor for even one hour a day may quickly add up. With exposure to native-speaking adults, your hearing is preserved. This issue may be mitigated by consistently engaging in the Anki activities and by listening to and reading native French resources on a daily basis.

No Subtitles, But How?

Train your ears to listen with your full attention and find the words that are both unknown to you and that are repeated frequently. The moments that you desire to understand the most can also be learned. Simply jot down the video times for later reference and don't press pause.

In case there are irremovable English subtitles in a video, you can block them from view by cutting out and placing a wide and thick but short piece of paper in front of your computer screen.

Keeping English subtitles out can be fairly difficult for some folks. You will be tested. You'll need hope and drive to break the pattern of always speaking English. The belief that you need to know everything in order to fully appreciate something will grow if even a little bit of time is spent on it.

However, this assumption is not always correct when you factor in the pleasure you get as your French comprehension expands day by day. The joy of witnessing genuine development in oneself is unparalleled. It's a great way to boost your confidence.

Starting out with familiar content will help you adjust to the language barrier while still enjoying the story.

It can be frustrating to watch the same episode or video five or more times in a week, even if doing so is beneficial for listening practice. The same rules for watching and reading in your native language apply. One and finished. And if you find the information particularly interesting, you can always go back and read it again, just like you would in your first language.

Pursue making it a habit to consume media without interrupting your flow. Do not keep pausing to check things up in the dictionary. It's stressful to try something new and not comprehend it right away, but learning takes off when you finally get your hands on something that piques your interest and makes sense to you. Realizing that you can still enjoy your favorite works even if you don't grasp every nuance of the language used is a huge step forward.

Choose Easy

Let's make sure your Anki passages are appropriate for your level. You can still break down vocabulary and grammar in scenarios with four or more unknown words. If these challenging paragraphs from your high-frequency word list keep coming up, you may wish to skip them. Too many new words, phrases, and grammar points might slow down learning and need a lot of research.

These portions can frustrate Anki's activities. Too much difficulty in Anki and in general might make learning and practicing French boring.

Easy choice makes learning French entertaining and addictive. Selecting contexts with one, two, or three new words accelerates learning. When the difficulty is right, we can enter a flow-like condition and enjoy learning.

Double Check Your Work

Once you have broken down your high frequency word list and looked up the new vocabulary and grammatical information, you will have a far better understanding of the meaning of the context they came from. But sometimes it's hard to get a firm grasp on the meaning of the words themselves. When translating from one language to another, it's possible to lose the nuance and nuanced meaning of a sentence. Maybe you've seen the humorous outcomes of this on pictures of badly translated Asian signage or T-shirts. You obviously don't want it to happen to your French speech or writing!

If so, refer to the English subtitles or translations to make sure you understand everything. That said, you shouldn't rush toward speaking English when exposed to local French media. The English subtitles and translations can be checked after the initial 20 minutes of immersion to better understand the underlying tone and meaning of the speech. Before attempting to put what you are learning into practice, be sure you have a solid grasp of the material. This is why English translations are typically included in language textbooks.

This discussion of subtitles and translations may seem confusing at first, so let me try to clarify things. Reading and listening to the original sources is a great way to improve fluency and comprehension. The short-term, high-intensity study is best accomplished with subtitles and translations.

Where to Find French Subtitles

Obtaining the subtitles and transcripts for specific audio and video materials is not always possible. Yet once they are in your hands, learning straight from the material that you love becomes possible.

Perhaps the most readily available source of French and English subtitles for TV shows and movies can be found on Netflix (https://www.netflix.com). The former days of desperately hunting down subtitles for days has come to an end, as Netflix offers Closed Captioning (CC) for virtually any French TV show and movie in their library. In order to fully access these French subtitles and even French-dubbed materials, you will need to change Netflix's language settings to French under "Account" and "My Profile".

Searching the internet for "French subtitles" will net you all kinds of interesting ideas to try out. For example, the website Simpsons Park (http://www.simpsonspark.com) offers French transcripts for full episodes of The Simpsons dubbed in French. These can be accessed by finding the web page for the episode that you are interested in watching and then clicking "Voir le script de l'épisode en VF".

If you are looking for something more inspirational and uplifting, TED Talks in French can be found on YouTube as well by searching YouTube for "Ted Talks français".

And if you are interested in news, politics, and foreign affairs, Euronews (http://fr.euronews.com) provides news coverage in French via video along with full transcripts.

Working Towards Immersion

The secret to being consistent in reading and listening to native French everyday lies in finding the French hobbies that you truly care about. For example, if what you love to do is play video games in your free time, change the language settings to French and don't look back. In fact, it may help to envision yourself as someone from France. It may sound silly, but this kind of creative thinking will enable you to replace your old English hobbies one by one permanently.

Take the things you do in English that truly interest you and stir excitement from deep within and refuse to do them unless they are in French instead. Advanced reading, listening, speaking, and writing skills will come as a natural result of spending thousands of hours living through the language.

Switch your primary source for learning to French books, websites, music, or whatever got you interested in the language in the first place. Let this material become your new textbook. Learning from native French materials that you truly love to read, watch, and listen to for fun makes it an absolute joy to put in those thousands of hours.

Foreign pop culture and TV do not have to be the end goal in learning a language. There is so much more to a language than what you might find on TV. Regardless of the language and culture, low-quality TV programs can numb the mind rather than excite it.

You will know exactly when you find the best native material for you to learn from. How? It will be addicting, and you won't want to put it down even after reading and listening to it all day.

This may require searching far and wide to find native French materials that you genuinely care for, but we do this in our native language all the time. We try new things, and if we don't like them, we look elsewhere. So learn from everything you come across, and when you find yourself continually growing bored, move on to the next thing. There's literally an entire French speaking world to explore.

Some folks may just wish to meet, befriend, and be proficient in communicating with people in French. In this case, Facebook, Twitter, and other social media platforms provide instant gold mines of reading material to dissect.

You may also find new topics to read up on through social media. Press the "Like" button on French pages and groups that pique your interest. Follow famous people that you admire. Immerse your social feed in only French.

If what you truly enjoy is found mostly in reading, all the better. In short, some of the world's most impressive polyglots like Alexander Arguelles and Luca Lampariello claim a strong habit of extensive reading is one of the secrets to their amazing language abilities.

And finally, going full immersion in your home environment is not required by any means, but it offers ample opportunities to get yourself used to relying less on English by reading and listening to more French at all hours of the day. Some of these steps towards immersion you can immediately get used to, but others may take years in order to overwrite old habits that are strongly rooted in your native language.

Here are some ideas. Start your day by reading and watching the weather forecast for France in French. Delete all songs in English from your music library and replace them with French music. Change your computer and phone's language to French. Use French to learn a skill completely new to you like cooking a new dish for example.

Chapter 6 - Negation

Crafting negative sentences in the French language is quite simple. You merely need to use "*ne... pas*" around the verb, while leaving the rest of the sentence unchanged.

For instance:

Original: *Je mange du gâteau.* (I eat cake)

Negative: *Je ne mange pas de gâteau.* (I don't eat cake)

Keep in mind that if the verb starts with a vowel or a silent "*h*," you should use "*n'... pas*" instead.

In colloquial French, the "*ne*" is often dropped. However, the "*ne*" is exclusively used with sentences that include a verb. If a sentence lacks a verb, the negative word stands alone.

For example:

Original: *Ceci n'est pas vrai.* (This is not true)

Colloquial: *Ceci pas vrai.*

Original: *Je ne comprends pas.* (I don't understand)

Colloquial: *Je comprends pas.*

Apart from "*pas*," you can use other negation expressions after "ne":

non:

Typically used as a negative response to a question.

Original: *Marc: A-t-il répondu?* (Did he respond?)

Response: *Sonja: Non, il n'a pas répondu.* (No, he didn't respond)

ne... plus ("no longer"):

The opposite of *encore* (still/yet) and *toujours* (always).

Original: *Elle a décidé de ne plus fumer.* (She decided to no longer smoke)

ne... pas encore ("not yet"):

The negation of *déjà* (already).

Original: Bénédicte: *A-t-il terminé son travail?* (Has he finished his work?)

Response: Nadine: *Non, pas encore.* (No, not yet.)

ne... personne (no one)

Original: *Ils ne voient personne.* (They don't see anyone)

ne... jamais (never):

The negation of *toujours* (always), *quelquefois* (sometimes), *souvent* (often), and *parfois* (occasionally).

Original: *Marie: Vas-tu à la bibliothèque régulièrement?* (Do you go to the library regularly?)

Response: Paul: *Non, je n'y vais jamais.* (No, I never go there)

ne... ni... ni... ("neither... nor"):

The negative form of *et* (and) and *ou* (or).

Original: *Je n'aime ni le café ni le thé.* (I like neither coffee nor tea)

ne... rien (nothing)

Original: *Non merci, je ne veux rien.* (No thank you, I don't want anything)

que (only): Signifies "only" in a sentence.

Original: *Je n'ai que des livres.* (I only have books).

Exercise

Change the following statements into the negative form.

- *Je vais souvent au Canada.*
- *Nous marchons ensemble tout le temps.*
- *J'ai encore faim.*
- *Elle a déjà une voiture.*
- *Il veut toujours se baigner ici.*
- *Elle a beaucoup d'enfants.*
- *Jon Snow sait tout.*
- *Les étudiants ont classe.*
- *Je peux parler français et allemand.*
- *J'aime aller à la plage tous les étés.*

Solutions

- *Je ne vais jamais au Canada*
- *Nous ne marchons jamais ensemble*
- *Je n'ai plus faim.*
- *Elle n'a pas encore de voiture.*
- *Elle ne veut jamais se baigner ici.*
- *Elle n'a pas beaucoup d'enfants.*
- *Jon Snow ne sait rien*
- *Les étudiants n'ont pas classe.*
- *Je ne peux ni parler français ni parler allemand.*
- *Je n'aime pas aller à la plage tous*

Chapter 7 - French Travel And Business Words

In this chapter, you will learn some of the most commonly used French words when traveling and on business.

Travel Terms

<u>The Airport and Plane:</u>

"Quelle est la raison de votre voyage?": What is the reason for your trip?

"Combien de temps restez-vous à/ en/ au/ aux...?: How much time are you staying in...?

Départs: departures

Arrivées: arrivals

Enregistrement des bagages: baggage check

"Pouvez-vous ouvrir votre sac?": Can you open your bag?

Décoller: to take off

Atterrir: to land

Faire une escale: to stop over

Attachez votre ceinture: fasten your seatbelt

Ne fumez pas or Interdiction de fumer: do not smoke or no smoking

Restez assis: remain seated

Éteignez tout appareil électronique: turn off all electronic devices

<u>The Bus:</u>

Le bus: the bus

Quartiers: neighborhoods

Les lignes de bus: bus routes:

Des excursions en bus: bus tours

Un billet: a ticket

Le conducteur de bus: the bus driver

Distributeur automatique: automated ticket vending machine

Le guichet: the ticket window

<u>Entertainment:</u>

L'opéra: the opera

Le concert: the concert

Le ballet: the ballet

Le cinéma: the movies

Le théâtre: the theater

La soirée: the party

Tourist Spots:

La Joconde: The Mona Lisa

Châteaux: castles

Défense d'entrer: no admittance

Photos avec flash interdites: no flash photography

Theater:

Les costumes: the costumes

La pièce: the play

La représentation or Le spectacle: the performance

Monter un pièce: to put on a play

Le rideau: the curtain

La scène: the stage

Le balcon: the balcony

La tragédie: tragedy

La comédie: comedy

L'entracte: the intermission

Business Terms

The Professionals:

Le président-directeur général: the CEO, managing director, or chairman

Le directeur or la directrice: manager of a company or business

Le gérant or la gérante: hotel, shop, or restaurant manager

Le/ la propriétaire: the owner

Le personnel: the employees or staff

Snail Mail and Phone Calls:

Un mobile or un portable: a cellphone

Une carte téléphonique : a calling card

"Allô": "Hello" on the telephone

Dring dring: the French version of "ring ring"

Computers and the Worldwide Web:

L'ordinateur: computer

Le portable: laptop

Le pseudo: username

Le mot de passe: password

Le navigateur: web browser

Surfer sur le Web: to surf the Web

Télécharger: to download

Pièce jointe: an attachment

Envoyer: Send

Insertion: Insert

Fichier: file

Exercise

Construct French sentences based on the following scenarios.

- You need to look for the Louis Vuitton manager.
- You need to borrow a computer and surf the internet.
- Answer the telephone and tell them that you want to speak with the caller's company CEO.
- Tell your friend that you are going to watch a tragedy play first, then a comedy.
- Ask the bus driver about the price of the ticket and the route of the bus.
- Answer this question using French: "Quelle est la raison de votre voyage?"
- You want to know the directions to the museum that holds the Mona Lisa.

Chapter 8 - Socializing in French

Learn these essential phrases for interacting with others:

- Yes in the French language is translated to *oui*

- No in the French language is translated to *non*

- Please in the French language is translated to *s'il vous plait*

- Thank you. in the French language is translated to *Merci.*

- You are welcome. in the French language is translated to *Je vous en prie.*

- Excuse me. in the French language is translated to *Excusez-moi.*

- Sorry in the French language is translated to *pardon*

Salutations

In France, it is customary to kiss someone on both cheeks while welcoming them. However, males are more likely to shake hands with one another. When a man meets a woman for his initial time, he is held to the same standard.

- Hello in the French language is translated to *bonjour*

- Hi in the French language is translated to *salut*

- Good morning or good afternoon in the French language is translated to *bonjour*

- Good evening in the French language is translated to *bonsoir*

- See you later. in the French language is translated to *à bientôt.*

- Goodbye in the French language is translated to *au revoir*

- How are you? in the French language is translated to *Comment allez-vous?* (formal) or *Ça va?* (informal)

- Fine, thank you. in the French language is translated to *Bien, merci.*

- What is your name? in the French language is translated to *Comment vous appelez-vous?* (formal) or *Comment tu t'appelles?* (informal)

- My name is... in the French language is translated to *Je m'appelle...*

- I would like to introduce you to... in the French language is translated to *Je vous présente...*

- I am pleased to meet you. in the French language is translated to *Enchanté* (masc.) or *Enchantée* (fem.)

You may also find that French people are formal when speaking to someone they do not know well. In situations when an English speaker may not know someone, you are likely to hear someone address another as *"monsieur," "madame,"* or *"mademoiselle."* There is no difference between using *"Monsieur"* as for Mister and Sir. Referring to a Mrs. or Miss (in a formal sense) as *"Madame"* is common. A "Miss" is referred to as a *"Mademoiselle"* in French.

Doing Conversations

Conversations about culture and sports are often safe bets during social gatherings. It's better to avoid discussing money, particularly income, and costs, but chatting about food is a surefire method to get a French person talking.

– Do you speak English? in French can be expressed as "*Parlez-vous anglais?*"

– Do you live here? in French can be translated to "*Vous habitez ici?*"

– Do you like it here? in French can be rendered as "*Est-ce que cela vous plaît ici?*"

– I love it here. in French can be said as "*J'adore cet endroit.*"

– Where are you going? in French can be conveyed as "*Où allez-vous?*"

– What are you doing? in French can be stated as "*Que faites-vous?*"

– Are you waiting (for a taxi)? in French can be said as "*Attendez-vous un taxi?*"

– Can I have a light? in French can be expressed as "*Puis-je emprunter un briquet?*"

– What do you think (about…)? in French can be asked as "*Que pensez-vous de…?*"

– What is this called? in French can be translated to "*Comment cela s'appelle-t-il?*"

– Can I take a photo (of you)? in French can be asked as "*Est-ce que je peux prendre une photo (de vous)?*"

– That is beautiful, is it not? in French can be expressed as "*C'est beau, n'est-ce pas?*"

– Are you here on a holiday? in French can be said as "*Êtes-vous ici en vacances?*"

– I am here for a holiday. in French can be conveyed as "*Je suis ici en vacances.*"

– I am here on business. in French can be expressed as "*Je suis ici pour affaires.*"

– I am here to study. in French can be translated to "*Je suis ici pour étudier.*"

– I am here with my family. in French can be stated as "*Je suis ici avec ma famille.*"

– I am here with my partner. in French can be said as "Je suis ici avec mon partenaire" (masc.) or "Je suis ici avec ma partenaire" (fem.).

– This is my first trip (to France). in French can be translated to "*C'est mon premier voyage (en France).*"

– How long are you here for? in French can be asked as "*Pour combien de temps êtes-vous ici?*"

– I am here for… days/weeks. in French can be expressed as "*Je reste ici pendant… jours/semaines.*"

– Have you ever been (to England)? in French can be asked as "*Êtes-vous déjà allé(e) en Angleterre?*"

– Do you want to come out with me? in French can be translated to "*Voulez-vous sortir avec moi?*"

– This is my son. in French can be stated as "*Voici mon fils.*"

– This is my daughter. in French can be expressed as "*Voici ma fille.*"

– This is my friend. in French can be conveyed as "*Voici mon ami*" (masc.) or "*Voici mon amie*" (fem.).

– This is my husband. in French can be translated to "*Voici mon mari.*"

– This is my wife. in French can be said as "*Voici ma femme.*"

Some common French expressions are as follows:

- Hey! in the French language is translated to *He!*

- Great! in the French language is translated to *Formidable!*

- No problem. in the French language is translated to *Pas de problème.*

- Sure. in the French language is translated to *D'accord*

- Maybe. in the French language is translated to *Peut-être.*

- No way! in the French language is translated to *Pas question!*

- It is alright. in the French language is translated to *C'est bien.*

- OK. in the French language is translated to *Bien.*

- Look! in the French language is translated to *Regardez!* (formal)

- Listen (to this)! in the French language is translated to *Ecoutez (ceci)!* (formal)

- I am ready. in the French language is translated to *Je suis prêt(e).* (masc. or fem.)

- Are you ready? in the French language is translated to *Vous êtes prêt(e)?* (formal) or *Tu es prêt(e)?* (informal)

- Just a minute. in the French language is translated to *Une minute.*

- Just joking! in the French language is translated to *Je blaguais!*

- I am pulling your leg! in the French language is translated to *Je te fais marcher!* (informal)

Nationalities

- Where are you from? in the French language is translated to *D'où êtes-vous?* (formal) or *D'où es-tu?* (informal)

- What part of (Africa) do you come from? in the French language is translated to *D'où est-ce que vous venez (en Afrique)?* (formal) or *D'où est-ce que tu viens (en Afrique)?* (informal)

- I am from (Singapore). in the French language is translated to *Je suis de (Singapour).*

Age

- How old are you? in the French language is translated to *Quel âge avez-vous?* (formal) or *Quel âge as-tu?* (informal)

- I am (20) years old. in the French language is translated to *J'ai (vingt) ans.*

- Too old! in the French language is translated to *Trop vieux/vieille!* (masc. or fem.)

- I am younger than I look. in the French language is translated to *Je ne fais pas mon âge.*

- He/She is... years old. in the French language is translated to *Il/Elle a... ans.*

Occupations and Study

- What is your occupation? in the French language is translated to *Que faites-vous comme métier?* (formal) or *Tu fais quoi comme métier?* (informal)

- I am a businessperson. in the French language is translated to *Je suis un(e) homme / femme d'affaires.* (masc. or fem.)

- I am a chef. in the French language is translated to *Je suis cuisinier / cuisinière.* (masc. or fem.)

- I am a drag queen. in the French language is translated to *Je suis un(e) travesti(e).* (masc.)

- I work in education. in the French language is translated to *Je travaille dans l'enseignement.*

- I work in health. in the French language is translated to *Je travaille dans la santé.*

- I work in sales and marketing. in the French language is translated to *Je travaille dans la vente et le marketing.*

- I am retired. in the French language is translated to *Je suis retraité(e).* (masc. or fem.)

- I am self-employed. in the French language is translated to *Je suis indépendant(e).* (masc. or fem.)

- I am unemployed. in the French language is translated to *Je suis chômeur/chômeuse.* (masc. or fem.)

- What are you studying? in the French language is translated to *Que faites-vous comme études?* (formal) *Que fais-tu comme études?* (informal)

- I am studying engineering. in the French language is translated to *Je fais des études d'ingénieur.*

- I am studying French. in the French language is translated to *Je fais des études de français.*

- I am studying media. in the French language is translated to *Je fais des études mediatiques.*

Family

- Mother in the French language is translated to *une mère*

- Father in the French language is translated to *un père*

- Husband in the French language is translated to *un mari*

- Wife in the French language is translated to *une femme*

- Sister in the French language is translated to *une sœur*

- Brother in the French language is translated to *un frère*

- Child in the French language is translated to *un/une enfant* (masc. or fem.)

- Boyfriend in the French language is translated to *un petit ami*

- Girlfriend in the French language is translated to *une petite amie*

- Family in the French language is translated to *une famille*

- Partner in the French language is translated to *un/une partenaire* (masc. or fem.)
- Do you have a...? in the French language is translated to *Vous avez...?* (formal) or *Tu as...?* (informal)
- I have a... in the French language is translated to *J'ai...*
- I do not have a... in the French language is translated to *Je n'ai pas...*
- This is my... in the French language is translated to *Voici mon/ma/mes...* (masc., fem., or plural)
- Are you married? in the French language is translated to *Est-ce que vous êtes marié(e)?* (masc. or fem.) or *Est-ce que tu es marié(e)?*
- I am married. in the French language is translated to *Je suis marié(e).*
- I am single. in the French language is translated to *Je suis célibataire.*
- I am separated. in the French language is translated to *Je suis séparé(e).*

Sentiments

Emotions can be expressed via a noun or an adjective in French. Add "have" before the word, as in "I have thirst." Adjectives require the "be" verb, precisely like in English.

- I am cold. in the French language is translated to *J'ai froid.*
- I am not cold. in the French language is translated to *Je n'ai pas froid.*
- Are you cold? in the French language is translated to *Vous avez froid?* (formal) or *Tu as froid?* (informal)
- I am hot. in the French language is translated to *J'ai chaud.*
- I am not hot. in the French language is translated to *Je n'ai pas chaud.*
- Are you hot? in the French language is translated to *Vous avez chaud?* (formal) or *Tu as chaud?* (informal)
- I am hungry. in the French language is translated to *J'ai faim.*
- I am not hungry. in the French language is translated to *Je n'ai pas faim.*
- Are you hungry? in the French language is translated to *Vous avez faim?* (formal) or *Tu as faim?* (informal)
- I am thirsty. in the French language is translated to *J'ai soif.*
- I am not thirsty. in the French language is translated to *Je n'ai pas soif.*
- Are you thirsty? in the French language is translated to *Vous avez soif?* (formal) or *Tu as soif?* (informal)
- I am tired. in the French language is translated to *J'ai sommeil.*
- I am not tired. in the French language is translated to *Je n'ai pas sommeil.*
- Are you tired? in the French language is translated to *Vous êtes fatigué?* (formal) or *Tu es fatigué?* (informal)

- I am OK. in the French language is translated to *Je vais bien.*

- I am not OK. in the French language is translated to *Je ne vais pas bien.*

- Are you OK? in the French language is translated to *Ça va?*

Opinions

- Did you like it? in the French language is translated to *Cela vous a plu?*

- What did you think of it? in the French language is translated to *Qu'est-ce que vous en avez pensé?*

- I thought it was... in the French language is translated to *Je l'ai trouvé...*

- It is... in the French language is translated to *C'est...*

- Beautiful in the French language is translated to *beau*

- Better in the French language is translated to *mieux*

- Bizarre in the French language is translated to *bizarre*

- Great in the French language is translated to *formidable*

- Horrible in the French language is translated to *horrible*

- OK in the French language is translated to *bien*

- Strangein the French language is translated to *étrange*

- Weird in the French language is translated to *bizarre*

- Worse in the French language is translated to *pire*

Degree Levels

- A little in the French language is translated to *un peu*

- I am a little sad. in the French language is translated to *Je suis un peu triste.*

- Really in the French language is translated to *vraiment*

- I am really sorry. in the French language is translated to *Je suis vraiment navré.*

- Very in the French language is translated to *très*

- I feel very vulnerable. in the French language is translated to *je me sens très vulnérable.*

If You're Having Trouble

- Do you speak English? in the French language is translated to *Vous parlez anglais?*

- Does anyone speak English? in the French language is translated to *Y a-t-il quelqu'un qui parle anglais?*

- Do you understand? in the French language is translated to *Vous comprenez?*

- I understand. in the French language is translated to *Je comprends.*

- I do not understand. in the French language is translated to *Je ne comprends pas.*

- I speak a little. in the French language is translated to *Je parle un peu.*

- What does 'fesses' mean? in the French language is translated to *Que veut dire 'fesses'?*

- Could you please repeat that? in the French language is translated to *Pourriez-vous répéter, s'il vous plait?*

- Could you please speak more slowly? in the French language is translated to *Pourriez-vous parler plus lentement, s'il vous plait?*

- Could you please write it down? in the French language is translated to *Pourriez-vous l'écrire, s'il vous plait?*

- How do you...? in the French language is translated to *Comment...?*

- How do you pronounce this? in the French language is translated to *Comment le prononcez-vous?*

- How do you write "bonjour"? in the French language is translated to *comment est-ce qu'on écrit "bonjour"?*

Chapter 9 - Advanced Sentences

French Advanced sentences:

1. *Je travaille dans un bureau de poste.*

Êtes-vous un facteur?

Non, je suis un employé des postes.

2. *Greg travaille dans une banque.*

Est-il un caissier?

Oui il l'est.

3. *Ils vivent à Washington.*

Sont-ils des sénateurs?

Non, ils ne le sont pas.

4. *Je déjeune à 8 heures du matin.*

Qu'est-ce que tu manges?

(Je mange) des œufs, du bacon et du pain grillé.

5. *Elle va au travail à 10heures.*

Où travaille-t-elle?

À la cafétéria.

6. *Danny joue au basket tous les jeudis.*

Où joue-t-il?

À la salle de sport.

7. *Penny commence les cours à 10 heures.*

Quand finit-elle?

À 11 heures

8. *Je ne bois pas de bière.*

Pourquoi (pas)?

Je n'aime pas.

English version of the previous sentences:

1. I work in a post office.

Are you a letter carrier?

No, I'm a postal clerk.

2. Greg works in a bank.

Is he a teller?

Yes, he is.

3. They live in Washington.

Are they senators?

No, they aren't.

4. I eat breakfast at 8 a.m

What do you eat?

(I eat) eggs, bacon, and toast.

5. She goes to work at 10 a.m.

Where does she work?

In the cafeteria.

6. Danny plays basketball every Thursday.

Where does he play?

At the gym.

7. Penny starts class at 10:00.

When does she finish?

At 11:00.

8. I don't drink beer.

Why not?

I don't like it.

Presentation:

Here, we will first discuss the verbs used in the above sentences, then the placement of the pronouns when they act as objects in a sentence, and the adverbs of affirmation and negation.

The new verbs to be noted here are the verbs "*DEJEUNER*" (to eat breakfast/ to have lunch, depending on the time), the verb "*MANGER*" (to eat), the verb "*JOUER*" (to play), the verb "*COMMENCER*"(to start), the verb "*FINIR*" (to finish), the verb "*BOIRE*" (to drink) and the verb "*AIMER*" (to like/love).

Conjugation of the verb "*DEJEUNER*" (To eat breakfast/To have lunch)

Je déjeune – I eat breakfast/lunch

Tu déjeunes – You eat breakfast/lunch

Il/Elle déjeune – He/She eats breakfast/lunch

Nous déjeunons – We eat breakfast/lunch

Vous déjeunez – You eat breakfast/lunch

Ils/Elles déjeunent – They eat breakfast/lunch

Conjugation of the verb "*MANGER*" (To eat)

Je mange is translated to I eat

Tu manges is translated to You eat

Il/Elle mange is translated to He/She eats

Nous mangeons is translated to We eat

Vous mangez is translated to You eat

Ils/ Elles mangent is translated to They eat

Conjugation of the verb «*JOUER*» (To play)

Je joue is translated to I play

Tu joues is translated to You play

Il/Elle joue is translated to He/She plays

Nous jouons is translated to We play

Vous jouez is translated to You play

Ils/Elles jouent is translated to They play

Conjugation of the verb "*COMMENCER*" (To start)

Je commence is translated to I start

Tu commences is translated to You start

Il/Elle commence is translated to He/She starts

Nous commençons is translated to We start

Vous commencez is translated to You start

Ils/Elles commencent is translated to They start

Conjugation of the verb «*FINIR*» (To finish)

Je finis is translated to I finish

Tu finis is translated to You finish

Il/Elle finit is translated to He/ She finishes

Nous finissons is translated to We finish

Vous finissez is translated to You finish

Ils/Elles finissent is translated to They finish

Conjugation of the verb «*BOIRE*» (To drink)

Je bois is translated to I drink

Tu bois is translated to You drink

Il/Elle boit is translated to He/She drinks

Nous buvons is translated to We drink

Vous buvez is translated to You drink

Ils/Elles boivent is translated to They drink

Conjugation of the verb «*AIMER*» (To like/love)

J'aime is translated to I like

Tu aimes is translated to You like

Il/Elle aime is translated to He/She likes

Nous aimons is translated to We like

Vous aimez is translated to You like

Ils/Elles aiment is translated to They like

Placement of pronouns

The placement of pronouns when they act as the object in a sentence: Before we tackle this topic, it is important that we describe the types of personal pronouns in detail. We have personal pronouns that act as subjects, which means they perform the action in that sentence e.g *je, tu il, elle nous et*;, then we have personal pronouns that act as a direct objects e.g *me, te, le, la* etc., this is where the subject directly acts upon the object without a preposition(Example: *Je vois ma mère*/I see my mother=*Je la vois*); we also have personal pronouns that act as indirect objects e.g *me, te, lui, leur* etc., this is where the subject only act on the object through a preposition (Example: *Je parle à Jean* /I speak to John=*Je lui parle*/I speak to him). Then we have the reflexive personal pronouns, e.g *me, te, se, nous* etc., these show actions that the subject performs on itself e.g *Je me lave* – I bathe myself.

Detailed personal pronouns in tabular format:

Person	Subject Pronoun	Object Pronoun (direct)	Object Pronoun (indirect)	Reflexive Pronoun
1st person singular	*Je* - I	*me* - me	*me* - me	*me*
2nd person singular	*Tu* - You	*te* - you	*te* - you	*te*
3rd person singular (masc.)	*Il* - He	*le* - him	*lui* – him	*se*

3rd person singular (fem.)	*Elle* - She	*la* - her	*lui* - her	*se*
1st person plural	*Nous* - We	*nous* - us	*nous* - we	*nous*
2nd person plural	*Vous* - You	*vous* - you	*vous* - you	*vous*
3rd person plural	*Ils/Elles* - They	*les* - them	*Leur* - them	*se*

When we have nouns functioning as the subject and the object in a sentence, the normal placement is Subject – Verb – Object. Example: *Anna aime le riz* – Anna likes rice. Here, Anna is the subject that is performing the action of like in the sentence, while rice is the object that is being acted upon. If we change the noun 'rice' to a pronoun like 'it', the position of the object will change to become Subject – Object – Verb. Therefore rice (represented by the pronoun 'le' or l') will now come before the verb *'aime'* (like), the sentence will become *"Anna l'aime"*.

Adverbs of affirmation and negation

Adverbs of affirmation in French are words that are used to confirm if an action or a statement is true.

Some are: *Oui*/Yes, *si*/yes, really/*vraiment*, absolutely/*absolument*, *certainement*/certainly, *sans doute*/undoubtedly, *certes*/certain, *bien sur*/of course, *sûrement*/surely etc.

Example:

Vous travaillez demain? –Oui, bien sûr! / Are you working tomorrow? –Yes, of course!

Adverbs of negation are words that oppose the action or the statement given.

Some are: *Non*/No, *ne...pas*/not, *ne...jamais*/never, *ne...rien*/nothing, *ne...plus*/no more.

Examples:

Je suis une femme, je ne suis pas un homme/I am a woman, I am not a man.

When writing a sentence in the negative, the verb is placed between '*ne.....and..... pas*, or between *ne....and....rien*, or between *ne...and...jamais*, e.g, *je ne mange pas de pain*/I am not eating bread, *elle ne sort jamais*/she never goes out, *je ne veux rien*/I want nothing or I don't want anything, *je ne chante plus*/I don't sing anymore or I'm singing no more.

Chapter 10 - Questions And Objects

We're going to knock out two seemingly unrelated birds with one very big stone in this chapter. In French, questions and objects actually intertwine in a way. I suppose that they intertwine in any given language, really. In a lot of conversations, you'll be talking about a given subject, and in order to carry on the conversation, you'll find it necessary to ask questions about what the other person is saying. So questions like "When did you see it?" or "How did you get in there?" or "How was it?" will naturally crop up.

That is to say that any budding French conversationalist will need both of these concepts quite handily, and I'm prepared to set you up with them.

Questions

French questions are rather easy. Every question is composed of question words. Much like in English, every proper question has a word which designates what exactly we're asking about.

In English, these words are what, why, how, with whom, who, which, how many, and where.

In French, the words are as follows:

Quoi is translated to What

Quand is translated to When

Pourquoi is translated to Why

Quel(le)(s) is translated to Which

Combien de is translated to How many

Comment is translated to How

Où is translated to Where

Qui is translated to Who

Avec qui is translated to With whom

These, of course, function just like they do in English --- they can be parts of normal statements, or they can be used in questions.

If used in questions, there's another phrase you need to know: *est-ce que* (pronounced EST kuu). This literally translate to "is it that?". When combined with other question words, or on its own, it signals that the statement following it is a question.

Est-ce que tu l'aimes?

Do you love him?

(literally "is it [the case] that you love him?")

Où est-ce que tu chantes?

Where do you sing?

(literally "Where is it that you sing?")

This phrase already is powerful, but sometimes you don't want such a clunky phrase. Sometimes, in fact, you can say more with less. This is when inverted questions become the go-to.

And indeed, they're a little familiar to us as English speakers. Think of it this way: let's say you walked into your living room wanting to watch a certain show, but your brother or child was there watching TV, though absentmindedly since they're also playing on their DS and seem mostly preoccupied with that. You want to change the channel. What do you do?

Well, so long as you aren't a barbarian, you'll normally ask something along the lines of:

Are you watching the TV?

Which is an inverted question. What if you just wanted to say that they were watching TV? You would instead say:

You are watching the TV.

So the "you" and the "are" were inverted in order to make the sentence into a question. French questions work similarly to this mechanism.

Let's say the same scenario happened. With the little est-ce que trick we just learned, we might be tempted to say this:

Est-ce que tu regardes la télé?

But we can make this a lot shorter and snappier. We can just invert the question:

Regardes-tu la télé?

This kind of inversion will serve you very well and explain a lot of potentially confusing sentences you'll run into.

Direct object pronouns

This is a really tedious but very necessary lesson to give. We use direct object pronouns constantly. Think about it: have you ever been talking about something with a friend, and then you something like "Yeah, I saw them" or "Yeah, I heard it."? The answer, of course, is yes. It would be incredibly monotonous, slightly robotic, and ultimately very creepy if we didn't have direct object pronouns. It would feel absolutely unnatural to say the name of something every time we brought it up. Of course, it wouldn't if that were just the way we spoke, but from our perspective and speaking the way we do, it sounds odd. Besides, it saves time. Replacing a multi-syllable name or phrase with the simple

"it" or "them" or "him" saves a lot of time and effort in terms of speaking and writing.

So how do direct object pronouns in French work? Well, I'm assuming that you know how they work in English already.

In French, you correlate the previously mentioned object to the correct direct object pronoun based on perspective (is it first person? second person? third person?) and plurality (singular? plural?). Then you just throw it before the noun. (Notice how I just said "throw it before the noun" -- direct object pronouns at work!)

The French direct object pronouns are as follows:

me is the first person singular

te is the second person singular

le, la, l' is the third person singular

nous is the first person plural

vous is the second person plural

les is the third person plural

So let's say that I wanted to say "I'm giving it to Jeffrey." How would I do so?

Well, I first recognize the "direct object". Here, it's it. Then I analyze to see which word fits it: it refers to a singular third person object, so I'll use the third person singular. Then, we have to figure out the gender of the noun. Let's say we're giving Jeffrey a papaya. This translates to *une papaye*, which is feminine. So it's a feminine third person singular direct object. Perfect. The word is la.

So to say "I'm giving it to Jeffrey", knowing "it" is la, I just have to translate the rest, and throw the la before the verb, like so:

Je la donne à Jeffrey.

Honestly, explaining it makes it sound so much more difficult than it really is. In practice, it's a very easy concept to grasp and there's not a whole lot of genuine difficulty involved in it.

Indirect object pronouns

Now comes the part where things start to get more complicated. The use of direct object pronouns as opposed to indirect object pronouns is marked by a significant difference. The object that is immediately impacted by a certain verb is known as the direct object of that verb. The object to which the bulk of the action of the verb is transferred is referred to as the indirect object.

The way I like to put it is this: without the direct object, there is no verb. Full stop. If you throw a ball, you can't detach the ball from the concept of throwing. Either you're throwing a ball, or there is nothing to be thrown. The same with sending a letter. You can't just send nothing. You have to have something to be sending. You can absolutely not detach the concept of the letter from the notion of sending.

However, this is where indirect objects are different. You can detach the indirect object from the rest. The indirect object is non-essential. You can throw a ball without throwing it to somebody. You can send a letter without sending it to somebody (though it may not go anywhere.) You can do these things without the existence of the indirect object. But since the indirect object is there, it serves to give context to the verb and the direct object, by giving them an end goal and, indeed, a thing for which and to which they're performed.

The French indirect object pronouns are as follows:

me is translated to to me

te is translated to to you

lui is translated to to him/to her

nous is translated to to us

vous is translated to to you all/to you (f.)

leur is translated to to them

So let's go back to that sentence from the direct object pronoun section: "I'm giving it to Jack". We ended up getting the following:

Je la donne à Jack.

So how do we get the indirect object pronoun here? We first find the preposition, which will indicate to/for whom or what the action is being performed. The preposition here is à, and the prepositional phrase is "à Jack." Thus, the indirect object is Jack. So that's a third person singular indirect object, and it's gender neutral in the indirect object form, so we can just take *lui* and stick it behind our verb too.

Je la lui donne.

This literally means "I'm giving it to him." Not too shabby, no?

The general rule for placement of direct and indirect object pronouns, when you have both, is that they go in alphabetical order.

Adverbial pronouns

There are a couple of other pronouns you need to be aware of. They are as follows:

y --- replaces "there"; also replaces "*à*" and a noun.

en --- replaces either a partitive article and noun ("*Je mange des pommes*" becomes "*J'en mange*") or replaces de followed by an indefinite article and a noun ("*J'ai envie d'une banane*" becomes "*J'en ai envie*") which makes it particularly useful for shortening phrases of verbs which traditionally are followed by de (*se souvenir de* --- to be reminded of, *avoir besoin de* --- to need, *avoir envie de* --- to want, and so on...)

These are called adverbial pronouns, and will turn out to be quite useful as you go forward with French. You'll understand the usage of them more as you practice with them and read/hear more and more French.

Ce, cela, celui, and so on

One of the most important French phrases you'll ever encounter is c'est (sey). It's somewhat of a catchall. For example, "*C'est mon chien!*" means "This is/that is/it is my dog!". "*(Ça,) c'est mon ami, [name]*" can be used to introduce one friend to another. "*(Ça,) c'est intéressant!*" means "That's interesting!". The French have such a love affair with "*ça, c'est*" that they'll use it places where it really doesn't belong, but you'll figure that out on your own.

C'est is a contraction of the pronoun ce and the verb est. It means approximately "it is", "this is", or "that is" depending upon the context. "*Ce*" just means "this" or "that". You can use it before a noun, too, to indicate a specific one. For example, "*ce chien*" means this dog. If you do this, you have to pay attention to your spelling. If it's used before a masculine noun with a vowel, you have to use cet instead of *ce*. If it's before a feminine noun, you must use *cette*. If it's before a plural noun, you must use *ces*.

There are some other forms, too. *Ceci* and *cela* are important for you to know - they both mean approximately "this" and "that", but can be used somewhat interchangeably. *Cela* contracts to the popular *ça*.

Then, there's *celui* and *celle*. *Celle* is the feminine form of celui. They both mean "this one" or "that one" dependent upon context, and refer to one of a specific group of different people or things in a given set.

These are important pronouns for you to know just because they're so prolific in French usage.

Chapter 11 -- Formulating Questions

You saw in the first part of this section a very powerful tool that will be essential during any language learning journey: questions. Indeed, being able to understand and ask questions is the crux of any learning experience. Whether you need to ask for clarifications or simply demonstrate your newly-acquired French skills, questions are an easy way to make connections much faster and to get you acquainted with much more French wherever you go.

First, the major difference between English and French, which should be the crux of your learning for now: French doesn't employ auxiliaries in questions. It means that any mark of a tense should instead be seen on the verb and that you may find the verb in the place of the English auxiliary in some questions:

Does he like coffee? – *Aime-t-il le café*? [Likes-he coffee, literally]

Do you want to grab a coffee? – *Voulez-vous qu'on aille prendre un café*? [Like-you...]

When will he arrive here? – *Quand arrivera-t-il ici*? [When will-arrive-he here]

As the third example demonstrates, interrogative pronouns, when used, are automatically at the beginning of the question.

Next, are some formal questions, as they are the ones most resembling English—and probably the most useful when introducing yourself to new people in French.

Formal questions: (Interrogative Adverb) + Verb + Subject + complement

Will he be able to be there on time? – *Sera [V être, 'to be']-t-il* [subject 'il'] *en mesure d'être là à l'heure*? [complement]

When do you think he'll come back? – *Quand* ['when'] *crois-tu* ['think-you' literally] *qu'il reviendra*? [complement]

While the lack of an auxiliary in French may lead you astray, don't worry! Simply report your attention to the verb in all previous questions—you will notice it is at the very beginning of the sentence, similarly to where the English auxiliary would be. This particular question structure is considered formal and is seldom used in everyday speech. However, addressing someone politely, and asking them questions with *vous*, tends to require the use of a formal question as seen above: *Voulez-vous qu'on aille prendre un café*, or "Would you like us to go grab a coffee?"

A quick notice before you proceed: *voulez-vous* indeed links the verb directly to the subject with a hyphen; it is, of course, never pronounced out loud, but has to be there in every written formal question. The structure changes a bit for *aime-t-il* and *sera-t-il* because all three singular pronouns *il, elle, on*—and the plural *ils* and *elles*—would sound clunky if directly appended to the verbs with no adjacent consonant. Try to pronounce *sera-il* or *aime-il* to see how weird that would be! For these three pronouns only, an additional 't' surrounded by two hyphens is required for the whole sentence to flow naturally—unless, importantly, the verbal form already ends with a 't', thus making the whole process redundant and unnecessary:

Aime-t-il – aime-t-elle – aimerons-nous – aimerez-vous – aimeraient-ils (no additional 't')

Sait-il (no additional 't') – *savent-ils*

Formal questions: long subjects

In all the formal questions shown, the subject of the question was simply a pronoun (*tu, je, nous,* etc...). Of course, longer subjects may be used (*nos amis, cet homme, mon oncle*), but they require some structure changes.

You may only use a longer subject to replace 'he', 'she', 'it', or 'they'. Of course, it would be hard to replace 'I', 'we', or 'you', and any attempt at adding information would only go next to it: with you, it could only be 'Will you, my dear friend, agree to...?', but simply using 'My dear friend' would automatically refer to someone else, a 'he' or a 'she'.

What happens is as follows: the pronoun *'t-elle'* or *'t-ils'* remains in place after the verb, and the subject inserts itself between the interrogative adverb and the verb, or simply before the verb:

- no interrogative adverb (what, who):

Will he be able to be there on time? – *Sera-t-il en mesure d'être là à l'heure?*

Will our teacher be able to be there on time? – *Notre professeur sera-t-il en mesure d'être là à l'heure?*

- with an interrogative adverb:

When will she come back? – *Quand reviendra-t-elle?*

When will your aunt come back? – *Quand ta tante reviendra-t-elle?*

Please pay attention to two particular phenomena that only take place in formal questions:

First of all, in questions where 'not' or the French ne... *pas* is present, *ne* goes to the very beginning of the question:

Can't he at least try to speak some French? – *Ne peut-il pas au moins essayer de parler français?* (Not can-he (not) at least try to speak French?)

Shouldn't you be in class right now? – *Ne devrais-tu pas être en classe en ce moment?* (Not should-you be...)

Secondly, in the presence of indirect pronouns, they should automatically be in the very beginning of the question, or right after the interrogative adverb if there is one. For now, simply train yourself to recognize and understand that structure, as it will naturally crop up later in your learning journey:

'I need' may translate in French as *'il me faut...'* (lit. to me is required...). 'I' or me is an indirect pronoun and not the subject of the sentence in that construction; hence, the placement of the indirect pronoun in the following questions:

Do you need any more sugar for that cake? – *Te faut-il plus de sucre pour ce gâteau?* [to you 'te' + needed-is *'faut-il'* more sugar for that cake?]

What do you need to repair that wall? – *Que te faut-il pour réparer ce mur?* [What *'Que'* + to you needed is to repair that wall?]

more (water, sugar, people...) – *plus de + noun*

Again, these sentences draw on knowledge that you will only be exposed to in the following sections. It may be more useful to start writing them down if you wish to master the art of producing flawless French as the word order might be confusing at first.

One could say that formal questions in French still harbor some difficulties that can seem overwhelming for foreign learners; however, rest assured that is actually not the case! The most important point is that the subject and the verb are switched and tied together with a hyphen. For now, you can easily create small formal questions to ask strangers and recognize them easily thanks to their structure. As for the unforeseen difficulties of that section, they will be useful when advancing into greater depths within the French language—but for now, they should only be interesting points at most. Remember, subject and verb are switched, and there you go!

Now you will learn the most common structure for questions, used in both formal and informal contexts (even with *vous*):

Most common structure with '*est-ce que*':

Below is a complete line to deconstruct the important sentence structure:

(Interrogative adverb, if any) + *est-ce que / qu'* + Subject + Verb + Object / complement...?

This is what it looks like:

-   When did he come back? – *Quand est-ce qu'il est revenu?*

[Quand, 'when' + '*est-ce qu*' + subject '*il*' + '*est revenu*', verbal group]

-   Will you be able to memorize all those words? – *Est-ce que tu seras capable de mémoriser tous ces mots?*

['*Est-ce que*' + subject '*tu*' + verb '*seras*' + adjective 'capable' + ...]

-   Wouldn't it be better to just not plan anything? – *Est-ce que ça ne serait pas mieux de ne rien planifier?*

[*Est-ce que* + subject '*il*' + '*ne serait pas mieux*' (lit. wouldn't be better) + ...]

The whole structure can look intimidating to learners, but it is simply a matter of learning it by heart and remembering that, in this case, the normal word order Subject + Verb is respected, whereas it isn't in formal questions. It is all about adding a couple of words in front of a normal sentence, in short! If you wish to see the two question structures contrasted directly:

-   Wouldn't it be better to just not plan anything? *Est-ce que ça ne serait pas mieux de ne rien planifier? Ne serait-ce pas mieux de ne rien planifier?*

As to how to pronounce est-ce que, there is nothing to be afraid of—its full pronunciation (assuming you are speaking at a normal pace) would be /èse-ke/, but the French more commonly drop the first 'e' sound— remember, it sounds a bit like a schwa (er in 'butter')—and therefore tend to say /èske/ really fast.

Informal questions: speaking like a real native

Of course, you will hardly be able to use this sentence in a formal business meeting where you should at least demonstrate a bit of politeness, but the most relaxed or informal questions do happen to be the easiest of all. There is no change to the word order compared to an affirmative sentence; only the interrogation point—or an ascending tone at the end of the sentence—makes it clear it is a question. It follows the same structure as informal questions in English:

You want some sugar with your tea? – *Vous voulez / Tu veux du sucre avec ton thé?*

You think he'll come around eventually? – *Tu penses qu'il finira par changer d'avis*? (lit. 'You think he'll end up coming around?')

- to come around – *changer d'avis*

See: forming questions turned out pretty straightforward after all! It may prove confusing to English learners who are used to getting into the "meat of it" without so many gymnastics, but where would the unmistakable charm of French be otherwise?

To recap everything:

- For formal questions, get your conjugated verb and your pronoun together, inverse them (*voulez-vous*), and add a hyphen in between—which will not change anything in the pronunciation, except for *il, elle*, and *on* where there is an additional 't' that is always pronounced.

- For *est-ce que* questions, which are by far the most useful and used questions in French, simply add these words at the beginning of your question, this time keeping a normal word order with the subject before its verb. *Est-ce que cette section vous a appris beaucoup de choses?*

- Finally, if you want to use more informal questions, when offering some tea to a good friend of yours, for example, you'd switch to: "*Tu voudrais du thé*?" (You'd like some tea?), or even: "*Tu veux du thé*?" (You want some tea?). That one has the bonus of not requiring any change at all compared to an affirmative question.

Here is a useful visual reminder: *penses-tu / est-ce que tu penses / tu penses?*

In short, just remember: there is no need to use inversed questions everywhere you go, but using them in French denotes a professional relationship or demonstrates politeness when addressing a person you might not know.

Now you will see interrogative pronouns that tie many questions together:

When, where, what, why, how: harder than they may seem…

Here is a concise overview of how to translate those useful interrogative adverbs:

When: *Quand?*

When will you be available for a meet-up? – *Quand seras-tu disponible pour un rendez-vous?*

When should your new project start? – *Quand ton nouveau projet devrait-il commencer?*

Where: Où? / D'où?

Whereas English balances questions so that provenance is often indicated with a final preposition:

Where do you come from? – *D'où venez-vous/viens-tu?*

French instead modifies the adverb: if you are referring to where someone is or will be, use *où*; if you are referring to the someone's geographical origin, or the place they are arriving from, use *d'où* (*de + où*).

Where is your cat? – *Où est ton chat?*

Where did he go? – *Où est-il allé?*

Where did he come from with all these bags? – *D'où venait-il avec tous ces sacs?* (from where did he come...)

Why / What for: Pourquoi? / Pour quoi?

Why should I consider your advice? – *Pourquoi devrais-je tenir compte de ton conseil?*

Why is everything always closed on Sundays? – *Pourquoi est-ce que tout est toujours fermé le dimanche?*

'What for' is probably the interrogative pronoun you should pay most attention to here since it introduces a particularity of French that has just been shown with "Where...from". Whereas prepositions are commonly found at the very end of questions in English, they have to be introduced right before the interrogative adverb in French:

What are you actually cleaning the whole house for? – *Pourquoi* ('for what') / *Pour quelle raison* ('for what reason') *es-tu en fait en train de nettoyer toute la maison?* A more 'acceptable' way to phrase it would be – *Pourquoi est-ce que tu nettoies toute la maison en fait?*

What: Quoi / Qu'est-ce que, que / De quoi, par quoi / Quel, quelle, quels, quelles?

Who would have thought that such a small word could conceal such nuances in French! What is great about them, though, is that each possibility is only used in specific circumstances, so they are easy to apply once you recognize the right structure:

- *Quoi*: /kwa/

You may only encounter quoi in two contexts:

- when it is the only word in the question:

I heard my aunt is going to remarry next year. – What?

J'ai entendu que ma tante va se remarier l'année prochaine. – Quoi?

- in informal questions, it places itself after the verb, such as in:

What do you want? – *Tu veux quoi?* [You want what?]

What am I supposed to do now? – *Je suis supposé(e) faire quoi maintenant?* [I do what now?]

For the more formal or traditional counterparts, you may encounter the following: *Qu'est-ce que tu veux? / Qu'est-ce que je suis supposé faire maintenant?*:

- *Qu'est-ce que*, or more formally *que*:

You will find qu'est-ce que or simply que when it replaces the direct object of a verb in a sentence. Pay attention to how French questions are constructed, as the syntax isn't the same in both variants. Qu'est-ce que is the most common variant while que has become quite formal and will likely only be found in classical books or the like.

Remember: you can easily identify the direct object of a sentence if you can replace it with 'that':

What are you going to do tomorrow? – I'm going to do that (mow the lawn, put up some wallpaper...)

This is opposed to indirect objects, which may be, for instance, the person you are doing an action for or that is indirectly concerned: What do you need of me? – I need this of you. In the previous sentence, both a direct and indirect object are present. The examples below are guides to distinguish them:

What do you need for lunch? – *Que te faut-il pour le déjeuner?* (lit. What to you is needed for lunch?) / *Qu'est-ce qu'il te faut pour le déjeuner?* (lit. What is to you needed...)

What does he think will happen when they'll know about it? – *Que croit-il qu'il se passera quand ils le sauront?* / *Qu'est-ce qu'il croit qu'il se passera quand ils le sauront?*

What are you doing on such a sunny morning? – *Que fais-tu par un matin si ensoleillé?* / *Qu'est-ce que tu fais par un matin si ensoleillé?*

lunch – *un déjeuner* (m)

know about something / know it – *le savoir, invariable pronoun* (pronoun + verb)

sunny – *ensoleillé*(e)

In short: que, being more formal and seldom used compared to qu'est-ce que, keeps the Verb + Subject order commonly found in formal questions; on the other hand, qu'est-ce que retains the normal Subject + Verb order when used in a question.

- *Quel, quelle, quels, quelles?*

There is no need to recoil before all of these declensions: *quel* and all of its compounds are used in questions when you are referring to objects, concepts, or non-human creatures, and each ending only indicates gender and/or number:

What is this sound? – *Quel est ce bruit?* (masculine singular)

What was that book you recommended me? – *Quel était ce livre que tu m'as recommandé?* (masculine singular)

What are the current regulations here? – *Quelles sont les régulations en vigueur ici?* (feminine plural)

What is the reason for such a mess? – *Quelle est la raison pour un tel bazar?* (feminine singular)

You would oppose quel to the *qui* form that corresponds to 'who', which will be touched upon in a later subsection in this chapter:

Who is that woman standing there? – *Qui est cette femme qui se tient debout là-bas?*

current (rules, standards) – *règles, normes en vigueur* (en vigueur is invariable)

sound – *bruit (m)* /brui/ ('u' sound is shorter that in '*pendule*' /pãdul/)

to stand – *se tenir debout; être debout*

Golden nugget: English and French possess a similar construction when saying, "What a..." in affirmative sentences.

What a beautiful creature! – *Quelle créature magnifique!*

What lovely puppies! – *Quels beaux chiots!* (Remember: *beau,* along with other common adjectives, regularly places itself before the noun rather than after it).

- *De quoi, par quoi:*

Do you remember what was earlier detailed about the multiple translations for 'where' depending on prepositions which, in English, are relegated to the end of the sentence? The same principle applies here.

For instance, you may have in English:

What will we start with?

'To start with' is *commencer par* in French: given how French builds questions, the word order will literally have to be 'With what will we start', or:

Par quoi commencerons-nous?

Here are other equivalencies between the two languages to get you even more acquainted with how this works in French—having you crack the code early in your language learning journey will soon have you reach a similar level to that of natives!

What are you afraid of? – *De quoi as-tu / avez-vous peur?*

What would you need if there was a tsunami? – *De quoi aurais-tu / auriez-vous besoin s'il y avait un tsunami?*

- to be afraid of something – *avoir peur de quelque chose*
- need something – *avoir besoin de quelque chose*

Who: *Qui? / Quel?*

Here is some good news: the pronoun *qui* is invariable, and thus works for masculine, feminine, singular, and plural subjects. Of course, depending on whether are not the subject is assumed to be singular or plural, the verb will be conjugated differently:

Who ate my slice of pie? – *Qui a mangé ma part de tarte?*

Who is the man you met yesterday? – *Qui est l'homme que tu as rencontré hier?*

Who is that superb woman walking down the street? – *Qui est cette femme magnifique qui marche dans la rue?*

Who's in charge here? – *Qui est aux commandes ici?*

Who are the most renowned French poets who lived here? – *Qui sont les poètes français les plus renommés qui ont vécu / à avoir vécu ici?*

- to be in charge – *être aux commandes*, idiomatic; if you wish to be even more idiomatic, *être aux manettes* (manettes are 'levers' or 'controllers' for machinery or video gaming)

- *Qui ont vécu ici / à avoir vécu ici*: that second structure is very idiomatic and requires the preposition as well as an unconjugated verb or auxiliary right after it. You may still use the first formulation, but the second one will definitely impress your acquaintances.

Quel, on the other hand, is influenced by the subject's gender and number, and hence possesses the following forms: *quel, quelle, quels, quelles*. It is used only when the person asking the question already has an idea of who he or she is addressing. For instance, work out an alternative translation to the first question:

Who is the one who ate my slice of pie? – *Quel est celui / Quelle est celle qui a mangé ma part de tarte?*

In this case, French puts forth more distinctions than English: *Quel est celui* clearly states that the person asking believes it is a man or a boy who ate the slice of pie; similarly, the second structure specifically targets a woman or a girl.

If they were to think that several people were involved, they would resort to:

Quels sont ceux / Quelles sont celles qui ont mangé ma part de tarte? (lit. Who are the ones...)

Here, the same distinction is present: the second sentence clearly targets several female subjects, while the first one may rather target only men or a group of men and women—remember that, as far as gender is concerned, one single masculine person or object takes precedence and sets the pronoun as masculine automatically.

Who(m): *à qui?*

Just as 'whom' is built on 'who' in English, *qui* and *à qui* are linked by the same relationship:

To whom am I speaking? – *Qui est à l'appareil?* (this one is idiomatic; translating literally as *A qui suis-je en train de m'adresser?* while grammatical in French and understandable by natives, it isn't common at all)

To whom it may concern... – *A qui de droit...*

Whose: *à qui?*

Expressing possession in French has yet to be conveyed, but here is the most important piece of information you need to remember: when expressing possession with a pronoun (it belongs 'to him' as opposed to 'to my brother'), the pronoun *à* has to be used. As to the whole structure in French, it is the literal equivalent of the English 'To whom does/do... belong?':

Whose shorts are they? – *A qui appartient ce short? / A qui est ce short?*

Whose car is parked in the alley? – *A qui appartient la voiture dans l'allée? / A qui est la voiture...?*

- belong to someone – *appartenir à quelqu'un*

- shorts – *short* (m), preferably in the singular in French

Remember that French questions do not rely on an auxiliary but instead on a verb; this is why it places itself right after à qui.

Note: not only can 'be' be used in those questions in both English and French but using the verb/auxiliary *être* instead of *appartenir* will single you out as a very good French speaker! Don't refrain from using this idiomaticism when you can.

Which one: lequel, laquelle, lesquels, lesquelles

As much as French can be described as a complicated language, these forms remain straightforward—being taken from quel and all of its declensions, as you have seen as translations for what: plus, in this case, 'which one' and lequel can both refer to people or inanimate objects in their respective languages, so that you only have to remember these four forms to start building the sentence. Here it is in more detail:

(members of a male football team) Which one of them should I choose? – *Lequel (d'entre eux) devrais-je choisir?*

(coats, manteaux (m)) Which of them suits me better? – *Lequel (d'entre eux) me va le mieux?*

(songs, chansons (f)) Which one sounds best? – *Laquelle (d'entre elles) sonne le mieux?*

The reason why *d'entre eux / elles* is in parentheses is that when what you are referring to is obvious, they can be omitted. If you are pointing at a batch of coats and asking a friend for their opinion, it is unnecessary to repeat it. *D'entre eux* being, literally, "from among them" (*de + entre + eux*), it undergoes a slight transformation when referring to an item directly instead of using a pronoun. Again, the construction remains similar to English:

Which one of these songs do you like the most? – *Laquelle de ces chansons* (of + these + songs) *aimes-tu le plus?*

Which ones of these women delivered the best performance? – *Lesquelles de ces femmes ont livré la meilleure performance?*

- to deliver a performance – *livrer une performance*

How: *Comment?*

How do you intend to complete this drawing in less than 24 hours? – *Comment comptes-tu compléter ce dessin en moins de 24 heures?*

- to intend to do something – *compter faire quelque chose*

How many: *Combien de...?*

How many languages are there in the world? – *Combien y a-t-il de langues dans le monde? / Combien de langues y a-t-il dans le monde*

How much (debating or asking for a price): *Combien?*

How much is this dress worth? – *Combien coûte cette robe?*

- He told me to deposit 5,000 dollars in cash tomorrow. – *Il m'a demandé de faire un versement de 5000 dollars en liquide demain.*

- How much? – *Combien?*

How much (water, salt): *Combien de / Quelle quantité de...?*

Without going into the nitty-gritty of things here, *combien de* will preferably be used for grains and other 'palpable' materials, while *quelle quantité de* will be used for liquids; when in doubt, use *Quelle quantité de*, which perfectly works for both.

How much salt should I consume per day? – *Quelle quantité de sel devrais-je consommer par jour?*

How much water does an entire forest need? – *De quelle quantité d'eau une forêt a-t-elle besoin?*

- *De quelle*: to need, or in French *avoir besoin de*, requires the preposition in any sentence. It is why, in this case, de has to come before *quelle quantité*, similarly to what you have been shown regarding "what" (*De quoi as-tu peur?* – What are you afraid of?)

Exercise:

Fill in the gap with the appropriate pronoun:

- .... *(pl) de ces plages (f) sont les moins visitées en été?*

Which ones of these beaches are least visited in summer?

- *Je ne sais pas .... (sg) de ces cravates (f) choisir.*

I don't know which one of these ties to choose.

- .... *(sg) de ces professeurs (m) fait cours aujourd'hui?*

Which one of these teachers has a lecture today?

<u>Exercise: Correction</u>

- *Lesquelles de ces plages sont les moins visitées en été?*

- *Je ne sais pas laquelle de ces cravates choisir.*

- *Lequel de ces professeurs fait cours aujourd'hui?*

Learning objectives: You have now seen that

- French places interrogative pronouns at the beginning of a question, just like English.

- There are three ways of phrasing questions: the formal one (*est-il possible*), the common one so to speak (*est-ce qu'il est possible*), and the informal one (*il est possible*).

- For questions that in English would end with a pronoun (What are we doing this for?), the pronoun has to go before the interrogative adverb in French (*Pour quoi faisons-nous ça?*)

- French tends to draw finer lines when it comes to the meaning of certain adverbs (what, for example), making it crucial to understand the context of the sentence to use the right word(s)

But how do I answer questions?

Quickly and efficiently! There are not that many differences between English and French, and you will soon find yourself fully capable of bridging the language gap.

- With simple Yes or No answers:

Did you clean up your room? – Yes.

As-tu rangé ta chambre? – Oui.

Can you please stop reading that book? – No.

Peux-tu arrêter de lire ce livre, s'il te plaît? – Non.

- 'I do', 'I didn't' answers: how do we do it?

You saw in a previous section that French also uses auxiliaries—for example, when using *passé composé* in lieu of the English Preterite most of the time— but they are not used as an integral part of questions just as in English:

When did you complete your studies? --- *Quand as-tu fini tes études?* (literally: When have-you completed your studies?)

Why does he always leave at night? --- *Pourquoi part-il toujours la nuit?* (literally: Why leaves-he always at night?)

Therefore, you will often need to repeat the subject and the verb when using 'I do's:

Did you take your credit card with you? – I did. / Yes, I did. / Indeed. / Of course.

As-tu pris ta carte bleue avec toi? --- Je l'ai prise. / Oui, je l'ai prise. / En effet. / Bien sûr.

Do you believe he's really French? – I don't. / No, I don't. / I don't think so.

Penses-tu qu'il soit vraiment français? --- Je ne le pense pas. / Non, je ne le pense pas. / Je ne crois pas.

As you have just been shown, French also has many different ways of answering—both short and long—simple questions. While English has an emphasis on the auxiliary to drive the question forward, French not use any and instead relies on the verb.

Chapter 12 - Let's make some negative questions

So, that's how you make the going future tense into a question. Now, let's have a look at how we can turn it into a negative question. Well, it's pretty easy; all you do is take the question form of the going verb and put a "*ne*" in front and a "*pas*" on the end. You can then chuck an infinitive onto the end of that. Also, just be aware that the word "*ne*" turns into "*n*'" in front of a vowel.

ne vais-je pas is translated to: am I not going

ne vas-tu pas is translated to: isn't he going

ne va-t-elle pas is translated to: aren't we going

n'allez-vous pas is translated to: aren't you going

ne vont-ils pas is translated to: aren't they going

ne vont-elles pas is translated to: aren't they going

So, see if you can put these short questions into French:

Group 1

1. Are they not going to ask?
2. Am I not going to establish?
3. Am I not going to show?
4. Is she not going to see?
5. Is he not going to lose weight?
6. Are you not going to lose weight?
7. Am I not going to give?
8. Are you not going to understand?
9. Am I not going to lose?
10. Are they not going to write?

Group 1 --- answers

1. *Ne vont-ils pas demander?*
2. *Ne vais-je pas établir?*
3. *Ne vais-je pas montrer?*
4. *Ne va-t-elle pas voir?*
5. *Ne va-t-il pas maigrir?*
6. *N'allez-vous pas maigrir? / ne vas-tu pas maigrir?*
7. *Ne vais-je pas donner?*
8. *N'allez-vous pas comprendre / ne vas-tu pas comprendre?*
9. *N'allez-vous pas perdre / ne vas-tu pas perdre?*
10. *Ne vont-ils pas écrire?*

Group 2

1. Are we not going to fill up?
2. Are we not going to read?
3. Is he not going to fill up?
4. Am I not going to write?
5. Is he not going to do?
6. Are we not going to give back?
7. Is he not going to drink?
8. Are they not going to grow old?
9. Are you not going to succeed?
10. Are we not going to lose?

Group 2 --- answers

1. *N'allons-nous pas remplir?*
2. *N'allons-nous pas lire?*
3. *Ne va-t-il pas remplir?*
4. *Ne vais-je pas écrire?*
5. *Ne va-t-il pas faire?*
6. *N'allons-nous pas rendre?*
7. *Ne va-t-il pas boire?*
8. *Ne vont-ils pas vieillir?*
9. *N'allez-vous pas réussir? / ne vas-tu pas réussir?*
10. *N'allons-nous pas perdre?*

Group 3

1. Am I not going to say?
2. Are they not going to show?
3. Are you not going to answer?
4. Is she not going to lose weight?
5. Are they not going to open?
6. Are you not going to drive?
7. Am I not going to answer?
8. Is she not going to give?
9. Is he not going to succeed?
10. Are they not going to think about?

Group 3 --- answers

1. *Ne vais-je pas dire?*
2. *Ne vont-ils pas montrer?*
3. *N'allez-vous pas répondre? / ne vas-tu pas répondre?*
4. *Ne va-t-elle pas maigrir?*
5. *Ne vont-ils pas ouvrir?*
6. *N'allez-vous pas conduire / ne vas-tu pas conduire?*
7. *Ne vais-je pas répondre?*
8. *Ne va-t-elle pas donner?*

9. *Ne va-t-il pas réussir?*
10. *Ne vont-ils pas réfléchir?*

Group 4

1. Is she not going to think about?
2. Are we not going to say?
3. Are you not going to take?
4. Is she not going to understand?
5. Are we not going to understand?
6. Is she not going to speak?
7. Is he not going to lose?
8. Are you not going to see?
9. Are you not going to open?
10. Are we not going to learn?

Group 4 --- answers

1. *Ne va-t-elle pas réfléchir?*
2. *N'allons-nous pas dire?*
3. *N'allez-vous pas prendre? / ne vas-tu pas prendre?*
4. *Ne va-t-elle pas comprendre?*
5. *N'allons-nous pas comprendre?*
6. *Ne va-t-elle pas parler?*
7. *Ne va-t-il pas perdre?*
8. *N'allez-vous pas voir? / ne vas-tu pas voir?*
9. *N'allez-vous pas ouvrir? / ne vas-tu pas ouvrir?*
10. *N'allons-nous pas apprendre?*

Group 5

1. Are they not going to receive?
2. Are you not going to work?
3. Are we not going to give?
4. Are we not going to hear?
5. Are they not going to put?
6. Is he not going to give?
7. Are we not going to succeed?
8. Are we not going to speak?
9. Is he not going to establish?
10. Is he not going to make?

Group 5 --- answers

1. *Ne vont-ils pas recevoir?*
2. *N'allez-vous pas travailler? / ne vas-tu pas travailler?*
3. *N'allons-nous pas donner?*
4. *N'allons-nous pas entendre?*

5. *Ne vont-ils pas mettre?*
6. *Ne va-t-il pas donner?*
7. *N'allons-nous pas réussir?*
8. *N'allons-nous pas parler?*
9. *Ne va-t-il pas établir?*
10. *Ne va-t-il pas faire?*

Group 6

1. Are you not going to give?
2. Is she not going to grow up?
3. Is he not going to speak?
4. Is he not going to receive?
5. Is he not going to see?
6. Are they not going to grow up?
7. Is he not going to take?
8. Am I not going to understand?
9. Are we not going to receive?
10. Is she not going to receive?

Group 6 --- answers

1. *N'allez-vous pas donner? / ne vas-tu pas donner?*
2. *Ne va-t-elle pas grandir?*
3. *Ne va-t-il pas parler?*
4. *Ne va-t-il pas recevoir?*
5. *Ne va-t-il pas voir?*
6. *Ne vont-ils pas grandir?*
7. *Ne va-t-il pas prendre?*
8. *Ne vais-je pas comprendre?*
9. *N'allons-nous pas recevoir?*
10. *Ne va-t-elle pas recevoir?*

Group 7

1. Is she not going to visit?
2. Are they not going to understand?
3. Am I not going to learn?
4. Is he not going to drive?
5. Is he not going to grow old?
6. Are you not going to finish?
7. Are they not going to see?
8. Are they not going to lose weight?
9. Are we not going to make?
10. Am I not going to give back?

Group 7 --- answers

1. *Ne va-t-elle pas visiter?*
2. *Ne vont-ils pas comprendre?*
3. *Ne vais-je pas apprendre?*
4. *Ne va-t-il pas conduire?*
5. *Ne va-t-il pas vieillir?*
6. *N'allez-vous pas finir? / ne vas-tu pas finir?*
7. *Ne vont-ils pas voir?*
8. *Ne vont-ils pas maigrir?*
9. *N'allons-nous pas faire?*
10. *Ne vais-je pas rendre?*

Group 8

1. Is he not going to hear?
2. Are you not going to fill up?
3. Am I not going to find?
4. Am I not going to watch?
5. Is she not going to choose?
6. Are we not going to drink?
7. Are we not going to see?
8. Is he not going to think about?
9. Am I not going to put?
10. Is she not going to finish?

Group 8 --- answers

1. *Ne va-t-il pas entendre?*
2. *N'allez-vous pas remplir? / ne vas-tu pas remplir?*
3. *Ne vais-je pas trouver?*
4. *Ne vais-je pas regarder?*
5. *Ne va-t-elle pas choisir?*
6. *N'allons-nous pas boire?*
7. *N'allons-nous pas voir?*
8. *Ne va-t-il pas réfléchir?*
9. *Ne vais-je pas mettre?*
10. *Ne va-t-elle pas finir?*

Group 9

1. Are they not going to answer?
2. Are they not going to take?
3. Is he not going to read?
4. Am I not going to succeed?
5. Is she not going to grow old?
6. Are you not going to watch?
7. Are you not going to give back?
8. Is she not going to ask?

9. Are they not going to fill up?
10. Is she not going to write?

Group 9 --- answers

1. *Ne vont-ils pas répondre?*
2. *Ne vont-ils pas prendre?*
3. *Ne va-t-il pas lire?*
4. *Ne vais-je pas réussir?*
5. *Ne va-t-elle pas vieillir?*
6. *N'allez-vous pas regarder / ne vas-tu pas regarder?*
7. *N'allez-vous pas rendre / ne vas-tu pas rendre?*
8. *Ne va-t-elle pas demander?*
9. *Ne vont-ils pas remplir?*
10. *Ne va-t-elle pas écrire?*

Group 10

1. Is she not going to find?
2. Are we not going to grow old?
3. Am I not going to ask?
4. Are we not going to put?
5. Is she not going to work?
6. Is he not going to choose?
7. Am I not going to grow up?
8. Is she not going to put?
9. Is she not going to establish?
10. Are they not going to read?

Group 10 --- answers

1. *Ne va-t-elle pas trouver?*
2. *N'allons-nous pas vieillir?*
3. *Ne vais-je pas demander?*
4. *N'allons-nous pas mettre?*
5. *Ne va-t-elle pas travailler?*
6. *Ne va-t-il pas choisir?*
7. *Ne vais-je pas grandir?*
8. *Ne va-t-elle pas mettre?*
9. *Ne va-t-elle pas établir?*
10. *Ne vont-ils pas lire?*

Group 11

1. Are they not going to establish?
2. Are you not going to find?
3. Am I not going to wait?
4. Are we not going to find?

5. Are you not going to speak?
6. Is he not going to give back?
7. Are we not going to choose?
8. Is she not going to watch?
9. Are we not going to wait?
10. Is he not going to ask?

Group 11 --- answers

1. *Ne vont-ils pas établir?*
2. *N'allez-vous pas trouver? / ne vas-tu pas trouver?*
3. *Ne vais-je pas attendre?*
4. *N'allons-nous pas trouver?*
5. *N'allez-vous pas parler? / ne vas-tu pas trouver?*
6. *Ne va-t-il pas rendre?*
7. *N'allons-nous pas choisir?*
8. *Ne va-t-elle pas regarder?*
9. *N'allons-nous pas attendre?*
10. *Ne va-t-il pas demander?*

Group 12

1. Is he not going to learn?
2. Am I not going to work?
3. Are we not going to open?
4. Is she not going to take?
5. Am I not going to make?
6. Is she not going to learn?
7. Are they not going to lose?
8. Is she not going to lose?
9. Are you not going to offer?
10. Is she not going to open?

Group 12 --- answers

1. *Ne va-t-il pas apprendre?*
2. *Ne vais-je pas travailler?*
3. *N'allons-nous pas ouvrir?*
4. *Ne va-t-elle pas prendre?*
5. *Ne vais-je pas faire?*
6. *Ne va-t-elle pas apprendre?*
7. *Ne vont-ils pas perdre?*
8. *Ne va-t-elle pas perdre?*
9. *N'allez-vous pas offrir? / ne vas-tu pas offrir?*
10. *Ne va-t-elle pas ouvrir?*

Group 13

1. Are you not going to think about?
2. Are we not going to finish?
3. Are they not going to wait?
4. Are you not going to ask?
5. Are they not going to find?
6. Are we not going to do?
7. Is he not going to play?
8. Are we not going to watch?
9. Is he not going to put?
10. Are we not going to sell?

Group 13 --- answers

1. *N'allez-vous pas réfléchir? / ne vas-tu pas réfléchir?*
2. *N'allons-nous pas finir?*
3. *Ne vont-ils pas attendre?*
4. *N'allez-vous pas demander?*
5. *Ne vont-ils pas trouver?*
6. *N'allons-nous pas faire?*
7. *Ne va-t-il pas jouer?*
8. *N'allons-nous pas regarder?*
9. *Ne va-t-il pas mettre?*
10. *N'allons-nous pas vendre?*

Group 14

1. Are you not going to drink?
2. Is he not going to understand?
3. Am I not going to sell?
4. Am I not going to finish?
5. Is she not going to answer?
6. Are we not going to drive?
7. Are we not going to take?
8. Is she not going to wait?
9. Is he not going to sell?
10. Are you not going to visit?

Group 14 --- answers

1. *N'allez-vous pas boire? / ne vas-tu pas boire?*
2. *Ne va-t-il pas comprendre?*
3. *Ne vais-je pas vendre?*
4. *Ne vais-je pas finir?*
5. *Ne va-t-elle pas répondre?*
6. *N'allons-nous pas conduire?*
7. *N'allons-nous pas prendre?*
8. *Ne va-t-elle pas attendre?*

9. *Ne va-t-il pas vendre?*
10. *N'allez-vous pas visiter? / ne vas-tu pas visiter?*

Group 15

1. Am I not going to grow old?
2. Are we not going to play?
3. Am I not going to drink?
4. Are we not going to show?
5. Are they not going to speak?
6. Are you not going to play?
7. Are you not going to write?
8. Are they not going to do?
9. Are we not going to ask?
10. Am I not going to lose weight?

Group 15 --- answers

1. *Ne vais-je pas vieillir?*
2. *N'allons-nous pas jouer?*
3. *Ne vais-je pas boire?*
4. *N'allons-nous pas montrer?*
5. *Ne vont-ils pas parler?*
6. *N'allez-vous pas jouer? / ne vas-tu pas jouer?*
7. *N'allez-vous pas écrire? / ne vas-tu pas écrire?*
8. *Ne vont-ils pas faire?*
9. *N'allons-nous pas demander?*
10. *Ne vais-je pas maigrir?*

Group 16

1. Is he not going to wait?
2. Am I not going to hear?
3. Am I not going to receive?
4. Is she not going to make?
5. Are they not going to give?
6. Is he not going to write?
7. Am I not going to play?
8. Is she not going to read?
9. Am I not going to offer?
10. Are we not going to establish?

Group 16 --- answers

1. *Ne va-t-il pas attendre?*
2. *Ne vais-je pas entendre*
3. *Ne vais-je pas recevoir?*
4. *Ne va-t-elle pas faire?*

5. *Ne vont-ils pas donner?*
6. *Ne va-t-il pas écrire?*
7. *Ne vais-je pas jouer?*
8. *Ne va-t-elle pas lire?*
9. *Ne vais-je pas offrir?*
10. *N'allons-nous pas établir?*

Group 17

1. Are they not going to learn?
2. Are we not going to grow up?
3. Are we not going to visit?
4. Are you not going to establish?
5. Is she not going to offer?
6. Are they not going to give back?
7. Are they not going to play?
8. Is she not going to sell?
9. Are they not going to offer?
10. Is he not going to show?

Group 17 --- answers

1. *Ne vont-ils pas apprendre?*
2. *N'allons-nous pas grandir?*
3. *N'allons-nous pas visiter?*
4. *N'allez-vous pas établir? / ne vas-tu pas établir?*
5. *Ne va-t-elle pas offrir?*
6. *Ne vont-ils pas rendre?*
7. *Ne vont-ils pas jouer?*
8. *Ne va-t-elle pas vendre?*
9. *Ne vont-ils pas offrir?*
10. *Ne va-t-il pas montrer?*

Group 18

1. Is she not going to show?
2. Is he not going to watch?
3. Are you not going to show?
4. Is he not going to visit?
5. Is he not going to grow up?
6. Are they not going to watch?
7. Is she not going to say?
8. Is he not going to finish?
9. Are they not going to hear?
10. Am I not going to take?

Group 18 --- answers

1. *Ne va-t-elle pas montrer?*
2. *Ne va-t-il pas regarder?*
3. *N'allez-vous pas montrer? / ne vas-tu pas montrer?*
4. *Ne va-t-il pas visiter?*
5. *Ne va-t-il pas grandir?*
6. *Ne vont-ils pas regarder?*
7. *Ne va-t-elle pas dire?*
8. *Ne va-t-il pas finir?*
9. *Ne vont-ils pas entendre?*
10. *Ne vais-je pas prendre?*

Group 19

1. Am I not going to see?
2. Is she not going to succeed?
3. Are they not going to say?
4. Is he not going to find?
5. Is she not going to fill up?
6. Are you not going to wait?
7. Is she not going to do?
8. Am I not going to open?
9. Are you not going to say?
10. Are we not going to write?

Group 19 --- answers

1. *Ne vais-je pas voir?*
2. *Ne va-t-elle pas réussir?*
3. *Ne vont-ils pas dire?*
4. *Ne va-t-il pas trouver?*
5. *Ne va-t-elle pas remplir?*
6. *N'allez-vous pas attendre? / ne vas-tu pas attendre?*
7. *Ne va-t-elle pas faire?*
8. *Ne vais-je pas ouvrir?*
9. *N'allez-vous pas dire? / ne vas-tu pas dire?*
10. *N'allons-nous pas écrire?*

Group 20

1. Am I not going to choose?
2. Are we not going to work?
3. Am I not going to drive?
4. Am I not going to do?
5. Are they not going to work?
6. Am I not going to speak?
7. Is she not going to drive?
8. Are you not going to receive?

9. Are they not going to succeed?
10. Is he not going to offer?

Group 20 --- answers

1. *Ne vais-je pas choisir?*
2. *N'allons-nous pas travailler?*
3. *Ne vais-je pas conduire?*
4. *Ne vais-je pas faire?*
5. *Ne vont-ils pas travailler?*
6. *Ne vais-je pas parler?*
7. *Ne va-t-elle pas conduire?*
8. *N'allez-vous pas recevoir? / ne vas-tu pas recevoir?*
9. *Ne vont-ils pas réussir?*
10. *Ne va-t-il pas offrir?*

Group 21

1. Are you not going to sell?
2. Are we not going to lose weight?
3. Am I not going to think about?
4. Are they not going to drive?
5. Are you not going to put?
6. Are you not going to grow up?
7. Is he not going to work?
8. Is he not going to open?
9. Are we not going to think about?
10. Is he not going to say?

Group 21 --- answers

1. *N'allez-vous pas vendre? / ne vas-tu pas vendre?*
2. *N'allons-nous pas maigrir?*
3. *Ne vais-je pas réfléchir?*
4. *Ne vont-ils pas conduire?*
5. *N'allez-vous pas mettre? / ne vas-tu pas mettre?*
6. *N'allez-vous pas grandir? / ne vas-tu pas grandir?*
7. *Ne va-t-il pas travailler?*
8. *Ne va-t-il pas ouvrir?*
9. *N'allons-nous pas réfléchir?*
10. *Ne va-t-il pas dire?*

Group 22

1. Am I not going to fill up?
2. Is she not going to drink?
3. Is she not going to play?
4. Are they not going to choose?

5. Are you not going to grow old?
6. Are you not going to read?
7. Are they not going to drink?
8. Are you not going to hear?
9. Are they not going to finish?
10. Are you not going to choose?

Group 22 --- answers

1. *Ne vais-je pas remplir?*
2. *Ne va-t-elle pas boire?*
3. *Ne va-t-elle pas jouer?*
4. *Ne vont-ils pas choisir?*
5. *N'allez-vous pas vieillir? / ne vas-tu pas vieillir?*
6. *N'allez-vous pas lire? / ne vas-tu pas lire?*
7. *Ne vont-ils pas boire?*
8. *N'allez-vous pas entendre? / ne vas-tu pas entendre?*
9. *Ne vont-ils pas finir?*
10. *N'allez-vous pas choisir? / ne vas-tu pas choisir?*

Group 23

1. Is she not going to hear?
2. Are they not going to visit?
3. Am I not going to visit?
4. Are they not going to make?
5. Are they not going to sell?
6. Are you not going to make?
7. Are you not going to do?
8. Are you not going to learn?
9. Are we not going to answer?
10. Am I not going to read?
11. Are you not going to lose?
12. Is he not going to answer?
13. Are we not going to offer?
14. Is she not going to give back?

Group 23 -- answers

1. *Ne va-t-elle pas entendre?*
2. *Ne vont-ils pas visiter?*
3. *Ne vais-je pas visiter?*
4. *Ne vont-ils pas faire?*
5. *Ne vont-ils pas vendre?*
6. *N'allez-vous pas faire? / ne vas-tu pas faire?*
7. *N'allez-vous pas faire? / ne vas-tu pas faire?*
8. *N'allez-vous pas apprendre? / ne vas-tu pas apprendre?*
9. *N'allons-nous pas répondre?*

10. *Ne vais-je pas lire?*
11. *N'allez-vous pas perdre? / ne vas-tu pas perdre?*
12. *Ne va-t-il pas répondre?*
13. *N'allons-nous pas offrir?*
14. *Ne va-t-elle pas rendre?*

Chapter 13 - In Case of Emergency

We all dread the worst thing happening when we are abroad and unable to explain ourselves in our own home language. However, this section should be able to help you with any emergencies that you may face along the way. Whether you have rented a car and it has broken down, right through the spectrum to losing your spectacles, I have you covered. It's nice when you are able to have one section of a phrase book that will help you through these situations.

Remember that if you are in need of seeing a doctor, you should have your documentation with you. That includes your passport, any medical insurance that you have with you and also carry all medicines that you are currently taking so that the doctor has a good overall picture of your current state of health. For a generalist appointment, this costs you $23 and a little more than that if you call a doctor at weekends of if the doctor has to come and see you, but it's nothing to be that worried about as the doctors do not charge excessively. It's a better idea to let a doctor see you than to assume that your situation is an emergency because if you call out an ambulance unnecessarily, this may impact how much you get back from the expense of that ambulance, particularly if it is found that you didn't need it.

Illness

When you are in France, you may become ill. The first recourse when you are ill is to see a local doctor. Your hotel will be able to put you in touch with a doctor and if you are too ill to visit, will be able to arrange for a doctor to visit you at the hotel. You will need to explain your situation to the hotel and this is the easiest way to do it.

I am ill and need a doctor	Je suis malade et j'ai besoin d'un médecin	Juh swee mallad ay jay buzwan dun medsan
I feel very sick	Je me sens très malade	Juh muh ons tray mallad
I am dizzy	J'ai des vertiges	Jzay dé vair tij
I have a fever	j'ai de la fièvre	Jzay du la fee ev
My husband has had a heart attack	Mon mari a fait une crise cardiaque	Mon marry ah fay oon crease cardee ac
My wife has had a heart attack	Ma femme a fait une crise cardiaque	Ma Fam ah fay oon crease cardee ac
My son is very sick	Mon fils est très malade	Mon feece ay tray mallad
My daughter is sick	Ma fille est malade	Ma fee ay mallad

You can expect the cost of a visit to a doctor to be reasonable, so don't let this worry you for the time being. A doctor will be able to reassure you. Much of the time, it's merely a travel related thing, but even if it is not, the medical service in France is second to none and you can expect to be dealt with fairly fast. The hotel may decide that you need to go to hospital and again, don't let this worry you. In many cases, this is precautionary.

If you are taken ill away from your hotel and need medical assistance, the number that you need to dial will be 15. Speak slowly and concisely. They have a lot of patience, but will need to know several things:

Where are you?

What has happened?

Do you need an ambulance?

Thus, before dialing, try to establish where you are by looking at street names.

In the doctor's office

If you are sent to a doctor's office by your hotel or by arrangement made by phone, you can expect to be thoroughly examined. Your blood pressure will be taken and you will have a doctor who will check your heart rate and other things that are standard. If he feels that you need to be in hospital, he will arrange it. Many doctors speak English, but there are some words that you need to understand in order to help him.

That hurts	*ça fait mal*	Sa fay mal
I am having trouble breathing	*Je ne peux pas respirer*	Juh nuh puh pa respeeray
I feel terrible	*je me sens mal*	juh muh son mal
I can't swallow	*Je ne peux pas avaler*	Juh nu puh pa avallay
I am afraid	*J'ai peur*	Jzay pur

It helps to have a wide knowledge of body parts and this section will help you to find the right words to help you describe your illness.

My head hurts	*J'ai mal à la tête*	Jzay mal ah la tett
My neck is hurting	*mon cou me fait mal*	mon coo muh fay mal
I think that my leg is broken	*Je pense que ma jambe est cassée*	Juh ponss ku ma jomb ay cassay
I think I have broken a rib	*Je pense que j'ai une côte cassée*	Je ponss ku jzay oon cote cassay
I have stomach ache	*J'ai mal à l'estomac*	Jzay mal a lestoma
My back hurts	*Mon dos me fait mal*	Mon doe muh fay mal
My arm hurts	*Mon bras me fait mal*	Mon bra fay mal

More generally, you can tell the doctor that "IT HURTS HERE" and use your hands to show him where you are hurting.

| It hurts here | *ça fait mal ici* | sa fay mal ee see |

You may be interested to know that quite amusingly OUCH in English is said slightly differently in French as ACHH! However, the doctor will have the sense to recognize when something hurts!

When you have other emergencies

When you hire a car, you should be given a number of dial in the case of the car breaking down. These are some phrases that you will find helpful:

The car will not go	*La voiture ne roule pas*	La vwature nu rool pa
I don't know what to do	*Je ne sais pas quoi faire*	Ju nu say pa qwa faire
I hired the car	*J'ai loué la voiture*	Jzay loo ay la vwature
Can you call them for me?	*Pouvez-vous les appeler pour moi*	Poovay voo lays appellay por mwa

In most cases, this will be enough since garages all over France are accustomed to the hire car companies and most are friendly and helpful. Once the garage has the go ahead from the company to repair the car, they may also be able to replace the car and will let the garage know. They will pass this news on to you and may even be in association with the hire car company.

In the case of Loss or Theft

If you have lost something of value, then your best bet is to first approach your embassy. It's a good idea to have their number at hand. If, however, this is not possible, you will need to contact the Gendarmerie Nationale especially if you believe that foul play is at work in the loss of your items. The phrases that you may need are included here and will help you to move forward with your situation.

Where is the police station?	*Où est la gendarmerie?*	Ooh ay la jhondarm ah ree
My passport has been stolen	*Mon passeport a été volé*	Mon pass port a ettay volay
My handbag has been stolen	*Mon sac à main a été volé*	Mon sack ah mahn ah etay volay
My money has been stolen	*Mon argent a été volé*	Mon arrjon ah etay volay

Once they have established that something has been stolen, you may have to report where this happened and give them as much detail as you can. This means knowing when you first noticed that it was gone. If you were robbed by people and can describe them this will help the police in their inquiries. Here are some phrases that may help you to describe the thieves.

They were young	*Ils étaient jeunes*	Eels ettay jhun
There were three of them	*Il y en avait trois*	Eel yon avay twa
There were two of them	*Il y en avait deux*	Eel yon avay duh
There was only one man	*Il n'y avait qu'un seul homme*	Eel nyavay kun sool hom
He followed me	*Il m'a suivi*	Eel ma sweevay

342

Can you ring the US embassy please?	*Pouvez-vous appeler l'ambassade des États-Unis, s'il vous plait?*	Poovay voos appellay lembassade days etat ooni see voo play?

Or if you want them to ring the British Embassy you use the same phrase but replace the name of the embassy thus:

Can you ring the British embassy please?	*Pouvez-vous appeler l'ambassade Britannique, s'il vous plait?*	Poovay voos appellay lembassade britanneek see vous play

The important thing to let people know when you are in an emergency situation is that you don't speak French and that you need to speak to someone who understands English. Getting in touch with your embassy will help you because members of staff at the embassy will be able to translate for you so that you are better served by the emergency services.

The phrases that are shown below will help you with this, but you need to try and keep calm in an emergency situation and it helps to have details of your embassy with you so that these can be called straight away to get the help that you need.

I don't speak French	*Je ne parle pas français*	Juh nuh parl pa froncay
I am American	*Je suis américain(e)* the e explains you are feminine but doesn't matter in speech too much.	Juh swees amairican
I am English	*Je suis anglais(e)*	Juh swees onglay(z)

Most emergency services these days in France will be able to put you in touch with someone who speaks your language. With the opening up of Europe, English is the second language to most French. However, be patient if it takes them a little time to get a translator to the scene so that you can use that person to explain your predicament.

You will find that the emergency services are very prompt and that your call to them will be answered quickly. The emergency number for the Police is 17 or if you are calling from a mobile, the number is 112 which will then filter your call either for fire, ambulance or police. On the 112 number, you should have no difficulty talking to someone in English, since the international operators who answer these calls talk in up to 40 languages.

Things emergency services will need:

They will need your name. Try to learn the alphabet letters that make up your name because they are pronounced differently in French. However, if you are going to call and do not have this information use the 112 number.

They will need a note of where you are, so try to have this ready for them. Street names are usually shown on the wall of buildings, especially at junctions with other roads.

They may ask your date of birth. Usually this is stated day/month/year.

They will need to ask you what the situation is that you have found yourself in and explaining this to the 112 number should not be a problem, once you have told them that you only speak English.

Phrases that will be of use:

Je m'appelle .... My name is ....

Pronunciation: Juh mapelle

Mon sac a été volé .... My purse has been stolen

Pronunciation: Mon sac a ettay volay

Je suis perdu .... I am lost

Pronunciation: Juh swee perdoo

You should have no trouble getting your problems sorted out and can always ask your hotel owner to telephone for you in the case of emergency happening while going to your hotel. This is usually the best way because the hotel owner will know the language and will also know what to do to help you through difficult circumstances.

Quiz Time!

Here we are at the end of the third lesson!. Are you ready for quiz number three? Let's see!

1) What is the emergency number for the police?

2) What is the mobile emergency number for police?

3) How would you say "It hurts here"?

4) How would you say "the care will not go"?

5) How do you say "I am sick and need a doctor"?

Answers:

1) *17*

2) *112*

3) *Ça fait mal ici*

4) *La voiture ne va pas*

5) *Je suis malada et j'ai besoin d'un médicin*

Chapter 14 - Creating a Simple Learning Plan

Your Core Daily French Practice

We have looked at a variety of techniques and tips for learning French in this book, but how much and how often should you actually study? I have learnt that success in language learning depends largely on being consistent, and that going for days (or even weeks) without studying makes it difficult to progress. Therefore, I try to make language learning a part of my lifestyle and this means aiming to study every day. Now, in reality, I do take days off --- sometimes a few days off! However, when you consider that learning a language is a long-term project, it seems smarter to set out with the intention of studying every day and to allow yourself some flexibility within that, than to do the opposite, which is to "fit it in" whenever you have time.

To make sure language learning is part of my lifestyle, I have a daily core study time. This is a session of around 45 minutes (sometimes more, sometimes less) which I like to do first thing in the morning, before my day begins. Having my core study time early in the morning helps make sure the study gets done, because once the working day begins it is hard to carve out time for anything else! I sit in a quiet room where I will not be distracted and I use the time to do what you might call the "hard work" --- concentrated and focused study, as opposed to activities such as browsing language videos on YouTube, which is usually a shallow activity full of distraction.

Now, the key is to make your core study time regular, because it is in the act of revisiting the language every day that you learn new things and deepen your understanding of what you already know. Along with consistency, the other most important aspect of this approach to learning languages is the creation of time for in-depth study. You may have plenty of dead time throughout your day --- on the bus, during your lunch hour --- and this can be useful time for extra practice, but dead time is often short and prone to distraction. I have found nothing to be as valuable as quiet, uninterrupted time for language learning in which you can truly focus, and that is why I create this core study time every day and make it a priority.

What I have described here is the routine that works particularly well for me --- I can focus well in the morning, and 45-60 minutes is a productive amount of time. However, I would be the first to say you should adapt this to fit your personal preferences. If the most practical and productive study time for you is 15 minutes in the evening before bed, then that is precisely what you should do. The important thing is to study consistency and to create an environment in which you can focus.

Finding Time to Speak

The way I view speaking practice is not so much for learning new things (although you certainly will), but rather to consolidate what you have already learnt. Speaking with people is your opportunity to take the language you have learnt on your own and put it into practice, so that speaking starts to become natural and you learn to express yourself better in French. Once you feel ready to start speaking and have experienced your first conversations in French, you may well become addicted to the feeling of communicating in another language, which is a wonderful thing!

However, the practicalities of creating the time to speak French with people is not always easy, and for this reason there is an ongoing risk that you go for weeks or months without speaking with anyone, for no reason other than you do not get around to organising it. Unless you are lucky enough to be surrounded by French speakers, you will have to be proactive in creating your own opportunities to speak French. In my own learning, I realised a long time ago that if I do not schedule my speaking time, it will not happen!

Therefore, I have a rule of scheduling multiple lessons and language exchanges at a time, usually deciding on the next four or five dates in advance, so that they go into my diary and are fixed. As a consequence, my speaking happens. I recommend you do the same.

Studying in Your Dead Time

If you have adopted the principle of core study time, then you are off to a great start. The good news, though, is that there is almost certainly plenty of extra time throughout your day which you can take advantage of to spend more time with French. Dead time refers to those moments in the day when you cannot be productive and have no choice but to wait. Commuting is the classic example, but you may also spend time walking, eating, or waiting for meetings to start. People use this time differently, but there is a fair chance that in such situations you either reach for your phone, daydream, or some combination of the two!

Periods of dead time throughout your day can add up to considerable amounts of time --- easily an hour or more per day --- and this time can be a great asset for your language learning if you make use it in smart way. While your core study time is best used for focused study, your dead time is ideal for less intense, more entertaining activities. For most people, the trick to taking advantage of your dead time is to use your smartphone or tablet to make your language learning material portable. By all means, you can carry your textbook around with you all day, but technology has given us many options for accessing the material we want anywhere:

- Download podcasts in French
- Use electronic flashcards to review your vocabulary
- Read the news in French on Le Monde website
- Buy French short story books for your Kindle
- Take pictures on your phone of the chapter you are currently working on in your textbook so you always have it with you
- Take a picture of the grammar tables you are trying to memorize

The great thing about using your dead time to study French is that everyone has dead time, it does not have to be scheduled, and it can quickly add up to large amounts of time. The trick is to develop the habit of recognizing when you are at a loose end and to use the time for French rather than Facebook!

What Should the First Year of French Look Like?

Let's imagine you have a goal of achieving a good level of proficiency in French in one year. What would that year look like, and how would you need to study differently over the course of that year in order to reach your goal? This is a frequently-asked question which is helpful for developing the mindset of a good language learner, and so in this closing section I will describe my experience of how the study process changes as your level improves.

Getting Started: The First Three Months

It is preferable to be fairly superficial at this stage, as the value lies in getting a general picture of the language rather than memorizing every detail.

After this, you will need to move on to a more complete textbook that will give you a good grounding in all aspects of French, including pronunciation, vocabulary, grammar and so on. The majority of your time should be spent listening and reading to the dialogues in the textbook, referring to grammar explanations where necessary to help you understand the contents of the dialogues. (you will learn the most French by reading and listening, not by learning rules).

At this stage, you should start to learn any key verbs, useful expressions and basic verb conjugations that you have not yet mastered, as these will allow you to start speaking and communicating with people. At the same time, I recommend starting to work with a teacher or language partner, and the best way to use your speaking time is to practice the material you have learnt from your textbook.

This is an exciting phase in which you learn a lot, quickly, and your progress is tangible.

Building on Your Foundations: Months 3-6

At this stage, you should have a strong foundation in French and be able to hold a basic conversation on simple topics. This next phase might last for another three months, but will feel very different to the first phase: at this point, despite having studied for a few months already, you will still struggle to understand spoken French, and you will grow frustrated at not being able to express yourself as well as you would like.

The main goal of this phase is to grow your vocabulary as much and as fast as possible, because without enough words you will not be able to speak or understand enough to hold enjoyable conversations. In order to grow your vocabulary, you need to give yourself as much exposure as possible to French, and this means doing a lot of listening and reading. The problem you face in doing this, however, is that your comprehension is not yet good enough to read interesting content; you will struggle with newspapers, novels, radio, or any material intended for native speakers. Therefore, you will likely be restricted to learner material such as intermediate level textbooks or graded readers, and may have to compromise on the "fun factor"!

It is also vital at this stage to begin to speak more. I recommend at least three speaking sessions a week of 30-60 minutes, but ideally more. In these speaking sessions, you should talk about a variety of topics, and it is helpful to use your study material as inspiration for this. For example, if you have been reading a story about World War II, you can discuss the story with your speaking partner, which allows you to review the new vocabulary you have learnt, and gain more and more confidence in your speaking.

Pushing on Towards Fluency: From Month Six Onwards

After around six months of regular study, you should have developed a good conversational level in French, and now be able to understand a fair amount --- although you will still feel out of your depth when given native-level material. At this stage, you will want to move away from studying the language and start using it in your daily life, with real people and for real purposes. You will still find it hard, but this is the stage where you need to take a step up, and learn by doing.

Your aim for this period is to do everything possible to integrate French into your daily life. Attend events where people speak French, join French Meetup groups, watch TV in French instead of in English, read the news in French rather than English, read magazines and books. In short, replace everything you normally do in English with French. The more immersion you can create for yourself, the faster and more effective your learning will be. When choosing material to read, the guiding principle is to choose things you are genuinely interested in. If you like cycling, read French books on cycling. If you like healthy eating, read blogs or watch YouTube channels that talk about healthy eating in French. There is no greater source of motivation than spending your time doing things that interest you.

Finally, you may consider using more advanced tools such as a frequency dictionary. This is a dictionary that lists words in French in their order of frequency in daily life. When browsing through the dictionary, any unknown words you encounter will be the most useful for you to learn. In this way, you can use the frequency dictionary to "plug the holes" in your French. You might also study an advanced grammar textbook, for example, in order to improve your grammar in a targeted way. Perhaps ironically, the more advanced you get, the more you will find studying grammar to be useful.

This phase lasts longer than the other two phases combined, the reason being that mastering the most advanced areas of a language is inevitably harder than learning the basics. In this phase, you shift your approach to learning French dramatically, away from studying and towards living the language.

If you can follow the spirit of this three-phase structure for a year, you will find yourself with a good level of French, able to cope well in daily life, and fully able to meet new people and make friends. I hope this prospect is exciting for you --- it should be! Of course, for many people, doing this in one year will be too intensive, but the balance of the journey looks the same whether you do it in one year or ten years.

Chapter 15: Strategies in Language Learning

Staying Motivated

Learning a language takes some time. You may have heard advertisements claiming to make you fluent in a language in one month or three months; don't believe them. Depending on your goal you will have hundreds of hours of language learning ahead. Therefore it is important that you mentally prepare yourself to put the time and effort required to attain the desired level of proficiency in your target language. As I have mentioned earlier, a good percentage of learners abandon their language-learning program before even reaching an intermediate level. Don't be like them. Without persistence and determination it is not possible to gain mastery in anything. In projects that takes a longer period of time, people may go through phases where they feel reluctant to continue their learning and become tempted to let everything go down the river. Setbacks are part of the learning process. Keep yourself motivated in times you feel like giving up.

Grab a pen and paper and write down what motivated you for learning a foreign language. You can maintain a journal to write down your goal, your progress and your success. Sometimes we are very quick to forget our past success and get frustrated with our pursuit. Journaling will be helpful to look back, remind us of our past success and get ourselves back on the track. A journal can be a lifesaver in down times, and will be helpful to refresh your motivation and enthusiasm. The visual imagery exercise is also an excellent technique for keeping you motivated in your language learning.

Identifying Your Learning Style

Since birth, we have all been learning, and throughout our lives, our innate ability to learn anything efficiently will stay constant. Before beginning your second language study, you need to know your 'learning style' more than anything else. Everyone has their own unique process when it comes to learning a new language. There are four distinct learning styles that every one of us falls into.

- Visual/Verbal
- Visual/Non-Verbal
- Auditory/Verbal
- Tactile/Kinesthetic

To find out whether you are a visual, auditory or tactile learner, you can follow a simple technique: Pick two random words and read them over a few times; try to remember the words the next day, if you can, then you are probably a visual learner. If not, pick another two words and have someone to read you a few times without you seeing them. On the next day, try to remember those words, if you can, you are most likely an auditory learner. If both techniques fail, pick another two words, write them, repeat them out loud, relate them to your memories, feelings or sound-alikes, then try to remember the next day. If you can, most likely you are a tactile learner.

You have now identified the style that works best for you. Now it is time to move on.

Immersing Yourself

Although we have discussed earlier that living in the country of your chosen language does not always guarantee that you will learn the correct usage of grammar and pronunciation, there are still some great advantages. The biggest advantage is, the environment will always keep you motivated and you will learn naturally. Some people create a language bubble shield around themselves from the local tongue while living in a foreign country; they don't bother to change their faulty grammar and pronunciation. But to get the most out of your immersion strategy here are the suggestions you can follow:

Live with native speakers if you want to develop your conversational skill within the quickest time possible. You may look for a family with a spare room or student house share, the point of this strategy is to spend a good amount time of your day with native speakers. By living with native speakers under the same roof, you will not only practice language skills, but also gain a good cultural understanding. This technique will work better if they don't speak English.

When you are living in a foreign country, you may discover people trying to practice their English with you. It won't always be easy to ignore their demand, but don't be tempted. Continue to speak the local language.

Immersion technique often fail because people feel reluctant to formal study. Without studying the grammar you will keep making mistakes without knowing it. Check language learning websites; try verb drills; soon you will start enjoying it.

Always keep a notebook with you. If you hear a word and don't understand it, note it down even if it's the phonetic guess of the right spelling. It is an amazing technique to build up your own vocabulary in a natural setting and pick up colloquialisms.

Don't get disappointed if you are not living in the country of your language of interest. Find the native speakers and communities in your country and communicate with them. Foreigners staying in your country are most often flattered if people make attempts to learn their languages, and show eagerness to help you correcting your pronunciation. They may even teach you slang which you most likely won't find in any language course.

Memorizing Words and Phrases

Memorization is half the battle, and there are some powerful techniques to memorize words quickly. A typical language has hundreds of thousands even millions of words; a large portion of them won't be immediately relevant to you in the beginning. Even natives know only a fraction of the entire vocabulary. Therefore it is wise to opt for the most useful words. In every language, there are few words that are used quite frequently. For example, you can cover a quarter of whatever you say or write in English by only nine words: and, be, have, it, of, the, to, will, you. Typically in a given day, a native speaker uses between 3000 and 4000 frequent words that covers 90-95% of the language. These are the words, which you absolutely need to know to get the most minimum idea of what is written or spoken. Therefore make sure you pick up the vocabulary that is universally useful and not necessarily what you think may be useful some day if you are in an extremely particular situation.

In order to memorize selected words, you have to build a context. If you try to absorb words in absence of context, you may soon forget them.

Here and example on how to create a context. Let's say you want to remember a Spanish word "caber" which means, "to fit". With repetition you will certainly manage to memorize the word. But, there is an easy way; break down the word: caber = cab + bear; now imagine fitting a bear in a cab. You will only need to recall this hook a couple times to create a lasting memory. One of the popular methods to memorize words is mnemonic link system, which involves creating a meaningful story and link together the successive words in the list. Here is the list of eleven words: Monkey, Apple, Bear, Twig, Tornado, Train, Airplane, Eagle, Sahara, ice cream and hat. Let us put those words in the story and visualize.

Our first word is monkey. So imagine a funny looking Monkey is sitting on a tree. The next word is apple, so the monkey is sitting on an apple tree and eating an Apple. A lazy Bear is sleeping under the apple tree. As the monkey finished with eating the apple, he noticed the bear lying under the tree. So he thought to have some fun. He grabbed a Twig and approached the bear cautiously. Then he tickled inside the bear's nose with the twig. The bear woke up and started to sneeze so heavily, that it caused a Tornado. The tornado wind was so strong that it pulled a Train and lifted it up in the sky. There was an Airplane flying along; the train got in the way and crashed into the airplane. A big Eagle was passing by. She noticed the incident and came into rescue. She held the train in one claw and the plane in another and flew towards the Sahara desert. In the Sahara desert there was an ogre eating an Ice cream. He was wearing a strange big Hat. The eagle landed on his hat. This story may sound absurd. But the human brain can remember absurd stories quicker. Don't forget to keep practicing the words once you move on to memorizing other words.

Listening Comprehension and Pronunciation

Spend some time paying attention to the sound and rhythm of the language. You can watch movies or TV shows or the native speakers in your neighborhood. Listen to things that interest you; if you don't enjoy something, you will find it hard to continue; you will feel bored and quit. Listening to songs is a wonderful way to boost your listening comprehension, especially when you have lyrics written so that you can follow along while listening.

Language learners often work tirelessly on their pronunciation skill, spending hours to attain native level perfection. But it is extremely difficult for an adult learner to imitate a flawless accent; it takes years of practice. Accent will improve in time. Instead of putting too much emphasis on perfecting the accent, it will be wise if you stress on honing your pronunciation so that it's clear to understand.

Embracing Mistakes

Fear of making mistakes will hinder your progress. Every mistake is an opportunity to learn. Don't feel embarrassed if you make mistakes while speaking. Instead learn to embrace the mistake. Mistakes aren't the monsters that we make them out to be. Use your mistakes to ask yourself some thought provoking questions like what can be done to correct them.

Start acting like a child while learning a new language. Like children go for something they want, they don't really care what people think. Embrace your mistakes and your quality of learning will be an unstoppable force.

Stay motivated

The acquiring of a second language is an enjoyable and rewarding endeavor that can be pursued at any age. It is beneficial in many ways, including intellectually, practically, and aspirationally. However, it takes time and dedication – and the primary factor contributing whether a learner will succeed or not is Motivation.

At the commencement of any second language learning, the learner thinks that he will do the utmost to learn and communicate effectively in the target language, however, without motivation the learner may simply give up before even trying.

When the learner pursues a learning activity for the pure enjoyment of it – for example with regard to language learning, he wishes to connect with people with various cultures, access to the worlds of fashion, gastronomy, and arts, etc. – that is called Intrinsic Motivation.

On the other hand – the learner is learning the language for his career growth or to find meaningful employment – it is called Extrinsic Motivation which is rewards-based and determined by external factors.

Set SMART goals

Goals setting along with motivation are an important aspect of achieving the desired result that the learner envisions. An effective way to set goals is to use SMART which stands for Specific, Measurable, Attainable, Relevant, and Time-Bound.

Keep in mind that having clarity in mind is important for setting a goal, and for the mind to respond best and immediately the goals are written in the present tense which makes them more believable. Goals should be set within a 3 to 6 months time frame.

Now with regard to language learning, take a look at the following goal assuming we are in the month of January:

It is the last day of the month of May. I can speak and write confidently about myself and someone else for 5 minutes using the Présent, Passé composé, and Futur Simple tenses in French. I can confidently ask questions using the following interrogative words : quoi, qui, quand, où, qui, qui, qui, pourquoi, comment et combien

- Specific as it focuses on specific tenses and specific interrogative words.

- Measurable as it focuses on 3 tenses and 10 interrogatives words.

- Ambitious as it focuses on Speaking and Writing which are fundamental means through which we learn new information.

- Realistic as the goal was set in the month of January and has to be achieved by the month of May.

- Time-Bound as the goal's deadline is the last day of the month of May.

Buddy up

When a student starts learning a language, the first thing he must do is to pair up with a language partner. Connect with people is easier now as advancements in technologies have afforded us the ability to communicate no matter where we are in the world.

Meeting new people who know another language can be life-changing and full of extraordinary adventures. Personally, this led me to make friends on several continents, to visit cities or even entire countries.

Reward yourself

Children aren't the only ones who love rewards - adults too!

Using rewards as a source of motivation is one of the most effective tools in achieving goals, but also one of the least used. For example, once you reach a milestone, treat yourself to a night at the movies or special food, or buy that new top that has caught your eye.

Remember that rewards and motivation go hand in hand. Whether it is a gold star reward, a congratulatory note, or a prize, the next time you feel stuck or in need of help, reward yourself.

Conclusion

I want to praise you and congratulate you on continuing down my journey from start to finish. I sincerely hope that I managed to set you up for success in the course of this book. I truly believe that I do, but the proof will be in the pudding of learning and using French in your daily life. I expect you to do that.

This is not all about the French language, grammar or vocabulary, but if you have done so far, you should have laid a strong foundation on which to base your future studies of the French language and be well on your path to fluency. It doesn't take ten years, or even one, to learn French. You might be shocked to discover that you already know a lot of French.

French grammar can be a hassle, even for a native speaker, but if you pay attention to this guide, you can quickly realize that English and French are much more similar than you may have guessed at first. As a native English speaker, French is a surprisingly easy language to understand. Or it ought to be, rather.

FREE AUDIO OF "LEARN FRENCH for advanced users"

Download your fee audio from our website:

www.dupontlanguageinstitute.com

or follow this QR code:

To download the file:

Username: book-4-AC
Password: +]RzE&CFw,T,

To open the file:

Password: Ycr/85)74H0?2!45

French
short stories

11 compelling short stories for

intermediate and advanced users

Introduction

Are you ready to dive in to French short stories? If yes, then keep reading...

This book presents short stories that you can read to practice French language. Each story has its own topic, where important vocabulary is presented before the story. Then, you have the story, which you can read at your own leisure.

The most challenging part of learning a foreign language is making yourself study regularly. When studying a language, repetition and regularity are vital. You could do small sessions in a week, but if you leave off until the next week, much of it will be forgotten. However, if you study a little each day and practice regularly, you'll easily remember and retain the information that you've covered. The French language is not difficult, you just have to know the basics. Once you get them, it will just be a matter of practice.

The first few times you try to speak French, you'll probably get it wrong. And that's okay!

Learning French is easy, especially if you have the opportunity to talk to native speakers They don't articulate as much, so you've got to listen carefully, but you'll get used to it with time.

The best tip I can give you is to never give up. It may sound cliché, but it is the best way to accomplish your goal..

Also, start speaking French with friends. Get them involved, because explaining your new favorite words will help consolidate your learning.

Or, if your friends aren't interested, just speak to yourself! There are so many ways to learn spoken French nowadays, such as listening to French music, watching French movies (be sure to watch the original version with English subtitles though. You need to understand it, too). An excellent way to learn is to record yourself reading or speaking French, then listen to the recordings while you walk or travel, etc. You'll improve day by day, so don't give up.

And one more thing...

Learn French at your own pace. It's easier to learn a language with passion!

1. Fin des vacances

Histoire 1

Henry est au camp d'été et c'est aujourd'hui le dernier jour des vacances où Peter peut faire tout ce qu'il veut avant de retourner au travail comme enseignant la semaine prochaine.

Peter emmène Charlie faire une longue promenade. Ils se rendent au parc, puis se promènent dans les champs et rentrent chez eux après huit kilomètres. Charlie s'allonge pour un long sommeil.

Peter va dans la cuisine pour préparer un déjeuner et s'arrête pour réfléchir à ce qu'il veut vraiment faire pendant l'après-midi.

Henry is at summer camp and today is the last day of the holidays when Peter can do whatever he wants to do before he goes back to work as a teacher next week.

Peter takes Charlie for a long walk. They go to the park and then walk through the fields and arrive home after eight kilometres. Charlie lies down for a long sleep.

Peter goes into the kitchen to prepare an early lunch and stops to think about what he really wants to do during the afternoon.

Quelles sont ses options?

Il peut rester à la maison et regarder la télé. Non, il peut le faire quand il veut.

Il peut aller faire les courses afin d'acheter de la nourriture pour la semaine prochaine. Non, il peut acheter de la nourriture en ligne quand il le veut.

Il peut aller jouer au golf. Non, il préfère avoir de la compagnie pour le faire, il n'aime pas jouer seul.

Il peut aller nager. Non, il ne veut pas encore retourner au centre sportif.

What are his options?

He can stay at home and watch TV. No, he can do that whenever he wants to.

He can go shopping to buy food for next week. No, he can shop online for food whenever he wants to.

He can go and play a round of golf. No, he would rather have company to do that, he doesn't like playing on his own.

He can go for a swim. No, he doesn't want to go back to the sports centre yet.

Il peut tondre la pelouse, nettoyer la maison, laver la voiture et nettoyer les toilettes. Non, il le fera demain avec l'aide d'Henry. Ce sera plus amusant.

Il peut aller acheter de nouveaux vêtements de travail.

En fait, ce n'est pas une mauvaise idée.

C'est alors qu'il a une autre idée. Il appelle Sarah.

"As-tu déjà déjeuné?"lui demande-t-il lorsqu'elle répond au téléphone.

"Pas encore. Je prends mon déjeuner dans une demi-heure environ"répond-elle.

"Fantastique. Déjeunons ensemble alors", lui dit Peter."Je viens en ville pour acheter de nouveaux vêtements. Nous pouvons déjeuner tranquillement ensemble, car mes vacances sont presque terminées."

"Ce serait sympa", répond Sarah de manière positive."Je te retrouverai au restaurant italien au coin de la rue High Street. J'ai vraiment hâte d'y être!"

Peter est très heureux et court à l'étage pour se changer.

He can mow the lawn, clean the house, wash the car, and clean the bathrooms. No, he will do that tomorrow with Henry's help. That will be more fun.

He can go shopping for some new work clothes.

Actually, that isn't a bad idea.

Then he has another idea. He phones Sarah.

"Have you had lunch yet?"he asks her as she answers the phone.

"Not yet. I take my lunch in about half an hour,"she replies.

"Fantastic. Let's have lunch together then,"Peter says to her."I'm coming to town to buy some new clothes. We can have a quiet lunch together as my holiday is nearly over."

"That would be lovely,"Sarah replies, positively."I will meet you at the Italian restaurant on the corner of the High Street. I am really looking forward to it!"

Peter is very pleased and runs upstairs to get changed.

Quiz

1) Quel est le métier de Peter?
a) Cuisinier
b) Enseignant
c) Fermier
d) Babysitter
1) What is Peter's job?
a) Cook
b) Teacher
c) Farmer
d) Babysitter

2) Qu'est-ce que Peter n'aime pas faire seul?
a) Regarder la télé
b) Faire du shopping
c) Jouer au golf
d) Nager
2) What does Peter not like to do alone?
a) Watch TV
b) Go shopping
c) Play golf
d) Swim

3) Pourquoi Peter va t-il en ville?
a) Pour acheter de nouveaux vêtements
b) Pour aller travailler
c) Pour visiter la ville

d) Pour retrouver un ami

3) Why does Peter go to town?

a) To buy new clothes

b) To go to work

c) To visit the city

d) To meet a friend

Answers:

1) B

2) C

3) A

Histoire 2

Peter et Henry prennent le petit déjeuner ensemble le dernier jour des vacances. Sarah est partie travailler tôt.

"Henry, aujourd'hui nous devons faire tous les tâches ménagères afin de laisser la maison propre et en ordre lorsque nous retournerons à l'école la semaine prochaine", dit Peter.

Henry sourit et dit:"Je sais papa. Je sais que nous devons travailler dur aujourd'hui. On pourra faire de la pâtisserie après?"

Peter and Henry are having breakfast together on the last day of the holidays. Sarah has gone to work early.

"Henry, today, we need to do all the household jobs so that we leave the house clean and tidy when we go back to school next week,"says Peter.

Henry smiles and says,"I know, Dad. I know we have to do some hard work today. Can we do some baking afterwards though?"

Peter est d'accord pour un après-midi de cuisine quand ils auront fini de faire leur travail.

Henry propose de nettoyer à nouveau la voiture --- il a apprécié cela et l'a bien fait la dernière fois.

Peter lui dit qu'il doit d'abord s'assurer que sa chambre est bien rangée et que son sac d'école et son uniforme sont prêts.

Henry n'est pas content d'avoir à ranger sa chambre et monte lentement.

Peter agrees to a baking afternoon when they have finished doing all their jobs.

Henry offers to clean the car again – he enjoyed that and did it well last time.

Peter tells him that first, he has to make sure that his bedroom is tidy, his school bag is packed, and his uniform is ready.

Henry isn't happy at having to tidy his bedroom, and goes upstairs slowly.

Peter met la vaisselle dans le lave-vaisselle, nettoie la cuisine et le sol de la cuisine. La cuisine est maintenant plus ou moins finie.

Peter monte ensuite vers la salle de bain pour commencer à nettoyer. Il n'aime pas nettoyer les toilettes.

Quand il a fini, il se souvient qu'il doit mettre du linge dans la machine à laver. Ensuite il change les draps.

Peter dit à Henry qu'il sort pour tondre la pelouse. Il le trouve dans sa chambre et lui dit que sa chambre est assez rangée et qu'il peut maintenant aller nettoyer la voiture.

Peter puts the dishes in the dishwasher, cleans the kitchen, then mops the kitchen floor. Now, the kitchen is more or less done.

Peter then walks upstairs to the bathrooms to start cleaning there. He doesn't like cleaning the bathrooms.

When he finishes that, he remembers to put some washing in the washing machine. Then he changes the beds.

Peter tells Henry that he's going outside to mow the lawn. He finds him in his bedroom and tells him that his bedroom is looking tidy so he can go and clean the car now.

Peter et Henry descendent ensemble. Peter tond la pelouse et Henry nettoie la voiture.

Encore une fois, Henry fait un très bon travail et la voiture brille une fois qu'il a terminé.

Le jardin a également l'air bien quand Peter finit.

Ils se rendent compte que c'est l'heure du déjeuner, ils s'assoient alors ensemble dans le jardin et mangent un sandwich.

Ils pensent joyeusement à ce qu'ils ont fait ce matin et conviennent qu'ils vont faire de la pâtisserie tout l'après-midi.

"Lequel devons-nous faire en premier? Le gâteau au chocolat ou les scones?", demande Peter à Henry.

Henry réfléchit un instant et dit:"Maman adore le gâteau au chocolat, faisons les scones en premier. Le gâteau sera plus chaud quand maman rentrera à la maison elle va l'adorer!".

Peter and Henry go downstairs together. Peter mows the lawn and Henry cleans the car.

Again, Henry does a very good job and the car is very shiny when he finishes.

The garden looks good when Peter finishes, as well.

They realise it's time for lunch now so they sit down together in the garden and eat a sandwich.

They reflect happily on what they have done this morning, and agree that they are going to do some baking in the afternoon.

"Which shall we make first? The chocolate cake or the scones?" Peter asks Henry.

Henry thinks for a moment and says," Mum loves chocolate cake so let's make the scones first. The cake will be warmer when Mum gets home and she will love it!".

Quiz

1) Qu'est-ce qu'Henry n'aime pas faire?
a) De la pâtisserie
b) Laver la voiture
c) Ranger sa chambre
d) Nettoyer les toilettes
1) What does Henry not like doing?
a) Baking
b) Wash the car
c) Tidying his room
d) Cleaning the toilets

2) Que fait Peter pendant qu'Henry nettoie la voiture?
a) Il nettoie la cuisine
b) Il nettoie les toilettes
c) Il tond la pelouse
d) Il change les draps
2) What does Peter do while Henry washes the car?
a) He cleans the kitchen
b) He cleans the toilets
c) He mows the lawn
d) He changes the beds

3) Quelle pâtisserie la mère adore t-elle?
a) Le gâteau au chocolat
b) Le pain d'épices
c) Les gaufres
d) Les scones
3) Which pastry does the mother love?
a) Chocolate cake
b) Gingerbread
c) Waffles
d) Scones

Answers:

1) C
2) C
3) A

Vocabulaire / Vocabulary

- *Camp d'été* --- summer camp
- *Promenade* --- walk
- *Faire les courses* --- to do shopping
- *Tondre la pelouse* --- to mow the lown
- *J'ai hâte de --- avoir hâte de* --- to look forward to
- *Tâches menagères* --- household jobs
- *Pâtisserie* --- baking
- *Ranger sa chambre* --- to tidy his bedroom
- *Vaiselle* --- dishes
- *Lave-vaiselle* --- dishwasher
- *Salle de bain* --- bathroom
- *Linge* --- washing
- *Machine à laver* --- washing machine

2. Jour De Marché

Tous les mercredis matins, Jacqueline parcourt les quelques centaines de mètres qui la séparent du square Montsouris pour se rendre au marché. C'est un marché de fruits, de légumes, de viandes, de poissons, de fleurs...

Every Wednesday morning, Jacqueline travels the few hundred meters separating her from the square Montsouris to go to the market. It is a market of fruits, vegetables, meat, fish, flowers ...

Cela fait des années qu'il existe, et il n'a jamais changé de lieu, ni d'horaires. Jadis, ses parents venaient faire leurs courses au même endroit, et certains commerçants sont restés les mêmes.

It's been years, and it has never changed places or schedules. In the old days, his parents came to shop at the same place, and some traders stayed the same.

Le marché était un moment agréable. Arrivée sur place, Jacqueline aime toujours autant se sentir embarquée dans un mouvement vivant, les stands s'offrant aux yeux de tous, les marchands criant, les clients tâtant les produits, les sentant.

The market was a nice moment. Arrived on the spot, Jacqueline still likes to feel as if she is embarked on a living movement, the food stalls are open to everyone's eyes, the merchants shouting, the customers feeling the products, feeling them.

Aujourd'hui, Jacqueline a prévu de passer à la poissonnerie. Du poisson tout frais y était exposé. Le vendeur est un petit jeune, Lucas, qui vient de reprendre l'activité après la maladie de son père qui l'a obligé à tout délaisser, et à se reposer. Lucas est plutôt beau, vêtu de son tablier blanc. Il est très dynamique, ses yeux marron toujours alertes. Ses cheveux blonds dépassent d'un béret gris qui le coiffe. Sa joue gauche est ornée d'un grain de beauté qui, selon Jacqueline, a la forme d'un cœur. Il sait manier les compliments. Mais il est un peu jeune pour elle, et en plus elle a déjà son Marcel à la maison qui l'attend et la chérit depuis des années.

Today, Jacqueline is planning to go to the fish market. Fresh fish was exposed. The salesman is a young boy, Lucas, who has just returned to work after his father's illness which forced him to leave everything behind and to rest. Lucas is pretty handsome, dressed in his white apron. He is very dynamic, his brown eyes always alert. His blond hair is protruding from a gray beret that caps him. Her left cheek is decorated with a mole which, according to Jacqueline, has the shape of a heart. He knows how to handle compliments. But he is a little young for her, and in addition she already has her Marcel at home who waits and cherishes her for years.

Lucas l'apostrophe:

Lucas quotes him:

– Bonjour ma belle Jacqueline, qu'est-ce que vous prendrez aujourd'hui?

- Hello my beautiful Jacqueline, what will you take today?

– 4 filets de cabillaud s'il vous plaît.

- 4 cod fillets please.

– On reçoit la famille ce soir?

- Are we getting the family tonight?

Jacqueline sourit. Lucas est toujours attentif, attentionné. C'est un chouette garçon. Il faudrait qu'elle

366

le présente à sa petite-fille Caroline, qui reste toujours célibataire.

Jacqueline smiled. Lucas is always attentive, attentive. It's a nice boy. She should introduce him to his granddaughter Caroline, who remains single permanently.

Il sert les filets de cabillaud à Jacqueline, ainsi qu'une lotte. Il les enveloppe précautionneusement dans du papier. Alors qu'elle quitte l'étal, il l'interpelle:

He serves the cod fillets to Jacqueline, as well as a monkfish. He wraps them carefully in paper. As she leaves the stall, he calls her:

– Jacqueline, voilà pour vous. Je sais que vous en raffolez.

- Jacqueline, this is for you. I know you're crazy about it.

Il lui tend un petit sachet en papier. Chaque mercredi, il lui offre des petites crevettes roses. Elle rougit, elle sourit et en sort une du sachet. Elle adore le croustillant et la saveur un peu sucrée de ces bestioles.

He hands her a little paper bag. Every Wednesday, he offers her small prawns. She blushes, she smiles and pulls out one of the bag. She loves the crispy and sweet flavor of these critters.

Elle se dirige ensuite vers le stand du boucher charcutier traiteur. Monique et son mari viennent depuis plus de vingt ans vendre leurs produits préparés par leurs soins dans leur ferme familiale.

She then goes to the butcher's butcher's stand. Monique and her husband have been coming for more than twenty years to sell their prepared products on their family farm.

– Bonjour Jacqueline, je te sers comme d'habitude?

- Hello Jacqueline, I serve you as usual?

– Oui Monique, et ajoute un peu de boudin noir s'il te plaît, Marcel en avait envie hier soir.

- Yes Monique, and add a little black pudding please, Marcel felt like it last night.

Monique a toujours l'air heureuse de servir ses clients, elle aime bavarder avec tout le monde, prend son temps. Elle récupère le pâté de campagne que Jacqueline apprécie tout particulièrement, et en coupe deux larges tranches. Des morceaux de champignons se révèlent aux yeux de tous. Cette recette forestière est la même depuis des lustres. Et elle a un succès incroyable auprès de toute la famille de Jacqueline. Préparée à base de porc, de foie de volaille, de persil, d'échalotes, de champignons, et surtout de cognac, elle fait saliver les papilles des plus grands aux plus petits. Monique s'empare ensuite de deux beaux boudins, qu'elle enveloppe dans du papier. Le sac de Jacqueline est prêt.

Monique always looks happy to serve her clients, she likes to chat with everyone, takes her time. She recovers the pie that Jacqueline particularly likes, and cuts two large slices. Pieces of mushrooms are revealed to everyone. This forest recipe has been the same for ages. And she has incredible success with all of Jacqueline's family. Prepared with pork, poultry liver, parsley, shallots, mushrooms, and especially cognac, it makes the taste buds salivate from the largest to the smallest. Monique then seized two beautiful pudding, which she wrapped in paper. Jacqueline's bag is ready.

– Cela fera 8 euros ma Jacqueline.

- That will make my Jacqueline 8 euros.

Une fois l'achat réglé, il est temps de se rendre au dernier stand. Il s'agit du stand de la boulangerie-pâtisserie. Un régal pour les yeux: des gâteaux, de la crème. Un régal pour le nez: l'odeur du pain chaud, du chocolat. Un régal pour l'estomac: les baguettes aux céréales, les boules de campagne, les torsades, les feuilletés au fromage... Jacqueline a toujours envie de tout prendre, mais elle doit faire attention à sa ligne, et à celle de Marcel. Ses yeux pétillent comme si elle avait dix ans. Elle choisit deux gros pains de campagne, et quatre parts de tarte au citron.

Once the purchase is settled, it's time to go to the last stand. This is the stand of the bakery. A feast for the eyes: cakes, cream. A treat for the nose: the smell of hot bread, chocolate. A treat for the stomach: cereal baguettes, country balls, twists, cheese puffs ... Jacqueline always wants to take everything, but she must pay attention to his line, and that of Marcel. Her eyes sparkle as if she were ten years old. She chooses two large country breads and four slices of lemon pie.

– Et avec ceci? Lui demande la boulangère.

- And with this? Ask him the baker.

– Je souhaiterais vous acheter quelques feuilletés, au fromage, aux olives, et aux lardons.

- I would like to buy you some puff pastries, cheese, olives, and bacon.

– Vous avez de la chance, ce sont mes derniers!

- You're lucky, these are my last!

Les bras chargés, Jacqueline reprend tranquillement la route de son appartement. Sur le chemin, elle croise Gérard. Il semble plier sous le poids de ses sacs. Comme toujours, il a acheté une dizaine de fromages, des saucissons, et des pains. Toutes les personnes qui repartent du marché arborent de magnifiques sourires satisfaits.

Arms loaded, Jacqueline quietly resumes the road to his apartment. On the way, she meets Gerard. He seems to be bending under the weight of his bags. As always, he bought a dozen cheeses, sausages, and breads. Everyone who leaves the market has beautiful, satisfied smiles.

C'est aussi pour cela que Jacqueline ne rate jamais ce rendez-vous du mercredi matin. Cela la rend heureuse!

This is also why Jacqueline never misses this meeting on Wednesday morning. It makes her happy!

Quiz

1) Quel est le nom du square sur lequel le marché est situé?
a) Montsouris
b) Montchat
c) Montchien

2) De quelle couleur sont les yeux de Lucas, le vendeur de la poissonnerie?
a) bleus
b) gris
c) marron

3) Monique a toujours l'air _____ de servir ses clients:
a) agacée
b) heureuse
c) pressée

4) La tarte que Jacqueline a acheté est une:
a) Tarte aux pommes
b) Tarte aux figues

c) Tarte au citron

Answers

1) a
2) c
3) b
4) c

Vocabulaire / Vocabulary

- *agréable* --- enjoyable
- *alertes* --- awake
- *arborent* --- *arborer* — to wear
- *attentif* --- paying attention
- *attentionné* --- considerate
- *baguettes aux céréales* --- french baguette made of cereal
- *bavarder* --- to chitchat
- *beau* --- handsome
- *béret gris* --- grey beret
- *boucher* --- butcher
- *boudin noir* --- blood sausage
- *cabillaud* --- cod
- *ceci* --- this
- *célibataire* --- single
- *centaines* --- hundreds
- *champignons* --- mushrooms
- *charcutier* --- butcher
- *chérit* --- *chérir* — to cherish
- *cheveux* --- hair
- *cœur* --- the heart
- *comme d'habitude* --- as usual
- *commerçants* --- retailers
- *crevettes* --- shrimps
- *croustillant* --- crispy
- *délaisser* --- to abandon
- *derniers* --- lasts
- *des lustres* --- a long time ago
- *dix* --- ten
- *échalotes* --- shallots
- *embarquée* --- *être embarqué* — to be carried by
- *endroit* --- a location
- *enveloppe* --- envelope
- *étals* --- market stalls

- *faire leurs courses* --- to go grocery shopping
- *fait saliver* --- *faire saliver* — to make someone salivate
- *feuilletés* --- type of salty pastry
- *fleurs* --- flowers
- *foie de volaille* --- chicken liver
- *fromage* --- cheese
- *fruits* --- fruits
- *gâteaux* --- cakes
- *grain de beauté* --- beauty spot, mole
- *horaires* --- opening and closing schedule
- *jadis* --- A long time ago
- *joue* --- cheek
- *l'achat* --- the purchase
- *l'apostrophe* --- *apostropher* — to shout at
- *l'estomac* --- the stomach
- *l'odeur* --- the smell
- *lardons* --- bacon
- *le chemin* --- the way
- *légumes* --- vegetables
- *lieu* --- location
- *lotte* --- monkfish
- *magnifiques* --- magnificent
- *maladie* --- a disease
- *marché* --- market
- *mêmes* --- same, similar
- *mercredis* --- Wednesdays
- *papier* --- paper
- *pâté de campagne* --- country-style pâté
- *persil* --- parsley
- *petite-fille* --- granddaughter
- *poissonnerie* --- fishmonger's
- *poissons* --- fishes
- *porc* --- pork
- *précautionneusement* --- with care
- *raffoler* --- to love
- *reposer* --- to rest
- *sachet* --- bag
- *sachet en papier* --- paperbag
- *saucissons* --- sausages
- *séparent* --- séparer — to split
- *succès* --- success
- *tablier* --- apron
- *tarte au citron* --- lemon pie
- *traiteur* --- caterer
- viandes --- meats
- *victuailles* --- food, provision

3. Une Panne De Voiture

Vers dix heures, je quitte le travail et je m'arrête devant l'appartement de Laura. Elle ne vit qu'à quelques pâtés de maisons de chez moi. Ce n'était pas difficile de trouver. Elle se tient sur le trottoir, vêtue d'un jean et d'un t-shirt. Ses cheveux sont tirés en queue de cheval. Cette fois-ci, elle ne porte pas de maquillage. Je me rends compte qu'elle a des taches de rousseur, comme moi. C'est mignon.

I took off from work and stopped in front of Laura's apartment around 10pm. She lived only a few blocks away from my house. It wasn't hard to find at all. She stood on the sidewalk, dressed in jeans and a t-shirt. Her hair was pulled back in a ponytail. She was not wearing makeup this time. I noticed she had freckles, just like me. I find it cute.

"Tu es en retard.", me dit-elle en ouvrant la porte passager. Elle affiche une mine renfrognée.

"You're late,"she said while opening the passenger door. She looked grumpy.

"Juste de quelques minutes, dis-je.

"Only of a couple of minutes,"I said.

– Quelles bonnes manières!", dit-elle. C'est exactement ce que je lui avais dit la première fois que nous nous étions rencontrés. Je lui souris.

"What good manners!"she said. It was exactly what I'd told her the first time I've met her. I grinned at her.

"Touché.", dis-je. Elle entre dans la voiture et met sa ceinture.

"Touché,"I answered. She got into the car and put her seatbelt on.

Nous sommes silencieux pendant un moment, avec seulement la radio pour briser le silence. La voix féminine du GPS interrompt la chanson de temps en temps.

We drove in silence for a while, with just the radio to break the silence. The female voice on the GPS was the interrupting the tune every now and then.

"Qu'est-ce que tu fais dans la vie? lui demandais-je finalement.

"So, what do you do?"I finally asked.

– Je suis juriste, étudiante pour le moment.", répond-t-elle.

"I'm a lawyer, still studying,"she said.

Je hoche la tête. Elle ressemble plutôt au type qui préfère travailler avec des nombres.

I nodded. She looked like the type that would rather work with numbers.

"Et toi?", demande-t-elle.

"What about you?"she asked.

Je jette un coup d'œil dans le rétroviseur et change de voie. La voiture fait un bruit étrange, je fronce les sourcils en regardant sur le tableau de bord.

I glanced in the rearview mirror and changed lanes for the upcoming turn. The car made a scraping sound and I frowned, looking confused at the dashboard.

"Je suis en communication.", dis-je.

"I'm studying communications,"I said.

Elle hausse les épaules sans réponse. Nous sommes à un feu rouge.

The car spluttered and the engine cut for a second before roaring.

Le feu passe au vert, je redémarre la voiture. Il faut un moment pour qu'elle se lance, je fronce d'autant plus les sourcils. Je retente une deuxième fois, au cas où. La voiture vrombit, le moteur coupe pendant une seconde avant de rugir.

The light goes green, I restart the car. It takes a moment for her to start, I frown all the more. I retry a second time, just in case. The car roars, the engine cuts for a second before roaring.

"Woah.", dis-je. Ça recommence. Le volant frémit dans mes mains. Un autre bruit sourd et la voiture est foutue. Je tourne les roues et la guide sur le bord de la route. Je m'arrête lentement.

"Woah,"I said. Not again. The steering wheel shuddered in my hands. One more muffled sound and the car died. I turned the wheel and pulled onto the emergency lane of the road while the car still rolled. I stopped the car slowly.

"Qu'est-ce qui ne va pas? interroge Laura.

"What's wrong?"Laura asked.

– Je ne sais pas. Tire sur le levier du capot, tu veux bien? C'est en-dessous de la boîte à gants."

"I don't know. Could you please pull the lever for the hood? It's below the glove compartment."

Laura se penche en avant. Je sors de la voiture et j'entends le capot s'ouvrir lorsqu'elle trouve le levier. J'ouvre le capot et je regarde l'état du moteur.

Laura leaned forward. I got out of the car and heard the hood click open as she found the lever. I opened the hood and looked at the engine.

"Tu vois quelque chose?", demande-t-elle en sortant de la voiture.

"Do you see something? She asks as she gets out of the car.

Je secoue la tête.

"Je ne connais que les bases. Je vais devoir appeler quelqu'un."

Elle lève les yeux au ciel.

I shake my head.

"I only know the basics. I will have to call someone."

She rolls her eyes.

"Fantastique.", dit-elle avec sarcasme. Je sors mon téléphone et je téléphone aux services d'urgence.

"This is just fantastic,"she said sarcastically. I pulled out my phone and dialed emergency services.

Laura s'appuie contre la voiture. Je referme le capot et la rejoins. Nous regardons les voitures passer devant nous sans vraiment les regarder. Je sors de ma poche un paquet de cigarettes et j'en allume une.

Laura leaned against the car. I closed the hood again and joined her. We watched cars passing by without really watching anything. I fished in my pocket for a pack of cigarettes and lit one up.

Laura fronce les sourcils.

Laura frowned at me.

"Tu fumes?"

"Do you smoke?"

"De temps en temps. Quand les choses sont stressantes. Quand je m'ennuie. Ou quand ça me dit." J'inhale profondément. La fumée remplit mes poumons. Je m'éloigne de Laura pour expirer.

I shrugged."Here and there. When things are stressful. Or if I'm bored. Or if I feel like it." I inhaled deeply. Smoke filled my lungs. I exhaled away from Laura.

"Crois-tu au mariage, Mathieu?", me demande-t-elle tout d'un coup.

"Do you believe in marriage, Mathieu?", she asked out of the blue.

Je suis un peu surpris par sa question.

I am surprised by her question.

"Eh bien... Je pense que le mariage cause beaucoup de problèmes. Des problèmes qui auraient pu rester loin. La vie de couple est géniale, bien sûr, mais le mariage? Je ne sais pas."

"Well... I believe marriage brings a lot of problems. Problems that could have been avoided. Being in a relationship is great, of course, but marriage? I don't know about that."

Je lui lance un clin d'œil. Ce n'est pas du tout la personne que j'ai rencontrée à l'anniversaire de Zack. Celle-ci est douce, gentille et réfléchie. OK, elle pense beaucoup. Mais elle n'est pas agaçante du tout.

I wink at her. She wasn't the girl I'd met at Zach's party at all. She is sweet, kind and thoughtful. Sure, she overthinks stuff. But she doesn't sound annoying at all.

"Pourquoi ne crois-tu pas au mariage?", demande-t-elle.

"Why don't you believe in marriage?"she asked.

Je hausse les épaules et reprends ma cigarette. J'expire la fumée et fais tomber la cendre.

I shrugged, pulling on my cigarette again. I blew out the smoke and tapped off the ash.

"Je ne sais pas. Je pense que je croirai au mariage le jour où je rencontrerai quelqu'un qui en vaut la peine, avec qui je voudrai passer ma vie. Je n'ai pas encore trouvé cette personne, tu vois?"

"I don't know. I guess I'll believe in it one I'll meet someone who's really worth it, someone I would want to spend the rest of my life with. I haven't found anyone like that yet, you see?"

Quiz

1. Comment s'appellent les personnages de l'histoire?
a. Les personnages s'appellent Mathieu et Laura.
b. Les personnages s'appellent Marc et Laura.
c. Les personnages s'appellent Mathieu et Clara.

2. Quelle heure est-il quand Mathieu passe chercher Laura?
a. Il est 11 heures.
b. Il est 10 heures.
b. Il est 15 heures.

3. Quels vêtements portait Laura?
a. Laura portait un jean et une capuche.
b. Laura portait un jean et un t-shirt.
c. Laura portait une robe.

4. Que fait Laura dans la vie?
a. Laura est danseuse.
b. Laura est écrivain.
c. Laura est cartographe.
d. Laura est juriste.

5. Que fait Mathieu dans la vie?
a. Mathieu est étudiant en communication.
b. Mathieu est cartographe.
c. Mathieu est enseignant.

6. Que se passe-t-il en chemin?

7. Que fait Mathieu quand il est stressé?

8. Que font Mathieu et Laura en attendant la dépanneuse?

9. Que penses Mathieu de Laura?

10. Pourquoi Mathieu ne croit-il pas au mariage?

Answers

1 --- a
2 --- b
3 --- b
4 --- d
5 --- a
6 --- La voiture tombe en panne en chemin.
7 --- Mathieu fume quand il est stressé.
8 --- Mathieu et Laura parlent pendant qu'ils attendent la dépanneuse.
9 --- Mathieu pense que Laura est douce, gentille et réfléchie. Elle pense beaucoup.
10 --- Mathieu ne sait pas pourquoi. Il suppose que si c'est pour passer sa vie avec quelqu'un, il veut que ce soit avec quelqu'un qui en vaut la peine. Il n'a pas encore rencontré une telle personne.

Vocabulaire / Vocabulary

- *travail* --- work
- *appartement* --- apartment
- *pâtés de maisons* --- blocks
- *trottoir* --- sidewalk
- *queue de cheval* --- ponytail
- *maquillage* --- make up
- *taches de rousseur* --- freckles
- *voiture* --- car
- *ceinture* --- seatbelt
- *radio* --- radio
- *GPS* --- GPS
- *cartographe* --- cartographer
- *rétroviseur* --- rearview mirror
- *virage* --- turn
- *moteur* --- engine
- *rugir* --- roaring on
- *roues* --- wheels
- *levier* --- leaver
- *capot* --- hood
- *sarcastiquement* --- sarcastically
- *paquet de cigarettes* --- pack of cigarettes
- *clin d'œil* – wink of an eye
- *fumée* --- smoke
- *cendres* --- ashes

4. Rira Bien Qui Rira Le Dernier

Stéphane et Charlène sont frère et soeur. Ils s'entendent plutôt bien, mais se disputent de temps en temps, c'est normal. Charlène a quinze ans, et Stéphane neuf ans. Ils n'ont pas les mêmes centres d'intérêt. Ce soir, leurs parents sont sortis au restaurant italien tous les deux. D'habitude, ils sortent en famille, mais c'est leur anniversaire de mariage. Ils veulent faire quelque chose de plus romantique. Alors, ils ont demandé à Charlène de garder son petit frère.

Stephane and Charlene are brother and sister. They get along pretty well, but fight every once in a while, that's normal. Charlene is fifteen, and Stéphane is nine. They do not have the same interests. Tonight, their parents went out to the Italian restaurant. Usually, they go out with their family, but it's their wedding anniversary. They want to do something more romantic. So, they asked Charlene to babysit her little brother.

Stéphane n'est pas content. Il dit qu'à neuf ans, il n'a pas besoin de baby-sitter. Il dit qu'il sait très bien se débrouiller tout seul, sans Charlène. En plus, il sait que Charlène va l'obliger à faire ses devoirs. Stéphane n'aime pas l'école, il a souvent des mauvaises notes.

Stéphane is not happy. He says that at nine, he does not need a babysitter. He says he knows very well on his own, without Charlene. In addition, he knows that Charlene will force him to do his homework. Stéphane does not like school, he often has bad grades.

Charlène n'est pas contente non plus, elle ne peut pas aller au cinéma avec ses amis. Ce soir, tous ses amis vont voir le nouveau Star Wars. Demain, ils vont tous parler du film au lycée. Charlène va être la seule à ne pas l'avoir vu. En plus, Stéphane ne veut pas l'écouter.

Charlene is not happy either, she can not go to the movies with her friends. Tonight, all his friends will see the new Star Wars. Tomorrow, they will all talk about the movie in high school. Charlene is going to be the only one who has not seen it. In addition, Stéphane does not want to listen to him.

Leurs parents sont partis vers 18 heures. Ils ont dit à Stéphane de faire ses devoirs et d'écouter sa grande soeur. Stéphane ne veut pas faire ses devoirs. Il a des exercices de géométrie et une leçon d'histoire à apprendre. Il dit que c'est trop difficile. Charlène essaie de l'aider. Elle lui explique les exercices. Stéphane ne veut pas l'écouter. Il finit par jeter son stylo. Charlène est énervée, elle le laisse tout seul dans sa chambre, et va regarder la télévision dans le salon.

Their parents left around 18 hours. They told Stephane to do his homework and listen to his older sister. Stéphane does not want to do his homework. He has geometry exercises and a history lesson to learn. He says it's too difficult. Charlene tries to help him. She explains the exercises. Stéphane does not want to listen to him. He ends up throwing away his pen. Charlene is angry, she leaves him alone in his room, and goes to watch television in the living room.

Charlène regarde son programme préféré à la télé. C'est une série pour adolescents qui passe tous les soirs sur TF1. Charlène ne manque jamais un épisode.

Charlene is watching her favorite program on TV. This is a series for teenagers who spend every night on TF1. Charlene never misses an episode.

Stéphane arrive dans le salon et change de chaîne. Il met le match de foot. Charlène s'énerve:

Stéphane arrives in the living room and changes channels. He puts the football match. Charlene gets upset:

«Va regarder la télé dans ta chambre! Laisse moi tranquille!"dit-elle à son frère.

"Go watch TV in your room! Leave me alone! She said to her brother.

"Je préfère la télé du salon, elle est plus grande!"lui répond Stéphane d'un air insolent.

"I prefer the TV in the living room, it's bigger! Replied Stephane, insolently.

Charlène essaie de lui reprendre la télécommande des mains, mais Stéphane part en courant et en riant! Maintenant Charlène est très énervée. Il cache la télécommande de la télévision. Impossible de la retrouver. Charlène finit par abandonner, et lit un magazine.

Charlene tries to take the remote control from her hands, but Stéphane runs off and laughs! Now Charlene is very upset. He hides the TV remote control. Can not find it. Charlene ends up giving up, and reads a magazine.

Stéphane décide qu'il ne veut plus regarder le match de football à la télévision. Il veut embêter Charlène au maximum. Il retourne dans sa chambre.

Stéphane decides that he no longer wants to watch the football game on television. He wants to annoy Charlene to the maximum. He returns to his room.

"Enfin, un peu de calme!"pense Charlène.

"Finally, a little calm! Charlene thinks.

Stéphane allume sa console de jeux vidéos. Il choisit un jeu violent et met le son très fort. Charlène crie:

Stéphane turns on his video game console. He chooses a violent game and puts the sound very strong. Charlene shouts:

"Baisse le son! C'est beaucoup trop fort!"

"Turn down the sound! It's way too strong!"

"Non! Je préfère jouer avec le son, c'est plus réaliste!"

"No! I prefer to play with sound, it's more realistic!"

Stéphane continue à jouer à son jeu avec le son au volume maximum.

Stéphane continues to play his game with the sound at maximum volume.

D'un seul coup, après avoir été insupportable pendant trois heures, Stéphane vient voir sa soeur dans le salon. Il sourit, et parle à Charlène gentiment.

All of a sudden, after being uncomfortable for three hours, Stéphane comes to see his sister in the living room. He smiles, and talks to Charlene nicely.

"Coucou ma grande soeur adorée."dit-il d'un air joyeux.

"Cuckoo my big sister adored. He said cheerfully.

"Toi, tu veux quelque chose, j'en suis sûre!"répond Charlène. Elle est très énervée. Stéphane a été insupportable depuis que leurs parents sont partis. Elle n'est pas allée au cinéma avec ses amis. Elle n'a pas regardé sa série préférée. Il fait du bruit et l'empêche de lire depuis des heures. Charlène est de très mauvaise humeur.

"You want something, I'm sure of it! Charlene answers. She is very upset. Stéphane has been unbearable since their parents left. She did not go to the movies with her friends. She did not watch her favorite series. It makes noise and prevents it from reading for hours. Charlene is in a very bad mood.

"Nos parents sont sortis. On commande une pizza?"Stéphane fait un grand sourire. Il prend l'air innocent.

"Our parents are out. We order a pizza? Stephane makes a big smile. He looks innocent.

Stéphane adore les pizzas. Il dit souvent qu'il pourrait manger des pizzas à tous les repas. Il aime les pizzas au jambon, les pizzas au fromage, les pizzas calzone... il aime tous les types de pizza, sauf une. Charlène a soudainement une idée... Stéphane l'embête depuis des heures, et il a gaché sa soirée. Alors, elle décide de se venger...

Stéphane loves pizzas. He often says he could eat pizzas at any meal. He likes ham pizzas, cheese pizzas, calzone pizzas ... he likes all types of pizza except one. Charlene suddenly has an idea ... Stéphane has been bothering him for hours, and he spoiled his evening. So, she decides to take revenge ...

"Pas de problème!"répond Charlène. Elle prend l'air joyeux, comme si rien ne s'était passé."Je commande tout de suite!"

"No problem! Charlene answers. She looks happy, as if nothing had happened."I order right away!"

Stéphane a l'air un peu surpris. Il ne pensait pas que ce serait si facile de convaincre sa soeur. Après tout, il sait bien qu'il l'a ennuyée toute la soirée! Charlène sourit, elle n'a pas l'air énervée. Bon, tant mieux! Ils regardent la télé tous les deux en attendant. Stéphane rend la télécommande à Charlène. Il la laisse choisir le film. Il est ravi que la pizza arrive bientôt.

Stéphane looks a little surprised. He did not think it would be so easy to convince his sister. After all, he knows he has been bored all night! Charlene smiles, she does not look upset. Good, all the better! They are watching TV while waiting. Stéphane returns the remote control to Charlene. He lets her choose the movie. He is delighted that the pizza is coming soon.

Une demi-heure plus tard, le livreur de pizzas est à la porte. Stéphane est surexcité, il court vers la porte d'entrée, dit à peine bonjour au livreur, prend la boîte à pizza, court à toute vitesse dans la cuisine, et ouvre la boîte immédiatement.

Half an hour later, the pizza delivery man is at the door. Stephane is excited, he runs to the front door, barely says good morning to the delivery man, takes the pizza box, runs at full speed in the kitchen, and opens the box immediately.

"Noooon!"Stéphane crie."Tu as commandé une pizza jambon-ananas! La seule que je déteste!"

"Noooon! Stéphane shouts."You ordered a ham-pineapple pizza! The only one I hate!"

C'est la seule pizza que Stéphane ne mange pas. Stéphane adore toutes les pizzas, sauf une: la pizza à l'ananas. Il dit que les fruits ne devraient jamais être sur une pizza.

It's the only pizza Stéphane does not eat. Stéphane loves all pizzas except one: pineapple pizza. He says fruits should never be on a pizza.

Charlène est bien contente de son coup. Elle rit, elle rit sans s'arrêter, elle rit tellement qu'elle en a les larmes aux yeux. Stéphane la regarde d'un air dépité. Il sait qu'il l'a bien mérité.

Charlene is happy with her turn. She laughs, she laughs without stopping, she laughs so much that she has tears in her eyes. Stephane looks at her with a disappointed expression. He knows he deserved it.

"Allez, ne t'inquiètes pas: il reste des légumes au frigo!"

"Come on, do not worry, there are still vegetables in the fridge!"

Quiz

Careful! There might be more than one option.

1. How old is Charlène?
a. Fifteen
b. Twelve
c. Thirteen

2. How old is Stéphane?
a. Ten
b. Nine
c. Twelve

3. "Son petit frère" means:
a. Her big brother
b. Her little brother
c. His little brother

4. Where are Charlène and Stéphane's parents?
a. At the cinema
b. At the pizzeria
c. At the restaurant

5. What did Charlène want to do?
a. Go to the restaurant with her parents
b. Go to the cinema with her friends
c. Have pizza at home

6. What is Stéphane doing?
a. He does his homework.
b. He plays videogames.
c. He hides the remote control.

7. "Elle est très énervée" means:
a. She's very bored.
b. She's very annoyed.
c. She's very patient.

8. What does Stéphane ask his sister?
a. He wants to play more video games.
b. He wants her to do his homework.
c. He wants to order pizza.

9. What pizza does Charlène order?
a. Ham and cheese
b. Ham and mushrooms
c. Ham and pineapple
10. "il reste des légumes au frigo!" means:
a. There are still leftovers in the fridge!

b. There are still fruit in the fridge!
c. There are still vegetables in the fridge!

Answers:

1. a
2. b
3. b
4. c
5. b
6. b and c
7. b
8. c
9. c
10. c

Vocabulaire / Vocabulary

- *romantique* -- --- romantic
- *content* --- happy
- *devoirs* --- homework
- *jeu video* --- video game
- *empêche* --- prevents
- *bruit* --- noise
- *ordre* --- order
- *sourit* --- smiles
- *des rires* --- laughs
- *désappointé* --- disappointed

5. Aventure Africaine

Christine ne sait pas ce qui l'attend ce matin de juillet lorsque Patrick lui dit de se dépêcher de monter dans un taxi. Direction inconnue. En fait, Patrick a voulu faire une belle surprise à Christine pour leurs vingt ans de mariage: un voyage au Kenya! Maintenant que les enfants sont grands, ils peuvent enfin se permettre d'êtres spontanés et de partir où ils le souhaitent, quand bon leur semble. Un luxe qui leur était dénié depuis l'arrivée des enfants.

Christine does not know what awaits him this morning in July when Patrick tells him to hurry up in a taxi. Direction unknown. In fact, Patrick wanted to make a nice surprise to Christine for their twenty years of marriage: a trip to Kenya! Now that children are grown up, they can finally afford to be spontaneous and leave wherever they want, whenever they want. A luxury denied to them since the arrival of the children.

Christine, passionnée de photo, adore les animaux sauvages. Patrick est fou de nature. Le Kenya est donc une destination idéale pour le couple, une manière de lier deux passions et de profiter ensemble de la beauté et de l'exotisme d'un nouveau pays. Patrick a comme toujours très bien organisé le voyage. Une voiture de location les attend à leur arrivée, et ils partent immédiatement vers leur hôtel situé à deux cents kilomètres. Ils sortent rapidement de la ville, puis l'aventure commence.

Christine, passionate about photography, loves wild animals. Patrick is crazy about nature. Kenya is therefore an ideal destination for the couple, a way to link two passions and enjoy together the beauty and exoticism of a new country. Patrick always organized the trip very well. A rental car is waiting for them on their arrival, and they leave immediately for their hotel located two hundred kilometers away. They leave the city quickly, then the adventure begins.

Le désert. Tellement différent de ce qu'ils ont pu voir du désert marocain lors de leur voyage l'année précédente. Ni dunes ni dromadaires, mais une route à n'en plus finir. Quelques buissons par-ci, par-là, un sol craquelé par la sécheresse et... pas d'animaux. Christine, appareil photo à la main, est pourtant prête à mitrailler.

The desert. So different from what they saw in the Moroccan desert during their trip the year before. Neither dunes nor camels, but a road to no end. A few bushes here and there, a soil cracked by drought and ... no animals. Christine, camera in hand, is yet ready to strafe.

D'après Patrick, ils auront plus de chances de voir des animaux demain, lorsqu'ils partiront en safari avec les"rangers"de l'hôtel. Christine n'a aucun souci à se faire; elle pourra prendre toutes les photos qu'elle souhaite.

According to Patrick, they will be more likely to see animals tomorrow, when they go on safari with the"rangers"of the hotel. Christine has no problem to be made; she can take all the photos she wants.

À la grande joie de Christine, les animaux ne se font pas attendre: deux magnifiques zèbres les attendent devant leur bungalow. N'osant pas déranger ces superbes créatures, l'installation prendra plus longtemps que prévu, mais les photos ne manqueront pas d'être spectaculaires. Le silence de la nuit tombante n'est dérangé que par le réveil des criquets et ce qui ressemble au hululement lointain d'un hibou. Presque une heure plus tard, ils peuvent enfin sortir de la voiture et découvrir ce qui sera leur pied-à-terre, leur base pour la semaine à venir. Ils ne sont pas déçus.

To the delight of Christine, the animals are not long in waiting: two beautiful zebras are waiting in front of their bungalow. Not daring to disturb these beautiful creatures, the installation will take longer than expected, but the photos are sure to be spectacular. The silence of the falling night is disturbed only by the awakening of the locusts and what resembles the distant hooting of an owl. Almost an hour later, they can finally get out of the car and discover what will be their pied-à-terre, their base for the week ahead. They are not disappointed.

La chambre est spacieuse, avec un espace salon donnant sur une terrasse ouverte sur une plaine qui semble s'étendre à perte de vue, mais pour l'instant, l'éclairage seul de la lune montante ne suffit pas; la surprise demain matin n'en sera que meilleure. Christine cherche la salle de bain... introuvable! Aucun signe de porte donnant vers une salle de bain dans la chambre. La tension monte, jusqu'à ce que Patrick fasse la trouvaille du jour: la salle de bain est en fait sur le côté de la terrasse, à ciel ouvert.

The bedroom is spacious, with a sitting area opening onto a terrace overlooking a plain that seems to extend as far as the eye can see, but for now, the only illumination of the rising moon is not enough; the surprise tomorrow morning will only be better. Christine is looking for the bathroom ... not found! No sign of a door leading to a bathroom in the room. The tension goes up, until Patrick makes the find of the day: the bathroom is in fact on the side of the terrace, in the open air.

Le bain à remous est très tentant après une telle journée, mais Patrick a faim. Il n'a rien mangé dans l'avion, trop occupé à lire son guide des animaux d'Afrique. Entre gazelles, zèbres et éléphants, il a établi une liste des animaux qu'il compte bien approcher dans leur habitat naturel. Christine, elle, préfère s'en tenir aux photos.

The hot tub is very tempting after such a day, but Patrick is hungry. He did not eat anything on the plane, too busy reading his guide to African animals. Between gazelles, zebras and elephants, he has drawn up a list of animals he intends to approach in their natural habitat. Christine, she prefers to stick to the photos.

Les bungalows sont reliés à la réception et au restaurant par une sorte de chemin surélevé en bois, qui offre une certaine sécurité et protection contre les animaux que l'on pourrait rencontrer, surtout la nuit. Une agréable marche de quelques minutes plus tard, le couple s'installe au restaurant. Le décor est très africain: masques de bois, armes traditionnelles, peaux de bêtes au sol et trophées au mur. Dépaysement garanti! Les immenses baies vitrées longeant la salle intriguent beaucoup Christine, qui se demande quelle sera la vue le lendemain matin, pendant que Patrick déguste des plats qu'il ne mangera certainement jamais ailleurs.

The bungalows are connected to the reception and restaurant by a kind of elevated wooden path, which offers some security and protection against animals that one might encounter, especially at night. A pleasant walk a few minutes later, the couple moved to the restaurant. The decor is very African: wooden masks, traditional weapons, skins of animals on the ground and trophies on the wall. Change of scenery guaranteed! The huge picture windows along the room intrigue Christine a lot, who wonders what will be the view the next morning, while Patrick is eating dishes that he will probably never eat elsewhere.

Le repas terminé, retour au bungalow par le même chemin. Tout est plus calme maintenant. La lune éclaire le paysage, et Patrick devine la nature qu'il a hâte de découvrir demain. Avant de profiter d'un repos bien mérité: une douche sous les étoiles.

The meal finished, return to the bungalow by the same way. Everything is quieter now. The moon illuminates the landscape, and Patrick divines the nature he is eager to discover tomorrow. Before enjoying a well-deserved rest: a shower under the stars.

Christine, qui malgré son amour des animaux n'est jamais très friande de reptiles, ne semble pas sourciller lorsque deux petits lézards se faufilent derrière le porte-savon, à la grande surprise de Patrick. Le calme est cependant de courte durée. Patrick, connaissant la phobie de Christine, s'empresse d'attraper une serviette pour attraper les deux monstres avant qu'elle ne s'en aperçoive, mais Christine prend peur et hurle, déchirant le silence si apaisant de la nuit. Plus de peur que de mal et quelques bouteilles renversées plus tard, le calme revient et c'est au tour de Patrick de prendre une douche bien méritée avant de se coucher et être prêt pour la longue journée de découvertes qui s'annonce le lendemain.

Christine, who despite his love of animals is never very fond of reptiles, does not seem to frown when two small lizards sneak behind the soap dish, much to Patrick's surprise. The calm is however short. Patrick, knowing the phobia of Christine, hastens to catch a towel to catch the two monsters before she realizes it, but Christine gets scared and screams, tearing the soothing silence of the night. More fear than harm and a few bottles spilled later, the calm returns and it's Patrick's turn to take a well-deserved shower before going to bed and be ready for the long day of discoveries that will be announced the next day.

Réveillé aux aurores pour ne pas rater le lever de soleil, Patrick court ouvrir les rideaux, curieux et rempli d'enthousiasme à l'idée d'enfin découvrir la vue qui promettait d'être superbe. Il n'est pas déçu. À quelques mètres de la terrasse, un troupeau de zèbres et une sorte de gros taureau absorbent les premiers rayons de soleil en paissant.

Awake at dawn so as not to miss the sunrise, Patrick runs to open the curtains, curious and full of enthusiasm to finally discover the view that promised to be superb. He is not disappointed. A few meters from the terrace, a herd of zebras and a kind of big bull absorb the first rays of sun while grazing.

– Christine! Réveille-toi! Regarde!

- Christine! Wake up! Look!

Christine, réveillée en sursaut, attrape son appareil photo et court sur la terrasse pour ne rien rater, lorsque quelqu'un frappe à la porte. Patrick ouvre la porte et tombe nez à nez avec un homme qui pousse une petite table recouverte d'un drap blanc. Il s'excuse de déranger, puis lui demande s'il souhaite prendre son petit-déjeuner à l'intérieur ou sur la terrasse. La réponse ne se fait pas attendre: la terrasse, évidemment!

Christine, awake with a start, catches her camera and runs to the terrace to miss nothing, when someone knocks on the door. Patrick opens the door and comes face to face with a man who pushes a small table covered with a white sheet. He apologizes for disturbing, then asks if he wants to have breakfast inside or on the terrace. The answer is not long in coming: the terrace, of course!

Il ne faut cependant pas traîner: le safari commence dans une heure. Une fois le petit-déjeuner avalé, le sac rempli de l'appareil photo, jumelles, guide des animaux et autres accessoires indispensables à l'aventure, Patrick et Christine se dirigent vers la réception où les attendent leur véhicule et leur guide Moses.

However do not hang out: the safari starts in one hour. Once the breakfast has been swallowed, the bag is filled with the camera, binoculars, guide animals and other accessories essential to the adventure, Patrick and Christine head for the reception where their vehicle and their guide Moses await them.

Quelques minutes plus tard, ils sont sortis de l'enceinte de l'hôtel et sont immédiatement plongés dans un autre monde: le désert. Autour d'eux se trouvent des arbustes, du sable durci, un sol craquelé par des années de sécheresse, quelques rochers, mais pas d'animaux. Christine est un peu déçue, mais le guide la rassure. Les animaux sont bien là, mais les trouver fait partie du plaisir de l'aventure. Elle se demande toutefois: comment?

A few minutes later, they came out of the hotel and are immediately immersed in another world: the desert. Around them are shrubs, hard sand, soil cracked by years of drought, some rocks, but no animals. Christine is a little disappointed, but the guide reassures her. The animals are there, but finding them is part of the pleasure of adventure. She wonders, how?

C'est là que la nature va nous éclairer et nous aider à traquer les animaux. Tous ces plantes, arbres, arbustes, oiseaux, traces de pas en tout genre et même les rochers nous donnent des indices sur les animaux qui pourraient être dans les environs. Comment reconnaître une trace de gazelle d'une trace de léopard? Comment distinguer une autruche d'un phacochère?

This is where nature will enlighten us and help us track down animals. All these plants, trees, shrubs, birds, footprints of all kinds and even the rocks give us clues about the animals that might be in the vicinity. How to recognize a trace of gazelle from a leopard print? How to distinguish an ostrich from a warthog?

Patrick est tout ouïe, et Christine est à l'affût de la moindre trace de pas susceptible d'indiquer le passage récent d'un animal intéressant. Il ne faut surtout pas faire de bruit; le chauffeur roule lentement pour ne pas effrayer les animaux. La voiture s'arrête, puis le guide attrape ses jumelles. Christine dirige immédiatement son objectif dans la direction indiquée par le guide et aperçoit un troupeau d'éléphants au loin. Changement de cap. Objectif: se rapprocher du troupeau qui, d'après Moses, se dirige vers un point d'eau.

Patrick is all ears, and Christine is on the lookout for any trace of footsteps likely to indicate the recent passage of an interesting animal. It is important not to make noise; the driver rolls slowly so as not to frighten the animals. The car stops, then the guide catches his binoculars. Christine immediately directs her goal in the direction indicated by the guide and sees a herd of elephants in the distance. Change of direction. Objective: to approach the flock that, according to Moses, goes to a water point.

Nouvel arrêt. Moses explique que l'arbrisseau à quelques mètres est très prisé des girafes, et l'absence de feuilles dans les hautes branches fraîchement cassées indique une visite récente. Le retour ne se fait pas attendre, et un petit groupe de girafes arrive bientôt terminer son repas, suivi de quelques zèbres et d'un buffle. Une fois que Christine a terminé sa série de clichés, le véhicule repart et rencontre rapidement une famille de phacochères.

New stop. Moses explains that the shrub a few meters away is very popular with giraffes, and the absence of leaves in the freshly broken branches indicates a recent visit. The return is not long, and a small group of giraffes arrives soon to finish his meal, followed by some zebras and a buffalo. Once Christine finishes her series of shots, the vehicle leaves and meets quickly a family of warthogs.

Quels drôles d'animaux, les phacochères! Des pattes disproportionnées par rapport à la longueur du corps, un air menaçant, mais les petits sont si mignons que Christine ne peut s'empêcher de les photographier sous toutes leurs coutures.

What funny animals, warthogs! Legs disproportionate to the length of the body, a threatening look, but the little ones are so cute that Christine can not help but photograph them in all their seams.

Patrick profite de l'instant et repère avant tout le monde les girafes qui se dirigent vers leur véhicule. En un instant, le troupeau les entoure. Le chauffeur s'arrête pour éviter de les blesser ou de les apeurer. Le convoi continue et les dépasse bientôt. Le véhicule repart lentement et les suit pendant quelques centaines de mètres, jusqu'à ce que les girafes décident de bifurquer et de repartir dans la savane. Un dernier cliché"pour la route": Christine ne peut s'en empêcher.

Patrick takes advantage of the moment and sees before all the world the giraffes who go to their vehicle. In an instant, the flock surrounds them. The driver stops to avoid hurting or frightening them. The convoy continues and will overtake them soon. The vehicle starts slowly and follows them for a few hundred meters, until the giraffes decide to fork and go back to the savannah. A last shot"for the road": Christine can not help it.

Toujours en route vers le point d'eau, notre équipe traverse une rivière asséchée qui apparemment abritait des crocodiles; ceux-ci n'ont malheureusement pas survécu à la détérioration de leur habitat. La végétation a repris ses droits dans le lit de la rivière, et Christine profite de cette perspective pour prendre encore quelques photos. Moses décide de s'y arrêter quelques instants et d'attendre, car certains animaux y reviennent parfois.

Always on the way to the water point, our team crosses a dry river that apparently harbored crocodiles; these have unfortunately not survived the deterioration of their habitat. Vegetation has regained its rights in the bed of the river, and Christine takes advantage of this perspective to take some more photos. Moses decides to stop for a few moments and wait, because some animals come back sometimes.

Quelques minutes plus tard, ce dont tous les visiteurs rêvent: deux lionnes, un lion et 3 lionceaux arrivent et se couchent. Christine n'est pas très rassurée, mais Moses la rassure bien vite. Ils se trouvent à une distance raisonnable et sont en sécurité. À condition de ne pas sortir de la voiture, bien sûr. Le chauffeur redémarre quand même le moteur au cas où...

A few minutes later, what all visitors dream: two lionesses, a lion and three cubs arrive and go to bed. Christine is not very reassured, but Moses reassures her very quickly. They are within a reasonable distance and are safe. As long as you do not get out of the car, of course. The driver still restarts the engine just in case ...

Un bruissement de l'autre côté attire l'attention de Moses: une trentaine de gazelles marchent lentement; celles à l'arrière du groupe se déplacent un peu plus vite et sautent par-dessus les branches au sol. Moses explique que ce ne sont pas des gazelles: ce sont en fait des nyalas, une espèce indigène de l'Afrique subsaharienne. La première s'arrête, le troupeau aussi. Elles ont repéré les lions. Le véhicule se trouvant maintenant entre les prédateurs et les proies potentielles, le chauffeur avance doucement. Patrick et Christine ne perdent pas une miette du spectacle. Les lions n'ont possiblement pas remarqué les nyalas ou sont déjà repus, car ils ne bougent pas. Les nyalas, ayant certainement senti le danger, font rapidement demi-tour.

A rustle on the other side draws Moses' attention: thirty or so gazelles walk slowly; those at the back of the group move a little faster and jump over the branches on the ground. Moses explains that they are not gazelles: they are actually nyalas, a species native to sub-Saharan Africa. The first stops, the flock too. They spotted the lions. With the vehicle now between predators and potential prey, the driver moves slowly. Patrick and Christine do not lose a crumb of the show. The lions may not have noticed the nyalas or are already sated because they do not move. The nyalas, having certainly felt the danger, quickly turn back.

Le groupe est presque arrivé au point d'eau vers lequel les éléphants se dirigent; il ne reste plus qu'une immense plaine à traverser. Ils ne croisent pas beaucoup d'animaux, seulement quelques zèbres et un troupeau de buffles. Cette traversée fait pourtant le délice de Patrick, qui profite de la leçon de botanique de Moses: comment les aloès, fougères et autres fleurs de sable poussent en toutes saisons; comment les animaux les utilisent pour se nourrir, se soigner et s'abriter; pourquoi leur hauteur est importante pour chaque espèce; comment les insectes s'y installent pour s'y nourrir des excréments des animaux... une mine d'informations que Patrick emmagasine avec la plus grande joie.

The group has almost arrived at the water point towards which the elephants are heading; there remains only an immense plain to cross. They do not cross many animals, only a few zebras and a herd of buffaloes. This crossing, however, is the delight of Patrick, who takes advantage of Moses' botanical lesson: how aloes, ferns and other flowers of sand grow in all seasons; how animals use them to feed, heal and shelter; why their height is important for each species; how insects settle there to feed on the excrement of animals ... a wealth of information that Patrick stores with great joy.

Enfin arrivés au point d'eau. Les éléphants les ont devancés, mais quelle merveilleuse surprise! Le troupeau au grand complet est dispersé autour du point d'eau, et un énorme mâle se tient en retrait pour surveiller les alentours, selon Moses. Les éléphanteaux jouent dans l'eau, s'aspergeant les uns les autres avec leur trompe. Certaines éléphantes lavent et rafraîchissent leurs petits, d'autres boivent et s'arrosent eux-mêmes. Un gros éléphant se roule dans la boue sur la rive avant d'aller se rincer dans l'eau qui semble assez profonde, puisqu'il s'y enfonce de moitié. Un spectacle aussi naturel que merveilleux pour un couple qui, il y a encore vingt-quatre heures, faisait son chemin dans le métro de Paris!

Finally arrived at the water point. The elephants have preceded them, but what a wonderful surprise! The entire flock is scattered around the water point, and a huge male stands back to watch the surroundings, according to Moses. The elephants play in the water, splashing each other with their trunks. Some elephants wash and refresh their young, others drink and water themselves. A big elephant rolls in the mud on the bank before going to rinse in the water that seems quite deep, since it sinks in half. A show as natural as it is wonderful for a couple who, twenty-four hours ago, was sailing their way in the Paris metro!

Le soleil commence à descendre sur ce tableau féérique, il est temps de rentrer à l'hôtel.

The sun begins to descend on this magical picture, it is time to return to the hotel.

La plaine traversée à l'aller est presque déserte, à l'exception de deux hyènes. Éclairées uniquement du soleil couchant, seules au milieu de nulle part, le spectacle est envoûtant. Puis un cri strident déchire le silence: ce sont les hyènes. L'envoûtement et la féérie sont rapidement remplacés par des frissons et un sentiment d'inconfort général. Christine profite de ce moment pour filmer; le son apportera certainement une dimension supplémentaire à la scène.

The plain crossed on the way out is almost deserted, with the exception of two hyenas. Lit only by the setting sun, alone in the middle of nowhere, the show is mesmerizing. Then a strident cry breaks the silence: these are the hyenas. The spell and the magic are quickly replaced by chills and a feeling of general discomfort. Christine takes advantage of this moment to film; the sound will certainly bring an extra dimension to the scene.

Les cris des hyènes s'éloignent, le retour se fait dans le silence. Tout le monde profite des couleurs changeantes du paysage, des sensations et des émotions ressenties pendant cette journée. De retour au bungalow, Christine s'empresse de trier ses photos pendant que Patrick se délasse dans la baignoire à ciel ouvert avant de partir dîner.

The cries of hyenas move away, the return is in silence. Everyone enjoys the changing colors of the landscape, the sensations and the emotions felt during this day. Back in the bungalow, Christine hastens to sort her photos while Patrick relaxes in the open-air bath before leaving for dinner.

Patrick a prévu bien d'autres aventures pour Christine les jours suivants: demain, ils partiront pour deux jours de randonnée et camping sauvage accompagnés d'un groupe. Encore une nouvelle expérience qui promet d'être mémorable.

Patrick has planned many more adventures for Christine the following days: tomorrow, they will leave for two days of hiking and wild camping accompanied by a group. Another new experience that promises to be memorable.

Quiz

1. Quelle est la passion de Patrick?
a) la nature
b) la photographie
c) la chasse
d) les voyages

2. Quel est le premier animal rencontré par le couple?
a) lions
b) gazelles
c) zèbres
d) éléphants

3. Quelle est la particularité de la salle de bain de l'hôtel?
a) elle n'a pas de fenêtre
b) elle est dans les arbres
c) elle est à ciel ouvert
d) il n'y a pas d'eau

4. Comment Christine trouve-t-elle les petits du phacochère?
a) terrifiants
b) apeurants
c) dangereux
d) mignons

5. Quel troupeau d'animaux trouvent-ils autour du point d'eau?
a) lions
b) gazelles
c) zèbres
d) éléphants

Answers

1. a
2. c
3. c
4. d
5. d

Vocabulaire / Vocabulary

- *à ciel ouvert* --- open air
- *à condition de* --- under the condition of
- *à perte de vue* --- for as far as the eye can see
- *agréable* --- nice, pleasant
- *air* --- appearance
- *aloès* --- aloe
- *animal sauvage* --- wild animal
- *apeurer* --- to scare, to frighten
- *arbre* --- tree
- *arbrisseau* --- very small tree
- *arbuste* --- small tree
- *arme* --- weapon, gun
- *arrivée* --- arrival
- *attrape* --- *attrapper* – to catch, to grab
- *au cas où* --- in case
- *aurore* --- aurora, dawn
- *autruche* --- ostrich
- *avion* --- plane
- *baie vitrée* --- bay window
- *baignoire* --- bath tub
- *bain à remous* --- bubble bath
- *bifurquer* --- to bifurcate, to branch off
- *blesser* --- to hurt
- *botanique* --- botanical
- *boue* --- mud
- *bouteille* --- bottle
- *branche* --- branch
- *bruit* --- noise, sound
- *buffle* --- buffalo
- *buisson* --- bush
- *cap* --- course, direction
- *chambre* --- bedroom
- *chemin* --- path
- *craquelé* --- cracked
- *créature* --- creature, animal
- *criquet* --- grasshopper, cricket
- *cri* --- scream
- *dénié* --- *dénier* --- to deny, to refuse
- *dépaysement* --- change of scene
- *détérioration* --- wear
- *dispersé* --- scattered
- *douche* --- shower
- *dromadaire* --- dromedary
- *dune* --- sand dune
- *emmagasine* --- *emmagasiner* --- to store, to accumulate

- *en sursaut* --- with a start
- *enceinte* --- enclosure
- *environs* --- surroundings
- *envoûtant* --- captivating, enchanting
- *est tout ouïe* --- être tout ouïe – to be all ears
- *étoile* --- star
- *excrément* --- faeces
- *exotisme* --- exoticism
- *féérique* --- magical, enchanting
- *feuille* --- leaf
- *fougère* --- fern
- *friand/friande* --- fond of
- *frisson* --- shiver
- *girafe* --- giraffe
- *habitat* --- housing
- *hauteur* --- height
- *hibou/chouette* --- owl
- *hululement* --- hooting
- *hurle* --- hurler – to scream
- *hyène* --- hyena
- *inconnu* --- unknown
- *indispensable* --- vital, essential
- *introuvable* --- nowhere to be found
- *jumelles* --- binoculars
- *lézard* --- lizard
- *lier* --- to tie together
- *lion/lionne* --- lion
- *lionceau* --- baby lion
- *lit de la rivière* --- river bed
- *masque* --- mask
- *miette* --- crumb
- *mignon/mignonne* --- cute
- *mitrailler* --- to snap away at (photo)
- *monter dans un taxi* --- to hop in a taxi
- *se font attendre* --- *se faire attendre* – to keep someone waiting
- *nuit tombante* --- falling night, dusk
- *objectif* --- objective (photo)
- *oiseau* --- bird
- *patte* --- paw
- *peau de bête* --- animal skin, fur
- *phacochère* --- warthog
- *pied-à-terre* --- short-term housing
- *plaine* --- plains, prairie
- *plante* --- plant
- *point d'eau* --- watering hole
- *porte* --- door
- *porte-savon* --- soap dish

- *prédateur* --- predator
- *proie* --- prey
- *quand bon leur semble* --- whenever it suits them
- *raisonnable* --- reasonable
- *réveil* --- waking
- *rideau* --- curtain
- *rocher* --- rock
- *s'aspergeant* --- *s'asperger* --- to spray, to spritz
- *sable* --- sand
- *salon* --- living room
- *savane* --- savannah
- se délasse --- se délasser --- to relax
- *sécheresse* --- dryness
- *sol* --- ground
- *soleil couchant* --- setting sun
- *souci* --- worry
- *spectaculaire* --- spectacular
- *spontané* --- spontaneous
- *strident/stridente* --- ear-splitting
- *surélevé* --- raised, elevated
- *susceptible* --- easily offended, touchy
- *taureau* --- bull
- *terrasse* --- terrace, balcony
- *trace de pas* --- footprint
- *traquer* --- to hunt down
- *trier* --- to sort
- *trompe* --- trunk
- *trophée* --- trophy
- *troupeau* --- herd
- *végétation* --- vegetation
- *voiture de location* --- rental car
- *zèbre* --- zebra

6. Les Années Passent.

Kevin est grand, il a maintenant quinze ans. Isabelle, sa sœur, est grande aussi. Elle a maintenant dix-sept ans. Son père travaille toujours à l'écurie. Et la mère de Kevin est toujours là pour la famille. Elle cuisine, fait le ménage et s'occupe de la lessive. C'est les vacances. Kevin peut tous les jours aller à l'écurie. Le matin, Kevin se lève de bonne heure. Il va à l'écurie. La première chose à faire, c'est donner à boire aux chevaux. Il change la litière de Rosa. Ensuite, il change la litière de Champion. Quand il arrive, Champion et Rosa hennissent tous les deux. Ils sont contents de voir Kevin. Et le petit poulain, Champion, a trois ans. C'est un grand cheval. Ses jambes sont en bonne condition. Tous les jours, Kevin l'emmène pour s'entraîner sur le champ de course derrière l'écurie. Tous les jockeys sont là aussi. Et tous les autres chevaux de monsieur Petit. Sur le champ de course, les jockeys entraînent les chevaux. Ils galopent. Les chevaux sont très rapides. Parfois, Kevin court aussi avec Champion. Champion est très rapide.

Kevin is tall, he is now fifteen years old. Isabelle, her sister, is great too. She is now seventeen years old. His father still works at the stables. And Kevin's mother is still there for the family. She cooks, cleans and takes care of laundry. It's the holidays. Kevin can go to the stables every day. In the morning, Kevin gets up early. He goes to the stable. The first thing to do is give the horses a drink. He changes Rosa's litter. Then he changes Champion's litter. When he arrives, Champion and Rosa both neigh. They are happy to see Kevin. And the little foal, Champion, is three years old. It's a big horse. His legs are in good condition. Every day, Kevin takes him to train on the race track behind the team. All the jockeys are there too. And all the other horses of Monsieur Petit. On the race course, the jockeys train the horses. They gallop. The horses are very fast. Sometimes Kevin also runs with Champion. Champion is very fast.

Pour l'anniversaire de ses quinze ans, les parents de Kevin lui offrent une tenue d'équitation de course. De belles bottes neuves et une cravache. Une superbe casquette aussi. Kevin est très fier. Il peut maintenant monter son cheval comme un vrai jockey. Monsieur Petit lui explique les ficelles du métier. Tous les autres jockeys sont très gentils avec Kevin. Ils sont fiers de lui, car il soigne bien son cheval, Champion.

For the birthday of his fifteen years, Kevin's parents offer him a race riding outfit. Beautiful new boots and a whip. A superb cap too. Kevin is very proud. He can now ride his horse like a real jockey. Mr. Petit explains the ropes. All the other jockeys are very nice to Kevin. They are proud of him because he looks after his horse, Champion.

Un jour, Kevin demande à monsieur Petit de courir sur le grand champ de courses.

One day, Kevin asks Mr. Petit to run on the big racetrack.

– Si tu veux, mon garçon, dit monsieur Petit, mais fais bien attention.

"If you want, my boy,"said Monsieur Petit,"but be careful.

– Oh, oui, monsieur. Je vais faire bien attention, répond Kevin.

- Oh, yes, sir. I'll be careful, Kevin answers.

Il est très content. Courir sur le grand champ de course avec les autres chevaux est un honneur. Il est très fier. Il rentre à la maison, le soir, et il le raconte à son père, sa mère et sa sœur. Ils sont tous les trois très fiers de lui.

He is very happy. Running on the big race course with the other horses is an honor. He is very proud. He goes home at night and tells it to his father, his mother and his sister. They are all three very proud of him.

Plusieurs fois, Kevin va courir avec Champion sur le grand champ de courses. Champion est rapide. Il court aussi vite que les autres chevaux. Monsieur Petit a une idée. Un matin, il appelle Kevin.

Many times, Kevin will run with Champion on the big racetrack. Champion is fast. He runs as fast as other horses. Mr. Petit has an idea. One morning, he calls Kevin.

– Dis donc, mon garçon, viens me voir à mon bureau quand tu auras fini les litières. Je veux parler avec toi un moment.

"Say, my boy, come see me at my office when you have finished the litter. I want to talk with you for a moment.

Kevin a un peu peur. Il pense que, peut-être, il a fait une bêtise. Il se demande ce que monsieur Petit veut lui dire. Il va au bureau et frappe à la porte. Son cœur bat très fort.

Kevin is a little scared. He thinks maybe he's done something stupid. He wonders what Mr. Petit wants to tell him. He goes to the office and knocks on the door. His heart beats very hard.

– Entre, dit monsieur Petit. Assieds-toi sur la chaise.

"Come in,"said Monsieur Petit. Sit on the chair.

Il montre une chaise à Kevin devant le bureau. Kevin est très impressionné. C'est la première fois qu'il vient dans le bureau de monsieur Petit. Sur les murs, il y a beaucoup de photos de chevaux. Ce sont les chevaux de monsieur Petit. Des chevaux qui gagnent des courses. Des champions. Il y a aussi des photos de jockeys de l'écurie. Kevin les reconnaît. Il voit aussi une photo de son père. Monsieur Petit voit Kevin qui regarde les photos. Il lui dit:

He shows Kevin a chair in front of the desk. Kevin is very impressed. This is the first time he has come to Mr. Petit's office. On the walls, there are many pictures of horses. These are Monsieur Petit's horses. Horses who win races. Champions. There are also pictures of the team's jockeys. Kevin recognizes them. He also sees a picture of his father. Mr. Petit sees Kevin looking at the pictures. He tells him:

– Tu vois, mon garçon. C'est les photos de mes jockeys et de mes chevaux. Ce sont des champions. Des vrais champions. Et la photo de ton père parce qu'il s'occupe des chevaux. Tu penses que ta photo sera bientôt là?

- You see, my boy. It's the pictures of my jockeys and my horses. They are champions. Real champions. And your father's picture because he looks after the horses. Do you think your picture will be here soon?

– Je ne sais pas monsieur, répond Kevin.

- I do not know sir, Kevin answers.

– Tu penses que ton Champion est un vrai champion?

- Do you think your Champion is a real champion?

– Oh, oui, monsieur, je pense qu'il est un champion.

- Oh, yes, sir, I think he's a champion.

– Alors, nous allons voir. Dans un mois, il y a la course pour les trois ans. Nous allons inscrire Champion.

- So, let's see. In a month, there is the race for three years. We will register Champion.

– C'est vrai? demande Kevin fou de joie.

- It is true? Kevin asks for joy.

– Oui, mon garçon. Ton père est d'accord. Tu vas courir pour le prix. Il faut apprendre. Allez va vite. Il

y a du travail.

- Yes, my boy. Your father agrees. You will run for the price. You need to learn. Go go quickly. There's work.

Kevin court tous les jours avec Champion. Le matin de bonne heure, il est sur le champ de course. Champion fait de grands progrès. Il est prêt pour la grande course.

Kevin runs every day with Champion. In the early morning, he is on the racetrack. Champion is making great progress. He is ready for the big race.

Kevin danse presque. Il est si content. Il saute de joie.

Kevin almost dances. He is so happy. He is jumping for joy.

Le mois passe rapidement et le grand jour arrive.

The month passes quickly and the big day arrives.

La mère, le père et la sœur de Kevin sont tous les trois dans les tribunes. Kevin a mis sa belle tenue de jockey avec les couleurs officielles de monsieur Petit. Il porte les bottes offertes par ses parents, avec une chemise bleue et verte, une casaque. Sa sœur, Isabelle, lui donne un porte-bonheur: une chaîne avec un cheval. Kevin tient sa cravache dans la main gauche. Mais Kevin n'utilise jamais sa cravache. Il parle toujours à Champion pour le faire courir plus vite.

Kevin's mother, father and sister are all in the stands. Kevin put on his beautiful jockey outfit with Mr. Petit's official colors. He wears the boots offered by his parents, with a blue and green shirt, a coat. His sister, Isabelle, gives him a lucky charm: a chain with a horse. Kevin holds his whip in his left hand. But Kevin never uses his whip. He always talks to Champion to make him run faster.

Il y a vingt chevaux sur la ligne de départ. Le juge baisse le drapeau et c'est le départ de la course. Tous les chevaux partent en même temps. C'est une course de deux kilomètres sur un terrain plat. Champion sait sauter les obstacles, mais les courses pour les jeunes chevaux sont sur terrain plat. Champion fait un départ lent. Il est quatrième. Mais, petit à petit, il est troisième, puis deuxième et il gagne la course.

There are twenty horses on the starting line. The judge lowers the flag and it is the start of the race. All the horses leave at the same time. It's a two-kilometer race on flat ground. Champion knows how to jump the obstacles, but the races for young horses are on flat ground. Champion makes a slow start. He is fourth. But, little by little, he is third, then second and he wins the race.

– *Bravo, crient les amis et les parents de Kevin. Tout le monde applaudit.*

- Well done, shout Kevin's friends and relatives. Everyone applauds.

Monsieur Petit félicite Kevin. Il reçoit une grande couronne de fleurs. C'est un jour merveilleux pour Kevin. Tout le monde est fier de lui. Champion est un champion.

Mr. Petit congratulates Kevin. He receives a large wreath of flowers. It's a wonderful day for Kevin. Everyone is proud of him. Champion is a champion.

Quiz

1. Quel âge Kevin a-t-il maintenant?
a. Dix-sept ans.
b. Quinze ans.
c. Seize ans.

2. Quand Kevin arrive à l'écurie, que fait-il en premier?
a. Il donne à boire aux chevaux.
b. Il change la litière de Champion.
c. Il change la litière de Rosa.

3. Sur les murs du bureau de monsieur Petit, il y a:
a. Des photos de ses enfants.
b. Des tableaux.
c. Des photos de ses chevaux.

4. Pourquoi Kevin est-il fou de joie?
a. Champion est inscrit pour la course.
b. Il a des bottes neuves.
c. Sa sœur lui donne un porte-bonheur.

5. Pourquoi Champion ne saute-t-il pas les obstacles?
a. Il ne sait pas sauter les obstacles.
b. C'est une course sans obstacles.
c. Il n'a pas le droit de sauter les obstacles.

Answers

1. b
2. a
3. c
4. a
5. b

Vocabulaire / Vocabulary

- *les années passent* in English is translated to years go by
- *quinze ans* in English is translated to fifteen years old
- *dix-sept ans* in English is translated to seventeen years old
- *la famille* in English is translated to the family
- *le matin* in English is translated to in the morning
- *Kevin se lève de bonne heure* in English is translated to Kevin gets up early
- *la première chose à faire* in English is translated to the first thing to do
- *ensuite* in English is translated to then
- *quand il arrive* in English is translated to when he comes in
- *en bonne condition* in English is translated to in good shape
- *derrière* in English is translated to behind
- *ils galopent* in English is translated to they gallop
- *rapides* in English is translated to fast
- *parfois* in English is translated to sometimes
- *l'anniversaire de ses quinze ans* in English is translated to his fifteenth birthday
- *offrent* in English is translated to offer
- *une tenue d'équitation* in English is translated to riding clothes
- *bottes neuves* in English is translated to new riding boots
- *une cravache* in English is translated to a crop
- *casquette* in English is translated to cap
- *les ficelles du métier* in English is translated to the tricks of the trade
- *gentils* in English is translated to kind
- *fais bien attention* in English is translated to take care
- *honneur* in English is translated to honour
- *raconte* in English is translated to tell
- *plusieurs fois* in English is translated to several times
- *viens me voir* in English is translated to come to see me
- *à mon bureau* in English is translated to at my office
- *un peu peur* in English is translated to a little afraid
- *peut-être* in English is translated to maybe
- *une bêtise* in English is translated to a stupid thing
- *frappe à la porte* in English is translated to knock at the door
- *son cœur bat* in English is translated to his heart beats
- *entre* in English is translated to come in
- *assieds-toi* in English is translated to sit down
- *devant le bureau* in English is translated to in front of the desk
- *impressionné* in English is translated to impressed
- *c'est la première fois* in English is translated to it is the first time
- *sur les murs* in English is translated to on the walls
- *bientôt* in English is translated to soon
- *alors, nous allons voir* in English is translated to then we'll see
- *dans un mois* in English is translated to in a month from now
- *inscrire* in English is translated to to register
- *fou de joie* in English is translated to overjoyed
- *le prix* in English is translated to the prize

- *danse presque* in English is translated to almost dances
- *il saute* in English is translated to he jumps
- *prêt* in English is translated to ready
- *rapidement* in English is translated to quickly
- *les tribunes* in English is translated to the gallery
- *une casaque* in English is translated to a casague
- *un porte-bonheur* in English is translated to a lucky charm
- *la main gauche* in English is translated to the left hand
- *Kevin n'utilise jamais* in English is translated to Kevin never uses
- *la ligne de départ* in English is translated to the starting line
- *le juge baisse le drapeau* in English is translated to the judge lowers the flag
- *en même temps* in English is translated to at the same time
- *un terrain plat* in English is translated to a flat ground
- *lent* in English is translated to slow
- *petit à petit* in English is translated to gradually
- *applaudit* in English is translated to applauses
- *félicite* in English is translated to congratulates
- *il reçoit* in English is translated to he receives
- *une grande couronne de fleurs* in English is translated to a big wreath of flowers
- *merveilleux* in English is translated to marvellous

7. La Salle De Sport

Comme tous les jours, Anne se lève à six heures du matin. Elle bois un grand bol de café accompagné de tartines de confiture. Elle se rue à la salle de bain, se déshabille et prend sa douche. Or, ce matin semble différent pour Anne. En enfilant sa paire de collants, elle réalise qu'elle a pris du poids. Ses formes semblent bien plus généreuses qu'autrefois. À l'aube de ses trente ans, Anne n'a plus la silhouette filiforme de ses vingt ans...

Like every day, Anne gets up at six in the morning. She has lunch with a large bowl of coffee and toast with jam. She rushes to the bathroom, undresses and takes a shower. But this morning seems different for Anne. By pulling on her pair of tights, she realizes she has gained weight. Its forms seem much more generous than before. At the dawn of her thirties, Anne no longer has the slender silhouette of her twenty years ...

-Mon Dieu! s'exclame-t-elle en se scrutant dans le miroir. Il faut que je fasse quelque chose.

-My God! she exclaims, scrutinizing herself in the mirror. I have to do something.

Anne est très gourmande et l'assume. Elle se refuse à entamer tout régime. Hors de question de se laisser mourir de faim! Elle n'est pas non plus une très grande sportive. Elle se souvient encore de ses années collège où elle imaginait tous les prétextes possibles pour être dispensée de cours de gymnastique! Mais il fallait se rendre à l'évidence, trois, quatre séances de sport par semaine ne lui feraient guère de mal.

Anne is very greedy and assumes it. She refuses to start any diet. No way to let yourself starve! She is not a very big sportswoman either. She still remembers her college years where she imagined all the pretexts possible to be dispensed from gymnastics classes! But it had to be clear, three, four sports sessions a week would not hurt him.

C'est l'esprit résigné qu'elle franchit la porte de la salle de sport du quartier. Elle est accueillie, à l'accueil, par une jeune femme athlétique et toute de couleurs fluo vêtue.

It is the resigned spirit that she walks through the door of the neighborhood gym. She is greeted, at the reception, by a young athletic woman and all in fluorescent colors.

—Bonjour, j'aurais aimé profiter d'une journée d'essai. J'ai pour objectif une petite perte de poids.

-Hello, I would have liked to enjoy a test day. My goal is a small weight loss.

—Bienvenue au club. Nous vous offrons l'accès au club pour la journée. Les vestiaires se situent sur votre droite. N'hésitez pas à demander des conseils aux coachs présents dans la salle. Nous vous souhaitons une bonne séance!

-Welcome to the club. We offer you access to the club for the day. The locker rooms are on your right. Do not hesitate to seek advice from the coaches present in the room. We wish you a good session!

Anne regarde autour d'elle, la salle de sport regorge d'hommes et de femmes aux silhouettes athlétiques. Elle file se mettre en tenue de sport et parcourt le club à la recherche d'un sport qui pourrait lui convenir. Elle s'essaie à la musculation, s'allonge sur le banc et entreprend de soulever la barre lestée. En vain... Elle observe la barre de plus près:

Anne looks around her, the gym is full of men and women athletic silhouettes. She goes to wear sportswear and runs the club in search of a sport that could suit him. She tries to bodybuilding, lying on the bench and begins to lift the bar weighted. In vain ... She looks at the bar more closely:

-50 kg? Il y a vraiment des personnes qui arrivent à soulever ce poids?!

-50 kg? Are there really people who can lift this weight?!

Anne se lève et part à la découverte des autres machines.

Anne gets up and goes to discover the other machines.

Elle s'essaie au tapis de course. Les réglages sont fastidieux. Elle sélectionne le premier programme qui apparaît à l'écran. Aussitôt, le tapis se met en marche:

She tries the treadmill. The settings are tedious. It selects the first program that appears on the screen. The carpet starts immediately:

-3 km/heure... Ce n'est pas si difficile que ça au final!

-3 km / hour ... It's not that difficult in the end!

Elle décide d'augmenter la cadence, mais fait une mauvaise manipulation. Soudain, le tapis s'emballe. Anne panique en voyant 14 km/heure au compteur! Elle pousse le bouton d'arrêt d'urgence pour échapper à ce rythme infernal.

She decides to increase the pace, but does a bad job. Suddenly, the carpet is racing. Anne panics seeing 14 km / hour on the meter! She pushes the emergency stop button to escape this hellish pace.

Anne jette son dévolu sur le vélo elliptique. Ses bras et ses jambes bougent en rythme. Elle sent ses muscles travailler. La sensation n'est pas désagréable, l'effort n'est pas surhumain non plus, mais qu'est-ce qu'elle s'ennuie! Chaque minute lui semble durer une éternité! Lassée, elle décide à nouveau de changer d'appareil.

Anne sets her sights on the elliptical trainer. His arms and legs move rhythmically. She feels her muscles working. The sensation is not unpleasant, the effort is not superhuman either, but what is it bored! Every minute seems like an eternity! Tired, she decides to change her camera again.

Stepper, rameur, vélo classique, machine à adducteurs et abducteurs en passant par la presse à cuisse. Aucune de ces machines ne trouve grâce à ses yeux.

Stepper, rower, classic bike, adductor and abductor machine through the thigh press. None of these machines find grace in his eyes.

Anne s'octroie donc une pause. Toutes ces émotions, ça creuse! Des pommes et du thé détox sont mis à disposition dans un petit espace cosy. Anne s'en délecte avec plaisir. Elle s'accorde même une micro sieste!

Anne gives herself a break. All these emotions, it digs! Apples and detox tea are available in a cozy little space. Anne enjoys it with pleasure. She even gives herself a nap!

—Allez! C'est reparti! Je vais bien finir par trouver un appareil qui me corresponde.

-Go! Here we go again! I will eventually find a device that suits me.

Anne se relève, toute requinquée et plus motivée que jamais quand soudain des cris se font entendre. Intriguée, Anne laisse le son de la musique la guider. Les cris proviennent de la salle de sport collectif. Anne entrouvre la porte et découvre un groupe de femmes surexcitées sautant et dansant sous une musique tambourinante. De la Zumba! Son entrée est immédiatement remarquée par la coach.

Anne gets up, all shark and more motivated than ever when suddenly screams are heard. Intrigued, Anne lets the sound of the music guide her. The cries come from the collective gym. Anne opens the door and discovers a group of excited women jumping and dancing under a drumming music. Zumba! His entry is immediately noticed by the coach.

—Hé toi là-bas! Allez! Allez! Rejoins-nous!

-Hey you there! Go! Go! Join us!

Anne intimidée, obéit et se met à suivre les mouvements de la coach. On ne peut pas dire qu'Anne a le rythme dans la peau, ses gestes ne sont pas coordonnés, manquent de grâce... Mais qu'est-ce qu'elle s'éclate! Anne rigole, transpire, s'essouffle, mais y prend beaucoup de plaisir! La séance de Zumba s'achève. Anne est épuisée. En sueur comme jamais, mais néanmoins ravie!

Anne is intimidated, obeys and starts following the movements of the coach. We cannot say that Anne has the rhythm in her skin, her gestures are not coordinated, lack grace ... But what is it fun! Anne laughs, sweats, is out of breath, but it takes a lot of fun! The Zumba session ends. Anne is exhausted. Sweaty as ever, but still delighted!

Elle part se doucher et se changer au vestiaire. Elle ne manque pas de prendre un abonnement au cours de Zumba et rentre, satisfaite, tranquillement chez elle.

She goes to shower and change in the locker room. She does not fail to take a subscription to the Zumba class and returns, satisfied, quietly at home.

Arrivée à la maison, c'est le sourire aux lèvres et le cœur léger, qu'elle s'affale devant la télé pour regarder son feuilleton favori et savourer sa crème glacée préférée.

Arriving home, it's with a smile on her face and a light heart, that she slumps in front of the TV to watch her favorite soap opera and enjoy her favorite ice cream.

Quiz

1) A quelle heure Anne se lève-t-elle?
a) 5h
b) 6h
c) 7h

2) Quelle âge Anne a-t-elle?
a) 28 ans
b) 30 ans
c) 32 ans

3) Quel snack Anne mange-t-elle après la première partie de sa séance?
a) Des pommes
b) Des fraises
c) Des poires

4) Complétez la phrase:"Après sa séance de sport, Anne _____".
a) Se douche en rentrant chez elle.
b) Ne se douche pas.
c) Se douche dans les vestiaires.

Answers

1) b
2) b
3) a
4) c

Vocabulaire / Vocabulary

- *à la recherche* --- looking for
- *à nouveau* --- once again
- *appareil* --- machine
- *aucune* --- none
- *autrefois* --- formerly
- *bienvenue* --- welcome
- *bol de café* --- bowl of coffee
- *bouton d'arrêt d'urgence* --- an emergency button
- *cadence* --- pace
- *ce matin* --- this morning
- *comme jamais* --- like never before
- *conseil* --- advice
- crème glacée --- icecream
- *déjeune --- déjeuner* — to have breakfast
- *dispensée* --- exempted from
- *en vain* --- in vain
- *enfilant --- enfiler* — to wear
- *fastidieux* --- tedious
- *feuilleton* --- a soap opera
- *filiforme* --- skinny
- *fluo* --- fluorescent, neon
- *gourmande* --- someone that enjoys eating
- *guider* --- to guide
- *hors de question* --- no way it is an option
- *intriguée* --- intrigued
- *jambes* --- legs
- *journée d'essai* --- a one day trial
- *l'accès* --- the access to
- *léger* --- light
- *miroir* --- mirror
- *motivée* --- motivated
- *mourir de faim* --- starve to death
- *musculation* --- weight-lifting
- *objectif* --- objective
- *paire de collants* --- tights
- *panique* --- a panic
- *perte de poids* --- weight loss

- *pommes* --- apples
- *porte* --- a door
- *prétextes* --- pretexts
- *pris du poids* --- *prendre du poids* — to gain weight
- *rameur* --- rowing machine
- *ravie* --- enchanted
- *régime* --- a diet
- *réglages* --- settings
- *rendre à l'évidence* --- accept the obvious truth
- *requinquée* --- replenished
- *s'affale* --- *s'affaler* — to slouch
- *s'ennuie* --- s'ennuyer — to be bored
- *salle de bain* --- bathroom
- *salle de sport* --- the gym
- *se doucher* --- to shower
- *se font entendre* --- *se faire entendre* — to be heard
- *séance* --- session
- *son* --- sound
- *son entrée* --- her entry
- *sportive* --- athletic
- *surexcitées* --- overly excited
- *surhumain* --- superhuman
- *tapis de course* --- treadmill
- *tartine de confiture* --- toast with jam
- *tenue de sport* --- sport attire
- *thé detox* --- cleansing tea
- *trente* --- thirty
- *une éternité* --- an eternity
- *vélo elliptique* --- elliptical bike
- *vestiaire* --- the locker room
- *vingt* --- twenty

8. Ville Et Métropole

Avant de retrouver Laura aujourd'hui pour leur rendez-vous, Louis avait quelques courses à faire pour s'assurer que tout était prêt. Pour commencer, il devait se rendre à la banque pour retirer suffisamment d'espèces pour la journée bien remplie qui s'annonçait. Sur le chemin de la banque, il s'est arrêté dans son café préféré pour récupérer la caféine dont il avait grand besoin pour bien débuter la journée.

Before his big date with Laura today, Louis had a few errands to run to make sure everything was ready. First of all, a trip to the bank was needed, so he could withdraw enough cash for the busy day ahead. Along the way to the bank, he stopped by his favorite coffee shop to pick up some much needed caffeine to jump-start the day.

Il devait ensuite se rendre au bureau de poste et déposer plusieurs courriers tardifs et pratiquement en retard. Après ça, il s'est rendu au centre commercial pour trouver une nouvelle tenue pour son rendez-vous. Il a examiné les articles dans deux magasins de vêtements et il a même trouvé le temps de s'offrir une nouvelle coupe de cheveux chez le barbier.

Next, he had to make a run to the post office and drop off some mail that was overdue and nearly late. After that, it was off to the mall to find a new outfit to wear on today's date. He perused two clothing stores and even had enough time to get himself a new haircut at the barber shop.

A 14 heures, Louis et Laura se sont retrouvés et ils étaient prêts pour une ballade en ville. Ils ont commencé par se promener dans le parc pour se tenir au courant des évènements qu'ils avaient vécus pendant la semaine. Le parc abritait une grande place où le couple a pu assister au petit concert d'un groupe de rock. Après avoir écouté quelques chansons, ils ont quitté le parc et se sont rendus dans un parc d'attractions local en voiture.

At 2:00 pm, Louis and Laura met up, ready to take a tour around town. They started by walking around the park, catching up on what happened with each other during the week. Inside the park was a large plaza, where the couple found a small concert by a rock band. After hearing a few songs, they left the park and drove towards a local amusement park.

Le parc d'attractions a dû fermer à cause d'un grave accident de la route, le couple a donc décidé d'opter pour un plan de secours, et d'aller au cinéma. Pour le plus grand plaisir de Laura, un film d'horreur était diffusé cette semaine-là. Il y avait une heure d'attente avant de voir le film, ils ont donc décidé de dîner tôt dans un restaurant des environs, ce qui leur a permis de revenir au cinéma juste à temps. Le film s'est avéré plutôt banal et prévisible, mais il incluait tout de même un jump scare qui a vraiment beaucoup effrayé Louis et Laura.

Due to a large accident, the amusement park had to be shut down, so as a back-up plan, the couple decided to go to the movie theater instead. To Laura's luck, they were able to find a horror movie playing that week. It would be an hour-long wait for the movie, so they grabbed an early dinner at a nearby restaurant with just enough time to make it back to the theater. The movie turned out to be fairly generic and predictable, but there was one jumpscare that got both Louis and Laura really, really good.

Le soir venu, Louis, tout comme Laura, ne souhaitait pas rester tard en ville, mais ils ont décidé ensemble de prendre un verre dans le seul bar qui était indiqué sur leurs smartphones. Il s'agissait d'un bar à thème château médiéval et il était décoré avec des bannières, des armures et des sièges qui ressemblaient à des trônes. Ils ont repris leur conversation, qui les a amenés à commander d'autres boissons par la suite.

As the evening came, the couple had a mutual feeling of not wanting to stay out too late in the city, but they agreed to have one drink at a unique bar they found searching on their smartphones. It had a medieval castle theme and was decorated with banners, suits of armor, and chairs that looked like thrones. The conversation picked up between the two and along with it came more drinking.

A présent, ils étaient tous les deux trop ivres pour pouvoir rentrer en voiture sans encombre! Ils n'avaient pas envie d'aller danser toute la nuit et ils ont donc décidé de patienter pendant deux heures pour dégriser avant de rentrer chez eux en voiture. Appeler un taxi constituait une option vraiment très coûteuse et d'ailleurs, ils n'avaient pas longtemps à attendre. Pour passer le temps, ils ont marché le long de la promenade et ils se sont arrêtés dans une supérette pour prendre une collation rapide.

Now they were both too intoxicated to drive home safely! Not feeling up for a night of clubbing, they would wait two hours to sober up before driving home. Calling a taxi would be a crazy expensive option, and it wasn't all that much of a wait to begin with. To pass the time, they walked along the boardwalk and stopped by the convenience store for a quick snack.

Chacun appréciait vraiment beaucoup la présence de l'autre, les heures ont donc passé plus rapidement qu'ils ne le pensaient, mais il était temps de se séparer. Le rendez-vous s'est achevé lorsque Louis et Laura ont échangé un baiser rapide et quelques sourires coquins, avant de rentrer chez eux en voiture.

Louis and Laura thoroughly enjoyed each other's presence, so the hours passed quicker than expected, but it was time to part ways. A brief kiss was shared, along with a couple of cheeky smiles, and that was it before they both drove home.

Quiz

1. Quel terme désigne le fait d'ajouter de l'argent sur un compte bancaire?
A) Faire un retrait
B) Consulter le solde
C) Ouvrir un compte
D) Faire un dépôt

2. Qu'a fait Louis au centre commercial?
A) Il a joué aux jeux vidéo dans la salle de jeux.
B) Il a passé du temps avec ses amis et il a acheté des vêtements.
C) Il a acheté des vêtements et il s'est fait couper les cheveux.
D) Il s'est fait couper les cheveux et il a déjeuné dans l'aire de restauration.

3. Où Louis et Laura sont-ils allés directement après avoir quitté le parc?
A) Le parc d'attractions
B) Chez eux
C) Le cinéma
D) Le restaurant

4. Comment le couple a-t-il trouvé le bar à thème médiéval?
A) Ils se sont promenés en ville pour trouver un bar.
B) Il leur a été recommandé par un ami commun.
C) Ils ont cherché les bars disponibles dans les environs en utilisant leurs smartphones.
D) Ils ont vu une affiche publicitaire du bar.

5. Si vous êtes ivre, il est dangereux de...
A) boire davantage.
B) conduire une voiture.
C) parler au téléphone.
D) marcher dans les lieux publics.

Answers

1. D
2. C
3. A
4. C
5. B (A could be true also)

Vocabulaire / Vocabulary

- *ville et métropole* --- town and city
- *courses* --- errands
- *banque* --- bank
- *retirer des espèces* --- to withdraw cash
- *café* --- coffee shop
- *caféine* --- caffeine
- *bureau de poste* --- post office
- *courrier* --- mail
- *tardif* --- overdue
- *centre commercial* --- mall
- *tenue* --- outfit
- *magasins de vêtements* --- clothing stores
- *coupe de cheveux* --- haircut
- *barbier* --- barber shop
- *se retrouver* --- to meet up
- *une ballade en ville* --- a tour around town
- *parc* --- park
- *évènement* --- event
- *grande place* --- large plaza
- *couple* --- couple
- *petit concert* --- small concert
- *assister* --- to go to, to attend
- *groupe de rock* --- rock band
- *chansons* --- songs
- *parc d'attractions* --- amusement park
- *accident de la route* --- traffic accident
- *être fermé* --- to be shutdown
- *plan de secours* --- back-up plan
- *cinéma* --- movie theater

- *film d'horreur* --- horror movie
- *une heure d'attente* --- an hour-long wait
- *dîner tôt* --- early dinner
- *des environs* --- near-by
- *restaurant* --- restaurant
- *banal* --- generic
- *prévisible* --- predictable
- *jump scare* --- jump scare
- *rester tard* --- to stay late
- *un verre* --- one drink
- *le seul bar* --- a unique bar
- *château médiéval* --- medieval castle
- *thème* --- theme
- *être décoré* --- to be decorated
- *bannières* --- banners
- *armures* --- suits of armor
- *sièges* --- chairs
- *trônes* --- thrones
- *conversation* --- conversation
- *ivre* --- intoxicated
- *rentrer en voiture* --- to drive back home
- *danser toute la nuit* --- to dance the night away
- *dégriser* --- to sober up
- *appeler un taxi* --- to call a taxi
- *vraiment très coûteuse* --- crazy expensive
- *passer le temps* --- to pass the time
- *promenade* --- boardwalk
- *supérette* --- convenience store
- *une collation rapide* --- a quick snack
- *présence* --- presence
- *se séparer* --- to part ways
- *baiser rapide* --- brief kiss
- *sourires coquins* --- cheeky smiles

9 - Shopping and Ordering

De la vitrine à l'écran --- From the Window to the Screen

Julie rentre, exténuée, d'un après-midi de lèche-vitrine. Elle se couche sur le canapé, retire ses chaussures et laisse ses sacs de courses par terre. Elle a l'impression qu'elle vient de courir un marathon. Ses pieds brûlent. Elle a les bras sans vie et elle est ruinée! C'est ter-mi-né. Fini le shopping! C'est bien parce qu'elle n'avait plus rien à se mettre qu'elle s'est infligé ce supplice. Il n'est plus question de marcher des kilomètres, d'entrer et de sortir de cinquante magasins différents, d'essayer dix pantalons pour en acheter un, de faire la queue devant les cabines d'essayage et la file indienne devant la caisse, tout ça pour, à la fin de la journée, se retrouver sans un sou!

Julie returns, exhausted, from an afternoon of window shopping. She lies down on the couch, takes off her shoes, and leaves her shopping bags on the floor. She feels like she's just run a marathon. Her feet are burning. Her arms feel lifeless, and she's broke! It's over. No more shopping! She endured this ordeal because she had nothing left to wear. There's no more talk of walking for kilometers, entering and exiting fifty different stores, trying on ten pairs of pants to buy one, waiting in line in front of fitting rooms, and queuing in a single file line at the cash register—all of that, only to end up with not a penny by the end of the day!

C'est le vingt et unième siècle après tout, nous n'avons plus à nous infliger une épreuve pareille. C'est décidé. Désormais, Julie fera son shopping en ligne. Plus de temps à perdre avec ces bêtises. En plus, c'est certain, elle fera des économies et ne sera pas tentée d'acheter ce dont elle n'a pas besoin. Économique et pratique: vive la technologie.

It's the twenty-first century, after all. We no longer have to subject ourselves to such a trial. It's decided. From now on, Julie will do her shopping online. No more time wasted on these foolish activities. Plus, it's certain, she'll save money and won't be tempted to buy things she doesn't need. Economical and practical: long live technology.

Deux mois plus tard, Julie a tenu bon et n'a pas fait de nouvelles séances de shopping. Par contre, la période des soldes commence aujourd'hui. Impossible de passer à côté de ces soldes et de ces offres promotionnelles! Julie est bien décidée à faire les soldes loin de la foule et de la frénésie acheteuse: elle va faire ses achats sur son ordinateur, bien confortablement assise sur son canapé, en pyjama, et elle va se contenter d'acheter ce dont elle a besoin. Elle a une liste! C'est parti!

Two months later, Julie held strong and refrained from any new shopping sprees. However, the sales period starts today. Impossible to ignore these sales and promotional offers! Julie is determined to take advantage of the sales far away from the crowds and shopping frenzy. She's going to do her shopping on her computer, comfortably seated on her couch, in pajamas, and she's only going to buy what she needs. She has a list! Let's get started!

Pour commencer, il lui faut une nouvelle paire de baskets. Sa marque préférée fait une démarque à moins 50 %. C'est le moment d'en profiter. Elle sait quel modèle elle veut, elle connaît sa pointure et elle a déjà calculé la ristourne. Il ne reste plus qu'à commander... mais voilà: le modèle qu'elle voulait n'est déjà plus disponible. Elle en trouve un autre, mais il n'y a plus sa taille. Et finalement, ce n'est pas 50 % de remise, c'est 20 %. Tant pis. C'est mieux que rien.

To begin with, she needs a new pair of sneakers. Her favorite brand has a markdown of 50%. This is the time to seize the opportunity. She knows the model she wants, she knows her size, and she has already calculated the discount. All that's left is to place the order... but here's the issue: the model she wanted is already unavailable. She finds another one, but her size is no longer in stock. And ultimately, it's not a

50% discount, it's 20%. Oh well, it's better than nothing.

Prochaine étape: trouver un cadeau pour la fête des Mères. La boutique en ligne a justement une section «Fête des Mères». Le marketing est bien fait, il n'y a pas à dire: sur Internet, on a le sens du commerce! Après de longues minutes à parcourir la boutique en ligne, Julie réalise avec horreur qu'il y a beaucoup trop de choix. Elle ne sait pas quoi prendre. Des milliers de références, c'est beaucoup plus de choix que dans les magasins. Elle finit par se décider pour un collier fantaisie fait main. Elle clique, et hop, dans le panier... mais ça ne semble pas marcher. Alors elle reclique, reclique... Ah! Finalement le panier est activé! Elle va pouvoir payer la note, laisser son adresse de livraison et valider la commande. Elle précisera sur le bon de commande qu'il s'agit d'un cadeau: elle voudrait un emballage et que le prix soit caché. Merveille de la technologie, le vendeur en ligne est relié à sa carte bancaire: paiement automatisé par virement. Julie clique sur «valider», mécaniquement... mais quelle horreur! 270 euros! Comment ça se fait? Le collier vaut 27 euros. Elle retourne vérifier, puis c'est bien 27 euros qui étaient indiqués sur l'étiquette.

Next step: find a gift for Mother's Day. The online store has a "Mother's Day" section. The marketing is well done, there is no denying it: on the Internet, we have a sense of commerce! After long minutes browsing the online store, Julie realizes with horror that there are far too many choices. She doesn't know what to take. Thousands of references means much more choice than in stores. She ends up deciding on a fancy handmade necklace. She clicks, and poofs, into the basket... but it doesn't seem to work. So she clicks again, clicks again... Ah! Finally the basket is activated! She will be able to pay the bill, leave her delivery address and validate the order. She will specify on the order form that it is a gift: she would like packaging and the price to be hidden. A marvel of technology, the online seller is linked to his bank card: automated payment by bank transfer. Julie clicks on "validate", mechanically... but what horror! 270 euros! How come? The necklace is worth 27 euros. She goes back to check, then it is indeed 27 euros that were indicated on the label.

Malheureusement, Julie a été trop impatiente et a cliqué dix fois: elle a commandé dix colliers! Elle passe l'heure qui suit à essayer de contacter le vendeur pour annuler sa commande et modifier les quantités. Elle a de la chance, le commerçant accepte. Ouf. Plus de peur que de mal.

Unfortunately, Julie was too impatient and clicked ten times: she ordered ten necklaces! She spends the next hour trying to contact the seller to cancel her order and adjust the quantities. Luckily, the merchant agrees. Phew. All's well that ends well.

Le dernier achat des soldes, ce sera la superbe offre promotionnelle deux en un, sur une machine à laver et un sèche-linge de qualité, à un prix défiant toute concurrence. Pas besoin de négocier, le prix est fabuleux. Acheté, commandé, validé et... paiement refusé. Comment ça? Julie appelle immédiatement sa banque. Elle apprend que c'est à cause des 270 euros qu'elle vient de dépenser: elle a atteint son maximum de débit et elle est à découvert. Impossible de continuer ses achats tant que le vendeur du collier n'a pas annulé la transaction. Quel cauchemar. C'était l'affaire du siècle. Et demain, c'est sûr qu'il n'y aura plus de machines en stock, le vendeur aura été dévalisé.

The last purchase of the sales will be the fantastic two-in-one promotional offer on a quality washing machine and dryer, at an unbeatable price. No need to negotiate, the price is fabulous. Bought, ordered, confirmed, and... payment declined. How come? Julie immediately calls her bank. She learns that it's because of the 270 euros she just spent: she has reached her maximum debit limit and is overdrawn. She can't continue her purchases until the necklace seller cancels the transaction. What a nightmare. It was the deal of the century. And tomorrow, for sure, there won't be any machines left in stock; the seller will have been cleaned out.

À la fin de sa journée de soldes sur Internet, Julie est de nouveau couchée sur son canapé, épuisée, les oreilles rougies par les heures au téléphone pour débloquer son moyen de paiement, avec une migraine à cause de l'écran et des crampes dans le doigt qui tenait la souris.

At the end of her day of sales on the Internet, Julie is again lying on her sofa, exhausted, her ears reddened by the hours on the phone to unlock her means of payment, with a migraine because of the screen and cramps in the finger holding the mouse.

Trois jours plus tard, Julie trouve des avis de passage dans sa boîte aux lettres. Le facteur et les livreurs sont venus pour lui remettre ses colis, mais elle était absente. Il va donc falloir qu'elle aille chercher par ses propres moyens : une paire de chaussures au bureau de poste, un collier dans un point-relais à l'autre bout de la ville et... une machine à laver et un sèche-linge «à retirer en magasin»! Le cauchemar n'est donc pas terminé.

Three days later, Julie finds delivery notices in her mailbox. The postman and the delivery people came to deliver her parcels, but she was absent. So she will have to go get her own way: a pair of shoes at the post office, a necklace at a pick-up point at the other end of town and... a washing machine and a dryer. to be picked up in store! The nightmare is not over.

Cette fois c'est sûr, Julie est déterminée. Les achats en ligne c'est ter-mi-né! Désormais, elle ira faire ses achats en magasin, comme tout le monde. Ce sera beaucoup plus simple et moins fatigant.

This time for sure, Julie is determined. Online shopping is over! From now on, she will go shopping in physical stores like everyone else. It will be much simpler and less tiring.

Résumé de l'histoire

Julie est une acheteuse compulsive. Elle aime parcourir les boutiques et acheter des choses, pour elle-même ou pour faire des cadeaux. Mais elle se rend vite à l'évidence: le shopping est une activité épuisante ainsi qu'une grande perte d'argent! Elle prend donc la décision de ne plus aller courir d'un magasin à un autre, mais de faire les prochaines soldes sur Internet, en faisant ses achats en ligne. Elle se dit que cela lui permettra d'économiser de l'argent et de gagner du temps... mais est-ce que ce sera vraiment le cas?

Summary of the Story

Julie is a serial shopper. She loves to visit the shops and buy various things for herself or as presents for others. But she soon faces the facts: shopping is both exhausting and a waste of money! She then decides to stop running from one shop to the other and starts taking advantage of online deals by shopping on her computer. She believes it will be much better this way, as she will save time and money... but will she really?

Quiz:

1. Quel est le cadeau que Julie a prévu pour sa mère?
a) des baskets
b) un lave-linge
c) un collier

2. Quel est le véritable prix du cadeau de Julie pour sa mère?
a) 27 €
b) 270 €
c) 54 €

3. Le problème rencontré par Julie avec ses baskets est que...
a) la taille ne va pas
b) le prix a changé
c) le modèle qu'elle voulait n'est plus disponible

4. Julie devra aller chercher son sèche-linge...
a) en magasin
b) au bureau de poste
c) au point-relais

5. Pour les prochaines soldes, Julie a décidé de faire ses achats...
a) en magasin
b) sur Internet
c) à crédit

Answers

1. C
2. A
3. C
4. A
5. A

Vocabulaire / Vocabulary

- *à découvert* --- overdrawn
- *retirer* --- to collect
- *achat* --- purchase
- *acheter* --- to buy
- *annuler* --- to cancel
- *avis de passage* --- delivery notice
- *banque* --- bank
- *baskets* --- running shoes
- *bon de commande* --- purchase order
- *boutique en ligne* --- online shop
- *bureau de poste* --- post office
- *cabine d'essayage* --- dressing room
- *cadeau* --- gift
- *caisse* --- checkout
- *carte bancaire* --- debit card
- *clique* --- *cliquer* – to click (computer)
- *colis* --- parcel
- *collier fantaisie* --- fashion necklace
- *commande* --- order

- *commerçant / commerçante* --- seller
- *commerce* --- shop
- *débloquer* --- to unlock
- *défiant toute concurrence* --- highly competitive
- *démarque* --- mark down sale
- *dépenser* --- to spend
- *deux en un* --- two-in-one
- *dévalisé / dévalisée* --- robbed (in this case, figuratively)
- *disponible* --- available
- *doigt* --- finger
- *économies* --- savings
- *économique* --- economical
- *écran* --- screen
- *emballage* --- wrapping
- *en ligne* --- online
- *en stock* --- in stock
- *essayer* --- to try on
- *étiquette* --- label, price tag
- *facteur* --- postman
- *faire la queue* --- to wait in line
- *fait main* --- handmade
- *file indienne* --- single line
- *frénésie acheteuse* --- shopping frenzy
- *journée de soldes* --- sales day (ex. --- Black Friday)
- *lèche-vitrine* --- window-shopping
- *livraison* --- delivery
- *livreur / livreuse* --- delivery man / delivery woman
- *magasin* --- shop
- *marque* --- brand
- *modèle* --- model, design
- *moins 50%* --- half price
- *moyen de paiement* --- payment method
- *négocier* --- to negotiate
- *offre promotionnelle* --- special offer
- *oreille* --- ear
- *paiement automatisé* --- automated payment
- *paiement refusé* --- payment declined
- *panier* --- basket, cart
- *pantalons* --- pants, trousers
- *payer la note* --- to pay the bill
- *plus de peur que de mal* --- no harm done
- *point-relais* --- delivery relay
- *pointure* --- shoe size
- *prix* --- price
- *profiter* --- to benefit from
- *quantité* --- quantity, amount

- *rien à se mettre* --- nothing to wear
- *ristourne* --- rebate
- *ruiné /ruinée* --- broke
- *sac de courses* --- shopping bag
- *sans vie* --- lifeless
- *sèche-linge* --- dryer (for clothes)
- *soldes* --- sales
- *sou* --- penny, cent
- *souris* --- mouse (computer)
- *taille* --- size
- *vaut* --- valoir – to be worth
- *vendeur / vendeuse* --- seller
- *virement* --- bank transfer
- *vitrine* --- window

10. Job D'été

"Choisissez votre nom d'utilisateur et votre mot de passe".

"Choose your username and password".

*David réfléchit un instant, puis il tape "Davidberlin" sur le clavier de son ordinateur portable tout neuf. Ensuite, il entre son mot de passe. Il utilise le même à chaque fois, pour tous les différents sites internet et pour toutes les applications, bien que pour des raisons de sécurité, cela soit strictement déconseillé: "ichbineinberliner375*12".*

David thought for a moment, then he typed"Davidberlin"on the keyboard of his brand new laptop. Then he enters his password. It uses the same every time, for all the different websites and for all applications, although for security reasons, this is strictly not recommended:"ichbineinberliner375 * 12".

*Oui, c'est quand même bien plus facile de mémoriser un unique mot de passe. Dès qu'il essaye de changer, c'est la même chose: à chaque fois, il oublie ce qu'il avait choisi, et bien sûr il ne prend jamais le temps de noter l'information sur un petit bout de papier. "ichbineinberliner375*12", c'est très bien.*

Yes, it's still easier to memorize a single password. As soon as he tries to change, it's the same thing: each time, he forgets what he chose, and of course he never takes the time to write the information on a piece of paper."Ichbineinberliner375 * 12"is very good.

La page du site change. Maintenant, David doit entrer ses informations personnelles: son âge, son lieu de naissance, son parcours scolaire et professionnel. Bon, comme David n'a que 20 ans, il n'a pas encore eu beaucoup d'emplois différents. Bien sûr, il aide son père au restaurant familial depuis qu'il a 15 ans et il a déjà travaillé dans plusieurs cafés de la ville où vit sa mère; mais cette fois-ci, David n'a pas envie de travailler dans la restauration. Il a envie d'essayer autre chose pour changer.

The site page changes. Now, David has to enter his personal information: his age, his place of birth, his educational and professional background. Well, since David is only 20, he has not had many different jobs yet. Of course, he has been helping his father at the family restaurant since he was 15 and he has already worked in several cafes in the city where his mother lives; but this time, David does not want to work in the restaurant business. He wants to try something else to change.

Il aimerait beaucoup travailler dans le secteur culturel. Dans un musée ou dans un théâtre, par exemple. Travailler dans un cinéma indépendant, cela serait aussi vraiment pas mal, car, après tout, comme il s'apprête à commencer des études dans l'audiovisuel, il a tout intérêt à essayer de récolter quelques expériences qui soient au moins légèrement en rapport avec ce domaine. Il paraît que ce n'est vraiment pas facile de trouver du travail dans ce secteur, et qui sait, si jamais il travaille dans un cinéma, il va peut-être pouvoir rencontrer des personnes intéressantes qui pourront lui donner des conseils ou l'aider à trouver des stages...

He would very much like to work in the cultural sector. In a museum or in a theater, for example. Working in an independent cinema, that would also be really not bad, because, after all, as he is about to start studies in the audio-visual, it is in all interest to try to collect some experiments which are at least slightly related to this domain. It seems that it is not really easy to find work in this sector, and who knows, if he ever works in a cinema, he may be able to meet interesting people who can give him advice or help him to find internships ...

Toutefois, nous sommes seulement en mai et ses études ne vont pas commencer avant le mois d'octobre. Non, ce n'est vraiment pas le moment de penser à tout cela.

However, we are only in May and his studies will not start until October. No, it's really not the time to think about all this.

David essaie de se concentrer sur ses objectifs: gagner un peu d'argent tout en approfondissant ses connaissances en langues étrangères. Il adore le français (il a vu des tas et des tas de films français depuis qu'il est tout petit) et il veut absolument améliorer son niveau cet été. Alors, ce mois-ci, il doit absolument trouver un travail en France, et il doit se dépêcher: il a lu sur des forums français que la meilleure période pour trouver un emploi d'été, c'est maintenant!

David tries to focus on his goals: to earn some money while deepening his knowledge of foreign languages. He loves French (he has seen lots and lots of French films since he was little) and he really wants to improve his level this summer. So, this month, he must find a job in France, and he must hurry: he read on French forums that the best time to find a summer job is now!

Quand il a parlé de son projet à son père, celui-ci était d'abord un peu sceptique:

When he spoke about his project to his father, he was initially a bit skeptical:

– Comment ça, tu ne resteras pas travailler avec moi cet été? Tu veux partir et me laisser me débrouiller au restaurant? Tu sais bien que les clients apprécient beaucoup ta présence et qu'ils te laissent toujours plein de pourboires. Tu veux vraiment laisser passer cette chance?

- How are you, you will not stay with me this summer? You want to leave and let me manage at the restaurant? You know that customers really appreciate your presence and they always leave you plenty of tips. Do you really want to miss this chance?

Mais David était déjà plus que décidé. Cette année, son père allait devoir embaucher un autre étudiant, mais il pouvait lui conseiller plein de bons copains à lui. Cela n'était absolument pas un problème. Devant sa détermination, le père de David ne pouvait que plier et commencer à encourager son fils.

But David was already more than decided. This year, his father was going to have to hire another student, but he could give him lots of good friends. It was absolutely not a problem. In front of his determination, David's father could only bend and start encouraging his son.

– Bon. Tu as raison après tout. C'est très bien de ta part de vouloir améliorer ton niveau en langue et découvrir un peu mieux la culture française. Moi, quand j'étais jeune, j'ai adoré aller travailler dans des grands restaurants à Paris. C'était une super expérience, et j'ai toujours conservé un excellent niveau de français ensuite. Tu sais quoi? J'aimerais bien pouvoir te soutenir dans ton projet. Alors, j'ai déjà réfléchi, et j'ai contacté ta tante Louise. Tu te souviens de Louise? On lui avait rendu visite deux, trois fois à Toulouse quand tu étais petit. Eh bien, elle a directement proposé de t'héberger cet été si jamais tu arrives à trouver un petit travail sur place. Elle m'a même donné le nom d'un site internet qui aide les jeunes à trouver du travail. Il s'appelle "taffétudiantàtoulouse.com". Apparemment, c'est un très bon moyen de trouver quelque chose. Il y a plein de petites annonces diverses sur le site. Il suffit de se faire un profil complet avec un bon CV et de commencer à répondre aux annonces. Il y a même un forum pour répondre à toutes tes questions.

- Good. You are right after all. It is very good of you to want to improve your level in language and discover a little better French culture. When I was young, I loved going to work in great restaurants in Paris. It was a great experience, and I have always maintained an excellent level of French. You know what? I wish I could support you in your project. So, I already thought about it, and I contacted your Aunt Louise. Do you remember Louise? He had been visited two or three times in Toulouse when you were little. Well, she directly offered to host you this summer if you ever find a little job on the spot. She even gave me the name of a website that helps young people find work. His name is"taffétudiantàtoulouse.com". Apparently, it's a very good way to find something. There are plenty of various ads on the site. Just get a complete profile with a good resume and start responding to ads. There is even a forum to answer all your questions.

– Taff étudiant à Toulouse? Mais, papa, ça veut dire quoi"taff"? Je ne suis pas bien sûr de comprendre.

- Taff student in Toulouse? But, dad, what does"taff"mean? I'm not sure I understand.

–"Taff", c'est un mot d'argot qui veut dire"travail". Tu sais bien que les jeunes Français utilisent énormément d'argot. D'ailleurs, si tu veux utiliser le site, il va sans doute falloir que tu fasses quelques recherches. J'ai déjà jeté un coup d'œil au forum et il est plein d'expressions en argot.

-"Taff"is a slang word that means"work". You know that young French people use a lot of slang. Moreover, if you want to use the site, it will probably have to do some research. I have already taken a look at the forum and it is full of expressions in slang.

– Ah OK, je comprends. Franchement papa, merci beaucoup! Avec ça, je suis sûr de réussir à trouver un travail et de passer un été au soleil à Toulouse chez Louise. C'est génial. Je vais m'y mettre tout de suite!

- Ah ok I understand. Frankly dad, thank you very much! With that, I'm sure to find a job and spend a summer in the sun in Toulouse at Louise's. It's awesome. I'll get started right away!

Alors, maintenant, David se retrouve devant son écran. Il commence à consulter les petites annonces. Il s'apprête à trouver le travail de ses rêves. Il clique sur la première page:"Travail de juin à septembre dans un camping près de Toulouse". Tiens, ce n'est pas si mal, ça. Peut-être qu'il faut faire de l'animation sur le camping, organiser des jeux ou des concours… Il lit la description du travail. Oh non, le travail consiste uniquement à nettoyer les toilettes et les douches… en plus, il faut commencer à six heures tous les matins, six jours par semaine… Il n'est vraiment pas certain de vouloir faire un tel travail.

So, now, David is in front of his screen. He starts to look at the classifieds. He is about to find the job of his dreams. He clicks on the first page:"Work from June to September in a campsite near Toulouse". Well, it's not that bad. Maybe you have to do animation on the campsite, organize games or contests … He reads the description of the work. Oh no, the job is only to clean the toilets and the showers … besides, you have to start at six o'clock every morning, six days a week … It is not really sure to want to do such a job.

David fait défiler son écran avec sa souris et consulte les autres annonces. Mince alors, se dit-il, il n'y a que du travail pour nettoyer des toilettes ou faire la vaisselle… ce n'est pas très excitant.

David scrolls his screen with his mouse and consults the other ads. So slim, he thought, there is only work to clean toilets or do the dishes … it's not very exciting.

Il décide d'aller faire un tour sur le forum, histoire de trouver plus d'informations. Il y a plusieurs utilisateurs connectés, dont une"Lolaberlin"qui l'intrigue. Peut-être qu'il s'agit aussi d'une allemande qui cherche un travail en France. Peut-être qu'elle a de bons conseils à lui donner. Il lui envoie un message et attend sa réponse.

He decides to go for a ride on the forum, just to find more information. There are several connected users, including a"Lolaberlin"intriguing. Maybe it is also a German looking for a job in France. Maybe she has good advice to give him. He sends a message to him and awaits his answer.

En attendant, il part faire un tour sur les réseaux sociaux. Il publie un statut et décrit l'objet de sa recherche. Il connaît quelques Français et il a beaucoup d'amis qui sont à l'étranger. On ne sait jamais, c'est peut-être un moyen de trouver quelque chose. Matthieu, un jeune parisien qu'il a connu à une soirée dans un bar du coin et avec qui il avait très vite sympathisé, lui répond presque aussitôt:

In the meantime, he goes for a ride on social networks. He publishes a status and describes the purpose of his research. He knows some French people and he has many friends who are abroad. You never know, maybe it's a way to find something. Matthieu, a young Parisian whom he knew at a party in a local bar and with whom he had quickly sympathized, answered him almost immediately:

– *Tu sais, David, ce n'est pas toujours facile de trouver du travail en France. Même les petits boulots sont assez demandés, alors il ne faut pas trop faire le difficile. Pour trouver rapidement, le mieux est d'être déjà sur place. Tu devrais demander à ta tante si elle n'a pas des contacts intéressants. En tout cas, moi je serai à Paris cet été et c'est seulement à quelques heures en voiture de Toulouse. Peut-être que je viendrai y passer quelques jours, comme ça on pourra se revoir et moi je pourrai avoir un peu d'air frais! L'été, à Paris, on étouffe parfois!*

- You know, David, it's not always easy to find work in France. Even odd jobs are quite in demand, so do not do too hard. To find quickly, the best is to be already there. You should ask your aunt if she does not have interesting contacts. In any case, I'll be in Paris this summer and it's only a few hours drive from Toulouse. Maybe I will come to spend a few days, so we can meet again and I can get some fresh air! Summer in Paris sometimes suffocates!

David est content. Si Matthieu vient le voir, ils vont passer des bons moments. En plus, il est passionné de cinéma tout comme lui. Ensemble, ils vont pouvoir aller voir plein de films à Toulouse!

David is happy. If Matthew comes to see him, they will have a good time. In addition, he is passionate about cinema just like him. Together, they will be able to see lots of movies in Toulouse!

David commence à regarder la liste de tous les cinémas indépendants de la ville, quand soudain il reçoit une notification. Ah, Lola lui a répondu. Super! Il regarde dans sa boîte de réception. Elle lui a envoyé un long message où elle lui explique sa situation: non, elle n'est pas allemande, mais elle vient de terminer une année d'étude à Berlin et elle est maintenant rentrée à Toulouse, sa ville natale. Elle adore l'Allemagne et elle est vraiment triste d'être partie, mais elle a terminé ses études et elle a déjà trouvé un stage à Paris pour l'an prochain, alors elle ne pouvait pas rester. Là, elle cherche un travail dans un café pour gagner un peu d'argent et pour financer ses projets. Elle serait toutefois vraiment très heureuse de rencontrer David, car cela lui permettrait de pouvoir continuer à parler allemand. En échange, elle pourra l'aider en français et lui faire découvrir Toulouse.

David begins to look at the list of all independent cinemas in the city, when suddenly he receives a notification. Ah, Lola answered him. Great! He looks in his mailbox. She sent him a long message where she explains his situation: no, she is not German, but she just finished a year of study in Berlin and she is now back in Toulouse, her hometown. She loves Germany and she is really sad to be gone, but she has finished her studies and she has already found an internship in Paris for next year, so she could not stay. There, she looks for a job in a café to earn some money and to finance her projects. She would be very happy to meet David, however, because that would allow her to continue speaking German. In exchange, she can help him in French and make him discover Toulouse.

David lui répond avec enthousiasme. Vraiment, quelle bonne idée d'avoir utilisé ce site internet! Non seulement il va peut-être pouvoir trouver un travail, mais en plus il commence déjà à rencontrer des gens avant même d'être sur place! Il veut savoir ce que Lola a étudié et quels sont ses projets.

David responds enthusiastically. Really, what a great idea to have used this website! Not only will he be able to find a job, but he's already starting to meet people before he's even there! He wants to know what Lola has studied and what his plans are.

Lola lui dit:

Lola tells him:

– *Alors moi, c'est un peu compliqué, car j'ai commencé par des études de commerce pour ensuite aller vers l'audiovisuel. Cet été, je vais aider une amie à réaliser un clip musical pour une de ses chansons. C'est un très bon exercice pour moi, mais il faut absolument que je mette un peu de sous de côté pour pouvoir acheter une nouvelle caméra. C'est pour ça qu'il faut que je commence un nouveau travail le plus vite possible!*

- So me, it's a little complicated, because I started with business studies and then go to the audiovisual. This summer, I'm going to help a friend make a music video for one of her songs. This is a very good exercise for me, but I must absolutely put a little money aside to buy a new camera. That's why I have to start a new job as soon as possible!

Quelle coïncidence, se dit David! Il faut absolument qu'il rencontre cette fille! Ils vont pouvoir échanger sur plein de sujets et peut-être même qu'il va pouvoir participer à son projet cet été. Aussitôt, il lui propose son aide et lui explique que lui aussi veut faire des études dans l'audiovisuel.

What a coincidence, David thought to himself! He must meet this girl! They will be able to discuss a lot of topics and maybe even be able to participate in his project this summer. Immediately, he offers his help and explains that he too wants to study in the audiovisual.

– *Ah ouais srx? Lui dit Lola, c'est ouf, j'ai trop hâte de faire ta connaissance, je suis encore plus déter maintenant!*

- Oh yeah srx? Said Lola, it's ok, I can not wait to meet you, I'm even more determined now!

David est un peu perplexe. Il n'a pas compris grand-chose à ce message.

David is a little puzzled. He did not understand much about this message.

– *Hum, excusez-moi Lola, mais il y a plusieurs mots que je n'ai pas compris. Tu sais, je n'ai encore jamais vécu en France, alors je suis un peu perdu parfois... Cela veut dire quoi"srx"? Et"c'est ouf", et"je suis déter"?*

- Um, excuse me Lola, but there are several words that I did not understand. You know, I've never lived in France before, so I'm a little lost sometimes ... What does"srx"mean? And 'it's whew', and 'I'm determined'?

– *Oh mince, pardon David. Tu écris tellement bien français, je n'ai plus fait attention aux mots que j'utilisais. Alors,"srx"c'est simplement l'abréviation de"sérieux", ce que je voulais dire c'est"Ah oui, vraiment?","ah oui, c'est vrai?". C'est"ouf", c'est un mot d'argot qui veut dire"c'est fou". En fait, le mot est simplement dit à l'envers. Quant à"déter", c'est un raccourci pour dire"je suis déterminée", ça veut dire que je suis trop contente et trop motivée, quoi. Tu comprends? Je vais faire un peu plus attention par la suite!*

- Oh thin, sorry David. You write French so well, I did not pay attention to the words I used. So,"srx"is simply the abbreviation of"serious", what I meant was"Oh yes, really?","Oh yes it's true?". It's"phew", it's a slang word that means"it's crazy". In fact, the word is simply said in reverse. As for"determine", it is a shortcut to say"I am determined", it means that I am too happy and too motivated, what. You understand? I'll do a little more attention later!

– *Oh non, ne t'en fais pas! C'est trop cool de pouvoir apprendre de nouvelles expressions. Bon, je vais devoir te laisser maintenant, car il faut absolument que je trouve un petit travail, sinon je n'aurai pas d'argent et je ne pourrai pas venir à Toulouse! Maintenant que je sais que je vais pouvoir participer à des projets intéressants, je m'en fiche de devoir faire le ménage! Après tout, il s'agit juste d'un travail de quelques mois! Je vais commencer à répondre à des annonces.*

- Oh no, do not worry! It's so cool to learn new expressions. Well, I'll have to leave you now, because I absolutely have to find a little job, otherwise I will not have money and I will not be able to come to Toulouse! Now that I know I will be able to participate in interesting projects, I do not care about cleaning up! After all, it's just a few months work! I will start responding to ads.

– *Oui, tu as raison David. D'ailleurs, je suis déjà en contact avec un café qui a l'air plutôt pas mal. Il me semble qu'il recherche plusieurs personnes. Je peux te donner leur adresse e-mail et tu pourras leur écrire pour leur demander. Je vais sans doute faire un essai mercredi. Je pourrai te dire si l'endroit à l'air sympa! Qu'en penses-tu?*

- Yes, you're right David. Besides, I'm already in touch with a coffee that looks pretty good. It seems to me that he is looking for several people. I can give you their e-mail address and you can write to them to ask them. I will probably give it a try on Wednesday. I can tell you if the place looks nice! What do you think?

– Génial, c'est parfait Lola! Merci à toi!

- Great, it's perfect Lola! Thanks to you!

David éteint son PC et va faire un tour.

David turns off his PC and goes for a ride.

Vraiment, internet, pour se faire des contacts, c'est top!

Really, internet, to make contacts, it's great!

Quiz

1. Dans quel domaine professionnel David veut-il étudier l'an prochain?
a) audiovisuel
b) restauration
c) tourisme
d) langues étrangères

2. Qui habite à Toulouse?
a) Matthieu
b) Lola
c) le père de David
d) la tante de David

3. D'habitude, où est-ce que David travaille pendant l'été?
a) il anime des soirées
b) il fait du ménage
c) il fait des sites internet
d) il aide son père au restaurant

4. D'après Matthieu, trouver un emploi en France est...
a) facile
b) long
c) difficile
d) impossible pour un allemand

5. Qu'est-ce que David et Lola ont en commun?
a) ils sont tous les deux allemands
b) ils connaissent tous les deux sa tante
c) ils sont au chômage
d) ils étudient l'audiovisuel

Answers

1. a
2. b, d
3. d
4. c
5. d

Vocabulaire / Vocabulary

- *à l'envers* --- upside-down, inside-out
- *abréviation* --- abbreviation
- *adresse e-mail* --- email address
- *âge* --- age
- *améliorer* --- to improve
- *animation* --- animation
- *approfondissant* --- *approfondir* – to deal with something in depth
- *argot* --- slang
- *aussitôt* --- as soon as
- *avoir tout intérêt* --- to be wise to do something
- *boîte de réception* --- inbox
- *boulot* --- job
- *bout de papier* --- paper note
- *clip musical* --- music video
- *clique* --- *cliquer* – to click
- *connaissance* --- knowledge
- *connecté/connectée* --- connected
- *conservé/conservée* --- preserved, stored, kept
- *copain/copine* --- friend, pal, buddy
- *cv* --- curriculum vitae, resume
- *des tas* --- many, plenty of
- *déterminé/déterminée* --- determined, decided
- *divers/diverses* --- various
- *emploi* --- employment, job
- *études de commerce* --- business studies
- *faire le difficile* --- to be picky
- *faire un essai* --- to try
- *faire un tour* --- to go for a stroll
- *fait défiler* --- *faire défiler* – to scroll down
- *héberger* --- to host
- *informations personnelles* --- personal information
- *intrigue* --- plot, scheme
- *jeu* --- game
- *jeune* --- young
- *langue étrangère* --- foreign language
- *légèrement* --- lightly

- *lieu de naissance* --- place of birth
- *m'en fiche* --- *s'en ficher* --- to not care
- *m'y mettre* --- *s'y mettre* --- to get started
- *mette des sous de côté* --- *mettre des sous de côté* --- put some money aside
- *motivé/motivée* --- motivated
- *moyen* --- average
- *nom d'utilisateur* --- username
- *noter* --- to write down
- *notification* --- pop up notification
- *objectif* --- goal
- *page du site* --- webpage
- *parcours scolaire* --- school career
- *Parisien/Parisienne* --- Parisian, who lives in Paris
- *pas mal* --- not bad
- *période* --- era (time of the year)
- *petite annonce* --- classified ad
- *plier* --- to fold
- *pourboire* --- tip (money)
- *qui sait* --- who knows
- *raccourci* --- shortcut
- *récolter* --- to harvest
- *restaurant familial* --- family restaurant (business)
- *restauration* --- catering, food industry
- *s'apprête à* --- s'apprêter à – to get ready to
- *sans doute* --- most likely
- *se concentrer* --- to focus
- *se dépêcher* --- to hurry
- *secteur culturel* --- cultural domain
- *si jamais* --- if ever
- *site internet* --- website
- *soleil* --- sun
- *statut* --- status
- *strictement* --- strictly
- *sur place* --- on site
- *sympa* --- nice, friendly
- *sympathisé* --- *sympathiser* --- to make friends
- *taff* --- job (slang)
- *tape* --- *taper* --- to hit, to press a key
- *utilisateur/utilisatrice* --- user

11- Everyday Tasks

David vient rendre visite à son père à la maison de retraite. Le vieil homme a 85 ans et il est là depuis 2 ans. David a le cœur lourd chaque fois qu'il voit son père.

David comes to visit his father at the nursing home. The old man is 85 years old and has been there for 2 years. David's heart is heavy every time he sees his father.

Il y a encore deux ans, il allait très bien. Il était en bonne santé, il vivait normalement. Et puis, quand la mère de David est décédée, la santé de son père a commencé à décliner. La famille s'est rendu compte que le veuf perdait la tête. Il avait des pertes de mémoire, de plus en plus graves.

Just two years ago, he was doing very well. He was in good health, living his life normally. And then, when David's mother passed away, his father's health started to decline. The family realized that the widower was losing his mind. He experienced memory loss, increasingly severe.

Au début, le père oubliait la date, ou simplement qu'il avait pris un rendez-vous chez le coiffeur ou le médecin. Après, il a commencé à oublier qu'il avait mis un plat au four ou qu'il avait allumé le gaz. Cela aurait pu créer des accidents, mais heureusement, rien de grave ne s'est produit. Un jour, David a remarqué que son père ne savait plus se faire à manger. Il avait mis n'importe quoi dans une casserole, puis commençait son repas par le dessert. Il allait acheter du pain à la pharmacie. Il avait plaisanté en lui disant que si ça continuait comme ça, son père allait s'habiller en mettant ses chaussures avant d'enfiler ses chaussettes...

In the beginning, the father would forget the date, or simply that he had made an appointment with the hairdresser or the doctor. Later, he started forgetting that he had put a dish in the oven or turned on the gas. This could have caused accidents, but fortunately, nothing serious happened. One day, David noticed that his father no longer knew how to cook for himself. He would put anything in a pot and sometimes start his meal with dessert. He would go to the pharmacy to buy bread. David had joked with him, saying that if things continued like that, his father would start dressing by putting on his shoes before his socks...

La situation est devenue plus inquiétante lorsque David a remarqué que son père oubliait de se laver et de s'habiller. Il ne se rasait plus, ne savait plus se brosser les dents. David avait été pris de panique à l'idée que son père oublie de boire ou de manger.

The situation became more alarming when David noticed that his father would forget to wash and dress himself. He stopped shaving and couldn't remember how to brush his teeth. David had been struck with panic at the thought of his father forgetting to drink or eat.

Un jour, la sœur de David est venue rendre visite à son père. Il ne l'a pas reconnue. Il fallait alors se rendre à l'évidence: ce que ses enfants avaient pris pour de la dépression était beaucoup plus grave que cela. Le médecin devrait le soigner pour la maladie d'Alzheimer. Il devrait réapprendre à faire les choses du quotidien, comme se doucher, ouvrir et fermer sa porte à clé. Pour le reste, les enfants du vieil homme avaient engagé une dame pour faire le ménage et ranger un peu, puis une autre pour faire les courses. Une infirmière passait de temps en temps s'assurer qu'il prenait ses médicaments, se nourrissait et s'hydratait convenablement.

One day, David's sister came to visit their father. He didn't recognize her. It was then evident that what his children had initially thought was depression was much more serious. The doctor would have to treat him for Alzheimer's disease. He would need to relearn everyday tasks like showering, locking, and unlocking his door. As for the rest, the old man's children had hired a lady to do some cleaning and tidying, and another to do the grocery shopping. A nurse would occasionally visit to make sure he was taking his medications and eating and drinking properly.

David essayait de passer le plus souvent possible pour aller se promener avec son père et regarder la télévision avec lui. Il se disait que parler des actualités et jouer aux cartes avec lui entretiendrait son esprit. Puis, David a remarqué que son père ne parlait plus que des actualités... d'il y a vingt ans en arrière. Si on lui demandait ce qu'il s'était passé la veille, il n'en avait aucune idée et changeait de sujet. David a été vraiment très étonné un jour en croisant la voisine alors qu'il sortait avec son père prendre l'air. Il avait dit à celle-ci: « venez boire un café, ma femme sera contente de vous voir. Nous n'avons pas beaucoup de visites ». Son père avait simplement oublié que la femme qu'il avait épousée et avec qui il avait vécu pendant 60 ans était décédée.

David tried to visit his father as often as possible, taking walks together and watching television. He thought that discussing current events and playing cards with him would keep his mind engaged. Then, David noticed that his father only talked about news events from twenty years ago. If asked about what happened the day before, he had no idea and would change the subject. One day, while taking a walk with his father, David was truly surprised when he ran into their neighbor. He had said to her, "Come have coffee with us, my wife will be happy to see you. We don't have many visitors." His father had simply forgotten that the woman he had married and lived with for 60 years had passed away.

Alors, toute la famille s'était réunie pour décider qu'il fallait déménager le vieil homme et le laisser vieillir dans un endroit où il serait protégé et surveillé, là où on s'occuperait bien de lui. C'est comme ça que son père s'était retrouvé à la maison de retraite, avec une mémoire qui diminuait un peu plus chaque jour. Depuis environ 2 mois, il avait oublié le prénom de son fils. David, c'est pourtant un prénom simple. Le père confondait son fils David avec son petit-fils Joseph et parfois avec son frère André, mais il était toujours content d'avoir de la visite et de le voir. C'est pourquoi David continuait à y aller.

So, the whole family had gathered to decide that they needed to move the old man and let him age in a place where he would be protected and monitored, where he would be well taken care of. That's how his father ended up in the nursing home, with a memory that was diminishing a little more each day. For about 2 months, he had forgotten his son's name. David, a simple name. The father would confuse his son David with his grandson Joseph and sometimes with his brother André, but he was always happy to have visitors and see him. That's why David kept going.

En prenant une grande respiration et en serrant contre lui la boîte de chocolats qu'il venait lui apporter, David frappa à la porte et entra.

Taking a deep breath and holding the box of chocolates he had brought tightly, David knocked on the door and entered.

- *Bonjour papa.*

- Hello dad.

- *Bonjour monsieur.*

- Hello Sir.

- *Comment vas-tu aujourd'hui?*

- How are you today?

- *Ça va très bien! Ils ont ouvert la fenêtre, changé les draps et planté des arbres dans le jardin.*

- I'm very good! They opened the window, changed the sheets and planted trees in the garden.

- *Je t'ai apporté des chocolats.*

- I brought you some chocolates.

Le vieil homme s'approche, prend la boîte de chocolats et s'assied en la posant sur ses genoux. Il l'ouvre délicatement et en tend un à David.

The old man walks over, takes the box of chocolates, and sits down, putting it on his lap. He gently opens it and hands one to David.

- *Non papa, c'est pour toi. Mange-les.*

- No dad, this is for you. Eat them.

- *Prends-en un, allons. Ce sont tes préférés.*

- Take one, let's go. These are your favourites.

- *Tu... tu te souviens de ça? Lui dit David très ému et étonné.*

- Do you... do you remember that? Said David very moved and surprised.

- *Tu sais, j'ai peut-être oublié ton prénom. J'ai sans doute le cerveau qui déraille par moment, mais il y a une chose que je n'oublierai jamais. C'est le jour où mon petit garçon avec sa première pièce d'argent de poche gagnée en lavant la voiture est rentré à la maison tout fier en nous montrant le chocolat qu'il était allé s'acheter. Tu l'as gardé près de toi sous ton oreiller pendant plusieurs jours avant de le manger! Pour qu'il dure plus longtemps, j'imagine!*

- You know, maybe I forgot your name. My brain may be out of whack at times, but there's one thing I'll never forget. It was the day when my little boy with his first pocket money earned by washing the car came home proudly showing us the chocolate he had gone to buy. You kept it close to you under your pillow for several days before eating it! To make it last longer, I imagine!

David se mit à pleurer.

David began to cry.

Il avait complètement oublié.

He had completely forgotten.

Résumé de l'histoire

David rend visite à son père à la maison de retraite, où il vit depuis qu'il a la maladie d'Alzheimer. Sur le chemin, il repense aux quelques mois qui ont précédé l'installation de son père dans cet endroit, à la façon dont la santé du vieil homme avait décliné depuis la mort de sa mère. Il est nostalgique et se demande avec nervosité combien de temps il lui reste avant que son père oublie qui il est. Il a déjà oublié son prénom. Que reste-t-il du lien père-fils lorsque la mémoire s'efface?

Summary of the Story

David visits his father at the retirement home, where the old man lives since he was diagnosed with Alzheimer's disease. On the way to his father's room, David recalls the previous months that lead to his father being moved there, and how his memory faded away after the passing of his wife. He is nostalgic and anxiously wonders how much time is left before his own father forgets about him. He had already forgotten his name a few times in the past. What remains of the father-son bond when memory fades away?

Quiz

1. Depuis combien de temps le père de David est-il en maison de retraite?
a) 2 mois
b) 2 ans
c) 2 semaines

2. Par quoi le père de David commençait-il ses repas?
a) le vin
b) le pain
c) le dessert

3. Quel cadeau David apporte-t-il à son père?
a) un jeu de cartes
b) des chocolats
c) une télévision

4. Comment David a-t-il gagné son premier argent de poche?
a) en jouant aux cartes
b) à l'école
c) en lavant une voiture

5. Où David avait-il caché son chocolat?
a) sous son oreiller
b) sous son lit
c) dans sa poche

Answers

1. B
2. C
3. B
4. C
5. A

Vocabulaire / Vocabulary

- *acheter du pain* --- to buy some bread
- *allait très bien* --- *aller très bien* --- felt very well
- *allumé le gaz* --- *allumer le gaz* --- to switch on the gas cooker
- *apporter* --- to bring
- *boire un café* --- to drink a coffee
- *changé les draps* --- *changer les draps* --- to change the bedsheets
- *changeait de sujet* --- *changer de sujet* --- to change the subject
- *croisant la voisine* --- *croiser la voisine* --- to bump into the neighbor
- *décider* --- to decide
- *déménager* --- to move (to a new home)
- *déraille* --- *dérailler* --- to lose your marbles
- *enfiler ses chaussettes* --- to put on some socks
- *était en bonne santé* --- *être en bonne santé* --- to be in good health
- *faire le ménage* --- to tidy up, to clean
- *faire les courses* --- to buy groceries
- *fermer sa porte à clé* --- to lock the door
- *gardé / gardée* --- kept
- *infirmier / infirmière* --- nurse
- *jouer aux cartes* --- to play cards
- *ouvre* --- *ouvrir* --- to open
- *lavant la voiture* --- *laver la voiture* --- to wash the car
- *maison de retraite* --- retirement home
- *manger* --- to eat
- *mémoire* --- memory
- *mettant ses chaussures* --- *mettre ses chaussures* --- to put shoes on
- *mis un plat au four* --- *mettre un plat au four* --- to put a dish in the oven
- *oreiller* --- pillow
- *oubliait* --- *oublier* --- to forget
- *ouvert la fenêtre* --- *ouvrir la fenêtre* --- to open the window
- *parler des actualités* --- to discuss or debate about the news
- *perdait la tête* --- *perdre la tête* --- to lose your mind
- *planté des arbres* --- *planter des arbres* --- to plant some trees
- *pleurer* --- to cry
- *posant* --- *poser* --- to put something somewhere
- *prenait ses médicaments* --- *prendre ses médicaments* --- to take his medicine
- *prendre l'air* --- to breathe some air
- *prénom* --- first name
- *pris un rendez-vous* --- *prendre un rendez-vous* --- to make an appointment
- *quotidien* --- daily
- *ranger* --- to clean up, tidy up
- *regarder la télévision* --- to watch television
- *rendre visite* --- to pay a visit
- *rentré à la maison* --- *rentrer à la maison* --- to come back home
- *s'acheter* --- to buy oneself something

- *s'assied* --- *s'asseoir* --- to sit down
- *s'est rendu compte* --- *se rendre compte* --- to realize
- *s'habiller* --- to get dressed
- *se brosser les dents* --- to brush your teeth
- *se doucher* --- to shower
- *se faire à manger* --- to cook, make something to eat
- *se laver* --- to wash oneself, to take a bath
- *se nourrissait* --- *se nourrir* --- to eat
- *se promener* --- to take a stroll
- *se rasait* --- *se raser* --- to shave
- *se rendre à l'évidence* --- to recognize, to acknowledge
- *serrant* --- *serrer* --- to hold tight
- *soigner* --- to take care
- *souvenir* --- memory
- *vieillir* --- to get older
- *vivait* --- *vivre* --- to live

Conclusion

Learning a new language is a journey, and we are glad to accompany you along the way. You can come back to these stories any time you like, and take the quizzes again to see if your skills have improved.

In fact, may we suggest you go back to the first story and answer the questions again? You will be surprised to find out how much you remember and how much you've learned!

Congratulations! You have just read 16 short stories in French and in the process, you have learned French vocabulary and stored numerous expressions in your brain which you can use in day to day conversations. We hope you enjoyed reading our characters' adventures and taking the quizzes at the end of each section.

After reading through all the stories and doing the researches from the reading comprehension part, you should now have a much wider French vocabulary than when you first started. You have also learned some interesting facts about French culture and expressions along the way.

FREE AUDIO OF "FRENCH SHORT STORIES"

Download your fee audio from our website:

www.dupontlanguageinstitute.com

or follow this QR code:

To download the file:

Username: 005-book-AC
Password: If8,V~U~]AMn

To open the file:

Password: M_òFh@!f$5g6huRT

Speak French

Typical French way of saying and sentences to use in your daily life and speak like a native.

Includes cultural habits and tips on how to behave in different situations

Introduction

One of the most frustrating things at the intermediate stage of learning a new language is that often, you quite simply don't have enough words to say what you need to or want to. A great way of getting rid of this frustration, and progressing in your fluency and building of your confidence, is to have a bigger store of words at your disposal. And it's not the most technically complex thing to do, but does involve a certain amount of rote learning... and, therefore, an investment of time.

The great news is that there are a ton of vocabulary lists out there often organized by theme, or with a "1000 most useful words in Urdu" or "100 most useful verbs in French" theme at least. However, although you do need to put the time in, this is the kind of work or study that you can do in "temps mort" or otherwise wasted time—on public transport, waiting in a queue, walking, or in a waiting room. Depending on the format, you may even be able to use your commute by car in a constructive way.

So, prepare your lists, in paper or audio format, and start learning. But vary this "passive" kind of reading/listening to kind of learning, with something more active. Try writing the words out, then cover them and test yourself or have somebody else test you, or use them in sentences. And make sure that you are prioritizing learning things that are useful and or interesting for you.

If you have no use for and no interest in, say, different kinds of trees, perhaps start with another theme first. You can even make your own vocabulary lists. If you are a wrestling fan, you may not find something specific enough ready-made, but you could list in English all the words that you would be interested in knowing in French, then look them up in a dictionary (on-line dictionaries are so quick), and make your vocab list.

- Work on your grammar – rote learning

While on the subject of learning by heart, there is often not a shortcut to learning irregular verbs. Working on these will really boost your fluency. You may think you are only working on one part of speech, but honestly, once you have the verbs "done", you have done most of the hard work. There are books, or even audio, available with irregular verb tables (and while you're at it, make sure the regular forms have really sunk in and that you have them at your fingertips to use!). And again, while downtime is useful for the rote learning aspect, make sure you don't forget to test yourself so that you can use them—mix up the tenses, make sure you can use them in a sentence, etc.

- Work on your grammar – understanding new concepts

In this guide, you have seen an overview of many important aspects of grammar, but its aim was never to be a comprehensive grammar. Students who really want to take their French to a new level will really need to invest in a complete grammar course—either online or in book form, and work their way through it, making sure they understand the concepts in-depth. The good news is that you have touched on a lot of stuff here, so much of it will be "revision" or perhaps going into certain subjects in more depth, and also, you are well-prepared for any new material.

- Listen!

If you want to speak and understand a new language, you really need to listen to it. Find YouTube videos on subjects you are interested in, and even if the level is initially a little advanced (and perhaps fast!) for you, the main thing is to listen, as this will help your pronunciation, tuning in your ear for better understanding in real-life conditions, and you may pick up some expressions and vocabulary along the way. Watch a film or a TV series in French with French subtitles, or if this is not possible, a film or a series where you know what is happening so that you are not completely lost. And speak! Even if you are on your own, try reading some texts, vocab lists, verb conjugations out loud, or even better find an app/website that allows you to repeat words/phrases as you go along, or even one of those sites that corrects your pronunciation.

Chapter 1 - Meeting and Greeting

When it comes to meeting people or running into people on the street, there are some common things you will say as a formality. We will look at these below.

Phrases You Need to Know

If you need to ask someone how to say a certain thing in French, you can ask them, *Comment dit-on … en français?* And then insert the thing that you are asking them about. For example, you can ask them, "*comment dit-on banana en français?* [coh-mon][dee-t][ohn]banana[oh-n][f-ron-say], how do you say banana in French.

In French, if we want to say see you later, we would say *à toute à l'heure* [ah][too-t][ah][l-err]. If you want to say see you later, on a specific day, we would say, for example, "see you Tuesday," *à mardi!* [ah][mah-r-dee].

If you want to ask someone for help for anything you can say "*Est-ce que vous pouvez m'aider?*" [ess-kuh][voo][poo-vay][m-eh-day] which means "Can you help me?"

If a person asks a question but you are unsure of the answer, you can say "*Je ne sais pas*" [j-uh][nuh][say][pah] which means "I don't know."

If you want to ask someone about something, what something is, or if you need clarification about something specific you can say "*Qu'est-ce que c'est?*" [k-ess][kuh]say], this means "What is it?" Or It can also mean what is _____. You then will insert whatever you are wondering about such as

Qu'est-ce que c'est, ça? "Which means what is that?"

Qu'est-ce que c'est (insert word in French that you aren't sure of the meaning of), this could be something like *Qu'est-ce que c'est l'hiver?* Say this if you aren't sure what they said. Then, they will tell you that *l'hiver* means winter.

Répétez, s'il vous plaît or Répète s'il te plaît, Can you repeat that please?

This is a way of asking someone to repeat themselves. If you want to directly ask them to repeat themselves instead of just saying "sorry?" you can ask them this. As we learned earlier, using *vous* is a polite way, and using *tu* is a less formal way that you would use with friends.

Plus lentement [p-loo][lon-tuh-mon-t], slower. You can use this phrase to ask someone to speak slower for you if you are having trouble understanding them because of a different accent than you are used to or if they are speaking too fast for you to understand. *Plus, lentement* directly translates to "more slowly." If you want to make it even more polite you can say *s'il vous plaît* at the end of this phrase and form it as a question.

Encore Une fois [on-k-or][oo-n][f-wah], one more time. This can be used similarly to the above phrase, but this one is used to ask someone to repeat themselves in a different way. This way doesn't mean that you want them to speak slower, it's more for when you just simply did not hear someone. If you want them to repeat themselves but in a slower voice, be sure to use the previous phrase instead. This one can be used if you are in a loud place and cannot hear someone or if they mumbled their words. Someone may say this phrase to you if they are having some trouble understanding your accent but not to worry, just press on and repeat yourself.

Greetings

Common greetings that you will use in French when you first meet someone or when you encounter someone and begin a conversation. This will help you to know how to get a conversation started.

The first word we will begin with is how to say hello or hi. This you will use quite often, so spend some time practicing this word and its pronunciation. In French, hello is *Bonjour* [bon-j-oor].

Another one that is similar to hello that you may use often is *Bonsoir* [b-ohn-s-wah], which means "good evening." This one can be used both formally and informally, depending on the circumstances.

There are a few other ways to say hello, some that are less formal and are more of a casual way to greet someone that is usually reserved only for your friends or family members. They are as follows;

Salut [sah-loo], which can mean either hello or goodbye and is quite informal, like saying "hey" and "see ya," but with a single word that can be used anytime.

Coucou [k-oo-k-oo] this one is a silly greeting that means "hey!" for close friends and people like your siblings.

Allô [ah-loh], which is usually used when you pick up a phone call or when you call someone. This is primarily used in Canadian French; it is a sort of combination of both English and French in one.

If you are meeting someone for the first time and you want to introduce yourself, you would say *Je m'appelle* [j-uh][m-ah-p-el]. This directly translates to mean, "I am called." You would say *Je m'appelle* _____ (insert your name).

To introduce someone else, like if you bring a friend to a party or something of the sort, you would say *Je te présente* _____ (insert their name) [j-uh][tuh][pr-eh-s-on-tuh]. If you want to say this more formally like if you are introducing someone in a work-related meeting, you would say *Je vous présente* _____ (insert their name) [j-uh][v-oo][pr-eh-s-on-tuh].

When asking someone their name, you would say one of two things. Remember how, in the introduction to this book, I introduced the concept of addressing someone using different words depending on if they are your friend or if they are an acquaintance to whom you want to show respect? This is where that concept will come to life, and I will show you the different options and examples of this. Firstly, if you are speaking to a friend or someone who is deemed an equal of yours, you would say *Comment t'appelles-tu?* [k-ohm-on][t-app-el][too]. Tu is a less formal and more casual way of addressing a person. If however, you want to show them respect or if they are an elder or something like this, you would say *Comment vous appelez-vous?* [k-ohm-on][v-oo-z][app-el-ay][v-oo]. In English, we would ask "what is your name?" or "...and you are?" or something along those lines, regardless of who we are asking, but in French this distinction is important.

After you have introduced yourself to someone and you have exchanged names, either you or the other person will say, *enchanté* [on-sh-on-tay], which is how we say, "Nice to meet you," or it is a pleasure to meet you. It directly translates to mean "Enchanted to meet you."

There are also a couple of other options that are more similar to what we would say in English such as *C'est un plaisir de faire votre connaissance*, which means it's a pleasure to meet you, as well as, *C'est un plaisir de vous connaître*, which means it's a pleasure to know you.

Whether you have just met someone or you meet up with someone who you know already, you can ask them how they are by saying *Comment allez-vous?* [coh-mon][ah-lay][v-oo-z], which means "how are you doing." This is a nice way of asking someone how they are doing. This would be used as a nicer and slightly more formal way of saying this, and if you want to ask your friend how they are by saying something more like "hey, how are ya?" or "what's up?" you would say *Ca va?* [sah][vah], this is used very commonly in French between friends as a replacement for "hi" and "how are you" at the same time. Similar to what we would say in English. If you want to ask someone specifically "what's new?" or "what's up?" you can ask this by saying *Quoi de neuf*? [k-wah][duh][n-uff], which directly translates to mean what is new? As a response to any of these, you can say the following;

Bien, et toi? Good, you? (less formal)

Bien, et vous? Good, you? (more formal)

Mal, et toi? Bad, you? (less formal)

Mal, et vous? Bad, you? (more formal)

Rien, et toi? Nothing, you? (less formal)(these 2 last answers can only be used to answer to "*quoi de neuf*?" and the first 4 answers to "*ça va*?" or the other form to say "how are you?")

Rien, et vous? Nothing, you? (more formal)

As you begin the conversation with the person you have just met, you can say

Je suis [j-uh][s-wee], which means "I am." This would come in handy when you are getting to know someone, and you want to tell them more about yourself. This can be followed by just about anything that you want to say. For example, a feeling, an adjective or it can simply begin a sentence. An example is below.

Je suis heureux [j-uh][s-wee][euh-r-uh], which means "I am happy"

You can also begin a sentence by saying what you do for work or by asking the person what they do. *Je travaille comme dentiste*, which means "I work as a dentiste" or *je suis dentiste* "I am a dentist." You can ask them by saying *qu'est ce que vous faites comme travail* or *qu'est ce que tu fais comme travail*? The first example is a more formal way of asking, as it uses *vous* and the second is more casual.

If you are initiating a conversation with someone to whom you have not been introduced, you can get their attention by saying *Excusez-moi* [ex-k-you-z-ay][m-wah], which means "excuse me." This is a polite way to get someone's attention, and can also be used to ask someone to move aside politely if you need to get by them or if they are in your way. From this, a conversation may ensue which is when you would then introduce yourself and may ask them how they are doing, as you have learned above.

Thank You

There are several options for expressing gratitude in French, based on the recipient. Depending on the context and the listener, you can use more or less formal language.

Merci [meh-r-see], Thank you

Merci beaucoup [meh-r-see][b-oh-k-oo], Thanks a lot, thank you so much

Merci bien [meh-r-see][bee-yen], Thank you very much

If you want to be more formal, you can say thank you, sir, or thank you, *ma'am*.

Merci Madame [meh-r-see][mah-dah-m], Thank you ma'am

Merci Monsieur [meh-r-see][moh-see-uh-r], Thank you Sir

You're Welcome

To say you're welcome in French, we say "it's nothing" instead of saying you're welcome, but it means the same thing. Just like saying thank you, there is a variety of ways of saying you're welcome, depending on how formal or informal you prefer to be.

De rien, It's nothing.

Avec plaisir, with pleasure.

For the next two examples, you can see that there are two forms. The first is a less formal form because it uses the word *tu*. It looks different as it is made into a conjunction as t' instead *of je t'en prie*. The second example is more formal as it uses the word *vous* which is more formal

Je vous en prie

Je t'en prie

Chapter 2 - Pronouns and Adverbs

You have seen the subject pronouns – *je, tu, il*..., and the reflexive pronouns – *me, te, se*... Now, you will look at two other kinds of pronouns.

Direct pronouns:

Here is a list of these pronouns with rough English equivalents. Below, you will also find notes and examples on how to use them.

Me – me (as opposed to I).

Te – you (as an object) (cf. the French subject pronoun when "you" is the subject of the sentence – *tu*).

Le/la – him or her (i.e., not he and she) – used for animate and inanimate things, depending on the gender of the word.

Nous – as in "us", as opposed to "we", even if both are "*nous*" in French.

Vous – you (pl) – again, it is identical to the subject pronoun.

Les – them, for both masculine and feminine, when *ils* and *elles* become the object of a sentence.

To explain it simply, the "object" (or sometimes referred to as "accusative") of a sentence is the person or thing having something done to them, as opposed to the person or thing doing the doing.

If you take the verb "manger" in a sentence, such as "*il mange le gâteau*" – he (subject) eats the cake (object), the cake is the (direct) object of the sentence, and can be replaced with a pronoun, like "it" in English – so it would become (and watch the word order!) "*il le mange*" – he eats it.

You may even have several cakes being eaten, so "*il mange les gâteaux*" can be shortened to "*il les mange*" – he eats them.

If you have a cannibal situation, the guy in the sentence (or replace the guy with a shark as the "he") could be eating a person. So, decline this sentence using all the personal pronouns (and again, keep an eye on the word order):

Il me mange in English is translated to he eats me

Il te mange in English is translated to he eats you

Il le mange/Il la mange in English is translated to he eats him/he eats her

Il nous mange in English is translated to he eats us

Il vous mange in English is translated to he eats you (plural or polite)

Il les mange in English is translated to he eats them.

And just in case you need an easy example to remember the difference between the personal and reflexive pronouns, compare the difference between "*il le mange*" – he eats him, and "*il se mange*" – he eats himself.

Indirect object pronouns:

This is when there is an object of the sentence, but not a direct object.

English has something similar, although the construction is not always the same. For example, Anne gave a present to him. The him is an object but not a direct object (the present is the direct object, being the thing that has the "giving" done to it, the "him" indirectly benefitting from this giving).

Here are the indirect object pronouns declined.

"*Me*" is the same as a reflexive, direct or indirect object pronoun, although its meanings are different, so if tomorrow you decided to be a translator, you would translate them differently, as in "myself", "me" and "to me", respectively.

Te in English is translated to "to you"

Lui in English is translated to "to him/to her"

Nous in English is translated to "to us"

Vous in English is translated to "to you"

Leur in English is translated to "to them"

So, do that all with Anne giving a present (and again look at the word order). Both common forms of saying it in English are given, although the "to someone" formulation is more useful to remember when dealing with an indirect object:

Anne me donne un cadeau – Anne gives a present to me, or Anne gives me a present

Anne te donne un cadeau – Anne gives a present to you, Anne gives you a present

Anne lui donne un cadeau – Anne gives a present to him/her, Anne gives him/her a present

Anne nous donne un cadeau – Anne gives a present to us, Anne gives us a present

Anne vous donne un cadeau – Anne gives a present to you (plural or polite), Anne gives you a present

Anne leur donne un cadeau – Anne gives a present to them (male, female, mixed, animate, inanimate, as long as it is third person plural), Anne gives them a present

You can be even more concise: she gives him a present – "*elle lui donne un cadeau*", or even go one step further to "she gives it to him", and watch the word order – *elle le lui donne*. Here the *elle* (she) is a subject pronoun, the "*le*" (it), referring to the present, is a direct object pronoun, and the "*lui*" (to him) is the indirect object pronoun.

All of this might seem like a lot to remember, but it is best to deal with "direct" and "indirect" together, as it's so much easier to see the relationship and ask yourself the question of "Is it direct or indirect?" before getting into bad habits.

If this all seems a little confusing, this is relatively high-level stuff, so feel free to go over it as many times as you need, and try out examples for yourself—have different people giving different things to different people until you are comfortable with it. Once you have done enough examples, you'll be very at ease using it when the need arises, and also recognizing it when you hear it.

Mine, yours

You learned previously how to say "my something"; now, you will look at saying "mine, yours", etc., as opposed to "my, your", which avoids using the noun.

It follows a format that is quite familiar. There is a speaker, but the "mine" agrees in number and gender with the noun that it replaces, or the thing it is talking about.

Le mien/la mienne/les miens/les miennes corresponds to English: Mine

Le tien/la tienne/les tiens/les tiennes corresponds to English:Yours (sing, familiar)

Le sien/la sienne/les siens/les siennes corresponds to English:His/hers

Le nôtre/la nôtre/les nôtres/les nôtres corresponds to English:Ours

Le vôtre/la vôtre/les vôtres/les vôtres corresponds to English:Yours (plural or polite)

Le leur/la leur/les leurs/les leurs corresponds to English:Theirs

Examples:

C'est le mien corresponds to English:it's mine

Ce sont les tiens corresponds to English:they're yours

C'est la leur corresponds to English:it is theirs (referring to a feminine singular noun)

Adverbs

Just as an adjective describes or qualifies a noun, an adverb qualifies a verb, allowing you, for example, not only to say you do something, but how well, quickly, badly, slowly, etc., you do something, or at least that you do it quickly, slowly, etc.

As in English, there are regularly adjectives (quickly, slowly) and irregular (well…)

To construct a regular adverb, take the feminine form of the adjective and add -*ment* to the end (a bit like the -ly ending in English).

So "*lent*" – slow, is "*lente*" in the feminine singular, then add the ending/suffix "-*ment*" at the end, and you get "*lentement*" – slowly.

Try it with "*rapide*" for fast. The feminine adjective is "*rapide*", add "*ment*" and you have "*rapidement*" – quickly (although you will also hear "*vite*", as in "fast", used as an adjective).

Here are a few common ones:

Tristement – sadly

Absolument – absolutely

Brusquement – abruptly

Certainement – certainly (also probably)

Complètement – completely

Dernièrement – lately

Doucement – gently, slowly

439

Énormément – hugely

Gentiment – kindly

Franchement – honestly

Heureusement – fortunately

Immédiatement – immediately

Largement – greatly

Légèrement – lightly, slightly

Naturellement – naturally

Parfaitement – perfectly

Précisément – precisely

Premièrement – firstly

Profondément – profoundly, deeply

Rapidement – quickly, rapidly

Rarement – rarely

Sérieusement – seriously

Seulement – only

Simplement – simply

Tellement – so (much)

Vraiment – really

There are also some irregular and often very common ones: "*bien*" for well and "*mal*" for badly.

Parce que (explain yourself!)

You may, when talking about interests, or in many other areas, be asked to explain why you do something, why you feel a certain way, why things are a certain way, etc. "*Pourquoi*" will be the question word, and you will use "*parce que*" and then carry on your sentence as normal with normal word order. *Parce que* is, of course, contracted to *parce qu'*, if followed by a word with a vowel.

Here are some examples:

-   *Pourquoi tu aimes la musique classique?* (Why do you like classical music?)

-   *Parce que je trouve cela reposant.* (Because I find it relaxing.), or you can even say the full sentence, "*j'aime la musique classique parce que je trouve cela reposant.*"

-   *Pourquoi tu habites à Londres?* (Why do you live in London?)

-   *Parce que mon travail est à Londres/parce que j'aime les grandes villes.* (Because my job is there/because I like big cities.)

Possession is nine-tenths of the law...

There may come a time when you want to denote possession, say something belongs to you or someone else.

There is no 's for the possessive in French, always remember it as "of", as in "the dog of Marie", "the door of the house", "the monuments of Paris", etc.

This is relatively easy in French: you use *de* + the noun (a person, place, or thing, including proper nouns).

Of course, remember that "*de*" is declined according to what follows it, and becomes *du, de la, de l', des*, depending on whether the noun is masculine or feminine (or indeed begins with a vowel for de l'), or "*de*" on its own if it is followed by a city or person without an article, Paris.

Here are some examples:

The group U2's music/The music of the group U2 – *la musique du groupe U2*

The dog's dinner/the dinner of the dog – *le dîner du chien*

The lady's hat/the hat of the lady – *le chapeau de la dame*

The side of the table – *le côté de la table*

The entrance to (of) the opera – *l'entrée de l'opéra*

The boys' coats/the coats of the boys – *les manteaux des garçons*

The lights of Paris – *les lumières de Paris*

Marie's cat/the cat of Marie – *le chat de Marie*

Pierre's friends/the friends of Pierre – *les amis de Pierre*

Bear in mind that countries are often used with an article, as in "*la France*", so the population of France would be "*la population de la France*".

Possessive pronouns

Pronouns are handy and used a lot in English too. They are second nature in people's language, but the work you put into them in a foreign language will definitely pay dividends—not least because it will make things easier to say in the long run, and much more natural.

You want to say that something is "my" or "your" or "his", etc., so reach for a possessive pronoun! Here they are:

Mon (m sing)/*ma* (f sing)/*mes* (pl) – my

Ton (m sing)/*ta* (f sing)/*tes* (pl) – your

Son (m sing)/*sa* (f sing) /*ses* (pl) – his or her

Notre (sing)/*nos* (plural) – our

Votre (sing)/*vos* (plural) – your (plural or polite)

Leur (sing)/*leurs* (plural) – their

The slightly tricky bit here is that you need to know the gender of the person who is speaking to know whether to use a form of "my" or "our", etc., AND you also need to know the gender and number of the thing you are talking about, to be able to select between "*mon/ma/mes*" forms.

Also, one of the things most confusing to learn is the "his/her" part. In French, the choice of "*son*" or "*sa*" is not the gender of the person owning the thing like it is in English (his or her denotes the gender of the person doing the owning), but the thing owned. So "his table" – is not "*son table*" just because "his" is male, but "*SA table*" because the table, the thing owned, is feminine. Once you have grasped this, the rest is easy.

Here are some examples for each

My pencil – *mon crayon* (whether the my is a man or a woman speaking, the pencil, the thing owned, is masculine, hence "*mon*").

My fountain pen – *ma plume* (again it could be a man speaking, but the plume/fountain pen is feminine, so it has to be "*ma*").

Mes chiens. Mes affaires – "dogs" and "things" are both plural, one is masculine and the other feminine, but both take "*mes*" for my dogs, my things, because there is only one plural form for my. Also, again, it really is important to get this—it doesn't matter if the person doing the owning here, the person whose dogs or things they are, is a man or a woman, the "*mes*" refers to the gender, or in this case number (plural) of the things owned.

Ton chat – your cat (chat/cat being masculine).

Son stylo – his pen, but also her pen. You cannot tell whether it is "his" or "hers" from this phrase, but "*stylo*" is masculine, so it has to be "son".

To make it clearer whether it's him or her, or even between several hims or hers, or for emphasis, if there are several people present, or just if you want to really emphasize it, you can say "*à elle*" for hers at the end, or "*à lui*" for his, so it would be "*son stylo à elle*" – her pen or "*son stylo à lui*" – his pen). You can also add "*à moi*", "*à toi*", "*à nous*", "*à vous*", "*à eux*", "*à eux*" for the other *je, tu, nous, vous, ils/elles* forms for emphasis or clarity.

Ses affaires – his or her things. *Ses affaires à lui* – his things

Ses chiens – his or her dogs – *ses chiens à elle* – her dogs

Notre cahier, notre gomme – our exercise book, our eraser—one is masculine and one is feminine, but for "*notre*" – our, you just need to know that it is singular, so "*notre*". Or *notre cahier à nous* (for emphasis)

Nos affaires, nos chiens – our things, our dogs (again, it's always irrespective of the gender of the speaker/the owner)

Votre chat, votre gomme – your cat, your rubber—the same principle as above

Leur chien – their dog

Leurs chiens – their dogs

And *leurs chiens à eux* to denote that the owners are masculine (or mixed) and *leurs chiens à elles* to denote that they are female.

Just to repeat the notion of emphasis, or of making clear who the owner is, you saw "*à lui*" and "*à elle*", but you can do this with all of the pronouns.

So – mon/ma/mes X à moi

Ton/Ta/Tes X à toi

Son/sa/ses X à lui (his) or à elle (her)

Notre/nos X à nous

Votre/vos X à vous

Leur/leurs X à eux (their – masculine plural – or mixed) and *à elles* (their feminine plural).

Example: *leur chien à eux* – their dog (the "they" being masculine or mixed company), *leur chien à elles* (their dog, belonging to a group of females). Likewise, *"leurs chiens à elles"*, *"leurs affaires à elles"*, *"leurs affaires à eux"*, *"leurs chiens à eux"*.

Chapter 3 - Word order, Imperfect and Conditional tense

Putting Sentences Together: Word Order

In simple sentences, French word order is more or less the same as in English which follows a structure known as subject-verb-object. For example:

- *la fille lit le livre* --- the girl (subject) reads (verb) the book (object)

The first difference comes when we add an adjective to the sentence, since adjectives usually follow the noun they describe:

- *la fille lit le livre rouge* --- the girl reads the red book

Some adjectives usually come before the noun, la *jolie fille*, the "pretty girl" and yet others have different meanings depending on whether they are placed before the noun or after. For example, the word *propre* before a noun means "own" (as in "my own"), whereas after the noun it means "clean". As such:

- *ma propre chemise* --- my own shirt

- *ma chemise propre* --- my clean shirt

You can even have *ma propre chemise propre* which would mean "my own clean shirt"!

Things start to get a little more involved when we throw words like "me", "you", "him", "it" (object pronouns) into the mix, because in French these words go before the verb instead of after as in English. For example:

- *je vois David* --- I see David

- *je le vois* --- I see him

In the above example, can you see how David not only changes to *le* ("him"), but also moves its position in the sentence?

Sometimes, other pronouns might be thrown into the sentence if there is more than one person or thing involved. Take the sentence "I give the book to David". In this sentence, we can replace both "the book" and "to David" with pronouns, which we might do in order to avoid repetition, giving us a sentence like: "I give it to him". Here is how we arrive at this sentence in French:

- *je donne* --- I give

- *je le donne* --- I give it

- *je le lui donne* --- I give it to him

In the above example, *le* means "it" and *lui* means "to him". What is more interesting than a technical explanation at this point is to simply point out that a lot of information can come before the verb in French, whereas in English the information would come after the verb.

When it comes to asking questions in French there are some similarities with English. In English, it is possible to make a question just using the intonation of your voice, so "you have a girlfriend" (statement) becomes "you have a girlfriend?" (question) just by raising the tone of your voice. This way of asking a question is even more common in French than in English, and is probably the most colloquial way of asking a question: *Tu as une copine*? You might even notice that French people often tend to use this device when speaking English rather more than native English speakers!

Another way to form a question in French is to invert the verb and the subject, giving:

- *voulez-vous...?* --- do you want...? (lit: want you)

- *pensez-vous...?* --- do you think...? (lit: think you)

A third way to form a question is to add *est-ce que* to the beginning of a statement, so *vous voulez un café*, "you want a coffee" (statement) becomes:

- *Est-ce que vous voulez un café?* --- Do you want a coffee? (question)

With language learning more broadly, it is often tempting to ask "why?" and to want to understand why something is the way it is, especially if you are an analytical person. However, you can often get all the communicative benefits of learning a new phrase without necessarily knowing the grammar that lies behind the phrase.

In fact, we have found that learning useful set phrases is extremely helpful, because it exposes you to natural grammar regardless of whether you understand the grammar or not. Over time, you find that the grammar from the phrases you have learnt begins to make sense to you, even though you may never have analyzed it. We describe this as "free grammar" and it is far more effective than carrying out a deep analysis of everything you learn at the beginner stages --- there are other more important activities to be doing!

The purpose of this chapter has been to show you the fundamental building blocks of French grammar that allow you to understand the most basic workings of the language, so you can begin to understand and speak French yourself. Needless to say, there is far more to French grammar than the contents of this chapter, and I fully expect you to have further questions about grammar at this stage.

One of the biggest mistakes made by students of foreign languages is to place too much importance on grammar in the early stages of learning. This is not to diminish the importance of grammar, but rather to say that grammar does not have to be mastered at the beginning. As a beginner, unable to read or understand much in French, the only way you can learn grammar is by studying abstract rules. However, once you can read and understand French you will be able to learn grammar naturally --- as you find it being used in the real world --- which gives you a far deeper understanding of the grammar than if you had learnt it as "rules", and also happens to be far easier.

When learners place too much importance on grammar at the beginner stages, and insist on "getting it right" before moving on, there is a significant danger of paralysis in learning. I have seen so many people fall out of love with a language simply because they develop a negative mindset towards grammar, frustrated by the number of rules to learn and the exceptions to those rules. With the grammar you have learnt in this chapter, you are already equipped not only to understand basic French, but also to make simple sentences yourself. Above all, with just a basic knowledge of grammar you can already make yourself understood, and that is the key --- get started today and the rest will come with time!

Imperfect tense (usage)

The imperfect tense is a past tense, which is used to describe what things were like and how people felt in the past.

For example, it was raining – *il pleuvait* (compare this to "it rained" – *il a plu*).

For example, I was very sad when she left (the "I was sad" is in the imperfect, but the "she left" was a single action at a moment in time so it will take the perfect tense – *j'étais très triste quand elle est partie*).

We used to get up very early to go to school. *Nous nous levions très tôt pour aller à l'ecole.*

I was reading a book when the phone rang. *Il était en train de lire quand le téléphone a sonné.*

You always used to wear long dresses. *Tu portais toujours de longues robes.*

We were living in London at that time. *Nous vivions à Londres à cette époque.*

You can often recognize an imperfect tense in English because it will use a form like "was reading" or "was raining".

(A tip on how to know when to use the imperfect and when to use the perfect tense: Think of yourself as a film director or a theater director. Anything that is already happening when the camera starts rolling is imperfect, and any action that is a stage direction after the camera is rolling is the perfect tense. This is perhaps not 100 percent foolproof, but it's a very logical way to work out whether what you want to say is imperfect or perfect. In any case, with use, you will start to hear what sounds right for each situation and will naturally reach for the right tense.)

Imperfect tense (construction)

This is a relatively easy tense to construct, as it is just a matter of taking the stem of the verb and adding endings. As always, there are a couple of exceptions or things to learn, but first, look at the three regular verb groups.

The imperfect tense for -ER verbs.

Take the stem (remove the -*er*) and add the following endings:

Je -ais

Tu -ais

Il -ait

Nous -ions

Vous -iez

So, with the verb *donner* (to give), that will give:

Je donnais – I gave, I was giving, I used to give

Tu donnais

Il donnait

Nous donnions

Vous donniez

Ils donnaient

For -IR verbs, again remove the -*ir* to form the stem and add the following endings:

Je -issais

Tu -issais

Il -issait

Nous -issions

Vous -issiez

Ils -issaient

So, with *finir*, that will be:

Je finissais – I finished, I was finishing, I used to finish

Tu finissais

Il finissait

Nous finissions

Vous finissiez

Ils finissaient

(If it is easier for you to remember this way, you can always think of -ir verbs having a different root for the imperfect, -iss. For example, *finiss*, and then they just take the same endings as -er verbs.)

And for -RE verbs, again find the stem, by removing the *-re*, and then add the following endings:

Je -ais

Tu -ais

Il -ait

Nous -ions

Vous -iez

Ils -aient

(Note that these are the same endings as for the -er verbs.)

With *attendre*, this will give:

J'attendais – I waited, I was waiting, I used to wait

Tu attendais

Il attendait

Nous attendions

Vous attendiez

Ils attendaient

And for regular verbs, that is (almost) all there is to it.

There are a few verbs (often -er verbs) that change spelling to keep a sort of coherence in pronunciation. Here are a few examples:

Lancer – to throw

Je lançais

Tu lançais

Il lançait

Nous lancions

Vous lanciez

Ils lançaient

(Note the appearance of the cedilla in the forms that now have an -a at the start rather than an *-e* or *-i*, so that you still get the "s" sound and not the "k" sound.)

The verb "*manger*" is similar, but as no cedilla is possible with a "g", you add an "e" to keep the g soft where necessary (zh rather than a hard gue sound).

Manger – to eat

Je mangeais

Tu mangeais

Il mangeait

Nous mangions

Vous mangiez

Ils mangeaient

And here is the really good news—there is only one verb that is irregular in the imperfect tense – the verb '*être*'.

Être – to be

J'étais – I was, I used to be

Tu étais

Il était

Nous étions

Vous étiez

Ils étaient

(Note that the stem is irregular, but the endings are as for -er and -re verbs, so the main thing is to make sure that you have learned the stem.)

So, "I was happy," or "I used to be happy" is "*J'étais heureuse.*"

Ma mère était vendeuse – My mother used to be a teacher, or my mother was a teacher.

The pluperfect tense (or *plus-que-parfait*)

This is one of the easiest tenses, as you already know all the elements that you need to form it.

It is used to say that something happened even further back in the past. The English equivalent is "I had done something" (as opposed to I have done something or I did something).

This sentence is constructed in French by the imperfect form of the auxiliary verb (avoir or être) plus the past participle of the verb (the same as in the perfect tense):

J'avais + pp

Tu avais + pp

Il avait + pp

Nous avions + pp

Vous aviez + pp

Ils avaient + pp

OR

J'étais + pp

Tu étais + pp

Il était + pp

Nous étions + pp

Vous étiez + pp

Ils étaient + pp

Some examples:

I had been – *J'avais été.*

You had gone – *Tu étais allé*, or, as agreements still apply in this case, if it is a woman, *tu étais allée.*

With reflexive verbs, it looks like this:

We had got up – *Nous nous étions levé.*

She had washed herself – *Elle s'était lavée.*

In the negative, it looks like this:

Je n'étais pas allé – I hadn't gone.

Je n'avais pas été … – I had not been.

You can often find it in combination with other past tenses:

Il pleuvait et je m'étais déjà lavé, mais je suis sorti quand même.

So, the idea here is: it was raining, and I had already washed, but I went out anyway.

Conditional tense

The conditional verb tense describes what might happen or could be real in particular circumstances (which may or may not be explicit). For instance, I would help you if I could.

It can also be used for saying what it is that you would do or needed. For example, could you give me the bill? I would like to go swimming.

Often, you can hear a conditional in English from the "would" form (or shortened to d).

So that is what you would use it for (note the conditional there!), and in some ways, it is one of the easiest tenses to learn because you have all the elements already—you just put them together differently.

For *-er* and *-ir* verbs, you take the infinitive, so *donner* and *finir*, and for *-re* verbs, you use the infinitive without the final *-e* (Is this looking familiar? If so it is because it's the same form as the future tense).

Then add the following endings for all three verb groups:

Je -ais

Tu -ais

Il -ait

Nous -ions

Vous -iez

Ils -aient

Do these look familiar, too? They are the imperfect endings for -er verbs.

So, if you do not want to have to learn anything new, just remember—same basic form as the future tense + the imperfect endings from -er verbs. Not a thing to learn!

Now look at what it looks like with the three "favorite" verbs:

Je donnerais – I would give

Je finirais – I would finish

J'attendrais – I would wait

Tu donnerais

Tu finirais

Tu attendrais

Il donnerait

Il finirait

Il attendrait

Nous donnerions

Nous finirions

Nous attendrions

Vous donneriez

Vous finiriez

Vous attendriez

Ils donneraient

Ils finiraient

Ils attendraient

There are some spelling exceptions, where double letters or accents change, again to keep pronunciation consistent, but these are not covered here. If you want to be absolutely perfect on the subject, you can find any of them in any good grammar book or verb table (and in any case, this is only important in written French—when you speak, you will not hear these differences in spelling). A few examples of verbs in these categories are "*appeler*" – to call, "*jeter*" – to throw, "*lever*" – to raise (or to get up when used reflexively), "*peser*" – to weigh, and also verbs that end in -*yer*, like *nettoyer, payer, essayer*.

Here is the really good news with this tense—you do not need to learn any irregular verbs. That is not to say that there are no irregular verbs, just that you have already learned all the elements. The root form for the conditional tense is the same as that for the future tense, and then you just add the regular conditional endings.

So *être* has a root of ser- (like the future tense) and takes the ais, ais, ait, etc., endings, giving: *je serais, tu serais, il serait, nous serions, vous seriez, ils seraient*.

Likewise, with aller, it has the root ir- like the future tense, and with the conditional endings, it becomes: j'irais, tu irais, il irait, nous irions, vous iriez, ils iraient. Savoir is saur-, avoir is aur-, faire is fer-, etc.

(Note: Although the spelling is different, some of these in spoken French will sound identical to the future tense, but you should be able to work out very easily which one is being used from the context.

When you are expressing something that you want using the form *"je voudrais"*, you can follow this either with a noun, for example, *je voudrais un kilo de pommes*, or with a verb, for example, *je voudrais aller au parc*.

You can have a kind of conditional perfect, again built up using elements that you have already seen. So, I would like – *je voudrais*; I would have liked – *j'aurais voulu*; You would know – *tu saurais*; and You would have known – *tu aurais su*.

Verbs that take *"être"* in the perfect tense will also in conditional perfects, so *je serais allé* – I would have gone, and *je me serais lavé* – I would have washed myself.

You can do the same thing with the future tense, giving a future perfect: *je serai allé* – I will have gone; *il aura su* – he will have known; and *nous aurons donné* – we will have given.)

Now you really do have everything you need to manipulate any tense that you may need in French. Congratulations! Now it is really just a question of practice!

Avoiding libel (Conditional tense in a newspaper, etc.)

Here is just a little usage note on a specific use of the conditional that you will be sure to see if you pick up a French newspaper or listen to the French news, or you may even come across it in general conversation.

The conditional tense can be used to express something that has not been proven to be true, but which is reported as such, or which you believe to be the case. It is roughly the equivalent of adding "allegedly" to a sentence.

Here are some examples: *l'homme serait parti en courant* – allegedly the man ran away. *Le voleur serait une femme de 22 ans de la region Parisienne* – the thief is said to be a 22-year-old woman from the Paris area.

So now you will not be surprised if you come across this specific use of the conditional tense, and you can even start to use it yourself to express "facts" that have some doubt attached to them or which need confirming, or which you wish to distance yourself from in a sense.

Chapter 4- Personal Relationships

Sometimes you might be introduced to people who are related to each other either by family, friendship, or love, that may help you hone your French language skills. You may also make new friends while speaking French.

Family

Let's start with close friends and relatives.

1. *famille* translates to family

2. *parents* translates to parents (masculine)

3. *parentes* translates to parents (feminine)

4. *père* translates to father

5. *mère* translates to mother

6. *enfant* translates to child

7. *enfants* translates to children

8. *frères et soeurs* translates to siblings

9. *frère* translates to brother

10. *sœur* translates to sister

11. *fils* translates to son

12. *fille* translates to daughter

13. *épouse* translates to spouse (feminine)

14. *époux* translates to spouse (masculine)

15. *mari* translates to husband

16. *épouse* translates to wife

17. *demi-frère* translates to half-brother

18. *demi soeur* translates to half-sister

19. *les grands-parents* translates to grandparents

20. *grand-père* translates to grandfather

21. *grand-mère* translates to grandmother

22. *petits enfants* translates to grandchildren

23. *petit fils* translates to grandson

24. *petite fille* translates to granddaughter

25. *oncle* translates to uncle

26. *tante* translates to aunt

27. *cousin* translates to male cousin

28. *cousine* translates to female cousin

29. *neveu* translates to nephew

30. *nièce* translates to niece

31. *beau-père* translates to stepfather

32. *belle-mère* translates to stepmother

33. *beau-fils* translates to stepson

34. *belle fille* translates to stepdaughter

35. *beau-frère* translates to stepbrother

36. *demi-soeur* translates to stepsister

37. *beaux-parents* translates to parents-in-law

38. *beau-père* translates to father-in-law

39. *belle-mère* translates to mother-in-law

40. *beau-frère* translates to brother-in-law

41. *belle-soeur* translates to sister-in-law

42. *beau fils* translates to son-in-law

43. *belle-fille* translates to daughter-in-law

Friends and Other Close Relationships

44. *fiancé*– fiancé

45. *fiancée* – fiancée

46. *amie*– friend (feminine)

47. *ami* – friend (masculine)

48. *meilleur ami* – best friend

49. *confidente* – confidante

The following phrases and/or sentences may prove useful while seeking out human interaction. You can use them to introduce people or recount stories about your friends and relatives. You can use them to have private conversations with loved ones as well.

Ce fut un plaisir de vous rencontrer – It was a pleasure to meet you

Voulez-vous sortir avec nous? – Do you want to hang out with us?

Puis-je vous demander un rendez-vous? – Can I ask you out on a date?

Je t'aime, ours câlin – I love you, cuddle bear

Veux-tu être mon petit ami? – Do you want to be my boyfriend?

Veux tu devenir ma copine? – Do you want to be my girlfriend?

Veux-tu être mon ami? – Will you be my friend?

Veux-tu m'épouser? – Will you marry me?

Je suis éperdument amoureux – I am head over heels in love

Tu es l'amour de ma vie – You are the love of my life

Je suis tellement en toi – I am so into you

Je ne t'aime pas – I do not like you

Embrasse-moi, ma chérie – Kiss me, my darling

Vous êtes belle – You are beautiful

Tu as de beaux yeux bleus – You have beautiful blue eyes

Avez-vous des projets samedi? – Do you have plans on Saturday?

Nos vacances en famille – Our family vacation

Mon père est mort quand j'étais jeune – My dad died when I was young

Ma mère s'est remariée quelques années plus tard – My mom remarried a few years later

C'est mon mari – This is my husband

C'est mon fiancé - This is my fiancé

Votre frère vient-il avec nous? – Is your brother coming with us?

Ma soeur est gentille – My sister is kind

Mon beau-fils s'appelle John – My stepson's name is John

Ma fille a cinq ans – My daughter is five years old

J'ai trois grands frères – I have three older brothers

Jane est ma soeur – Jane is my sister

Je suis très excité pour notre mariage – I am very excited for our wedding

Ma mère est originaire de France et mon père est originaire des États-Unis. – My mom is from France, and my Dad is from the United States

Ma famille est américaine, mais mes frères et soeurs et moi avons grandi à Paris – My family is American, but my siblings and I grew up in Paris

Mes grands-parents étaient mariés depuis soixante ans – My grandparents were married for sixty years

Mon père et ma mère sont divorcés – My father and mother are divorced

Mes parents sont divorcés – My parents are divorced

James est mon mari – James is my husband

Avez-vous des frères et sœurs? - Do you have any siblings?

J'ai un frère – I have one brother

J'ai un frère et une soeur – I have one brother and one sister

J'ai une demi-soeur – I have a half-sister

Ma mère a 55 ans – My mother is 55 years old

Mon père s'appelle Joe – My father's name is Joe

C'est mon mari – He is my husband

Elle est ma femme – She is my wife

Mon ami d'enfance vient visiter – My childhood friend is coming to visit

Toute ma famille élargie est venue à mon mariage – My entire extended family came to my wedding

Ma soeur était ma demoiselle d'honneur – My sister was my maid of honor

Mon fils est maintenant un bambin – My son is now a toddler

J'ai eu des bébés jumeaux – I had twin baby girls

J'ai nommé ma fille d'après ma grand-mère – I named my daughter after my grandmother

Mon cousin avait une liaison illicite avec une femme rencontrée au travail – My cousin had an illicit affair with a woman he met at work

J'ai une famille nombreuse et heureuse – I have a large and happy family

En grandissant, j'étais l'enfant préféré de ma mère – Growing up, I was my mother's favorite child

Mes frères et moi nous battions beaucoup quand nous étions enfants – My brothers and I used to fight a lot when we were children

J'ai toujours voulu un petit garçon – I have always wanted a baby boy

Ma fille a les cheveux roux comme son père – My daughter has red hair just like her father

Mes jumeaux sont nés à dix minutes d'intervalle – My twins were born ten minutes apart

Chapter 5 - Street Directions

Addresses

We will now look at the way we say addresses in French. When we are talking about street addresses, there many things that are different between French and English. First, we will break it up into pieces and look at each section contained in an address.

Streets

Rue [roo], Street

Route [roo-t], Road

Chemin [sh-uh-m-an], Trail, Path

Allée [ah-lay], Driveway

Ruelle [roo-el], Alley

Parking (we use the same word as English), Parking lot

Numbers

You already know the numbers from one to beyond in French, and in this section, we will put that into practice. If you forget how to say the larger numbers that we learned in an earlier chapter, then for your purposes as long as you can say the numbers themselves you will be fine. I will show you an example of what I mean below.

325 Example St.

Instead of having to say Three hundred and twenty-five example street, as long as you can say "three two five example street," you will be able to adequately get your point across to whoever you are asking like a taxi driver or a person from whom you are asking directions. As you now know, numbers from 1 to 20 and multiples of 10 from 20 to 100 (from learning about numbers in chapter 4), you will be able to say many many address numbers. If you aren't sure, however, you can simply state the numbers that you see that you do remember and the person you are talking to will likely be able to understand what you are trying to say. As a refresher, the numbers from 1 to 10 are again below for your reference.

1, 2, 3, 4, 5, 6, 7, 8, 9, 10

Un (one), deux (two)

trois (three), quatre (four)

cinq (five), six (six)

sept (seven), huit (eight)

neuf (nine), dix(ten)

As an example, we will use the following address and look at it in more detail;

9 Rue Ste. Catherine

In French, when there is the word Saint, or St. in an address, like the street name St. Catherine Street or St. Andrew street, It is written as *Ste* for feminine and *St.* for masculine. This is because the proper word "*Sainte*" for a feminine noun (which becomes "*Ste.*") an "*Saint*" for a masculine noun ("*St.*"). So when talking about any word or street with the word Saint in it, it will be written in this way.

Ste. Catherine, Sainte Catherine

St. Andrew, Sainte Andrew

Address Examples

When we write addresses, we write them in this order; number + street type (road, crescent, etc.) + street name. It is a bit of a different order than in English as the word street is moved to the front of the street name instead of after it.

9 St. Catherine Street is what we would say in English. In French, this would be written as *9 Rue Ste. Catherine* and said as *neuf, rue sainte Catherine, à Paris, en France.*

13 Chemin Georges, treize chemin georges. 13 Georges Street

100 chemin arbres, québec, québec, Canada. Cent chemin arbres, à québec, québec au Canada. 100 Arbres Trail, Quebec, Quebec, Canada.

À Kansas Vs. Au Kansas

When we are talking about being or having been someplace, there are different ways to say this, depending on what type of place it is you're talking about. For example, in the United States, there are two different places called Kansas. One is a state, and the other is a city. When speaking in English, we can tell which of these a person is talking about because if they are talking about the state they will say Kansas State. In French, we don't do this, but there is another way that we can actually tell which of these somebody is talking about based on the word that precedes it. If we are talking about a city or town, we would say "*À Kansas*", which would indicate to the person we are speaking to that we are talking about the city. If we are talking about the state, we would say "*Au Kansas*".

One more thing to note is that if the province, state or country we are talking about begins with a vowel, then using au would be quite a mouthful. In this case, we would say *en*. For example, "*Je suis allé en France*" which means I went to France. If you were talking about going to Paris, which is a city you would say "*Je suis allé à Paris.*"

Asking For Directions

This section will focus on the phrases you will need when you are travelling. These are related to transportation and directions so that you can get around with ease.

If you need to ask someone where something is, you can ask them in the following way;

Excusez-moi, où est ____? This means Excuse me, where is _____? You will then insert something like *La Tour Eiffel*, The Eiffel Tower.

Like you learned earlier in this book, you could also say *Est-ce que vous pouvez m'aider à trouver _____?* Which means, "could you help me find _____?"

Alternatively, you could also say *Est-ce que vous savez où est* _____? Which means, "Do you know where _____ is?"

After asking this, you will likely hear one of the following responses;

C'est à côté de [s-eh][ah][k-oh-tay][duh], It's beside (something)

C'est près de [s-eh][pr-eh][duh], It's close to (something)

C'est près d'ici [s-eh][pr-eh][d-ee-see]], It's close to here

C'est loin de [s-eh][l-w-ah-n][duh], It's far from (something)

C'est loin d'ici [s-eh][l-w-ah-n][d-ee-see], It's far from here

Left And Right

Gauche, Right

Droite, Left

C'est..., It is/ It's...

C'est à gauche, It's to the left

C'est à droite, It's to the right

N,S,E,W

Below you will see the French terms for the compass directions North, South, East, and West. When using these in a sentence, you will say the word *vers*, which means toward or in the direction of. This is like saying "to the west" for example, in English.

North, le nord, [l-uh][n-or]

South, le sud, [l-uh][soo-d]

East, l'est, [l-ess-t]

West, l'ouest, [l-oo-ess-t]

Upstairs/Downstairs

When talking about directions in a house or a building, we will use the following terms.

En haut, Upstairs

En bas, Downstairs

We will now look at sentence examples of this.

Elle est allée en haut. She went upstairs.

Il aime aller en bas. He likes to go downstairs.

Chapter 6 - Interests and Entertainment

Sightseeing

Do you have a guidebook/map? *Avez-vous un guide (touristique)/une carte?*

Tourist information – *office (m) de tourisme*

What should I see while I'm here? – *Qu'est-ce que je devrais voir pendant que je suis là?*

What's that? – *Qu'est-ce que c'est?*

Can I take photos? – *Puis-je prendre des photos?*

To sightsee – *faire du tourisme*

Guided tour – *visite (f) guidée*

What is there for children to do? – *Qu'est-ce qu'il y a à faire pour des enfants?*

Admission – *l'entrée (f)*

How much is admission? – *Combien coûte l'entrée?*

Ancient – *ancien*

Archaeological – *archéologique*

Castle – *château* (m)

Cathedral – *cathédrale* (f)

Cemetery – *cimetière* (m)

Church – *église (f)*

Concert hall – *salle (f) de concert*

Library – *bibliothèque* (f)

Main square – *place* (f) *principale*

Market – *marché (m)*

Modern art – *art* (m) *moderne, art* (m) *contemporain*

Monastery – *monastère (m)*

Monument – *monument (m)*

Mosque – *mosquée*(f)

Natural history – *histoire* (f) *naturelle*

Old city – *vieille ville* (f)

Palace – *palais (m)*

Opera house – *opéra (m)*

Ruins – *ruines* (f, pl)

Shrine – *lieu (m) de pèlerinage, autel* (m)

Statue – *statue (f)*

Temple – *temple (m)*

Tomb – *tombe (f)*, *tombeau (m)*

Typical --- *typique*

University – *université (f)*

X marks the plural

Although many regular plurals in French take *-s* to denote the plural form (for both the noun and the adjective), there are some cases where the plural is denoted by a *-x*. Often these are words which end in -*au* or -*eau* in the singular.

Examples: water – "*eau*" becomes "*eaux*" in the plural; "*chateau*" – castle becomes "*chateaux*", and for an adjective, "*beau*" – beautiful, handsome becomes "*beaux*" in the plural.

This might be the time to do a little zoom in on the adjective "*beau*", which becomes "*beaux*" in the masculine plural, but also, its feminine forms are "*belle*" and "*belles*" for singular and plural, respectively.

Going Out

What is there to do here in the evenings? – *Qu'est-ce qu'il y a à faire ici le soir?*

Are there any nightclubs around here? – *Y a-t-il des boites (de nuit) par ici?*

Where can I find a bar? – *Où est-ce que je peux trouver un bar?*

Can you recommend a restaurant for me? – *Pourriez-vous me conseiller un restaurant?*

How much does it cost to get in? – *Combien coûte l'entrée?*

Is there a dress code? – *Y a-t-il un code vestimentaire?*

Cinema – *cinéma (m)*

Concert – *concert (m)*

Nightclub – *boîte (f) (de nuit)*

Theater – *théâtre (m)*

Bar – *bar (m)*

Coffee shop – *café (m)*

Pub – *pub (m)*

Music – *musique (f)*

Live music – *musique (f) live*

What?

If you want to ask what in a question (as opposed to "which" – "*lequel*"), use "*qu'est-ce que*".

460

Sports and hobbies

Sport – *sport (m)*

Hobby – *passe-temps (m), loisir (m)*

Free time – *temps (m) libre*

What sports do you play? – *Quels sports faites-vous? Or pratiquez-vous?*

What are your interests? – *Quels sont vos loisirs/ passe-temps?*

What do you like doing in your free time? – *Qu'est-ce que vous aimez faire pendant votre temps libre?*

I like – *j'aime*

I love – *j'adore*

I don't like – *je n'aime pas*

I hate – *je hais/ j'ai horreur de*

To play at something

All of the above—liking, hating, loving—can be used with a noun or verb, so *"J'aime jouer au football"* – I like to play football, or *"J'aime le football"* – like football.

The one thing that is a little trickier to grasp is that the French language often does not have you playing something, but playing "at" something. So, take football – not *"j'aime jouer le football"* or worse still, like nails down a blackboard to a French person, *"j'aime jouer football"* – non, non, non. But rather *"j'aime jouer AU football,"* literally "I like playing at football," even if you are a professional! The playing "at" is just a figure of speech, and casts no aspersions on your ability as a player or your amateur status. Similarly, *"j'aime jouer aux échecs"* – I like playing chess, as chess is plural in French (à becomes au when it would be *à le, à la* when it is *à la* with a feminine noun, and aux with a plural, rather than *à les*).

Also compare that some sports are not *"jouer"* – played, so much as *"faire"* – done. For example, *"faire du ski"* – to ski, go skiing, or *"faire du shopping"* – to go shopping (for leisure).

And although you *"jouer d'un instrument"* – play an instrument, once you specify which instrument, it becomes *"jouer du"* as in *"jouer du piano, de la guitare"*.

So, as a reminder, *"de"* when followed by a masculine singular (*"de le"*) becomes *"du"*, by a feminine singular stays *"de la"*, and by a plural (*"de les"*) becomes *"des"*.

Art – *l'art (m)*

Basketball – *basket-ball (m)*

Chess – *échecs (m, pl)*

To collect – *collectionner, faire une collection de*

Coins – *pièces (f, pl)*

Stamps – *timbres (m, pl)*

To dance – *danser*

Food – *nourriture* (f), or you will hear the slang *'la bouffe'* for food quite often

To cook – *cuisiner*

461

Football – football (m), or foot (m)

Play football – *jouer au foot*

Hiking – *randonnée (f), faire de la randonnée*

Martial arts – *arts (m, pl) martiaux*

Spending time with friends – *passer du temps avec des amis*

Movies – *films (m, pl)*

Going to the cinema – *aller au cinéma, often shortened to aller au ciné*

Action film – *film (m) d'action*

War film – *film (m) de guerre*

Rom-com – *comédie (f) romantique*

Music – *la musique (f)*

Band/group – *groupe (m)*

Rock – *rock* (m) – noun or adjective – NB as an adjective, it does not decline – so '*la musique rock*'

Classical – *Classique* – adjective

Pop – *pop* (m) noun or adjective – NB as an adjective, it does not decline – so '*la musique pop*'

Jazz – *jazz (m)*

Listen to music – *écouter de la musique*

Play music – *faire de la musique*

Play an instrument – *jouer d'un instrument*

Piano – *piano (m)*

Flute – *flûte (f)*

Guitar – *guitare* (f)

Violin – *violon (m)*

Cello – *violoncelle* (m)

Nightclubs – *boîtes* (f, pl), *boîtes de nuit*

Photography – *photographie* (f)

To take photos – *prendre des photos*

Portrait – *portrait (m)*

Landscape – *paysage (f)*

Reading – *lecture (f)*

To read – *lire*

Novel – *roman (m)*

Detective novel – *roman (m) policier*

Classic novel – *roman classique*

Historical novel – *roman historique*

Biography – *biographie* (f)

Autobiography – *autobiographie* (f)

Fiction – *fiction (f)*

Literature – *literature (f)*

Magazine – *revue (f)*

Shopping – *faire du shopping*

Skiing – *faire du ski*

Swimming – *natation (f)*

To swim – *nager*

Tennis – *tennis* (m)

Play tennis – *jouer au tennis*

Squash – *squash (m)*

Play squash – *jouer au squash*

Handball – *handball* (m), or shortened to '*hand*' (m)

Play handball – *jouer au hand*

Rugby – *rugby (m)*

Play rugby – *jouer au rugby*

Traveling – *voyager, faire des voyages* (m pl)

Travels – *voyages* (m, pl)

TV – *télévision* (f), or shortened to '*la télé*' (f)

Watch TV – *regarder la télé*

Program – *émission* (f)

Favorite – *préféré*

Series – *série (f)*

Soap opera – *feuilleton (m) (à l'eau de rose)*

Documentary – *documentaire* (m)

Current affairs – *actualités (f, pl)*

News (program) – *informations* (f, pl), *infos* (f, pl), *journal* (m) (*télévisé*)

Internet – *internet (m)*

Surf the internet – *surfer sur internet*

Social media – *réseaux sociaux* (m, pl)

Dinners with friends – *dîners* (m, pl) *entre amis*

To go out – *sortir*

To surf – *surfer, faire du surf*

Windsurfing – *planche* (f) *à voile*

To windsurf – *faire de la planche à voile*

Karate – *karaté (m)*

Judo – *judo (m)*

Draughts – *dames* (f, pl)

Play cards – jouer aux cartes

Poker – *poker (m)*

Knitting – *tricot (m)*

To knit – *faire du tricot*

Sewing – *couture* (f)

Sew – *faire de la couture*

Crafts – *travaux (m, pl) manuels, artisanaux*

Play golf – *jouer au golf*

Play snooker – *jouer au snooker*

Sports center – *centre (m) sportif*

To sing – *chanter*

Horse riding – *équitation (f)*

Fencing – *escrime (m)*

Rock climbing – *escalade (m)*

Ice-skating – *patinage (m)*

Ice rink – *patinoire* (f)

Skateboarding – *skate (m)*

Water skiing – *ski (m) nautique*

Water sports – *sports (m, pl) aquatiques*

Reality TV – *télé-réalité (f)*

Sailing – *voile (f)*

Film star – *vedette (f)*

Celebrity – *célébrité (f)*

Volleyball – *volley (m)*

To know (*connaître and savoir*): conjugations and usage

The concept of "knowing" in other languages, including French, is often tricky. To know a person or a place is "*connaître*", but to know a fact is "savoir", as is to know a skill, to know how to do something, to be able to do something.

The construction is simple to say you know how to do something: *savoir* + infinitive. For example, *Je sais jouer aux échecs* – I know how to play chess.

Or in the case of "*connaître*", you just add the noun, as a direct object, so "*je connais Paris*" – I know Paris; "*je connais Annabel*" – I know Annabel; "*je le connais*" – I know it, or I know him; and "*je la connais*" – I know it, or I know her.

The only thing is that they're irregular…

Savoir translates to to know (how to), to be able to

Je sais translates to I know how to, I am able to, I can (with a skill), I know (a fact)

Tu sais translates to You know

Il/elle sait translates to He/she knows

Nous savons translates to We know

Vous savez translates to You know

Ils/elles savent translates to They know

You will also come across this quite often for "I know" translates to *je sais*; "I don't know" translates to *je ne sais pas*; and "you know/do you know" – *tu sais*, or *vous savez*.

Connaître

Je connais translates to I know (a person, a place…)

Tu connais

Il/ elle connait (connaît with the circumflex accent on the "I" is also correct)

Nous connaissons

Vous connaissez

Ils/ elles connaissent

Here is a way of summing up their differences: "*je connais le hand, mais je ne sais pas jouer au hand*" – basically "I know about handball intellectually speaking," "I am familiar with handball/the concept of handball," but "I don't know how to play it."

Or try "*je connais Londres, mais je ne sais pas comment y aller*" – meaning, I know London, but I don't know how to get there. Or "*je connais Marie, mais je ne sais pas quel âge elle a*" – I know Maria (as a person, who she is), but I don't know the fact/information of what age she is.

Faire or jouer

In the list of words above, there are several sport nouns, but how do you go about saying that you "practice" them? Here is a quick rule, which will keep you right most of the time:

If it is a team sport, you will often use "*jouer*" – for example, *je joue au foot, je joue au rugby, elle joue au volley*.

Note that it is "*jouer à*" + a sport.

Also note that although racket sports are not technically team sports, you also "*joue*" them – *je joue au tennis, je joue au bad, je joue au squash*. Likewise, golf, chess, and some others.

For many of the other sports, you will use the verb *"faire"*, and more specifically, *"faire de"*. For example: *Je fais du judo, je fais du ski, je fais de la voile*.

To say that you can manage to do something in a very idiomatic way

There are two ways of saying that you can do something, that you manage to do something, which will automatically boost your fluency points.

They are: *réussir à and arriver à* (+ infinitive)

So: *j'arrive à jouer au piano* – I can play piano, I manage to play the piano.

J'arrive à jouer au golf deux fois par semaine – I manage to play golf twice a week.

Je réussis à jouer la nouvelle chanson de Pink au piano – I can/I can manage to play Pink's next song on the piano.

Chapter 7 - So Many Roads and So Many Places

I personally love to walk. When I was younger and single, I would put my earphones in and walk through any new city I got the chance to visit. Now, with my girlfriend, I put the headphones away and we enjoy long chats while walking and looking around. Sometimes she takes pictures, and they are mostly of me taking pictures of her or the landscape. But I enjoy watching her under all the different shades and lights. Have you ever noticed how every city has different colors and vibes?

Back to business. Tell me, what do you typically want to visit first when exploring a new city? Wherever you want to go, I am here to help you. Why don't we start with a few basics?

Museum	*Musée*
Where is the Louvres Museum?	*Où se trouve le musée du Louvres?*

Mu-zé

Square	*Place*
How can I get to Saint-Georges Square?	*Comment puis-je me rendre à la place Saint-Georges?*

Pla-ssuh

Avenue	*Avenue*
What can I find on the main avenue?	*Que puis-je trouver sur l'avenue principale?*

Ah-veh-nuh

This one should not be a problem. The pronunciation is very similar to the English "avenue".

Monuments	*Monuments*
Paris is rich in history and monuments.	*Paris est riche en histoire et monuments.*

Moh-nuh-men

Park	*Parc*
Park Buttes-Chaumont is in Paris.	*Le Parc Buttes-Chaumont se situe à Paris.*

Par-k

Church	*Eglise*
They gave me this church as a reference.	*Ils m'ont donné cette église comme référence.*

Ee-glee-zuh

Not to be disrespectful, but travelling is not just about history and monuments. It is also about having fun and experiencing the true local culture, as well as going to bars and clubs.

Bar	Bar
Where is this bar?	Où se trouve ce bar?

See? Globalization scores again!

Now that you have learned the name of some places, let's go there together.

Across	En face
You can find them across the avenue.	Vous pouvez les trouver en face de l'avenue.

En fah-suh

In front of	Devant
He is waiting in front of the statue.	Il attend devant la statue.

Deh-van

Opposite	Opposé
We were walking in the opposite direction.	Nous étions en train de marcher du côté opposé.

Oh-poo-zé

Street	Rue
You can find it down the street.	Vous pouvez trouver ça en bas de la rue.

ruh

Subway	Métro
We can get there by subway.	Nous pouvons nous y rendre en métro.

Meh-troh – This word comes from "Metropolitain" which as you can guess, means "Metropolitan".

Mall	Centre commercial
What kind of mall would you like to visit?	Quel type de centre commercial souhaiteriez-vous visiter?

Cen-truh ko-mer-sial

Recommend	Recommander
What can you recommend?	Qu'est-ce que vous recommandez?

Re-co-men-déh

"*Recommander*" is a general word for "suggestions". So, whenever you are out of ideas, just remember this one.

In terms of tourism, you should already be an expert at getting around. You learned how to request a cab, rent a car, and ask for directions and recommendations. You are almost done with this section, so why don't we practice a little more?

Front desk (*Reception*):	Hello! How can I help you?
	Bonjour! Comment puis-je vous aider?
Allen:	I would like some recommendations for places to visit.
	J'aimerais avoir des recommandations d'endroits à visiter.
Front desk:	Very well. What type of place did you have in mind? A club, a museum?
	Très bien. Quel type d'endroit aviez-vous en tête? Un club, un musée?
Allen:	I heard that you have beautiful squares and monuments in this city.
	J'ai entendu que vous aviez des places et des monuments magnifiques dans la ville.
Front desk:	That is true. Sadly, most cultural attractions are across town.
	C'est vrai. Malheureusement, la plupart des attractions touristiques sont de l'autre côté de la ville.
Philip:	Oh, I see. Could you give me some directions, please?
	Oh, je vois. Pouvez-vous m'indiquer comment m'y rendre, s'il-vous-plaît?
Front desk:	Sure! Would you like to travel by car or take the subway?
	Bien-sûr! Vous préférez vous y rendre en voiture ou plutôt prendre le métro?
Philip:	I would rather take a subway and walk.
	Je préfèrerais prendre le métro et marcher.
Front desk:	Very well. The subway is only 300m away.
	Très bien. Le métro se trouve à seulement 300m d'ici.
Philip:	Perfect! How do I get there?
	Parfait! Comment puis-je m'y rendre?
Front desk:	You only have to go down this street, take a right, and walk straight for 200m.
	Vous avez seulement à descendre la rue, prendre à droite puis marcher tout droit pendant 200m.
Philip:	That sounds easy. Thank you very much!
	Ça à l'air facile. Merci beaucoup!
Front desk:	All right, then. After you get to the subway, go to the mainline and take a train to

étoile station.

D'accord, alors, en arrivant au métro, allez à la ligne principale et prenez le métro jusqu'à la station étoile.

Philip: Very good. I appreciate your help.

                 Très bien. Merci pour votre aide.

Front desk: My pleasure. Have a nice day.

                 Avec Plaisir. Bonne journée.

Allen: Likewise. Bye.

                 Egalement. Au revoir.

Ready to walk around the city and get lost in its little streets? I'm sure you can't wait. Then you'd better get ready. Go out and have fun. Who knows how many funny stories you will be able to tell once back from your trip!

Chapter 8 - Rent and Car driving

Routes / Roads's Vocabulary

Whether you are moving there or just visiting on holiday, be sure to learn this list of key phrases relating to hiring a car in France, French road signs and other key phrases relating to driving in France.

La route principale / the main road

Le périphérique / a bypass

Un cul-de-sac / a dead-end street

Un péage / a toll road

Une autoroute / a motorway (Am. freeway)

Une nationale / an A-road (Am. highway)

Une piste cyclable / a cycle lane/a cycleway

Une route / a road (between towns)

Une route à quatre voies / a dual carriageway (Am. divided highway)

Une route à sens unique / a one-way street

Une route régionale / a B-road (Am. secondary road)

Une voie / a lane

Car Rentals

Conditions you should know:

In France, to be able to rent a car, you must be: 21 years, have a 1 year old license, be able to present proof of identity (passport, identity card) to the tenant and also provide the original copy of your driver's license.

Here are the key car rental agencies in France: Europcar, Avis, Hertz, Sixt, Rentacar

Hire car glossary

I would like to rent a car. / *Je voudrais louer une voiture.*

How much is it per day? / *C'est combien par jour?*

Is insurance included in the price? / *Est-ce que l'assurance est comprise?*

I made a booking last month. / *J'ai fait une réservation le mois dernier.*

I need a transfer from the city to the airport. / *J'ai besoin d'un transfert ville-aéroport.*

I need a 4×4 for the mountains. / *Il me faut un 4×4 (quatre-quatre or 'cat-cat' phonetically) pour la montagne.*

Do you have a camper-van available in Provence next week? / *Avez-vous un camping-car disponible en*

Provence la semaine prochaine?

Is it possible to have a car with a driver? / *Est-ce possible d'avoir une voiture avec chauffeur?*

I would like to modify/change an existing reservation. / *Je voudrais modifier une réservation existante.*

I have to cancel my reservation. / *Je dois annuler ma réservation.*

Where is your office? / *Où se trouve votre agence?*

Key Words And Phrases When Driving:

Some essential French road signs

Follow the signs. / *Suivez les panneaux.*

Agricultural vehicles have right of way. / *Priorité aux véhicules agricoles.*

You do not have right of way. / *Vous n'avez pas la priorité.*

Exit for vehicles. / *Sortie véhicules*

Parking prohibited. / *Stationnement interdit.*

Slow down (for our children). / *Ralentissez (pour nos enfants).*

Exit / *Sortie*

Give way / *Cédez le passage*

One way / *Sens unique*

Town centre / *Centre ville*

Diversion / *Déviation*

All exits must be kept clear. / *Toutes les sorties doivent rester dégagées.*

Railway station / *Gare SNCF*

Narrow lanes / *Files étroites*

Keep in lane. / *Ne changez pas de file.*

Get in lane. / *Mettez-vous dans/sur la bonne file.*

No overtaking. / *Interdiction de doubler/dépasser.*

Deliveries / *Livraisons*

No loading or unloading. / *Interdiction de charger ou de décharger.*

Restricted parking zone / *Zone bleue*

Pedestrian precinct / *Zone piétonne/piétonnière*

Traffic / *La circulation*

A traffic jam / *Un embouteillage*

Reminder of the speed limit. / *Rappel de limitation de vitesse*

An estate car / *Un break*

A touring-car / *Une voiture de tourisme*

At the gas station:

La voiture n'a plus d'essence.	This car is out of gas.
Où est-ce qu'il y a une station-service près d'ici?	Where is there a gas station near here?
Le plein, s'il vous plaît.	Fill it up, please.
Vingt litres, s'il vous plaît.	20 liters, please.
Cette voiture utilise de l'essence ordinaire.	This car uses regular gas.
Cette voiture utilise de l'essence sans plomb.	This car uses unleaded gas.
Cette voiture utilise du diesel.	This car uses diesel.
Est-ce que c'est la bonne route pour Paris?	Is this the right road for Paris?
Voici mon permis de conduire.	Here is my driver's license.
Est-ce que je roulais trop rapidement?	Was I driving too fast?
la location de voitures	car rental
louer une voiture	to rent a car
réserver une voiture	reserve a car
prendre la voiture	to take / pick up the car
rendre la voiture	to return the car

Car's Renting

J'aimerais louer une voiture, s'il vous plaît.	I'd like to rent a car please.
Avez-vous une voiture manuelle?	Do you have a manual shift car?
Avez-vous une voiture automatique?	Do you have an automatic (car)?
C'est combien pour louer par jour, s'il vous plaît?	How much is it to rent per day, please?
C'est combien pour louer par semaine, s'il vous plaît?	How much is it to rent per week, please?
Je voudrais....	I would like....
...une voiture compacte.	...a compact car.
...une voiture intermédiaire.	...a mid-sized car.
...une grosse voiture.	...a big car.
...une petite voiture.	...a small car.
...un quatre-quatre.	...a 4 x 4.
...un camion.	...a truck.

...une voiture de luxe.	...a luxury car.
...une voiture hybride.	...a hybrid car.
...une voiture électrique.	...an electric car.

Vehicle Parts:

Le frein	Brake
Le frein à main	Hand brake
Le siège conducteur	Driver seat
La ceinture de sécurité	Seat belt
Le klaxon	Horn
Le tableau de bord	Dashboard
Le clignotant	Indicator / blinker
Le phare	Headlight
Les feux de route (plein phare)	Full beam lights
Les feux de croisement	Dipped headlights
Le rétroviseur	Rearview mirror / side mirror
L'embrayage	Clutch
Le volant	Steering wheel
L'accélérateur (m)	Accelerator / Gas pedal
Un champignon	Accelerator (informal)
L'allumage (m)	Ignition system
La boîte de vitesses	Gear box
Le levier de vitesses	Gear stick
La boîte manuelle	Manual transmission / Stick shift
La transmission automatique	Automatic transmission
Le toit ouvrant	Sky-light
La décapotable, le cabriolet	Convertible
L'appui-tête (m)	Headrest
Le moteur	Motor
Le capot	Hood
Le coffre arrière	Rear boot
L'aile (f)	Wing
Le réservoir	Petrol/gas tank
De l'essence (f)	Gas / petrol

Du sans plomb (essence)	Unleaded gas
Du super (essence)	Premium gas
Le gasoil, gazole	Diesel
La jauge à huile	Oil dip stick
La bougie (=candle)	Spark plug
Le piston	Piston
Le cylindre	Cylinder
Le carter	Sump
La soupape	Valve
Le radiateur	Radiator
La courroie de ventilation	Fan belt
La roue de secours	Spare wheel
La roue	Wheel
L'enjoliveur (m)	Wheel hub
La tête de delco	Distributor cap
La batterie	Battery
Le pare-brise	Windscreen
La lunette arrière	Rear windscreen
Le cric	Jack
Les feux de détresse	Warning/distress lights
L'essuie-glace (m)	Windscreen wiper
Le pneu	Tyre
Le pneu neige	Snow tyre
Le pneu clouté	Studded tyre
La boîte à gants	Glove box
La serrure de portière	Door lock
La vitre	Window
Le pot d'échappement	Exhaust pipe
L'amortisseur (m)	Shock absorber
Le permis de conduire	Driving license

Other Driving Expressions:

Conduire	to drive
Démarrer le moteur	to start the engine

Se mettre en marche (m)	to start moving
Changer de vitesse	to change gear
Rouler	to move forward
Dépasser	to pass
Accélérer	to accelerate
Doubler	to overtake
Freiner	to brake
S'arrêter	to stop

Chapter 9 - Eat, Travel, Love

Food is one of my favorite parts of traveling. Eating is an awesome way to learn a bit more about the culture and history of each place. Your nose and tongue become guides that can lead you through unknown passages, allowing you to enjoy the aromas of France in a glass of Cabernet; or to experience the culinary revolution in Paris, in the shape of a sweet and crusty croissant. Flavors are unique everywhere you go, and that is what makes them a huge part of traveling.

For this reason, I want to be sure I am giving you the opportunity to have the best experience. Plus, ordering food is a recurrent activity, which means you will have many chances to practice. I can also assure you something: some of the best typical food places will not have a translator. With that in mind, let's start this chapter.

Restaurant	*Restaurant*
Let's go into that restaurant.	*Rentrons dans ce restaurant.*

Rehs-to-ran

It is very similar to the English word, except for the intonation (Also, French people don't pronounce the "t" at the end.)

Table	*Table*
Table for four, please.	*Une table pour quatre, s'il-vous-plaît.*

Once again, the word is the same but the pronunciation is not. The French way to pronounce is: Tah-bluh".

Suggestions	*Suggestions*
Do you want to hear today's suggestions?	*Vous voulez voir les suggestions du jour?*

Suh-gest-eeon

Portion	*Portion*
I want a portion of fries.	*J'aimerais avoir une portion de frites.*

Pors-eeon

Quite easy, huh?

Fork	*Fourchette*
I dropped my fork.	*J'ai fait tomber ma fourchette.*

Foor-chett

Spoon	Cuillère
Can I get a spoon?	Puis-je avoir une cuillère?

Cu-ee-eh-ruh

Knife	Couteau
I will need a meat knife.	J'aurais besoin d'un couteau à viande.

Koo-toh

Plate	Assiette
Can you bring an extra plate?	Pouvez-vous apporter une assiette en plus?

Ass-ee-et

Entry	Entrée
Do you want an entry?	Voulez-vous une entrée?

An-tré

Main dish	Plat principal
For the main dish, I want the chicken.	En plat principal, j'aimerais le poulet.

Pla-prehn-si-pal

Well-cooked	Bien cuit
I want my steak well-cooked.	J'aimerais mon steak bien cuit.

Bee-n koo-ee

"Bien" (Bee-n) means "good".

Medium	A point
Medium is fine for me.	A point, ça me convient.

Ah poo-ehn

Dessert	Dessert
Of course, I want a dessert.	Bien-sûr que j'aimerais avoir un dessert.

Deh-ssehr (The "s" is pronounced as "s", not as a "z", like the English way.)

Vegan	*Végétalien*
Do you have a vegan menu?	*Est-ce que vous avez un menu végétalien?*

Veh-geh-tal-ee-ehn (Note that French people also say "vegan" sometimes, so they will probably understand this word, especially in restaurants).

Check	*Addition*
I want the check, please.	*J'aimerais avoir l'addition, s'il-vous-plaît.*

Ah-dee-ssion

Are you excited to order your first dish? Why don't we go practice a bit more first.

Waiter (*serveur*):	Good afternoon! Welcome to our restaurant. My name is Shawn. How many are you?
	Bonjour! Bienvenue dans notre restaurant. Mon nom est Shawn. Vous êtes combien?
Mike:	Hello! We have a reservation under Paulson. Table for four.
	Bonjour! Nous avons une réservation sous le nom de Paulson, table pour quatre.
Waiter:	Yes, here you are. Come with me, please.
	Oui, je vois. Venez avec moi, s'il-vous-plaît.
Mike:	I would like to order right away. We are starving.
	J'aimerais commander maintenant. Nous sommes morts de faim.
Waiter:	Perfect. What would you like to order?
	Parfait. Que voulez-vous commander?
Mike:	What are your suggestions?
	Quelles sont vos suggestions?
Waiter:	The lobster ceviche as an appetizer. For the main dish, we have a beef tartare which is excellent.
	Le ceviche de homard en entrée. En plat principal, nous avons un excellent tartare de boeuf.
Mike:	Sounds great! I want one of each. Also, a salad and two beef dishes.
	Ça a l'air fabuleux! Je voudrais un de chaque. Aussi, une salade et deux plats à base de boeuf.
Waiter:	Do you want extra plates to share?
	Vous voulez des assiettes pour partager?
Mike:	Yes, please.
	Oui, s'il-vous-plaît.
Waiter:	Perfect. I will be back in a second with your plates, forks, and meat knives.

	Parfait. Je reviens dans une seconde avec vos assiettes, fourchettes et couteaux à viande.
Mike:	Thank you very much.
	Merci beaucoup.
Waiter:	I'll be right back.
	Je reviens tout de suite.

I bet this chapter was easy. How did you feel after repeating that last dialogue? Look... I do not want to freak you out, but you are about to feel a bit under the weather.

Chapter 10 - To the Grocery Store - *À l'épicerie*

Gunter détestait faire les courses. Il y avait toujours trop de monde, et il finissait toujours par partir avec beaucoup plus que ce qu'il avait l'intention d'acheter.

Gunter hated going grocery shopping. There were always too many people, and he always ended up leaving with way more than he had intended to buy.

Il supposait que c'était probablement de sa faute puisqu'il n'avait pas fait de liste, mais il ne pouvait pas s'en faire. Il s'est dit qu'il savait assez bien ce qu'il avait à la maison et qu'il réussissait toujours à obtenir ces articles... ainsi qu'une dizaine d'autres dont il n'avait pas besoin.

He supposed that was probably his own fault for not writing a list, but he could not be bothered. He figured he knew well enough what he was out of at home and did always manage to get those items...along with ten or so more that he did not need.

Il a blâmé leur publicité.

He blamed their advertising.

Et le fait qu'il ne faisait ses courses que quand il avait faim. Une mauvaise idée? Oui. Aura-t-il vu cela changer dans un proche avenir? Probablement pas.

And the fact that he only ever found himself shopping when he was hungry. A bad idea? Yes. Did he see that changing in the near future? Probably not.

Gunter s'est rendu à l'entrée de l'épicerie, prenant un chariot avant d'entrer.

Gunter made his way to the grocery store entrance, grabbing a cart before entering.

Il s'est immédiatement rendu à l'arrière du magasin, comme il l'a toujours fait, et s'est mis à avancer. Il parcourait généralement toutes les allées pour ne rien rater de ce dont il avait besoin --- même si c'est certainement ainsi qu'il finissait avec tant d'articles supplémentaires dans son chariot.

He immediately made his way to the back of the store, as he always did, and proceeded to work his way forward. He generally walked through all of the aisles so that he would not miss anything he needed – though this was certainly how he ended up with so many extra items in his cart.

Il n'y avait rien à faire, cependant. Il s'était résigné à partir avec plus qu'il n'était venu à la seconde où il avait décidé qu'il devait aller à l'épicerie en premier.

It could not be helped, though. He had resigned himself to leaving with more than he came for the second he decided he needed to go grocery shopping in the first place.

Gunter marchait dans l'allée des fruits et légumes, se souvenant vaguement qu'il avait besoin de légumes et de fruits.

Gunter walked through the produce aisle, vaguely remembering that he needed vegetables and fruit.

Il a choisi quatre pommes, deux pamplemousses, cinq pêches, un sac de raisins et trois bananes, les mettant tous dans son chariot. Il hésita un moment entre mûres et fraises avant de se décider à prendre les mûres.

He picked out four apples, two grapefruits, five peaches, a bag of grapes, and three bananas, putting them all in his cart. He debated between blackberries and strawberries for a moment before settling on the blackberries.

Il s'est ensuite dirigé vers les légumes. Il savait qu'il avait besoin de choux-fleurs, de pommes de terre, d'oignons et de haricots verts, mais il ne pouvait s'empêcher d'ajouter des épinards, de la laitue et des carottes aussi.

He then made his way toward the vegetables. He knew he needed cauliflower, potatoes, onions, and green beans, but could not stop himself from adding spinach, lettuce, and carrots too.

Il secoua la tête, n'étant pas impressionné par le fait qu'il ajoutait déjà des extras. Cela n'était certainement pas de bon augure pour le reste de ces courses.

He shook his head at himself, not impressed that he was already adding extras. This certainly did not bode well for the rest of this trip.

Gunter s'est ensuite dirigé vers les réfrigérateurs. Il avait besoin d'œufs, de beurre, de lait et de crème fraîche. Après avoir pris ceux-là, il a regardé le yaourt à la fraise et a décidé de l'acheter aussi.

Gunter then headed toward the fridges. He needed eggs, butter, milk, and cream cheese. After grabbing those he looked at strawberry yogurt, deciding to get it as well.

Il cherchait de la saucisse de foie, mais il n'arrivait pas à en trouver. En regardant autour de lui, il a vu une employée remplir les étagères un peu plus loin de lui et a décidé de lui demander.

He was searching for liverwurst, but could not seem to find it anywhere. Looking around, he spotted an employee filling shelves a bit further away from him and decided to ask her.

"Savez-vous où est la saucisse de foie?"

"Do you know where the liverwurst is?"

"Oh, ouais. On vient de les déplacer. C'est juste ici." dit-elle, en montrant du doigt la viande de charcuterie qu'elle stockait.

"Oh, yeah. We just moved it. It is right here." She said, pointing next to the deli meat she was stocking.

"Merci." dit-il, en l'attrapant et continuant à se frayer un chemin dans le magasin.

"Thank you." He said, grabbing it and continuing to make his way through the store.

Il s'est retrouvé dans l'allée voisine à choisir entre deux sortes de céréales différentes. L'homme à quelques mètres de lui semblait faire la même chose, et au bout d'un moment, ils ont ri tous les deux.

He found himself in the next aisle deciding between two different kinds of cereal. The man a few feet away from him seemed to be doing the same thing, and after a moment they both laughed.

"On pourrait penser que ce n'est pas si difficile à décider." dit Gunter, en repensant aux options qui s'offraient à lui.

"You would think it would not be this hard to decide." Said Gunter, looking back at the options in front of him.

L'homme hocha la tête: "D'habitude, ma copine fait l'épicerie, mais elle n'est pas là pour la semaine."

The man nodded, "My girlfriend usually does the grocery shopping, but she is out of town for the week."

"Alors, vous êtes tout seul."

"So, you are on your own."

Il rit et acquiesça, "Exactement. C'est vraiment plus difficile que je ne le pensais."

He laughed and agreed, "Exactly. It is really ending up being more difficult than I thought."

"Avez-vous essayé celui-ci?" demanda Gunter en montrant un de ses paquets de céréales préférées.

"Have you tried this one?" asked Gunter, pointing to one of his favorite cereals.

L'homme secoua la tête.

The man shook his head.

"J'essayerais bien." Lui a-t-il répondu:"C'est une bonne idée."

"I would give it a try." He encouraged, "It is definitely a good one."

"Merci," dit-il en prenant une boîte sur l'étagère et en la jetant dans son chariot,"Souhaitez-moi bonne chance."

"Thanks," he said, taking a box from the shelf and tossing it into his cart, "Wish me luck."

L'homme est sorti de l'allée, laissant Gunter décider de ses propres céréales. Suivant ses propres conseils, il prit les mêmes céréales qu'il venait de recommander et se dirigea vers l'allée suivante.

The man headed out of the aisle, leaving Gunter to decide on his own cereal. Taking his own advice, he took the same cereal he had just recommended and made his way to the next aisle.

Il a ramassé des choses au hasard dans les deux allées suivantes --- du mélange à gâteau, du chocolat Milka et un paquet de chewing-gum.

He picked up random things from the next two aisles – cake mix, Milka chocolate, and a pack of gum.

Dans l'allée suivante, Gunter a ajouté des pâtes et du riz à son chariot, ainsi que quelques boîtes de haricots, du maïs et des haricots verts. Il avait l'intention de faire un ragoût de haricots verts, alors il a aussi pris un pot de cubes de bouillon.

In the next aisle, Gunter added pasta and rice to his cart, along with a few cans of beans, corn, and green beans. He was planning to make green bean stew, so he grabbed a jar of bouillon cubes as well.

Il a décidé de prendre un paquet de boeuf et s'est assuré d'avoir tout ce qu'il fallait pour son dîner de ce soir. Une fois qu'il était sûr, il avait tout ce qu'il voulait dans le magasin.

He decided to grab a package of beef and made sure he had everything for his dinner tonight. Once he was sure, he had everything he continued through the store.

Il a décidé de se procurer du pain frais et du fromage dans la petite boulangerie de l'épicerie.

He decided to get some fresh bread and cheese from the little bakery inside the grocery store.

Après avoir examiné les options pendant un moment, il avait pris sa décision.

After looking over the options for a moment, he had made up his mind.

"Je peux avoir quatre petits pains et une demi-livre de brie?" demanda Gunter au vieil homme derrière le comptoir.

"Can I get four rolls and half a pound of brie?" Gunter asked the older man behind the counter.

"Bien sûr." dit-il en prenant un sac en papier et en le remplissant de petits pains avant d'aller chercher le fromage derrière la vitrine. Une fois qu'il l'avait tranché, emballé et mis dans le sac, il a tout donné à Gunter.

"Of course." He said, grabbing a paper bag and filling it with the rolls before getting the cheese from behind the glass case. Once he had sliced it, wrapped it, and added it to the bag, he handed everything to Gunter.

"Voilà pour toi. Passez une bonne journée."

"There you go. Have a nice day."

483

"Je vous remercie. Vous aussi." Dit Gunter, en se dirigeant vers la section des congélateurs.

"Thank you. You too." Said Gunter, making his way to the freezer section.

Il a pris quelques plats congelés, des bâtonnets de mozzarella et de la crème glacée à la vanille avant de finalement se rendre à la caisse.

He grabbed a few frozen dinners, mozzarella sticks, and vanilla ice cream before finally making his way to the register.

La file d'attente était assez longue, mais elle s'est rétrécie assez rapidement, et assez rapidement, il a placé ses articles sur le comptoir.

The line was fairly long but moved pretty quickly, and soon enough he was placing his items onto the counter.

"Bonjour! Vous avez tout trouvé? demanda la jeune femme derrière la caisse enregistreuse au moment où elle commençait à scanner ses objets.

"Hello! Did you find everything okay?" asked the young lady behind the register as she began scanning his items.

Il hocha la tête: "Plus que ce dont j'avais besoin, comme d'habitude."

He nodded, "More than I needed, as usual."

Elle rit, "J'entends cela toute la journée. Vous n'êtes certainement pas le seul."

She laughed, "I hear that all day. You are certainly not the only one."

"Vous avez besoin de sacs?"

"Do you need any bags?"

Gunter secoua la tête en tirant trois sacs en tissu de son sac à dos: "Non, je les ai."

Gunter shook his head, pulling three cloth bags from his backpack, "No, I have got these."

"Votre total est de 98,45 euros."

"Your total is 98.45 Euro."

Gunter a sorti 100 euros en billets de 20 euros et les a remis à la caissière.

Gunter pulled out a hundred in the twenties and handed them to the cashier.

Une fois qu'elle lui avait rendu sa monnaie, il a poussé son chariot jusqu'au comptoir opposé pour charger ses provisions dans ses sacs. Après quelques minutes, il a tout emballé et a poussé le chariot avec ses trois sacs hors de l'épicerie.

Once she had given him his change, he pushed his cart over to the opposite counter to load his groceries into his bags. After a few minutes, he had everything packed away and pushed the cart with his three bags back out of the grocery store.

Il a chargé ses sacs sur le panier à l'avant de sa bicyclette et a commencé le retour rapide à la maison.

He loaded his bags onto the basket on the front of his bike and began the quick ride home.

Chapter 11: Numbers and Pronunciation

Say the numbers aloud many times for each group before moving on to the next group.

One to Ten

1 is pronounced [uhhn], 2 is pronounced duuh], 3 is pronounced [t-r-wah] (rolled r), 4 is pronounced [cat-ruh](rolled r), 5 is pronounced [sank], 6 is pronounced [see-s], 7 is pronounced [set], 8 is pronounced [wee-t], 9 is pronounced [nuuf], 10 is pronounced [dee-s]

Let's have a look at the French spellings of these numerals. While reading, you may come across written numbers rather than just the numbers themselves. The spelling is different from the example above, but the pronunciation is the same.

Un - deux - trois - quatre - cinq - six - sept - huit - neuf - dix

One - two - three - four - five - six - seven - eight - nine - ten

Check the pronunciations of these numerals alongside their written French counterparts. You may now use what you learned here in conjunction with what you learned about the alphabet in the previous section. You may have noticed that although the number 6 is written the same way in both French and English, it is pronounced considerably differently. You may also try to find regularities in the way that different combinations of letters modify the final sound. Consider the French words deux and dix; they both start with a d and end with an x, but are pronounced differently. Now let's have a look at the range from 11 to 19.

Eleven to Nineteen

11 is pronounced [oh-n-z], 12 is pronounced [doo-z], 13 is pronounced [t-r-ez](rolled r), 14 is pronounced [cat-or-z], 15 is pronounced [k-an-z], 16 is pronounced [s-ez], 17 is pronounced [dee-set], 18 is pronounced [dee-sweet], 19 is pronounced [dee-s-nuf]

Despite sounding very different from their English counterparts, there are cues in the pronunciation that help identify which digit is being spoken. If you look at the words for eleven through nineteen and compare them to the words from one through ten, you'll realize that the lower number is frequently contained within the larger one.

11 - 12 - 13 - 14 - 15 - 16 - 17 - 18 - 19

Onze - douze - treize - quatorze - quinze - seize - dix sept - dix huit - dix neuf

Except for starting with the identical letters as one and two, onze and douze have no pattern. Remember those two. Quinze since it has no pattern, it must be memorized like these two. Notice that treize begins with t and r, which are also the first letters of the French number 3, *trois*. Quatorze and seize also start with *quatre* and *six*, respectively. As long as you know numbers one to ten, this method will help you guess what number is being uttered or written. *Dix-sept, dix-huit, and dix-neuf* all include ten. These are ten-seven, ten-eight, and ten-nine. Reducing any number from eleven to nineteen can help you identify it. To analyze the number, find the smaller number (1–10) inside the larger number (11–19). Now that you know numbers 1–19, we'll go on to 20–100. Once you grasp the pattern of these numbers, you can say anything in French!

Twenty to Sixty

20 (Twenty) is translated to French *vingt* and pronounced [v-ain-t].

30 (Thirty) is translated to French and pronounced *trente* [t-ron-t] (with a rolled r)

40 (Forty) is translated to French and pronounced *quarante* [ka-ron-t] (with a rolled r)

50 (Fifty) is translated to French and pronounced *cinquante* [s-ain-k-ont]

60 (Sixty) is translated to French and pronounced *soixante* [s-wah-s-ont]

We'll discuss each group of numbers between these terms after you learn them. Repeat until you're comfortable.

Every number in the range from twenty to sixty-nine, including twenty-one and forty-three, follows the same pattern. As an illustration, let's take a look at the numbers between twenty-one and twenty-nine.

21, *vingt et un*. Any number between twenty and sixty-one with a one at the end starts with a multiple of 10 (vingt, trente, quarante, cinquante, or soixante) and ends with et un, which means and one in English. This rule is simple.

21, 31, 41, 51, 61.

Twenty-one, thirty-one, forty-one, fifty-one, sixty-one.

Vingt et un, trente et un, quarante et un, cinquante et un, soixante et un

is pronounced [v-ain-t][eyy][uhhn], is pronounced [t-ron-t](with a rolled r)[eyy][uhhn], is pronounced [ka-ron-t] (with a rolled r)[eyy][uhhn], is pronounced [s-ain-k-ont][eyy][uhhn], is pronounced [s-wah-s-ont][eyy][uhhn].

We will now look at the patterns and rules for all the numbers between twenty and sixty-nine that finish in a digit other than zero or one, assuming you are already familiar with the preceding material. All of these numerical values are simple to understand. *Vingt, trente, quarante, cinquante,* or *soixante* are all good places to start. The following digit will be indicated by a hyphen. Numbers 22 to 29 shown below provide an illustration of this.

22, vingt-deux, 23 vingt-trois, 24 vingt-quatre, 25 vingt-cinq, 26 vingt-six, 27 vingt-sept, 28 vingt-huit, 29 vingt-neuf.

Any number between one and ten can be constructed using this rule if one knows the multiples of ten from twenty to sixty. To use, simply replace the first or second numeral with the appropriate word. Since the digits following the hyphen do not change, hearing or reading these numbers is straightforward; all you have to do is add the two digits together. Here are some practice exercises you can use to see how much you remember from our discussions thus far. Say the numbers out loud so you do them to obtain optimal results.

Seventy to Ninety-Nine

Seventy through ninety-nine are next. Before proceeding to this part, make sure you're comfortable with the numbers above, especially 11–19. Always read these numbers loudly and go over them several times before going on.

70 Seventy is written in French *Soixante-Dix* and is pronounced [s-wah-s-ont] [dee-s]

80, Eighty is written in French *Quatre-Vingts* and is pronounced [cat-ruh](rolled r)[v-ain-t]

90, Ninety is written in French *Quatre-Vingt-Dix* and is pronounced [cat-ruh](rolled r)[v-ain-t][dee-s]

The names of these three digits may be difficult to keep straight at first glance. However, if we dissect them, we can see that they make a lot of sense and will actually tell us which number they are referring to.

As a starting point, let's examine the number 70 (or *Soixante-Dix* in French). *Soixante* combines the words for "sixteen" and "nine" to form this composite number. *Soixante* means sixty, and we now know that *dix* means ten. Adding up the digits, we get 70, which is the result of adding 60 and 10. I'll now explain how this rule applies to the other two digits.

The name *Quatre-Vingt* is a combination of the French words for four and twenty, respectively. Thus, eighty can be written as *Quatre-Vingt*, which literally translates to "Four-Twenty," since four twenties equals eighty. Since 80 is 4 x 20, this makes sense.

Therefore, the meaning of *Quatre-Vingt-Dix* is derived from a synthesis of the latter two approaches. *Dix* and *Quatre-Vingt* both translate to ten and four twenties, respectively. Four twenties plus ten is the result of adding these together. 4x20+10=90. That makes 90 altogether. These last three numbers, and the ones before them, are useful because they allow us to determine which number we are looking at by dissecting the names into their component parts and analyzing them separately before reassembling them into a whole.

70 is written *Soixante-Dix* and is pronounced [s-wah-s-ont] [dee-s]

Seventy, we have already examined as sixty plus ten. Below are the numbers between seventy-one and seventy-nine.

71 is written *Soixante-et-onze* and is pronounced [s-wah-s-ont][ayy][oh-n-z]

Similar to the other numbers we've looked at that end in one, the pattern for 71 involves inserting the word and(et) between the first and second digits. Here, however, we say "sixty and eleven" instead of "seventy and one," just as we do with the numbers 21, 31, 41, 51, and 61. It wouldn't sound very nice to say sixty-ten and one, or *Soixante-Dix et Un*, because the number seventy is pronounced as sixty-ten. That's just too much to chew on and say in one go. Therefore, sixty-and-eleven is pronounced as soixante-et-onze. We aim to avoid expressing a number with too many extra syllables, so if you remember that they all make sense if you break them down into smaller bits, you'll have no trouble comprehending them!

72 is written *Soixante-douze* and is pronounced [s-wah-s-ont][doo-z]

73 is written *Soixante-treize* and is pronounced [s-wah-s-ont][t-r-ez](rolled r)

74 is written *Soixante-quatorze* and is pronounced [s-wah-s-ont][cat-or-z]

75 is written *Soixante-quinze* and is pronounced [s-wah-s-ont][k-an-z]

76 is written *Soixante-seize* and is pronounced [s-wah-s-ont][s-ez]

77 is written *Soixante-dix-sept* and is pronounced [s-wah-s-ont][dee-set]

78 is written *Soixante dix-huit* and is pronounced [s-wah-s-ont][dee-sweet]

79 is written *Soixante-dix-neuf* and is pronounced [s-wah-s-ont][dee-s-nuf]

The numbers here, like the number Seventy-One or *Soixante-et-onze*, take the *Dix* or the Ten from the term *Soixante-Dix* (70) and replace it with the numbers that come following ten (eleven, twelve, thirteen, etc.). This is very similar to how the number Seventy-One or *Soixante-et-onze* is written. As was the case earlier, this is done to prevent one's mouth from becoming too full. When you consider them separately, for instance as sixty-two (72) or seventy-two (73), it becomes clear why we chose to call it in this fashion. The same holds true for the numbers between ninety and ninety-nine, which we will examine right now while this idea is still very fresh in your memory because we want to make sure that you have a complete understanding of it.

90 is written *Quatre-Vingt-Dix* and is pronounced [cat-ruh](rolled r)[v-ain-t][dee-s]

91 is written *Quatre-Vingt Onze* and is pronounced cat-ruh](rolled r)[v-ain-t][oh-n-z]

92 is written *Quatre-Vingt Douze* and is pronounced [cat-ruh](rolled r)[v-ain-t][doo-z]

93 is written *Quatre-Vingt Treize* and is pronounced [cat-ruh](rolled r)[v-ain-t][t-r-ez](rolled r)

94 is written *Quatre-Vingt Quatorze* and is pronounced [cat-ruh](rolled r)[v-ain-t][cat-or-z]

95 is written *Quatre-Vingt Quinze* and is pronounced [cat-ruh](rolled r)[v-ain-t][k-an-z]

96 is written *Quatre-Vingt Dix Seize* and is pronounced [cat-ruh](rolled r)[v-ain-t][dee-s-ez]

97 is written *Quatre-Vingt Dix-Sept* and is pronounced [cat-ruh](rolled r)[v-ain-t][dee-set]

98 is written *Quatre-Vingt Dix-Huit* and is pronounced [cat-ruh](rolled r)[v-ain-t][dee-sweet]

99 is written *Quatre-Vingt Dix-Neuf* and is pronounced [cat-ruh](rolled r)[v-ain-t][dee-s-nuf]

Chapter 12 - Accommodation

Where can I find a cheap/good/nearby hotel? – *Où est-ce que je peux trouver un hôtel pas cher/ un bon hôtel/ un hôtel près d'ici?*

Hotel – *hôtel (m)*

Guesthouse/B&B – *maison (f) d'hôte, pension, bed and breakfast*

Apartment – *appartement (m)*

Gîte/ holiday house – *gîte (m)*

Room – *chambre (f)*

Do you have a room available? *Est-ce que vous avez une chambre disponible?*

I have a reservation – *J'ai une réservation*

In the name of – *au nom de*

Suite – *suite (f)*

Single room – *chambre simple*

Double room – *chambre double*

Family room – chambre familiale

I would like a room with... – *Je voudrais une chambre avec...*

Shower – *douche (f)*

Bath – *baignoire* (f)

Balcony – *balcon (m)*

Patio – *terrace* (f)

Smoking – *fumeur*

Non-smoking – *non-fumeur*

Air con – *climatisation/ clim*

One night – *une nuit (f)*

One week – *une semaine* (f)

Two nights – *deux nuits*

How much is this room per night/per person? – *Combien coûte cette chambre par nuit/ par personne?*

Can I see the room, please? – *Est-ce que je peux voir la chambre, s'il vous plaît?*

Very good, I'll take it – *très bien, je la prends.*

Fully booked – *complet*

Key – *clef* (f)

Keycard – *carte-clef* (f)

Minibar – *minibar (m)*

One star – *une étoile*

Two star – *deux étoiles*

Is there a swimming pool/gym? – *Y a-t-il une piscine/ un gymnase?*

Is there a restaurant? – *Y a-t-il un restaurant?*

I would like to dine here this evening – *Je voudrais dîner ici ce soir*

What time is check-out? – *A quelle heure faut-il libérer la chambre?*

I would like to have breakfast tomorrow morning – *Je voudrais prendre le petit déjeuner demain matin*

Do you take credit cards? – *Est-ce que vous prenez les cartes de credit/ cartes bleues?*

I've left my key in my room – *J'ai laissé ma clef dans ma chambre*

Are towels provided? – *Est-ce que les serviettes sont fournies?*

Room service – *service (m) d'étage*

Meal – *repas* (m)

Half-board – *demi-pension* (f)

Full board – *pension* (f) *complète*

All-inclusive – *all inclusive*

Tourist tax – *taxe* (f) *de séjour*

Included – *inclus*

On what floor? – *A quel étage?*

Breakfast included – *petit déjeuner compris*

That will suit me – *cela me convient*

Is there a lift? – *Y a-t-il un ascenseur* (m)?

Could you take my baggage up, please? – *Pourriez-vous faire monter mes bagages, s'il vous plaît?*

What time is breakfast/lunch/dinner? – *A quelle heure est le petit déjeuner/le déjeuner/le dîner?*

Where is the dining room? – *Où est le restaurant?*

My key is not working – *ma clef ne fonctionne pas*

Wi-Fi code – *code (m) Wi-Fi*

The Wi-Fi is not working – *le wifi ne fonctionne pas*

Could you print something out for me, please? – *Pourriez-vous imprimer quelque chose pour moi, s'il vous plaît?*

Could you call a taxi for me? – *Pourriez-vous appeler un taxi pour moi?*

Can you recommend a... – *pourriez-vous me conseiller un/ une...?*

Is it far from here? – *Est-ce loin d'ici?*

Chambermaid – *femme (f) de chambre*

Do not disturb – *ne pas déranger*

You can make up the room – *vous pouvez faire la chambre*

Wake-up call/alarm – *réveil*

Shower curtain – *rideau (m) de douche*

Towel – *serviette (f)*

Bathrobe dressing gown – *robe (f) de chambre*

Bidet – *bidet (m)*

Blanket – *couverture* (f)

Pillow – *oreiller* (m)

Hairdryer – *sèche-cheveux* (m)

Paper – *papier (m) (à écrire)*

Toilet paper – *papier (m) toilette*

Newspaper – *journal (m)*

Envelope – *enveloppe* (f)

Linen – *linge (m)*

Pen – *stylo* (m)

Direct line – *ligne (f) directe*

Telephone – *téléphone (m)*

Sheet – *drap (m)*

Sheets – *draps* (m, pl)

Could you change the sheets, please? – *Pourriez-vous changer les draps s'il vous plaît?*

This is not clean – *ceci n'est pas propre*

Could you take this away, please? – *Pourriez-vous emporter ceci s'il vous plaît?*

Laundry service – *service (m) blanchissage (f)*

When will it be ready? – *Quand sera-t-il prêt?*

Bill – *note* (f), *facture* (f)

Receipt – *facture (f)*

Breakfasts at... – *petits déjeuners à...*

Paid, settled – *payé, acquitté*

Tourist tax – *taxe de séjour*

Do you want to pay now? – *Voulez-vous régler maintenant?*

Deposit – *accompte* (m)

Could I see your passport, please? – *Pourrais-je voir votre passeport s'il vous plaît?*

Could I take an impression of your credit card, please? – *Pourrais-je prendre une empreinte de votre carte de credit s'il vous plaît?*

To pay – *à régler*

Balance – *solde (m)*

Did you take anything from the minibar? – *Avez-vous pris quelque-chose au mini-bar?*

Snack – *en-cas (m)*

Do you want the bill made out to a company name? – *Voulez-vous la facture au nom d'une société?*

Do you want the bill made out to any time in particular? – *Voulez-vous la facture à un nom en particulier?*

Do you want the bill in your name? – *voulez-vous la facture à votre nom?*

The booking name – *le nom de la reservation*

Check-out – *depart (m), check-out (m)*

There is a mistake here – *il y a une erreur ici*

I did not take this – *je n'ai pas pris ceci*

I am leaving today/tomorrow/in the morning – *je pars aujourd'hui/demain/demain matin*

Please could you bring my luggage down? – *Pourriez-vous faire descendre mes bagages, s'il vous plaît?*

Can I leave my bags somewhere for the day? – *Est-il possible de laisser mes bagages quelque part pour la journée?*

I will be back at… – *je reviendrai à…*

Is there somebody at reception 24 hours a day? – *Y a-t-il quelqu'un à la réception 24 heures sur 24?*

Bed & breakfast – *pension (f)*

Lodging – *hébergement* (m)

Accommodation – *logement (m)*

I will be back in an hour – *je reviens dans une heure*

Do you want a deposit? – *voulez-vous un acompte?*

Apartment hotel – *aparthotel (m)*

Spa – *spa (m)*

Swimming pool – *piscine (f)*

Beauty treatment – *soins (m, pl) esthétiques*

Massage – *massage (m)*

Steam room – *hammam (m)*

Sauna – *sauna* (m)

Hot water – *eau* (f) *chaude*

There is no hot water – *il n'y a pas d'eau chaude*

Snack-bar, bistro – *bistrot (m)*

Package – *formule (f)*

Irregular verb '*prendre*' (to take)

Je prends – I take, am taking, do take

Tu prends – You take

Il/elle prend – He/she takes

Nous prenons – We take

Vous prenez – You take

Ils prennent – They take

This next one is really useful. It means to "need to" or "be necessary", and is often only found in the third person: il faut + infinitive:

Il faut faire – It is necessary to do

Il faut sortir – It is necessary to leave

Il faut libérer la chambre – Guests need to leave the room/check-out

Time expressions

It is always handy to say when you want to/need to/are going to have done something. Here are some time expressions:

Today – *aujourd'hui*

Tomorrow – *demain*

Yesterday – *hier*

Morning – *matin (m)*

Afternoon – *après-midi* (masculine, although this one stumps even the French sometimes when it comes to gender. You will hear "*une après-midi*," but technically, it is masculine)

Evening – *soir (m)*

Night – *nuit (f)*

Tomorrow night – *demain soir*

This evening – *ce soir*

Yesterday evening – *hier soir*

This morning – *ce matin*

Tomorrow morning – *demain matin*

Last night – *la nuit dernière*

At the same time --- *À la fois*

In the future – *à l'avenir*

The day after tomorrow – *après-demain*

Formerly, in the past – *auparavant*

The day before yesterday – *avant-hier*

493

First – *d'abord*

From time to time – *de temps en temps, de temps à autre*

Again – *de nouveau*

Once again – *encore une fois*

Next day – *lendemain (m)*

Sometimes – *parfois*

Rarely – *rarement*

Recently – *récemment*

Century – *siècle (m)*

Every day – *tous les jours*

All of a sudden – *tout à coup*

Suddenly – *soudain*

Telling the time

What time is it? – *Quelle heure est-il?*

It is... – *Il est...*

One o'clock – *une heure*

Two o'clock – *deux heures*

Etc. up to 23 o'clock (the French are very fond of using the 24-hour clock).

Midnight – *minuit (m)*

Midday – *midi (m)*

In the morning – *du matin*

In the afternoon – *de l'après-midi*

In the evening – *du soir*

The easiest way to use the minutes is to say 1 o'clock 30. For example: "*une heure trente.*" This is possible with any number. "*Une heure vingt-trois,*" deux heures cinquante-neuf," etc.

If you want to use the other form—half past, quarter to, etc.:

Half past one – *une heure et demie*

Quarter past one – *une heure et quart*

Quarter to one – *une heure moins le quart*

Ten (minutes) to one – *une heure moins dix*

Note: there is no equivalent of "ten past one"—it would simply be "*une heure dix.*"

Camping

Tent – *tente (f)*

Caravan – *caravane (f)*

Camper van – *camping car (m)*

Space – *emplacement (m)*

Mobile home – *mobile home (m)*

Bungalow – *bungalow (m)*

Sheets – *draps (m, pl.)*

Towels – *serviettes (f, pl.)*

Backpack – *sac (m) à dos*

Can opener – *ouvre-boîte (m)*

Compass – *boussole (f)*

Firewood – *bois (m) de chauffage*

Campfire – *feu (m) de camp*

Mattress – *matelas (m)*

Sleeping bag – *sac (m) de couchage*

Water bottle – *gourde (f)*

Requests and Complaints

Could I have an outside line? – *Puis-j'avoir une ligne vers l'extérieur?*

Is there Wi-Fi? – *Y a-t-il du Wi-Fi?*

Do you have a Wi-Fi code? – *Avez-vous un code Wi-Fi?*

Could I have some more towels, please? – *Pourrais-je avoir des serviettes supplémentaires, s'il vous plaît?*

Would it be possible to…? – *Serait-il possible de…?*

Chapter 13 - Health

Body – *corps* (m)

Head – *tête (f)*

Neck – *cou (m)*

Back of neck – *nuque (f)*

Shoulder – *épaule (f)*

Arm – *bras* (m)

Elbow – *coude (m)*

Lower arm – *avant-bras* (m)

Wrist – *poignet* (m)

Hand – *main (f)*

Finger – *doigt (m)*

Thumb – *pouce (m)*

Index finger – *index (m)*

Middle finger – *majeur (m)*

Ring finger – *annulaire (m)*

Little finger – *petit doigt* ("*auriculaire*" is the formal name but we use a lot "*petit doigt*")(m)

Joint – *articulation* (f)

Chest – *poitrine* (f)

Breast – *sein (m)*

Tummy – *ventre* (m)

Pelvis – *bassin (m)*

Back – *dos (m)*

Lower back – *bas (m) du dos*

Upper back – *haut* (m) *du dos*

Upper part – *partie (f) supérieur*

Lower part – *partie (f) inférieure*

Bone – *os (m)*

Shoulder blade – *omoplate (f)*

Collar bone – *clavicule (f)*

Side – *côté (m)*

Rib – côte (f)

Hip – *hanche* (f)

Leg – *jambe* (f)

Knee – *genou* (m)

Ankle – *cheville* (f)

Foot – *pied (m)*

Toe – *doigt (m) de pied, orteil (m)*

Big toe – *gros orteil* (m)

Shin – *tibia* (m)

Thigh – *cuisse* (f)

Calf – *mollet* (m)

Spine – *colonne (f) vertébrale*

Vertebra – *vertèbre*

Ligament – *ligament (m)*

Tendon – *tendon (m)*

Muscle – *muscle (m)*

Skull – *crâne (m)*

Eye – *oeil* (m) – plural *yeux* (m, pl)

Ear – *oreille* (f)

Nose – *nez (m)*

Chin – *menton* (m)

Mouth – *bouche* (f)

Tooth – *dent (f)*

Lip – *lèvre* (f)

Jaw – *mandibule* (f)

Cheek – *joue (f)*

Forehead – *front (m)*

Eyebrow – *sourcil (m)*

Eyelash – *cil (m)*

Nail – *ongle* (m)

Heart – *Coeur (m)*

Stomach – *estomac (m)*

Liver – *foie (m)*

Lung – *poumon* (m)

Kidney – *rein (m)*

Diaphragm – *diaphragme* (m)

My X hurts... – *J'ai mal à...*

Nausea – *nausée (f)*

Headache – *mal de tête, céphalée* (f)

Migraine – *migraine (f)*

I have a migraine – *J'ai la migraine*

To suffer from... – *souffrir de...*

Allergy – *allergie* (f)

To be allergic to – *être allergique à*

Food allergy – *allergie (f) alimentaire*

Peanut allergy – *allergie aux cacahuètes*

Intolerance – *intolérance (f)*

Symptom – *symptôme* (m)

Weight – *poids (m)*

Height – *taille (f)*

Blister – *ampoule (f)*

Burn – *brûlure* (f)

I burnt myself – *Je me suis brûlé/ brûlée*

I burnt my X... – *Je me suis brûlé le/la...* (Example: *Je me suis brûlé la main*)

Sunburn – *coup de soleil*

I got sunburnt – *j'ai pris un coup de soleil*

Sunstroke – *insolation* (f)

Cold – *rhume* (m)

To have a cold – *avoir un rhume*

Catch cold – *prendre froid*

To catch a cold – *attraper un rhume, s'enrhumer*

The flu – *grippe (f)*

Constipation – *constipation (f)*

Constipated – *constipé*

Cough – *toux (m)*

To cough – *tousser*

Sore throat – *mal de gorge, angine* (f)

Tonsillitis --- *Angine (f) rouge*

Diarrhea – *diarrhée (f)*

To have diarrhea – *avoir la diarrhée*

Fever – *fièvre* (f)

Feverish – *fiévreux, febrile*

To have a fever – *avoir de la fièvre*

Blood pressure – *tension* (f) (*artérielle*)

Take someone's blood pressure – *prendre la tension (artérielle) de quelqu'un*

Have high blood pressure – *faire de l'hypertension (f)*

Have low blood pressure – *faire de l'hypotension (f)*

Pain – *douleur* (f)

Indigestion – *indigestion (f) (crise (f) de foie* is old, so now, most of the time it's the old persons who use it)

Food poisoning – *intoxication (f) alimentaire*

Venereal disease – *maladie (f) vénérienne*

Illness – *maladie (f)*

Vomit – *vomir*

Doctor – *médecin, docteur*

Hospital – *hôpital (m)*

Practice – *cabinet (m)*

Dentist – *dentiste* (m)

Toothache – *rage (f) de dent*

Filling – *plombage* (m)

Cavity – *carie (f)*

Extraction – *extraction (f)*

Crown – *couronne* (f)

Bridge – *bridge (m)*

Braces – *appareil (m, sing) dentaire*

Gum – *gencive* (f)

Painkiller – *antidouleur* (m)

Injection – *piqûre (f)*

Vaccination – *vaccin (m)*

Vaccinated – *vacciné*

Treatment – *soin (m)*

Health records --- *Carnet de santé*

Vaccination records – *carnet de santé*

Medical history, antecedent – *antécédents médicaux (m, pl)*

Pregnant – *enceinte (f)*

I am pregnant – *Je suis enceinte*

I am X weeks/months pregnant – *Je suis enceinte de X semaines/mois*

I have gone into labor – *Le travail a commencé*

Sting – *piqûre* (f)

Wasp – *guêpe* (f)

Bee – *Abeille* (f)

Mosquito – *moustique* (f)

Bite – *morsure* (f) (dog, snake)

Bite – *piqûre* (insect)

Nettle – *ortie (f)*

Hive – *urticaire* (f)

Blood test – *prise (f) de sang*

Blood – *sang*

Bleeding – *saignant*

X is bleeding – *X saigne*

Sprain, strain – *entorse (f)*

Rest – *repos* (m)

Broken – *cassé*

I broke my leg – *Je me suis cassé la jambre*

I sprained my ankle – *Je me suis tordu la cheville*

I got stung – *Je me suis fait piquer*

I think it's broken – *Je crois que c'est cassé*

Anesthetic (general, local) – *anesthésie (f) générale/locale*

Under anesthetic – *sous anesthésie (f)*

Give a local anesthetic – *faire une anesthésie locale à quelqu'un*

Appointment – *rendez-vous*

Reception – *réception*

Waiting room – *salle d'attente*

Chapter 14 - The doctor

Going to the doctor in France: What you need to know

Going to the doctor in France is a little bit different. The doctor himself (or herself) will greet you in the waiting room instead of a nurse calling your name and doctors here rarely wear the traditional white doctor coats we're used to seeing in the US. Keep that in mind.

More or less, going to the doctor in France is the same as in the US. You make an appointment, you go see the doctor, he/she examines you, diagnoses you, gives you a prescription if necessary, and you're on your way. I said more or less the same. There are some nuances you might want to take note of if you're going to the doctor in France. Let's take a look.

Making the appointment

When you call the *cabinet médical* to make an appointment, you will talk to the secretary who may or may not be in a good mood.

Phrase to use:

"Je voudrais prendre rendez-vous s'il vous plaît." (I'd like to make an appointment please).

Upon arrival

Normally you don't fill out 10 papers for insurance/new patient forms when going to the doctor in France like you would in the US, so don't show up early for paperwork. Doctors all over the world run late and it's not specific to France, but I must say no one is ever on time here. Upon arrival, let the secretary know you're there and if there's no secretary, go to the *salle d'attente* (waiting room) for your particular doctor. In most cases, the door will be marked as such and in a practice with multiple doctors, again go to the waiting room for your particular doctor.

Greet everyone in there with a "*bonjour*" and then sit down. The doctor will personally come and call you when it's your turn. There is no nurse visit to check your vitals or get your history first.

At the appointment

When going to the doctor in France, you'll first be asked by the doctor to present your *carte vitale* (insurance card) and to pay (this can also be done at the end). If you don't yet have your *carte vitale*, you'll get a *feuille de soins* (health form/receipt) to submit yourself to the *sécurité sociale*.

Once that's out of the way, you'll explain why you're there and the doctor will fully examine you. There's no nurse who comes to see you in advance, so be thorough.

Common dialog:

Cabinet du docteur Philippe, bonjour. / Good morning, Doctor Philip's Clinic.

Bonjour, excusez-moi de vous déranger, je voudrais prendre rendez-vous avec le docteur Philippe s'il vous plaît. /Good morning, sorry for disturbing you. I wanted to make an appointment with Doctor Philipe, please.

Quelles sont vos disponibilités? (=quand?) / When would you like to make an appointment?

Je préfère mercredi matin. OU Tous les jours après 17h. OU Le plus tôt possible. OU Tout me va. / I prefer Wednesday morning. OR any day after 5pm. OR As early as possible. OR Anything will do.

Je vous propose le jeudi 12 à 10h. / Is Thursday the 12 at 10 am convenient?

Merci beaucoup, c'est très bien. / That's good. Thank you very much.

OU – Non, je ne suis pas disponible ce jour-là. Avez-vous autre chose (à me proposer)? / No, I'm busy on that day. Could you suggest another vacant time slot?

Vous pouvez me donner votre nom? / Could you give me your name?

Tout à fait. (Say your name) / Certainly. (Your name)

If it is urgent

C'est une urgence, est-ce que vous pourriez me prendre plus tôt? / It's urgent, can you please give me an appointment at the earliest?

Non, désolé. Tout est plein. / No, sorry. We are full.

Est-ce que vous auriez un autre collègue à me recommander? J'ai absolument besoin de voir quelqu'un. / Can you suggest any other doctor? I desperately need to see one.

Or if it is very urgent:

Est-ce que je dois me rendre aux urgences? / Do I have to go to the E.R?

Oui./Non. / Yes./No.

Merci madame/monsieur, à bientôt. / Thank you, Madam/sir.

Note:

You don't require your French papers to visit a doctor or the emergency ward.

You have to pay the full consultation fee and the bill for the medicines.

Don't forget to ask for the price when you book!

If you can't afford to pay the gynecologist's fee, go to Planning Familial.

Emergency French phrases:

You may come across an operator who speaks English but there is no guarantee of this. If you do not speak French, it is best to find a French-speaker whom you can trust.

- Police: *La Police Nationale or gendarmerie*
- Fire brigade: *Les sapeurs pompiers*
- Emergency services/ambulance: *Service d'Aide Médicale d'Urgence or SAMU*

- Poisoning emergency: *Centre antipoison*

- Road emergency services: *Services d'urgence routière*

- Emergency numbers: *Numéros d'urgence*

- It's an emergency: *C'est une urgence.*

- My name is...: *Je m'appelle...*

- My telephone number is...: *Mon numéro de téléphone est le...*

- I live at...: *J'habite à...*

- Help!: *Au secours!*

- Ambulance: *une ambulance; J'ai besoin d'une ambulance. (I need an ambulance.)*

- Heart attack: *une crise cardiaque; Mon mari fait une crise cardiaque. (My husband had a heart attack.)*

- Stroke: *un AVC (= accident vasculaire cérébral); Je pense que ma femme a souffert d'un AVC.* (I think my wife suffered a stroke.)

- Choke: *s'étouffer; Mon bébé s'étouffe.* (My baby is choking.)

- Difficulty breathing/gasping: *haleter or difficulté à respirer; J'ai du mal à respirer.* (I have difficulty breathing.)

- To bleed: *saigner; Je saigne beaucoup.* (I am bleeding a lot.)

- Hemorrhage: *une hémorragie; Mon mari fait une hémorragie.* (My husband had a hemorrhage.)

- Concussion: *une commotion cérébrale; Mon enfant est tombé. A-t-il une commotion cérébrale?* (My child fell. Does he have a concussion?)

- Diabetic: *diabétique; Je suis diabétique. J'ai besoin d'insuline.* (I need insulin).

- Labor: *accouchement/accoucher; Ma femme accouche; la poche des eaux s'est percée.* (My wife is giving birth. Her water has broken.)

- To be poisoned: *s'empoisonner; Mon enfant s'est empoisonné.* (My child has been poisoned.)

Headaches, colds, sore throat

Je tousse.

I have a cough.

Vous auriez quelque chose contre la toux?

Do you have medicines for cough?

Toux grasse ou toux sèche?

Do you have a cough with mucus or dry? (They often ask it)

J'ai mal à la tête. / Vous pourriez me donner quelque chose contre le mal de tête?

I have a headache. / Can you give some medicines for headaches?

J'ai un rhume.

I have a cold.

Je me mouche tout le temps. / J'ai le nez qui coule.

I have a running nose.

J'éternue tout le temps.

I sneeze all the time.

J'ai mal à la gorge.

I have a sore throat.

J'ai la gorge très sèche.

I have a parched throat.

J'ai des glaires.

I have mucus.

J'ai de la fièvre.

I have a fever.

Pharmacy:

The pharmacist is called *le pharmacien* here. And a pharmacy is called *la pharmacie*. There are pharmacies everywhere, and you find them by looking for a big green cross. It is usually a big neon sign. They are open during the day, like other French shops. In case you need any special medication that cannot wait till the morning, you have to find *une pharmacie de nuit*, also called *pharmacie de garde*, which would be open at night.

The pharmacist sells the medicines.

Ask for a doctor:

Est-ce que je dois aller voir un médecin? / Should I see a doctor?

Est-ce que vous avez un médecin à me recommander? / Do you have a doctor to recommend?

Vous avez son numéro? / May I have the phone number of the doctor you recommend?

Vous avez quelque chose contre les allergies? / Do you have medicines for allergy?

Medicine Vocabulary:

Un cachet --- a tablet

Un comprimé --- a pill

Une pastille --- a lozenge

Aspirine --- aspirin

Le dosage --- the dosage

Une goutte --- a drop

Le médicament --- the medicine

Un pansement --- a bandage

Prescrire --- to prescribe

Ordonnance --- the prescription

Chapter 15 - Exploring the City

When you are in the city, you will find that large roads usually have a pelican crossing and you are permitted to cross the road when the light is green. You may take the metro to travel from one place to another, or in some cities may take the tram. There are special prices available for people who are going to be in the city for a set number of days and buying these tickets can be advantageous to you when wishing to discover as much as you can within the limits of your stay. A *Carte Orange* is one such special priced ticket for the Paris Metro and it will save you a lot of money on having to pay individual fares each time you catch the metro. Look on the bulletin boards and then you can ask for the specific promotional ticket.

For example, if you choose to buy the *Carte Orange* you would say:

One Carte Orange please	*Une carte orange s'il vous plaît*	Oon cart oronge see vous play

You will always be able to get a tourist map from the Tourist Information Office in any large city in France. You will first need to find the tourist information office.

Where is the tourist information offices please?	*Où est l'office de Tourisme?*	Ooh aye loffiss duh tourisme?

As you are going to a town that you don't know, it is quite possible that you will need to ask for a lot of directions. It is wise to have your map with you because someone can easily show you on the map how to get somewhere, whereas their explanation in French may be difficult to understand. The basics of directions include these phrases:

where is...?	*Où est*	Ooh ess
straight on	*Tout droit*	Too dwat
to the right	*à droite*	Ah dwaht
to the left	*à gauche*	Ah goash

You may be told to take the second turn on the right. Let's look at the words that denote first (*premier*), second (*Deuxième*) or third (*Troisième*). As you can see these are fairly easy words to memorize. If you already know the French numbers, this helps too.

Let's take a moment to review these useful phrases for exploring the city.

Do you know where the metro is?	*Est-ce que vous savez comment aller au métro?*	S kay voo sah-vay koh-mahn ah-lay oh meh-tro?
the park	*le parc*	luh pahrk
the train station	*à la gare*	ah lah-gahr
the travel agency	*l'agence de voyage*	lah zahn duh vwah-yaj
the grocery store	*l'épicerie*	lay pee-suh-ree

the shopping center	*le centre commercial*	luh sahntr koh-mehr-shal
the town hall	*la mairie*	lah mar-ree
the town center	*le centre-ville*	luh- sahntr-veel
the public bathrooms	*les toilettes publiques*	lay twa-let puh-bleek
the bar	*le bar*	luh bahr
Where can I park my car?	*Où puis-je garer ma voiture?*	Ooh pweez gah-ray mah vwah-tyur?
Where is the nearest restaurant?	*Où est le restaurant le plus proche?*	Ooh eh luh rehs-toh-rahn lun plyu prosh?
Is there a bank nearby?	*Est-ce qu'il y a une banque près d'ici?*	S-keel-ya oon bahnk preh dee-see?
Is it very far?	*Est-ce que c'est loin d'ici?*	S-kuh seh lwehn dee-see?
It's far.	*C'est loin.*	Seh lwehn.
Is it close by?	*Est-ce que c'est près d'ici?*	S-kuh seh preh dee-see?
It's close by.	*C'est près d'ici.*	Seh preh dee-see.
Can I go on foot?	*Est-ce que je peux y aller à pied?*	S kuh zay puh ee yah-lay ah piay?
Take the next left.	*Prends la prochaine à gauche*	Prahn lah proh-shain ah gosh.
Take the next right	*Prends la prochaine à droite.*	Prahn lah proh-shain ah dwaht.
cross the...	*traverse le...*	trah-vehrs luh...
follow the...	*suis les...*	swee lay
until you reach the...	*jusqu'au...*	zhyus-koh...
It's on the left.	*C'est à gauche.*	Seh tah gosh.
It's on the right.	*C'est tout droit.*	Seh too dwa.
It's next to ...	*C'est à côté...*	Seh tah koh-tay
It's in front of...	*C'est devant*	Seh duh-vahn
It's behind...	*C'est derrière*	Seh deh-riair
It's to the North	*C'est au nord.*	Seh toh nor
It's to the South	*C'est au sud.*	Seh toh syud.
It's to the East	*C'est à l'est.*	Seh tah lest.
It's to the West	*C'est à l'ouest*	Seh tahl-west.

Now let's look at some of the things that you are likely to want to find in the city. This includes museums and places of interest to tourists.

The Museum --- *le musée* – Pronounced: Luh Muzay

It's a good idea to know which particular museum and to have the name of the museum at hand so that you can ask the directions specifically for that museum. Paris is so filled with Museums that you can use your map to point to the exact museum that you are looking for and get help to get there.

| The Eiffel tower | la tour Eiffel | Lah toor eefelle |

Simply by adding the name of the place that you are looking for to the question, where is (Où est) you will be able to find your way around. This is pronounsed as oow ay.

| Where is the Eiffel tower? | Où est la tour Eiffel? | Oow ay lah toor eefelle |

Looking for somewhere for a coffee and a break? You can ask people locally if they can recommend a good coffee shop. If you stop someone on the street to ask something, it is polite to say excuse me before you ask them what it is that you want to know.

Excuse me --- *Excusez-moi*

You would then qualify this by saying *Madam* (to a lady), *Monsieur* (to a man), *mademoiselle* (to a young lady).

Excuse me, please but can you tell me where I can get a good coffee?

Excusez-moi, Madame, Connaissez-vous un bon café ici?

One of the best verbs that you can learn in French when you are hitting the town is the verb *CHERCHER* which means to look for. You can use this in the street when you are looking for a particular shop, to pinpoint a tourist spot or to even ask when you are in a shop or a pharmacy for a particular product.

I am looking for the Eiffel Tower	Je cherche la tour Eiffel	Jzuh Share sh la toor eefell
I am looking for the station	Je cherche la gare	Jzuh Share sh la garr
I am looking for a gift for my mother	Je cherche un cadeau pour ma mère –	Ju share sh un cadow pour ma mare

Chapter 16 - Dictionary of Simple Phrases

You may have seen some of these words and phrases in previous chapters, but in this chapter and the next we will put them all together, so you have a quick reference guide.

You will notice that many of these phrases have multiple forms depending on how formal you want to be. As a rule of thumb, when addressing someone who you want to be more formal with or who you want to show respect to, you should use *vous* anything you are talking to them. Alternatively, if you are speaking to a friend or a family member, you can use *tu* when addressing them as this is more casual. In English we do not have different ways to speak formally and informally like this, so their translations to English are the same. Note this difference in French though as it will help you to avoid seeming rude if you call someone you just met *tu*.

Basic Phrases For Everyday Conversations

Bonjour [bon-j-oor], Hello, hi

There are two different ways to say please in French. One of them is more formal than the other. As you learned previously in this book, there are two ways to say you as well. The word *vous* means you and is used in a much more formal way than *tu*. *Vous* can also be used in a plural sense to talk about people in terms of you as a pair or a group of people. If you have just met someone or if they are someone that you want to show respect to and be more formal with, then you will use the first example below. If you are friends with them and you want to say please in a more casual and less formal way, then you can use the second one.

S'il vous plaît [seel][v-oo][play], please

S'il te plaît [seel][t-uh][play], please

Je suis [j-uh][s-wee], I am.

This can be followed with just about anything that you learned in the previous chapters. You can follow it with a feeling, an adjective or it can simply be the beginning of a sentence.

Tu es [too][ay], you are.

This is similar to the previous example that means I am, but when you are speaking to someone in a less formal and more casual way you would say you are. For a more formal and respectful way of saying you are, you can use the word *vous* instead of *tu* and adjust the verb *être* accordingly, making it *Vous êtes* [voo-s][eh-tt-s].

Je m'appelle [j-uh][m-ah-p-el], My name is. This directly translates to mean "I am called".

Enchanté [on-sh-on-tay], Nice to meet you. You would say this right after meeting someone new, just like how we say nice to meet you or it was a pleasure to meet you in English.

Pardon? [pa-r-doh-n] (rolled r), *Pardon?*, Sorry? Sorry. This can be used in a variety of ways, either to ask someone politely to repeat themselves or as a statement if you wish to apologize to someone. You can use this when you are squeezing by someone at the movie theatre when you go to the bathroom during the film, if you want someone to repeat what they said because you didn't hear them or if you want to apologize to someone.

Comment t'appelles-tu? [coh-mon][t-app-el][t-oo], What is your name? This is similar to the above examples where *vous* can be switched out if you are speaking to a group of people or if you want to be more formal. In this case you would say *comment vous appelez-vous*? [coh-mon][v-oo-z][app-el-ay][v-oo-z], though the English translation of these is the exact same.

Oui [wee], yes

Non [noh], no

Comment allez-vous? [coh-mon][ah-lay][v-oo-z], How are you? This is a nice way of asking someone how they are doing, as it uses the word *vous*.

Ça va? [sah][vah] is used when we want to ask someone how they are, but this is more like saying, "hey, how are ya?" or "what's up?" This would be used with friends.

Excusez-moi [ex-k-you-z-ay][m-wah], excuse me. This can be used to get someone's attention in a polite way, and can also be used to ask someone to move if you need to get by them or if they are in your way. This is a polite way of saying either of these things.

Je ne comprends pas [j-uh][nuh][k-om-p-ron-d][pah], I don't understand. I hope you won't need to use this one too much, but if you don't understand someone's French when they are speaking too fast, or if you don't understand a concept in general aside from the language you can say this to them.

If you need to ask someone how to say a certain thing in French, you can ask them, *Comment dit-on ... en français*? And then insert the thing that you are asking them about. For example, you can ask them "comment dit-on banana en français? [coh-mon][dee-t][ohn]banana[oh-n][f-ron-say], how do you say banana in French.

In French, if we want to say see you later, we would say *à toute à l'heure* [ah][too-t][ah][l-err]. If you want to say see you later, on a specific day we would say for example, "see you tuesday", *à mardi*! [ah][mah-r-dee].

If someone asks you a question and you don't know the answer you can say *"Je ne sais pas"* [j-uh][nuh][say][pah] which means "I don't know".

If you want to ask someone about something, what something is or if you need clarification about something specific you can say *"Qu'est-ce que c'est?"* [k-ess][kuh]say] which means What is it? Or It can also mean what is _____. You then will insert whatever you are wondering about such as

Qu'est-ce que c'est ça? "Which means what is that?"

Qu'est-ce que c'est (insert word in French that you aren't sure of the meaning of), this could be something like *Qu'est-ce que c'est l'hiver*? If you don't know the word that they just said. Then, they will tell you that *l'hiver* means winter.

Plus lentement [p-loo][lon-tuh-mon-t], slower. You can use this phrase to ask someone to speak slower for you if you are having trouble understanding them because of a different accent than you are used to or if they are speaking too fast for you to understand. *Plus lentement* directly translates to "more slowly". If you want to make it even more polite you can say *s'il vous plaît* at the end of this phrase and form it as a question.

Restaurant Phrases

If you go to a restaurant in a French speaking place, chances are you will have to read French on the menu, order in French and ask for anything you may need in French. This section will teach you all of that.

When you enter the restaurant, or if you are to seat yourself, there will likely be a sign saying *Asseyez-vous* [ah-say-yay][voo][m-eh-m] which means seat yourselves. If you don't see this, someone will likely seat you. When they do, if you need a menu or if you are checking out a restaurant to see if you'd like to eat there, you can ask for a menu by saying *La carte, s'il vous plaît* [lah][k-ar-t][seel][voo][p-l-ay], the menu please. La carte means the menu. You can say it as a question or as a statement. Once you are eating, you can ask for something by saying any one of the following followed by *s'il vous plaît* [seel][voo][p-l-ay], which means please.

Le sel [luh][s-el], The salt

Le poivre [luh][p-wah-v-ruh], The pepper

Des serviettes [day][s-air-vee-et-s], Napkins

De l'eau [duh][l-oh], Some water

Du café [doo][kah-fay], Some coffee

Du thé [doo][tay], Some tea

Le ketchup [luh]ketchup, The Ketchup

La sauce piquante [luh][soh-s][pee-k-ont], The hot sauce

When you finish eating and you are ready for your bill you can say *L'addition, s'il vous plaît* [lah-dee-see-on][seel][voo][p-l-ay]. *L'addition* is the bill or the check.

After they bring you anything, or when you are leaving and you want to thank them you will say,

Merci bien [meh-r-see][bee-yen], Thank you very much

If you want to be more formal, you can say thank you sir or thank you ma'am.

You can combine any of the above ways of saying thank you with sir or ma'am to be extra polite for example;

Merci Beaucoup Madame [meh-r-see][b-oh-k-oo][mah-dah-m], Thank you so much ma'am.

Try an exercise now to practice this;

You walk into a restaurant and there is a sign saying "*Asseyez-vous*". You walk into the dining room and seat yourself. When you see a waiter walk by you want to ask her for the menu so you say _____. After looking at the menu, you decide that you want to order a coffee. When the waiter comes by again you say _____. Then, you need some Sugar (*du sucre* [soo-k-ruh]) so you say _____. You finish your coffee and you are ready for your bill. You ask her by saying _____. Then, you pay and you are ready to leave so as you walk out the door you say _____.

Les Textos

In French, when you are texting it is called "*un texto*" [t-ex-toh]. There are some short-forms you can use when texting in French, and French speaking people will know what you mean. If you are texting a French speaking person, you may see some of these short forms if they are sending you text messages.

Bjr, Bonjour, hi, hello

Bsr, bonsoir, good evening, good night

biz, bisous, kisses

511

ça va, ça va? Or *ça va.*

If it's used as a question, it means are you good? Or how are you?

If it is used as a statement, it means i'm good or it's going well.

b1, bien , good

é twa, et toi, and you?, how are you?

dsl, je suis désolé, I'm sorry

Both of the next two short forms mean see you later or see you soon, but one is a little more polite than the other. The second form would be used more casually when texting friends.

a tt, à toute à l'heure, see you soon, see you later

a +, à plus, see you later

The next two examples are two ways of saying please, just like we learned earlier. One of them, the one that uses *vous* is a more formal way. Sometimes you may be texting someone with whom you want to be a bit more respectful and this is when you would use this one. The one that uses *tu* is a less formal form and one that you would use with a friend.

stp, s'il te plaît, please (informally)

svp, s'il vous plaît, please (formally)

Phone Conversation Phrases

If you are going to be speaking on the phone with people in French, say, if you are calling a hotel to ask a question about your reservation or if you are calling a museum's front desk to ask them about an attraction that you've been wanting to see, you will need to know some common phrases to use on the phone. Below are all of the things you need.

This set of phrases is to do with phones and the actual hardware that you use when you are on the phone. You will need to know some of these terms if you are waiting on hold and being asked to press certain keys, or if you are wanting to mention something to someone about the phone itself.

Un téléphone fixe, landline

Un téléphone mobile, un portable, a cell phone

Une boîte vocale, voicemail, voice-mailbox

Allumer, Allumer le téléphone, to turn on the telephone Or *Allumer mon téléphone*, to turn on MY phone

Brancher, verb meaning to plug in.

Je vais brancher mon téléphone, I will plug in my phone

Recharger, to recharge

If you are on hold and you need to press a key that the voiceover is asking you to press, you may hear one of these terms;

Une touche, a key

Appuyer, verb meaning to press

Appuyer sur la touche, press the key/ the button

La touche dièse, the hashtag key

Appuyer sur la touche dièse, press the hashtag key

Appeler quelqu'un, to call someone

For example, *Je vais appeler Marie*, I will call Marie

Téléphoner à quelqu'un, to telephone someone

For example, *Je vais téléphoner à Jean*

Passer un coup de fil, To make a phone call

Passer un coup de téléphone, to make a telephone call

Un appel téléphonique, A phone call

Un coup de fil is a less formal way of saying a phone call, and if you want to be a bit more correct in terms of vocabulary, you can say the word telephone instead. We would say *"Un appel téléphonique"* if we want to reference a phone call in a formal way, for example if you are working in an office and you want to say to your boss that you will make a phone call, you would say *"Je vais passer un appel téléphonique."* Which means "I'm going to make a phone call" But you would not want to say *"Je vais passer un coup de fil"* as that would come off too informal and almost rude.

Décrocher le téléphone, the verb *décrocher* which means to pick up, but which is only used when speaking about the telephone and not when talking about picking up anything else.

Composer un numéro [k-om-poh-say][uhn][noo-meh-row], to dial a number. This directly translates to mean "to compose a number" which can help you to remember when you are dialing a number on your phone, you are essentially composing something.

ça sonne [sa][soh-nuh], it's ringing

ça sonne occupé [sa][soh-nuh][ok-you-pay], it's ringing the busy tone. This one doesn't translate as well into English as we don't have an exact way to say this, but it essentially means that the phone is sounding the busy tone. The word *"occupé"* means occupied, which means that the phone line is occupied or busy.

Personne ne répond [p-air-soh-n][nuh][r-eh-poh-nd], nobody is answering. This does not translate into English but it means that nobody has picked up the phone.

Pierre répond, Pierre answers

Pierre a répondu, Pierre answered

Pierre décroche, Pierre picks up the phone

Pierre a décroché, Pierre picked up the phone

Allo [ah-loh]

This word is used only on the telephone, but it is a way of saying hello, hi or of initiating conversation over the phone. Both people can initiate a conversation using this word, regardless of who called who.

C'est Madame _____, It's Mrs. _____ speaking

C'est Monsieur _____, It's Mr. _____ speaking

C'est de la part de qui?, Who is calling?

Qui est à l'appareil?, This directly means "Who is on the phone?" It is another way of asking "Who is calling?

These are used only over the phone to ask who is calling or when taking a message for someone else over the phone and you are wondering whose name to write down.

Est-ce que je peux parler à..., may I speak to...

Bonjour, c'est Jean, un ami de Pierre. Pourrais-je lui parler s'il vous plaît? Hi, this is Jean, a friend of Peter. May I speak to him please?

The above is a polite way of asking for someone on the phone and stating your intentions at the same time. This is a nice way to call a landline whether it is a friend or something business related. If this is a work-type call, you can remove *"un ami de Pierre"* and simply say *"bonjour, c'est Jean. Pourrais-je parler avec Pierre s'il vous plaît?"* This way you do not have to state your relationship to the person you are calling, but you can still ask for them in a polite way.

If the person is unavailable and you want to ask them if you can leave a message for someone you can say, *"Je peux lui laisser un message?"* May I leave a message for him or her?

Je vous la passe, I'll put her on

Je vous le passe, I'll put him on

These two directly translate to mean "I pass you to her/him" Which makes sense from a literal standpoint as you are in the phone in a sense and you are being passed to the person you want to speak with.

Ne quittez pas, don't hang up

Un instant s'il vous plaît, One moment please

Est-ce qu'il peut me rappeler? Can he call me back?

Est-ce que vous pouvez lui demander de me rappeler? Can you ask him to call me back?

Je rappellerai plus tard, I will call back later

The following are used when you have some type of problem on the phone and you want to clarify or resolve the issue:

On a été coupés, we got cut off, we got disconnected

Vous avez le mauvais numéro, You have a wrong number

This is a polite way of telling someone that they have the wrong number.

Il n'y a pas de réseau, there is no reception, there is no service

Je n'ai plus de batterie, I have no more battery, my battery is dead

Je t'entends mal, directly translates to mean "I hear you bad" but this means that you cannot hear the person, or that the reception is choppy and the person is cutting out. To tell someone that they are cutting out you can also say *"La connexion est mauvaise"* which directly translates to mean "the connection is bad".

If you missed someone's call you can say to them *"Je n'ai pas entendu la sonnerie"* Which means that you did not hear your ringer. If you want to be a bit more formal and apologetic, you can say *"Je suis desolé, je n'ai pas entendu la sonnerie"*. Remember, *je suis desolé* [j-uh][s-wee][d-eh-soh-lay] means "I am sorry". So this means "I'm sorry, I didn't hear the phone/ I did not hear the phone ring/ I did not hear my ringer." If you are on the other side of this, you can ask the person if they heard their phone ring by saying *"Est-ce que tu as entendu la sonnerie?"* If you want to know if they got your message you can ask them by saying *"As-tu reçu mon message?"* Which means"did you receive my message?"

Chapter 17 - The French Culture

When you think about French culture, what is the first thing that comes into your mind? Some people would associate it with images of the Eiffel tower and the Louvre, while others would think of fashion, food, and art. Naturally, there is a lot more to the French culture than what you might get out of movies and the television.

It would be impossible to summarize the entirety of the French culture in a single chapter, so take the following tidbits as a simple overview.

One thing to remember about the French culture is that the French are very proud of their government and nation, and any negative comments toward these would be seen as offensive.

French cuisine is esteemed worldwide and has influenced many other cuisines from around the world. Some of the most famous dishes that the French have contributed to the world and have become classics are the *coq au vin, boeuf bourguinon*, and of course, the *creme brulee*.

The French are also passionate and romantic by nature, and by this they are open towards the concept of extramarital affairs. In fact, approximately 50 percent of the children in France are born to parents who are unmarried.

Art and France have been married for centuries, especially in the major cities. The public buildings and cathedrals in France clearly display this. The Venus de Milo and the Mona Lisa, two of the most famous works of art, are displayed in the Louvre Museum.

Paris is the most prominent beacon of high-end fashion and has shared to the world the works of Louis Vuitton, Dior, Chanel, and Hermes. You can even see it in such fashion words as *"chic"*, *"haute couture"*, and *"avant garde"*.

As for the holidays in France, keep in mind that most of the French are Catholics and therefore celebrate Christmas, Easter, and other traditional Christian holidays. The 1st of May is the Labor Day of the French, while on May 8 they celebrate the Victory in Europe Day. July 14 is when they celebrate Bastille Day.

Whatever your passion may be, you will find it in the culture of the French. By allowing yourself to sink deeper into their culture you will find that learning the language is simply a bonus in the entire experience.

Exercise

Create a list of the aspects of the French culture that you like the most. It may be their cuisine, fashion, food, art, or even their passion and romance. After that, make an" inspiration board" by compiling pictures and French phrases that are associated with the items on your list. Use this to help keep you determined to learn the French language.

Conclusion

Wow! It seems like we just got started and we are already at this point. It has certainly been an interesting trip. We hope that the contents and materials in this book have helped you to improve your overall French Speaking skills. We are certain that you have put in your best effort in order to do so.

That is why our recommendation is to go back to any of the chapters which you feel you need to review and go over the content. Of course, the more you practice, the better your skills will be. Indeed, your overall skills will improve insofar as you continue to practice.

So, do take this opportunity to continue building on your current skills. You will find that over time, you will progressively gain more and more understanding of the language you encounter on a daily basis.

Given the fact that there are a number of resources out there which can help you to practice your listening skills, such as movies, telenovelas and music, you will be able to put this content into practice right away.

Thank you once again for choosing this book. We hope to have met your expectations. And please don't forget to move to the next book in the series, **French Short Stories** (for intermediate and advance learners).

FREE AUDIO OF "SPEAK FRENCH"

Download your fee audio from our website:

www.dupontlanguageinstitute.com

or follow this QR code:

To download the file:

Username: 06-AudioAC
Password: jov&(dTR}_fG

To open the file:

Password: 4HTfvuTs365&&4$$1

NOTES

NOTES

NOTES

NOTES

NOTES

NOTES

NOTES

NOTES

NOTES